FAMILY THERAPY AND BEYOND

*A Multisystemic Approach to Treating the
Behavior Problems of Children and Adolescents*

FAMILY THERAPY AND BEYOND

A Multisystemic Approach to Treating the
Behavior Problems of Children and Adolescents

Scott W. Henggeler
United States International University

Charles M. Borduin
University of Missouri, Columbia

Brooks/Cole Publishing Company
Pacific Grove, California

Consulting Editor: *C. Eugene Walker, University of Oklahoma*

Brooks/Cole Publishing Company
A Division of Wadsworth, Inc.

Printed in the United States of America

10   9   8   7   6   5   4   3   2   1

Library of Congress Cataloging-in-Publication Data
Henggeler, Scott W., [date]
    Family therapy and beyond : a multisystemic approach to treating
  the behavior problems of children and adolescents / Scott W.
  Henggeler and Charles M. Borduin.
      p.   cm.
  Includes bibliographical references.
  ISBN 0-534-12432-1
    1. Family psychotherapy. 2. Child psychotherapy. I. Borduin,
  Charles M. II. Title.
  RC488.5.H47 1989
  616.89'156—dc20

Sponsoring Editor: *Claire Verduin*
Editorial Assistant: *Gay C. Bond*
Production Editor: *Marjorie Sanders*
Manuscript Editor: *Hal Straus*
Permissions Editor: *Carline Haga*
Interior Design: *Phyllis Larimore Publication Services*
Cover Design: *Vernon T. Boes*
Art Coordinator: *Cloyce Wall*
Typesetting: *Phyllis Larimore Publication Services*
Jacket and Cover Printing: *Phoenix Color Corporation*
Printing and Binding: *Arcata Graphics/Fairfield*

To Cindy and Bev, with all our love

PREFACE

During the past three decades, systems theorists and family therapists have changed the way that a vast number of mental health professionals conceptualize and treat behavior problems in children and adolescents. Most important, they consider that problem behavior is linked with patterns of interaction among family members and that these patterns are reciprocal and bidirectional. The conceptual advances brought about by family system theorists have led to substantial improvements in the treatment of children and families and to a proliferation of family therapy training programs. In fact, reviewers of the family therapy outcome literature have generally indicated that family-based interventions are more effective than traditional treatment approaches. Reviewers have also noted, however, that the positive results of family therapy outcome studies are relatively modest.

A primary supposition of this volume is that the generally modest results of family therapy outcome studies are due to certain limitations of most family therapy models. As discussed in Chapter 1, we believe that family therapists have taken unnecessarily narrow views of behavior problems and overly restrictive approaches to behavioral change. This is ironic, since family therapists tend to be justifiably proud of the fact that their conceptualizations and interventions are more comprehensive than those of mental health professionals who adhere to traditional models of psychotherapy. Nevertheless, most family therapy models have at least three significant limitations that reduce their effectiveness. First, these models often fail to appreciate the importance of key variables that pertain to individual family members and to the extrafamilial systems in which these members are embedded. Second, they fail to consider important individual developmental issues that should influence the therapist's understanding of problems and choice of intervention strategies. Third, they rarely utilize intervention strategies that are derived from other treatment paradigms (e.g., cognitive-behavioral therapy), but are of proven efficacy.

The limitations of mainstream family therapy approaches are addressed by the multisystemic treatment model that is discussed in this volume. Although the family is usually the most important system to which children and adolescents belong (Chapters 3 and 4), we discuss research and present case studies that show that extrafamilial systems, such as the peer group (Chapter 5) and school (Chapter 6), can also play significant roles in the development and maintenance of behavior problems. Moreover, individual characteristics of the child and adolescent, in conjunction with systemic factors, can substantially influence behavior (Chapter 2).

Throughout this volume we discuss the importance of child developmental issues in understanding behavior problems. This emphasis is consistent with the emerging field of developmental psychopathology, which seeks to relate developmental theory to childhood behavior problems. Likewise, we describe how intervention strategies must often be modified in accordance with the child's stage of cognitive/social development to increase the likelihood of a favorable therapeutic outcome. Similarly, we discuss ways to integrate effectively viable nonsystemic interventions into systemic treatment.

The most significant aspect of the multisystemic treatment model, however, is that its efficacy has been supported by three well-designed outcome studies. Each of these studies focused on clinical sample populations that have been traditionally regarded as difficult to treat. Our approach, however, is not limited to the problems experienced by the families in these samples; using the general guidelines discussed in this volume, we have treated hundreds of individuals and families in our own clinical practices. Moreover, we have supervised hundreds of cases seen by doctoral students and other trainees. Thus, our multisystemic model is based on both research and personal clinical experience.

In the first half of this volume, we provide general descriptions of the content and process of multisystemic therapy and supplement these descriptions with case studies to illustrate the application of this approach. In the second half of the volume, we apply the multisystemic model to the treatment of especially difficult problems in children and adolescents. These problems include delinquent behavior, chemical dependency, insulin-dependent diabetes mellitus, and incest.

We are extremely pleased that three colleagues have contributed the last three chapters in this volume: Milton Trapold, Memphis State University, on adolescent chemical dependency; Cindy L. Hanson, United States International University, on insulin-dependent diabetes mellitus (IDDM); and Pamela C. Alexander, University of Maryland, on incest. Each of these authors possesses extensive expertise and clinical experience in his or her respective field. Dr. Trapold is a widely respected experimental psychologist who has devoted the past decade to clinical work with chemically dependent individuals and their families. Dr. Hanson is a clinical psychologist who has been funded by the National Institute of Health to pursue her longitudinal research on the familial and extrafamilial determinants of emotional and physical well-being in youths with IDDM. Dr. Alexander is a clinical psychologist who has been funded by the National Institute of Mental Health to develop her innovative treatment programs for incest victims and their families. Although the approaches of these three chapters vary (e.g., the chemical dependency chapter is more clinically oriented and the IDDM chapter is relatively research oriented), their underlying themes are quite similar: Effective treatment must be broad-based and must consider a wide range of potentially important variables.

Several other colleagues have contributed indirectly to this book: Molly Brunk, Virginia Treatment Center for Children; Barton J. Mann, University of Missouri, Columbia; J. Douglas Rodick, private practice in Ontario, California; Jon R. Urey, University of Louisville; and James P. Whelan, Memphis State University. Throughout the past decade, these professionals have made extremely important contributions to both our research programs and our conceptualization of therapeutic processes. We are very appreciative of their assistance.

We would like to thank the reviewers, Alexandra L. Quittner, Indiana University, and Thomas V. Sayger, University of Wisconsin, Madison, for their constructive comments. In addition, we extend our most sincere appreciation to C. Eugene Walker, University of Oklahoma, for his helpful comments on earlier drafts of this volume, and to Claire Verduin and Marjorie Sanders at Brooks/Cole for their editorial assistance.

Finally, we must emphasize that this volume is not intended to offer a definitive description of our treatment approach. In fact, the volume is best understood as a groundbreaking effort to provide an overview of the multisystemic model. Continued research and clinical applications are needed before the complexity of the model can be fully delineated. Nevertheless, in light of the positive results of our controlled outcome studies and the agreement between the multisystemic approach and numerous research findings regarding the multidimensional nature of behavior problems, we believe that the time has come to provide a more extensive discussion of our treatment approach than has been possible in our journal articles and book chapters.

Scott W. Henggeler
Charles M. Borduin

CONTENTS

Chapter 1 **An Introduction to the Multisystemic Approach**   1

Distinguishing Features of the Multisystemic Model   4
The Theoretical Context of the Multisystemic Approach   12
The Basic Principles of Systems Theory   13
The Nature of Behavior Problems   18
The New Epistemology   20
Overview of the Multisystemic Clinical Approach   23
Summary   28
References   28

Chapter 2 **Individual Therapy with Children and Adolescents**   33

Individual Contributions to Contextual Problems   33
Cognitive-Behavioral Therapy   39
Situations and Case Examples in Which Individual Child Therapy Is
    Often Necessary   41
Summary   59
References   59

Chapter 3 **The Treatment of Parent-Child Difficulties**   62

Parental Control   64
Parental Affect   76
Parental Modeling   88
References   90

Chapter 4 **Changing Affective, Sexual, and Instrumental
Aspects of Marital Relations**   93

Philosophy of Marriage   94
Affective Relations   98
Sexual Relations   114
Instrumental Relations   117

Some Guidelines for Handling Special Problems   121
References   129

Chapter 5   **The Treatment of Difficulties in Peer Relations**   **131**

The Development of Children's Peer Relations   132
Assessment Strategies   133
Child Characteristics as Correlates of Peer Acceptance   137
Family-Peer Linkages   150
References   163

Chapter 6   **The School System and the Family-School Mesosystem**   **169**

Social Functioning   170
Cognitive Development   175
The Family-School Mesosystem   187
References   192

Chapter 7   **Issues and Interventions with Nonnuclear Families**   **194**

The Single-Parent Family   195
The Stepfamily   205
The Surrogate-Parent Family   212
References   216

Chapter 8   **Treatment of Delinquent Behavior**   **219**

Defining the Problem   219
Seriousness of the Problem   220
Correlates of Delinquent Behavior   221
Multidimensional Causal Models of Delinquent Behavior   222
Overview of Treatment Studies   224
Overview of Specific Intervention Strategies   231
References   242

Chapter 9   **Adolescent Chemical Dependency**   **246**
   Milton Trapold

Definitions   246
Assumptions About Chemical Dependency   248
Epidemiology   251
Symptomatology   252
Diagnosis   256
Intervention   261
Goals in Chemical Dependency Treatment   264
The Elements of a Good Treatment Program   270
Alternatives to Inpatient Treatment   271

References   275
Addendum   276

Chapter 10   **Understanding Insulin-Dependent Diabetes Mellitus
(IDDM) and Treating Children with IDDM and Their Families   278**
        Cindy L. Hanson

The Nature of IDDM   278
Overview of Therapeutic Process and Protocol   289
Multisystemic Correlates of Health and Their Implications for
        Treatment   291
References   318

Chapter 11   **Interventions with Incestuous Families   324**
        Pamela C. Alexander

Characteristics of Incestuous Families   325
Treatment   331
Conclusion   342
References   343

Name Index   345
Subject Index   353

CHAPTER 1

An Introduction to
the Multisystemic Approach

Reviewers of family therapy outcome research have reported that, in general, the results are respectable but not outstanding. For example, Hazelrigg, Cooper, and Borduin (1987) conducted a meta-analysis of 20 family therapy outcome studies and concluded that pragmatic family therapy had positive effects on family interactions and behavior ratings when compared with both no-treatment and alternative treatment controls. Similarly, Gurman and his colleagues (Gurman & Kniskern,1978a, 1978b, 1981; Gurman, Kniskern, & Pinsof, 1986) concluded that family therapy should be the treatment of choice for problems such as anorexia, juvenile delinquency, and sexual dysfunctions. Masten (1979), on the other hand, reported that there was little evidence to recommend family therapy as the treatment of choice for any childhood problems. She did suggest, however, that family therapy showed promise as a treatment for certain medical symptoms in psychosomatic illnesses. In a similar vein, Wells and Dezen (1978) concluded that family therapy is a legitimate treatment, despite the fact that the results of outcome studies have been generally disappointing.

A central thesis of this volume is that the generally mediocre results of family therapy outcome studies are due to certain limitations of most family therapy models. Although we believe that systems conceptualizations of behavior problems have significant advantages over traditional conceptualizations, we propose that family therapists have taken an unnecessarily narrow view of behavior problems and an overly restrictive approach to behavior change. The main limitations of most family therapy models are that: (1) they fail to appreciate the importance of key variables that pertain to the individual family members and to extrafamilial systems; (2) they fail to consider important individual developmental issues that should influence the therapist's understanding of problems and choice of intervention strategies; and (3) they rarely utilize proven intervention strategies that are derived from other treatment paradigms.

These general limitations are addressed by the multisystemic approach to the treatment of psychosocial problems. The multisystemic treatment model, labeled the "family-ecological systems approach" in some earlier writings (e.g., Henggeler, 1982), has been developed by Henggeler and a core group of family researchers and therapists during the past 12 years. These individuals have evaluated key assumptions of the approach, as well as its therapeutic efficacy with "difficult to treat" client populations.

The strengths of the multisystemic model are supported by three controlled outcome studies. Although we have applied the model to a wide range of cases in our private clinical work, each of the outcome studies focused on problems and client populations that are typically regarded as difficult to treat. We believe, therefore, that the results of these studies provide a conservative estimate of the efficacy of the multisystemic approach. Moreover, these studies meet almost all of the methodological criteria that Gurman and Kniskern (1978a) have established for evaluating the quality of outcome research (e.g., multiple dependent measures at multiple levels of systems, appropriate control groups). Similarly, the broad-based and multifaceted nature of the multisystemic approach is consistent with Kazdin's (1987) recommendation that researchers should broaden the scope of their interventions to address multiple domains that are pertinent to the youth's dysfunction.

Henggeler, Rodick, Borduin, Hanson, Watson, and Urey (1986) assessed the efficacy of the multisystemic approach with inner-city, delinquent adolescents who were predominantly male, lower class, Black, repeat offenders, and whose fathers were absent. Subjects included 57 juvenile offenders who received the multisystemic treatment, and 22 who received an alternative community-based treatment. The vast majority of these offenders had been arrested for relatively serious offenses such as assault or burglary. In addition, 44 normal adolescents served as developmental controls. The average length of multisystemic therapy was 20 hours per case, and the multisystemic therapists were doctoral students in clinical psychology. Subjects in the alternative treatment condition received an average of 24 hours of therapy, and their therapists were practicing professionals.

Research assistants conducted standardized pretreatment and posttreatment assessments of the adolescents and their parents. Personality inventories, behavior ratings, and self-report and observational measures of family relations were included to evaluate changes at several systemic levels (i.e., individual, parent-child, marital, peer). Multivariate statistical analyses revealed that the adolescents who received multisystemic treatment evidenced significant decreases in conduct problems, anxious-withdrawn behaviors, immaturity, and association with delinquent peers. The mother-adolescent and marital relations in these families grew significantly warmer, and the adolescent became increasingly involved in family interaction following treatment. In contrast, the adolescents who received the alternative treatment evidenced no positive change and, in fact, showed deterioration in family affective relations. The normal families manifested relationship changes that were consistent with those identified by investigators of normal adolescent development. Thus, the results of this first outcome study suggest that multisystemic therapy shows promise as a treatment of adolescent problems that have been traditionally considered as quite resistant to intervention (e.g., Henggeler, 1989; Romig, 1978).

In the second outcome study (Brunk, Henggeler, & Whelan, 1987), we contrasted the efficacy of the multisystemic approach to that of group parent training in the treatment of families that were referred for child abuse or child neglect. The theoretical foundations of these treatments are consistent with the two primary models of child maltreatment that have emerged in the literature: the ecological model (Belsky, 1980) and the social-situational model (Parke & Collmer, 1975).

Subjects in this study included 18 abusive families and 15 neglectful families who were randomly assigned to one of the two treatment programs. For both groups, therapy sessions lasted for 1.5 hours and were conducted once per week for eight weeks.

Multisystemic therapy was conducted by therapists trained in the multisystemic approach, and group parent training was conducted by therapists who were proponents of the social-learning approach. Pretreatment and posttreatment assessments evaluated functioning in three systems related to child maltreatment: individual, family, and community/social. Observational and standardized self-report measures were used to assess change from several perspectives.

Multivariate statistical analyses revealed that both parent training and multisystemic treatment were effective in improving the parents' emotional state, reducing stress, and decreasing the severity of identified problems. Multisystemic therapy, however, was more effective than parent training at restructuring parent-child relations. Neglectful families who received multisystemic therapy showed increased cohesion, and sequential analyses of observational measures revealed that multisystemic therapy was more successful at improving parental effectiveness, decreasing child passive noncompliance, and decreasing parental unresponsiveness. Importantly, these same types of parent-child interactions have been identified as dysfunctional characteristics of abusive families and neglectful families (e.g., Bousha & Twentyman, 1984). Thus, multisystemic therapy was most effective at changing the types of parent-child interactions that have been identified as most problematic in abusive families and neglectful families.

The third outcome study replicates and extends the findings of Henggeler et al. (1986). Borduin, Blaske, Mann, Treloar, Henggeler, and Fucci (1990) randomly assigned the families of 210 juvenile offenders to either multisystemic treatment or individual counseling that focused on personal, family, and school-related issues. Families in the multisystemic group received an average of 23 hours of therapy that was provided by doctoral students in clinical psychology. Families in the individual therapy group received an average of 28 hours of treatment provided by experienced masters level therapists. The juvenile offenders had an average of 4.2 arrests, indicating that, in general, they were chronic offenders. This is important because considerable evidence suggests that the antisocial behavior of chronic offenders is highly stable over time and is extremely resistant to change (Loeber, 1982).

We conducted pretreatment, posttreatment, and follow-up treatment assessments of the individual functioning of family members, family relations, peer relations, and school performance. Standardized instruments were used to assess the perspectives of family members and teachers, and observational measures of family interactions were obtained. Results at posttreatment assessment showed that, relative to the adolescents who received individual therapy, the adolescents in the multisystemic treatment group evidenced improved relations with peers, fewer behavior problems, more cohesive and adaptable family relations, and more positive mother-adolescent communication. In addition, multisystemic therapy was effective at reducing long-term rates of both self-reported and officially recorded delinquent behavior.

In summary, these three outcome studies show that the multisystemic treatment approach is a promising model for improving the relations of dysfunctional families and for decreasing the behavior problems of juvenile offenders. In addition to this empirical research, we have used the multisystemic model in our private clinical work and have supervised the therapy of hundreds of cases during the past decade. Through this experience, we have found that the multisystemic model provides the flexibility to intervene effectively with a wide range of problems, including depression, anxiety, and marital difficulties. Moreover, the approach seems to be accepted enthusiastically by trainees who possess the ability to master its complexity.

Succeeding chapters are devoted to a delineation of the approach and of the processes that we believe account for the efficacy of the multisystemic therapy. For the remainder of this chapter, however, we discuss four important aspects of the multisystemic model: First, we differentiate this model from other family system models. Second, we describe the theoretical underpinnings of the multisystemic model (i.e., the major tenets of systems theory). Third, we briefly review the epistemology debate in the field of family therapy and note where the multisystemic model fits within the "pragmatic versus aesthetic" context. Finally, we provide an overview of clinical aspects of the multisystemic appoach.

DISTINGUISHING FEATURES OF THE MULTISYSTEMIC MODEL

The multisystemic model was developed in response to three major weaknesses of existing family therapy approaches. The first and most important limitation is that these approaches do not sufficiently consider the role of individual characteristics and extrafamilial systems in the development and maintenance of behavior problems. Although some family theorists do consider the role of individual characteristics (Bogdan, 1984; L'Abate, 1985), and others have noted the importance of extrafamilial variables (Auerswald, 1968, 1987; Speck & Attneave, 1973), the field of family therapy as a whole has focused almost exclusively on a family system or subsystem level of analysis.

The second limitation is that family therapists typically ignore child development research findings that have important implications for understanding and changing behavior. Patricia Minuchin (1985) has argued that developmental psychology would greatly benefit from an increased understanding and utilization of the principles of systems theory. The reverse is also true: The field of family therapy would benefit from an increased awareness of child development conceptualizations and research findings.

The third limitation is the general lack of familiarity that family therapists have with nonsystemic treatment approaches. Family therapists tend to act as if any treatment derived from a reductionistic paradigm is inherently "bad." Although these approaches are often simplistic and linear, they can be used quite effectively within a systemic conceptual framework. For example, we believe that a good systems therapist can use the social learning treatment strategies developed by Gerald Patterson (1980) even more effectively than therapists directly trained in his model. Patterson's focus on the parent-child dyad, to the relative exclusion of other family subsystems, clearly limits the success of his otherwise well-conceived intervention strategies. We should note, however, that Patterson's recent work seems to be moving toward a systems paradigm (Patterson, 1986).

Multiple Interrelated Systems

Although the family is certainly the most influential system for the child, he or she directly interacts with, affects, and is affected by several other systems (see Bronfenbrenner, 1979, 1986). At the very least, these other systems include the peer group, school, and neighborhood. In addition, individuals are inherently predisposed to behave in certain ways. Children possess characteristics, such as sociability and intelligence, that have a genetic component and that will influence their transactions with family, peers, and workmates for their entire lives.

Other systems indirectly affect the child. For example, the parents' employment context and social support network can influence the quality of parent-child relations. The interaction of these different systems can also contribute to behavior problems. Different childrearing strategies, for example, are associated with different degrees of susceptibility to negative peer influences. Therefore, in order to fully understand children's behavior, it is necessary to consider the multiple, interrelated systems to which children belong.

To illustrate our point concerning the multisystemic nature of behavior, we outline below some of the key aspects of various systems that have been largely neglected by family therapy theorists.

Individual characteristics.   Genetically influenced qualities and learned response sets predispose individuals to engage in certain types of transactions. Physical characteristics, cognitive abilities, emotionality, and sociability have strong genetic components and interact with different systems in ways that relate to behavior (Goldsmith, 1983; Scarr & McCartney, 1983). For example, physically attractive people are initially perceived by others to possess more desirable personality and intellectual attributes, and, as a result, are responded to more favorably. Athletic skill is related to both self-concept and the quality of peer relations among children. Similarly, a child's cognitive ability strongly predicts academic performance and educational achievement, both of which, in turn, predict a myriad of future socioeconomic variables. Special cognitive problems, such as learning disability, relate to family and peer difficulties. Behavior problems are also associated with individual social skill deficits. Researchers have suggested, for example, that delinquent behavior is due, in part, to the adolescent's inability to respond appropriately in certain problem situations (Freedman, Rosenthal, Donahoe, Schlundt, & McFall, 1978).

As discussed in Chapter 2, individual characteristics of children can substantially mediate family influences on behavior. We are not suggesting that family variables are less important, but that certain inherent characteristics of individuals must often be considered in order to fully understand the systemic context of a behavior problem and to develop optimal interventions. This point has been discussed by L'Abate (1985), who has emphasized the important function of individual emotions and cognitions in family relations. Moreover, he recommended that investigators in the fields of family psychology and family therapy should study behavior at several levels of analysis, and not exclusively at a system level, as proposed by the new epistemologists. L'Abate believes that an excessive emphasis at any one level, or a commitment to any one "truth," will impede the progress of family science and therapy.

Family.   All models of family therapy are based on the premise that behavior problems are closely associated with the transactions among family members and the interrelations of family subsystems. Family systems theorists and researchers have provided extensive examination of these associations and have developed many strategies that are useful in the amelioration of behavior problems.

Although one must always be cognizant of the recursive nature of behavior, it seems that there are certain styles of childrearing that promote prosocial behavior, independence, and responsibility (Maccoby & Martin, 1983), and other styles that are related to childhood immaturity, behavior problems, and psychosocial difficulties. In the treatment of problematic parent-child relations, we use strategies that respect the parent as an authority, yet provide the child with the nurturance and freedom needed for successful development and emancipation (see Chapter 3).

Similarly, certain styles of marital interaction promote intimacy, whereas other styles seem to evoke hostility and conflict (Gray-Little & Burks, 1983). In the treatment of marital problems, interventions are aimed at enhancing positive reciprocity and providing the couple with the means to resolve conflicts. We teach the couple to appreciate each other's perspectives and to develop an interaction style that involves cooperation rather than competition (see Chapter 4).

Peers.   As children mature, peer influences become increasingly important. The peer group promotes socialization and influences children's social skills, emotional security, and understanding of social structure (Hartup, 1983). In addition, children's friendships are a learning ground for the development of equalitarian sharing, intimacy, and sensitivity in mutual decision making.

In our research and clinical work, we have found that adolescent behavior problems are sometimes related more strongly to dysfunctional peer relations than to family interactions. This is especially true for problems such as delinquency, drug use, and sexual behavior (Panella, Cooper, & Henggeler, 1982). In such instances, therapeutic interventions must involve the peer group either directly or indirectly. The parameters and nature of peer group interventions are discussed in Chapter 5.

Extrafamilial systems.   Dell (1984) has noted that the behaviors of systems such as the family should also be understood in terms of the behaviors of other systems of which they are a part. Although he draws conclusions with which we do not fully concur, we agree with his suggestion that, with certain exceptions, the larger systemic context has been largely ignored by family therapists.

School is one of the most important extrafamilial systems for children. Within the school context, children form relations with peers and adults and engage in extensive academic training and vocational planning. To a large extent, the success of these school-based transactions sets the tone for future peer relations and socioeconomic opportunities. We believe that every child should achieve up to his or her capabilities and learn to establish positive friendship networks and good relations with adults. Therefore, we have developed sets of intervention strategies for use with the child, family, and school to promote academic and social gains (see e.g., Rodick & Henggeler, 1980). As discussed in Chapter 6, many additional intervention strategies developed by other researchers can be used to enhance the child's gains within the school context.

The parents' primary extrafamilial systems include their places of employment, friends, extended families, and other social support networks. Researchers have observed that these extrafamilial systems are often related to family functioning. For example, the parent's job satisfaction has a direct bearing on parent-child relations (Henggeler & Borduin, 1981). Likewise, as discussed in Chapter 7, the availability of supportive adults such as friends and grandparents is an important factor in the single parent's ability to deal effectively with his or her children.

Many families are also involved with large social service, legal, or medical systems. Families with problems of child abuse and neglect, for example, are typically in contact with the local department of human services; the families of chronically ill or physically handicapped children spend considerable time involved with the medical system. Each of these systems possesses characteristics that influence the behavior of family members and transactions within the family system. Sometimes these characteristics can be used by the therapist to promote therapeutic gains; other times they can attenuate progress. In either case, however, the influences of these systems must be taken into account when designing and implementing treatment plans. In Chapters 10 and 11 the relevance of these systems and their place in treating chronic illness and sexual abuse are discussed.

Interrelations among systems.   Behavior problems are also associated with the interactions between these various systems. For children, problems commonly emerge between parents and school personnel. Sometimes, children will attempt to play one system against the other in an effort to avoid responsibility for misbehavior. The child may blame a suspension from school on a persecutory teacher, and the parent may storm to the school to defend his or her offspring. When the quality of the transactions between systems is contributing to a problem, the therapist must teach the family either to open intersystem communication channels and gain collaboration or to manipulate the system more effectively. Techniques that can be used to facilitate these processes are presented in Chapter 6.

The transactions among systems can also be governed by systemic principles. According to Hartup (1983), considerable research evidence shows that family relations and peer relations interact synergistically. Social skills are not simply transferred from one context to the other. Rather, an integrative coherence mediates the child's adaptation across these systems. For example, Henggeler, Edwards, Cohen, and Summerville (1990) found that the quality of perceived family relations and observed family interaction predicted increased child popularity during the school year.

The multidimensional and systemic nature of behavior has important implications for conceptualizing many different child and adolescent behavior problems. The primary implication is that therapists should not assume, *a priori,* that any one system is the most appropriate target for intervention. This contention is supported by the findings of several research groups concerned about the criminal activity of adolescents (e.g., Elliott, Huizinga, & Ageton, 1985; Hanson, Henggeler, Haefele, & Rodick, 1984; Patterson, 1986). These researchers have found that individual adolescent characteristics, parent-child relationship variables, peer factors, and school performance each contribute directly or indirectly to delinquent behavior. Such findings suggest that an exclusive focus on dysfunctional family relations, as advocated by many family therapists, might limit the efficacy of treatment of delinquent behavior. Effective treatment might need to focus on one or on some combination of these four systems.

Investigators have also demonstrated the importance of conceptualizing other types of behavior problems within a multisystemic framework. Brook, Whiteman, and Gordon (1983), for example, found that adolescent drug use is related to an interplay of personality attributes, family relations, and peer relations. Similarly, as frequently noted in the journal *Family Systems Medicine*, physical health is strongly linked to individuals' relations with family members and extrafamilial systems. For example, in a review of the correlates of glycemic control (Hanson & Henggeler, 1984) and in a preliminary causal model of the association between psychosocial variables and glycemic control (Hanson, Henggeler, & Burghen, 1987), we concluded that the metabolic control of adolescents with insulin-dependent diabetes was related to a variety of biological, psychological, health care behavior, familial, extrafamilial, and health care system variables (see Chapter 10).

Within the field of family therapy, several theorists have taken ecological perspectives regarding behavior change. As noted by Nichols (1984), Bowenian therapists and family network therapists often consider the role of individuals outside of the family system. Psychoanalytic, group-oriented, behavioral, and communication family therapists almost never consider extrafamilial variables. Structural and strategic therapists, as exemplified by Minuchin and Haley, respectively, give only brief mention to the larger context of families.

Auerswald's (1968) ecological approach and Aponte's (1976, 1986) eco-structural approach have emphasized the importance of collaboration among professionals who are involved with the same family. Both theorists dealt with the problems of impoverished families who were often in contact with several social service agencies at the same time. The main similarity between these ecological approaches and our multisystemic approach is that both emphasize the role of extrafamilial systems in the development and maintenance of behavioral problems. As such, both approaches include extrafamilial systems in their intervention schemes. As presented throughout this volume, however, the approaches differ substantially in defining the goals of treatment and in formulating actual intervention strategies.

The multisystemic approach presented in this book differs in a similar way with the family network therapy developed by Speck and Attneave (1973). Although both perspectives emphasize the importance of extrafamilial relations in the maintenance and resolution of behavior problems, the two approaches have very different treatment goals and intervention strategies. Speck and Attneave bring large numbers of family members, friends, neighbors, and significant others together in an attempt to open communication channels and to stimulate the potential of the network to resolve problems. The therapists use growth-oriented, group therapy techniques such as family songs, the empty chair, and family sculpting to achieve their goals. Our multisystemic approach is quite different, as discussed in subsequent chapters.

In summary, behavior problems are associated with many individual characteristics and extrafamilial variables, as well as with family transactions. To date, family therapists have generally devoted little attention to these characteristics and larger system variables. In many cases, however, we have found that such factors are instrumental in problem formulation and in evoking behavior change.

Developmental Variables and Research Findings

The second general distinction between multisystemic therapy and most other family therapy approaches pertains to the consideration of developmental variables. Family therapists have provided detailed descriptions of developmental processes in family systems (see e.g., Carter & McGoldrick, 1980). For example, they have addressed the compromises that newlyweds must make to maintain mutual satisfaction, the systemic changes that follow the birth of the first child and subsequent children, and the parental adjustments that follow adolescent emancipation and the return to a two-person family system. For many family therapists, understanding the developmental issues that are confronted at each of these stages is essential when planning treatment interventions for a given family. However, family therapists have largely ignored developmental processes in individuals. It is our contention that such processes can have significant implications for understanding and changing behavior.

The child's cognitive developmental abilities have a profound effect on behavior. Of particular importance in the area of cognitive development is the child's social perspective-taking ability (Henggeler & Cohen, 1984). "Social perspective-taking" refers to the ability to infer the thoughts and feelings of others. During the *preoperational* stage (approximately ages 2 to 7 years), the child is egocentric in the sense that he or she does not understand that the perspective of another person may differ from his or her immediate viewpoint. With the development of concrete *operational structures* (approximately 7 to 11 years of age), the child can accurately infer the thoughts and feelings of others. However, because the child fully understands only what is concretely present, the various possibilities and complexities of a situation are not appreciated.

With the attainment of adolescence and formal operational thought, the child begins to comprehend the functioning of distant systems and is able to explore a wide range of hypothetical solutions to problems. As suggested by the following examples, these Piagetian conceptions of cognitive growth have important implications for strategies of behavior change.

In working with a behavior problem child, it is not uncommon to find that the child has effectively alienated his or her classroom teacher. An appreciation of the child's level of social perspective-taking skill can help the therapist in deciding which school-related interventions have a reasonable chance of success, and which are probably doomed to fail. The child in the formal operational stage is capable of understanding the social hierarchy of the school system, the importance of maintaining that hierarchy, and the long-term disadvantages of antagonizing influential members of that hierarchy. Moreover, the formal operational adolescent can appreciate the impact that his or her classroom disruptions have on the feelings and professional relations of the teacher. Similarly, the adolescent is capable of comprehending and predicting the teacher's response to socially desirable behaviors. If motivated, the formal operational adolescent can learn how to "play the game" in order to create positive expectancies and eliminate negative ones. For example, the formal operational adolescent can use friendly greetings or the early completion of homework assignments to alter the adolescent-teacher relationship system.

The concrete operational child, on the other hand, is less capable of understanding and appreciating the teacher's motivations and the outside pressures that the teacher might be under. Although the concrete operational child is capable of learning the same interpersonal behaviors as the formal operational child, his or her use of these behaviors is less flexible and responsive. Consequently, teaching the child to alter the teacher's expectancies is more difficult than in the case of the formal operational adolescent. Finally, the preoperational child would not significantly benefit from knowing the teacher's perspective because such a child has less ability to assume the perspective of others. Thus, the therapist would be wise to consider another avenue for improving teacher-student relations.

The child's level of cognitive development is also an important consideration when intervening within the family system. For example, children whose parents have divorced within the past two years tend to present relatively high rates of conduct problems and are often jealous of the parents' dating partners. Treatment of these problems should incorporate intervention strategies that are consistent with the child's level of cognitive development. The preoperational child tends to be egocentric and has concerns that focus on material losses and decreased attention from the absent parent. In addition, because the preoperational child does not fully appreciate the meaning of divorce, he or she is often fearful that the custodial parent might also leave. Interventions for such conduct problems may appropriately include the setting of firm and consistent limits, in conjunction with parental reassurance and affection. Although some degree of limit-setting may also be appropriate for concrete operational and formal operational children who have behavior problems, these children are capable of understanding how their misbehavior aggravates an already difficult situation for the parent. Formal operational adolescents are especially able to appreciate their parent's need for support and involvement with other adults. The promotion of such understanding by the therapist often helps to change the interactions within the family system.

Several other aspects of child development are important to consider when treating families. Clearly, the therapist must use language that is consistent with the child's stage of receptive and expressive language development. Less apparent is the value of understanding the processes related to moral development, the development of self-control, and the development of altruism. Appreciation of the parameters of these processes can provide the therapist with the ability to see beyond the presenting problems and to identify styles of family interaction that may lead to deficits in sociocognitive development. For example, considerable developmental evidence shows that excessively harsh and authoritarian discipline strategies can contribute to negative child outcomes such as low self-esteem and poor internalization of moral values. Although such discipline strategies may not be directly related to the problems presented by the family to the therapist, we believe that these processes might nevertheless be considered appropriate targets for intervention. Throughout this book, we attempt to identify important issues that pertain to individual development and that relate to treatment efficacy.

"Nonsystemic" Therapeutic Interventions

The third distinctive aspect of multisystemic therapy is its use of "nonsystemic" interventions. Several family therapists have suggested that the field is long on therapeutic techniques and short on the validation of these techniques. Although there is some truth to this contention, family therapists have developed intervention strategies that are often quite effective at changing problematic sequences of behavior. The process of reframing (Watzlawick, Weakland, & Fisch, 1974), for example, is an excellent cognitive strategy that can set the stage for behavior change by altering the dysfunctional ways that family members may view their relations. Similarly, the use of paradox and symptom prescription can counteract some types of client resistance and lead to problem resolution. As discussed previously, however, the family therapy outcome literature suggests that many families do not benefit from traditional family therapy intervention strategies.

One of our main points in this volume is that it would be beneficial if family therapists also used certain nonsystemic intervention strategies; specifically, strategies that are of proven utility, but that have been derived from linear paradigms and are, therefore, nonsystemic. After all, family therapy has not cornered the market on the development of effective change techniques. Individual child therapy, for example, can alter the family system in numerous ways, as described by Montalvo and Haley (1973). They suggested that it is impossible for a therapeutic intervention to be truly nonsystemic. For example, a therapist may intend an intervention to focus solely on a child's intrapsychic processes, but the logistics and pragmatics of the therapeutic context are linked invariably to the child's ecology.

In this book, we take Montalvo and Haley's idea one step further and propose that certain nonsystemic strategies can significantly enhance a family therapist's ability to effect systemic change. Moreover, in light of the importance of extrafamilial systems and individual characteristics within the family-ecological framework, we propose that some cases of childhood problems do not reflect family dysfunction, and nonsystemic interventions can often be very helpful in treating such problems. For example, the temper tantrums of a first-born, 6-year-old girl would continue for almost an hour because the parents eventually acquiesced to whatever the child wanted. The parents had very permissive childrearing attitudes and did not know how to set appropriate, firm, and consistent limits for their daughter's behavior. In addition, even though the parents were very satisfied with their marriage, their daughter's tantrums were beginning to have a disruptive influence. The system changed immediately when the parents were taught child behavior management techniques (see Mash & Barkley, 1989, for a review of the child behavior therapy literature). The presenting problem was clearly circular: the girl's continued tantrums led to the eventual acquiescence of the parents, and their response promoted the girl's future tantrums. The intervention, however, had a clear linear component: the parents were taught to handle the tantrums differently. Although there were certainly recursive components in the therapist-parents interactions and in the parents' interventions with their daughter, the behavior therapy techniques were quite effective at ameliorating the problem.

Although behavior therapists tend to take narrow and linear views of behavior, they have developed sets of interventions that are extremely efficient for certain problems under certain circumstances. In the context of serious marital problems, interventions that were limited to these techniques would not be sufficient. In the hands of a systems therapist, however, behavior techniques such as parent training can serve a useful adjunctive role and are sometimes the only necessary intervention.

Cognitive behavior therapy is another nonsystemic intervention strategy that can serve a useful adjunctive role. During the past decade, researchers have developed strategies for treating child behavior problems that are directed toward children's internal cognitions (Meyers & Craighead, 1984). These cognitive behavior therapy techniques are used to teach children greater self-control, reflectivity, and problem-solving skills in academic and interpersonal contexts. Children learn to slow down, think, and plan behavioral alternatives before acting. These cognitive behavioral interventions have been repeatedly shown to be effective in helping to ameliorate problems such as learning disabilities and aggressive behavior.

There are several reasons why cognitive behavior therapy can be an effective intervention technique. First, individuals do possess certain traits that can contribute to behavior problems. Second, by changing the expectations and behavior of one member of the system, it is possible to change the expectations and behavior of other members. Third, expectations of change are especially likely when family and teachers know that the child is actively engaged in an attempt to remedy some of his or her problems. Although cognitive behavioral interventions address a limited segment of the child's ecology, they can be a valuable therapeutic tool when used in conjunction with systemic strategies (Henggeler & Cohen, 1984). In fact, many behavior therapists are beginning to recognize the systemic nature of behavior problems.

THE THEORETICAL CONTEXT OF THE MULTISYSTEMIC APPROACH

The theoretical foundation of the multisystemic model reflects a major paradigmatic shift that is occurring in the scientific community. This shift is from an analytic and reductionistic epistemology to one that is systemic and wholistic (deRosnay, 1979; Miller, 1978). Within the field of developmental psychology, P. Minuchin (1985) and Valsiner and Benigni (1986) have noted that researchers are beginning to move toward a systems paradigm. Similarly, Schwartz (1982) has proposed that the testing of the systemic model is the greatest challenge that faces the field of behavioral medicine. Within the behavioral sciences, however, the earliest proponents of this paradigmatic shift were the family therapists. As Hoffman (1981) has noted, family therapy is not simply a new therapeutic technique but is based on new assumptions about behavior and relationships. Many of these assumptions were developed in the 1950s by Gregory Bateson's schizophrenia research group that included individuals such as Jay Haley, Don Jackson, and John Weakland.

To discuss these new assumptions about human behavior, it is necessary to view them within the context of the "old" assumptions and to describe how they reflect different ways of viewing the world. In a summary of the four main epistemologies proposed by Pepper (1942), Schwartz (1982) has provided an excellent contrast of the old assumptions (characterized by formistic and mechanistic thinking) with the new assumptions (characterized by contextual and organistic thinking); this latter kind of thinking is the foundation of systems theory and of the multisystemic model.

Formistic thinking is binary in that things are presumed to fit into one category and not another (e.g., health vs. illness). Similarly, mechanistic thinking emphasizes single causes and single effects. Formistic and mechanistic thinking are complementary and incorporate the linear view that events have specific causes or are the result of some specific chain of causes. An example of such thinking in child clinical psychology is the idea that child behavior problems are caused by inoptimal parental discipline strategies. Research from this perspective is necessarily linear, reductionistic, and emphasizes the delineation of variables that influence the targeted behavior. From a formistic/reductionistic perspective, for example, research issues in the area of parenting might address questions such as: What types of discipline techniques are most effective? How should rewards and punishments be timed for the best results?

Contextual and organistic (systems) thinking are also complementary. Within a contextual framework, a given behavior is viewed as having multiple causes, and the significance of the behavior depends on the context of both the behavior and the observer of the behavior. Organistic thinking emphasizes wholeness, dynamic interactions of elements, and the system's transactions with its ecology. Different combinations of causes can lead to distinctly new outcomes. An organistic (systems) thinker would not only consider how parental discipline strategies affect child behavior, but also how the behavior of the child shapes and guides the behavior of the parents, and what function any misbehavior might serve in the environment. An organistic (systems) thinker might also ask how behavior within the parent-child dyad is associated with the parents' spousal relations, with the child's peer interactions, and with the extrafamilial relations of individual family members. Therefore, the organistic or systemic approach emphasizes the consideration of multiple, interrelated factors from multiple levels in the ecology.

Because systemic conceptualizations of behavior are fundamental aspects of the multisystemic model, it is important to review briefly the basic principles of general systems theory (Bertalanffy, 1968; Sutherland, 1973).

THE BASIC PRINCIPLES OF SYSTEMS THEORY

Patricia Minuchin (1985) has provided an excellent overview of the central principles of systems theory. Her outline is used as the starting point for the discussion of each principle.

1. **"Any system is an organized whole, and elements within the system are necessarily interdependent."**   The concept of organization means that the elements within the system have some type of consistent and predictable relationship with each other (Goldenberg & Goldenberg, 1985). In addition, the system has properties that cannot be discerned from the qualities of its individual elements. Just as water has properties that are very different from the qualities of its individual components, hydrogen and oxygen, the whole, the system, is more than the sum of its component parts.

An example of a living system is a cell. The cell is composed of several elements, including a nucleus, cytoplasm, and a semipermeable membrane. These elements are interdependent and have a consistent relationship with each other. Moreover, the system that comprises these elements is alive: it actively exchanges energy with the environment and it reproduces. These systemic properties are qualitatively greater than one would suppose by examining each of the elements in isolation.

This first principle of systems theory suggests that individual behavior can be understood only within the interpersonal context of the behavior. The immature temper tantrums of a 10-year-old boy make sense when it is learned that they are a very effective way of obtaining candy bars when his parents take him to the supermarket. Likewise, a wife's depression or aggressive outbursts are understandable behaviors within the context of a marriage in which her husband has placed family interests behind work, friends, sports, and television.

2. "Patterns in a system are circular rather than linear." Most theoretical approaches view behavior as the end product of one or more forces. From a psychoanalytic perspective, behavior is a direct function of the interplay between intrapsychic structures and basic psychosexual conflicts. Learning theorists view behavior as a predictable outcome of previous learning experiences that include exposure to certain reinforcement contingencies and behavioral models. Cognitive theorists emphasize the capacity of individuals to organize their environment and to develop behavioral strategies based on their hypotheses about how the world works. In each of these models, behavior is explained by an analysis of the causative forces in the internal or external environment.

Circular notions of causality emphasize the "fit" of the behavior into larger chains or sequences of interaction. As P. Minuchin (1985) noted, in systems theory, behaviors are viewed as interdependent components of a spiral of recursive feedback loops. The behavior of person A influences the behavior of person B, which in turn influences the behavior of person A, and so forth. One component of the spiral does not take priority over another component. Such a view argues against blaming problems on any one individual in the system.

Linear thinking is very prevalent in our society, especially in regard to emotionally charged issues, such as child abuse. Because child abuse is commonly viewed as a linear problem, caused by a disturbed parent, it can serve as a good example of circular processes. Researchers have shown that children who are physically abused tend to possess characteristics that elicit aversive responses from others. Compared to nonabused children, these children tend to be less mature and less socially and intellectually competent, and they generally present more behavior problems to their caretakers. Within certain contexts, such child behaviors can contribute to a cycle of abuse. This point is exemplified by a clinical case.

Mrs. Smith was a foster parent who was participating in a program for difficult-to-place foster children. She was an extremely successful single parent whose own children were away at college despite the financial poverty that characterized their neighborhood. Moreover, the neighborhood children regarded Mrs. Smith with great affection and spent many hours playing at her home. Her foster child, James, had experienced considerable abuse and neglect from his chemically dependent mother. One day, while watching Saturday morning wrestling or television, James "accidentally" broke a glass ashtray. Following the recommendations of the behavioral parent training that she had received, Mrs. Smith had James clean up the ashtray and sent him to his room for 15 minutes. Thirty minutes later, James accidently knocked over and broke a table lamp. This time, Mrs. Smith sent James to his room for 45 minutes. Shortly thereafter, James went into Mrs. Smith's bedroom and started to jump up and down on the bed while punching holes in the ceiling with a broom handle. Mrs. Smith ran into the room and proceeded to physically assault James.

We are not saying that the physical abuse of a child is ever justified. Our point is that to understand behavioral events, it is necessary to view them within their cycle or spiral. In the above case, did Mrs. Smith abuse James or did James abuse Mrs. Smith? On a theoretical level, it is impossible to lay blame on one person or another. On a practical level, however, adults must assume much greater responsibility than children. Nevertheless, it is still essential for the therapist to appreciate the systemic aspects of the case.

Such appreciation might require that interventions extend beyond the abusive parent's behavior to include problem child behavior and extrafamilial difficulties, such as unemployment and social isolation, that place stress on the family.

3. "Systems have homeostatic features that maintain the stability of their patterns." The interactions in any given family system are maintained within a range of functioning that is balanced or in equilibrium. When behavior deviates from this range, feedback serves to restore behavior to this central tendency. For example, most families have a range of acceptable child behavior. When a child transgresses this behavioral range, perhaps by becoming too aggressive, corrective feedback is given to restore acceptable behavior. A sibling might say, "If you don't stop hitting me, I'm going to tell Daddy." The parent might give the child a stern look or use a more intrusive discipline technique. Another family member might try to restore equilibrium by making the child laugh.

The behavioral equilibrium in a family system is dynamic rather than static. As external events require adaptations and as the system grows, the range of expected behavior changes. Concomitantly, the corrective feedback loops are modified. For example, parents may offer corrective feedback to their daughter for certain behaviors during high school years, but they may later tolerate these same behaviors when the daughter is away at college. Likewise, a wife may begin to closely monitor her husband's activities when she suspects that he is having an affair, but she may later detach emotionally from her husband when she decides to have her own extramarital relationship. Often, this change in the wife's behavior will prompt very different behavior from the husband in a process that restores the former equilibrium.

Richard Q. Bell, one of the first developmentalists to view behavioral interactions in circular terms, has developed the only model of dyadic homeostasis that is readily subject to empirical evaluation. Bell (1977) proposed that transactions between dyad members serve to maintain the two-person system in equilibrium and that each member has upper and lower limits regarding the intensity, frequency, and situational appropriateness of the other's behavior. When the upper limit of one member is reached, he or she exerts upper-limit controls (e.g., discipline) to reduce the other's excessive behavior and to restore equilibrium. When a member's lower limit is reached, he or she exerts lower-limit controls (e.g., encouragement) in an effort to stimulate increased behavior.

Bell's conceptualization of interpersonal reciprocity was evaluated by Brunk and Henggeler (1984), who postulated that anxious-withdrawn child behavior should elicit lower-limit adult controls, and that noncompliant-aggressive child behavior should prompt upper-limit controls. Two 10-year-old child actors were enlisted as confederates and were trained in anxious-withdrawn and noncompliant-aggressive roles. It was observed that when the children played the anxious-withdrawn role, adults responded with more helping and rewarding behaviors in an effort to stimulate child activity. When the children assumed the noncompliant-aggressive role, adults exerted more discipline, more direct commands, and ignored the child more frequently. This study supports Bell's model of dyadic reciprocity and provides a rare empirical test of the concept of homeostasis.

Some family theorists would consider our presentation of the concept of homeostasis to be flawed. As discussed later in this chapter, these theorists contend that it is erroneous to conduct empirical evaluations of systemic issues because such evaluations are derived from a reductionistic epistemology and are, therefore, incompatible with an organistic view. In addition, Goldenberg and Goldenberg (1985) note that Paul Dell has caused considerable controversy with his proposal that the concept of homeostasis has outlived its usefulness (Ariel, Carel, & Tyano, 1984; Dell, 1982, 1984). Dell argued that many family therapists view homeostasis as a trait of systems and that such a view is inconsistent with a systems paradigm. From a systems paradigm, neither individuals nor systems have inherent properties. Rather, all behavior and interactions are context-dependent and can only be understood in relational terms. Hence, from a systems perspective it is as incorrect to conclude that a family system has the trait of resisting change as it is to conclude that an individual has a passive-aggressive personality disorder.

4. "Evolution and change are inherent in open systems." Changes that occur with the development of living forms are readily apparent. Throughout the life span, individuals undergo change in their physical capacities and in their relations with the environment. Changes are triggered by genetic variables, as well as by the immediate and long-term environmental context of these variables (Scarr & McCartney, 1983). As immediate environmental contexts change, different behavioral strategies are required for successful functioning. For example, a 6-year-old boy who has learned to control his parents by whining and throwing tantrums (a successful strategy from the boy's point of view), finds that this style of interaction is not accepted by peers. Successful peer relations require different child behaviors. Likewise, successful functioning requires longitudinal changes in similar environmental contexts. Positive peer relations for a 6-year-old require very different behavioral interactions than for a 16-year-old, which should differ from those of a 26-year-old.

Behavioral change occurs, in part, as a function of the interplay between environmental feedback and the individual's internal structuring of the environment. Individuals are constantly exchanging information with the environment and, in the process, are modifying their internal rules that structure the world. As Piaget proposed (Neimark, 1975), each individual strives for adaptability and a full comprehension of experience. An imbalance between one's cognitive structures and experience results in a state of disequilibrium, which is intolerable. Through the processes of assimilation and accommodation, the individual is continuously reaching new levels of equilibrium. Hence, Piaget's perspective incorporates the dual processes of maintaining equilibrium and of continuous change.

The theories of Piaget are similar to those of family theorists in that both fall within an organistic paradigm. The conceptualizations of family theorists, however, pertain to the family system rather than to the individual. Families have a dual nature. On the one hand they are homeostatic, attempting to maintain constancy in the face of a changing environment. On the other hand, they are growing and changing their rules and structure in response to changing environmental circumstances. Over time, these changes in family structure and rules frequently lead to more complex and differentiated relationship patterns (P. Minuchin, 1985). Carter and McGoldrick (1980) have provided excellent descriptions of the ways that normal family transition periods and major environmental events mandate more complex and differentiated patterns of family reorganization. Similarly, Elkaim (1985) has described processes by which open systems that are far from equilibrium can evolve toward a different mode of functioning. Moreover, there is mounting evidence that families who do not function as "open" systems (i.e., who exchange little information with the outside world) are more likely to experience psychosocial difficulties such as incest (Alexander, 1985).

5. "Complex systems are composed of subsystems."   Subsystems are components of a larger system that carry out distinctive functions and that interrelate with other subsystems to maintain the larger system as a whole (Goldenberg & Goldenberg, 1985). On a biological level, the distinctive functions of the cardiovascular system, the central nervous system, and the digestive system are readily apparent. Yet, these subsystems are interactive and respond in a reciprocal and circular fashion to each other via feedback mechanisms.

Salvador Minuchin (1974) has emphasized the role that family subsystems play in the psychosocial functioning of family members. Subsystems are marked by generation, gender, age, and function. The most basic subsystem is the marital dyad. For effective family functioning, couples should have clear boundaries defining their relationship. Concretely, this means that spouses should engage in activities that are exclusively in their domain, such as having sexual relations and making important economic decisions. When the boundaries between subsystems are blurred, such as when one spouse aligns with a child against the other spouse, problems can arise.

The sibling subsystem also has its distinct boundaries and functions. Sibling relations provide the child with a training ground for the development of subsequent peer relations (Hartup, 1983). In large families, there are often subdivisions within the sibling subsystem. Some siblings make alliances against other siblings, and some are allowed greater status and privilege due to their age or special circumstances. Nevertheless, when the sibling subsystem is threatened, the members typically unite to defend each other. A 12-year-old boy who delights in hitting his 9-year-old brother, for example, usually protects the younger brother when he is attacked by a neighborhood bully.

Parent-child subsystems are also an integral aspect of the family system. These subsystems play a critical role in every aspect of child development. For example, parental sensitivity to child needs is associated with numerous positive child outcomes. On the other hand, certain types of parent-child relations have negative repercussions for the family system. Cross-generational alliances, for example, are more prevalent in families of delinquents than in families of well-adjusted adolescents (Mann, Borduin, Henggeler, & Blaske, 1990).

Each family member belongs to a number of different subsystems simultaneously, of course, and in each of these subsystems the family member plays a different role that requires different cognitive sets and behaviors. The role of husband is very different from the role of father, which is distinct from the role of adult son. When a therapist or researcher is attempting to understand family relations, it is essential to consider the meaning of these relations in the context of the different subsystems in the family.

6. "The subsystems within a larger system are separated by boundaries, and interactions across boundaries are governed by implicit rules and patterns." Subsystem boundaries are analogous to a semipermeable membrane. The membrane helps to distinguish the components of the subsystem from those of other subsystems and restricts the flow of information to and from the outside environment. However, if these boundaries are overly restrictive, the flow of information with the environment will be impeded, attenuating the ability of the system to adapt to changing environmental demands. For example, the relatively impermeable boundaries observed in many rural Appalachian families have made it difficult for them to adjust to changing economic fortunes (Urey & Henggeler, 1983). Conversely, boundaries that too readily allow the flow of information with the environment can fail to support the cohesion of the system. When a spouse involves a child in the couple's sexual difficulties, for example, the cohesion of the marital subsystem and of the entire family system is endangered.

Exchanges of information across boundaries are governed by implicit and explicit rules, which are responsible for the organized pattern and sequence that are observed in the interactions among family members (Jackson, 1965). The vast majority of these rules enable families to function normally. Indeed, well-functioning families often have rules that allow for adaptation to changing circumstances as well as rules that maintain the overall stability of the system (Goldenberg & Goldenberg, 1985). Dysfunctional families, however, have rules that maintain a cycle of problematic behavior. Examples of such rules are: "We must always take care of our own problems alone"; "It is the children's fault when father abuses them"; and "Family members should never discuss the fact that mother drinks excessively." In dealing with dysfunctional families, therefore, interventions might focus on changing the family rules with the intention of disrupting the recursive feedback loops that contain maladaptive interactions (Sluzki, 1983).

THE NATURE OF BEHAVIOR PROBLEMS

It should be apparent at this point that behavior problems are viewed very differently from a systemic perspective than from reductionistic models. From a systems perspective, symptoms are part of a circular and multicausal relationship system (Schwartz, 1982) and are not the product of mental illness or individual pathology. As Keeney (1979) has noted, a systemic conceptualization of behavior suggests that difficulties in one part of the relationship system might lead to symptoms in another part, and that relief of these symptoms might evoke new problems in a different part of the system. It is essential, therefore, that therapists consider the entire relationship system when designing interventions. Otherwise, the therapeutic change may only be superficial (Watzlawick, Weakland, & Fisch, 1974).

A good example of superficial change was presented in *Ordinary People*, the 1981 Academy Award winner for best motion picture. The therapist in this movie (Judd Hirsh) "successfully" treated the "emotional" problems of an adolescent boy (Timothy Hutton). These emotional problems were clearly connected to the boy's relationship with his parents (Donald Sutherland and Mary Tyler Moore), as well as to the parents' marital relationship. Yet, the therapist, who operated from a traditional epistemology, focused his attention almost exclusively on the boy's attitudes and beliefs. Although the boy's symptoms were eventually relieved, his mother became very distressed and his parents separated. A traditional therapist might consider the treatment of the boy to have been a success. A family systems therapist, however, would note that the family still had serious problems and that the family system achieved no net change.

If symptoms are not the product of emotional disturbance, how do they arise? Most family theorists (see e.g., Haley, 1976; S. Minuchin, 1974) believe that behavior problems are primarily the result of normal life stresses, transitions, or crises that were poorly managed by family members. From this perspective, it is noted that all individuals and families periodically experience normal problems in living and in adjusting to change. For example, marriage necessitates substantial accommodation regarding living habits, as well as emotional sharing and caring. Similarly, when the couple has their first child, additional relationship adjustments are needed. The couple can no longer devote as much energy to their own marriage or social life. As time goes by, families and family members experience many other changes that require modifications in behavior and relationships for the members to function effectively. When faced with these transitions, some families cope successfully, grow, and become more adaptive; other families use coping strategies that entail serious long-term costs and endanger the integrity of the family system.

Problem behavior often serves a functional purpose (Hoffman, 1981; P. Minuchin, 1985). Many family therapists have noted that child misbehavior can unite parents who are otherwise in conflict and help to maintain a family system that is otherwise unstable. Problem behavior is advantageous for the system—at least in the short run—in many other ways. In an examination of the literature on father-daughter incest, Hanson and Henggeler (1982) described the systemic nature of many incestuous relations, as well as the advantages that these relations give the various family members. The marital relationship in many preincestuous families is extremely conflictual. Rather than seek divorce, however, the parents remain together and pursue an active redefinition of the family roles. Mother and daughter often reverse roles. Concurrently, the father-daughter relationship is allowed to violate the sexual boundaries. These redefinitions permit the mother to continue receiving the material and economic advantages of being married while avoiding intimacy with her husband whom she disdains. The father fulfills his sexual fantasies and needs within the family and maintains his position of dominance. The daughter's behavior often defuses the extant marital conflicts, thereby stabilizing the family and avoiding disintegration. However, the family members, especially the daughter, experience serious long-term consequences. Sexually abused girls are at risk for developing emotional problems such as guilt and depression, as well as disturbed heterosexual relations characterized by promiscuity, distrust of men, involvement with unsuitable partners, and sexual dysfunctions. The treatment of incest is discussed extensively in Chapter 11.

Childhood aggression is another problem that can be highly functional in the short-run, but that is associated with serious problems in adolescence and adulthood. Aggression primarily gives the child control over the environment. Many aggressive children are very effective at bullying their parents, who will often yield to their child's demands in order to avoid an aggressive outburst. Among some peer groups, a high level of aggression can enhance a child's status. Similarly, a high level of aggressive behavior is needed to survive in some rough neighborhoods.

In summary, theories of family therapy generally assume that problem behavior (1) is intimately related to patterns of family interaction, (2) often occurs as a result of poorly managed life stresses and developmental transitions, and (3) has a functional component. Although incest and child aggression were used as examples to support these assumptions, other problem areas (such as depression, child abuse, anxiety) would also provide support. A case study that included a seemingly supernatural incident further clarifies the functional and systemic nature of symptoms.

James, a 13-year-old, and his 14-year-old sister, Rhonda, were referred to the therapist after setting fire to the tires of their father's pickup truck. The adolescents lived with their father, who was separated from their mother. The mother had recently moved to a distant city. A short time before the referral, the family had been visited by a poltergeist. According to television and newspaper accounts, the ghost had thrown knives, pillows, clocks, a frozen chicken, and the television set throughout the house and directly at family members. (It is interesting to note that solid objects often hit the father in the back, whereas the children were typically hit with the pillows.) After considerable coverage of the supernatural events in the local media, a psychologist informed a reporter that the occurrences were probably the product of unresolved psychosexual conflicts in the adolescents. Of course, only extensive psychoanalysis could confirm this hypothesis.

The systemic nature of the poltergeist was investigated and later confirmed by analyzing the functionality of the events. Both the father and the children strongly wanted the mother to return home. The parents' separation, however, had been very hostile, with much mutual bitterness. Moreover, both spouses were extremely proud, and neither counted forgiveness among their virtues. The poltergeist provided the perfect excuse for the mother to return home and for both spouses to save face: A mother must protect her children from the supernatural, even if her estranged husband lives in the same house. Similarly, through his collaboration in the children's hoax, the father set the stage for his wife's return without having to ask her directly.

Although most family therapists understand the nature of behavior problems through similar conceptual frameworks, family therapists do approach behavior change differently. Hoffman (1981) and Sluzki (1983), for example, noted that process-oriented family therapists tend to develop strategies that are specifically aimed at disrupting the repetitive interaction sequences of the symptomatic behavior. Structure-oriented family therapists, on the other hand, disrupt the problematic sequences of interaction by changing the hierarchies and boundaries within the system. Despite their different treatment strategies, both process-oriented and structure-oriented therapists are pragmatic in their primary goal of alleviating symptomatic behavior.

The value of these pragmatic approaches has been seriously questioned in recent years by the "new epistemologists," who take a more aesthetic perspective toward the field of family therapy. Keeney and Sprenkle (1982), for example, proposed that it may be inappropriate to view a symptom as something ugly that needs immediate removal. Consistent with the ideas of R. D. Laing, they suggested that a symptom may serve as a "motor for growth," and that the immediate alleviation of a symptom should be avoided and may even be unethical. The views of the new epistemologists have far-reaching implications for the treatment of families and for all research endeavors in the field.

THE NEW EPISTEMOLOGY

In the epilogue of her excellent text, *Foundations of Family Therapy*, Hoffman (1981) proposed that one group of family therapists are the vanguard of understanding the true meaning of systems theory. These theorists base their positions largely on the writings of Gregory Bateson (1972, 1977, 1978). As Hoffman described, Bateson viewed epistemology with a moral fervor and identified linear thinking and dualism as completely incompatible with a "true" systemic paradigm.

As noted earlier, linear thinking assigns a direct cause to problems and, consequently, assigns blame. An example of linear thinking is the view that a wife's depression is caused by her husband's infidelity and physical abuse or that a 5-year-old's temper tantrums are maintained by the parents' ineffective discipline strategies. A linear perspective implies that one part of the system is causing the problems of the other part. The new epistemologists argue that linear paradigms fail to consider how a particular symptom fits into the spiral of recursive interactions among family members. Because all behavior must be understood within its circular context, it is not valid to punctuate family interaction in a way that places cause on one component of the system (Dell, 1986).

Dualism is another way of demarcating the world that is seen as the antithesis of a "true" systems paradigm. As Dell (1984, p. 354) stated, based on Bateson's ideas, "the essence of the systemic paradigm (is that) individuals and families do not have inherent traits or properties." Dell (1982) proposed that conceptualizations such as family homeostasis, conflict, communication, and resistance are based on a dualistic world view. To assume that families possess such characteristics is to propose that families have traits that are context-independent. He believed that such a proposal is inconsistent with a systemic paradigm in which behavior must always be viewed as context-dependent.

As Hoffman (1981) indicated, the complete rejection of linear and dualistic conceptualizations has profound implications for therapy and research. The implications for therapy are aptly described by Keeney and Sprenkle (1982), who proposed that pragmatic therapists, such as Haley, are reductionistic in their emphasis on solving the presenting problem and, as such, fall outside of the "true" systemic paradigm. Moreover, they suggested that a short-term pragmatic approach to symptom alleviation may even be unethical because it precludes the opportunity for a long-term, holistic healing of self. They and others (e.g., Allman, 1982) also contended that the "aesthetic perspective," arising from phenomenological, psychodynamic, existential, and systemic theories, is characterized by a greater complexity, deeper sensitivity to holism, and higher level of abstraction than is pragmatic family therapy.

Aesthetic therapists view the therapy process as a journey that provides an opportunity to facilitate their own personal growth. Rather than viewing the therapist and family as two separate entities, aesthetic therapists see the therapist as one with the family. They argue, therefore, that direct and purposeful attempts to direct change should be avoided because they blind the therapist's awareness to the total ecology; rather than being in any hurry for change, the therapist should show infinite patience. Although Keeney and Sprenkle (1982) clearly implied that aesthetic approaches to family therapy more accurately reflect systemic "truth" than do pragmatic approaches, Keeney (1982) later noted that his paper with Sprenkle overemphasized aesthetics and gave the false impression that he and Sprenkle did not value pragmatic concerns. He argued that the field of family therapy should strive for a "whole" view—a combination of the aesthetic and pragmatic. Similarly, Kantor and Neal (1985) have proposed a more integrative approach to the field of family therapy.

Despite Keeney's (1982) disclaimer, the attitude of the new epistemologists toward empirical research (see e.g., Schwartzman, 1984) seems similar to their attitude toward pragmatic family therapy. This attitude is exemplified by Colapinto's (1979) discussion of the relative merit of empirical evidence. Colapinto challenged the assumption that empirical research can be used to validate key family therapy concepts and to assess the relative value of different therapy approaches. He argued that empirical research methods are derived from linear and reductionistic paradigms, and, therefore, cannot be used to evaluate a systemic paradigm. For example, traditional outcome research attempts to establish a cause-and-effect relationship. For Colapinto, this goal is problematic because any punctuation of behavioral sequences is dualistic and incompatible with a "true" systems paradigm. Conflicts between models of therapy, therefore, must be resolved through sociocultural evolution, rather than through well-designed research. Similarly, Colapinto discredited researchers' attempts to objectify their work through the use of operational definitions: operational definitions of behavior can never be considered truly "correct" because a different observer may ascribe a very different meaning to the behavior. Taken to their logical conclusion, Colapinto's arguments suggest that empirical research is not an important endeavor and that such research cannot be used to evaluate the relative benefits of different therapy approaches.

Several family systems theorists (Coyne, Denner, & Ransom, 1982; Falzer, 1986; Wilder, 1982) have been quite critical of the views of the new epistemologists. For example, in response to the criticisms of research methods that have been raised by the new epistemologists, Alan Gurman (1983) noted that, in light of the proliferation of dubious psychotherapy techniques in our society, family therapists have an ethical responsibility to continue research efforts to assess positive and harmful effects. Gurman viewed family processes as necessarily circular, but he noted that certain therapeutic subprocesses, including certain family interventions, are decidedly linear. He disagreed with the contention that it is completely erroneous to view the therapist and family in dualistic terms. Although Gurman concurred that the therapist is part of a circular system, he also noted that the therapist can function in a self-determined manner. Moreover, Gurman argued that the therapy outcome literature has already produced relevant findings. Based on his excellent reviews of this literature with Kniskern (Gurman & Kniskern, 1978a, 1978b, 1981), Gurman (1983) presented several general research findings that have already had an important impact on the field of family therapy.

Gurman also addressed the criticisms that Colapinto (1979) and Schwartzman (1984) have raised about the bias of operational definitions and the belief that a linear model of causality is implicit in empirical research methods. Though Gurman agreed that operational definitions cannot be completely objective and value-free, he noted that the virtue of operational definitions is that they make the researchers' biases more explicit. Regarding the issue of linear causality, Gurman suggested that psychotherapy researchers are thinking linearly only when they ask naive questions. Most current researchers ask more complex questions that acknowledge the importance of context, such as, "Which therapy is most effective with which families in which setting and according to which measures of change and from which perspectives?" By its nature, research can never be fully holistic, but merely because therapists and researchers are not capable of seeing the complete whole does not mean that they should stop examining the parts.

Without question, the multisystemic model of therapy that is presented in this volume is both pragmatic and research oriented. Our pragmatic approach is based on our belief that the primary purpose of therapy is to alleviate the problems of family members, not to provide a context for our personal growth. In our view, therapists should achieve personal growth through relationships with their own friends, colleagues, and families. Although our approach is usually directive, we recognize that in certain situations a more reflective therapeutic stance can better promote change. Nevertheless, we attempt to effect change within the shortest time possible and have found that, in most cases, brief therapy is all that is required to meet treatment goals.

As described in an earlier volume of literature reviews (Henggeler, 1982), the multisystemic model is grounded in research findings from the fields of developmental psychology, family therapy, and child clinical psychology. We possess a strong empirical bias and have devoted considerable energy toward the evaluation of various aspects of the model. As noted previously, the strength of our multisystemic model is that it takes a broader and more comprehensive systems approach to the transactions that family members have with each other and their environment. We believe, moreover, that the ultimate value of the model depends on the efficacy of the treatment that is derived from it.

OVERVIEW OF THE MULTISYSTEMIC CLINICAL APPROACH

In the chapters that follow, we describe the general nature of multisystemic therapy on a system-by-system basis. It should be noted, however, that the structure of this volume (i.e., devoting each chapter to interventions in a distinct system) is somewhat artifical. Indeed, interventions that target a particular system often have effects beyond that system. For example, marital therapy may not only enhance the quality of marital communications but may also lead to improvements in parent-child relations. It should also be emphasized that other systems may need to change to help maintain improvements in the targeted system. For example, the development of an adolescent's moral reasoning using individual therapy might be inconsequential if he or she continues to associate with deviant peers. In consideration of these factors, we have attempted to convey a sense of the complexity of seemingly "simple" interventions that occur within a single system.

Nevertheless, our demarcation of chapters may be troublesome. Often, while reading one chapter, the reader might get the impression that the described interventions are discrete rather than fitting within an overall mosaic of interventions (and noninterventions). Our hope is that the overall tone of the volume, and especially the final four chapters, provides the conceptual integration that is central to multisystemic therapy.

Kazdin (1987) has accurately noted that one of the limitations of broad-based treatment approaches, such as multisystemic therapy, is their minimal description of intervention strategies and treatment decision rules. This volume presents relatively extensive descriptions of the interventions that are used within and among the multiple systems in which behavior problems occur. The delineation of treatment decision rules, however, is more problematic. Although multisystemic therapists believe that such rules exist, they sometimes disagree over them. For example, the two authors of this volume do not always agree on the exact nature of the interventions that should be used with the systems in a particular case.

We do not believe, however, that complete agreement regarding treatment decisions is a necessary condition for effective multisystemic therapy. In fact, multiple therapeutic paths can lead to efficient and successful behavior change. From the multisystemic perspective, however, it is essential that therapists conceptualize behavior problems within a framework that considers the many individual, family, and extrafamilial variables that might be linked with the problems.

It is also essential that therapists appreciate the bidirectional influences between the child and his or her systems and that, as much as possible, interventions be conducted directly in the systems that have been targeted for change. School-based interventions, for example, should be orchestrated by the therapist (or the parents) *in* school, rather than simply suggested while the child is in the therapist's office. Finally, as emphasized throughout this volume, treatment should be relatively direct, pragmatic, and problem-focused.

Although the specifics of treatment may vary widely from one case to another, even for presenting problems that are alike, the initial therapy session(s) is conducted in the same manner and similar types of information are acquired. A brief overview of the content of the initial session(s) follows. Subsequent chapters offer more detailed suggestions for the assessment of specific problems.

The Initial Assessment

The first therapy session is usually conducted with the parents (or guardians), the identified "problem" youth, and his or her siblings. After exchanging introductions, the therapist typically begins the session by asking an open-ended question such as, "What can I do for you?" "What brings you in?" Or "What seems to be the problem?" Top priority is given to obtaining the parents' responses to this question, second priority is given to obtaining the "problem" child's response, and third priority is given to the siblings' responses. Thus, the therapist's first goal is to affirm the parents' authority while obtaining each family member's perspective about the presenting problems. The therapist should also identify, though not yet overtly, additional problems that may not have been mentioned by the family members (e.g., parental depression).

The therapist's second goal is to gain an understanding of the systemic context of the presenting problems. More specifically, the therapist should attempt to determine how these problems "fit" with the individual characteristics of the family members (e.g., attitudes, beliefs, cognitive level, social competence), the nature of family relations (e.g., affective qualities of parent-child and marital relations), and the many extrafamilial variables (e.g., the parents' social support networks, the child's peer relations) that can be linked with the presenting problems. Figure 1-1 presents a schematic drawing (adapted from Lerner, 1989) that shows the basic types of information to be obtained during the evaluation of systemic context. At first, this information is assessed through interviews with the entire family or through discussions with various family subsystems and individual family members. It should be emphasized that the nature of the information that is obtained will vary with the age of the child. Moreover, certain types of presenting problems (e.g., sexual abuse) require extensive assessment in special areas (see Chapter 11, for example). Nevertheless, several general areas should be assessed during the initial evaluation with the family.

To illustrate the fit between a presenting problem and its systemic context, Figure 1-2 presents the hypothesized correlates of the aggressive behavior of an 11-year-old boy. The strengths and weaknesses of the child and of the systems of which he is a part are identified, vis á vis his aggressive behavior.

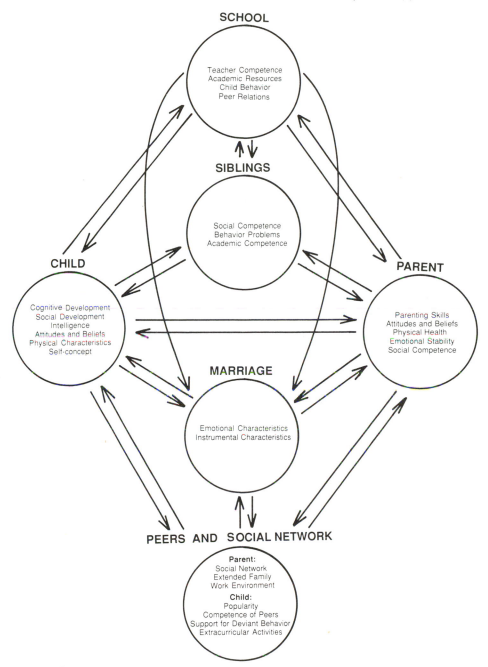

Figure 1-1 The multisystemic context of child behavior

As shown in Figure 1-2, the child's aggressive behavior was hypothesized to be linked with the problematic characteristics of several systems. These characteristics included the use of ineffective discipline strategies by the mother and the teacher, support

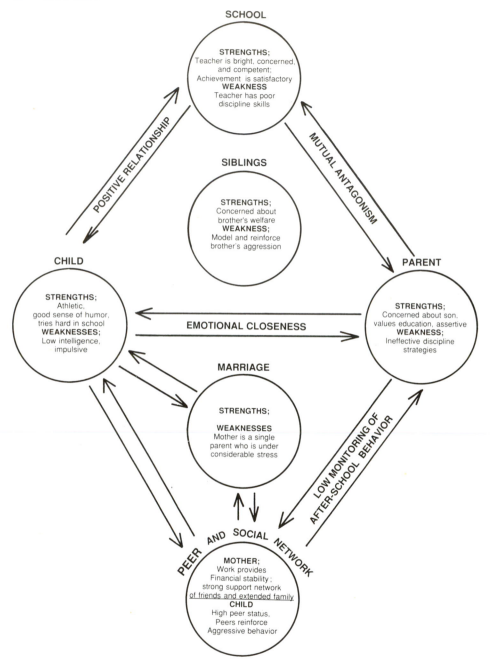

Figure 1-2   The context of the aggressive behavior of an 11-year-old boy

for aggressive behavior by peers and siblings, child impulsivity and low intelligence, and inadequate maternal monitoring of the child's behavior after school. Systemic strengths that could be used to promote therapeutic change included the mother's and teacher's general competence and concern for the child, the siblings' concern for their brother, the mother's strong social support network, the child's high status among his peers, and his athletic abilities and sense of humor. In addition, it can be seen that the interrelations among some of these systems either contributed to the aggressive behavior or could be used to help ameliorate this behavior. For example, the antagonism between the mother and the teacher exacerbated the boy's aggression, whereas the close affective relationship between the mother and her son could provide a useful lever for change.

In general, the therapist's task is to design interventions that build on the existing strengths of the various systems and/or that help to develop new strengths that can be used to promote behavior change. Before the interventions are recommended to the parent(s), however, the therapist should first organize the presenting problems into one or more general themes that are presented to the family. For example, if the behavior problems include stealing, fighting, lying, performing poorly in school, not doing chores, and noncompliance, the therapist might suggest that these problems fall into two general classifications: aggression and irresponsibility. The therapist can then describe the factors that seem to be contributing to these general problems and can discuss these factors with the parent(s) until a mutual agreement is reached regarding their validity. Such an agreement is usually easy to obtain for factors that have been described by the parents themselves (e.g., peer influences, parental inconsistency), but factors that have been identified by the therapist may need further elaboration (e.g., marital difficulties). In providing this elaboration, the therapist should make his or her points using material that has already been presented by the parents or with observations that have been made during the course of the interview. This strategy lends greater credibility to the therapist's perspective.

After the therapist and family have achieved a consensus regarding the general nature of the problems (and the ecological variables that are linked with these problems), the therapist's next task is to provide a coherent system of interventions that are logically associated with these problems and that build on the systemic strengths. In the case of the aggressive boy, the interventions might include: (1) finding a neighbor to monitor the boy after school (the mother has a strong social support network); (2) teaching the mother to use more effective discipline strategies (she is genuinely concerned about the child's behavior problems and future welfare); (3) finding ways to maintain the boy's peer status without the use of aggression (the boy is an excellent athlete and has a good sense of humor); (4) training the boy in the use of self-control strategies (the close mother-son relationship can be used to motivate him); (5) having the teacher reinforce the mother's new discipline strategies (the teacher is competent and concerned); and (6) discouraging the siblings' support of their brother's aggression (the siblings are concerned about their brother).

The specifics of these types of interventions are described in subsequent chapters. The essential point here is that the therapist should obtain a consensus with the parent(s) regarding the nature of the problems and of the possible determinants of these problems. Then, the proposed interventions follow logically. Throughout this volume, suggestions are presented for handling situations in which the parents show resistance to this process.

An experienced multisystemic therapist might be able to pull all this information together during the first session of a relatively simple case. When the therapist is inexperienced or in more difficult cases, it might take several sessions before the consensus between the therapist and parent(s) can be reached. We should emphasize, however, that we seek to intervene as soon as possible in most cases. This is accomplished by maintaining a therapeutic style that is usually informal and flexible, but one that also enables the therapist to determine the direction of conversations and the course of interventions. It is also important for the therapist to continuously review all treatment decisions. Each therapy session usually includes some modification or fine-tuning of ongoing interventions. In addition, as the therapist learns more about the family or obtains new information from sources such as peers or teachers, problems might need to be reconceptualized and new directions for interventions might need to be developed. Again, these changes should be validated with the parents.

In summary, the multisystemic approach emphasizes the evaluation of a broad range of factors that might contribute to behavior problems. The organization of these factors reveals how a particular behavior problem fits within the youth's systemic context and provides logical directions for therapeutic interventions. These interventions are pragmatic and problem-focused, and, whenever possible, they are conducted by the therapist directly with the systems that are targeted for change. The succeeding chapters present an overview of the types of interventions that are conducted within and among systems and provide general guidelines for deciding which types of interventions are appropriate in a particular case.

SUMMARY

Systemic models of behavior and of therapy have significant advantages over models that are based on formistic and mechanistic epistemologies. This is demonstrated by research findings that support systemic conceptualizations of behavior, by the increased use of family therapy by mental health professionals, and by some findings of family therapy outcome researchers. Existing family therapy models, however, generally include three shortcomings. First, they fail to fully consider the roles of individual characteristics and extrafamilial systems in the etiology, maintenance, and treatment of behavior problems. Second, they provide insufficient consideration of individual developmental variables that are pertinent to problem conceptualization and treatment. And, third, family therapists rarely use nonsystemic treatment approaches that are of proven efficacy and that can serve a very useful adjunctive role.

The multisystemic model was developed in response to these limitations. It is a pragmatic model that is based on extensive developmental and clinical literature, as well as on our own research and clinical work. Moreover, the results of three outcome studies with difficult-to-treat families have supported the efficacy of the multisystemic approach.

REFERENCES

Alexander, P. C. (1985). A systems theory conceptualization of incest. *Family Process, 24,* 79–88.

Allman, L. R. (1982). The aesthetic preference: Overcoming the pragmatic error. *Family Process, 21,* 43–56.

Aponte, H. J. (1976). Underorganization in the poor family. In P. J. Guerin, Jr. (Ed.), *Family therapy: Theory and practice.* New York: Gardner.

Aponte, H. J. (1986). "If I don't get simple, I cry." *Family Process, 25,* 531–548.

Ariel, S., Carel, C. A., & Tyano, S. (1984). A formal explication of the concept of family homeostasis. *Journal of Marital and Family Therapy, 10,* 337–349.

Auerswald, E. H. (1968). Interdisciplinary versus ecological approach. *Family Process, 7,* 205–215.

Auerswald, E. H. (1987). Epistemological confusion in family therapy and research. *Family Process, 26,* 317–330.

Bateson, G. (1972). Steps to an ecology of the mind. New York: Ballantine.

Bateson, G. (1977). Afterword. In J. Brockman (Ed.), *About Bateson.* New York: Dutton.

Bateson, G. (1978). Theory versus empiricism. In M. Berger (Ed.), *Beyond the double bind.* New York: Brunner/Mazel.

Bell, R. Q. (1977). Socialization findings reexamined. In R. Q. Bell & L. V. Harper (Eds.), *Child effects on adults* (pp. 53–84). Hillsdale, NJ: Erlbaum.

Belsky, J. (1980). Child maltreatment: An ecological integration. *American Psychologist, 35,* 320–335.

Bertalanffy, L. von. (1968). *General systems theory.* New York: Braziller.

Bogdan, J. L. (1984). Family organization as an ecology of ideas: An alternative to the reification of family systems. *Family Process, 23,* 375–388.

Borduin, C. M., Blaske, D. M., Mann, B. J., Treloar, L., Henggeler, S. W., & Fucci, B. R. (1990). *Multisystemic treatment of juvenile offenders: A replication and extension.* Manuscript submitted for publication.

Bousha, D. M., & Twentyman, C. T. (1984). Mother-child interactional style in abuse, neglect, and control groups: Naturalistic observations in the home. *Journal of Abnormal Psychology, 93,* 106–114.

Bronfenbrenner, U. (1979). *The ecology of human development.* Cambridge, MA: Harvard University Press.

Bronfenbrenner, U. (1986). Ecology of the family as a context for human development. *Developmental Psychology, 22,* 723–742.

Brook, J. S., Whiteman, M., & Gordon, A. S. (1983). Stages of drug use in adolescence: Personality, peer, and family correlates. *Developmental Psychology, 19,* 269–277.

Brunk, M. A., & Henggeler, S. W. (1984). Child influences on adult controls: An experimental investigation. *Developmental Psychology, 20,* 1074–1081.

Brunk, M. A., Henggeler, S. W., & Whelan, J. (1987). A comparison of multisystemic therapy and parent training in the brief treatment of child abuse and neglect. *Journal of Consulting and Clinical Psychology, 55,* 171–178.

Carter, E. A., & McGoldrick, M. (Eds.). (1980). *The family life cycle.* New York: Gardner.

Colapinto, J. (1979). The relative value of empirical evidence. *Family Process, 18,* 427–441.

Coyne, J. C., Denner, B., & Ransom, D. C. (1982). Undressing the fashionable mind. *Family Process, 21,* 391–396.

Dell, P. F. (1982). Beyond homeostasis: Toward a theory of coherence. *Family Process, 21,* 21–41.

Dell, P. F. (1984). Why family therapy should go beyond homeostasis: A Kuhnian reply to Ariel, Carel, and Tyano. *Journal of Marital and Family Therapy, 10,* 351–356.

Dell, P. F. (1986). In defense of "lineal causality." *Family Process, 25,* 513–521.

deRosnay, J. (1979). *The macroscope.* New York: Harper & Row.

Elkaim, M. (1985). From general laws to singularities. *Family Process, 24,* 151–164.

Elliott, D. S., Huizinga, D., & Ageton, S. S. (1985). *Explaining delinquency and drug use.* Newbury Park, CA: Sage.

Falzer, P. R. (1986). The cybernetic metaphor: A critical examination of ecosystemic epistemology as a foundation of family therapy. *Family Process, 25,* 353–364.

Freedman, B. J., Rosenthal, L., Donahoe, C. P., Schlundt, D. G., & McFall, R. M. (1978). A social-behavioral analysis of skill deficits in delinquent and nondelinquent adolescent boys. *Journal of Consulting and Clinical Psychology, 52,* 1448–1462.

Goldenberg, I., & Goldenberg, H. (1985). *Family therapy: An overview.* Pacific Grove, CA: Brooks/Cole.

Goldsmith, H. H. (1983). Genetic influences on personality from infancy to adulthood. *Child Development, 34,* 331–355.

Gray-Little, B., & Burks, N. (1983). Power and satisfaction in marriage: A review and critique. *Psychological Bulletin, 93,* 513–538.

Gurman, A. S. (1983). Family therapy research and the "new epistemology." *Journal of Marital and Family Therapy, 9,* 227–234.

Gurman, A. S., & Kniskern, D. P. (1978a). Research on marital and family therapy: Progress, perspective, and prospect. In S. L. Garfield & A. E. Bergin (Eds.), *Handbook on psychotherapy and behavior change* (2nd ed.). (pp. 817–901). New York: Wiley.

Gurman, A. S., & Kniskern, D. P. (1978b). Deterioration in marital and family therapy: Empirical, clinical, and conceptual issues. *Family Process, 17,* 3–20.

Gurman, A. S., & Kniskern, D. P. (1981). Family therapy outcome research: Knowns and unknowns. In A. S. Gurman and D. P. Kniskern (Eds.), *Handbook of family therapy.* New York: Brunner/Mazel.

Gurman, A. S., Kniskern, D. P., & Pinsof, W. M. (1986). Research on the process and outcome of marital and family therapy. In S. Garfield & A. Bergin (Eds.), *Handbook of psychotherapy and behavior change* (3rd ed.). New York: Wiley.

Haley, J. (1976). *Problem solving therapy.* San Francisco: Jossey-Bass.

Hanson, C. L., & Henggeler, S. W. (1982). The behavior disorders and problems of female adolescents. In S. W. Henggeler (Ed.), *Delinquency and adolescent psychopathology: A family-ecological systems approach* (pp. 117–138). Littleton, MA: Wright-PSG.

Hanson, C. L., & Henggeler, S. W. (1984). Metabolic control in adolescents with diabetes: An examination of systemic variables. *Family Systems Medicine, 2,* 5–16.

Hanson, C. L., Henggeler, S. W., & Burghen, G. A. (1987). A model of the linkages among psychosocial variables and health outcome measures of adolescents with IDDM. *Diabetes Care, 10,* 752–758.

Hanson, C. L., Henggeler, S. W., Haefele, W. F., & Rodick, J. D. (1984). Demographic, individual, and family relationship correlates of serious and repeated crime among adolescents and their siblings. *Journal of Consulting and Clinical Psychology, 52,* 528–538.

Hartup, W. W. (1983). Peer relations. In E. M. Hetherington (Ed.), P. H. Mussen (Series Ed.), *Handbook of child psychology: Vol. 4. Socialization, personality, and social development* (pp. 103–196). New York: Wiley.

Hazelrigg, M. D., Cooper, H. M., & Borduin, C. M. (1987). Evaluating the effectiveness of family therapies: An integrative review and analysis. *Psychological Bulletin, 101,* 428–442.

Henggeler, S. W. (Ed.). (1982). *Delinquency and adolescent psychopathology: A family-ecological systems approach.* Littleton, MA: Wright-PSG.

Henggeler, S. W. (1989). *Delinquency in adolescence.* Newbury Park, CA: Sage.

Henggeler, S. W., & Borduin, C. M. (1981). Satisfied working mothers and their preschool sons: Interaction and psychosocial adjustment. *Journal of Family Issues, 2,* 322–335.

Henggeler, S. W., & Cohen, R. (1984). The role of cognitive development in the family-ecological systems approach to child psychopathology. In J. B. Gholson & T. L. Rosenthal (Eds.), *Applications of cognitive development theory* (pp. 173–189). New York: Academic Press.

Henggeler, S. W., Edwards, J. J., Cohen, R., & Summerville, M. B. (1990). *Predicting changes in children's popularity: The role of family relations.* Manuscript submitted for publication.

Henggeler, S. W., Rodick, J. D., Borduin, C. M., Hanson, C. L., Watson, S, M., & Urey, J. R. (1986). Multisystemic treatment of juvenile offenders: Effects on adolescent behavior and family interaction. *Developmental Psychology*, *22*, 132–141.

Hoffman, L. (1981). *Foundations of family therapy*. New York: Basic Books.

Jackson, D. D. (1965). The study of the family. *Family Process*, *4*, 1–20.

Kantor, D., & Neal, J. H. (1985). Integrative shifts for the theory and practice of family systems therapy. *Family Process*, *24*, 13–30.

Kazdin, A. E. (1987). Treatment of antisocial behavior in children: Current status and future directions. *Psychological Bulletin*, *102*, 187–203.

Keeney, B. P. (1979). Ecosystemic epistemology: An alternative paradigm for diagnosis. *Family Process*, *18*, 117–129.

Keeney, B. P. (1982). Not pragmatics, not aesthetics. *Family Process*, *21*, 429–434.

Keeney, B. P., & Sprenkle, D. H. (1982). Ecosystemic epistemology: Critical implications for the aesthetics and pragmatics of family therapy. *Family Process*, *21*, 1–19.

L'Abate, L. (1985). The status and future of family psychology and therapy. In L. L'Abate (Ed.), *The handbook of family psychology and therapy* (Vol. 2, pp. 1417–1435). Pacific Grove, CA: Brooks/Cole.

Lerner, R. M. (in press). Developmental contextualism and the study of early adolescent development. In R. Cohen & A. Siegel (Eds.), *Context and development*. Hillsdale, NJ: Erlbaum.

Loeber, R. (1982). The stability of antisocial and delinquent behavior: A review. *Child Development*, *53*, 1431–1446.

Maccoby, E. E., & Martin, J. A. (1983). Socialization in the context of the family: Parent-child interaction. In E. M. Hetherington (Ed.), P. H. Mussen (Series Ed.), *Handbook of child psychology: Vol. 4. Socialization, personality, and social development* (pp. 1–101). New York: Wiley.

Mann, B. J., Borduin, C. M., Henggeler, S. W., & Blaske, D. M. (1990). *An investigation of systemic conceptualizations of parent-child coalitions and symptom change*. Manuscript submitted for publication.

Mash, E. J., & Barkley, R. A. (Eds.). (1989). Treatment of childhood disorders. New York: Guilford.

Masten, A. S. (1979). Family therapy as a treatment for children: Critical review of outcome research. *Family Process*, *18*, 323–335.

Meyers, A. W., & Craighead, W. E. (Eds.). (1984). *Cognitive behavior therapy with children*. New York: Plenum.

Miller, J. G. (1978). *Living systems*. New York: McGraw-Hill.

Minuchin, P. P. (1985). Families and individual development: Provocations from the field of family therapy. *Child Development*, *56*, 289–302.

Minuchin, S. (1974). *Families and family therapy*. Cambridge, MA: Harvard University Press.

Montalvo, B., & Haley, J. (1973). In defense of child therapy. *Family Process*, *12*, 227–244.

Neimark, E. D. (1975). Intellectual development during adolescence. In F. D. Horowitz, E. M. Hetherington, S. Scarr-Salapatek, & G. M. Siegel (Eds.), *Review of child development research* (Vol. 4). Chicago: University of Chicago Press.

Nichols, M. (1984). *Family therapy: Concepts and methods*. New York: Gardner.

Panella, D. H., Cooper, P. F., & Henggeler, S. W. (1982). Peer relations in adolescence. In S. W. Henggeler (Ed.), *Delinquency and adolescent psychopathology: A family-ecological systems approach*. Littleton, MA: Wright-PSG.

Parke, R., & Collmer, C. (1975). Child abuse: An interdisciplinary analysis. In E. M. Hetherington (Ed.), *Review of child development research* (Vol. 5, pp. 509–590). Chicago: University of Chicago Press.

Patterson, G. R. (1980). *Coercive family processes*. Eugene, OR: Castillia.

Patterson, G. R. (1986). Performance models for antisocial boys. *American Psychologist, 41,* 432–444.

Pepper, S. C. (1942). *World hypotheses.* Berkeley: University of California Press.

Rodick, J. D., & Henggeler, S. W. (1980). The short-term and long-term amelioration of academic and motivational deficiencies among low-achieving inner-city adolescents. *Child Development, 51,* 1126–1132.

Romig, D. A. (1978). *Justice for our children: An examination of juvenile delinquent rehabilitation programs.* Lexington, MA: Lexington Books.

Scarr, S., & McCartney, K. (1983). How people make their own environments: A theory of genotype-environmental effects. *Child Development, 54,* 424–435.

Schwartz, G. E. (1982). Testing the biopsychosocial model: The ultimate challenge facing behavioral medicine? *Journal of Consulting and Clinical Psychology, 50,* 1040–1053.

Schwartzman, J. (1984). Family theory and the scientific method. *Family Process, 23,* 223–236.

Sluzki, C. E. (1983). Process, structure and world views: Toward an integrated view of systemic models in family therapy. *Family Process, 22,* 469–476.

Speck, R. V., & Attneave, C. L. (1973). *Family networks.* New York: Pantheon.

Sutherland, J. W. (1973). *A general systems philosophy for the social and behavioral sciences.* New York: Braziller.

Urey, J. R., & Henggeler, S. W. (1983). Family relations in rural America. In A. W. Childs & G. B. Melton (Eds.), *Rural psychology.* New York: Plenum.

Valsiner, J., & Benigni, L. (1986). Naturalistic research and ecological thinking in the study of child development. *Developmental Review, 6,* 203–223.

Watzlawick, P., Weakland, J., & Fisch, R. (1974). *Change.* New York: Norton.

Wells, R. A., & Dezen, A. E. (1978). The results of family therapy revisited: The nonbehavioral methods. *Family Process, 17,* 251–274.

Wilder, C. (1982). Muddles and metaphors: A response to Keeney and Sprenkle. *Family Process, 21,* 397–400.

CHAPTER 2

Individual Therapy with Children and Adolescents

*T*he therapist who uses the multisystemic approach considers a broad range of variables that may be related to the problems presented by children and their families. The characteristics of individual family members are an extremely influential set of variables that must always be considered when planning therapeutic interventions. In some cases, a consideration of these variables may indicate that individual therapy is a necessary component of intervention.

The purpose of this chapter is to provide guidelines and a framework for deciding when individual interventions with children may be necessary. The first part of the chapter addresses individual contributions to contextual problems. Here, we describe ways in which individual child characteristics, such as cognitive developmental stage and attentional skills, are often associated with behavior problems. General treatment strategies for ameliorating individual child deficits are also discussed. These strategies include treatments that have been developed by clinicians from nonsystemic theoretical perspectives (e.g., cognitive behavior therapy). The second part of the chapter presents a number of situations in which individual child therapy is often necessary. Several examples are used to elaborate the process of therapy in these situations.

INDIVIDUAL CONTRIBUTIONS TO CONTEXTUAL PROBLEMS

Some family systems theorists have argued that all behavior must be understood within its systemic context. From this perspective, it is invalid to attribute a behavior problem to the characteristics of a particular individual. For example, child aggression or withdrawal is not viewed as an outgrowth of the child's personality. For a behavior to be judged as aggressive or withdrawn, it must occur in an interactional sequence and a social context that would enable such a judgment. For these theorists, it is inappropriate to say that a child "is" aggressive or withdrawn; rather, the child "shows" aggression or withdrawal as part of a circular pattern of family interactions. In other words, problem behavior must always be defined in contextual terms.

We agree with the view that it is impossible to understand any child behavior in isolation from its context. Even with a problem such as childhood autism, which is almost certainly the result of some biological abnormality, considerable evidence shows that the child's social competence and behavior problems are influenced by his or her family relations and school environment (Morgan, 1988). Moreover, even if the autistic child's behavior was fully driven by biological variables, the child's impact on his or her environment would still influence the therapist's conceptualization of the situation.

Hyperactivity is another behavior problem that seems to be biological in nature, which is one reason why psychostimulant drugs are the most frequently used therapeutic intervention. Indeed, research evidence strongly suggests that such drugs have beneficial effects on the ability of hyperactive children to concentrate in structured academic settings (Conners & Wells, 1986). Henker and Whelan (1980) have noted, however, that the use of psychostimulant drugs can have significant negative effects on the child's attributional system and social context. Therefore, even behavior problems that have a biological basis cannot be understood in isolation from their systemic context.

Although the contextual view of behavior problems has considerable merit, the multisystemic approach acknowledges the possibility that individual characteristics of system members can contribute *uniquely* to behavior problems. Relevant individual characteristics include biologically determined variables, as well as cognitive and behavioral characteristics that have been influenced by environmental experience. Although individual characteristics should not be viewed in isolation from the contexts in which they are expressed, these characteristics can have distinct implications for both the conceptualization and treatment of behavior problems.

The role of certain biologically determined variables in the incidence and expression of behavior problems is quite evident. Severe physical handicaps, for example, often evoke a range of problems at the family level and with extrafamilial systems. Similarly, adults who have been validly diagnosed as having schizophrenia or manic-depression are likely to experience a range of problems that are, at least in part, a function of their genetic makeup. While it is certainly true that family members, friends, and co-workers can influence the course of the psychosis, it is clear that genetically determined tendencies can directly influence the systems of which the individual is a member.

Scarr and McCartney (1983) have described three different mechanisms by which genotypes and environment combine to produce human development. First, the parents' genotype influences the type of environment in which they raise their child. Highly intelligent parents are more likely to provide intellectual experiences for their children, and athletic parents are more likely to provide recreational experiences. Second, different genotypes evoke different responses from the environment. Children and adults respond to attractive children very differently than to unattractive children. Third, through a process that Scarr and McCartney call "active niche-building," children construct the types of environments that fit their particular talents. Physically strong and aggressive children gravitate toward contexts that reward strength and aggression, and artistically talented children seek contexts in which their abilities are valued.

The therapist who believes that a child's individual characteristics may be contributing to certain problem behaviors should incorporate this knowledge into the treatment plan. For example, Sean W, the energetic 5-year-old son of a high school football coach, was referred for aggressive behavior in kindergarten. Sean, who was very large and strong for his age, assaulted other children when he did not get his own way and had become the class bully. Mr. and Mrs. W were very concerned about this behavior since they emphasized the value of self-discipline, especially in regard to physical activities. Both parents, who were former college athletes, had decided to channel Sean's aggressive tendencies into athletic activities. Sean attended karate classes twice a week and wrestled with his father each evening after dinner. From the parents' point of view, karate was teaching Sean self-discipline, and the nightly wrestling bouts helped to expend some of Sean's energy.

It is not necessarily problematic to have aggressive tendencies. In this case, however, the parents were handling such tendencies in a way that exacerbated the problem. Sean was too young to appreciate the self-discipline aspect of karate; instead, he simply learned more effective methods of fighting. Similarly, the father-son wrestling bouts were emotionally satisfying to the dyad, but implicitly encouraged Sean's assaultive behavior. A 5-year-old may not fully understand why fighting with dad is allowed, but fighting with a peer is not.

The therapist recommended interventions that recognized Sean's significant athletic potential, but also limited his opportunities for interpersonal aggression. Sean was removed from his karate class and enrolled in a gymnastics class. Gymnastics develops strength and athletic skill without concomitant combative behavior. Board games and sports such as basketball and teeball were substituted for the nightly wrestling bouts, thus preserving the special time that father and son spent together. In an effort to improve cooperative behavior, Mr. and Mrs. W encouraged Sean to join a soccer league. In addition, on days when Sean had been aggressive at school, he was not allowed to play with his father after dinner and was required to go to bed early.

It is important to note that the therapist chose interventions that were consistent with the parents' values and worldview. The therapist did not attempt to involve Sean in nonathletic activities such as arts and crafts. Although such activities would have provided nonaggressive peer experiences, they were not consistent with Sean's or his parents' interests. The therapist's suggestions were met with little resistance from the parents, and Sean's inappropriate classrooom behavior was almost completely eliminated within a month after the first therapy session.

Many other child characteristics besides aggression can contribute to behavior problems. As described in the next section, children's cognitive development and attentional skills are important determinants of behavior across multiple systemic contexts. These behavioral determinants need to be carefully considered in the selection and implementation of therapeutic interventions.

The Role of Cognitive Development

In this section we discuss how multisystemic interventions in the family and peer group are influenced by the child's cognitive developmental skills. The child's level of social cognition is especially important in this regard (Henggeler & Cohen, 1984). Social cognition involves the ability of the individual to infer the covert, psychological experiences of others. Consistent with Piaget's theory of development, Selman (1974) suggested that, before the age of about 6 years (preoperational stage), the child is egocentric in terms of role-taking and social cognition. The child recognizes that different perspectives exist but does not seem to understand the perspectives of those who do not share his or her immediate viewpoint. Between the ages of 6 and 10 years (concrete operational stage), the child can accurately infer the intentions, feelings, and thoughts of others. Although the child realizes that others can make such inferences about him or her, it is not until about age 10 or 11 years that this reciprocal or mutual role-taking is fully comprehended. Finally, after approximately 12 years of age (formal operational stage), the child has a sense of "generalized other." That is, it is known that both self and other can view a relationship in terms of a social system.

This developmental progression in role-taking abilities influences the child's understanding of the multiple systems of which he or she is a part. The egocentric preschooler and young elementary school child comprehend the world in relation to self. The impact of systems other than the family is not fully understood. In fact, the intentions, purposes, and feelings of those in the immediate family are not fully comprehended either. The concrete operational school-aged child, on the other hand, is much more susceptible to the influence of peers, schools, and any other social system that directly involves the child. The young concrete operational child understands the impact of these systems only when he or she is encouraged to reflect upon it. However, the older concrete operational child actively attempts to understand the effects of social systems. When the child reaches adolescence, he or she comprehends the operations of social systems, such as the parents' workplace and the teacher's family life, which exert indirect influences on the child's behavior.

As noted previously, the child's level of cognitive development is an important determinant of optimal treatment strategy. Stated somewhat differently, the effectiveness of an intervention often varies with the child's cognitive maturity. To delineate the role of cognitive development within the multisystemic treatment approach, two general examples are presented.

Treatment of sexually abused children. Females who were sexually abused during childhood have a greater likelihood of experiencing psychosocial difficulties as adults than do females who were not abused (Browne & Finkelhor, 1986; Hanson & Henggeler, 1982). These difficulties include depression, guilt, low self-concept, and heterosexual problems such as distrust of men and sexual dysfunctions. Females who were sexually abused at an early age, however, evidenced fewer negative effects as adults than females who were abused at a later age (Tsai, Feldman-Summers, & Edgar, 1979). This developmental difference in the psychosocial impact of abuse seems to be linked with the child's stage of moral development at the time of the abuse.

Kohlberg (1969) suggested that morality is largely a function of rule following. Moral feelings (e.g., pride and guilt), moral decision making, and moral behavior are related to the manner in which the individual conceptualizes transgressions and to the degree to which standards are violated. In Kohlberg's typology, the preconventional child (roughly comparable to Piaget's preoperational stage) who violates a moral rule experiences anxiety in the form of fear of consequences; that is, the transgression evokes anxiety because the preoperational child fears that he or she might be caught and punished. In contrast, the conventional child (i.e., concrete operational) who violates a moral standard experiences anxiety in the form of guilt. The conventional child recognizes the societal impact of his or her transgression more than does the younger, less sophisticated child.

The negative social consequences of sexual abuse, then, are less apparent to the preoperational child than to the concrete operational child. The preoperational child has not fully internalized societal mores and, consequently, experiences less guilt. When guilt is reported by such children, it is often related to the immediate consequences of the abusive act. For example, the child might feel that his or her behavior has caused parental upset or conflict between family members. Similarly, depression and perceptions of loss are less of a problem for the preoperational child because long-term consequences, such as the responses of future heterosexual partners, are less evident.

The preceding discussion suggests that the treatment of a sexually abused child must involve a careful consideration of the child's level of moral understanding. For the concrete operational child, it is frequently necessary to resolve feelings of guilt and to provide strong emotional support. It might also be important to address issues involving peer and heterosexual relationships. Social withdrawal, which often results from embarrassment and shame, can create a cycle that compounds existing problems. In contrast, the preoperational child does not necessarily need these interventions. Indeed, if well-meaning adults stress the traumatic aspects of the situation, difficulties might intensify. Emotional support is important, but the extent and quality of such support should be determined on an individual basis and not provided indiscriminately. More likely, the abused preoperational child has learned to fear a specific situation or person related to the abusive act. For example, the child might be afraid to enter a certain room in his or her home or a certain area of the neighborhood. In such cases, individual treatment might include traditional behavioral approaches, rather than involving peers and other social networks.

Treatment of conduct problem children.   Conduct problems in children and adolescents are often maintained, in part, by the negative expectancies of parents and teachers. Following repeated misbehavior, parents and teachers come to expect problematic behavior from the child. These expectations can then contribute to a cycle of defensive and hostile interactions that develops between the child and the adult.

With children who are motivated to change, it is possible to teach interpersonal strategies that can break the negative cycle and optimize positive responses from others. Formal operational adolescents are especially equipped to learn these strategies because they are capable of understanding complex hypothetical situations. Consequently, these adolescents can develop a wide range of interpersonal responses that enhance the probability of desirable outcomes.

Consider the example of a formal operational adolescent who has alienated a teacher with disrespectful behavior and poor academic effort. This adolescent is capable of understanding the social hierarchy of the school system and the long-term disadvantages of turning influential members of that system into enemies. Moreover, this adolescent can empathize with the fact that the teacher may be under pressure from school administrators to control disruptive student behaviors.

If the adolescent can adopt the teacher's perspective regarding classroom disruptions, the adolescent can also comprehend and predict the teacher's response to socially desirable behaviors. Thus, to eliminate the cycle of hostility and negative expectancies, the therapist can encourage the formal operational adolescent to "play the game." Specifically, the adolescent can be encouraged to apologize to the teacher, to initiate and persist in friendly interactions, to request after-school tutoring, and to turn in assignments before they are due. Despite initial skepticism, the teacher's attitude and behavior toward the student can eventually be altered in most cases. For this to occur, it is absolutely essential that the adolescent learn and use the verbal and nonverbal cues that communicate respect for authority. Frequently, a self-perpetuating cycle of positive interaction develops, and the teacher might even become the child's advocate.

The concrete operational child is not as proficient at generating positive interpersonal responses in complex or ambiguous situations. This child is less able to see beyond his or her immediate relationship with the teacher and appreciate the pertinence of outside pressures on the teacher. Although the concrete operational child can learn many of the same interpersonal skills as the formal operational adolescent, the use of these skills is not as flexible and the comprehension of the teacher's motivations is not as sophisticated. The preoperational child has even greater difficulty learning to consciously adopt many interpersonal skills because he or she is unable to assume the perspectives of others.

The Role of Attentional Processes

The preceding discussion focused on children's characteristics that have biological bases or that are tied to age-related changes in social cognition. Attention deficit disorder (ADD; hyperactivity) seems to be biologically based (Rosenthal & Allen, 1978; Solanto, 1984) *and* to include an important cognitive component; that is, children with ADD have difficulty attending selectively to environmental cues and modulating their motor behavior in accordance with situational demands. These attentional difficulties can affect various aspects of the child's psychosocial functioning and need to be considered when designing therapeutic interventions.

There is considerable evidence that ADD disrupts children's interactions within their social systems. Researchers have observed that mothers of hyperactive children provide relatively low rates of positive responses and high rates of negative responses and directive communications to these children (Cunningham & Barkley, 1979; Mash & Johnston, 1982). Similarly, reviewers (Campbell & Pavlauskas, 1979) have concluded that hyperactive children experience considerable difficulties in their relations with peers. The classroom and learning difficulties of ADD children have also been well documented (Conners & Wells, 1986).

The most common treatment of hyperactivity has been the prescription of psychostimulants, such as Ritalin. Reviewers (Conners & Wells, 1986; Whalen & Henker, 1976) have concluded that these drugs generally enhance the performance of hyperactive children on tests of vigilance, short-term memory, and learning. In addition, psychostimulants lead to improvements in the social adaptive behavior and psychosocial functioning of hyperactive children. In fact, psychostimulants seem to evoke positive bidirectional processes between hyperactive children and significant adults in their lives. For example, in a double-blind experiment, Whalen, Henker, and Dotemoto (1981) found that the in-class behavior of teachers became less intense and controlling toward hyperactive children placed on Ritalin than toward hyperactive children who received a placebo.

Although psychostimulants appear to provide an effective individual treatment for hyperactivity, Henker and Whalen (1980) have noted that the use of medication to address a behavioral problem may have a negative impact on the child's attributions of causality about that problem. The child may come to believe that behavior problems can only be controlled by medication and, thus, are not his or her direct responsibility. Such attributions can interfere with current coping strategies and with the long-term maintenance of behavior change by teaching the child that the answer to behavioral problems lies in medication rather than in individual effort.

There is also evidence that the use of medication for hyperactivity influences the expectations of others. Amirkhan (1982) found that teachers and classmates attribute the academic success of hyperactive children primarily to their medication, rather than to their ability or effort. Hence, hyperactive children who receive medication are placed in a situation that negates individual responsibility for both positive and negative behaviors.

In light of the negative ramifications of psychostimulant use, Henker and Whelan (1980) have recommended that children who receive psychostimulants should also receive some type of psychotherapeutic intervention. They suggest that any positive behavioral changes can then be attributed to the child's (and parents') efforts in therapy, rather than to the medication. This attribution promotes both internalization of behavior change and feelings of self-efficacy that may help the child to maintain desired behaviors when medication is terminated.

The most common behavioral interventions for hyperactivity are parent training and cognitive-behavioral therapy. As discussed in Chapter 3, parent training is often an effective intervention strategy in mildly dysfunctional families. Moreover, Dubey, O'-Leary, and Kaufman (1983) have shown that parent training can lead to many of the same positive changes that psychostimulants do, but without the negative side effects of such medication (e.g., nausea, sleep disturbance). As discussed next, cognitive-behavioral therapy can often have an adjunctive role in multisystemic therapy.

COGNITIVE-BEHAVIORAL THERAPY

The cognitive-behavioral approach to treating the behavior problems of children and adolescents is becoming widely used and accepted within the mental health community. This is evidenced by the fact that cognitive behavior therapy is the most frequently cited therapeutic preference among clinical psychologists who have recently received their PhDs and are working in academic settings (Klesges, Sanchez, & Stanton, 1982). Moreover, as described by Meyers and Craighead (1984), many behavior therapists have shifted from the use of operant treatment approaches to cognitive-behavioral approaches during the past 20 years. The impetus for this shift is based on several important developments, including new research findings and conceptual advances within the area of cognitive psychology, the rapid growth of self-control clinical interventions, and advances in cognitive therapeutic approaches.

Although it is beyond the scope of this book to address research and conceptual developments in the area of cognitive behavior therapy, cognitive-behavioral interventions can often have a valuable adjunctive role in multisystemic therapy. As detailed in other texts (e.g., Gholson & Rosenthal, 1984; Kazdin, 1988; Kendall & Hollon, 1979; Meichenbaum, 1977; Meyers & Craighead, 1984), two of the most promising and widely used cognitive-behavioral interventions in the treatment of childhood behavior problems are problem-solving skills training and self-control training. Each of these intervention strategies is briefly presented. It must be emphasized, however, that our presentation is only cursory and that the reader should refer to the references cited in this section for more complete information about these interventions.

Problem-solving.   D'Zurilla and Goldfried (1971) were the first researchers to develop problem-solving as a clinical intervention, and their approach has been widely used by other researchers and clinicians. Their problem-solving intervention program entails five basic steps (Kennedy, 1984; Meyers & Craighead, 1984).

1. The therapist helps the child to recognize the situations in which difficulties might arise and to develop a cognitive set that views these situations as opportunities for establishing greater competence and maturity. Concomitantly, the therapist helps the child to develop a cognitive set that inhibits his or her usual way of responding to the problem situation.

2. The therapist encourages the child to define the specifics of the problem and to decide what changes in behavior are needed. For example, 10-year-old Oscar, who is easily provoked into fighting with his peers, might say to himself, "I really have to watch out when Bobby and Jimmy start teasing me on the playground. They are trying to get me to fight so that I get into even more trouble at school. If they start teasing me today, I should be real cool about it and show them and my teacher that I am more grown up than they think."

3. The therapist assists the child in generating alternative responses to the problem situation. Using the same example, Oscar can be helped to see that he has several options for responding, aside from fighting. He can attempt to walk away from Bobby and Jimmy when they start to tease him. He can tell his teacher that the boys are teasing him and hope that she will intervene. He can try to ignore their comments. Or, he can tell Bobby and Jimmy that their teasing does not bother him anymore and that it is all right with him if they want to continue their teasing.

4. The child is taught to evaluate the advantages and disadvantages of each of the alternative responses that were formulated. In the example, Oscar would be asked to list the pros and cons of telling the teacher that Bobby and Jimmy are teasing him. On the positive side, such a response would probably inhibit the teasing in the short term. On the negative side, Oscar might develop a reputation as a tattletale, the teacher might not respond favorably, and/or the teasing might be increased the next day.

5. The efficacy of the solution that was implemented is evaluated. If the outcome was successful, self-congratulations are in order. If the outcome was unsuccessful, the child returns to a previous stage in the problem-solving process. Once again in the same example, if Oscar chose to ignore the teasing and Bobby and Jimmy escalated the conflict by pushing and shoving him, Oscar might again be faced with the same range of possible responses as when he was first being teased, but now the advantages and disadvantages of the responses could be very different. Telling the teacher, walking away, and even responding in kind become more viable alternatives. On the other hand, ignoring the pushing and prescribing the behavior become less realistic options.

As inferred from the complexity of this relatively straightforward case example, a problem-solving intervention may be difficult to implement in many situations. From our experience, the problem-solving approach is most helpful and time-efficient when used with children who are relatively sophisticated on both intellectual and interpersonal levels. It should be noted, however, that proponents of the approach have advocated its use, in simplified form, with children who possess low intelligence and poor interpersonal facility (e.g., Whitman, Burgio, & Johnston, 1984).

Self-instruction/self-control training.   Several childhood behavior problems have been linked with a response style that is impulsive. For example, research suggests that children who are learning disabled, hyperactive, or aggressive often approach academic and interpersonal situations in ways that interfere with successful coping (Meyers & Craighead, 1984). On academic tasks, such children may fail to follow directions that are essential for the successful completion of the task and may make premature and hasty decisions regarding the choice of correct responses for specific task items. In interpersonal situations, impulsive children often suffer the negative consequences that occur when individuals act before they think.

The goal of self-instruction training is to provide impulsive children with an internal cognitive framework that promotes a more reflective response style. When conducting self-instruction training, the therapist first rehearses the self-instruction protocol aloud for the child, and then the child repeats the self-instructions aloud for the therapist. After the instructions have been learned, the therapist whispers them while performing the task and has the child do the same. Finally, the therapist models the covert use of the instructions and has the child do the same. Training is complete when the child has internalized the use of on-task self-talk.

The following is an example of a self-instruction strategy that may be used by a child who is overly impulsive in solving arithmetic problems. The child may be taught to say: "Let's see, what am I supposed to do here? This is an arithmetic problem and I am supposed to figure out the correct answer. What type of arithmetic problem is this? The plus sign means that it is an addition problem so I must be sure to add the numbers. There are three numbers and each has three digits. I must remember to start from the right and to add down the entire column. Then, if the sum is greater than nine, I must remember to carry over to the tens column," and so on. Operationally, the effects of such training are judged by an increased response latency to test items and an increased percentage of correct responses.

Within the multisystemic approach, we have often used self-instruction techniques with children whose academic difficulties are associated with distractibility or impulsivity. These techniques have several attractive features. First, they are relatively easy to teach and can be applied to a variety of different academic tasks that demand planning and the use of an identifiable strategy. Second, researchers have shown that the use of self-instruction techniques can enable the child to improve school performance. We have observed that the benefits are especially favorable when the techniques are implemented along with systemic interventions (e.g., parental establishment of a "study" hour). Third, the techniques can be used in the classroom setting without placing any additional demands on the teacher.

SITUATIONS AND CASE EXAMPLES IN WHICH INDIVIDUAL CHILD THERAPY IS OFTEN NECESSARY

In this section we describe several general contexts in which therapy with the individual child is the intervention that has the highest probability of facilitating positive behavior change.

Individual Therapy When the Family Is Severely Dysfunctional

As discussed in Chapter 3, one of the therapist's primary responsibilities is to facilitate the development of a supportive and caring relationship between the target child and a responsible adult. In the vast majority of cases, this adult is a natural parent or a stepparent. In some instances, this adult might be another relative, such as an older sibling, aunt, uncle, or grandparent. In still other cases, this adult might be a neighbor, pastor, parent of a peer, or teacher.

Although the logistics of treatment are less complicated when the adult is also the child's parent, parenthood is not the primary criterion that should be used to identify a responsible adult. Most important is that the adult is someone who has adequate psychosocial adjustment, cares about the child, and can serve as a positive role model. Unfortunately, a small percentage of the parents of problem children do not demonstrate the capacity to serve as positive role models, nor have they developed a meaningful emotional attachment to the child. These parents tend to evidence serious psychiatric disturbances, chemical dependency, and/or extensive criminal activity. In addition, as one might expect, these parents usually have histories of very poor relations with their own parents. Despite this wide variety of personal difficulties, extreme egocentrism is often the core problem that prevents a healthy parent-child relationship; that is, these parents tend to be locked into their own (usually distorted) view of reality and have great difficulty appreciating and meeting the needs of their children.

As discussed in several other chapters in this volume, we have had some success in treating severely dysfunctional parenting behavior. For example, in our controlled outcome study with neglecting and abusive parents (Brunk, Henggeler, & Whelan, 1987) we promoted significant changes in parent-child relations. Following multisystemic treatment, neglectful parents became more responsive to their child's behavior, neglectful and abusive parents were more effective in their use of appropriate control strategies, and neglected and abused children showed less noncompliance. Nevertheless, in some cases our usual strategies are not successful in enlisting parental cooperation or support for treatment goals. In these cases, it may be necessary to identify another adult who can serve as a positive influence in the child's life. This adult should care about the child, already be in the child's natural environment, and be a mature and responsible individual. Sometimes, however, no such adult can be identified, or the identified adult does not wish to take on such a significant responsibility. In these cases, the only immediate avenue is the development of a therapist-child relationship that helps to meet the child's emotional needs. (In extreme cases, of course, out-of-home placements are another alternative.) In these situations, the therapist should develop a relationship with the child that serves several functions.

1. The therapist should emphasize the child's positive characteristics and personal strengths, an essential function in light of the significant rejection that the child has suffered from the adults in his or her world. Children tend to internalize parental rejection, and such internalization can permanently impair their psychosocial development.

2. The therapist needs to provide the child with a worldview that is positive and optimistic. Since children who live in severely disturbed families tend to view the world

as an unpleasant and punishing place, the therapist must attempt to engender hope by showing paths that the child can take to realistically achieve personal desires and goals.

3. The therapist should provide a model of a caring and supportive adult. The therapist need not become the child's peer or "buddy" but rather assume a role that is similar to the authoritative parent (Maccoby & Martin, 1983). Such a parent is emotionally positive in tone, encourages verbal give-and-take, and uses child-centered control strategies. The authoritative parent, however, also has high expectations for appropriate and responsible child behavior and is willing to assert authority when the situation dictates. Nevertheless, the therapist should be tolerant of noxious child behavior, even when this behavior is directed toward the therapist. The therapist must not take such behavior personally, nor should the therapist react in a highly emotional fashion. Rather, the therapist should understand that the child has had little experience in the development of close relationships and that considerable patience is required. The therapist should view noxious child behavior as an opportunity to broaden the child's social perspective-taking skills and interpersonal sensitivity.

4. The therapist should use the relationship with the child as a lever for change. The therapist should respond very favorably when the child shows positive efforts, such as studying hard for an exam or trying to befriend a socially desirable peer. Similarly, the therapist should show displeasure with maladaptive child behavior. The therapist should not totally withdraw positive affection but should clearly indicate the negative short-term and long-term consequences of the child's behavior.

5. The therapist should always recognize that his or her relationship with the child is not a permanent one. The child's long-term emotional needs will be best met within the context of an enduring relationship with another responsible adult. When such an adult is identified, the therapist should wean the child and do everything possible to promote the child's relationship with that adult.

The following examples describe the process of individual child therapy in cases where the family was severely dysfunctional.

Parents who reject the child.   Parental rejection presents one of the most serious emotional traumas that a child can experience. In some cases, the rejection is based on child behavior that displeases the parent. Here, parental responsivity can be increased in conjunction with steps that decrease the child's behavior problems. In other cases, parental rejection is based on factors that are not associated with the child's behavior. These factors are often tied to the parent's own social, emotional, and personality development and may never be fully understood by the therapist.

Kathy C was a 9-year-old girl who lived with her parents and younger sister. Kathy was referred for treatment by her fourth-grade teacher because of her depressive behavior in school. Although Kathy presented only minor behavior problems at home, her parents believed that she was severely disturbed and considered her to be a "bad seed." In such situations, the therapist usually attempts to change the parents' perceptions of the child by noting that some of the child's misbehaviors are developmentally normative (e.g., the rate of noncompliance is within the normal range) and that the child also has many positive characteristics. When this therapeutic maneuver was unsuccessful with Kathy's parents, the therapist attempted to deal with the parents' misperceptions in a more direct fashion. He suggested that Kathy might be the scapegoat for several problems that were evident (at least to the therapist) in the marriage. In addition, the therapist suggested that Kathy's depression might be linked with her perception that her parents did not love her.

The parents became extremely defensive at these suggestions and stated quite adamantly that except for Kathy neither they nor their family had any problems. They argued that Kathy was the one that needed treatment, not the marriage, and that they were tired of humoring the therapist by attending the family therapy sessions; they wanted him to either cure Kathy or refer them to someone who would.

At this point, the therapist had two apparent choices. He could treat Kathy individually, or he could terminate the case. A disadvantage of treating Kathy individually was that the therapist would be implicitly agreeing with the parents that Kathy was the problem. On the other hand, because she was the recipient of relatively severe parental rejection, she was a child who was clearly in need of emotional support. The therapist decided to see Kathy individually with the goal of initiating a process that would attenuate the deleterious effects of parental rejection. The therapist also hoped that individual treatment would initiate processes that would lead to systemic change. Indeed, as Montalvo and Haley have noted in their insightful essay (1973), it is never truly possible to treat a child in isolation from his or her family.

The therapist always greeted Kathy with enthusiasm in the clinic reception room. He also addressed Kathy with considerable respect, and was very supportive and positive in his emotional tone throughout the therapy sessions. During the first four therapy sessions, the therapist and Kathy exchanged their views on family, friends, school, and happiness. In the fifth session, the therapist gave Kathy a tour of the building in which he worked, and she was especially excited about playing with the rabbits in the animal laboratory. In the sixth session, Kathy and the therapist had a soft drink and cookie party, during which they decided on specific changes that Kathy was going to make in her interactions with classmates and in her school performance.

At the beginning of the seventh session, Mrs. C, who was responsible for transportation and always waited for Kathy in the reception room, asked if she could speak with the therapist. Reluctantly, the therapist stated that he would attempt to save some time at the end of the session. At the end of the hour, however, the therapist told Mrs. C that he and Kathy simply had had too much productive work to accomplish and that, unfortunately, he did not have time now to see Mrs. C.

At the beginning of the eighth session, Mrs. C insisted on meeting with the therapist immediately. She reported that Kathy was very excited about coming to therapy and that she and her husband had noticed a dramatic improvement in Kathy's behavior. Mrs. C then asked if she could do anything to facilitate Kathy's progress. The therapist responded that the situation was well in hand, and that he and Kathy were making substantial progress toward meeting their therapeutic goals. The therapist thanked Mrs. C for her offer, but politely refused to accept her assistance.

During each of the next several weeks, Kathy reported that both her mother and father were being very nice to her. She stated that her parents had played with her and had taken her shopping with them on several occasions. In addition, Mrs. C became involved in Kathy's school play, and Mr. C was teaching Kathy how to play softball.

After the twelfth individual therapy session with Kathy, the therapist asked Mr. and Mrs. C to attend the next session so that he could provide feedback regarding Kathy's behavior problems. During this session, it was clear that Kathy was no longer the family scapegoat. Marital communication and parent-child relations had become very positive, and increased family cohesion was evident. In light of the fact that neither the family members nor the therapist could identify any remaining problems, the case was terminated.

Curative therapeutic factors are not always easy to identify. In the case of Kathy C, it seems likely that her behavior at home did not change dramatically from the beginning of treatment to the end. Rather, the parents' perceptions of her behavior had changed. These perceptual changes were probably linked to the therapist's strategic moves. First, he made it obvious that he thought highly of Kathy and looked forward to spending an hour with her each week. This may have led the parents to recognize their daughter's positive characteristics. Second, as a result of the positive attention that the therapist gave to Kathy, she became emotionally attached to him and anxiously awaited their weekly sessions. In turn, the parents probably became jealous of Kathy's relationship with the therapist and, consequently, initiated efforts to win her back. Third, the therapist behaved as if the parents had little to contribute to the amelioration of Kathy's behavior problems. This paradoxical therapeutic strategy was used in light of the parents' initial resistance to conjoint treatment and may have prompted the parents to prove that the therapist was wrong. Fourth, the therapist devoted considerable energy toward providing Kathy with a more accurate view of herself and her capabilities. It is possible that as she came to feel better about herself, her depression decreased and others viewed her in a more favorable light.

Severely disturbed parents.   Although the treatment of severely dysfunctional families sometimes leads to the reunification of the family system, in other families the probability of change is minimal. Barry H was an 11-year-old boy who was referred by his school counselor. Barry was on the verge of a permanent expulsion from school because of aggressive behavior toward his fifth-grade teacher and principal. Barry was actively noncompliant, used profanity toward the teacher and principal, and threatened them with bodily harm.

The counselor's attempts to enlist family assistance in dealing with Barry's difficulties had been fruitless. Mr. H was unemployed and made his living from various criminal activities. One of Barry's older brothers was in prison, and another was in a juvenile correctional facility. Mrs. H was not a positive influence either. In fact, she told Barry that he did not have to take orders from anyone, including his teachers. It was not surprising, therefore, that following a long history of problems with the H children and their parents, the school personnel were anxious to expel Barry.

Yet the school counselor believed that Barry had considerable potential for prosocial behavior and success in life. Indeed, several factors supported this perception. Barry was the most popular child in his classroom. Interestingly, he did not maintain this status through intimidation of his peers. Rather, Barry was an extremely charming individual when interacting with his peers, and he used his charm to talk his classmates into a variety of misbehaviors. As an example of his charm, Barry shyly boasted that he had talked each of the girls in the class into kissing him. Additionally, although Barry's grades suffered due to his classroom behavior and attitudes toward school, he was, in fact, quite intelligent, scoring in the high average range on standardized intelligence tests. Barry was also a fine athlete, though he was no longer permitted to participate on local community youth teams.

In sum, Barry's main difficulties emerged when he interacted with authority figures. He had learned from his family that authorities are to be neither respected nor obeyed. Though Barry was talented in many ways, he was about to be permanently removed from the mainstream educational experience. Such removal would have had a very negative impact on Barry's future psychosocial and socioeconomic functioning.

The therapist's first goal was to find a way to motivate Barry to change his behavior toward authorities. To accomplish this, it was important that Barry did not perceive the therapist as an overt authority figure. Therefore, the therapist divided the therapy sessions into two parts. During the first part, the therapist responded in a nonjudgmental fashion and learned about Barry's perceptions of his family and school. During the second part, Barry and the therapist engaged in mutually enjoyable activities, such as playing pinball or throwing a football.

Because Barry was a bright, warm, and socially skilled child, the therapist quickly formed a relationship with Barry that was similar to that of an uncle. The next step in the therapeutic process was to show Barry the connection between his present behavior toward authorities and the high probability of incurring serious problems in the future. Because Barry held his family in high esteem and had learned his behavior toward authorities from his family, the therapist was very diplomatic in describing the connection between his behavior and future problems. The therapist noted that, although his older brothers and his parents were fine individuals in many ways, they each possessed one characteristic that led them to suffer many serious consequences. This characteristic—an unwillingness to form good relationships with individuals who possess power—was one that Barry shared with them.

Almost everyone is willing to admit to at least one family flaw, especially when the family is praised within the same context. In addition, the serious negative consequences of this particular family flaw could be easily understood. When Barry was able to recognize this flaw and link it to negative consequences, he experienced a change in his cognitive set that facilitated behavioral change. Nevertheless, because Barry had behaved antagonistically to authorities for many years, it would take more than this one cognitive change to modify the ways in which he interacted with the teacher and principal.

The remaining obstacle to behavioral change was Barry's reluctance to be placed in a situation in which he had little control. From Barry's perspective, children who followed adult directives were weak and inferior. The therapist's task, then, was to convince Barry that when he complied with an adult's directive, it did not mean that he was subservient or weak. In language appropriate to an 11-year-old, the therapist taught Barry the power of "going one down to become one up" (Haley, 1963). When his behavior change was reframed in this way, Barry no longer felt that he was simply obedient to authority but rather, that he was "tricking" his teacher and principal. It was much more satisfying for Barry to fool the authorities than to simply obey their rules, although the overt behavioral response was the same.

At the same time, the therapist also attempted to change the cognitive sets of the teacher and principal. These professionals had come to expect noxious behavior from Barry and, on several instances, had blamed him for classroom disruptions that were not his doing. Thus, even if Barry was very well behaved, it might take a long time before the teacher and principal recognized this improved behavior. To expedite the process of change, the therapist met with the teacher and principal and suggested that Barry spoke very highly of them during therapy sessions. The therapist also suggested that Barry was ready to straighten out his behavior and to pursue his education more seriously. Noting that he had no way of knowing whether Barry was following through on such changes, the therapist requested that the teacher and principal watch for positive social and educational efforts on Barry's part. The therapist also requested weekly feedback from the teacher and principal regarding Barry's progress. Thus, the therapist's maneuver altered the teacher's and principal's expectations and set the stage for early recognition and reinforcement of Barry's positive changes.

In summary, the therapist-child relationship in this case included several factors that facilitated positive behavioral change. It emphasized the child's strengths, provided the child with a more favorable worldview, used the therapeutic relationship as a lever for change, and was nonpejorative toward the child and his family. Finally, in light of the consistently negative influence of Barry's family and the transitory role of the therapist, it was important to link Barry with a positive adult influence. The school counselor, who was a neighbor of the H family, provided the perfect choice. She and Barry had already established a positive attachment; she lived in close proximity and was, therefore, readily available when Barry needed her guidance; and she had a good understanding of his family situation.

Exploitive Parents

Children are very vulnerable to parental exploitation for at least two reasons. First, children are almost always emotionally attached to their parents, even if the parents are not emotionally attached to them. Because of this attachment, children are usually eager to engage in behaviors that they believe will please the parents and eventually win the parents' love. Second, many children have an implicit faith that their parents are responsible individuals who have their children's best interests at heart. Similarly, children usually have an inherent respect for authority and are hesitant to challenge parental requests that may seem wrong or unfair.

The exploitation of children can occur on instrumental, emotional, and physical levels. On an instrumental level, for example, the child may be required to function as a servant. Because all children should have at least some responsibility for taking care of their own room and for performing chores that benefit the family as a whole, the judgment of whether the workload is excessive will vary from family to family. For example, the oldest child in a low-income, single-parent family will probably have more work responsibilities than his or her counterpart in a middle-income, two-parent family. Due to socioeconomic circumstances beyond their control, some children are forced to mature early, and it is unrealistic to view parental demands as exploitive. On the other hand, in a family where the father is employed and the mother is not employed, it is exploitive to require a 17-year-old daughter to grocery shop, plan and cook all of the meals, clean all of the pots and dishes, and assume major responsibility for caring for the younger children.

A more insidious type of exploitation can occur when parents turn their child into an emotional confidant. For example, a mother may tell a child personal secrets about the father or about marital difficulties. The child may feel privileged to provide the mother with emotional support, but the mother's behavior is detrimental to the child in several ways. First, it can interfere with the quality of the father-child relationship by drawing the child into a covert coalition with the mother against the father, and by undermining respect for the father as a parent. Second, the child probably does not possess the emotional maturity necessary to understand the mother's professed difficulties. Third, the child's emotional energy may be invested in his or her mother during a stage when development of peer relations and extrafamilial relations may be more important.

Another type of emotional exploitation occurs when the parent uses guilt to manipulate the child into believing that he or she is responsible for the parent's happiness. For example, the mother of a 20-year-old college student who still lived at home told her daughter, "After all the love that I have given you and all the sacrifices that I have made for you, how can you take a summer job with your brother in Los Angeles and leave me all alone?" For many parent-child dyads, this type of manipulation continues throughout the child's adult life.

Therapeutic interventions with children and adolescents who are being exploited in instrumental and emotional ways should focus on several general processes. On a systemic level, the therapist can attempt to alter the parent's perspective in a way that changes problematic parental behavior and arranges for the parent's needs to be met through more appropriate avenues. For example, the mother who is using her child as a confidant might be advised of the immediate and long-term negative effects on the child, and the therapist might recommend that the mother develop closer friendships with peers. On an individual child level, the therapist might provide the child with emotional support and a more realistic view of the situation. Returning to the above example, the child might need to learn that the mother's loneliness is best satisfied in a relationship with another adult, and that the child has many important psychosocial tasks to accomplish that are independent of the mother.

Sexual abuse represents an extreme, physical form of child exploitation. As noted earlier, incest is associated with many short-term and long-term negative consequences for the victim. Because treatment of child sexual abuse is discussed in detail in Chapter 11, the following discussion is focused on a particular type of cognitive intervention. This intervention is sometimes necessary in families that stay together after intrafamilial sexual abuse has become public.

The most common form of intrafamilial sexual abuse involves the father as the perpetrator and the daughter as the victim. In such situations, the mother's response to the abuse is a critical determinant of her daughter's adjustment. When the mother is highly supportive of her daughter and is overtly angry toward her husband, the daughter's ability to cope with the situation is enhanced. Although the daughter has been betrayed by her father, she is bolstered by the complete support that she receives from her mother. For example, in one case that was referred to us, the mother had gone so far as to attack her husband with a machete after learning that he had sexually abused their 14-year-old daughter. The wife then kicked her husband out of the house and pressed charges with the police. When the case was eventually referred to the therapist, the father was still out of the house, and the daughter was not experiencing emotional or interpersonal difficulties.

On the other hand, when the mother does not believe her daughter's allegations of abuse and is not emotionally supportive of her, the girl's adjustment can deteriorate dramatically. Not only has she been betrayed by her father, but she also has been rejected by her mother. Thus, through no fault of her own, she has lost her trust in the two most important people in her life.

Sharon J and her parents came for therapy three months after her stepfather had molested her for the second time. During the three months, Sharon's grades had dropped from mostly As and Bs to Cs and Ds. She had become noncompliant at home, had run away, and had been arrested for shoplifting. These behaviors were totally out of character for Sharon. At the first therapy session, Mr. J refused to acknowledge the incident, and Mrs. J refused to believe Sharon's reports of what had happened. Despite the therapist's best efforts, she could not succeed in persuading Mr. and Mrs. J to deal with the situation in an honest, direct fashion. Although Sharon was very angry at her stepfather, she was most distressed by what she perceived as her mother's rejection of her.

Because the parents were uncooperative, the therapist's goal was to provide Sharon with a different perspective regarding the situation. She hoped that this perspective would attenuate Sharon's level of hostility and distress. Although these emotional responses were certainly appropriate for the situation, they were beginning to have adverse effects on Sharon's capacity to fulfill her considerable intellectual and social potential.

The therapist met with Sharon individually and expressed complete confidence in the truthfulness of Sharon's reports of sexual abuse. The therapist also validated Sharon's feelings of anger and hurt toward her parents, especially in light of their denial of the abuse. When Sharon understood that the therapist was in full agreement with her perspective, the therapist then attempted to broaden Sharon's point of view. The therapist emphasized the difficult situation in which Sharon's mother found herself. Mrs. J was 45 years old and had few job skills. This was her second marriage, and she was responsible for the welfare of four children. If she supported Sharon in the face of her husband's denial, Mrs. J would either have to move out of the house or ask her husband to leave. In light of her limited resources, this would mean that the family would become very poor and that Mrs. J would probably have to spend the remainder of her life without a husband. The therapist indicated that she was not making excuses for Mrs. J's failure to support Sharon, only that she wanted Sharon to consider the situation from a different point of view. The therapist emphasized that she did not agree with Mrs. J's decision, but that she did sympathize with her no-win situation.

The therapist also tried to broaden Sharon's perspective regarding her stepfather's refusal to accept responsibility for his behavior. The therapist noted several ways in which Mr. J was trying to reconcile with Sharon and compensate her for what he had done. Although Mr. J would never explicitly state that restitution was the purpose of his new generosity toward Sharon, the therapist made this interpretation for Sharon. Therefore Sharon had no reason to be exasperated by her stepfather's denial because he was admitting to the abuse, albeit indirectly. In addition, the therapist explained that many individuals who abuse children are very reluctant to admit it, partly because society regards child sexual abuse as a reprehensible crime and child sexual abusers as severely disturbed individuals. In any event, the therapist stated that she could understand Mr. J's reluctance to be labeled a child sexual abuser, even though it may have been deserved.

As this case exemplifies, problems are rarely fully resolved in families that include exploitive, uncooperative, and defensive parents. The therapist, however, attempts to provide the child or adolescent with a way of viewing the situation that will attenuate the detrimental effects of the exploitation. In addition, when necessary, the therapist also attempts to link the child with an adult in his or her natural environment who is better equipped than the parents to meet the child's emotional needs. In extreme cases, of course, the child may be referred to the state for protective services and possible placement in an alternative living situation.

Individual Therapy When the Family Is Not Dysfunctional

When treating adolescents, the therapist sometimes grapples with problematic issues that are not necessarily linked with disturbed family functioning. Usually, the therapist can encourage the adolescent to discuss the issue with the parents. The therapist may even model or role play the discussion with the adolescent. We prefer, however, that family members use their own resources, whenever possible, to resolve difficulties that involve their children because the healthy growth of the family is partly based on the conjoint resolution of situational and developmental difficulties (Minuchin, 1974).

In certain situations, however, such conjoint discussions may create more problems than would be resolved. These situations usually involve a personal issue that the adolescent is justifiably hesitant to discuss with his or her parents. In general, we do not believe that heterosexual activity and drug use qualify as such issues. For example, we strongly encourage sexually active adolescents to discuss this issue with their parents, and we may mediate the discussion in a way that minimizes negative parental responses to the adolescent's openness. In fact, if the adolescent is seriously endangering him- or herself (e.g., through excessive drug use), we are ethically bound to violate confidentiality. When adolescents are informed of this fact, they usually decide to broach the topic with their parents.

In certain rare instances, however, the therapist might provide individual therapy to an adolescent who lives within a well-functioning family system. One case, for example, involved 16-year-old Tammy K, who had been referred by her parents for poor academic performance in a private girls' school. Tammy was functioning quite well in other aspects of her life, including peer relations and family relations. The academic difficulties were the result of her relatively low level of motivation. She was not interested in academics, never had been and would probably not be interested in the future. Although it was unfortunate that she was not achieving up to her intellectual abilities, she was satisfied with her performance, had no interest in improving, and was currently progressing toward her vocational goals in a technical field.

During the evaluation process, Tammy asked the therapist for feedback regarding a personal problem and requested assurance that their discussion would be confidential. The therapist responded that within certain limits, confidentiality would be maintained. Tammy explained that she thought that she might be homosexual and wanted to know the therapist's opinion. Her concern was based on the fact that she had had sexual interaction with two of her close girlfriends and that she had little interaction with boys. She found the prospect of a homosexual lifestyle depressing because she wanted to get married and raise children. In addition, she was cognizant of the discrimination that homosexuals suffer in our society.

The therapist learned that Tammy was sexually aroused by thoughts of sexual encounters with boys and that she was sexually attracted to some boys. Unfortunately, she was in a situation that was not conducive to heterosexual interaction. She attended a girls' school with rigorous academic requirements; she was not especially attractive; and she had a philosophical interpersonal style that was probably not appealing to 16-year-old boys.

The therapist's intervention was primarily educational. He informed Tammy that a high percentage of individuals have homosexual contact at some point during adolescence. While she might choose a homosexual lifestyle at some point in the future, at this point such a conclusion was premature. Because Tammy was sexually aroused by boys and had little opportunity to date them, she was probably going through a common phase of adolescence. The therapist pointed out that after Tammy graduated from high school, she would no doubt meet many more males who had similar interests and attitudes toward life. It would then be up to her to decide on a sexual orientation.

In this case, there was little to gain from family involvement; on the contrary, there was the risk of stirring up unnecessary emotional turmoil in the parents.

Analogous situations can be found with adolescents who are involved in normative alcohol or drug use. Although, as described in Chapter 9, we take a very firm approach when dealing with adolescent chemical dependency, we also realize that a certain degree of chemical experimentation is to be expected among most adolescents. Some parents, however, feel that *any* adolescent chemical use reflects severe dysfunction in their child, themselves, and their family. When adolescents in such families admit, in confidentiality, to chemical use, we determine whether such use is linked with the presenting problems. If it is, we follow the procedures discussed in Chapter 9. If the chemical use is nonproblematic, our interventions are educational in nature and we do not push for disclosure to parents.

In some well-functioning families, the child copes poorly with a problem that is beyond his or her control. (As described in Chapter 7, these situations often occur in single-parent families and stepfamilies.) In general, the adolescent may gain little relief from emotional distress even with family support and understanding. Debbie Y was a 15-year-old referred by her mother for problems that included verbal aggression toward family members, peer difficulties, mood swings, and isolation from family activities. Although Debbie had experienced a variety of behavior problems throughout her life, these difficulties had intensified since her father died of kidney failure seven months earlier. Mrs. Y believed that Debbie's difficulties were caused by her failure to resolve emotional aspects of Mr. Y's death.

Initially, the therapist attempted to determine whether the current family interactions were contributing in some way to Debbie's behavior problems. Although the family was not functioning perfectly, Mrs. Y and her other children seemed to be coping satisfactorily in a difficult situation. Mrs. Y ran the family business, met the emotional needs of her children, and used adequate parenting strategies when dealing with problem situations. Moreover, Debbie's siblings were doing well in school and were not presenting any significant behavior problems. The therapist concluded that

Debbie's behavior problems were not associated with any significant family dysfunction.

The therapist reconsidered Mrs. Y's interpretation of the cause of Debbie's problems and decided that there was substantial merit to the view that these problems were linked with a disturbed grief reaction. An interview with Mrs. Y revealed that Debbie was the first-born and had been favored by her father. She and her father shared the same sense of humor and had similar interests in sports and literature. During the two weeks that Mr. Y was comatose before he died, Mrs. Y visited him, but the children did not. When Debbie learned of her father's death, she evidenced considerable denial. Moreover, the casket was closed at the funeral, and the family did not travel to the cemetery for the burial. Other family members experienced the various stages of the grieving process, but Debbie did not. Thus, it seemed quite possible that Debbie had not fully dealt with the emotionality of her father's death.

On an emotional level, Debbie continued to use denial as a defense mechanism. She had cried only twice during the past seven months and had adopted a highly intellectualized way of coping with her loss. She reported that she had no logical reason to be depressed or to experience anger over the loss of her father. In fact, she was pleased that her father's suffering had been relieved and that she would meet him in heaven at some future time. With whom could she be angry? It wasn't her father's fault that he died; the doctors and her mother did all that they could; and God must have had His reason for taking her father. Debbie's denial of her father's death was further evidenced by the fact that she had never visited his grave.

The therapist's goal was to enable Debbie to deal with the death of her father on an emotional level. This goal was difficult to achieve because Debbie was a very resistant and intellectualized adolescent. The therapist initially broached the subject through discussions that focused on the positive aspects of Debbie's relationship with her father. Later, Debbie brought to the therapy sessions pictures of her father and a book that he had written. By learning the role that Mr. Y played in Debbie's life, the therapist was able to guide the discussion to topics that were certain to evoke feelings of sadness and depression. For example, Debbie had always turned to her father for emotional support when she experienced problems in her peer relations. Now, in her view, no one could understand her. Similarly, situations arose that would concretize the loss to Debbie. One such situation regarded a father-daughter dinner that was an important social event at her school.

After two months of individual therapy, Debbie had reached a point where she could discuss to some extent her father, his death, and its impact on her life. Although the therapist was not extremely satisfied with the progress, he was very pleased with Mrs. Y's reports that Debbie's behavior problems had decreased substantially and that she was becoming actively engaged in family activities. At this point, the therapist decided that the Y family should play a more active role in the remainder of therapy. It was important that certain aspects (e.g., emotional support) of Mr. Y's role in Debbie's life now be fulfilled within the present family structure. Other aspects (e.g., intellectual discussions) might never be replaced, but grieving through the past, present, and future losses would be an important part of Debbie's maturation.

Socially Isolated Children with Social Skill Deficits

Child social isolation often occurs in family contexts that include parental overprotection. Often, the child in such families has a disability or has experienced serious medical problems during early childhood. The parent, quite naturally, has responded to the child's limitations with overprotection, thereby further delaying the development of the child's social competence. In such cases, intervention often attempts to engage the overinvolved parent in extrafamilial activities (e.g., employment, charity work), and arranges for the child to become involved in peer activities that exclude the parents, but include an adult supervisor.

Although the therapist may orchestrate these therapeutic interventions, they are best implemented by individuals who will remain in the child's natural environment when the therapist is no longer present. Thus, in most cases of social isolation from peers, the therapist guides the parents in facilitating their child's development of peer relations. In some cases, however, individual therapeutic interventions are appropriate for children who are socially isolated from their peers. Parental involvement may be counterproductive, or the parents may not possess the requisite skills for teaching the child how to develop social relations. In such cases, the parents are encouraged to be supportive of treatment, but actual interventions are conducted by the therapist. Typically, these interventions are educational in nature and attempt to develop the child's social facility, as described in the following case.

Donnie O was a 15-year-old who had mild cerebral palsy. He was of average intelligence, but his speech was moderately distorted due to the cerebral palsy. He was ambulatory, but he walked with an awkward gait and was very clumsy. Donnie was referred by an educational consultant at the pediatric facility that he attended. The reason for the referral was that Donnie was extremely shy and had not spoken in school for two years.

Donnie's shyness was exacerbated by his family environment. Donnie was an only child, and his parents made few maturity demands. Both Mr. and Mrs. O were also extremely quiet individuals, and there was rarely any conversation in the home. Neither parent had any extrafamilial interests, and, except for an occasional dinner out, all of their nonworking hours were spent at home.

When the family did go out for dinner, Donnie was too shy to enter the restaurant. Consequently, the parents ordered for Donnie and brought his meal out to the car. In light of the parents' own social skill deficits, the therapist did not anticipate that they would be very helpful in providing the guidance that Donnie needed for the development of his peer relations. Nevertheless, Mr. and Mrs. O were very supportive of Donnie's therapeutic contacts and drove more than 100 round-trip miles to keep his appointment each week.

Donnie had been in therapy for a year before he was seen by the multisystemic therapist. During that year, Donnie had made great therapeutic progress and was now able to carry on a relatively appropriate conversation with the new therapist in his office. Previously, Donnie had made almost no eye contact and had minimal conversation skills. Unfortunately, Donnie had not generalized his new social skills to the outside social context, so this became the new therapist's primary goal. Although this was an extremely anxiety-arousing goal for Donnie, the therapist was assisted by the forces of nature. Puberty was in full swing, and Donnie's main goal in life was to have a girlfriend.

The therapist and Donnie jointly decided that the primary long-term goal of therapy would be to develop Donnie's social skills to the point that he could get a date, since this was a necessary step toward having a girlfriend. Getting a date may appear to be a relatively simple goal, but this case provided a valuable lesson regarding the complexity of even the simplest interpersonal communication.

The therapist was required to reduce each component of the social skills training into very small steps. At first, Donnie could not pretend that the therapist was a girl, face him, and say, "Hi, my name is Donnie." He could only say this if he was facing away from the therapist, and, even then, his speech was filled with anxiety. It took six therapy sessions before Donnie was able to accomplish this first step with the therapist.

Although there are thousands of ways to communicate the simplest message awkwardly, there are relatively few ways to communicate the message with social ease. Body posture must be appropriate, eye contact is necessary, the tone of the voice is important, and the pattern of speech must follow convention. Deficits in any single aspect of the communication can create the impression that the speaker is strange in some way. For adolescents, such an impression can readily contribute to poor peer relations.

After several months of practice in conversational skills with the therapist who was pretending to be a girl, Donnie was ready to try out his new social facility in vivo. The therapist informed Donnie that during the next session, they would leave the office and walk down the hall until they found a suitable female with whom he could use his conversational skills. Unknown to Donnie, the therapist arranged to have a 30-year-old female social worker at a convenient location. When Donnie saw her, he froze and refused to walk down the hall. The therapist, who was larger and stronger than Donnie, dragged him to the social worker, introduced him, and then excused himself so that he could read a bulletin board several yards away. Although Donnie struggled at first, the confederate was very responsive and Donnie's confidence started to grow. With increased confidence, Donnie's conversation became more animated and he began to enjoy the interaction immensely.

Conducting a five-minute conversation with a 30-year-old confederate is obviously a long way from having a date with a 15-year-old peer. Nevertheless, Donnie had made substantial progress toward his goal and deserved considerable credit for attempting to overcome a difficult problem. In addition, it is important to remember that for every Donnie, there is a Sally who is in a similar situation. For example, Sally might be a person who is disabled, longs to be loved and cared for, and believes that no one will ever want a long-term relationship with her because of her problems. Donnie and Sally could be a very compatible match. It is the therapist's task, therefore, to develop the child's cognitive and behavioral repertoires so that, when Donnie meets a Sally, he will be able to respond in a way that sets a spiral of positive reciprocity in motion. In the present case, Donnie wanted to date a cheerleader and was prejudiced against girls with physical disabilities. In light of the fact that his most frequent source of acculturation was television, it was not surprising that his views of heterosexual relations were unrealistic. The therapist spent considerable time reframing Donnie's perceptions of relationships, so that he came to believe that the important aspects of a girlfriend were personality, character, and emotional sensitivity, rather than physical appearance.

Several aspects of Donnie's case are pertinent to the multisystemic approach.

1. Individual therapy was used only when alternative options were not feasible.
2. The strengths of the adolescent (i.e., heterosexual desires, intellectual skills) were used by the therapist to facilitate therapeutic progress.
3. Emphasis was placed on extending treatment gains to the outside environment.
4. The outside environment was modified to promote the youth's acquisition and mastery of the social skills. If, for example, a female had been selected at random for the practice of social skills, Donnie might have experienced rejection and therapeutic progress would have been severely delayed. In addition, it was arranged that his eventual dating partner would be someone who would be receptive to an awkward adolescent and who was also intelligent and kind.

Motivating Appropriate Behavior in the Face of Short-Term Payoffs

The misbehavior of many children is motivated largely by the short-term consequences of that behavior. Some children are willing to engage in whatever tactics are necessary to achieve their desired goal. Younger children might cry, nag, and whine to achieve their ends, while adolescents might threaten to run away or otherwise harass their parents. In many cases, such noxious child behavior is maintained by intermittent parental acquiescence to child demands; that is, the child learns that if his or her pressures are tenacious enough, the parent will eventually give in.

As described in Chapter 3, concerning parent-child relations, the parents should set firm and consistent limits for child behavior and implement appropriate contingencies for both positive and negative behavior. It is also important to provide the parent with whatever cognitive and behavioral skills are needed to counter the variety of manipulations that the child might use to undermine the new set of limits.

Unfortunately, some parents are in situations that make it difficult for them to withstand the persistency of their children. For example, when single mothers arrive home after a long day of work, they typically face several additional hours of childcare and household responsibilities. These mothers may be extremely tired and, as a consequence, may not be able to hold firm against the persistent demands of a child who is well rested and has learned from previous interactions that mother will eventually give in.

Although the consistent implementation of contingencies for child misbehavior can alter the rate of that behavior, the therapeutic process can be very time-consuming and arduous. The parent training approach of Patterson and his colleagues (1980), for example, focuses on teaching parents how to use principles from social learning theory to decrease rates of negative child behaviors and to increase rates of positive behaviors. In one study of children with conduct disorders, Patterson (1974) reported a mean cost of 31.4 hours of professional time for family treatment, 28.6 hours for classroom intervention, and 1.9 hours for post-therapy retraining procedures. Moreover, since 44% of the children scored within normal ranges of behavior at baseline, time costs would likely have increased with a more seriously disturbed sample.

In order to expedite child behavior change in families where the parents have not enforced consistent limits, we have developed a motivational strategy that is utilized with the individual child. The goal of this strategy is to have the *child* decide to change the problem behavior, rather than to be forced to change by parental contingencies. This motivational strategy is used early in treatment, before any new contingencies are implemented.

The use of the motivational strategy is based on several assumptions and conditions.

1. Psychosocial development is enhanced when children believe that they have decided on their own to behave appropriately (Maccoby & Martin, 1983).

2. Children and adolescents typically wish to be treated by adults as if they are more mature than they actually are. Six-year-olds believe that they should be treated as 8-year-olds, and 16-year-olds believe that they should be treated as adults.

3. Despite the child's behavior problems, the parents love and support the child. Our motivational strategy is ineffective and inappropriate in the context of parental indifference toward or abuse of the child.

4. The child is attached to and loves the parent(s). The motivational strategy has little chance of success with children who are basically unattached to their parents.

The overriding goal of the motivational strategy is to help children to develop a more mature perspective regarding their role in the family. The process of the therapist's intervention aims at activating the child's social perspective-taking abilities and decreasing the child's egocentricity. The content of the intervention is best presented through a case example, which is typical of situations in which we have found this motivational strategy to be most effective.

Danny C was a 12-year-old boy who lived with his mother and younger brother and sister. Danny was referred by his mother for high rates of noncompliant behavior, poor school performance, and fighting with his siblings. Mrs. C was under considerable emotional and financial stress. She was lonely and socially isolated. Her ex-husband was not paying child support, she was employed for 50 hours per week, and she was barely paying the bills. In addition, the behavior problems presented by the children, especially Danny, were compounding the stress and causing much emotional turmoil. Consistent with the multisystemic perspective, interventions were developed to address the problems in Mrs. C's extrafamilial systems. Pertinent to the present discussion, however, the following strategy was used to motivate Danny to behave in a more responsible and mature manner.

The therapist met with Danny alone during the first half of the second therapy session. They chatted about sports, and the therapist speculated that given his size and apparent strength, Danny must be an exceptional athlete. The therapist also asked Danny if he had a girlfriend and learned that Danny had a crush on a classmate who also liked him. After paying Danny several other compliments pertaining to his maturity, the therapist asked Danny about an issue that had been bothering the therapist since last week. Throughout the subsequent discussion, the therapist was concerned, but was not pejorative at any point. He acted as if he simply did not understand how such a fine young man could behave so poorly toward his mother.

THERAPIST: "There is something that I really do not understand. Here you are, a bright, big, and strong teenager (the therapist knew that Danny was 12 years old) who is almost in high school and who almost has a girlfriend already. Also, now that your dad doesn't live with you any longer, in a way you are the man of the family. Your mom is still the boss, but you are the oldest child, though you're not really a child anymore. Are you with me so far; do you know what I'm saying?"

DANNY: "Yeah."

THERAPIST: "Well then, what is the story with how you are acting around the house? I mean, your mom is in a tough situation. Tell me, what is tough about the situation that she is in?"

At this point the therapist led Danny to use his perspective-taking skills to gain a better understanding of the stresses and difficulties that his mother was experiencing. Some children can readily appreciate their mother's situation. Other children need prompting and leading questions to understand the situation. When Danny had a good appreciation of the mother's difficult situation, the therapist proceeded as follows.

THERAPIST: "So here is the situation. Your mom is working hard every day so that she can make the money to pay the rent for the apartment, buy the food that she cooks you for dinner, and pay for all the other things that you and your brother and sister use. Also, she doesn't have anyone her own age to help her out, she's got to do it all by herself. Now here you are, a big, strong, healthy teenager. What do you do to make things better for your mom, who you love very much. You do love her, don't you?"

DANNY: "Yeah."

THERAPIST: "What do you do? Do you hug her when she comes home, cook the dinner, take care of the little ones, vacuum the carpet, clean up your room, sell newspapers to make some extra money? No, you hassle her. You talk back and treat her poorly. You don't do what you're told and don't do your chores. Even worse, you fight with your little brother and sister. Here you are big and mature, and you fight with them, rather than acting like a big brother and taking care of them to help your mom out. This is what I don't understand. If you were 6 years old, if you were not very smart, or if you just didn't love your mother, I could understand why you would act like this. But, look at you. You seem really nice, you are smart and talented, and you tell me that you love her. It just doesn't make any sense to me. So my question is, why do you act like this, what is the story?"

Rarely does the child have a response to this question.

THERAPIST: "I just don't know what to do. Your mom is very concerned about your behavior and I agree with her. I think that you really do need to start acting your age, but I don't know what to do about it. We can't make you act more mature; if you really want to act like a little kid, there isn't much we can do about it. What do you think about this whole situation?"

At this point, if the therapeutic manipulation has been well orchestrated, a high percentage of children will indicate that they are ready and willing to "act their age." These children will then consent to decrease their negative behaviors and to start behaving more responsibly. The therapist will accept the child's offer at face value and praise the child's decision. If the child's behavior is greatly improved by the next session, the therapist profusely praises the child. If the child's behavior has not improved, the therapist will implement a contingency system in an effort to provide external motivation for the desired behavior change.

Based on our clinical experience, approximately 30% of the children and adolescents who agree to change their behavior on their own follow through completely. Our assumption is that these individuals have acquired a different perspective regarding their role in the family. The old perspective was quite egocentric and concerned with the gratification of personal desires. The new perspective emphasizes the importance of their contributions to family functioning. The new perspective requires both increased maturity on the child's part and concomitant changes in the way that the child is treated in the family system: Increased maturity and responsibility should be rewarded with increased freedom and privileges. In such cases, therapy is often terminated after only three to four sessions.

In about 40% of the cases, the child's behavior has improved slightly, but it is still necessary to implement a contingency system through the parent(s). Our impression, however, is that reframing the child's role in the family facilitates further behavioral change and helps to limit the number of therapeutic sessions.

Finally, in approximately 30% of the cases, our cognitive intervention has virtually no discernable impact on the child. In such situations, we continue to attempt cognitive interventions, but we emphasize the development of firm and consistent parenting skills. If existing marital and extrafamilial problems can be resolved, we believe that it is usually possible to ameliorate the behavior problems of most children through the appropriate implemention of reinforcement contingencies. With adolescents, however, the situation can be more difficult because they are often able to function quite autonomously in relation to their parents. One 13-year-old boy, for example, responded to the therapist's motivational talk by saying, "I don't want to grow up and act mature and you can't make me." Strategies for dealing with seemingly unmotivated adolescents are discussed in Chapter 3.

In the case of Danny C, his egocentrism, together with the short-term payoffs that he received for his misbehavior, inhibited his ability to appreciate fully the negative ramifications of his problem behaviors for the family system. In other situations involving adolescents, egocentrism and short-term payoffs for dysfunctional behavior interfere with the ability of the adolescent to appreciate the long-term negative consequences of that behavior. In such cases, the therapist might use perspective-taking strategies, similar to those described for Danny C, to provide the adolescent with a broader view of self.

Kathy L, for example, was a 14-year-old ninth-grader who was referred because of sexually promiscuous behavior. During the first individual meeting with the therapist, Kathy reported that she was not popular and could not get a boyfriend before she became sexually active. She stated that her sexual activity, which had started a year ago, had led to considerable popularity and to many dates with boys. From a certain perspective, Kathy's promiscuous behavior was a logical solution to her peer problems.

The therapist's approach was to agree with Kathy's conceptualization of the situation. He knew, from her parents' reports, that moralizing would be counterproductive. The therapist noted, however, that although her point of view had merit, it was more typical of young adolescents than of older adolescents. The therapist explained that when most teenagers reach the tenth or eleventh grade, they realize that promiscuous behavior can have serious long-term negative consequences that more than make up for the short-term payoffs that she was currently receiving. Sexually promiscuous girls, the therapist pointed out, often develop a schoolwide reputation that greatly interferes with their chances of having the type of close heterosexual relationship that they desire. Therefore, by engaging in frequent sexual behavior, promiscuous girls actually decrease the probability of attaining future emotional intimacy. In addition, promiscuous individuals are at much higher risk for contracting diseases that can result in infertility or even death. While the therapist agreed that Kathy's sexual activity was largely her own business, he also enabled her to conceptualize her sexual behavior within a broader framework. This reconceptualization eventually enabled Kathy to reach her "own" decision to modify her sexual activity. Finally, it should be noted that several systemic problems were also treated in this case (e.g., a lack of parental monitoring).

SUMMARY

This chapter describes some of the most common contexts in which we recommend the use of individual child therapy, which is not viewed as theoretically incompatible with family therapy and other systemic approaches. In fact, as described in our case examples, the therapist's decision to use individual therapy is always based on a broad examination of the child's systemic context.

REFERENCES

Amirkhan, J. (1982). Expectancies and attributions for hyperactive and medicated hyperactive students. *Journal of Abnormal Child Psychology, 10*, 265–276.

Browne, A., & Finkelhor, D. (1986). Impact of child sexual abuse: Review of research. *Psychological Bulletin, 99*, 66–77.

Brunk, M. A., Henggeler, S. W., & Whelan, J. P. (1987). Comparison of multisystemic therapy and parent training in the brief treatment of child abuse and neglect. *Journal of Consulting and Clinical Psychology, 55*, 171–178.

Campbell, S. B., & Pavlauskas, S. (1979). Peer relations in hyperactive children. *Journal of Child Psychology and Psychiatry, 20*, 233–246.

Conners, C. K., & Wells, K. C. (1986). *Hyperkinetic children: A neuropsychosocial approach.* Beverly Hills, CA: Sage.

Cunningham, C. E., & Barkley, R. A. (1979). The interactions of normal and hyperactive children with their mothers in free play and structured tasks. *Child Development, 50*, 217–224.

Dubey, D. R., O'Leary, S. G., & Kaufman, K. F. (1983). Training parents of hyperactive children in child management: A comparative outcome study. *Journal of Abnormal Child Psychology, 11*, 229–246.

D'Zurilla, T. J., & Goldfried, M. R. (1971). Problem solving and behavior modification. *Journal of Abnormal Psychology, 78*, 107–126.

Gholson, J. B., & Rosenthal, T. L. (Eds.). (1984). *Applications of cognitive-developmental theory.* New York: Academic Press.

Haley, J. (1963). *Strategies of psychotherapy.* New York: Grune & Stratton.

Hanson, C. L., & Henggeler, S. W. (1982). The behavior disorders and problems of female adolescents. In S. W. Henggeler (Ed.), *Delinquency and adolescent psychopathology: A family-ecological systems approach*. Littleton, MA: Wright-PSG.

Henggeler, S. W., & Cohen, R. (1984). The role of cognitive development in the family-ecological systems approach to child psychopathology. In J. B. Gholson & T. L. Rosenthal (Eds.), *Applications of cognitive-developmental theory*. New York: Academic Press.

Henker, B., & Whalen, C. K. (1980). The many messages of medication: Hyperactive children's perceptions and attributions. In S. Salzinger, J. Antrobus, & J. Glick (Eds.), *The ecosystem of the "sick" child*. New York: Academic Press.

Kazdin, A. E. (1988). *Child psychotherapy: Developing and identifying effective treatments*. New York: Pergamon.

Kendall, P. C., & Hollon, S. D. (Eds.). (1979). *Cognitive-behavioral interventions: Theory, research, and procedures*. New York: Academic Press.

Kennedy, R. E. (1984). Cognitive behavioral interventions with delinquents. In A. W. Meyers & W. E. Craighead (Eds.), *Cognitive behavior therapy with children*. New York: Plenum.

Klesges, R. C., Sanchez, V. C., & Stanton, A. L. (1982). Obtaining employment in academia: The hiring process and characteristics of successful applicants. *Professional Psychology, 13,* 577–586.

Kohlberg, L. (1969). Stage and sequence: The cognitive-developmental approach to socialization. In D. A. Goslin (Ed.), *Handbook of socialization theory and research*. New York: Rand-Mc-Nally.

Maccoby, E. E., & Martin, J. A. (1983). Socialization in the context of the family: Parent-child interaction. In E. M. Hetherington (Ed.), *Handbook of child psychology, Volume IV: Socialization, personality, and social development*. New York: Wiley.

Mash, E. J., & Johnston, C. (1982). A comparison of the mother-child interactions of younger and older hyperactive and normal children. *Child Development, 53,* 1371–1381.

Meichenbaum, D. (1977). *Cognitive-behavior modification: An integrative approach*. New York: Plenum.

Meyers, A. W., & Craighead, W. E. (1984). Cognitive behavior therapy with children: A historical, conceptual, and organizational overview. In A. W. Meyers & W. E. Craighead, *Cognitive behavior therapy with children* (pp. 1–17). New York: Plenum.

Minuchin, S. (1974). *Families and family therapy*. Cambridge, MA: Harvard University Press.

Montalvo, B., & Haley, J. (1973). In defense of child therapy. *Family Process, 12,* 227–244.

Morgan, S. B. (1988). The autistic child and family functioning: A developmental-family systems perspective. *Journal of Autism and Developmental Disorders, 18,* 263–280.

Patterson, G. R. (1974). Interventions for boys with conduct problems: Multiple settings, treatments, and criteria. *Journal of Consulting and Clinical Psychology, 42,* 471–481.

Patterson, G. R. (1980). *Coercive family processes*. Eugene, OR: Castillia.

Rosenthal, R. H., & Allen, T. W. (1978). An examination of attention, arousal, and learning dysfunctions of hyperkinetic children. *Psychological Bulletin, 82,* 1113–1130.

Scarr, S., & McCartney, K. (1983). How people make their own environments: A theory of genotype-environment effects. *Child Development, 54,* 424–435.

Selman, R. L. (1974). Stages in role-taking and moral judgments as guides to social interventions. In T. Lockona (Ed.), *Man and morality*. New York: Holt.

Solanto, M. V. (1984). Neuropharmacological basis of stimulant drug action in attention deficit disorder with hyperactivity: A review and synthesis. *Psychological Bulletin, 95,* 387–409.

Tsai, M., Feldman-Summers, S., & Edgar, M. (1979). Childhood molestation: Variables related to differential impacts on psychosexual functioning in adult women. *Journal of Abnormal Psychology, 88,* 404–417.

Whalen, C. K., & Henker, B. (1976). Psychostimulants and children: A review and analysis. *Psychological Bulletin, 83,* 1113–1130.

Whalen, C. K., Henker, B., & Dotemoto, S. (1981). Teacher response to the methylphenidate (Ritalin) versus placebo status of hyperactive boys in the classroom. *Child Development, 52,* 1005–1014.

Whitman, T., Burgio, L., & Johnston, M. B. (1984). Cognitive behavioral interventions with mentally retarded children. In A. W. Meyers & W. E. Craighead (Eds.), *Cognitive behavior therapy with children.* New York: Plenum.

CHAPTER 3

The Treatment of Parent-Child Difficulties

*I*t is widely recognized by theorists, clinicians, and researchers that parent-child relations are closely associated with important aspects of children's emotional, social, and cognitive development. For example, most theories of socialization view parents as the primary facilitators of children's self-concepts, interpersonal skills, achievement motivation, and sex-role behavior. Moreover, empirical evidence suggests that children who evidence problematic relations with their parents are more likely to exhibit emotional, behavioral, and cognitive difficulties (Emery, 1982; Hetherington & Martin, 1986; Shinn, 1978). Although many factors affect child development, of course, the relationship between the developing child and parents probably represents the most significant influence during the course of the individual's life span.

During the past 15 years, numerous theorists have developed conceptual models for describing and explaining parent-child relations. The adoption of a given conceptual model represents an important starting point for the clinician because each model provides direction regarding the assessment and organization of information and the target and choice of interventions. For example, Olson and his colleagues (Olson, Russell, & Sprenkle, 1983; Olson, Sprenkle, & Russell, 1979) have developed the Circumplex Model of Marital and Family Systems in which the dimensions of cohesion (the emotional bonding between family members) and adaptability (the ability of the family members to reorganize in response to situational and developmental stress) are used to describe and identify 16 types of family systems. Olson and his colleagues assume that moderate levels of cohesion and adaptability are most desirable for effective family relationships and that extremes on either dimension are potentially problematic.

In a similar vein, Beavers and his associates (Beavers, 1981; Lewis, Beavers, Gossett, & Phillips, 1976) have proposed a model in which the dimensions of family competence in task performance and operating style are used to organize families into seven types. These theorists view family competence as including eight different components (e.g., efficiency in decision making, clarity of communication), and perceive family operating styles as ranging from centripetal (members are enmeshed) to centrifugal (members are disengaged). In this model, dysfunctional types of families include those who are less competent in meeting important developmental tasks and in balancing individual members' needs for intimacy with their needs for autonomy.

Other theorists have also attempted to delineate the basic dimensions that differentiate healthy from pathological families. Epstein, Bishop, and Levin (1978) have included six major dimensions of family relations in the McMaster Model of Family Functioning. These dimensions include (1) problem solving (the ability to resolve issues that threaten family integrity), (2) communication (information exchange), (3) roles (the development of behavior patterns for handling various family functions, such as the provision of economic resources), (4) affective responsiveness (the appropriateness of affective responses in individual family members), (5) affective involvement (concern for each other's activities and pursuits), and (6) behavior control (the way the family communicates and maintains behavior standards for each member).

Barnhill (1979) has suggested that family functioning can be described in terms of eight basic dimensions or continua, grouped according to the following four themes: identity (individuation vs. enmeshment, mutuality vs. isolation); change (flexibility vs. rigidity, stability vs. disorganization); information processing (clear vs. unclear or distorted perceptions, clear vs. unclear or distorted communication); and role structuring (role reciprocity vs. unclear roles or role conflict, clear vs. diffuse or breached generational boundaries).

Patterson (1982) has introduced a social learning model of family relations in which parental contingent responsiveness (defined as the ratio of contingent to noncontingent parental reinforcement) is viewed as an important determinant of child behavior. According to Patterson, parents who tend to respond noncontingently are likely to promote coercive cycles of interaction with their children.

In contrast to these theoretical efforts, several researchers have used factor analysis to identify basic dimensions of parent-child relations. The strength of this approach is that circumscribed domains of parent-child behavior can be determined from an empirical clustering rather than from an inductive conceptual clustering. Factor-analytic studies (for reviews, see Maccoby & Martin, 1983; Martin, 1975; Schaefer, 1959) have indicated that the majority of child-directed, parental behaviors represent two primary dimensions. The first dimension reflects parental *control* strategies that may range from permissiveness to restrictiveness. Permissive parents provide their children with little structure and discipline, make few demands for mature behavior, and take a tolerant attitude toward their children's impulses. Restrictive parents, on the other hand, are more directive, overcontrolling, and intrusive in regard to their children's activities. The second dimension, *affect*, reflects parental behaviors that are emotional in tone and that may range from warmth to rejection. Warm parents are relatively accepting and nurturing and use substantial positive reinforcement when interacting with their children. Rejecting parents, in contrast, are relatively hostile and low in nurturance and tend to use criticism and even aggression when interacting with their children. As discussed in this chapter, there are several possible configurations of parental control and affect (e.g., high permissiveness-high warmth, high restrictiveness-high rejection), and therapeutic interventions may be needed to target either or both of these behavioral dimensions.

This chapter provides a brief overview of the associations between parental control/affect and social development in children. Readers are encouraged, however, to supplement this overview with readings in the child development literature (e.g., Hetherington & Martin, 1986; Maccoby & Martin, 1983; Sigel, Dreyer, & McGillicuddy-DeLisi, 1984). This chapter also describes interventions that enable parents and children to change their problematic interaction styles in ways that promote positive development. Discussion of these interventions is intended only to provide general guidelines for treatment, with the recognition that every child and family deserves a highly individual-ized intervention plan that is designed to meet their specific developmental needs. A final purpose of this chapter is to discuss the effects of parental modeling on children and on parent-child relations.

PARENTAL CONTROL

Parental control strategies have several important functions in child development. One is to teach the child frustration tolerance. For example, when parents say "no" to their toddler, they are teaching the child that immediate gratification of impulses is not always possible and that successful interpersonal relations involve making some concessions. Unless a child learns to tolerate the occasional frustration of perceived needs, he or she will almost certainly experience later interpersonal difficulties.

Parental controls also teach children socially acceptable norms of behavior. Included among these social norms are the avoidance of aggression, cooperating with others, and showing respect for authority. When parents allow their child to behave aggressively toward them (or toward a sibling) or when they always give in to the child's selfish demands, they are teaching the child social norms that may promote aggression and noncooperation in the child's relations with peers. Similarly, when parents do not teach the child to respect their authority, the child is likely to have considerable difficulty interacting with adults outside of the home. Here, the child's lack of respect for authority (or the belief that he or she has the same rights and privileges as adults) may lead to problems in the child's interactions with teachers, adult leaders of children's groups (e.g., Scout leader, baseball coach), neighborhood residents, and, eventually, with the legal system. Hence, parental control teaches the child to manage emotions and behavior through the internalization of a socially sanctioned set of norms. This learning process prepares the child for interactions with peers and other adults throughout the life span. From this perspective, it is a primary responsibility of parenthood to implement reasonable controls over child behavior.

Research suggests that many child and adolescent behavioral disturbances are direct reflections of ineffective parental control strategies (Dornbusch et al., 1985; Olweus, 1980; Patterson & Stouthamer-Loeber, 1984). In the following section, a discussion of various styles of parental discipline and the likely impact of such styles on child psychosocial functioning are presented. Guidelines for altering factors that contribute to ineffective parental discipline are also provided. Following that, we discuss the role of parental consistency in the effective control of child behavior.

Discipline Strategies

The development of an effective intervention plan for childhood and adolescent behavior problems requires a careful assessment of the parents' discipline strategies—a determina-tion that can most reliably be made when the therapist obtains information from multiple vantage points. One source of information that we have found to be extremely useful when working with families of younger children is the direct observation of parental control strategies in the therapy setting. We typically request that everyone who lives in the home, including siblings and, when relevant, any live-in partner of the parent, attend the initial therapy meeting. By including all such individuals, the therapist has the opportunity to observe which adults attempt to exert control over the children and the method and effectiveness of this control.

A second important source of information is the parents themselves. The parents' decision to seek treatment is often precipitated by recent child misbehavior and is typically related to parental feelings of frustration regarding the control of such behavior. By initiating a discussion of the parents' typical disciplinary responses, the therapist can offer emotional support to the frustrated parents and obtain information that can be used to design more effective strategies.

It is also useful to obtain information regarding parental discipline from the children. Often, children will be quite candid regarding the severity and consistency of their parents' discipline. Numerous children and adolescents have told us, directly and indirectly, that their parents were too lax or inconsistent. On the other hand, many adolescents unrealistically feel that their parents are "too tough" on them. Sometimes, when the therapist suggests that more severe discipline might be needed to control the adolescent's misbehavior, the adolescent comes to view the parents' discipline as the lesser of two evils.

Early in the course of treatment, the therapist might also assign the parents homework tasks to obtain a clearer picture of parental discipline strategies. For example, the therapist can request that the parents keep a daily record of (1) child misbehaviors, (2) parental discipline in response to these misbehaviors, and (3) the child's compliance or noncompliance with each disciplinary attempt. The therapist can subsequently examine the parents' records to assess their disciplinary strategies and the perceived effectiveness of these strategies. Moreover, the parents' willingness to comply with the therapist's request, the quality of their record keeping, and their definition of child misbehavior can all provide the therapist with information that is relevant to the formulation of a therapeutic plan.

Style of discipline.   Parents may employ a wide variety of disciplinary techniques (e.g., room restriction, removal of select privileges, assignment of extra chores) in controlling a child's behavior, yet the style of the parent's discipline may remain consistent. Styles of parental discipline range from permissive to authoritative to authoritarian (Baumrind, 1967, 1978, 1983). A *permissive* discipline style is one in which the parent(s) makes few, if any, attempts to control the child's behavior, including those behaviors that are generally disapproved of by other members of society. In essence, the child has few rules to follow and is allowed to make his or her own decisions, and few maturity demands are placed on the child by the parent. In contrast, an *authoritarian* or power-assertive disciplinary style requires an unquestioning obedience to parental authority and provides the child with little opportunity to explain his or her behavior to the parent. When the child deviates from parental rules, fairly severe punishment (often physical) is likely to be used. The authoritarian parent uses a directive teaching style (i.e., physically taking over, or giving direct verbal orders) and does not invite the child's participation in decision making. An *authoritative* discipline style allows room for give-and-take between the parent and child, involves a high level of maturity demands, and includes the competent use of parental authority to control the child's inappropriate behavior. The authoritative parent recognizes that his or her parental status carries the responsibility to discipline the child, yet unlike the authoritarian parent, the authoritative parent does not ignore the child's feelings and opinions.

Although the concept of reciprocal parent-child influences must be remembered when interpreting results, research suggests that the authoritative discipline style is more likely to promote child psychosocial functioning than the permissive and authoritarian styles. Indeed, permissive parenting has been associated with impulsivity (Baumrind, 1967), aggression (Olweus, 1980; Yarrow, Campbell, & Burton, 1968), and a lack of social responsibility and independence in children (Baumrind, 1971). Similarly, authoritarian parenting has been linked to aggression (Eron, Walder, & Lefkowitz, 1971; Yarrow et al., 1968), social withdrawal from peers (Baumrind & Black, 1967), and low self-esteem in children (Coopersmith, 1967; Loeb, Horst, & Horton, 1980). In children of permissive parents, it seems likely that aggression and social incompetence are maintained by parental indifference toward child outbursts on the one hand, and by parental failure to make maturity demands of the child on the other. In contrast, among children of authoritarian parents, it seems that aggression and social incompetence are more likely the result of extreme parental punitiveness and demandingness, coupled with a lack of responsiveness to the child's needs. Thus, the high demandingness and low responsiveness associated with authoritarian parenting seem to have the undesirable effect of arousing or strengthening aggressive tendencies in the child. The mechanism by which these aggressive tendencies are created would appear to reside, at least in part, with the development of the child's moral reasoning skills. Hoffman and Saltzstein (Hoffman, 1976; Hoffman & Saltzstein, 1967; Saltzstein, 1976) have found that authoritarian (i.e., power-assertive) parents seem to hinder the moral development of their children. A likely explanation for this finding is that the child has only a relatively primitive model for interacting with another person, a "might makes right" model in which the other's needs and feelings are ignored. It would seem, then, that power-assertive parents impede moral reasoning and encourage aggression in their children because these parents may be discouraging the development of the child's social perspective-taking skills.

On the other hand, authoritative parents seem to facilitate the moral development of their children by explaining the consequences of the child's actions and being as responsive as possible to the child's reasonable demands and desires. In this case, it seems likely that the parent is teaching the child to consider the needs of others and to weigh the moral consequences of alternative courses of action before deciding on a given solution. Thus, authoritative parents may facilitate their children's moral development because these parents model social responsiveness and encourage the development of the child's perspective-taking skills.

Therapeutic guidelines.   These findings suggest that one important therapeutic task may be to help permissive and authoritarian parents develop more authoritative disciplinary styles. As a first step toward this goal, it is often helpful to point out some of the disadvantages that are associated with the parents' present style of discipline. Permissive parents might be told, for example, that impulse control problems and antisocial behavior can be a result of giving in to the child's demands or of allowing the child to behave disrespectfully toward authority. Similarly, to authoritarian parents, the therapist should explain how extreme punitiveness toward the child can evoke anger and resentment toward the parent. To those authoritarian parents who use physical discipline, the therapist should also explain that parental modeling of aggression can only exacerbate the child's aggressive behavior.

It may also be necessary to explain to authoritarian parents that physical discipline is inappropriate when used with adolescents (e.g., spanking a 14-year-old girl). More specifically, physical discipline is likely to be viewed by most adolescents as an invasion of their personal space and conveys a lack of respect for their emerging sense of adult sexuality. Thus, aside from the fact that physical discipline is unlikely to alter the adolescent's problematic behavior, such discipline may be humiliating to the adolescent and may have a negative effect on the adolescent's self-image. It should be noted, however, that some younger children will respond only to physical discipline, and that physical discipline may sometimes be required to prevent a younger child from engaging in some dangerous activity (e.g., running across a hazardous intersection).

As a second step in the development of new parental control strategies, the therapist should provide the parents with methods of handling behavior problems. There is extensive evidence (Patterson, 1982) that parents trained in behavior management procedures can ameliorate many behavior problems of young children. This training generally includes: (1) teaching the parents to set clearly defined rules for the child's behavior; (2) detailing how the parents can effectively monitor the child's compliance or noncompliance with the rules; (3) establishing contingencies for compliance (i.e., positive reinforcement) and noncompliance (i.e., punishment) to each rule; and (4) implementing the contingencies as outlined.

When the parents' rules and contingencies have been established, the therapist should emphasize that it is not the parents' responsibility to badger the child to follow the rules; instead, the decision about whether or not to comply with each of the rules is the child's alone. Thus, the parents should not remind the child 20 times to take out the trash, nor should they become emotionally upset when the child talks back. Rather, they should simply implement the previously established consequences for the child's specific misbehavior, leaving the child to deal with these consequences. Indeed, to the extent that the parents focus their efforts on monitoring the child's behavior and implementing the appropriate contingencies, the parents can avoid becoming involved in negative emotional interchanges with the child when he or she does not follow the rules.

Another set of guidelines that we offer to parents pertains to the types of discipline that they should use with their children. First, as a general rule of thumb, we advise parents to use shorter and more immediate punishments with younger children due to the child's more limited cognitive capacities. For example, with a preschooler, an immediate two-minute time out for throwing food is likely to be more effective in changing the child's behavior than is revoking the child's television privileges for the evening.

As the child becomes older and is increasingly able to reason beyond the immediate situation and to link events that are separated in time, the use of a wider range of punishments over a longer time period can be effectively used. For example, during the middle childhood years, the removal of privileges and activities that are important to the child (e.g., watching a particular television show, using the telephone for two evenings) can be very effective forms of punishment. During adolescence, discipline can be even more distal (e.g., being grounded for the next month).

Clearly, the therapist should carefully consider the child's cognitive skills when assisting the parents in implementing child control strategies. Failure to do so may exacerbate current behavior problems, contribute to more negative parent-child relations, and lead the parents to withdraw prematurely from treatment.

We also advise parents that an essential element of discipline is that it be aversive to the child, regardless of the child's age. If the punishment is not aversive, it is unlikely to counter the child's tendency to repeat the problem behavior. The therapist should help the parents select an aversive form of discipline that is tailored to the individual child. With older children and adolescents, we often guide the parents in finding a punishment that is both aversive and constructive (e.g., cleaning the toilet and bathtub, scrubbing the kitchen floor). The advantage of these punishments is that they provide a payoff for the parents (who would otherwise have to perform the chores), thus increasing the likelihood that the parents will enforce them.

The parents should not forget to reinforce positive and prosocial behaviors of the child or adolescent. Social reinforcement (e.g., praise), in particular, is highly valued by most children because it directly conveys parental approval and acceptance and serves to enhance the child's sense of self-efficacy. Examples of behaviors that should be socially reinforced include doing chores, being cooperative, playing well with siblings, completing homework, or bringing home a positive report from the teacher. If the parents use material reinforcers, the child's age and interests should be carefully considered when deciding on a particular reward. In addition, material reinforcements should not place undue hardships on the parents' finances.

Money is often a powerful reinforcer for older children and adolescents. When money is used as a reward, the therapist should attempt to ensure that the child does not have alternative sources of funds; that is, money may not be an effective motivator unless it is scarce. Thus, the therapist should encourage the parents to only provide money that is earned through appropriate behavior. Likewise, grandparents and other relatives should be discouraged from giving money noncontingently to the child. It should be reemphasized, however, that praise and special attention from the parents can be just as reinforcing as material rewards.

Returning to the general issue of discipline style, it should be noted that various individual and systemic factors may maintain authoritarian parental discipline. A parent who feels inadequate in various life areas that extend beyond parenting may attempt to adapt by adopting a rigid and inflexible lifestyle. A parent may justify a disciplinary stance on the basis of religious principles. Individual characteristics of the child (e.g., a difficult temperament, egocentrism, low educational achievement) may elicit harsh parental discipline in an effort to "correct" the child. A parent may adopt an authoritarian disciplinary stance when threatened by the apparent (or feared) negative impact of peers on the adolescent.

As the following case example suggests, an authoritarian control style is frequently accompanied by rejection and lack of warmth.

David Walker was a 15-year-old, eighth-grade student who was referred for therapy by a clergy member in his parents' church. David had taken his parents' car without their knowledge and crashed it into a parked vehicle. David had also been recently suspended for an entire year from a private, church-affiliated school, for repeated conflicts with peers. At the recommendation of the school principal, the parents decided to keep David at home for a year, with David's mother serving as his teacher.

The therapist requested that both David and his parents attend the therapy intake session. Although the parents agreed to this request, they canceled three consecutive intake meetings. In each instance, Mrs. Walker cited her husband's busy work schedule and family commitments to church activities as reasons for the cancellation. When Mr. and Mrs. Walker finally attended the fourth scheduled meeting, they informed the therapist that they had left David at home. They reported that in addition to his other misbehaviors, David had been found fondling the genitals of his 10-year-old female cousin one month ago. The parents were so angry at David that they refused even to talk to him. They were extremely concerned that the church leaders might learn of David's behavior and ask the family to leave the church. The therapist agreed that the parents had a serious problem but noted that avoiding David would not help them to deal with their concerns. Consequently, the therapist asked the parents to bring David to the next session.

During the next meeting with the family, the therapist learned that Mr. and Mrs. Walker were both former heroin addicts who had joined the church six years earlier in an attempt, as the parents stated, to "get hooked on God." The parents noted that they had provided David with little structure or discipline prior to joining the church. However, since joining the church, the Walkers had implemented a strict system of discipline and had enrolled David in the church-owned school at the suggestion of members of their congregation. Within this system of discipline, Mr. Walker had the ultimate say regarding the enforcement of rules, and David was not allowed to explain his behavior. Mrs. Walker supported this disciplinary structure and noted that it was consistent with the teachings of their church. Despite David's continued misbehavior, the parents believed that extreme punishment, together with the influence of the teachings of the church, would ultimately help to "straighten David out." Therefore, they had restricted David to his room for the next six months for "sexually molesting" his cousin. Nevertheless, the parents recognized that David was socially immature and that restricting him to his room, coupled with his suspension from school, would do little to enhance his social interactions with peers.

Although the parents' relatively extreme and rigid style of discipline had not been effective, the therapist reasoned that any initial attempts to modify this discipline would be met with extreme resistance. Because the parents valued the advice of their church members and might view any changes in disciplinary style as a rejection of the church itself, the therapist initially assisted the parents in defining goals for David that were consistent with the teachings of their church. Because David needed to learn to interact more appropriately with peers if he was to develop into a "responsible citizen," it was decided that David should be provided with a greater number of structured opportunities to interact with children from his church. Because it was also apparent that Mr. and Mrs. Walker had difficulty communicating with David, the therapist suggested that enhancing the family's communication skills might provide the parents with another important avenue for imparting valuable knowledge to David regarding morally acceptable behavior. The parents agreed that this was an important therapeutic goal.

During the next month, the parents reported that they had observed David engage in a number of positive interactions with his peers. The therapist coached the parents regarding ways to express their pleasure to David, and David was, in turn, encouraged to tell his parents how their support made him feel. Gradually, the parents learned to discuss their concerns with David regarding his past misbehaviors, and David was encouraged to respond to his parents. Although this process was difficult and highly emotional for the family members, the parents learned to respect David's feelings while still maintaining themselves as authority figures.

As positive feelings between David and his parents increased, the therapist suggested that it was unfortunate that David could not attend his school, as the school provided many valuable opportunities for peer interactions. Much to David's surprise, the parents admitted that they disagreed with the lengthy suspension given to David and believed that he should return to school. Following a number of unsuccessful attempts to have David readmitted to his church school, the parents decided to place David in a public school setting. Although the parents remained concerned about the moral impact of this nonparochial setting on their son, they agreed that David needed the benefits of formal education and of increased interaction with peers.

Approximately six months after the onset of treatment, David showed excellent academic performance in the public school and had developed a number of friendships. In light of David's continued progress, the therapist suggested that the parents consider allowing David greater freedom (e.g., a later curfew) in return for his accepting more adultlike responsibilities (e.g., part-time employment). The therapist assured Mr. and Mrs. Walker that David respected them and that their show of increased confidence would not lead to a diminished respect for their authority. The parents consented, and David readily found a part-time job.

The therapist terminated treatment after eight months, as parent-adolescent relations had improved significantly and David's behavior remained nonproblematic. At a follow-up six months later, the parents proudly informed the therapist that David had a girlfriend and was on the school honor roll. David still worked part-time and had volunteered to contribute a small amount of money each week toward room and board. The parents were saddened that David no longer attended their church, but they acknowledged that they had recently given him the freedom to make that decision for himself.

Therapist-parent alliance.   In this case, the therapist was able to help the parents shift from an authoritarian to an authoritative control style by appealing to the parents' belief in goals that were important to their son's development. The process of identifying mutual goals can be facilitated if the therapist acknowledges the parents' frustration with the child and emphasizes the emotional bond that the parents feel for the child. Because parents who seek the help of a therapist typically feel that they have somehow failed their child, the therapist who dwells on this sense of failure without pointing out the positive motives that were responsible for previous disciplinary attempts does little to facilitate the therapeutic process. It is essential that the clinician align with the parents from the outset of therapy to alleviate the parents' fears of failure and to establish a cooperative, rather than an adversary, relationship. When the therapist's efforts to align with the parents are unsuccessful, subsequent intervention strategies related to parental discipline will rarely succeed.

In cases where parental discipline is lax, the clinician may need to devote substantial and continued effort to the maintenance of a therapeutic alliance with the parents. In the absence of a supportive therapist, the parents may quickly abandon attempts toward discipline as child resistance mounts. Children with permissive parents typically resist parental efforts to implement new strategies of discipline. In addition, the factors that initially maintained parental permissiveness may continue to war against the implementation of disciplinary methods. For example, in a single-parent home, the task of controlling child behavior may be impeded by excessive work-related responsibilities and continued conflict with the ex-spouse. Similarly, in families with an adolescent, the peer group may exert a significant influence in promoting deviant adolescent behavior. (Chapter 5 discusses a number of strategies that the therapist can use to prepare the parents for disciplining the adolescent.)

As the following case demonstrates, some children will not respond to any form of discipline that is not backed by serious negative consequences. The parent may require substantial support in implementing such consequences.

Mrs. Davis was referred for treatment by a friend who had previously seen the therapist. Mrs. Davis had considerable difficulty in controlling her 17-year-old son, Michael, who had dropped out of school at age 15 and had a long history of minor delinquent offenses involving unruly conduct and habitual disobedience. For example, on several occasions, he had stayed out all night playing cards and gambling with his friends. On another occasion, he had driven his mother's car without her permission to visit a friend who had moved almost 200 miles away. More recently, he had sold several of his mother's gardening tools to a local pawn shop to obtain money to buy some new record albums. Although Michael had not yet been convicted for a more serious offense, several members of his current peer group had been incarcerated for burglary and grand larceny. According to Mrs. Davis, Michael refused to work or to help her with tasks at home.

Mrs. Davis, a successful real estate agent, had been divorced for almost six years at the time she came for treatment. In addition to Michael, she had three other children aged 15, 18, and 20 years, and all of these children lived at home. Mrs. Davis was a warm and nurturant parent to all of these children, but she lacked disciplinary skills. Fortunately, with the exception of Michael, Mrs. Davis's other offspring were well behaved. Two of Mrs. Davis's older children had jobs and assumed a number of the responsibilities related to household maintenance and upkeep.

The therapist decided to visit Mrs. Davis and her children at their home since Michael had reportedly refused to accompany his mother to the therapist's office. The home was well furnished and located in a relatively affluent middle-class suburb. All of the children, including Michael, were extremely courteous and well mannered. Michael was an attractive, interpersonally skilled adolescent who related warmly to everyone, including the therapist. When asked about his mother's complaints, Michael stated that he had been looking for a job and was willing to follow any rules that his mother established for him.

During the next two months, the therapist worked closely with Mrs. Davis and Michael in negotiating rules for his behavior. Because Michael valued spending time with his friends, listening to the family stereo, and watching TV, each of these activities was defined as a privilege that would be removed if he disobeyed Mrs. Davis's rules regarding curfew, household chores, and obtaining a job. However, despite Michael's verbal acknowledgment of these rules, he consistently ignored them and failed to comply with Mrs. Davis's disciplinary efforts. Michael was an apparent master at excuses, blaming his continued noncompliance on a poor memory and other circumstances that were beyond his control (e.g., he could not make curfew because he did not have a watch to keep track of the time). Similar excuses were offered for his failure to remain employed, despite the fact that the therapist had helped him to obtain two jobs. It was apparent that

Michael was not sufficiently motivated to behave responsibly, though he apparently wanted to be treated as an adult.

In cases such as this, the parent and therapist have relatively few means for enforcing child compliance. Mrs. Davis's warm parenting style had been ideally suited to enhancing her son's interpersonal skills, but her permissive style of discipline had not taught him to deal with frustration or to accept responsibility for his behavior. Consequently, Mrs. Davis's current efforts toward enforcing Michael's compliance were met with substantial resistance.

At this point, the therapist might have terminated treatment with the rationale that Mrs. Davis lacked the necessary fortitude and time (her job demanded long and irregular hours) to influence Michael's behavior. However, even in cases where the parent's ability to monitor the adolescent's behavior is quite limited, it is important to remember that the parent is usually providing the adolescent with resources (e.g., food, clothing, shelter) that are often taken for granted by the parent, the adolescent, and the therapist. Although removal of such resources might, at first glance, seem unduly harsh and even inhumane, the alternative is, arguably, even more unacceptable. Michael was headed for a life of crime and might seriously injure himself or others as a result. Moreover, he was a relatively bright, interpersonally skilled adolescent who had few intentions of using his abilities productively.

With the therapist's assistance, Mrs. Davis established a timetable during which Michael was to obtain a job and assume greater household responsibilities. Mrs. Davis allowed Michael five weeks (until his 18th birthday) to accomplish these tasks. Failure to accomplish these tasks would result in Michael's expulsion from the home. Because Michael was not expected to comply with his mother's requests, plans were established to assist Mrs. Davis in expelling and keeping Michael out of the home (e.g., the locks on the doors were changed, and Mrs. Davis informed Michael that she would call the police if he tried to force his way into the home). In addition, criteria were established for Michael's possible return into the home following his expulsion.

As expected, Michael was forced from the home on the date set by Mrs. Davis. For approximately three weeks, Michael lived in the homes of various friends. However, because neither these friends nor their parents wished to feed and clothe an 18-year-old adolescent who refused to provide financial reimbursement, Michael quickly wore out his welcome. Michael soon decided that it was in his best interests to obtain employment and to assist his mother with other household responsibilities. Michael returned home for one month, quit his job, and was again expelled from his mother's home. Two weeks later he again obtained employment and was permitted to move back into the home. One year later, he remained employed and was still living in the home. He was also attending night school in an effort to earn his high school equivalency diploma.

The expulsion of an adolescent from the home represents an intervention of last resort, but the psychosocial consequences are, in our experience, seldom negative. When considering such an intervention, the total cooperation of the parent(s) is an absolute necessity. Otherwise, the intervention is likely to fail and the behavior of the child will remain unchanged. In all cases, the therapist needs to assist the parents in exploring their options, and the likely consequences of each option should be carefully discussed. Usually, this discussion will make the parent less hesitant to impose the serious negative consequences. Throughout this process, the therapist should not underestimate the strength of the emotional bond that the parent feels for the child. The therapist needs to provide the parent with continued (even daily) emotional support to insure that the intervention will succeed.

Obviously, in many families, interventions involving extreme control procedures do not need to be implemented. In these families, the therapist may find that implementing relatively simple parent training procedures is effective in modifying maladaptive child behaviors. This is often the case with families in which the parents' knowledge of disciplinary techniques is limited. For example, the parents may become increasingly permissive as they find that certain forms of discipline (e.g., spanking) are no longer effective with an older child. Educating the parents about control strategies that are consistent with their child's developmental status may be all the therapeutic intervention that is needed.

Consistency

Children usually learn to behave appropriately through a process of repeated, reciprocal interchanges with their parents. Indeed, parents of young children frequently find that it is necessary to correct an inappropriate child behavior on many occasions before the child learns to abandon the behavior. This process may be time-consuming and, at times, frustrating for the parents, but it allows the child to learn that certain behaviors have predictable consequences. In the absence of such parental consistency, the child may repeat inappropriate behaviors time and time again.

When assessing the parents' efforts in disciplining children, the therapist must attend to both intraparental and interparental consistency. *Intraparental consistency* refers to the consistency in discipline that is evidenced by one parent, whereas *interparental consistency* refers to the consistency in disciplinary strategies that is evidenced between two parents. Frequently, parents of behavior problem children fail to recognize the importance of both types of consistency. Consequently, therapeutic interventions may be needed to address both of these areas.

Intraparental consistency.   Although most parents tend to adopt a general set of disciplinary procedures, the parent's application of these procedures is not necessarily consistent. For example, a parent may respond to a child's misbehavior by sending the child to his or her room on one occasion but may ignore the same misbehavior on a later occasion. In such instances, the parent may not recognize the inconsistency in discipline, but the child almost certainly will. The child will likely become confused by the parent's contradictory communications regarding the acceptability of the behavior. This confusion may be expressed in ways such as crying, withdrawal, anger, or some misbehavior that is directed toward the parent.

In some cases, child behavior problems can be ameliorated through educating the parents about the negative impact of erratic discipline on the child. As emphasized earlier, the therapist needs to accompany such an intervention with support for parental efforts and by engaging the parent in a cooperative relationship. Frequently, an intervention that teaches the parent to more carefully monitor and respond to both positive and negative child behaviors is most effective.

In other cases, it may be necessary to modify both the inconsistency of intraparental discipline and the style of that discipline. For example, Patterson (1982) has noted that the parents of many antisocial children tend to be more authoritarian and more inconsistent in their use of punishment than are parents of normal children. In the families of antisocial children, simply teaching the parents to be more consistent might have the undesired effect of actually promoting an authoritarian style of discipline. Thus, the parents of antisocial children may need to learn to adopt a more authoritative style of discipline as well as to be more consistent in dealing with child misbehavior when it occurs.

Interparental consistency.   In two-parent families, intraparental inconsistency in disciplinary strategies is typically accompanied by interparental inconsistency. Indeed, if one or both parents is erratic in the use of child control strategies, it is likely that the parents will at times subvert each other's authority regarding disciplinary decisions. The effective management of child behavior problems requires that the parents not only set and enforce clearly defined limits, but that they support *each other* in maintaining these limits. In the absence of such support, the child will usually avoid the more controlling parent and will turn to the less controlling parent to circumvent family rules. In fact, the child may become expert at controlling the parents and may "play one parent against the other," thereby diminishing the child's chance to learn responsible and appropriate behaviors.

Behavioral approaches to parent training have tended to emphasize both intraparental and interparental consistency in the management of deviant child behaviors. These approaches have typically utilized instruction and practice in behavior management procedures as primary therapeutic techniques. Unfortunately, with a few exceptions, behavioral parent training has not represented a particularly effective treatment for problem children and adolescents (Borduin, Henggeler, Hanson, & Harbin, 1982). In our view, this is because behavioral approaches to parent training have typically failed to address the marital difficulties that often underlie inconsistent interparental discipline. Such difficulties must be resolved before child behavior will change.

The assessment of parent-child relations can often provide the therapist with information that is relevant to marital relations. The marital coalition is the foundation of the family unit. As such, parental dissension or apathy should alert the therapist that marital difficulties are probably present. In fact, it is often possible to view the spouses' description of their relationship as parents as a metaphor for their marital relations. The following case exemplifies this point.

Mr. and Mrs. Rodriguez came for therapy to seek assistance in controlling their 14-year-old daughter, Angela. According to Mr. Rodriguez, Angela had become increasingly defiant of family rules (e.g., curfew), and the police had found her drinking liquor with an 18-year-old boy late one evening in a local park.

Mrs. Rodriguez described her husband as a harsh disciplinarian who had difficulty relating affectionately to Angela. She noted that her husband seldom spoke to Angela except to criticize her appearance and behavior. However, Mr. Rodriguez stated that he did not believe his daughter should be coddled. He also said that his wife did not recognize the importance of strict discipline and felt that he had been forced to carry the load of disciplining their daughter. Because, on a process level, it seemed that Mr. and Mrs.

Rodriguez were expressing some critical opinions about each other as persons and not just as parents, the therapist decided to shift the focus of therapy to the marriage. To accomplish this, the therapist asked Angela to leave the room, after which he asked Mr. and Mrs. Rodriguez to discuss their own relationship. Mrs. Rodriguez stated that her husband did not express his affection for her and seemed to care only about his work. She added that her husband never complimented her appearance or her efforts to maintain a clean house. In response, Mr. Rodriguez reported that he cared deeply about his wife but felt that his success as a provider, rather than his words, should be used to convey his feelings. Mr. Rodriguez added that although his wife frequently referred to him with affection, he was not certain that she really loved him, as evidenced by the fact that she frequently declined his invitations for sexual intimacy.

In the above case, each spouse's description of the other as a parent paralleled their descriptions of each other's behavior as a marital partner. For example, Mrs. Rodriguez saw her spouse as an unloving, critical father and as an emotionally distant, task-oriented husband. In both instances, she inferred her spouse's lack of affection from the fact that he seldom expressed any positive feelings. Similarly, Mr. Rodriguez saw his spouse as an indulgent mother who was fearful of confronting their daughter, and as an emotionally superficial wife who was fearful of sexual intimacy. Here, his inferences were based more on his wife's behavior than on her verbal statements.

Although we have found that child behavior problems often reflect marital problems, we do not believe that it is necessarily wise to immediately shift the focus of therapy to the marital relationship. Indeed, because the presenting problem that was defined by the family centered on the daughter's misbehavior, it is important that the therapist acknowledge this problem and set realistic goals for its amelioration. The therapist can assign tasks that require parental cooperation in dealing with adolescent behavior. This therapeutic strategy conveys respect for the family's definition of their problem and provides the therapist with opportunities to assess the marital difficulties.

In most instances, marital problems will impede the interparental cooperation and consistency needed for effective child discipline, and child behavior difficulties will continue. At this point, the therapist can then address possible reasons, including marital disagreements, for continued ineffective discipline. When marital problems are identified overtly, therapeutic interventions that are designed to increase marital satisfaction and to decrease marital conflicts can then follow. Some of these interventions may focus specifically on parenting, although we have frequently observed that marital therapy alone may lead to more effective parenting and to improved child behavior.

A small minority of parents are not willing to engage in marital therapy, despite the obvious effect of their marital difficulties on their parenting strategies. With these parents, it is nevertheless important to clarify the impact of the marital relationship on the child or adolescent. Although marital satisfaction may vacillate, the parents can be taught to unify their approach to discipline and to present a "united front" to their children. It is essential that the parents agree not to undermine each other's authority and to provide disciplinary consistency. The maintenance of this consistency will require continued and substantial effort on the parents' part, but this effort is absolutely essential for the psychosocial welfare of the children. Cognizant of this fact, some parents are able to maintain consistency despite continued marital discord. Others may subsequently return for marital therapy or may decide to divorce.

PARENTAL AFFECT

Parental affection, whether expressed verbally or nonverbally, provides an important communication from parent to young child. The expression of parental warmth affirms the emotional bond between parent and child in a way that can be understood by both. This affirmation provides a continued sense of emotional security for the child, who is likely to remain dependent on the parent for many years. Indeed, the expression of maternal warmth (e.g., through smiling and through holding the infant tenderly and carefully) seems to contribute to the development of a secure attachment (Ainsworth, Blehar, Waters, & Wall, 1978), which, in turn, is related to various indexes of positive emotional and social adjustment over at least the first five years of life (Arend, Gove, & Sroufe, 1979; Waters, Wippman, & Sroufe, 1979).

Parental warmth also plays an important role in establishing and maintaining a positive mood during interactions with the child. Parents establish positive mood states in their children through a variety of means, including play, humor, imitation, affectionate tones and gestures, and stressing positive rather than negative outcomes. As described by Maccoby and Martin (1983), the induction of positive mood states in the child is crucial because it sets the stage for the acquisition of conditioned empathic emotional responses. Assuming that children are innately capable of having their emotions classically conditioned, the signs of certain emotional states (e.g., warmth) in other persons will rapidly acquire the power to elicit the same emotions in the child. Thus, by conditioning the child's positive mood states to certain interpersonal situations and experiences, the parent shapes the child's emotional expressiveness and enhances the child's empathic responsiveness.

On the other hand, rejecting parents may teach their children to attach negative affective labels to a variety of early interpersonal experiences and, in the long run, to respond negatively to other persons. In addition, the behavior of these parents communicates the message that they are unwilling to meet their children's needs for nurturance. Consequently, the children quickly learn that they cannot depend on their parents for security and protection. This lack of emotional security can produce a state of fear and anxiety in the young child and is often associated with avoidant and resistant patterns of infant attachment (Hetherington & Martin, 1986; Maccoby & Martin, 1983).

All of this helps to explain why children who experience low levels of positive affection (i.e., emotional neglect) and high levels of negative affection (i.e., emotional rejection) are at risk for the development of emotional and behavioral difficulties. Emotionally neglected and rejected children frequently lack the requisite developmental experiences for learning to trust and to respond positively to familiar other persons. As a result, these children are likely to view interpersonal transactions in a negative light and may lack the emotional responsivity and social skills that are needed for initiating and maintaining positive interactions.

During the preschool years, these interpersonal difficulties are likely to become apparent as the child begins to interact with persons outside the immediate family. Indeed, Baumrind (1967, 1971) found that parents who were emotionally neglecting, as well as rigid and intrusive in their control attempts, had preschoolers who tended to be unhappy in mood, guileful, vulnerable to stress, and passively hostile toward age-mates. Moreover, George and Main (1979) found that preschoolers who were subjected to parental rejection and physical aggression were more likely to behave aggressively toward their teachers and their peers than were preschoolers who were not subjected to such parental behaviors. Considering our earlier discussion of the contribution of parental warmth to the development of empathic responsiveness, it is also not surprising to find that parental rejection is linked to conduct problems and aggressive behaviors in older children and adolescents (for a review, see Hetherington & Martin, 1986), and to marital problems and divorce in adults (for a review, see Rutter & Madge, 1976).

Parental Emotional Neglect

In light of the detrimental effects of emotional neglect and rejection on children, the therapist must carefully choose the interventions that are most likely to facilitate pertinent changes in the affective component of parent-child relations. The therapist must be aware that emotional neglect may be accompanied by varying degrees of parental rejection or hostility. At one extreme are parents who are openly antagonistic, belittling, and even aggressive toward their children; at the other extreme are parents who are relatively passive and do not take an actively hostile stance when relating to their children. Although parents at either extreme often fail to show love to their children, the family context that includes parental hostility is very different from one in which parental hostility is absent.

Several key factors can contribute singly or in combination to parental emotional neglect and rejection. These factors include characteristics of the child, parental knowledge/skill deficits, low commitment to parenting, and parental psychopathology.

Child characteristics.   As discussed in Chapter 1, theorists (e.g., Bell, 1968, 1977) have increasingly emphasized the reciprocal and circular nature of human interactions. Consistent with this emphasis, investigators of parent-child relations have shown that parents modify their behavior in response to various characteristics of their children (e.g., Brunk & Henggeler, 1984). If we apply this concept of reciprocal influences to the domain of parental affect, it becomes apparent that characteristics of the child represent a potentially important set of variables. For example, an infant with a difficult temperament may cry incessantly and may seem unresponsive to repeated parental attempts at calming and soothing. Over time, the parents may feel rejected by the child's apparent lack of responsivity and may decrease their attempts to behave affectionately toward the child. Similarly, children who evidence intellectual or physical handicaps may elicit less positive affection from their parents. Indeed, the parents of handicapped children are likely to face many disappointments, increased child care and financial burdens, social ostracism, and frequent demands for medical and educational interventions. As the following case demonstrates, parental rejection of a physically handicapped child may develop in response to the cumulative stress of attempting to meet the child's special needs over a prolonged period of time.

Carol Reese was an 8-year-old girl who had been paraplegic since she had been injured in a hit-and-run automobile accident at age 3. Although Carol had received intensive physical rehabilitation for several years, she remained confined to a wheelchair, and her physicians expressed doubt that she would ever walk again. The referral for treatment was made by a rehabilitation specialist at the local pediatric hospital who thought that Carol was very depressed.

The initial interview revealed that Mr. and Mrs. Reese were openly rejecting of Carol because of all the hardships that "she had put them through." Mr. Reese, who owned a modest hardware business, reported that his considerable financial difficulties were a direct result of Carol's medical bills. He noted that he needed a new truck for his business and a new car for the family, but that he could not afford to buy either vehicle. Mrs. Reese stated that she spent so much time caring for Carol at home and driving her to and from medical appointments that she had little time to do anything else. She added that she had all but abandoned her hopes of returning to college and pursuing a career of her own. As the parents blamed Carol for their problems, Carol felt that she was a burden to her family and had become withdrawn and uncommunicative.

Although Mr. and Mrs. Reese's behavior was having an adverse effect on Carol's well-being, it should be noted that, in many ways, the parents were trying to make the best of a very difficult situation. Consequently, the therapist emphasized that the parents had made many sacrifices for their daughter. Moreover, the therapist made an effort to align with the parents by demonstrating a good appreciation for the emotional strain of their situation. The therapist's supportive alignment with Mr. and Mrs. Reese helped them to relax their angry posture toward Carol and led to a discussion of several other pertinent aspects of their situation. The therapist learned, for example, that Mr. and Mrs. Reese felt extremely guilty about their resentment toward Carol. It also became apparent that Mr. and Mrs. Reese were very protective of Carol. Indeed, the parents described themselves as relatively independent people who did not like to ask others for favors and who worried about the ability of anyone else to provide adequate care for their daughter. Moreover, in light of their medical bills and strong sense of responsibility, the parents viewed spending any money on themselves as frivolous.

After considering the parents' feelings of guilt and responsibility, the therapist prefaced his recommendations to the family by emphasizing that the necessary changes were ultimately for Carol's benefit. Additionally, these changes would give the parents more energy and joy in their lives, help them to feel less resentful of Carol's burden, and lead to improved interactions between the parents and Carol. Although accomplishing these changes would demand a reallocation of some financial resources, the eventual impact of such changes on Carol would be more important than having the best possible medical care.

The therapist then presented several recommendations that were designed to help the parents build a regular social support network, pursue some of their own interests, and have time together apart from Carol. The therapist had the parents plan to set aside one weeknight and one weekend afternoon per week during which they would go out with other couples. The therapist also asked the parents to interview several responsible adults who were willing to stay with Carol during the parents' outings. The parents subsequently found a middle-aged widow in their church who was pleased to spend some time each week caring for Carol. At the therapist's suggestion, Mrs. Reese was also able to find a mature college student who agreed to stay with Carol after school one day each week so that Mrs. Reese could take a course of her choosing. In addition, the therapist helped the parents to locate a camp for handicapped children that Carol could attend for two weeks during the summer, thereby allowing the parents to take a vacation together.

The therapist also used individual and family interventions to help Carol overcome her feelings of rejection and to set the stage for more positive interactions with her parents.

At the individual level, the therapist provided Carol with emotional support and helped her to appreciate that she had many positive characteristics and personal strengths. With the family, the therapist assisted Mr. and Mrs. Reese in clarifying their feelings and behavior toward Carol. The parents helped Carol to understand that they loved her but that they sometimes did not show this love because of their self-imposed stress. This clarification of the parents' feelings, together with the other interventions, helped to foster a more affectionate pattern of parent-child relations and led to the amelioration of Carol's depression.

Another child characteristic that elicits parental rejection is repeated child misbehavior. In these cases, parents may mistakenly believe that their child is "mentally ill" or has some defective personality trait that motivates the bad behavior. One parent, for example, firmly believed that her daughter's misbehaviors were due to a "schizophrenia problem," even though the parent had minimal understanding of the term. In such cases, the therapist can sometimes change the parent's view of the child simply by teaching behavior management strategies to the parent. Implementing effective parental discipline and reward strategies may be all that is needed to show the parent that the child's negative behaviors can be controlled and that the child is capable of engaging in many positive relations.

It is important to recognize, however, that some parents are unwilling (or unable) to put forth the effort that is needed to control their child's problem behaviors. For these parents, viewing the child's misbehaviors as the product of some mental illness or personality flaw can be a convenient excuse for not attempting to develop a closer relationship. In these instances, rejection of the child probably reflects a lack of commitment to parenting and/or a serious psychiatric disturbance in the parent. Therapeutic strategies for dealing with these causes of parental rejection and low warmth are described in the next sections.

Knowledge/skill deficits.   Difficulties in parent-child affective relations are sometimes associated with parents not knowing how to express affection in ways that are developmentally appropriate for the child. Although most parents recognize that holding, touching, and smiling are appropriate ways of expressing affection to infants or young children, social norms for conveying love to older children are less well defined. Many adolescents, for example, are embarrassed by open displays of parental affection and may even discourage their parents from expressing affection toward them. Parents may interpret this discouragement as rejection or may come to believe that the adolescent does not need affection for continued emotional growth. Other parents may be unsure of appropriate ways to express affection to their children, particularly during adolescence, and so refrain from such expressions or attempt to express love in other ways, such as in the form of material rewards. Although parental displays of affection toward adolescents should typically involve less physical contact and verbal praise than are given to younger children, adolescents still need to receive parental communications that convey caring and respect. Such communications might include expressing approval and praise for the adolescent's accomplishments, showing respect for the adolescent's ideas and opinions, and giving the adolescent an occasional hug or kiss to demonstrate support (e.g., in times of sadness or disappointment) and love (e.g., in times of celebration or special accomplishment).

Because all children, regardless of age, rely on parental affection for continued emotional growth, deficits in parental knowledge and skill regarding the expression of affection can result in serious psychosocial consequences for the child. Moreover, older children who do not have warm relations with their parents are often likely to seek affection from persons outside of the family. Such relations may meet important emotional needs, but they may also lead to consequences for which the child is unprepared, such as sexual promiscuity and pregnancy (Hanson & Henggeler, 1982). Similarly, some evidence suggests that adolescents who receive weak emotional support from their parents are more susceptible to the influences of delinquent peers than are adolescents who receive strong emotional support (Poole & Regoli, 1979). The following case exemplifies this process.

Billy Cummings was a 15-year-old boy who was referred for therapy by the local juvenile court. Billy had been arrested five times in the last three years and was most recently arrested with several peers for physically assaulting an elderly woman and stealing her purse. Billy's parents were employed as kitchen staff in the local school system and had six other children ranging in age from 18 months to 10 years. At the therapist's request, the entire family attended the initial interview. Mr. and Mrs. Cummings reported that none of Billy's siblings had any behavioral or academic difficulties. They also noted that Billy had been "a perfect boy" until about age 11, when he began to associate with a group of "troublemakers." The parents attributed all of Billy's law violations to his susceptibility to peer influence and reported that Billy did not respond to any form of discipline. In fact, the parents had been referred for counseling at a local mental health center when Billy was 12, and they had received extensive training in behavior management procedures.

Although the presenting problem could be conceptualized in terms of the parents' failure to maintain control over their son's behavior, it appeared that Mr. and Mrs. Cummings had consistently attempted to control Billy's misbehaviors through the use of discipline. The parents had established a set of rules and privileges for all of their children, and they had demanded that Billy not associate with his delinquent peers. However, the therapist observed a vast discrepancy in the way the parents related to Billy and his 10-year-old male sibling versus the younger children in the family. Whereas the younger children were permitted to climb into the parents' laps and receive large doses of parental affection and attention, the older boys were expected to sit upright, did not make eye contact with the parents or the therapist, and received only harsh words from the parents. With some tactful probing from the therapist, the parents revealed that the older boys were expected to behave like "young men" and did not need "to be cuddled like babies." Other statements from the parents, particularly Mr. Cummings, revealed that they believed older children should be expected to "do right" and did not need praise from their parents.

The interventions in this case were designed to meet four primary therapeutic goals:

1. Help the parents see beyond their anger toward Billy. The therapist noted the apparent love and concern that the parents had shown for Billy and pointed out that the parents had not only set high expectations for Billy's behavior, but they had also jointly attended therapy in an effort to help their son overcome his problems.

2. Open lines of communication between the parents and the older boys. The therapist stated that such communication was needed for their transition into "manhood." The parents were taught not only to clarify their expectations for their boys' behavior, but to regularly praise their sons for their adultlike behaviors. Because Mr. Cummings initially resisted expressing positive feelings about his sons or their behavior, he was encouraged to offer only small compliments for work that the boys performed at home. The boys were also encouraged to report their feelings about receiving positive parental feedback. The parents were extremely surprised to learn of the impact of their praise on their sons, and the parents continued this praise in light of the obvious effect it had on the boys' behavior.

3. Improve the relationship between Mr. Cummings and his sons. The therapist helped Mr. Cummings and his two older sons plan weekly activities that were "for men only," including occasional trips to professional sporting events. The relationship between Mr. Cummings and his two sons showed substantial improvement, and Mr. Cummings changed his attitude about giving his sons an occasional hug or a pat on the back.

4. Help Billy find a few nondelinquent friends. This goal was largely accomplished by Mr. Cummings, who, at the therapist's request, helped Billy to find a part-time job in a grocery store where he established several new friendships.

Commitment to parenting.   Difficulties in parent-child affective relations can also be caused by a lack of commitment to parenting. Career aspirations are the first priority of many parents, who may work long hours and devote little emotional energy to their children. Although the professed intentions of the parents may be to provide their children with material and educational resources, a by-product of the parents' work schedule is that the parents have relatively little time to interact with their children. The parents may return from work feeling physically and emotionally exhausted, travel frequently, and use spare time to complete household tasks or to engage in leisure activities. The parents may view spending time with the children as a luxury that can be enjoyed occasionally, but not regularly. In these families, the children's emotional needs may go largely unmet.

Brian, a 9-year-old, and Shelly, a 7-year-old, were referred for therapy by their parents, Dr. and Mrs. Evans. The parents reported that their two children had become increasingly belligerent and unruly over the past eight months. At home, the children refused to complete their chores, deliberately spilled soft drinks and food on the parents' new furniture, called each other filthy names (e.g., "mother-fucker"), and drew pictures on the wallpaper in their bedrooms. The children's teachers reported similar incidents of uncooperative and disruptive behavior at school. For example, Brian often refused to complete his in-class assignments and had dropped several textbooks belonging to other children into the classroom fish tank. Shelly had announced to the class that her father had died and that her mother had brain cancer. She complained daily about feeling ill and wanting to go home (numerous medical exams confirmed that she was healthy). The parents stated that they were both extremely angry at the children for their disruptive behavior and had "begun to regret the day that they were born." In fact, during the initial interview, the father described the children as "a pain in the ass," and the mother noted that she had started spanking the children in an effort to "slap some sense into them" (the spankings were mild and, if anything, reinforced the children's negative behaviors).

The therapist later learned that each of the parents devoted approximately 60 hours per week to their respective careers. The father had established himself as a highly regarded specialist in internal medicine and had a lucrative practice. The mother had returned to graduate school to pursue her doctorate in biology. Thus, the children rarely saw either of their parents during the week, and the parents had largely turned over the task of raising the children to their hired nanny. Nevertheless, the parents reported that they were satisfied with their marriage and that they spent what little free time they had together at the country club. Unfortunately, these leisure activities did not include the children. In essence, then, the parents had largely abandoned the children in pursuit of their own careers and social activities; the children, in turn, had decided to stage a revolt in an effort to win back their parents.

Because Dr. and Mrs. Evans were behaving as if they had a right to ignore their children, the therapist decided to directly inquire about the parents' priorities in life. Both of the parents acknowledged that their careers were of primary importance to them, and both viewed childrearing as a relatively mundane and unimportant activity. Moreover, the therapist learned that Dr. and Mrs. Evans' own parents had also given higher priority to their careers than to their children. Thus, it was not surprising that Dr. and Mrs. Evans failed to recognize that their priorities were misplaced and that their children needed a greater share of their time and attention.

In such situations, it is essential that the parents change their attitudes and behaviors if the children's emotional needs are to be met. Providing for the child's physical needs is certainly an important part of commitment to parenthood, but spending time with the child on a regular basis is no less a responsibility of parenthood. Although much has been written in the past decade regarding the importance of the quality of parents' interactions with their children, we would argue strongly that parenting is first and foremost a commitment of *time* and *energy*. Without such a commitment, the quality of parent-child relations is likely to suffer.

In the case of Dr. and Mrs. Evans, the therapist took several steps that were designed to make it very difficult for the parents to maintain their present priorities. First, after talking further with the parents about some of their frustrations with the children's behavior, the therapist asked the parents to speculate about what the children might be trying to communicate to them. When the parents pleaded ignorance (this is not uncommon among parents whose commitment to their children is low), the therapist brought the children into the session and helped them to express what they had previously been unable to communicate directly: The children wanted to spend more time with their parents on a regular basis, whether it involved getting help with homework, watching television together, taking a walk, or going to the zoo.

Second, the therapist helped the parents to interpret the children's request in a positive light (i.e., as a loving request from their children who admired them, not as an angry demand from a pair of problem children). The therapist also pointed out that the children had a right to expect parental time and attention, and that the parents had much that they could teach to their children about the world around them.

Third, the therapist told the parents that total commitment to their careers commands a price: frequent behavior problems with both of their children, as well as long-term emotional maladjustment for each of them.

After considering the likely costs of maintaining their present priorities, the parents decided that they needed to develop a plan for balancing their responsibilities to their children with their careers. The remainder of therapy involved guiding the parents in implementing their plan, opening lines of parent-child communication (including the expression of positive affect), and crediting the parents for the amelioration of their children's behavior problems.

Other family situations demand an especially high level of commitment to parenting. For example, low-income families are generally larger than more financially advantaged families. Consequently, older and younger children must often compete for parental attention, with younger children typically receiving most of the available parental affection. In these families, the parents may need to set aside special time for interacting with the older children so that they receive sufficient emotional support. Single-parent family situations are another example. The special problems of single-parent families are discussed in Chapter 7, but it should be noted here that in these families, parental work demands may dictate that the older children serve as surrogate parents for their younger siblings. This child-care arrangement may be unavoidable, but it can have negative emotional consequences for the children if the parent is not strongly committed to spending time with each of the children during the limited time that the parent is at home. In the absence of a strong parental commitment to meeting the children's emotional needs, the children may seek nurturance outside of the family.

One source of emotional support in many Black, lower-income, single-parent homes is the extended family, usually the maternal grandmother (see Wilson, 1984). Unfortunately, when such parental support is not available, the single parent frequently has few positive alternatives. In the absence of support from extended family members, these single parents may seek joint living arrangements with other single parents and their children. Although these living arrangements represent an adaptation to a realistic problem, the large number of children and adults living under one roof can often create a chaotic living situation in which the adults are under constant tension and all but the youngest children are expected to independently care for their physical needs. In these environments, the emotional needs of children may go largely unmet.

When practical problems in living lead to low levels of parental commitment for meeting the children's emotional needs, a number of reality-oriented interventions are frequently required. In these instances, a working familiarity with the social service delivery system is a necessity if the family's basic financial needs are to be met and parent-child affective relations are to improve. In some cases, social service interventions must be implemented before the therapeutic procedures described earlier are likely to be effective.

Parental psychopathology.   As described in Chapter 2, some parents fail to develop a meaningful emotional attachment to the child because of a serious psychiatric disturbance. Most of these parents are immersed in an extreme egocentrism that results in emotional nonavailability, neglect, and a lack of responsiveness to the needs of the child. Such nonresponsiveness is especially prominent in depressed mothers (for reviews, see Burbach & Borduin, 1986; Hetherington & Martin, 1986) and has been associated with a broad range of child psychosocial difficulties, including depression, conduct disorders, and a lack of competence in peer relations and in school (Baldwin, Cole, & Baldwin, 1982; Weissman et al., 1984).

When parental psychopathology is a major factor in low levels of parent-child affection, the therapist should assess the various individual and systemic factors that may be maintaining the parent's psychosocial difficulties. On the individual level, a depressed parent may hold a number of irrational beliefs and attitudinal biases that contribute directly to his or her poor sense of self-efficacy. At a family level, severe stress such as marital discord or a recent divorce may have a negative impact on the parent's psychological adjustment. In addition, the absence of a supportive social network may contribute to the parent's inability to deal effectively with normal, everyday stresses and to maintain a positive self-image.

The direction of subsequent interventions should be determined by the results of the therapist's assessment. With a parent who is depressed, for example, the therapist might decide to use a cognitive-behavioral approach to challenge the parent's negative self-statements or attitudinal biases and to help the parent to build a more positive view of his or her capabilities. In addition, interventions that attempt to improve marital relations (see Chapter 4) or that encourage the parent to build a consistent system of extrafamilial social support (e.g., Parents Without Partners) may also be needed to ameliorate parental psychosocial difficulties. When these interventions are successful, the therapist can then try to improve the affective component of parent-child interactions. In some cases, the alleviation of the parent's emotional or interpersonal problems may be all that is needed to enhance parent-child affective relations.

Occasionally, the therapist's efforts to ameliorate parental psychosocial difficulites and to improve parental affect are unsuccessful. As one might expect, these instances often include those in which the parent has a history of psychiatric hospitalization and has come to accept the view that his or her behavior is the product of an incurable mental illness. Also included in this group are some parents who are chemically dependent or who are involved in extensive criminal activity, and who are unwilling to change this behavior. In these situations, after it has been determined that parental involvement is counterproductive, the therapist should attempt to identify another adult (e.g., an older sibling, an aunt or uncle, a grandparent, a teacher, a friend's parent) who is willing to serve as a surrogate parent for the child. It is extremely important that this adult be a responsible individual with adequate psychosocial adjustment, be able to act as a positive role model, and offer the child sound guidance. Moreover, the adult should be someone who cares about the child and is already in the child's natural environment. In some cases, such an adult is relatively easy to identify because he or she has already shown considerable interest in the child's welfare and spends a substantial amount of time with the child. In other cases, however, the therapist may need to do a good deal of investigative work before a surrogate parent can be identified.

When a surrogate parent is necessary, the therapist should be prepared to address the issue of transferring legal guardianship of the child from the biological parent to the surrogate parent. Although accepting legal guardianship is certainly not a necessary component of the surrogate parent's role, this issue is raised often enough by the biological parent and/or the surrogate parent that it is worth mentioning here. (In extreme cases, of course, the therapist may need to refer the case to the state protective services agency for possible termination of parental rights and placement of the child outside of the home.) When discussing this issue, the therapist should be aware that most children are emotionally attached to their parents, even if their parents are not emotionally attached to them. Depending on the circumstances, the therapist may wish to consider whether the transferral of legal guardianship would have a negative emotional impact on the child. On the other hand, in the absence of a legally established relationship with the child, the surrogate parent needs to exercise some caution regarding the legal boundaries of his or her actions toward the child. For example, the well-intentioned surrogate parent who frequently provides the child with food and shelter or who attempts to discipline the child may be faced, at some point, with legal action from the biological parent, whose action is motivated more by jealousy than by a desire to protect the child. The child may also attempt to play the biological parent against the surrogate parent when disciplinary issues arise. By clarifying some of these potential problems surrounding the issue of legal guardianship, the therapist can often help the biological parent and surrogate parent arrive at a decision that is satisfactory to both and that also serves the best interests of the child.

When a responsible adult cannot be identified or does not wish to assume the role of surrogate parent, we recommend that the therapist follow the guidelines discussed in Chapter 2 for engaging in individual therapy with the child. Briefly, this strategy entails the development of a therapist-child relationship that helps to meet the child's emotional needs. This is usually accomplished by emphasizing the child's positive characteristics and strengths, by providing the child with a worldview that is positive and optimistic, by broadening the child's social perspective-taking skills and interpersonal sensitivity, and by using the relationship with the child as a lever for changing the child's maladaptive behaviors.

Parental Overprotection

Whereas some parents lack commitment to the parenting role and are likely to neglect their children's emotional needs, others are so completely consumed by the parenting role that they become too involved in their children's emotional lives—a point when involvement becomes overprotection. Overprotective parental behavior is typically manifested in several ways, including restrictive control of the child's behavior, the exclusion of outside influences on the child, intrusion into the child's psychological and physical privacy, and active encouragement of dependency (Hetherington & Martin, 1986). Although this pattern of behavior may be motivated by the parent's beliefs about optimal childrearing, there is evidence that parental overprotection is related to anxiety-withdrawal disorders (e.g., school phobias, social phobias) and psychosomatic difficulties in children and adolescents (Hetherington & Martin, 1986).

Although prospective longitudinal research on the development of parental overprotection is lacking, several investigators have conducted correlational studies that provide a starting point in understanding the factors that may contribute to overprotective tendencies. One important factor may be parental anxiety. Eisenberg (1958) found that overprotective mothers tended to be highly anxious about their own unhappy childhood and/or about the circumstances surrounding their child's birth (e.g., the child was a late arrival after many sterile years). For these mothers, overprotective behaviors represented an effort to deal with the fear of becoming a "bad" parent or of losing the child through some accident. In addition, Parker (1983) found that, relative to other mothers and fathers, overprotective parents had higher levels of trait anxiety, suggesting that these parents may have an enduring personality tendency to be anxious about many things in life in addition to parenting. Other researchers (e.g., Ainsworth, Bell, & Stayton, 1971; Osofsky & Connors, 1979) have reported that high maternal anxiety reduces the mother's sensitivity to the infant's signals and is associated with the development of excessive attachment (e.g., crying when separated, low levels of exploratory behavior). Excessive attachment in the infant may be the forerunner of later anxiety disorders in the older child.

Other factors, such as stressful events involving family members, have also been linked to parental overprotection. For example, Waldron, Shrier, Stone, and Tobin (1975) found that school-phobic children (74% of whom had mothers who were rated as overprotective) tended to come from families who had experienced one or more significant life stresses in the previous year. These stresses included events such as a serious physical illness or injury to another family member, depression in a parent, or the absence of a parent. This finding raises the possibility that the occurrence of a serious family crisis may cause the mother to turn to her child for comfort and emotional support.

As suggested above, a number of different factors may be linked to overprotective parental behavior. The following example describes a case that is typical of those families in which a parent's overprotective behavior interferes with the psychosocial functioning of the child.

Mr. and Mrs. Walls and their 12-year-old daughter, Susan, were referred for treatment by Susan's school counselor. Susan was the couple's only child. She had evidenced a variety of somatic complaints over the past six months and had missed so many days of school that her grades had dropped significantly. During the initial interview, Mrs. Walls reported that she had taken Susan for a number of medical examinations and had been told on each occasion that there was no physical basis for Susan's complaints. Nevertheless, Mrs. Walls stated that she was extremely concerned about her daughter's physical complaints and noted that she had devoted her entire life to her daughter. The mother had involved herself in all of her daughter's activities, spent several hours each day helping her daughter with homework, and had very few friends or interests of her own. Likewise, her daughter had only one friend, and her peer relations generally seemed problematic; Susan was often teased by her classmates, and her teacher had described her as immature. Mr. Walls reported that he did not approve of his wife's extreme involvement with Susan, but because his wife did not work and enjoyed occupying her time with "her daughter," he had decided to leave the situation alone rather than fight it.

When evaluating the linkage between parental overprotection and child psychosocial problems, the therapist should carefully consider the changing developmental needs of the child. In this case, for example, an extremely close bond between the mother and child might not be problematic until the child's developmental status dictates the need for increased interactions with significant others outside of the family, such as peers. Indeed, it was apparent to the therapist that Mrs. Wall's extreme devotion to her daughter had begun to interfere seriously with Susan's needs for increased independence and responsibility. Although Mrs. Walls had a relatively warm relationship with her daughter, her continued involvement in Susan's activities did not encourage mastery of peer relations.

During the second interview with the family, several other pertinent aspects of the situation became apparent. First, Mrs. Walls believed that she was uniquely qualified to meet Susan's emotional and social needs. Moreover, because her husband had occasionally raised his voice toward Susan following minor transgressions, Mrs. Walls feared that her husband might actually strike Susan if he was ever left alone with her. However, when pressed on this issue by the therapist, Mrs. Walls acknowledged that her husband had never shown any signs of physical aggression toward Susan or herself. Second, although Mrs. Walls had always wanted to pursue a career and work outside the home, her husband had somehow convinced her that she was not capable of finding and holding down a job. Third, while Susan seemed emotionally immature, she was a relatively friendly and attractive girl who was certainly capable of building friendships and developing more positive relations given sufficient opportunities to do so. And fourth, the parents had grown apart over the past year in response to their repeated conflicts about raising Susan. Although they were still committed to the marriage, they were unhappy with the direction in which it was heading.

The therapist prepared the family for his recommended course of action in the following ways. First, he emphasized that it was not in Susan's best interest to spend so little time with peers and to continue to miss days at school. Susan needed to spend time with her parents, but the school's concerns about her peer relations and her grades also needed to be addressed. The therapist avoided blaming the parents for Susan's problems and stressed instead the important role that the parents might play in facilitating Susan's social and academic functioning. Second, the therapist noted that he appreciated Mrs. Walls's desire to be an excellent parent, but he did not believe that devoting her entire life to her daughter was in the best interests of anyone. He pointed out that Mrs. Walls seemed physically and emotionally exhausted from her parenting efforts and needed a well-deserved break. Moreover, she had a right to pursue her own career opportunities and personal interests. Third, the therapist challenged Mrs. Walls's belief that her husband was not a competent parent. Mr. Walls had worked hard for many years to help provide for Susan's physical needs, and his attendance and behavior during the first few interviews suggested that he cared deeply for Susan. Mrs. Walls simply needed to give her husband the benefit of the doubt in this instance. In the same way, Mr. Walls needed to stop doubting his wife's ability to find and hold a job.

Next, the therapist presented a course of action designed (1) to increase Susan's involvement with agemates, (2) to raise her grades, (3) to decrease Mrs. Walls's overprotective behavior, and (4) to promote harmony between the spouses both in terms of their parenting responsibilities and their marital relationship. The therapist recommended that, for the next month, Mr. Walls was to assume responsibility for seeing that Susan attend school each day and that she participate in at least one extracurricular club or group involving her peers. Mr. Walls was also directed to spend one evening each week with Susan outside the home in a mutually enjoyable activity. The therapist also recommended that Mrs. Walls spend a minimum of one hour per day exploring her career and employment options. The therapist emphasized that Mrs. Walls need not pursue a high-paying job, but rather some activity that she found enjoyable, regardless of the level of pay. Mrs. Walls was also instructed to serve as a consultant to her husband regarding his interactions and activities with Susan, but not to come to his rescue should some problem arise. Finally, the therapist recommended that Mr. and Mrs. Walls spend at least one weekend afternoon or evening together in some pleasant activity that did not involve Susan. After the parents had successfully followed these recommendations, the therapist guided the family to a pattern in which both parents shared more equally in childrearing.

Marital therapy is sometimes necessary to deal with an emotional rift between an overinvolved parent and the spouse. Although it was not necessary in this case to devote greater attention to the marital relationship, this course of action would have been implemented had the parents failed to comply with the therapist's recommendations or had they attempted to undermine each other's efforts to change.

In closing this section, we should emphasize that parental overprotection is almost invariably maintained by the entire family. As suggested in the preceding case, the husband of an overprotective mother has usually agreed, either implicitly or explicitly, with his wife about the nature of her relationship with the child. Similarly, the husband who is uninvolved in childrearing cannot maintain this lack of involvement in the absence of an implicit or explicit agreement with his wife. The agreement between husband and wife is evident in their complementary pattern of behavior. Thus, the therapist should never lose sight of the larger family system, or of other potentially relevant extrafamilial systems, when attempting to disengage an overinvolved parent and child.

PARENTAL MODELING

Parental behaviors that occur outside of the parent-child relationship may also have a profound impact on the quality of the child's psychosocial adjustment. Child behavior problems may persist if the parent fails to appreciate the influence that he or she has as a model for the child.

Children learn to behave as their parents behave. Even during the first year of life, children begin to imitate simple parental behaviors and sounds as a necessary step in the acquisition of more advanced social and language skills. During the preoperational period (beginning around 2 years of age), the child learns to imitate parental behaviors and words that are more complex and to reproduce these behaviors and words long after their initial presentation. However, it is not until the child acquires concrete operational structures (between 5 and 7 years of age) that he or she is able to accurately infer the intentions, thoughts, and/or feelings of others. This is an important developmental milestone because the child is now able to understand the intentions of behaviors that are modeled by the parent. Unfortunately, the parent may fail to recognize the child's increased cognitive capacities and may inadvertently model deviant behaviors. Consequently, the child may begin to imitate parental dishonesty as well as achievement, and parental aggression or hostility as well as emotional stability. Moreover, the child may begin to adopt the parent's coping strategies as his or her own. For example, children who experience parental discord and divorce are more likely to evidence conduct-disorder behavior, while children who experience the death of a parent are more likely to manifest the anxiety, depression, and withdrawal that are similar to the behaviors exhibited by the surviving parent (Emery, 1982; Felner, Stolberg, & Cowen, 1975).

When children adopt inappropriate or maladaptive parental behaviors, the child's behaviors frequently have a negative impact on important aspects of parent-child relations. For example, a child with an aggressive parent may assault other children on the playground. At the teacher's request, the parent may discipline the child in an attempt to stop the fighting in school. However, the child is likely to ignore parental advice or punishment that is not consistent with the parent's own behavior. The child may also receive a social benefit for the aggressive behavior (e.g., a reputation as the toughest child in the school) that he or she is unwilling to sacrifice. In response, the parent may view the child's defiance as a rejection of the parent's concern. The parent may then resort to more extreme forms of punishment or may lose some affection for the child.

The effects of parental modeling on child behavior and on parent-child relations extend to the child's future. Children whose parents model maladaptive behaviors such as drug and alcohol abuse, smoking, and overeating are likely to suffer serious long-term health, emotional, and social consequences if they adopt the parents' behaviors. In addition, children who are abused by their parents are more likely to later abuse their own children than are children who are not abused by their parents. In a similar vein, children raised in families that have few displays of affection often have later problems with emotional intimacy in their own marriages and relationships with their children.

As noted previously, parents who model inappropriate behaviors for their children frequently have problems in controlling their children. Often, however, these parents are unaware of the negative impact of their own behaviors on the child. Although this lack of awareness (or denial) may reflect a relative lack of sensitivity for the child's psychosocial needs, it is inadvisable for the therapist to suggest that the parent has caused the child's behavior problem. Although the parent will need to change his or her behavior, such change is best effected within the context of a supportive, parent-therapist relationship. A positive rapport should initially be established. This can often be accomplished by focusing on the parent's strengths (e.g., concern for the child, the parent's ability as a provider). Next, it is often useful to define the child's behavioral problems in terms of the child's extreme susceptibility to influence from others. Often, it is possible to identify examples in which individuals have influenced the child in negative ways. It can then be suggested that the parent may need to modify his or her behavior to benefit the "susceptible child." By focusing on the child's vulnerability and the parent's ability to help the child, parental cooperation is more likely to follow.

Following the enlistment of parental cooperation, the parent can be encouraged to discuss the maladaptive behavior with the child. The therapist should structure this interaction such that blame is avoided and the parent informs the child of the needed behavioral change in the family. Throughout this process, the therapist must exercise caution not to undermine the parent's position of authority with the child. The parent's authority can be made explicit by privately encouraging the parent to establish a set of positive and negative consequences that are contingent on the child's behavior. Moreover, the therapist should refuse to take credit for changes in the child's behavior and should emphasize the parent's effort as the primary contributing factor.

The therapist must also help to arrange contexts that promote more positive behaviors by the child and the parent. These contexts should provide the child and parent with consequences that are highly valued. For example, for the child who imitates parental aggression by fighting in school, the peer prestige gained from fighting might be obtained through prosocial activities. This child might be appointed, with the teacher's cooperation, as the unofficial sergeant-at-arms in the classroom. The entire class could earn a small reward (or points that are accumulated and applied toward some larger reward, such as a class party) for each day that no fighting occurs. Thus, the target child might maintain high peer status by playing an important role in helping all of his classmates to earn some benefit. In addition, the child could be encouraged to take a more active involvement in organized sports, where assertiveness and aggressiveness would be socially accepted. In a similar vein, the parent could be taught less aggressive coping strategies that lead to a smoother resolution of interpersonal problems and that ultimately enhance the parent's sense of self-efficacy. A consistent system of social support (e.g., Parent's Anonymous) could also be arranged to ensure that the parent has an appropriate context for discussing his or her frustrations and for obtaining emotional support.

REFERENCES

Ainsworth, M., Bell, S. M., & Stayton, D. J. (1971). Individual differences in strange-situation behavior of one-year-olds. In H. R. Schaffer (Ed.), *The origins of human social relations* (pp. 17–57). New York: Academic Press.

Ainsworth, M., Blehar, M., Waters, E., & Wall, S. (1978). *Patterns of attachment.* Hillsdale, NJ: Erlbaum.

Arend, R., Gove, F. L., & Sroufe, L. A. (1979). Continuity of individual adaptation from infancy to kindergarten: A predictive study of ego-resiliency and curiosity in preschoolers. *Child Development, 50,* 950–959.

Baldwin, A. L., Cole, R. E., & Baldwin, C. P. (1982). Parental pathology, family interaction, and the competence of the child in school. *Monographs of the Society for Research in Child Development, 47* (5, Serial No. 197).

Barnhill, L. R. (1979). Healthy family systems. *The Family Coordinator, 28,* 94–100.

Baumrind, D. (1967). Child care practices anteceding three patterns of preschool behavior. *Genetic Psychology Monographs, 75,* 43–88.

Baumrind, D. (1971). Current patterns of parental authority. *Developmental Psychology Monographs, 4* (1, Pt. 2).

Baumrind, D. (1978). Parental disciplinary strategies and social competence in youth. *Youth and Society, 9,* 239–276.

Baumrind, D. (1983). Rejoinder to Lewis's reinterpretation of parental firm control effects: Are authoritative families really harmonious? *Psychological Bulletin, 94,* 132–142.

Baumrind, D., & Black, A. E. (1967). Socialization practices associated with dimensions of competence in preschool boys and girls. *Child Development, 38,* 291–327.

Beavers, W. R. (1981). A systems model of family for family therapists. *Journal of Marital and Family Therapy, 7,* 299–307.

Bell, R. Q. (1968). A reinterpretation of the direction of effects in studies of socialization. *Psychological Review, 75,* 81–95.

Bell, R. Q. (1977). Socialization findings reexamined. In R. Q. Bell & L. V. Harper (Eds.), *Child effects on adults* (pp. 53–84). Hillsdale, NJ: Erlbaum.

Borduin, C. M., Henggeler, S. W., Hanson, C. L., & Harbin, F. (1982). Treating the family of the adolescent: A review of the empirical literature. In S. W. Henggeler (Ed.), *Delinquency and adolescent psychopathology: A family-ecological systems approach* (pp. 205–222). Littleton, MA: Wright-PSG.

Brunk, M. A., & Henggeler, S. W. (1984). Child influences on adult controls: An experimental investigation. *Developmental Psychology, 20,* 1074–1081.

Burbach, D. J., & Borduin, C. M. (1986). Parent-child relations and the etiology of depression: A review of methods and findings. *Clinical Psychology Review, 6,* 133–153.

Coopersmith, S. (1967). *The antecedents of self-esteem*. San Francisco: W. H. Freeman.

Dornbusch, S. M., Carlsmith, J. M., Bushwall, S. J., Ritter, P. L., Leiderman, H., Hastorf, A. H., & Gross, R. T. (1985). Single parents, extended households, and the control of adolescents. *Child Development, 56,* 326–341.

Eisenberg, L. (1958). School phobia: A study in the communication of anxiety. *American Journal of Psychiatry, 114,* 712–718.

Emery, R. E. (1982). Interparental conflict and the children of discord and divorce. *Psychological Bulletin, 92,* 310–330.

Epstein, N. B., Bishop, D. S., & Levin, S. (1978). The McMaster model of family functioning. *Journal of Marriage and Family Counseling, 6,* 19–31.

Eron, L. D., Walder, L. 0., & Lefkowitz, M. M. (1971). *Learning of aggression in children.* Boston: Little, Brown.

Felner, R. D., Stolberg, A., & Cowen, E. L. (1975). Crisis events and school mental health referral patterns of young children. *Journal of Consulting and Clinical Psychology, 43,* 305–310.

George, C., & Main, M. (1979). Social interactions of young abused children: Approach, avoidance, and aggression. *Child Development, 50,* 306–318.

Hanson, C. L., & Henggeler, S. W. (1982). The behavior disorders and problems of female adolescents. In S. W. Henggeler (Ed.), *Delinquency and adolescent psychopathology: A family-ecological systems approach* (pp. 117–138). Littleton, MA: Wright-PSG.

Hetherington, E. M., & Martin, B. (1986). Family factors and psychopathology in children. In H. C. Quay & J. S. Werry (Eds.), *Psychopathological disorders of childhood* (3rd. ed.; pp. 332–390). New York: Wiley.

Hoffman, M. L. (1976). Empathy, role-taking, guilt, and development of altruistic motives. In T. Lickona (Ed.), *Moral development and behavior: Theory, research, and social issues* (pp. 124–143). New York: Holt, Rinehart, & Winston.

Hoffman, M. L., & Saltzstein, H. D. (1967). Parental discipline and the child's moral development. *Journal of Personality and Social Psychology, 5,* 45–57.

Lewis, J. M., Beavers, W. R., Gossett, J. T., & Phillips, V. A. (1976). *No single thread: Psychological health in family systems.* New York: Brunner/Mazel.

Loeb, R. C., Horst, L., & Horton, P. J. (1980). Family interaction patterns associated with self-esteem in preadolescent boys and girls. *Merrill-Palmer Quarterly, 26,* 203–217.

Maccoby, E. E., & Martin, J. A. (1983). Socialization in the context of the family: Parent-child interactions. In E. M. Hetherington (Ed.), P. H. Mussen (Series Ed.), *Handbook of child psychology, Vol. 4: Socialization, personality, and social development* (pp. 1–101). New York: Wiley.

Martin, B. (1975). Parent-child relations. In F. D. Horowitz, E. M. Hetherington, S. Scarr-Salapatek, & G. M. Siegel (Eds.), *Review of child development research* (Vol. 4, pp. 463–540). Chicago: University of Chicago Press.

Olson, D. H., Russell, C. S., & Sprenkle, D. H. (1983). Circumplex model of marital and family systems: VI. Theoretical update. *Family Process, 22,* 69–83.

Olson, D. H., Sprenkle, D. H., & Russell, C. S. (1979). Circumplex model of marital and family systems: I. Cohesion and adaptability dimensions, family types, and clinical applications. *Family Process, 18,* 3–27.

Olweus, D. (1980). Familial and temperamental determinants of aggressive behavior in adolescent boys: A causal analysis. *Developmental Psychology, 16,* 644–660.

Osofsky, J. D., & Connors, K. (1979). Mother-infant interaction: An integrative view of a complex system. In J. D. Osofsky (Ed.), *Handbook of infant development* (pp. 519–548). New York: Wiley.

Parker, G. (1983). *Parental overprotection: A risk factor in psychosocial development.* New York: Grune & Stratton.

Patterson, G. R. (1982). *Coercive family process*. Eugene, OR: Castalia Publishing.

Patterson, G. R., & Stouthamer-Loeber, M. (1984). The correlation of family management practices and delinquency. *Child Development, 55,* 1299–1307.

Poole, E. D., & Regoli, R. M. (1979). Parental support, delinquent friends, and delinquency: A test of interaction effects. *Journal of Criminal Law and Criminology, 70,* 188–193.

Rutter, M., & Madge, N. (1976). *Cycles of disadvantage: A review of research.* London: Heinemann.

Saltzstein, H. D. (1976). Social influence and moral development: A perspective on the role of parents and peers. In T. Lickona (Ed.), *Moral development and behavior: Theory, research, and social issues* (pp. 253–265). New York: Holt, Rinehart, & Winston.

Schaefer, E. S. (1959). A circumplex model for maternal behavior. *Journal of Abnormal and Social Psychology, 59,* 226–235.

Shinn, M. (1978). Father absence and children's cognitive development. *Psychological Bulletin, 85,* 295–324.

Sigel, I. E., Dreyer, A. S., & McGillicuddy-DeLisi, A. V. (1984). Psychological perspectives on the family. In R. D. Parke (Ed.), *Review of child development research* (Vol. 7, pp. 42–79). Chicago: University of Chicago Press.

Waldron, S., Shrier, D. K., Stone, B., & Tobin, F. (1975). School phobia and other childhood neuroses: A systematic study of the children and their families. *American Journal of Psychiatry, 132,* 802–808.

Waters, E., Wippman, J., & Sroufe, L. A. (1979). Attachment, positive affect, and competence in the peer group: Two studies in construct validation. *Child Development, 50,* 821–829.

Weissman, M. M., Prusoff, B. A., Gammon, G. D., Merikangas, K. R., Leckman, J. F., & Kidd, K. K. (1984). Psychopathology in children (ages 6–18) of depressed and normal parents. *Journal of the American Academy of Child Psychiatry, 23,* 78–84.

Wilson, M. N. (1984). Mothers' and grandmothers' perceptions of parental behavior in three-generational black families. *Child Development, 55,* 1333–1339.

Yarrow, M. R., Campbell, J. D., & Burton, R. (1968). *Child rearing, an inquiry into research and methods.* San Francisco: Jossey-Bass.

CHAPTER 4

Changing Affective, Sexual, and Instrumental Aspects of Marital Relations

In this chapter we address issues and problems that pertain to the marital dyad. The marital relationship is the foundation of the family system. When couples are emotionally bonded and have the ability to resolve conflicts, there are positive ramifications for the entire family system. Family members are provided with secure emotional attachments, and periodic crises do not threaten the integrity of the system. Conversely, when the husband and wife are emotionally distant or in continued conflict, family members can suffer in both the short-term and long-term. For example, children who are raised in cold or emotionally unstable homes have difficulty developing the positive perceptions of self and the interpersonal skills that are needed for intimacy as adults.

Consistent with our multisystemic perspective, the marital dyad is viewed within the context of the multiple systems of which it is a part. Marital difficulties are often associated in a cyclic and reciprocal fashion with extrafamilial transactions. Problems at work can lead to marital difficulties, and marital difficulties can lead to further problems at work. Marital disagreements can promote conflicts with extended family, and conflicts with extended family can provoke marital disagreements. Similar cycles of problematic interaction can revolve around financial issues, relations with friends, and associations with organizations such as churches and clubs.

Although extramarital systems certainly affect marriage and vice versa, treatment plans for marital problems should usually be targeted at the marital dyad. This is because we view the marital dyad as a critical subsystem that, to a significant degree, must function as a distinct, separate entity with clear, well-defined boundaries. A successful marital relationship should have qualities that distinguish it from all other interpersonal relations discussed in this volume. These distinctive qualities include sexual intimacy, a long-term commitment, and an agreement to share in the emotional and instrumental efforts that are needed to raise a family, maintain a household, and provide a respite from outside stress. The present chapter, therefore, is devoted to the treatment of problems that are most often within the domain of the marriage.

Many couples come to therapy with the explicit goal of resolving problems with their marriage. In fact, marital difficulties are the most frequently reported problem for which people seek professional counseling (Gurin, Veroff, & Feld, 1960). By the time that the couple has decided to enter therapy, their relationship has usually deteriorated, they are unhappy, and they want an objective third party to help them save their relationship and avoid a divorce. Such couples are relatively easy to work with. They tend to be motivated, open to suggestions, and willing to work on difficult issues. Much of this chapter is devoted toward descriptions of strategies that are useful for ameliorating some of the common problems presented by motivated couples.

Some spouses, however, come to therapy for reasons other than to build their marital relationship. They may have been coerced by the threat of divorce or may have a hidden agenda. Some couples, for example, have already decided to separate but seek marital therapy so they can tell their friends and family that they did everything possible to save the marriage. Others spouses have decided to leave their mate but want to arrange for him or her to have a ready-made source of emotional support. If such processes are not identified early, they can present the therapist with considerable frustration. We will discuss ways to identify individuals who are serious about change, as well as those who are not. We will also present strategies for dealing with covert agendas and their aftermath.

Many cases of marital therapy start with a presenting problem that does not pertain to the marriage. Marital difficulties are often at the root of child behavior problems. Similarly, many individual clients are experiencing psychosocial difficulties, such as depression and anxiety, that are directly related to their marriage. In these situations, it is imperative that the therapist recognize the implications that a presenting problem might have for the marriage. We will discuss how to assess the interplay between presenting problems and marital relations in a way that minimizes resistance and defensiveness. We will also suggest how to shift the focus of therapy, when necessary, to the marriage.

Before the treatment strategies are described, a general overview of our philosophy of marriage is presented. This overview includes some assumptions about human nature, and about the roles of men and women in our society. Because such issues stimulate considerable disagreement, the reader should be aware of our biases and the reasons for them.

PHILOSOPHY OF MARRIAGE

Consistent with the ideas presented by ethologists, we believe that humans are genetically predisposed to form certain types of social relationships. People tend to form monogamous heterosexual bonds that are based on shared affections and mutual instrumental interests. The nature of these bonds has considerable evolutionary significance. Heterosexuality is necessary for the propagation and survival of the species. Because the child is not capable of independent functioning for many years, it is essential that parents develop a stable and long-term commitment to each other and the child. Similarly, survival is enhanced by the ability of the parents to adapt to environmental changes in a flexible manner. There are undoubtedly many contemporary exceptions to our view of the basic nature of people. Nevertheless, we feel that the innate predisposition to form long-term, monogamous, heterosexual bonds has important implications for the treatment of marital problems.

The implications of this human biological predisposition pertain to four general components of a successful marriage: love, monogamy, quid pro quo, and flexibility. Although some theorists could argue cogently against the inclusion of one or more of these components, the absence of any one component can greatly increase the probability of an eventual breakdown in the integrity of the marital dyad or in the psychosocial functioning of an individual family member.

Love

People have a strong desire to love and to be loved. A warm and stable relationship provides the spouses with feelings of worth and belonging that enhance esteem and security. Intimacy also provides a context in which the couple can relax and recover from the stress of work and other responsibilities. Similarly, the giving of love, understanding, and support to someone who needs and appreciates these gifts, enhances both the recipient and the giver.

Despite the strong propensity to form intimate relationships, many couples never move beyond "roommate" status. We have observed several consistent themes when trying to understand why some people have difficulty forming close relationships. Most commonly, one or both spouses were raised in families that were low in displays of verbal and nonverbal affection. Usually, the parents were emotionally distant, and the children were not provided with models of marital love and giving. In other marriages, the difficulty forming a close relationship is a function of troublesome experiences in the spouses' lives. For example, adults who were abused or neglected as children may believe that the world is not a caring place and that people are not to be trusted. Likewise, persons who have been deserted by someone they loved may be hesitant to develop another close attachment. They often build an emotional barrier to protect themselves from being hurt again. Another common factor that maintains emotional isolation is chemical dependency. Chemically dependent individuals, who are still using drugs, are usually incapable of maintaining close relationships that are based on mutual love, respect, support, and understanding.

Monogamy

We believe that monogamy is an important factor in the development and continuation of successful marital relations. Our definition of a successful marriage is one in which the partners share intimacy, feel valued and respected, weather the normal crises of living, and jointly build for the future. When one or both partners become intimately involved with another person, there are invariably negative ramifications for the marriage. In our view, "intimate involvement" refers to any relationship that includes strong emotional ties; sexual familiarity is not a necessary component.

In light of the ongoing sexual revolution, why do we consider monogamy to be important? The primary reason is that extramarital relations severely disrupt the marriage on several levels. First, the spouse who is having an affair is less motivated to devote the emotional energy that is needed to maintain a successful marriage or to solve extant marital problems. When a sympathetic ear is available elsewhere (one that does not have to deal with the inherent problems of running a household and having a long-term commitment), it is much easier to turn to that person during a marital conflict than to extend the serious effort that is needed to resolve the conflict. Solving marital problems can require a substantial amount of work, and this work may not be forthcoming if there is a ready avenue of escape. This is one important reason why we do not treat couples when one or both members are having affairs that they refuse to terminate completely.

The existence of an extramarital relationship also sends a powerful negative message to the spouse. Minimally, the implicit communication is: "You are not meeting my emotional and/or sexual needs. I do not respect you and I may not even care about you any more." When the loyal spouse is prone toward internalization of blame (especially likely when the cheating mate is a good manipulator), he or she can suffer a significant loss of self-esteem and security. The spouse may engage in self-depreciation and may search for reasons to explain the affair, such as, "I'm old, fat, and ugly. I'm not smart enough. I don't make enough money. I nag too much." Moreover, the thought of solitude if the mate leaves can be extremely frightening for many people. Such interpersonal dynamics, quite obviously, are not conducive to building a marriage based on respect, love, and reciprocity.

Some individuals choose to avoid monogamous relationships. Sometimes this is done on philosophical grounds, as illustrated by the "open marriage" trend of some years ago. For reasons similar to those described above, these marriages were rarely successful. In addition, we believe that individuals who choose open relationships tend to possess characteristics that do not facilitate the development of emotional intimacy. Many of these individuals seem to use promiscuity as a way to avoid real closeness. When someone is having two or more sexual relationships, interactions tend to stay at a relatively superficial level. These individuals, moreover, tend to be emotionally imma-ture, egocentric, and concerned with immediate gratification of desires. As discussed later in this chapter, people avoid intimacy for many reasons, and self-centeredness is a leading cause of marital problems.

Quid Pro Quo

A successful marriage requires a tremendous amount of work. On an instrumental level, couples must decide who is responsible for various household and childrearing tasks, and how they will deal with the division of labor for future tasks. On an emotional level, spouses need support, understanding, and love. When one spouse is tired from a hard day of work, it can be difficult to extend the necessary effort. Nevertheless, the fulfillment of such needs is at least as important as the completion of the more obvious instrumental tasks.

Most spouses want to feel that they are getting out at least as much as they are putting in the marriage. In fact, the equitable exchange of positive behaviors is such an important aspect of marital relations that some theorists have made it the cornerstone of their approach (Jacobson & Margolin, 1979). Clearly, marital satisfaction is linked to the perception that the benefits of the relationship outweigh the disadvantages.

Dissatisfaction arises when one spouse feels that he or she is making much more of an emotional or instrumental effort than is the other spouse. A common example of this problem may occur in families in which the wife is employed *and* has full responsibility for child care and housekeeping. Numerous 80-hour workweeks can lead the wife to resent her "lazy" husband. Another example may be found when one spouse is expressive and empathetic, and the other is more emotionally distant. Dissatisfaction often results when the emotional needs of the expressive spouse are not met.

Our perspective on this issue is that the marital workload should be a 50/50 split, unless both partners truly want it otherwise. The split, however, should be based on an agreement that considers the respective values of the spouses. One spouse may wish the other to give mainly instrumental assistance. He or she may not desire greater affection and understanding, but would appreciate help in taking care of the house. Another spouse may desire a daily hour of time alone with his or her mate to talk about the events, problems, and worries of the day. It is imperative that each spouse understands and appreciates that what is important to himself or herself may not be as important to the other spouse, and vice versa. Giving, or the exchange of positive behaviors, should be conceptualized within a relativistic framework.

Flexibility

Flexible relationships have a better chance of passing the tests of time. Throughout the course of a typical marriage, many instances of crisis and transition occur. To deal successfully with these instances, spouses must often alter their viewpoints and behavior. Couples who are flexible in their relations are more likely to make the changes that enable a functional solution to new problems.

Intellectual or interpersonal rigidity, on the other hand, can make it very difficult to resolve crises and make transitions. Rigid viewpoints are adaptive in that they can help individuals to organize and understand their environment (e.g., religious or political dogma provide rules that enable people to make clear moral and behavioral decisions), but when individuals are locked into viewing the world from a particular perspective, they have trouble in situations where that perspective does not provide productive solutions. A common marital impasse is presented here to exemplify the importance of flexibility. This case is typical of many couples who are in a crisis of "roles."

For the first few years of marriage, Jack was the breadwinner and carried the bulk of the decision-making authority. Pam acted as his primary support system, but had secondary status in some important ways. For example, she could not write checks for more than $20 without his approval, nor could she visit her friends without his permission. Yet, both parties were perfectly content with this arrangement. As time passed, however, Pam's perspective on the situation changed, and she began to favor a more equalitarian view of marriage. Consequently, she made attempts to enhance her status, such as enrolling at a local college. In turn, Jack resisted these changes because he viewed them as challenges to his authority. His resistance further accentuated Pam's secondary status and made her even more determined to change her role. By the time the couple sought therapy, they were engaged in a full-blown conflict in which each spouse used whatever personal resources were available (e.g., sex, money, jealousy).

Therapeutic interventions in this case might have aimed to increase rates of positive behavior exchange or to develop problem-solving skills. The conflicts, however, seemed to reflect overriding philosophical differences and appeared inevitable as long as the spouses had such divergent perspectives regarding their roles. The most productive solution to the problem appeared to center on the couple's capacity to be flexible in their worldviews. Because it was clear that Pam would not return to her earlier status, Jack had to chose whether to modify his beliefs about marital roles, or to maintain a rigid stance and eventually lose his wife. Jack decided to yield to Pam's beliefs, and as he did, Pam was able to limit her role redefinition to those issues that were most important to her.

Our notion of flexibility is very similar to the adaptability dimension of family relations that has been described by Olson, Russell, and Sprenkle (1979, 1983). According to these authors, adaptability is the capacity of the family system to change its power structure, role relations, and relationship rules in response to situational and developmental stress. These authors have proposed that healthy families need a balance between too much change (chaotic system) and too little change (rigid system). Based on our clinical work and research (Rodick, Henggeler, & Hanson, 1986), we strongly support the conceptualizations of Olson and his associates. Families and couples who engage in too much change tend to be so disorganized that members rarely attain their goals. In contrast, rigid families and couples do not allow the freedom that is needed for successful independent functioning, nor do they provide a means for coping with changing circumstances.

Now that we have stated our biases, we will turn to the task of marital therapy. We have divided our discussion into three main areas: affective relations, sexual relations, and instrumental relations. Within each area, we describe ways to assess the quality of the relations and recommend strategies for effecting change. Finally, near the end of the chapter, we suggest guidelines for handling special problems including the aftermath of an extramarital affair, prolonged indecision regarding a commitment to the relationship, spousal abuse, and problems with the extended family.

AFFECTIVE RELATIONS

Affection and warmth are necessary components of a successful marriage. Indeed, feelings of attraction and emotional sharing are the factors that usually bring about the couple's initial bond. Although love does not necessarily conquer all, it certainly helps couples to get through the hard times. Conversely, an absence of love can make it very difficult for a marriage to survive.

It is important for the therapist to determine the quality of the spouses' feelings for each other because these feelings have significant implications for both treatment and prognosis. The outlook can generally be considered more positive when, in the context of marital problems, the husband and wife still feel a genuine caring and affection for each other. In such instances, the relationship usually possesses some important strengths, and the couple is often motivated to extend the serious effort that is needed for successful therapy. When the love is gone, however, spouses are less motivated to struggle with the difficult tasks of treatment, and success is not likely. Stated simply, it takes two to tango. One permanently disenchanted spouse can mean the end of the marriage.

Assessing Affective Relations

We recommend that the therapist determine the affective status of the marriage during the initial interview. After the introductions and social exchanges, the couple usually needs little encouragement to describe the reasons they have come for counseling. These reasons typically pertain to difficulties that the two spouses are having in relating with each other. During this description, the therapist can begin to assess the affective quality of the marriage by attending to the couple's nonverbal cues and tone of voice. The therapist can observe, for example, how close the spouses sit to each other, and whether they attend respectfully to each other's description of the problem.

Information regarding marital affect can also be obtained by asking the spouses to describe each other's positive characteristics. Often, during this task, the spouses attribute an impressive array of positive qualities to each other. Such reports are a favorable prognostic sign and should be acknowledged as such by the therapist. In addition, the delineation of positive qualities can help to create expectations of change. A spouse can be pleasantly surprised to learn that despite the recent conflicts, the other still feels that he or she has many attractive qualities.

In judging the significance of the spouses' reports of each other's positive qualities, the therapist should remember that sociocultural differences are sometimes a factor. Middle-class individuals tend to focus on the personal qualities of their spouse, such as kindness, generosity, a sense of humor, and sensitivity. Lower-class individuals, on the other hand, tend to emphasize functional and pragmatic concerns. A husband might say, for example, that his wife is a good cook and does a good job of taking care of the house and children. His wife might appreciate the fact that he brings home his paycheck and does not beat her. From a therapist's middle-class biases, such responses might appear dysfunctional. When viewed within the couple's sociocultural context, however, these responses may have very favorable implications for the marriage.

If either spouse has extreme difficulty in describing positive aspects of the other, it may mean that the spouse truly feels that the other has little redeeming value. It may also indicate, however, that the couple's difficulties have temporarily biased the spouse's perceptions about the relationship. One problem associated with prolonged conflict is that spouses begin to devote so much attention to the negative aspects of the relationship that they ignore the positive aspects. Another problem is that, in the context of long-term conflict, many spouses come to believe that their partners view them entirely in a negative light.

In assessing the affective nature of the marital relationship, the therapist can also ask the couple to describe what their relationship was like when they first dated, what first attracted them to each other, or what they currently do together for fun. If the answers are positive in nature, the therapist should comment on and emphasize these strengths. Again, the therapist's goal is to promote feelings of optimism. If the answers are negative (e.g., "We had to get married, she was pregnant"; "We have never spent much time having fun with each other"), the therapist should probably avoid commenting on the implications of these messages until later in the therapy process.

An additional index of the couple's affective relationship is the frequency of their lovemaking. Couples who rarely make love tend to be distant, and those who have an active love life tend to be more intimate. There are, however, many exceptions to this rule of thumb. For example, we have known several couples with extremely active sex lives who also had miserable relationships on emotional and instrumental levels.

When the therapist has a general impression about the affective nature of the relationship, an attempt should then be made to confirm this impression. Confirmation is important because the direction of therapy is based, in part, on the couple's affective status. Next, guidelines that can be used for confirming impressions of positive feelings and negative feelings are presented.

Positive messages.   The easiest situation for the therapist to deal with is when both spouses are implicitly communicating that they care very much about each other. The following interaction, which occurred during the beginning of an initial therapy session, suggests such a situation.

WIFE: I just don't know what's the matter with us. I know that we love each other, but we are also at each other's throats a lot of the time. We call each other nasty names and really try to hurt each other. I know that he doesn't mean what he says, but it still hurts. Sometimes we make up in a couple hours, other times the fights last for days.

HUSBAND: Yeah, I'll come home and I can tell that she is just itching for a fight. If I'm in a bad mood, I just don't have any tolerance for her nonsense. Other times, I think we have a wonderful marriage, but those times are becoming few and far between.

WIFE: The fighting is really wearing me down. We used to spend a lot of time together and really enjoy each other. Now all we do is fight.

HUSBAND: We've got to find some way out of this or I'm going to go nuts.

This printed version of the conversation does not do justice to the nonverbal cues (e.g., hand holding, mutual smiles) and the verbal intonations that reflected positive emotional feelings. The content of the conversation does, of course, reveal several positive aspects about the couple's relationship. First, at some previous time, the spouses' interactions were much more satisfying. Second, the spouses seem willing to share responsibility for their problems. And, third, they are very anxious to find a solution to their problems. In this type of situation, we suggest that the therapist temporarily place the delineation of the presenting problems on hold. The therapist might say something like this.

THERAPIST: Let me just stop you for a second and get clear on a couple of points. I want you to interrupt me if I say anything that is not on target. First off, it seems that you both had a pretty good relationship until about six months ago. You spent a lot of time together and enjoyed being with each other. Also, just from the way that you talk and the fact that you are sitting close to each other makes me think that you are still close. Is that true?

WIFE: Yes, but we fight so much now.

HUSBAND: (nods yes)

THERAPIST: I know about the fighting, but I want to make the point that you still have a lot of close feelings between you. That makes me optimistic about making the changes we'll be talking about later.

HUSBAND: I don't think we've doubted our love for each other, but the constant conflict is tough to live with.

THERAPIST: The other point I wanted to make is that neither of you are into blaming each other for all the problems. You might point fingers at each other during the heat of the argument, but after you calm down, you realize that you are both partly at fault. This is very positive to me because it shows a certain maturity and an ability to appreciate the other person's point of view. These qualities will be very helpful in resolving the areas of disagreement that you both have.

On a process level, the therapist has emphasized the couple's strengths and has attempted to create positive expectancies regarding the course of treatment. Because considerable time and energy in therapy are devoted to resolving problems, it is important to begin treatment by addressing the couple's strengths and to accentuate these strengths throughout treatment. By beginning treatment in this way, the therapist communicates respect for the couple. Such communication can enhance the spouses' self-image, and can facilitate the development of a productive therapist-couple relationship.

Mixed messages.   Many couples who seek therapy are not certain that they want to continue the marital relationship. After months or years of hostile interactions, one or both spouses may reasonably doubt that the marriage will improve. Such doubt will often be communicated by the spouses' attitudes and demeanor during the first minutes of the initial session. The therapist who perceives significant doubt should investigate the issue before proceeding with the conjoint interview. There is no reason to set up treatment goals when it is unlikely that both spouses are willing to extend considerable effort. Rather, the issue should be dealt with directly.

In contexts that include extensive mixed messages, we have found that spouses are more likely to tell the therapist how they truly feel when their mate is not in the same room. The following example shows how the therapist might deal with a perception that the wife has already decided to disinvest from the marriage, even though she has come to the initial interview with her husband. In this case, the therapist had been attempting to assess marital affect, but was having a difficult time getting closure. Approximately ten minutes after the conjoint interview began, the therapist decided to speak with each spouse separately.

THERAPIST: What I would like to do now is to speak with each of you alone for a little while. After that, we'll get back together at the end of the session and talk about where to go from here. It doesn't matter to me who I start with. (The husband leaves the room.)

THERAPIST: One thing that I wanted to ask about was a feeling I have that you don't really want to be here, and that, maybe, you have more or less given up on the marriage.

WIFE: (nods in agreement) A couple of years ago this might have helped us. Many times I asked Jim if we could see a counselor. He always refused, and I was just too weak to leave.

THERAPIST: If it is too late for counseling, why did you decide to come in now?

WIFE: Last Friday I had finally saved enough money to take the kids and move out. He refused to leave the house, so I had no other choice. Jim really didn't believe that I would do it, but I wasn't going to live like that any more.

THERAPIST: I understand, but why did you decide to come in here today?

WIFE: He pleaded and cried. He promised that he would change and that things would be better. After fourteen years of marriage, he said that I owed him one more chance. I don't agree; I don't owe him anything after all he has put me through. But he is extremely persistent, and I know that he would continue to hound me until I came here.

THERAPIST: So what you are saying is that you really came just to get your husband off your back, and that you have no intention of attempting a reconciliation?

This last inquiry is the key question. If the spouse answers "yes" at all levels of communication (i.e., verbal, nonverbal, tonal), the therapist should probe the firmness of the decision. If the decision is firm, the therapist's interventions should no longer be based on saving the marriage, but rather on helping the husband to understand and cope with the situation, and on helping the children to adjust to their parents' divorce. The wife probably does not need therapeutic attention. She has been preparing for the divorce for at least two years and has already made many of her emotional and pragmatic adaptations.

It is much more likely, however, that the spouse will respond to this last inquiry with a highly ambivalent "yes." In this case, the therapist needs to examine the ambivalence.

THERAPIST: You're saying that you have decided on the divorce, but I'm not certain that you really mean it.

WIFE: Things have been so bad for so long that I just don't believe that he can change. Sometimes he is nice for a couple of weeks, but then, as soon as he has me back, he returns to his old obnoxious self.

THERAPIST: I'm not sure that he can change either. If he did change though, and the change lasted, what would you think about staying with him?

WIFE: If he really changed it would be all right. It's not that I don't care about him anymore, it's just that I'm not going to put up with being fourth on his priority list.

The wife's last statement has opened the door for marital therapy. She is understandably doubtful about the potential success of treatment, but she still seems to be connected to her husband on an emotional level. Next, the therapist needs to frame the wife's feelings in a way that emphasizes her willingness to work on the relationship under specific terms.

THERAPIST: It sounds to me that you're saying you would consider staying in the marriage if you felt that Jim was really serious about the changes, and not just trying to manipulate you again?

WIFE: I think that's true.

THERAPIST: If that is the case, we will definitely be able to see how serious he is if you both decide to continue counseling.

WIFE: I don't know. How will you ever be able to tell?

THERAPIST: It is easy to see who is serious about change and who is not. We'll get together once a week to decide on some changes that would make you both more satisfied with the marriage. Then, we will work out ways to implement these changes, and you will both be responsible for specific efforts during the week. On a day-by-day basis, you will be able to see how much each of you is trying. If Jim stops trying after a couple weeks, he was probably not serious about changing his relations with you. It might also mean that his decision to come for counseling was just another manipulation to get you back. If, on the other hand, he is serious, you will see his efforts and they will make you want to work harder too.

WIFE: I don't mean to sound like it's all his fault. I have my problems as well. It's just mostly his fault.

THERAPIST: No, I know what you mean. I'm sure that both of you can work on lots of things to help out. How does the general game plan sound to you?

WIFE: I suppose it's worth a try.

THERAPIST: Good, we'll do the best we can and maybe things will work out this time. Often it takes a real crisis, like leaving home, before people start to deal with their problems. Let me talk with Jim now, and we'll get back together at the end of the hour.

The therapist has attained the wife's tentative agreement to work on the marriage. The therapist has also attempted to set positive yet realistic expectations regarding the probability of success. The course of treatment will be determined largely by how hard the husband and wife are willing to work. The therapist should convey this supposition to both spouses in very clear terms.

Predominantly negative messages.   After probing the apparent ambivalence, the therapist sometimes learns that one spouse no longer wants the marriage. This is usually an implicit decision that has been made over the course of one or more years. Typically, the spouse has not acted on these feelings or made the decision overt for a variety of reasons (e.g., fear of losing custody of the children, fear of losing economic advantages or of losing face with relatives and in-laws). In such cases, when the therapist is certain that the spouse's decision is firm, we recommend that the therapist encourage the spouse to be more open to his or her mate and not drag out the process any longer.

The therapist might also attempt to allay any of the spouse's fears. For example, the therapist might tell the husband that as long as he maintains close contact and puts the necessary energy into the children, he can continue to have a close relationship with them. Moreover, if he and his wife can avoid extended bitterness, it is unlikely that the children will experience any significant emotional difficulties, though some economic deprivation is usually unavoidable. Regarding the mate who is being left, the therapist's primary task is to ensure that there is an adequate social support network and that this network will be used to cope with the crisis. Also, the therapist might note that in the long-run, the person will be better off than in his or her current marriage after eventually developing a relationship with someone who shows love and caring.

Setting the Stage for Change

Before making specific interventions, the therapist might think about creating a cognitive set in the couple that will facilitate change. We have already noted the value of emphasizing the positive aspects of the couple's marriage. Change will also be facilitated if the therapist stresses the idea that the couple's problems will significantly improve if they extend their best effort, and that the spouses will extend this effort if they truly want the relationship. The first assumption puts considerable responsibility on the therapist and assumes a directive style of treatment. This assumption also requires that the therapist is able to accurately analyze relationship problems and to implement effective interventions. The second assumption places substantial responsibility on the couple. A lack of effort is interpreted to mean that the spouse does not want the relationship enough to make sacrifices. Few individuals will allow this interpretation to be made if it is not true. If the interpretation is true, a resolution of the motivational issue should become an immediate priority.

We have also found it useful for the therapist to describe some general guidelines that the couple should follow throughout therapy. These guidelines communicate to the couple that treatment is not a frivolous, once-a-week task, and, again, that with serious effort and work the couple will be able to significantly improve their relationship. First, the couple is told that they must begin to emphasize mutual giving and cooperation. The shift away from a competitive orientation will be promoted when the spouses are able to appreciate each other's perspectives on problem issues, and to communicate this appreciation. Second, the spouses must learn how to resolve the conflicts, resentments, or frustrations that naturally arise. Because of the fear of starting a full-scale fight, many spouses hold in their frustrations and become more and more aggravated until they explode. The conflict resolution strategies that we use emphasize nondefensive communication and compromise. A third guideline stresses the importance of providing more frequent recognition of the other spouse's positive efforts. A spouse whose efforts are appreciated is more likely to continue them. A fourth guideline is that the couple must make the marriage their number one priority. This may mean that time and energy will be taken from other activities (e.g., the children, work, golf, TV) and devoted to the relationship.

Finally, the therapist sets the stage for future sessions. In general, the couple is told that these sessions will address the issues and problems that the couple presents and that the therapist delineates. Solutions that are mutually acceptable will be worked out, and these solutions will then be implemented by the couple during the week. The therapist should always remember that, although problems will be addressed one at a time, he or she should conceptualize the problems at a meta-level and should structure the interventions at that level. The therapy process does not involve merely working out solutions to specific problems, but also the use of identified problems as vehicles for teaching the couple more effective ways of coping.

Improving Affective Relations

When the cognitive set for change has been developed in the couple, it is time to start making these changes. An efficient way to begin this portion of therapy is to simply ask the couple for several changes that they would like to see in their relationship.

In listening to the spouses' responses, the therapist should try to conceptualize these requests at a meta-level, rather than focusing at a purely content level. The differences between content and meta-level conceptualizations are similar to the distinctions that theorists have made between digital and analogic communication (Haley, 1976), and between the report and command aspects of messages (Lederer & Jackson, 1968). *Content* refers to the literal meaning of the communication. The *content message* is the one that would be conveyed if the communication was typed and read silently. An understanding of *meta-level meanings* requires greater attention to the context of the communication, including nonverbal cues, tone of voice, and the place of the communication in the overall sequence of ongoing transactions.

As described next, therapeutic strategies are guided by meta-level interpretations. It is very important, therefore, that the therapist always remains open to the possibility that his or her meta-level interpretations are not entirely accurate. The highly subjective nature of meta-level conceptualizations results in considerable room for error. The best sign that the therapist has made an erroneous meta-level judgment is when therapy has not progressed significantly, despite considerable effort. At this point it is best if the therapist attempts to reconceptualize the situation, or consults with a colleague in order to obtain a fresh perspective. Some examples are presented to clarify the distinction between content and meta-level messages.

The therapist asked the Smiths for changes that they would like to see in their marriage. Charlotte requested that her husband, Roger, stop playing golf every Sunday with his friends and start going to church again. The therapist should not necessarily take these requests literally. A meta-level interpretation may be that Charlotte is actually saying that she feels left out of her husband's life and that she wants to spend more time with him alone. If such is the case, the therapist should design an intervention that addresses this meta-level issue. If Roger's golf game is very important to him, it might provoke unnecessary conflict to intervene in that one area. On the other hand, Charlotte would probably not be bothered by her husband's weekend golfing if the couple shared a significant amount of positive time with each other during the week. What is justifiably upsetting to Charlotte is that Roger devotes little attention to her during the week *and* avoids her on weekends. The avoidance and lack of sharing are the problem, not golf. Another example of the need to consider the meta-level message is provided in the following case.

Frank and Debbie Jackson were happily married for the first nine years of their relationship. Their overt problems began when Debbie decided that she was tired of being a housewife and wanted more out of life. She found a job and planned to enter a management training program. Frank was very dissatisfied with this change and demanded that Debbie stop working and start devoting more time to the household and to the children. Debbie refused to comply, thus intensifying the conflict between herself and Frank.

On a content level, the central issue was Debbie's job versus household responsibilities. At a meta-level, however, Frank's underlying concern was that Debbie was moving away from him emotionally, and that he and the family were no longer a high priority. Frank was afraid that Debbie would become increasingly independent and self-sufficient and that she would eventually leave him. Therefore, the therapist decided that the most productive solution would be to help Frank feel more secure in the relationship, but not to ask Debbie to drop her new interests. The meta-level issue was commitment to the marriage, not the performance of housework.

Once the meta-level issues are identified, it is time to intervene. Again, it may be helpful to ask the spouses for specific changes that they would appreciate. For example:

THERAPIST: What types of things could Debbie do that would show you that she really was committed to you and the family?
HUSBAND: Quit work and stay home.
(Nonproductive answers should be countered by the therapist.)

THERAPIST: I don't think that is a good idea for two reasons. First, the job and the positive feelings that it provides are very important to your wife. Part of having a successful marriage is that both partners should feel good about each other *and* themselves. Second, the real issue is not Debbie's job, it's that you and Debbie have both grown apart and you are afraid that you might lose her. I think it would be much better if you could come up with some other ways that she might show her love for you.

The therapist is not hesitant to give this message even though the wife has probably given it 100 times before. The therapist is in a position to define what is "good" and what is "bad" for the marriage and to push the husband for satisfactory alternatives to his request for change. If the therapist is not directive in this type of situation, it will lead to fight 101.

If the couple comes up with changes that are mutually agreeable and fit their meta-level problems, the therapist should compliment them on their good judgment and help arrange the specifics. Returning to the Smiths:

WIFE: It would make me happy if we could spend more time together. Just you and me, without the kids. That would make me think that golf and your buddies aren't all that matter to you.

HUSBAND: Sure, I'd be willing to do that.

THERAPIST: That is an excellent idea. It's very positive that you're so agreeable. How, exactly, do you want to arrange things?

HUSBAND: Well, maybe we could go out on Friday or Saturday night.

THERAPIST: How does that sound to you, Mrs. Smith?

WIFE: Fine, if he sticks to it.

THERAPIST: He just said he would, and I would give him a chance. It might be a good idea, however, if you both talked about exactly how and when you will make the decision, and about where to go and that kind of stuff.

At the beginning stages of therapy, it is important to make agreements very explicit. If the agreement breaks down, it will then be much easier to determine which spouse has not lived up to the bargain. As we shall discuss later, breakdowns and unkept agreements represent important topics of conversation in subsequent sessions.

The therapist should also be prepared to provide the couple with suggestions for increasing their mutual involvement. One of our most common suggestions is that the couple structure their schedules so that they can spend time together on a daily basis. Many couples who are experiencing problems have structured their time in a way that minimizes interaction. One spouse may read while the other spouse watches television, or the couple might devote their free time to club or civic activities. Although this arrangement may limit the amount of pain that each spouse suffers in the relationship, it also impedes the development of cycles of positive reciprocity. During their newly arranged times together, the spouses might share their experiences of the day. Indeed, it is important that couples who have grown apart become more involved in each other's careers and outside interests. By actively sharing the experiences of the day, several positive messages are implicitly communicated. The most important is: "I want you to be involved in my life." Other messages may include: "I am interested in learning about the matters that concern you during the day," and "I respect and value your opinion." Such messages can have very favorable effects on the marital relationship because they are clear, though implicit, communications of caring and concern.

Couples who frequently use sarcasm and other put-downs should be requested to limit their initial communications to ones that are positive. Relationship problems will receive extensive attention throughout treatment, and will be resolved more easily if the couple is able to first focus on the positive. For example, the therapist might request that each day the couple spend 15 to 20 minutes writing down the positive things that the other did during the day. Each spouse should then verbally express appreciation for the other's efforts to build the relationship. This task enables the spouses to receive overt recognition for their efforts and helps to delineate the actions that each spouse views as positive and rewarding. From the therapist's perspective, the couple's efforts on the task also reflect their commitment to change.

Another way to facilitate positive affective change is to have the couple "date" during the weekend. Many couples with marital problems no longer engage in the joint activities that they enjoyed during the early part of their relationship. An important part of close relationships, however, is the pursuit of mutual enjoyment. The dates might entail going out to dinner and a movie, riding bicycles, or any other form of recreational activity that both spouses view as attractive. The meta-level goal of the task is to provide a context in which the couple can relax and become reacquainted with each other's favorable qualities. Typically, these are the qualities that first attracted the spouses to each other.

Dealing with Negative Affect

When the spouses have been able to attend to their positive feelings for a week or two, it is time to teach them how to handle negative feelings and emotions effectively. Although this is a very difficult process to learn, it is applicable to several common situations that cause great distress in many marriages.

Some distressed couples engage in cycles of negativity. Each spouse responds to the real or perceived aggressions of the other until there is a traumatic blowup. The blowup is followed by apologies and promises, but not by the resolution of pertinent issues, and so the cycle is repeated at a later point in time. Other spouses do everything possible to avoid the traumatic blowup. They learn that the best way to avoid conflict is never to discuss anything that is bothering them, so they hold in their frustrations and dissatisfactions. Again, however, the pertinent issues are not resolved and the frustrations are expressed out of context in the form of sarcasm, derogatory comments, passive aggression, or withdrawal.

Our suggestions for intervention assume that the couple is committed to the relationship and that they share a positive affective bond. The suggestions also presume a level of cognitive development that is near the stage of formal operations (Neimark, 1975). Significant social perspective-taking skills and introspective abilities are required for the interventions to succeed.

Five general steps are helpful in teaching couples how to deal with their frustrations and negative emotions: (1) recognizing that a concern exists, (2) informing the spouse that there is a concern, (3) explaining the concern to the spouse in a nonattacking way that minimizes defensive reactions, (4) gaining an understanding of the spouse's perspective of the concern and learning that the spouse appreciates your perspective, and (5) working out a mutually agreeable solution to the concern.

Recognizing that a concern exists.   This is usually an easy step for the couple to learn because most people readily identify when they are becoming upset. A certain tension and "ill" feeling typically accompanies aggravation with a spouse. Moreover, the aggravation is cued by thoughts such as: "The house was a mess for the fortieth day in a row. That woman has got to be the laziest slob in the universe. I wish she would get off her ass." Or, "He is such an insensitive jerk, totally wrapped up in his own pitiful little world. The man is incapable of any real feeling." When such thoughts are expressed openly, they tend to evoke mutual hostility. When the thoughts are not expressed openly, they still impede positive marital relations. It is hard to be warm and giving to someone you resent, or to whom you attribute extremely negative characteristics. Because of the intensity of the emotions that are stirred by such concerns, it is not difficult for individuals to recognize when they occur. The difficult part, as we will address shortly, is handling the negative emotions in a productive way.

When working with couples who engage in open battles, the therapist should initially help the couple to identify the conflict in its early stages, before it develops into a full-blown fight. Couples almost always know when a disagreement is beginning to escalate. At this point, each spouse usually has thoughts that amount to: "How dare that dirty rat say that to me, I'm going to nail him (her) to the wall." Although the spouses usually realize that a full-blown fight is brewing, they are willing to pay the price of intense conflict in order to deliver their blows. People often choose short-term gratification of impulses at the expense of long-term negative consequences. It is important, therefore, that the therapist notes that the long-term and eventual consequences of this high-conflict situation are further marital distress and divorce.

The first step in the conflict resolution process is teaching the spouses to recognize when tensions are beginning to escalate. Early during the spouses' initial exchange of barbs, one or both of them needs to think: "Look out, we're starting to get into it again." As a vehicle to promote this process, the therapist might ask the spouses to monitor closely their daily hostilities in an attempt to identify them as early as possible. In a moderate percentage of cases, we have observed that such monitoring alone greatly decreases the frequency of conflicts. Paradoxically, in such instances, we usually inform the spouses that it is important for them to have fights, otherwise it will be more difficult to teach them the necessary conflict resolution strategies.

Even when conflicts do not decrease, the monitoring serves valuable functions. Before the couple can fully learn the remaining steps in conflict resolution, it is important that they develop an increased awareness of the contexts of their conflicts. Monitoring also provides a more adaptive contextual frame for the couple's conflicts. The previous frame was: "My mate is being a pain again and I'm not going to put up with it." The new frame should be: "I'm starting to get angry and this is one of the situations that the therapist said I should pay close attention to." The intensity of a conflict can be reduced when the spouses devote their energy to analyzing their emotions, rather than to preparing for combat.

Informing the spouse that a concern exists.   Informing can take place either before or in the early stages of an argument. It is very important that the informing is not power-assertive in nature. Otherwise, the receiver could take the request as an order. To minimize defensiveness, it can be helpful if the informer takes a one-down position. For example: "Sally, something is bothering me and I was wondering when would be a good time to talk about it?" The tone of voice and body language must be congruent with the one-down verbalization.

During the early stages of an argument, the informing step involves a similar approach. Again, the style must be nonaggressive, for example: "Burt, I think we are starting to get hostile with each other. How about if we take a time-out and get back together later? Would that be okay with you?" It is also important that the couple learns to make requests that do not convey superiority. Some couples will use what they learn from the therapist to deliver more subtle blows to each other. For example, the preceding request could be said in this way: "Burt, you are obviously getting out of control again. I, on the other hand, am in firm control of my emotions and am doing my best to follow the doctor's suggestions. Perhaps we should take a few minutes off so that you can regain your composure."

Explaining the nature of the concern.   This step is not the solution to the problem, but it can set the groundwork for a communication process that will enable the couple to derive a satisfactory solution. The therapist should emphasize that the most important part of this step is to avoid any message that is personally attacking or blaming. When a spouse feels that he or she is being attacked or blamed, it is likely that the response will be defensive or hostile. Such a response can aggravate an already tense situation and lead to further escalation of the conflict. In order to minimize defensiveness, we usually suggest that the concerned spouse express the frustration in a way that emphasizes its impact on his or her own feelings. Some case examples are given to clarify this point.

Marilyn's major complaint was that when her husband, Tom, smoked marijuana, he became apathetic and ignored her. (An evaluation had determined that he was not chemically dependent; see Chapter 9.) During the second therapy session, Tom agreed to stop smoking marijuana to facilitate some of the changes that both spouses saw as desirable in their marriage. Three days after this agreement, Marilyn returned home from work and found a messy house that smelled of marijuana smoke, with Tom asleep on the couch. Marilyn ordered Tom to clean up his mess. In response, he demanded that she immediately cook dinner. Marilyn called Tom a slob, and he called her a whore. One thing led to another, and soon Marilyn walked out the door and Tom threatened divorce.

When teaching a couple how to address their concerns in a more productive fashion, it is important for the therapist to conceptualize issues at the meta-level. In the preceding example, the therapist should recognize that Marilyn was not really concerned about the messy house; her meta-level concern was the message communicated by Tom's behavior. The message was that Tom was not committed to their relationship and that he cared more about getting high than about their marriage. This communication made Marilyn feel rejected and unloved, which, in turn, elicited a hostile retaliation. The therapist's task is to teach the couple ways to address their concerns without exacerbating the situation. At several points, either spouse could have responded in a way that attenuated the conflict. For example:

MARILYN: I am very upset and need to talk with you about what's bothering me.
TOM: Go on.

MARILYN: I have been very happy over the last couple of days because I thought that
we were finally making the changes that would help our marriage. I love you very
much and our marriage is very important to me. When I got home today, though, I
saw that you had been smoking marijuana again. This makes me very sad and angry.
Sad because it means that you must not want me and don't care enough to change
your habits. Mad because it was an agreement that we had made and I felt that I was
living up to my end.

This example highlights several points that we believe are important. First, Marilyn
expressed her concern to Tom but did not attack him in the process. Second, she focused
on how the concern made her feel. In so doing, her words were more likely to evoke
apology and regret than an attack. Third, her response required considerable self-restraint
and maturity. It is not a coincidence that these same qualities are important components
of a successful marriage.

It can be extremely difficult for individuals to learn how to respond in the reflective
style that is needed to minimize defensiveness. In some cases, several therapy hours may
be needed to teach this response style. During these hours, the therapist can model the
reflective style, discuss examples with the couple, and utilize role play as a vehicle for
teaching reflectivity. Examples and role play should be taken from actual conflicts that
the couple has had in the past. Couples will view such examples as pertinent to their own
context and will be more likely to transfer the learning to present conflicts.

For further clarification of how spouses should explain the nature of their concern,
examples of two common problems follow.

The husband was upset because his wife came home from work an hour later than
expected. In this situation, many husbands in dysfunctional marriages tend to think in
one of two different ways. He may think: "That inconsiderate bitch, making me worry
whether something has happened to her." Alternatively, the husband may wonder: "What
is she up to? Who is she with?" In either frame of mind, it is likely that the husband's
initial comments when the wife returns would be hostile.

How might the husband present his concerns in a way that promoted a productive
solution to the problem? In the situation where the husband was concerned for his wife's
safety, he might say: "It is so good to see that you are all right. I was so worried that
something had happened to you. For the past forty minutes I've been on pins and needles
and was getting ready to call the police." When the concern is expressed in this way, it
is much more likely that the wife will reciprocate by apologizing and saying that in the
future she will be certain to call when she is going to be late.

In the situation where the husband thought that his wife might be cheating on him,
he might say: "I'm getting worried about us. We seem to spend hardly any time together,
and today you didn't come home from work until late. I am afraid that you are pulling
away from me or are upset with me about something." These comments focus on how
the concern makes the husband feel and do not denigrate the wife. Such an expression
sets the groundwork for change.

The context of the following example is one in which the husband uses sarcasm and
put-downs to dominate his wife. She has gradually become both insecure about her
abilities and resentful of her husband's attempts to control the relationship. To address
her concern in a positive way, the wife might say: "Sometimes I think that you feel that

I'm a complete idiot and that you are much smarter than me. The put-downs make me feel unloved and unrespected. They tell me that you don't like me or care about my feelings. This is very difficult for me because I respect your opinion and look up to you in many ways. It makes me feel worthless and incompetent when someone I value keeps putting me down." Again, the expression of concern focuses on how the wife feels, not on the husband's character flaws.

Gaining an understanding of the spouse's perspective.   Interpersonal conflict is exacerbated when one spouse perceives that the other is not listening to his or her point of view and does not appreciate his or her perspective. In this context, marital partners do not reciprocate with understanding. Instead, they respond with counterpoints and often demean the other's viewpoint. Such transactions do not enhance the couple's ability to derive mutually satisfactory solutions to their conflicts. Gaining an appreciation of the other spouse's perspective, therefore, is a pivotal step in learning how to resolve arguments and ameliorate negative situations.

This step is also extremely difficult. It requires that each spouse temporarily put aside arguments and justifications for certain behaviors. When in conflict, spouses usually entrench in their own points of view. Their arguments focus on how correct their perspectives are, and how erroneous the other's viewpoint is. Energy is devoted to developing rationales, rather than to understanding and appreciating the mate's point of view.

The following strategy is recommended for diminishing the intensity and longevity of marital conflicts. After the couple is able to identify when a cycle of negative reciprocity is beginning to develop, we suggest that they call a 5 to 10 minute time-out. This time-out is useful for two reasons. First, it breaks the couple's usual sequence of escalating negative transactions. From a systems theory perspective, when behavioral sequences that include problematic behavior are changed, individual cognitions and interpersonal relations frequently improve (Haley, 1976). Second, the time-out provides the opportunity for each spouse to demonstrate clearly a willingness to put relationship interests above personal interests. Such a demonstation promotes the view that each is actively working toward building the relationship. When dysfunctional couples begin to develop this view, constructive change can become self-perpetuating.

What should the couple do during the time-out period? After moving to separate rooms, we encourage each spouse to try to understand the other's point of view and to appreciate the validity of the other's arguments or behavior. Even those individuals who are exceptionally intelligent and interpersonally skilled can find it difficult to make this change in behavior. It is especially difficult when the issue is emotionally charged. Nevertheless, we feel that this change is a critical step toward resolving marital problems. The difficulty of the change requires that the therapist devote substantial effort toward teaching the process. It is helpful if the therapist models the process using actual conflicts that the couple has had. Role play and coaching during the session can also be used to convey the process.

Immediately following the time-out, the couple should come back together. The central task for the spouses is to demonstrate that each appreciates the other's perspective. To accomplish this, the first spouse describes the other's point of view and feelings about the issue. The presentation is *not* evaluative; it is purely descriptive (e.g., "You are angry at me because I have ignored your attempts at conversation today."). The spouse devotes no attention to his or her own perspective in the conflict. The word *but* is never used (e.g., "You feel that I was not showing you respect, but I didn't mean my comment that way."). The presentation should also be uninterrupted. The sole intention is to let the other know that he or she understands the other's viewpoint.

Immediately after the presentation of the first spouse, the second spouse should then clarify his or her feelings. The second spouse should acknowledge the perceptions of the first spouse that were accurate: "It is good to know that you understand why I felt angry when you flirted with that woman at the picnic." Next, the second spouse should elaborate on impressions that were not entirely accurate, and describe views and feelings that were omitted: "Although I was angry at you, I also felt really bad about myself. I thought that maybe I wasn't attractive anymore after gaining so much weight." During this phase, the first spouse tries to acquire a more complete understanding of the second spouse's perspective. When this has been achieved, the roles are reversed: The second spouse explains the perspective of the first spouse, and the first spouse provides nonjudgmental feedback regarding accuracies and inaccuracies.

Once this interaction sequence has been completed, most couples are no longer in a state of intense hostility. An interaction style that emphasizes perspective-taking and cooperation has been substituted for one that emphasizes power plays and competition. Although competition may be adaptive in work and some extrafamilial relations, competition in marriage advances one spouse at the expense of the other.

An individual can become extremely frustrated when his or her spouse refuses to listen to a concern. This frustration is eliminated when the spouse not only listens but actively demonstrates an appreciation of the individual's perspective. In addition, an individual has no reason to argue and repeatedly present his or her views when the spouse has already demonstrated a good understanding of these views. With reduced frustration and anger, the couple is ready to negotiate a mutually satisfactory solution to the issue.

The preceding description pertains to situations in which couples openly battle. Battles, however, usually arise because one or both spouses are frustrated or upset about some behavior of the other. Dealing with these frustrations on a daily basis is preferable to waiting for the eventual full-blown conflict to develop.

Our interventions for addressing marital frustrations are very similar to the procedures that we have already described. The concerned individual requests that the mate listen to the concern, which is expressed in a nonattacking manner to minimize defensiveness and counterattack. Next, the mate should acknowledge the spouse's concern. This acknowledgment does not necessarily signify that the mate agrees with the spouse's perceptions, but it does indicate that the spouse appreciates the mate's point of view regarding the concern. Next, the spouse explains his or her perspective on the concern. This is also done in a way that facilitates understanding and minimizes aggression. Similarly, the concerned spouse should then demonstrate an appreciation of the other's position. When the spouses learn that the other truly appreciates their perspective, patterns of behavior can change dramatically.

Some couples, however, are not able to achieve this kind of mutual appreciation. Some individuals have not attained the level of cognitive development that is necessary for social perspective-taking. In such cases, interventions should remain as concrete as possible, avoid abstractions, and utilize operant techniques to increase the exchange of positive behaviors and to decrease negative interactions (Jacobson & Margolin, 1979). Individuals who are chemically dependent will also have great difficulty in developing and using perspective-taking skills. Such skills require a clear head, tolerance, reflectivity, and thought processes that are not egocentric.

Spouses who are not truly committed to saving the marriage will also experience difficulty in perspective-taking. If that commitment is not present, it is extremely important that the therapist recognize this fact. The willingness to "try" then becomes the central issue that must be resolved before therapy can progress. The therapist might note, for example, that the process message of minimal effort is that the spouse feels that marriage is "not worth the work." If this is true, the other spouse will have to decide whether to remain in a one-sided relationship. In addition, the therapist should point out that the spouse's lack of effort also has important implications for treatment, that is, there is little purpose to continuing marital therapy without significant effort from both spouses.

Finally, extremely self-centered or stubborn individuals will have difficulty learning the perspective-taking process. Successful marriages require emotional and instrumental giving, as well as the yielding of some personal needs for the good of the relationship. When one of the partners refuses to attempt such changes, the prognosis can be bleak.

Working out a mutually acceptable solution.   The process of compromise and negotiation is quite different when resolving marital conflicts than when resolving extrafamilial conflicts in such areas as labor relations. In the latter, each side attempts to maximize its own benefits through the use of argument, ploys, and manipulation. In a marital conflict, however, the goal is not for one spouse to "win." In fact, if one spouse does consistently win, the relationship will probably fail. Rather, the goal is for both spouses to feel that they give as much as they receive. Therefore priority is placed on each spouse doing whatever is reasonable to make the other comfortable with the outcome.

To achieve this end, the therapist attempts to develop a cognitive set in the couple that can be generally described as follows: "I believe that I am right, but I understand his (her) perspective too. This conflict is having a negative effect on our relationship, and the marriage is more important than any one disagreement. The best way to handle the situation, therefore, is to be giving." If both spouses are willing to adopt this cognitive set, the therapist has little need to teach techniques of compromise. We have observed consistently that attitudinal change about the relationship, together with the feeling that one's views are respected, lead to a ready willingness to compromise. This is because couples with a strong emotional bond usually wish to return to their "normal" satisfied state. Marital conflict not only presents aversive situations, but it also interferes with the positive interactions that normally characterize the relationship. In the vast majority of cases, the spouses make their own compromises when this step is reached.

When the couple still has difficulty reaching compromise solutions, the therapist can serve as an arbitrator. Assuming that the spouses have an accurate understanding of each other's requests for change, the therapist can nudge and cajole the couple toward equitable compromises. For example, with one couple who spent little time together, the therapist convinced the husband to agree to play cards with his wife in return for her help in refinishing his fishing boat. In a similar impasse, the therapist convinced the husband to provide his wife with a complete breakdown of the family's financial assets and liabilities in return for her agreement to adhere to a mutually developed family budget.

SEXUAL RELATIONS

Marital dissatisfaction is often associated with complaints about sexual relations. These complaints may be related to sexual inadequacies, a low frequency or inoptimal style of making love, and difficulties following an extramarital affair. The treatment of these problems involves similar processes.

Sexual Dysfunctions

In the early 1970s, the research of Masters and Johnson (1966, 1970) and others (e.g., Kaplan, 1974) revolutionized the treatment of sexual dysfunctions. Before that time, our empirical knowledge regarding sexual functioning was sparse, and treatment strategies for sexual problems were not well developed. Masters and Johnson based their therapeutic approach on many years of experimental research, together with clinical trial and error. Although researchers have subsequently modified some of Masters and Johnson's ideas, we feel that their core approach remains extremely relevant. In general, we follow their approach in the treatment of sexual problems such as premature ejaculation, impotence, and orgasmic dysfunction, and we strongly recommend that therapists who treat couples should study their research.

A core premise of Masters and Johnson's approach is that sexual problems occur within the context of a relationship. It is, therefore, the relationship that is the focus of treatment. Their treatment of relationships emphasizes the development of open communication, especially regarding sexual matters. However, the Masters and Johnson approach does not focus narrowly on sexual problems. It also addresses other relationship issues that might be associated with the couple's difficulties.

Masters and Johnson's model is also multidimensional. At a biological level, it is important to determine whether the sexual problems are related to any physical difficulties. Therefore, therapists should make appropriate medical referrals to eliminate the possibility of physiological causes or complications. At a cognitive level, their approach assesses the sexual beliefs and values of the spouses. Individuals develop attitudes from their family of origin that can significantly impede sexual development (e.g, the belief that sex is dirty and bad). Moreover, experiences such as molestation during childhood can disrupt sexual development as an adult. It is important, therefore, that the therapist obtain a complete history from the husband and wife and, when necessary, provide educational and therapeutic experiences to instill alternative viewpoints.

One cognitive variable, fear of failure, is viewed as particularly significant in the development of sexual problems. Masters and Johnson have shown that this fear develops and is maintained within the context of the couple's reciprocal transactions. They also describe a strategy labeled "sensate focus" that can be used to eliminate this cycle of self-perpetuating anxiety. Sensate focus helps the couple to reexperience the positive sensations that are associated with physical contact in a loving relationship. A paradoxical component of sensate focus is that more intimate sexual contact is strictly prohibited. It is this prohibition that eliminates the fear of failure and sets the stage for problem resolution.

The Masters and Johnson approach also attends to the dyadic and extradyadic levels of the couple's system. As noted previously, therapy focuses on enhancing marital communication and interaction. Moreover, interventions are used to reduce stress that may be related to any problems outside the marriage. Sources of stress may include problems presented by the children, or difficulties related to a spouse's employment situation.

In summary, we believe that Masters and Johnson provide a comprehensive approach to treating sexual dysfunctions that is conceptually consistent with the multisystemic model presented in this volume. We have found their methods to be extremely useful in ameliorating sexual difficulties. Rather than detailing these methods, we feel that it is more sensible to refer the reader to their volumes, which present the empirical basis for their approach, describe a general therapeutic model, and delineate specific strategies for specific problems. In addition, other clinicians such as Kaplan (1974) and LoPiccolo (LoPiccolo & Friedman, 1985) have provided many useful suggestions for the treatment of sexual difficulties.

Low Frequency or Inoptimal Style of Lovemaking

Healthy sexual relations come in many forms. Some couples make love rarely; others make love twice a day. Some couples prefer their lovemaking to be relatively conservative; others employ an array of sexual aids and positions. On a purely content level, we feel that such differences among couples are largely irrelevant to the maintenance of successful marital relations. What is important to the success of the marriage, however, is that each spouse is satisfied with a particular frequency or style of lovemaking. When sexual dissatisfaction is present, it usually signals other meta-level problems in the relationship, as the following examples show.

Priscilla came alone to the therapist's office for the first session. She wanted to know whether her sexual relationship with her husband, Dick, was normal. She was 29 years old, Dick was 46, and they had been married for 14 years. During sexual relations, she was required to act out her husband's fantasies, which usually included sadomasochistic or pedophilistic themes. Because Priscilla had married an older man at a very young age, and because she was socially isolated, she did not know whether her sexual relationship was typical of most marriages. She felt uncomfortable in her role, but her husband had convinced her of its validity.

When the presenting problem in the marriage involves a sexual issue or complaint, the therapist's decision regarding an appropriate treatment strategy should always include a consideration of nonsexual aspects of the marriage as well. If, for example, Priscilla was satisfied with the general level of affection and with the instrumental aspects of the relationship, her discomfort regarding sexual behavior would not necessarily reflect any serious disturbance in the marriage. Intervention might aim toward a clarification of how each spouse feels about the situation, and a negotiation of mutually acceptable changes in sexual interaction. If, on the other hand, Priscilla was also unhappy about some nonsexual aspects of the marriage, her sexual concerns might reflect a more serious disturbance in the relationship.

In this case, Priscilla was also upset because Dick would not allow her to leave the house alone, would not permit her access to the family finances, was extremely critical of her behavior, and was physically abusive toward one of the children. Within this context, her discomfort with their sexual relations was only one indication of a much more serious problem. Attempts at marital therapy failed, however, because Dick refused to comply with Priscilla's request that he attend therapy sessions and attempt to change his behavior toward her and the children. Nevertheless, the situation warranted relatively extensive intervention, beginning with the therapist's report of the child abuse to the Department of Human Services, as required by law. On a cognitive level, the therapist supported Priscilla's emerging personal beliefs about marital values and norms. In light of her subsequent decision to separate from Dick, Priscilla was taught effective behavior management strategies (her husband had been the primary disciplinarian), and was encouraged to develop an extrafamilial support network that would promote her self-esteem.

In some situations, sexual dissatisfactions do not reflect any serious meta-level problems. Often the parameters of the dysfunction can be understood when the therapist examines the couple's sex life within the ecological context of their marriage, as the following example reveals.

John and Mary were a young and attractive couple who came for therapy because of a fear that they were growing apart. The most salient aspect of this fear was that their previously enjoyable love life had entirely disappeared. John was a business executive who was very successful, but who also worked 70 hours per week. During his few hours of leisure time, he attended to numerous home maintenance tasks or slept. Mary had a masters degree in art history and was also very active. She took care of their 18-month-old son and participated in several aerobics classes and athletic events each week. As a consequence of their lifestyles and the fact that each spouse was physically exhausted by 9:00 P.M., it was not difficult to understand why their sexual relationship was not going well.

John and Mary's decreased sexual activity reflected a general disengagement. They had made a mistake (at least in terms of marital relations) that often befalls upwardly mobile young couples. Their energies were being devoted primarily to career advancement and to the pursuit of physical conditioning. In a very real sense, they were taking their marriage for granted, believing that it would take care of itself. This belief was based on the fact that they had already developed a very positive relationship and tended to be successful at whatever they tried.

Treatment was relatively simple and direct. The therapist suggested that the couple needed to discuss and to reestablish their priorities. As with any accomplishment (e.g., business promotion, physical conditioning), marital satisfaction necessitates considerable motivation, commitment, and effort. Therefore, if the couple wished to save their relationship, it would be necessary to devote considerably more attention to their marriage. If this meant delaying a promotion by two years, or gaining ten pounds, so be it. With this couple, it was simply a question of priorities. After obtaining agreement from the couple, specific plans were made for ways in which they could find the time to get reacquainted. One of the vehicles for this goal was to plan some time in which they would not be tired and could be alone together.

In several ways, the process of treating sexual dissatisfaction is similar to the process of alleviating dissatisfaction with any aspect of marital relations. It is, however, especially difficult to avoid defensive reactions to concerns that are expressed by either spouse. Spouses tend to be much more sensitive about their sex lives than about household chores. Nevertheless, the process is much the same. The concerned individual must learn to express the concern in a self-effacing style that minimizes the likelihood of a defensive reaction. In addition, the spouses should attempt to appreciate each other's perspective on the issue. Then, the couple should arrive at a solution that represents some mutually agreeable compromise. Clearly, the therapist needs to provide the impetus to overcome any stumbling blocks. Such obstacles might include difficulty with discussing sexual matters, inappropiate attitudes and expectations about sex, and poor sexual technique. The following case included these obstacles.

Phillip and Nancy were experiencing several sexual difficulties. One of Nancy's primary complaints was that foreplay lasted only two minutes. One of Phillip's major complaints was that he and Nancy rarely had sex. However, it was only after several meetings with the couple that these complaints were expressed to the therapist, and even then these complaints were communicated with great hesitation. The couple needed the presence of an objective and supportive third party before they could bring up any sexual issues. With the therapist's help, Phillip was able to appreciate how the brevity of his lovemaking produced a negative set in Nancy's mind. She felt that Phillip used her and that he viewed her as an object, not as a partner. Similarly, Nancy was able to realize that her frequent refusal of Phillip's sexual advances represented a personal rejection to Phillip. He felt insecure in the marriage and thought that Nancy might be involved with someone else. When they arrived at a mutual understanding, they were then able to make plans for specific changes in their love life. These plans included descriptions of exactly what Nancy wanted to happen during foreplay, and how Phillip (and Nancy) should initiate sexual activity.

In conclusion, we believe that sexual relations can be best understood within the overall context of marital relations. In cases where sexual dysfunctions are related to problematic sexual beliefs or sexual techniques, we strongly recommend that therapists follow the guidelines developed by specialists in sex therapy such as Masters and Johnson, Kaplan, and LoPiccolo. It is always important, however, for the therapist to evaluate the couple's affective relations, as discussed previously, and the couple's instrumental relations, which are discussed next. It is difficult for many couples to have a good love life when one partner is not emotionally connected or feels exploited on an instrumental level.

INSTRUMENTAL RELATIONS

Raising a family requires a tremendous amount of physical and emotional work. Money must be earned to pay the bills. The house has to be vacuumed, dusted, and cleaned. Someone must take care of the laundry, lawn, and car. The children require continuous nurturance and periodic discipline. Someone must take them to their dance lessons, ballgames, and other social events. Groceries must be purchased, and the meals must be prepared. In light of the numerous and sometimes unpleasant tasks that must be completed in a typical household (few adults actually enjoy cleaning the bathtub or disciplining the children), it is not surprising that marital conflicts frequently involve instrumental issues.

Incongruent role expectations provide one of the most common sources of serious marital friction. Although the situation has changed somewhat during the past 20 years, many men and women hold the belief that the wife should assume primary responsibility for taking care of the home and the children, and that the husband should assume responsibility for generating income. This attitude often prevails even when the wife is employed. When both spouses are satisfied with such an arrangement, it is a perfectly acceptable division of labor. With distressed couples, however, one spouse commonly feels exploited. This feeling usually evokes resentment and can be associated with behaviors that disrupt the marital relationship, as the following case example suggests.

Immediately after Bob and Alice graduated from high school, they married because she was pregnant. Both had been raised in blue-collar homes and held traditional values concerning marriage and family. Although Bob was bright and hard-working, his lack of marketable skills limited his employment opportunities to low-paying jobs. Consequently, Alice took a minimum wage position in a department store to help make ends meet. During the next five years, both spouses advanced rapidly at their respective places of employment. Concomitantly, Alice became increasingly dissatisfied with certain aspects of the marriage. She valued Bob's warmth and affection but felt that he was extremely selfish in some ways. Finally, Alice threatened Bob with divorce if he did not come for counseling.

During the first interview, Alice reported that she was very depressed and thought that it had to do with the marriage. Bob reported that he was fairly happy and had no major complaints about the marriage. A description of their instrumental relations revealed why one was dissatisfied and the other was content. Alice worked 40 hours per week and also had full responsibility at home for preparing the meals, doing the housework, and taking care of their son. When she came home from her job, she still had to accomplish household tasks for several hours and, consequently, went to bed exhausted. When Bob came home from his job, he usually played with his son or watched television. During the weekends, he would go hunting or fishing with his friends, and Alice would try to catch up on the housework and also get some rest. It was not difficult to understand how this might lead Alice to feel depressed.

Although Bob emerged as the "heavy" in this marriage, it was important for the therapist to recognize the reasons for (though not necessarily the validity of) Bob's position. The couple was very young, and their primary groundwork for learning marital roles had come from their parents. In both households, the mother had raised several children and had performed all the chores. Based on the couple's experience, therefore, it was understandable that Bob should expect Alice to fill a similar role and that Alice should feel a similar obligation. The qualifier was, however, that the spouses' mothers had not been employed 40 hours per week. A second aspect of Bob's perspective was that he earned twice the salary of his wife and felt that this entitled him to be excluded from any household responsibilities. His third argument for why Alice should do all the housework was because men do not do housework. This belief might be an object of derision in certain circles, but it was consistent with the worldview of his peers and family. Fourth, like most persons, Bob wished to avoid menial tasks whenever possible. In his situation, he had a wife who had continued to perform these tasks without major objection, at least until the present time.

What are the treatment objectives in this context? In some respects, Alice had probably already made the major therapeutic move. She had said, in effect, "I am not going to put up with this anymore." By threatening divorce, she had gotten Bob's full attention. The therapist's task, assuming that Bob wanted to save the marriage, would be to help Bob find a graceful way to make the changes that his wife demanded. However, if the changes were purely the result of Alice's coercion, serious difficulties would probably arise in the future. If Bob also had complaints about the relationship, it would be possible to make tradeoffs. After the spouses understood each other's positions, Bob could agree to some changes and Alice could agree to others. Bob, however, had no major complaints. Therefore, the therapist focused on modifying Bob's attitudes that exacerbated the problem.

The therapist began the discussion with the comment that he considered marriage to be a 50-50 proposition. Not surprisingly, few clients will disagree with this statement. Next, the therapist proposed that 50-50 means equal effort, time, and energy. Consequently, someone who is working for $5.00 per hour for 40 hours per week is contributing as much as someone who is earning $50.00 per hour for 40 hours per week. (It is necessary, of course, that the therapist have a better counterpoint for every argument that the client might develop.) When Bob agreed to this point, the logical conclusion was that the childcare and household responsibilities should be evenly divided between him and Alice, who were both working full time.

Bob still believed, however, that men should not have to perform housework. The therapist agreed and took the notion one step further: Women should not have to do housework either. Indeed, no one likes to clean the toilet or wash the kitchen floor. The reality of the situation was, however, that unless the couple was wealthy, some adult in the family had to perform these chores. The therapist explained that it would be better for the marriage if the misery was divided, rather than assumed by just one person. Because the therapist was a male, he used a personal example to show Bob that his belief that men did not do housework was not entirely accurate. Bob's only alternative would have been to say that because the male therapist did housework, he could not be a man. We have not met a client who was willing to openly draw this conclusion. Moreover, it is irrelevant to the course of therapy that Bob might not have "truly" agreed with the belief that real men do housework too. What mattered was that he had given tacit approval of this belief within the therapy context. The therapist could then use such approval as a lever of change throughout the treatment process.

The therapist could have also talked with Bob about the importance of flexibility in a marriage. The therapist might have explained that if people are to adapt to changing times, it is important that they remain open to new ways of thinking and behaving. Again, few young adults will disagree with this premise. Bob's agreement with the flexibility premise would promote the development of a cognitive set that would facilitate attitudinal and behavioral change.

The therapist could have also focused on the pragmatic side of the issue. The therapist might point out that Bob loves his wife and that she is an extremely important part of his life; however, if he continued in his present stance, there was a distinct possibility that she would leave him. Even if she stayed, she would be very dissatisfied, and his relationship with her would suffer. From this perspective, Bob could avoid serious problems if he would just agree to devote several hours a week to household chores. It would be a small price to pay for keeping his marriage and family.

Whether the therapist discusses his own housework responsibilities, the importance of spousal flexibility, or the husband's love for his dissatisfied wife, it is important to note that the therapeutic process underlying the discussion of each issue is the same: to convince the couple that they will need to alter their conceptualizations of the relationship in order to resolve their difficulties. This meta-level process, rather than the specific content of the argument, is a critical component of therapy. The therapist frames the rationale for this change in a way that is most useful for motivating the particular couple. The reframing has direct and logical implications for behavior change. Thinking about the situation in a new way does not necessarily result in behavior change, but it does set the stage for such change.

Making the Behavioral Changes

When each spouse has consented to the new conceptualizations and has agreed to extend serious effort toward resolving problems, the therapist's next tasks are to concretize the changes, develop a daily monitoring system, and deal with any breakdowns in the process.

It is important that the desired behavioral changes are defined in such a way that they can be observed and monitored. For example, doing the dishes, fixing the porch, cooking dinner, and taking the children to their recreational activities are all observable behavioral events. If the requests are poorly defined, the therapist should modify the requests to make them specific. For example, the wife might request that her husband help her out with the cooking. To introduce greater specificity, the therapist might ask whether the husband should cook one meal per week, do the dishes five nights per week, set the table every evening, buy all the groceries, or combinations of these tasks. When the request is made more specific, it is then possible to determine whether the spouses have lived up to their agreements during the week. If the therapist allows the request to remain vague, it is possible that the couple will subsequently disagree regarding their completion of the tasks.

When the tasks have been specified, the therapist should ask whether the spouses are willing to commit to such changes. If the answer is no, the therapist should help the couple to reach a mutually acceptable compromise. It is rarely difficult to reach a compromise because each spouse realizes that he or she will also be getting something in return.

Therapeutic progress requires that the therapist is accurately informed of the spouses' efforts. It is important, therefore, that the therapist asks the spouses whether the designated tasks were completed during the previous week. Because completion of these tasks is essential to positive change in the relationship, the therapist should address this issue at the beginning of the session. Depending on the couple's response, the therapist can proceed accordingly. If both spouses have lived up to their promises, the therapist should congratulate them. The therapist can also make the interpretation that the couple's behavior shows that they are sincere in their desire to resolve their marital conflicts, and that the outlook is very optimistic. It is also helpful if the therapist prompts the couple to describe how each other's efforts made them feel about the marriage.

After the positive feelings are shared, it is time to move on to the additional changes that are requested. These changes should be negotiated during the session and added to the list for the upcoming week. This process is then repeated until all instrumental issues are resolved. With some couples, treatment may be completed within three to four sessions. When couples also have affective difficulties or are not sincere in their commitment to work and to compromise, more extensive treatment may be needed.

One impediment to therapeutic progress occurs when either or both spouses believe that the other is not sincerely willing to change. This issue can be addressed in two ways. First, by definition, the successful completion of tasks demonstrates the sincerity of the individual. This is, of course, qualified by the fact that the changes must be maintained and are not accompanied by whining or complaining.

Second, we have found that it is very useful to have the couple grade themselves on a daily basis. At the end of the day, the spouses sit down and discuss their view of each other's efforts on the agreed goals. This provides an opportunity to receive positive recognition for attempts to build the relationship, and immediate feedback for a lack of effort. Positive recognition is important because it can help to break the cycles of negative reciprocity that often develop between distressed spouses.

The daily feedback can also help spouses to put "bad" days in perspective. For example, some couples overgeneralize and feel that the entire week is a disaster if they have had one bad day. If a written grading system reveals that six out of seven days were good, it is possible for the therapist to make a more realistic interpretation of therapeutic progress and interpersonal commitment.

Negative feedback (or a low grade) can also serve a useful purpose. Some individuals cope with marital conflict by withdrawing and by surrounding themselves with an emotional wall. The wall protects them from further insult, but it also impedes effective problem solving and reconciliation. When the partners come together each night to grade the day's efforts, it provides an opportunity to let the wall down. Moreover, each party knows that if he or she has made a mistake, but then devotes an extra effort during the day, these efforts will probably be recognized. Many times such efforts are an indirect way of saying "I'm sorry for my mistake."

The grading system also teaches the couple that successful marriages require effort and feedback. As we noted earlier, many people are willing to work 50 hours per week on a career, but balk at putting 10% of that time into their marriage. These individuals seem to feel that a good marriage should somehow evolve naturally, with little direct effort. We believe that it is more productive if couples conceptualize the goal of having a successful marriage the same way that they would conceptualize other life goals, such as career advancement or physical fitness. It is unlikely that a runner who trains only three hours per week will successfully complete a marathon. The same logic can be applied to the development of successful marital relations.

SOME GUIDELINES FOR HANDLING SPECIAL PROBLEMS

The preceding guidelines are applicable to most situations that involve distressed couples. Some situations, however, are especially problematic and may require a modified approach.

Aftermath of an Extramarital Affair

One of the most difficult problems for a couple to resolve is an extramarital affair. Typically, the spouse who has been faithful feels betrayed, angry, and depressed. Because the faithful spouse has typically been told a series of lies, he or she also usually experiences a complete lack of trust and confidence in the relationship. If the unfaithful partner is a skilled manipulator, the faithful spouse may also feel responsible for somehow "driving" the partner to have the affair.

The emotions and interpersonal dynamics of this situation make it very difficult for the therapist to proceed "as usual." As we have noted, the resolution of marital conflicts requires considerable effort, understanding, and appreciation for the other's perspective. However, the spouse whose mate has been unfaithful is usually in no mood to cooperate in relationship building. In most cases, the spouse would rather learn the gory details of the affair and make the mate pay dearly for being unfaithful. As a payback, some spouses immediately go out and have their own affair. Others attempt to evoke tremendous guilt (e.g., "How could you ever do this to me, I've been so good to you and loved you so much?"). Other spouses attack, attack, and attack some more.

Throughout this period of anger, the spouse who has had the affair is usually willing to receive a significant amount of retaliation (this assumes that he or she wants to continue the marriage and that the affair was not a signal of impending divorce). The retaliation may alleviate the guilt of the unfaithful spouse and may allow the other spouse to feel that he or she has gotten even. Retaliation, therefore, is not necessarily a counterproductive meta-level process, even if it appears quite vicious from a content perspective.

As long as the faithful spouse emphasizes retaliation, the therapist is limited in ways to effect change. It is usually most advantageous if the therapist aligns with both spouses and validates the emotions and perceptions of each. The therapist can reflect the pain and anger that one is experiencing, as well as the regret and guilt of the other. Within several weeks, however, the time must come for the couple to deal with their differences. The unfaithful spouse will not submit to retaliation for an unlimited period of time. Similarly, the other spouse must decide at some point that it is more important to save the marriage than to continue to gain revenge.

We use several guidelines for promoting reconciliation. First, the unfaithful spouse must answer all questions that the mate has about the affair. If the spouse stonewalls, the other spouse will always be uncertain. As long as uncertainty exists, the offended spouse will have considerable difficulty leaving the past behind and building toward the future. Rather than learning the details of the affair bit by bit, it is better if the couple has one or two prolonged question-and-answer sessions.

The rebuilding process cannot begin until the anger of the offended spouse has decreased substantially. When anger and resentment are still high, they continually attenuate therapeutic progress. Although we do not adhere to a cathartic model of behavior change, we have found that within the present context, anger does not decrease until it is fully expressed. Therefore, as an additional guideline, we encourage the offended spouse to be as hostile as he or she pleases, short of physical violence. We also suggest that one to two weeks of intense hostility will probably be sufficient. The unfaithful spouse is told that he or she deserves the hostility and will have to accept it.

This intervention has a paradoxical flavor in that it is usually more difficult for a spouse to continue venting hostility when he or she is encouaged to do so by the therapist.

Within one or two sessions, the offended spouse is usually ready to begin marital therapy. Although this spouse may still have feelings of anger, the therapist should remind the spouse that the anger has been adequately expressed and that the primary task at hand is to rebuild the marriage so that future problems are avoided. It is more productive, therefore, to control the anger and focus attention on the present. If the unfaithful spouse is expending serious effort in therapy, this should be interpreted as a very positive sign. If, on the other hand, the unfaithful spouse is not extending serious effort, such behavior has very negative implications and must be addressed directly in therapy.

Some offended spouses continue to display intense anger for a prolonged period. Although the anger is understandable, it can be very counterproductive in terms of saving the relationship. Consequently, the therapist can suggest that the offended spouse can only go in two directions (excluding an immediate divorce). First, the offended spouse can continue to punish the unfaithful mate and eventually risk the relationship. We usually inform the offended spouse that this strategy represents a rather inefficient way to pursue a divorce. Second, the offended spouse can try to leave the past behind and focus on solving underlying marital difficulties in a way that helps to ensure the successful resolution of future problems.

Finally, the issue of "trust" almost always arises when a mate has had an extramarital affair. We believe that the offended spouse *should* feel a loss of trust, and that the therapist should describe this as a natural consequence of an extramarital affair. Moreover, it may take many years before the trust returns completely. Only one context promotes the return of trust: The unfaithful spouse must continually and consistently demonstrate a commitment to the relationship. Trust will grow slowly in response to a successful track record.

The preceding discussion of the issue of extramarital affairs has been conceptualized within a unidirectional perpetrator-victim framework. Although this perspective has some validity, most of the time both spouses are culpable; the offended spouse has usually behaved in ways that promoted the mate's behavior. For example, it is common for the offended spouse to have devoted little emotional energy to the marital relationship. We have found, however, that couples who enter treatment during the crisis following the discovery of the affair rarely respond favorably to a framework that emphasizes shared responsibility. The offended spouse is in no mood to "share blame." For pragmatic reasons, therefore, we initially employ a unidirectional model, unless the couple responds otherwise. There is nothing to lose by taking this approach initially because therapeutic interventions regarding expressive, sexual, and instrumental issues follow the same guidelines as presented earlier in this chapter. Although the affair might be blamed on one spouse, the reciprocal nature of all other relationship problems is emphasized.

Indecision

Sometimes therapy does not progress because one spouse is uncertain about wanting to save the marriage. This uncertainty can be very frustrating for both the therapist and the other spouse. Although the therapist may have developed an ideal set of interventions, progress will be slow because an uncommitted spouse is usually not willing to extend the consistent effort needed to resolve serious marital problems. Likewise, it is difficult for the other spouse to maintain a prolonged commitment when faced with mixed messages. In earlier sections of this chapter, we discussed ways to address mixed messages. In this section, we present strategies that the therapist can use to resolve overt and extended indecision.

One strategy is called "The 80% Rule." Many people cannot make an important life decision until they are 99% certain of their choice and so waver for an indefinite period of time. (We have seen individuals take 10 to 12 years to make a decision to end an unsatisfactory relationship.) During this fence sitting, the status quo of the relationship is maintained. These individuals hope that some new information will come to light or that some life circumstance will occur to provide the certainty that allows a "correct" choice. The new information, of course, rarely comes in a nonambiguous form.

Decisions that are emotionally charged, such as reconciliation versus divorce, are almost never accompanied by 99% certainty. We recommend, therefore, that clients should base their decisions on 80% certainty. This is not to suggest that the decision should be made impulsively. It is assumed that the therapist and client have spent sufficient time discussing the pros and cons of the various possibilities. Rather, the 80% rule is viewed as a cognitive strategy that can be used to traverse a therapeutic impasse. In a surprisingly high percentage of cases, this cognitive shift prompts movement in therapy.

Some clients, however, feel that their decision is a 50-50 toss-up. This perception seriously impedes change in either direction. When the other spouse is giving, the individual wants the relationship. When tensions arise, the individual does not want the marriage. In the 50-50 situation, the therapist needs to alter the individual's perceptions of the available choices. The therapist should explain that the individual who sits on the fence is actually making a decision to commit to the emotional instability that accompanies fence-sitting. Continued indecision will make it impossible for the spouses to build the marital relationship or to develop emotionally satisfying lifestyles as single adults. The therapist can make helpful interventions if the client moves in either direction, but little can be accomplished otherwise.

The following case illustrates the resolution of a wife's indecision in a marriage that included physical abuse. Although the therapist felt that the husband was a "con artist," the therapist attempted to safeguard the interests of both spouses.

After three years of physical abuse, Rosemary had left Tony and had moved in with a friend. The couple's cycle had been one in which Tony would become extremely jealous and beat Rosemary, she would threaten to leave him, and he would become repentant and promise that the abuse would never happen again. Tony was a smooth-talking insurance salesman and had always been able to convince Rosemary that he was going to "really change." It was not difficult for Tony to convince Rosemary because she loved him very much. Throughout the marriage, Rosemary had frequently asked Tony to seek counseling, but he had adamantly refused.

Tony came to the first session alone. This was primarily a maneuver to show Rosemary that he was more serious than ever in his desire to change. Both spouses came to the second session. During this session, Tony pressured Rosemary to move back home. He professed to have finally recognized his "problem," and he felt that he was developing the insight that was needed to solve it. The therapist believed that Tony was not being candid, but kept that view to himself. Rosemary was encouraged by Tony's words, but she was uncertain whether she wanted to risk another letdown. It had taken her many months to find the courage to leave, and she was certain that she would no longer submit to his attacks. On the other hand, her most important goal in life was to have a happy marriage with Tony.

The therapist tried to handle Rosemary's uncertainty in a way that supported the interests of both spouses. He told the couple that in light of their history, it was best that Rosemary stayed with her friend, but that she and Tony should spend a significant amount of time together. The therapist also stated that Tony's willingness to enter therapy, in combination with Rosemary's follow-through on her threat to leave, might provide the impetus needed to resolve the violence problem and the couple's other marital difficulties. Finally, the therapist noted that the therapeutic sessions would provide the perfect context for Tony to demonstrate his commitment to the marriage and to learn alternative methods for dealing with his anger and jealousy.

The therapist's strategy was essentially to place Rosemary in a "no-lose" position. If Tony was serious about changing, he would have ample opportunity to show his newly acquired self-control and social perspective-taking skills. In addition, the couple would be able to resolve their extant problems and build a foundation for dealing with future concerns. On the other hand, if Tony was not serious about changing, that would become evident within a relatively brief period of time. If Tony remained aggressive or if he did not extend serious effort toward resolving marital conflicts, it would be extremely unlikely that he would ever change his behavior patterns. In such a case, Rosemary's path would become quite clear.

Some spouses who report that they are uncertain about the marriage have actually made a decision. Typically, they have decided to get a divorce but want to let their mate down easy. Unfortunately, unless the mate also wants a divorce, it is impossible to shield him or her from extreme pain. The mate will either suffer through the prolonged anguish that accompanies uncertainty about the marriage, or through a briefer but more intense pain that follows the decision to divorce. We believe that one partner should inform the other of the decision in clear and direct terms. The spouse should not leave a door open if there is no chance of reconciliation. Although we sympathize with the spouse's desire to save his or her mate from intense pain, we also feel that when the decision is firm, it should be carried out as quickly as possible. The sooner the emotional disengagement, the sooner both spouses will adjust to life as single adults.

Occasionally, despite all therapeutic moves, a spouse will not commit one way or the other. The therapist has three apparent choices, and we recommend either of the latter two. First, the therapist can continue to see the couple with no particular goals in mind. Though this choice may have certain financial advantages for the therapist, it is counter-therapeutic and not in the couple's best interests. Second, the therapist can terminate the case until the spouse reaches a decision. This choice is usually not harmful because it leaves the couple in the same position that they have occupied for some time. Third, the therapist can refer the couple to a colleague who might have an alternative strategy to resolve the impasse.

Physical Abuse

Physical abuse is frequently related to alcohol or drug use. Therefore, the therapist *must* conduct an evaluation for chemical dependency whenever aggressive behavior is part of the presenting problem. If the abusive spouse is chemically dependent, this problem must be resolved before it will be possible to address other marital issues. Chemical dependency requires a specialized set of interventions that pertain to several systemic levels. Moreover, the low frustration tolerance that usually accompanies physical abuse is often ameliorated by continued sobriety.

Abusive spouses do not usually enter therapy voluntarily. They most often come under threat from the legal system or because they believe that their mate will leave unless the problem is resolved. It is not necessarily negative that abusive spouses come to treatment involuntarily. In fact, pressure from the legal system or from the mate can provide a more effective lever for change than just a personal desire to become less aggressive. The legal system and the mate can apply severe negative sanctions for continued aggression. When the major impetus for change is personal desire, feelings of guilt for aggressive acts may not provide motivation that is sufficient for lasting change.

Although marital violence occurs within a systemic context, the therapist must give priority to safeguarding the well-being of the abused spouse. The abused spouse may have behaved in a way that exacerbated the situation, but there is no justification for physical violence. It is essential, therefore, that the therapist immediately address the issue of violence from the victim's perspective. We suggest that concrete plans be made that allow victimized spouses to protect themselves from future dangers. For example, we might encourage a wife to immediately leave the house and drive to a friend's home or a women's shelter at the first sign of a physical threat.

The prearranged plan can serve other purposes in addition to the protection of the spouse. There is less opportunity for the conflict to escalate when the spouse leaves at the first sign of a threat. The perpetrator is also provided with direct feedback and knows exactly what the result of the threats will be. We have found that such knowledge promotes self-control because abusive spouses strongly wish to keep their aggression a secret from third parties, such as friends of the spouse. Because the plan has been advocated by the therapist, the abusive spouse cannot blame the mate for leaving, and the abused spouse has no reason to feel guilty about leaving. Finally, a discussion of the situation that led the spouse to feel threatened can be used constructively during the next therapy session. The material can provide a vehicle for teaching more adaptive ways of dealing with emotional distress.

After the violence issue has been addressed and a mutually satisfactory safety net has been developed, it is then possible to proceed with therapy. In general, interventions can follow the guidelines presented in the other sections of this chapter. The therapist should be especially sensitive to interactional styles that are manipulative in nature. Abusive couples tend to have little experience in using direct, honest, and straightforward communication. Consequently, considerable time must usually be devoted to teaching a nondefensive communication style, social perspective-taking skills, and compromise strategies.

Control and dependency issues are often very salient in abuse cases. The abusive spouse typically uses violence or the threat of violence as a way to achieve his purposes. The following case exemplifies this process. Danny and Kim were referred from the court after Kim was hospitalized with serious injuries sustained from her husband. Danny was extremely jealous of any contact his wife had with other adults. In order to keep her isolated, he forbade her to leave the house alone and would beat her if she even made eye contact with a man. On a meta-level, Danny was very insecure regarding Kim's feelings for him, and his violence was the most effective way that he knew to keep Kim with him. On the other hand, Kim had tolerated Danny's abuse for several years because she was socially isolated and had become financially and emotionally dependent on him. The problem in this situation was clearly cyclic. Danny's violent behavior kept Kim in the system, yet her inability to say, "I'm not putting up with this anymore," perpetuated the problem. Therapeutic interventions, similar to those described previously, were used to address the problems in the marriage. Moreover, interventions that focused at individual and extrafamilial levels were also an important component of treatment, as discussed in the final section of this chapter.

Two additional types of interventions can be quite useful when treating spousal violence. The first set of interventions focuses on the abuser. The abusive spouse can be taught cognitive self-control strategies that help to reduce feelings of frustration and to enhance impulse control. In Chapter 2, these strategies are discussed in regard to aggressive adolescents. In treating aggressive adults, the content of these strategies is different, but their general process is the same.

The second set of interventions provides peer support for both the abused and the abusive spouses. In recent years, self-help groups for abusers and their spouses have been formed in many cities across the nation. In the same way that AA provides continuous support for sobriety, spouse abuse groups can provide helpful emotional and instrumental assistance to participants. Couples learn that they are not alone with this problem and that others have overcome it. Weekly meetings provide a reliable source of encouragement and understanding and an opportunity for the couple to express their concerns and apprehensions.

The In-laws

Some marital problems are directly linked to the couple's relations with their parents. Difficulties can arise when one spouse feels that the mate's first allegiance is to the family of origin, not to the marriage. In such situations, the mate has usually failed to separate from the parents. The mate is often emotionally immature and has maintained a maladaptive interdependency with the parents.

Such interdependency is typically preserved in several ways. The parents may be extremely effective at inducing guilt or at otherwise manipulating their son or daughter. This guilt, together with the fear of hurting the parent, can prevent the married offspring from setting firm limits on acceptable parental behavior. For example, a mother of young children may allow her own mother to undermine her parental authority because the grandmother has convinced the daughter that she is not competent to deal with her own children's problems. Similarly, parents may attempt to maintain control over their adult children by giving them expensive presents, by lending them money, by employing them, or by promising them future wealth. In many cases, dependency and concomitant problems with in-laws are exacerbated by the emotional immaturity of the couple. The following case shows some common interpersonal dynamics of this process.

Martha had been married to Peter for five years. At first, she was attracted by the closeness of Peter's family because she had never had close relations with her own parents. After the birth of Martha and Peter's first child, however, Martha started to resent the role that her in-laws played in her new family. Peter and Martha had little time to be alone together. Every Saturday, Peter would play golf or go fishing with his father. Every Sunday, Peter, Martha, and the baby would go to church with his parents and spend the day at their house. Peter would also visit his parents each day after work, before he came home to Martha, and frequently requested his parents' input about decisions that affected Martha and the baby. Although Martha had confronted Peter about the amount of time he spent with his parents, Peter stated that he loved his parents and that he thought Martha did not appreciate the importance of close family ties.

This was a difficult couple to treat because neither spouse had matured much beyond the adolescent stage of development. As a child, Peter had been very pampered and overprotected by his parents. They had given him everything he wanted, had made few maturity demands of him, and had strongly discouraged his contact with anyone outside of the family. Martha was raised in an alcoholic family, and had little exposure to models of responsible behavior and little experience with emotional intimacy. From a therapeutic perspective, the problems that this couple presented were systemic, but they also had strong individual components. The immaturity of the spouses made it difficult for the therapist to promote martial changes because, as we have discussed throughout this chapter, successful marriages require considerable commitment and emotional maturity. Consequently, treatment was relatively long-term and emphasized the development of mature and responsible ways of conceptualizing problems and interacting with others. Significant attention was devoted to change at both individual and dyadic levels.

The next example describes a situation in which an emotionally mature daughter was taught to change the behaviors of her parents that were disrupting her marriage.

Melanie and Andy had been married against her parents' wishes. Andy was Jewish, and this was not a desirable ethnic group from Melanie's parents' perspective. At every opportunity, the parents would press for Melanie to leave Andy. When marital disagreements occurred, Melanie would involve her parents to obtain support, and they would side with her and encourage her to move back into their home. The parents also showered Melanie with expensive personal gifts that Andy could neither use nor afford to buy for Melanie. Andy was not pleased with this situation and informed Melanie that she needed to choose between him and her parents.

Getting married and establishing a separate residence do not insure that the parents and their adult child have agreed to redefine their relationship. In fact, the shift to an adult-adult relationship usually requires that the parties engage in a series of behavioral transactions in which each party attempts to establish rules for the relationship. This may mean that the son or daughter will have to set limits on the behavior of the parents. Moreover, these limits will need to be direct, clear, and firm.

In the case of Melanie and Andy, the marriage was unlikely to survive unless Melanie redefined her relationship with her parents. To promote this redefinition, the therapist asked Melanie to schedule a visit with her parents for a private conversation. She was coached to express the following: "Mom and dad, I need to talk with you about something that is bothering me very much. I love you both and do not want to hurt you, but it is very important for me to save my marriage. Andy and I have not been getting along and some of our problems are caused by my relationship with you. I feel that you need to stay out of our marriage, and that I need to stop dragging you into our problems. I know that you are only doing what you feel is best for me, but I am an adult now and I need to make these decisions for myself. I love Andy very much and want to do everything possible to help make our marriage successful."

Melanie also made specific requests that were backed by specific outcomes. These requests were stated as follows: "I would appreciate if you would treat Andy more respectfully when he is present. You both tend to ignore him and to make snide remarks that are directed toward him. You don't have to like him, but you should treat him with more courtesy. In addition, I will not tolerate any more negative comments about him or about our marriage. At the first sign of disrespect I am going to leave. I want to spend time with you both, but I will not accept any behavior that might disrupt our marriage. I will also not accept any gift that is not for the both of us, or that has any strings attached. I appreciate your generosity, but feel that it sometimes creates conflicts between Andy and myself. I hope that you understand. I want to remain close with you, but my marriage has to take first priority."

Spouses who have not separated from their parents will not be able to make the preceding statements without considerable thought, discussion, and role play. The therapist will need to provide a cognitive context that allows the dependent spouse to appreciate his or her mate's perspective on the situation. It is also best to avoid a forced choice between parents and mate. Rather, the dependent spouse can arrange the situation in a way that maintains positive relations with the parents, yet makes the marriage the first priority. If the parents refuse to accept the arrangement (which has rarely happened for more than a few weeks in our experience), the dependent spouse has no cause for guilt. All that she or he has requested is to be treated as an adult and for the mate to be treated with respect. These are not unreasonable demands.

Although it was not the case with Andy and Melanie, we have observed several cases in which the husband complained bitterly about the wife's parents, yet he accepted and used extravagant gifts that the parents gave the couple. In such instances, the wife was receiving mixed messages from her husband. Before conflicts concerning in-law relations can be resolved, the couple must jointly decide on what type of relationship they actually want to have with the wife's (and husband's) parents. If the couple is not willing to risk losing the benefits of the parents' generosity, the couple may need to tolerate parental interference into their own affairs. If, on the other hand, the couple wants to set limits on the parents' behavior, they will need to send clear and congruent communications to that effect and risk the loss of material rewards.

At this point, it is probably very clear that we believe that a couple's primary commitment should be to each other. Any other priority (e.g., career, friends) decreases the probability of a successful relationship. Right or wrong, spouses should support each other and then work out disagreements in private. When each spouse feels that the other is firmly committed to the marriage, it is much easier to resolve the conflicts that are an inevitable part of living together.

REFERENCES

Gurin, G., Veroff, J., & Feld, S. (1960). *Americans view their mental health*. New York: Basic Books.

Haley, J. (1976). *Problem solving therapy*. San Francisco: Jossey-Bass.

Jacobson, N. S., & Margolin, G. (1979). *Marital therapy*. New York: Brunner/Mazel.

Kaplan, H. S. (1974). *The new sex therapy*. New York: Brunner/Mazel.

Lederer, W. J., & Jackson, D. D. (1968). *The mirages of marriage*. New York: Norton.

LoPiccolo, J., & Friedman, J. M. (1985). Sex therapy: An integrated model. In S. J. Lynn & J. P. Garskee (Eds.), *Contemporary psychotherapies: Models and methods*. New York: Charles E. Merrill.

Masters, W. H., & Johnson, V. E. (1966). *Human sexual response*. Boston: Little, Brown.

Masters, W. H., & Johnson, V. E. (1970). *Human sexual inadequacy*. Boston: Little, Brown.

Neimark, E. D. (1975). Intellectual development during adolescence. In F. D. Horowitz, E. M. Hetherington, S. Scarr-Salapatek, & G. M. Siegel (Eds.), *Review of child development research* (Vol. 4). Chicago: University of Chicago Press.

Olson, D. H., Russell, C., & Sprenkle, D. (1983). Circumplex Model of marital and family systems VI: Theoretical update. *Family Process, 22*, 69–83.

Olson, D. H., Sprenkle, D., & Russell, C. (1979). Circumplex Model of marital and family systems I: Cohesion and adaptability dimensions, family types, and clinical applications. *Family Process, 18*, 3–28.

Rodick, J. D., Henggeler, S. W., & Hanson, C. L. (1986). An evaluation of the Family Adaptibility and Cohesion Evaluation Scales and the Circumplex Model. *Journal of Abnormal Child Psychology, 14*, 77–87.

CHAPTER 5

The Treatment of Difficulties
in Peer Relations

During the past 15 years, investigators have increasingly addressed the determinants and consequences of problematic peer relations in childhood and adolescence. The clinical significance of maladaptive peer relations was first established in longitudinal investigations by Cowen, Pederson, Babigian, Izzo, and Trost (1973) and Roff, Sells, and Golden (1972). In both studies, rejection by peers in the middle years of childhood predicted psychological adjustment problems in adolescence and adulthood. These findings have led to subsequent research efforts to discover the factors that are related to peer rejection and social isolation in childhood (for a review, see Parker & Asher, 1987). Although much remains to be learned about how negative and positive peer relations are established and maintained (for an extended discussion of this topic, see Asher, 1983; Hartup, 1983), current findings have important implications for clinical interventions.

Considering the significant impact of the peer group on the development of children's social growth, it is surprising that many professionals fail to appreciate the impact of peer relationship processes when planning therapeutic interventions. For example, among family therapists, it is commonly assumed that long-term change in maladaptive child behavior will occur only if dysfunctional family interaction patterns are changed. However, in many instances transactions within the child's peer group (or some other extrafamilial system) are more closely associated with problem behavior than are family relations.

The failure to consider peer group processes is also apparent in the policies of school systems and juvenile justice systems. In these systems, troublesome youth are frequently placed together in a special classroom or a treatment group. Although the intended purpose of such placements is to ameliorate problematic behavior, increased contact with problem peers often exacerbates the youth's difficulties. As noted by Elliott, Huizinga, and Ageton (1985), it seems unreasonable to expect that a group of behavior problem youth will somehow generate prosocial values and group norms by interacting with one another. We strongly believe that treatment interventions that ignore or underestimate the power of peer groups to influence the values and behaviors of group members will have considerable difficulty in achieving the desired behavioral change.

This chapter covers our approach in treating various problems that can arise in children's peer relations. To a large extent, our approach is based on developmental/clinical research that addresses normative age-related changes in children's peer relations and friendship expectations and the ecological correlates and causes of peer difficulties. A brief overview of this research begins this chapter, followed by several strategies that can be used by the therapist to assess peer relations. Then we discuss how problems in peer relations can be linked to characteristics of the child and of the child's family. Finally, general treatment strategies for ameliorating different types of peer relationship problems are discussed and case examples are presented.

THE DEVELOPMENT OF CHILDREN'S PEER RELATIONS

Peer interactions and friendships have a fundamental role in emotional, social, and cognitive development. At an affective level, peers influence the development of emotional security and self-esteem by providing the child with loyalty, affection, and a sense of belonging (Furman, 1982; O'Donnell, 1979). Instrumentally, peer interactions provide a proving ground in which children with incomplete but roughly comparable interpersonal skills can develop and enhance their skills through mutual exploration and feedback (Panella, Cooper, & Henggeler, 1982). Peer relations also promote cognitive growth and learning (Bruner, Jolly, & Sylva, 1976) and contribute to the child's acquisition of behavioral norms and moral values (Panella et al., 1982).

Given that peer interactions provide a wide range of essential experiences for the developing child, it is important to recognize that the nature of children's peer relations and the context for those relations change with age. Although it is probably not appropriate to say that infants have friends, the small but growing literature on infant-peer interactions suggests that infants are sociable with their peers from a very early age (Field & Roopnarine, 1982). In fact, even during the first few months of life, infants relate socially to mothers and peers in similar ways, namely, by looking, smiling, and cooing (Field, 1981; Fogel, 1980). Interestingly, some evidence shows that even 12-month-old infants engage in more proximal activity (proximity-seeking, body contact, touching) with familiar peers than with unfamiliar peers. During the age period of 10 to 24 months, involvement in play behaviors with peers (e.g., imitating, showing and offering toys, coordinated play) increases markedly, reflecting an increase in cognitive skills and attentional capacity. Thus, although infants and toddlers cannot be said to have friendships, many of the prerequisites for the establishment of friendships (e.g., discrimination between peers, greater attentional capacity) begin to emerge during this age period.

During the preschool years, the salient context for social interaction with agemates (usually neighbors or classmates) is coordinated, dyadic play (Gottman & Mettetal, 1987). Although preschoolers can be said to have friendships, their concept of a friendship does not go beyond the momentary physical interaction of shared play activities (Furman & Bierman, 1983; Selman, 1980). Thus, the friendships of preschoolers can change from day to day, are easily broken and reestablished, and tend to be short-lived. Nevertheless, as Furman (1982) has noted, these early relationships are important to children's social and emotional development. It is then that children begin to learn skills for becoming acquainted, for cooperating and sharing information about themselves, for resolving conflicts, and for dealing with negative emotions such as jealousy and rejection.

In middle childhood (around age 9), children become less egocentric in their conceptions of friendships as they begin to develop deeper relationships, or "chumships," that involve genuine affection and love for each other (Furman & Bierman, 1984;

Sullivan, 1953). These relationships typically emerge within the context of a same-sex peer group or clique and are thought to reflect, in part, the child's developing capacity for social perspective-taking (Furman, 1982; Selman, Lavin, & Brion-Meisels, 1982). For girls, these friendships tend to be more intense but fewer in number than for boys (Eder & Hallinan, 1978; Maccoby & Jacklin, 1974). Nevertheless, for both sexes, this more mature form of friendship can be viewed as a major milestone in socioemotional development because it provides children with a means to express interpersonal intimacy and trust, and it serves to validate their sense of self-worth.

In early-to-middle adolescence, same-sex friendships and cliques become even more intimate in nature, especially for girls (Buhrmester & Furman, 1987). Self-disclosure, commitment, respect, trust, and a similar system of attitudes and values are all important components of these friendships (Furman, 1982).

The adolescent's involvement in a same-sex clique also plays an important role in the transition to heterosexual relationships (Dunphy, 1963). Initially, the higher status members of the clique begin to break out of the same-sex constraints of the group to initiate heterosexual interaction. This results in the formation of heterosexual cliques from the membership of the same-sex cliques. Gradually, other members of the same-sex cliques participate in heterosexual transactions. The eventual formation of a heterosexual "crowd" gives rise to various social gatherings (e.g., parties, dances) and provides a context for involvement in dating and couples activities (Dunphy, 1963). These early heterosexual relationships tend to be quite superficial, however, and same-sex friendships are still the primary source of peer emotional support (Douvan & Adelson, 1966). Late adolescence is marked by a shift away from strong same-sex friendships toward the development of intimate relationships with members of the opposite sex.

This discussion suggests that as children mature, they change their friendship expectations, peer interactions, and salient contexts for those interactions. Knowledge of these developmental changes is essential for a valid clinical assessment of a child's peer competencies (Gelfand & Peterson, 1985). As noted later in this chapter, it is important for the therapist to recognize that social behaviors that can be problematic at one age may represent normal social activity at an earlier age.

ASSESSMENT STRATEGIES

This section discusses strategies that the therapist can use to assess children's peer relations. The assessment of peer relations should always go hand-in-hand with an assessment of the child's individual characteristics (e.g., cognitive skills) and family relations. Individual and family factors can play important roles in children's social competence with agemates.

Indirect Assessment

As a rule of thumb, the therapist should obtain information about the child's peer relations from several different sources. When conducting the first or second interview with the family, the therapist should assess each member's perceptions and beliefs about the child's social functioning. A good way to begin is to ask the parents about their impressions of their child's friends and about the amount of contact that the parents have with these children and their parents. The therapist should also assess whether the parents can describe their child's friendships in school versus those outside of school. Many children have close friends in the neighborhood whom they see only after school or on weekends, and they may have friends in their church or scouting organization. In fact, there are some children whose poor academic achievement in school may lead to low popularity in that setting, but whose satisfactory functioning outside of school (e.g., in a Four-H Club, a Little League, or a part-time job) may lead to more positive peer relations in the community.

These initial questions will usually reveal the extent to which the parents are informed and concerned about their child's peer relations. If these relations represent a source of concern for the parents, it is often helpful to determine the parents' attributions about the causes of the child's peer difficulties. For example, the parents may believe that their child is unfairly ridiculed by peers or is easily led by peers to engage in antisocial activities. It is also useful to assess whether the parents have attempted any interventions of their own in an effort to resolve the child's problems with peers. In some cases, the therapist may find that the parents' behavior is actually preventing a productive solution to the child's peer difficulties. In one family, for example, the mother reported that she had repeatedly threatened to sue her child's preschool if the teachers did not begin to "protect" her son (who had a speech impediment) from the cruel remarks of a few of his peers. In response to these threats, the preschool teachers had isolated the child from all of his peers for most of the day, thus keeping the boy from engaging in positive as well as negative interactions with the other children.

After obtaining information from the parents, we usually ask the child to tell us about his or her friends and about the types of activities in which they are interested. Information about the child's friends and their interests can be especially useful should the therapist decide to assess the child's social relations directly. For older children and adolescents, it is often informative to ask not only about peer group activities and interests, but also about peers' level of achievement in school and their families. Among older children who report having few or no friends, the therapist should assess the child's degree of concern for peer group acceptance. The rejected child who is not especially concerned about being accepted is less likely to respond to therapeutic efforts to improve his or her peer relations than is the rejected child who cares about peer acceptance. It should be noted, however, that some rejected children are not always truthful about their desire for peer acceptance; as a defense against the emotional pain of peer rejection, the child may adopt an "I don't care" attitude.

Although we have found that most children are quite open about their friends, in some cases children are very hesitant to discuss their friendships (or their difficulties with peer relations) during the therapist's interview with the family. In these situations, we recommend that the therapist respect the child's silence and not push for immediate disclosure. This silence should be taken as an indication that the child is distressed by the quality of his or her peer relations, or, as is more often the case with adolescents, that the child has friends of whom the parents strongly disapprove. In such instances, the parents have usually already provided the therapist with useful information about the child's peer relations. The therapist can use this information as a starting point for a private discussion with the child. Many children are willing to discuss information privately with the therapist that they are unwilling to discuss in the presence of their parents.

Teachers can also provide the therapist with a wealth of information regarding the child's peer relations (the assessment of children's social competence in school is discussed in Chapter 6). At this point, the therapist should keep in mind two general guidelines. First, when meeting with the child's teachers, the therapist should distinguish between the child's getting along well in the peer group (i.e., peer acceptance) and having close emotional ties with one or more agemates (i.e., having friends). A child can maintain friendships despite generally low peer regard; on the other hand, a child can have no friends and still be accepted by most peers. Second, when assessing the friendships of any child, but especially those of an older child or adolescent, the therapist should not limit the assessment to the child's friendships in a single classroom. Children often have friends in a number of different classes, as well as friends whom they see only at recess, lunchtime, or during extracurricular activities. Therefore, to obtain a fairly comprehensive evaluation of the child's friendships, the therapist should meet with as many of the child's teachers as is feasible. This strategy has the additional advantage of providing the therapist with a more balanced view of the child's interpersonal strengths and weaknesses than might be obtained from only one or two of the child's teachers.

The therapist might also wish to consider the use of a standardized assessment instrument to evaluate the child's peer relations. Because few such instruments are available, we have recently developed and validated the Missouri Peer Relations Inventory (MPRI; Borduin, Blaske, Treloar, & Mann, 1989). The MPRI includes a series of 5-point ratings that assess three primary dimensions of friendship and peer interactions: emotional bonding, aggression, and acceptance. We usually request that each teacher and individual family member (including the identified child) complete the MPRI for the purpose of comparison. A further advantage of this objective measure is that it provides the therapist with a useful tool for assessing changes in peer relations that occur during therapy.

Direct Assessment

If the information provided by teachers, parents, and the child suggests that the child's interactions with agemates are not problematic, direct assessment of the peer system is seldom necessary, and subsequent interventions should focus on other systems that are pertinent to the child's behavior problems. On the other hand, when the information regarding the child's peer relations is contradictory or difficult to obtain, we recommend that the therapist conduct a more direct evaluation of the child's peer relations.

For many young children, extended contact with peers first occurs in preschool or elementary school. Thus, it is within the school context that difficulties in their peer relations are most often observed. In such instances, the therapist can usually make arrangements to observe the child's peer interactions in the classroom and/or on the playground. We have found that younger children tend to habituate very quickly to the presence of classroom observers, such as parents, school administrators, community representatives (e.g., from Partners in Education programs), and other adults. Nevertheless, the therapist should be aware that some teachers may view a visit to their classrooms as an intrusion and as an evaluation of their competencies. Therefore, the therapist must develop positive rapport with the teacher and treat the teacher as a valued colleague when attempting to schedule a classroom visit. The therapist should go through normal administrative channels when arranging for a classroom observation. Ideally, the therapist should attempt to observe the child in those situations and at those times when the child's behavioral difficulties with peers are most apparent. The therapist must be flexible in scheduling to assure the cooperation of the teacher. See Chapter 6 for a detailed discussion of working with school systems.

The length of the therapist's visit to the child's school should be decided jointly with the teacher. In some cases, the therapist may need to visit the classroom and/or playground more than once to obtain an accurate picture of the child's problems with peers. Our charges for these visits are based on the same hourly fee that we use for assessment and treatment in the office.

Although therapists who are relatively inexperienced may feel a need to take notes while observing the child's classroom behavior, we usually advise against this practice for several reasons. First, note-taking can be very distracting to some children and may draw unwanted questions from those children. Second, despite the therapist's friendly demeanor and best intentions, note-taking can be anxiety-provoking for the teacher and may lead to less cooperation. Third, the therapist should be concerned primarily with observing and understanding the process of the child's interactions with peers rather than with obtaining a detailed account of the child's verbal and physical behavior.

Beginning in about the third grade, children's difficulties in relating to their peers are more likely to be observed in unstructured settings, such as the playground or neighborhood, than in the structured classroom. However, when an older child does evidence peer relationship difficulties in the classroom, these difficulties can usually be adequately described by the teacher because the pertinent behaviors are rather conspicuous (e.g., aggression or extreme withdrawal). Furthermore, most older children are very concerned about being accepted by their classmates (Sebald, 1981) and might feel quite embarrassed or humiliated if a therapist observes them in the classroom. Therefore, we usually recommend that, when necessary, the therapist observe the older child's behavior in a less structured setting.

In most elementary schools, the therapist can arrange to meet with the child's teacher on the playground periphery at a time when the child is engaged in a peer group activity, such as recess or a physical education class. Because children are accustomed to seeing adult supervisors at the playground, the presence of the teacher and the therapist together seldom draws notice. Still, prior to the therapist's visit to the school, the child should be told that the therapist plans to meet with the teacher to learn about the child's problems and accomplishments in school. Although some children may express displeasure when they are told about this visit, telling the child about it can help to avoid some potentially negative consequences. Indeed, not telling the child about the therapist's plans can lead the child to feel deceived by the therapist and the parents in the event that the child sees the therapist at the school.

The therapist can obtain important information even during a relatively brief observation of the child's playground behavior. The therapist might attend both to the child's attempts to initiate interactions with peers and to the peers' responses to these initiations. For example, the therapist might observe that the child moves from one peer to another in an effort to engage each peer, but that none of these peers seems interested in the child. Or, the child might initially elicit a positive response from one or more peers but then end up arguing with those peers. If the child associates primarily with a certain group of children, it may also be possible to determine the child's position in the peer group hierarchy by observing the nonverbal cues or behaviors of the group members. For example, the child might follow or lead his friends around the playground as they move from one place to another. During this process, the therapist can rely on the teacher's knowledge to clarify the social reputations, interests, and relative adjustment of the child's friends. Of course, the therapist might also observe that the child primarily engages in solitary activity and has little interaction with peers.

In some situations, the therapist might decide that it is more informative to interact directly with the child and one or two of the child's friends. To accomplish this task, the therapist will need to interact with the children on the basis of their interests or skills and in a setting that is comfortable to them. For example, the therapist can determine whether the child and a friend are interested in learning some card tricks (or how to juggle tennis balls), in meeting the therapist's pet dog, or in seeing the therapist's coin (or baseball card) collection. Then, with the parents' cooperation and assistance (this includes having the child's parents obtain consent from the friends' parents), the therapist can arrange to meet at the family's home with the child and his or her friends and can share the selected activity with them. By engaging the children in a meaningful activity, the therapist can obtain considerable information about the child's (and friend's) cognitive and behavioral skills. This information can provide the therapist with a general idea of the child's level of social competence and, consequently, can guide the formulation of treatment plans. If the therapist observed, for example, that an unpopular child was skillful when interacting with a good friend, the therapist would formulate different treatment plans than if the child did not get along even with children who were identified as friends.

A similar approach can be used to obtain a direct assessment of the friendships of adolescents. It is important to note that the therapist must be flexible when seeking direct access to the adolescent's peer system. Although adolescents' activities might differ from those of younger children, the process of the assessment is nearly identical, even though the emerging cognitive capacities of adolescents lead to qualitatively different ways of understanding interpersonal relationships. An evaluation of these capacities and of the prosocial/antisocial nature of the peer group is essential when the therapist directly accesses the adolescent's peer relations.

CHILD CHARACTERISTICS AS CORRELATES OF PEER ACCEPTANCE

Some children are well regarded by most of their peers and enjoy many friendships; other children are almost universally disliked and have no friends. To understand the differences in peer acceptance, developmental psychologists have begun to identify characteristics of children that are related to acceptance by peers. Next, we describe cognitive, behavioral, and other individual variables that have been identified as correlates and/or causes of children's social status. As shall be discussed, therapists should consider these variables when designing interventions for children with peer difficulties.

Cognitive Processes

Children's understanding of self and social relations goes through a period of rapid growth during the middle-childhood and preadolescent years (see Chapter 2). By the end of middle childhood, most children have attained a relatively sophisticated level of social perspective-taking (or role-taking) ability and can accurately infer the intentions, thoughts, and feelings of others. Investigations have suggested, for example, that older children and adolescents who exhibit conduct problems and delinquent behaviors show developmental lags and inconsistencies in perspective-taking ability (Chandler, 1973; Chandler, Greenspan, & Barenboim, 1974; Selman et al., 1982). Therefore, when working with older children, it is important to consider the extent to which peer difficulties may be a consequence of developmental lags in social perspective-taking skills. On the other hand, when working with youths who have *not* reached middle childhood, the therapist needs to consider the extent to which the youth's difficulties may be a function of his or her age-appropriate level of social understanding. The following excerpt from an interview with a 9-year-old boy demonstrates how normatively immature social perspective-taking skills can lead to difficulties in peer relations.

THERAPIST: Your teacher tells me that you have been hitting some of the children in your class. How do other kids feel when someone hits them?

CHILD: Well, they called me a dog and said I was stupid, so I hit them.

THERAPIST: I understand that you sometimes bark like a dog in class?

CHILD: Yeah, the boys laugh.

THERAPIST: And you sometimes tell the other children they are stupid?

CHILD: Well, they say I'm stupid.

THERAPIST: I bet that makes you feel bad.

CHILD: Yeah.

THERAPIST: How do other kids feel when someone says something like that about them?

CHILD: I don't know, but I'm not a dog.

THERAPIST: Maybe the other children call you a dog because you bark like a dog in class?

CHILD: I'm not a dog, but the other kids call me a dog.

THERAPIST: So you act like a dog sometimes, but you know you're only pretending to be a dog to make the other kids laugh?

CHILD: Well, sometimes I bark like a dog, and the boys laugh, but after my teacher yells at me I find out I didn't want to do it.

In addition to social perspective-taking, other cognitive skills play a significant role in the development of successful peer relations. Panella et al. (1982) suggested that an important component of adolescent peer relations is the ability to determine accurately the prevailing group norms or expectations in a given situation and to use this information in deciding which behaviors to perform. Interestingly, a similar cognitive ability seems to be an important component of the social competence of young children. Putallaz (1983) found that children who were successful at gaining entry into an ongoing group interaction in the summer prior to first grade and who later achieved high status in the classroom peer group, seemed to have the ability to "read" the social situation and to fit their behavior to the ongoing flow of interaction. Thus, to be socially accepted, it seems that the developing child needs to learn to accurately interpret the social behavior of others and to respond in a manner that is relevant to that behavior.

Another cognitive variable that is linked with children's peer competence is the ability to solve interpersonal problems. Research with behavior problem children and adolescents (Deluty, 1981; Platt, Scura, & Hannon, 1973; Platt, Spivack, & Altman, 1974) has indicated that deficits in problem-solving skills, including alternative thinking and means-end thinking, are related to interpersonal difficulties. *Alternative thinking* refers to the ability of the child to generate a variety of relevant solutions to problems. It is not unusual, for example, to find that a child who is easily provoked into fighting with his peers has difficulty in generating positive alternatives to aggression. *Means-end thinking* is a set of abilities that specify the individual steps necessary to reach a goal, the obstacles that might impede progress toward the goal, and the time needed to achieve the goal. According to Asher (1983), socially competent children seem to understand that interpersonal relationships develop slowly and that problems in relationships are not always solved quickly. In this regard, Asher has elaborated on the role of means-end thinking in the development of popularity.

> Socially competent children seem to have "a process view" of life in the sense that they appreciate that things take time and that the more effective way to attain a goal isn't always to go directly for it. Thus, in entry situations, popular children do not just start playing, or even always come right out and ask to play. Instead, they wait, they kibitz, and they work their way slowly into the group. Similarly, when children are interviewed about how they might get a child to become a friend, popular children take the more indirect process approach of suggesting an after-school bike ride or inviting a child to their house to play. Unpopular children are more likely to suggest the more direct approach and less process-oriented approach of simply requesting friendship (p. 1429).

Another element of cognitive processing that has received special research attention is children's appraisals of the social stimuli that they encounter. Children respond not only to the topography of their peer's behavior, but also to their perceptions of the peer's intentions or goals. Indeed, most children overlook a peer's "social errors" (e.g., irrelevant communication, uncooperative behavior) because the peer is assumed to be well-intentioned (Asher, 1983; Hymel, 1986). However, children who are both socially rejected and aggressive tend to attribute hostile intentions to peers in ambiguous conflict circumstances (Aydin & Markova, 1979; Dodge, 1980). Moreover, rejected-aggressive children (Dodge, Murphy, & Bushbaum, 1984; Nasby, Hayden, & DePaulo, 1980) and adolescents (Dodge & Newman, 1981) are also less proficient than other children at interpreting peers' intentions in unambiguous circumstances: Rejected-aggressive children tend to presume hostility when none exists, and they are particularly deficient at recognizing prosocial and benign intentions. In turn, these hostile attributional biases directly predict aggressive behavior toward peers (Dodge & Somberg, 1987). Aggressive children also appear to have distorted perceptions *of their own behavior*. Lochman (1987) recently found that aggressive fourth- and fifth-grade boys minimized perceptions of their own aggressiveness and perceived their peers as more aggressive than themselves. On the other hand, nonaggressive boys perceived that they were more aggressive than their peers. Lockman suggested that perceptions of other-blame, rather than self-blame, in the early stages of conflict may lead to less restraint of hostile impulses. Indeed, aggressive children tend to assume less responsibility for their aggressive behavior and do not take concrete steps to adaptively alter the situation.

Interventions.   To the extent that perspective-taking skills, problem-solving skills, and attributional processes can all mediate children's behavior toward peers, it is important for the therapist to identify the domains of greatest difficulty for a specific child. To accomplish this task, the therapist can begin by using one or more of the assessment strategies discussed earlier in this chapter. For example, interviews with the child, parents, and teachers can help the therapist identify contexts in which the child's problematic behavior toward peers is most evident. Next, the therapist may wish to obtain additional information about the child's peer relations through direct observation. When the therapist has acquired a relatively clear picture of the relevant contexts and behaviors that are associated with the child's peer difficulties, the therapist can then use role-play procedures to assess more directly the child's processing of social information. The enactment of various role-play scenarios can provide opportunities to discuss the child's problematic interchanges and to probe the child's thinking behind the behavior. The following case exemplifies this process.

Mason was a tall, muscular 13-year-old boy who was referred by his mother at the recommendation of his junior high school principal. According to the principal, Mason had a long-standing reputation for his quick temper and aggressive behavior toward other boys. Over the past four months, he had severely beaten up at least three of his male peers, one of whom had required eye surgery. Although assault charges had not been filed, it seemed only a matter of time before Mason's violent behavior would result in his arrest.

During the first few weeks of treatment, several pertinent aspects of Mason's peer difficulties became clear. The therapist learned that Mason was an exceptional athlete whose basketball and track skills had earned substantial recognition and had made him the envy of many of his male peers. On the other hand, Mason had relatively low intellectual abilities (a verbal comprehension IQ of 79), had a lisp (for which he received speech therapy), and was near the bottom of the achievement hierarchy in his classes (with a D+ average).

According to Mason's teachers, both his academic performance and his speech impediment were the targets of verbal taunts from several of his male peers. It was these taunts that usually provoked Mason's aggressive outbursts. Mason's school counselor reported that the majority of these peers had serious emotional and family problems, and that all of them had marginal academic and athletic skills.

In discussing the situation with the family, the therapist also learned that Mason had been exposed to considerable violence during his childhood. In fact, until the divorce of Mason's parents three years earlier, both Mason and his mother had been physically abused on numerous occasions by the father, who was chemically dependent. Therefore, it seemed likely that Mason was following his father's lead in adopting aggressive behavior as a coping strategy.

As a next step, the therapist decided to role-play a number of different scenarios with Mason in an effort to learn more about the cognitive factors that were contributing to his aggressive behavior. After Mason had described some of the interactions with peers that angered him, including the specific statements that his peers made to him, the therapist asked Mason to role-play a situation that involved verbal taunting about his academic abilities. The therapist explained that Mason should indicate when he was becoming very angry at the therapist (who played the role of a peer) so that the therapist could stop the role play at that point. Although Mason initially thought the idea of a role play was silly, the therapist enacted the role of a peer effectively enough to engage Mason in a series of angry interchanges.

Following each angry interchange, the therapist talked with Mason about his responses to the "peer's" statements. This discussion revealed that Mason did not recognize how readily he was baited by his peers, nor did he see that his peers might be envious of his athletic skills. Although he was unable to generate any positive alternatives to fighting with his peers, he reported that he did not enjoy fighting, nor did he like the fact that he had developed a reputation as a bully. The therapist also learned that Mason tended to interpret many physical signs of affection from peers (e.g., a pat on the back, a hand on the shoulder) in a hostile light. He stated that he did not want anyone "messing" with him, even if the person was someone he liked. When the therapist expressed puzzlement about Mason's apparent aversion to any physical show of affection, Mason went on to describe how his father "would be hugging me one minute and hitting me the next." In Mason's mind, physical contact inevitably led to physical violence.

The therapist's initial intervention in this case was to help Mason to identify some of the likely reasons behind the taunts of certain peers, and to understand some of the positive motives behind other peers' physical signs of friendship. Next, the therapist and Mason jointly developed some nonaggressive strategies for responding to both the negative and positive behaviors of his peers. For example, in response to peers' taunts about his academic performance and speech difficulties, Mason was instructed to kindly ask the peers whether they would like his help in developing their basketball and track skills (thus effectively silencing these nonathletic peers). In response to physical shows of affection from his peers, Mason was instructed to use a "high five" slap of the hands (used by many professional athletes that Mason admired) to convey his acceptance of the peers. These strategies were rehearsed and refined over a period of two months, and Mason's reputation as a bully was gradually diminished.

As described in Chapter 2, cognitive-behavioral interventions such as problem-solving training and self-instruction/self-control training can lead to important changes in children's cognitive mediational processes. Changes in these cognitive processes can alter the way in which the child views peers and can affect the child's self-concept and sense of personal efficacy. With some children, the therapist might find that certain elements of these interventions (e.g., didactic instruction, modeling, role playing, feedback, reinforcement) are sufficient to alter the relevant cognitive processes. The therapist should remember, however, that the role of other individual and systemic factors must also be considered when attempting to modify the child's peer relations. In the case of Mason, other interventions pertaining to parental discipline strategies and educational remediation (i.e., a resource class) were also used. Cognitive-behavioral interventions are usually most effective when used in conjunction with other pertinent interventions.

Behavioral Skills

Research on the behavioral correlates of children's sociometric status has been conducted for approximately 50 years (see Asher & Hymel, 1981, for an excellent review). In general, the early studies concluded that unpopular (i.e., low-status) children evidenced low rates of prosocial behaviors and high rates of aggressive and uncooperative behaviors toward peers, whereas popular (i.e., high-status) children evidenced a preponderance of friendly behaviors. Although this research provided an important foundation for subsequent research, it should be noted that most of these early studies suffered from two significant methodological limitations. First, the researchers used low scores on positive sociometric nomination items (e.g., "Name the children you like most") as the criterion for assignment to a low-status group. Because positive nomination scores tend to correlate quite poorly with negative nomination scores (-.20; Asher & Hymel, 1981), the use of only a positive score as the assignment criterion confounds two groups of low-status children: *rejected* children, who are not liked and are highly disliked; and *neglected* children, who are neither liked nor disliked (Gottman, 1977).

To address this methodological issue, researchers have begun to examine the behavior patterns that are associated with each of these groups. Rejected children report strong feelings of loneliness and social dissatisfaction (Asher & Wheeler, 1985) and are viewed by their peers and teachers as more aggressive and disruptive (Coie, Dodge, & Coppotelli, 1982; Dodge, Coie, & Brakke, 1982). Neglected children seem to experience no more of these problems than average children, although they tend to be somewhat shy and less interactive (Coie et al., 1982; Dodge et al., 1982). A growing body of evidence also shows that rejected children (but not neglected children) are at risk for later difficulties (Parker & Asher, 1987).

The second methodological problem with most early studies in this area is that they had correlational or post hoc designs. Thus, it is not possible to determine whether the observed behavioral differences associated with sociometric status were the causes or the consequences of the children's status. For example, children's aggressive behaviors might reasonably be viewed as the cause of low social status. Yet, it is also possible that low-status children behave aggressively because of the frustration and hurt that comes from being unpopular, and that their unpopularity stems from another cause, such as poor social cue-reading abilities.

In order to overcome the inherent limitations of correlational research, a small but growing number of researchers have begun to employ longitudinal techniques to investigate the causal connections between social behavior and sociometric status. To date, most of the published studies have focused on samples of grade school children. For example, in a well-designed study that has important implications for the assessment and treatment of young children's peer difficulties, Dodge (1983) examined the behavioral antecedents of peer rejection, neglect, and popularity. Forty-eight previously unacquainted second-grade children were brought together in six newly constructed play groups (eight children per group) for eight one-hour sessions. An observational method was used to record the interactive behaviors of each child. In addition, at the end of the eighth session, sociometric interviews were conducted to determine the status acquired in the group by each child. Several differences emerged between children who became actively rejected, those who became sociometrically neglected, and those who became popular. The rejected children showed relatively high frequencies of antisocial behavior (e.g., insults, threats, physical aggression), and their peers perceived them as poor leaders, highly aggressive, and unwilling to share. In contrast, the neglected children evidenced little antisocial behavior and were not viewed by their peers as aggressive; if anything, they were viewed as shy. Although these children approached their peers with a high frequency in early encounters, their peer interactions were generally inept and decreased over time. Children who became popular among their peers engaged in high rates of social conversation and cooperative behavior, they refrained from inappropriate and aggressive play, and they were viewed by their peers as good leaders who shared things. Interestingly, the popular children approached others less frequently than children in the other groups. When popular children did approach their peers, the popular children were more able to sustain their interactions, and they were unlikely to terminate social interactions.

The results of this study have important implications for the assessment and treatment of young children's peer relationship difficulties. First, it is essential to know how the child goes about the process of trying to establish friendships. Indeed, the child's social approach pattern may lead to a reputation with peers that shapes the quality of subsequent interactions. Clearly, children's peer group entry skills cannot be ignored in the design of therapeutic interventions.

Second, the factors that maintain low social status can vary widely from one child to another. Neither rejected nor neglected children are well liked by their peers, but the behavioral factors related to these two types of low peer status are quite different and have different implications for treatment. With a rejected child, it is usually crucial to eliminate the child's aggression toward peers and to promote the child's sense of positive give-and-take. With a neglected child, the awkward quality of the child's social approach toward peers often needs to be addressed, and the child must learn to develop ways to engage peers in mutually enjoyable activities.

Relatively little is known about the childhood behavioral antecedents of sociometric status during adolescence. In what is perhaps the only longitudinal study addressing this issue, Coie and Dodge (1983) found considerable stability in children's rejection by classmates over five-year periods starting from third grade as well as from fifth grade. Moreover, the behaviors predictive of later sociometric status were similar to those behaviors that were concurrently associated with sociometric status: Aggressive and immature behavior patterns predicted future rejection by classmates, while cooperative and prosocial peer interactions predicted future popularity. However, the reader should note that the subjects in this study were continuing classmates, rather than entirely new groups of peers each year. Thus, peer *reputations* that were established before the study began may have played a critical role in determining observed social behaviors during childhood and sociometric status during adolescence (see Hymel, 1986). Also, some of the adolescents identified as unpopular in this study might have had friends in other settings. Indeed, as children mature, they are more likely to form friendships outside the boundaries of their classrooms (Epstein, 1986). Of course, children's relationships with siblings, parents, and extended family members can act as emotional buffers when peer relationships in school are problematic (see e.g., Furman & Buhrmester, 1985), and these family relationships also provide important contexts for the development of social skills.

Interventions.   As detailed in other sources (e.g., Bierman, Miller, & Stabb, 1987; Oden & Asher, 1977), elementary school children can be effectively coached in their social skills for friendship making. Depending on the results of the therapist's assessment, the child can be instructed in one or more of the following areas: (1) participating (e.g., initiating a game, paying attention), (2) cooperating (e.g., taking turns, sharing materials), (3) asking questions (e.g., for information, clarification or invitation), (4) helping (e.g., giving encouragement, offering suggestions), (5) communicating (e.g., listening and talking to the other person), and (6) validating support (e.g., giving a smile, looking at the other person).

In most cases, the therapist can teach the child the requisite social skills in a few sessions using the following steps as general guidelines. The therapist should always outline these steps for the parents so that they can also coach the child when necessary.

1. The therapist tells the child that there are a number of things that are important to do when playing a game or participating in some other activity with another child. The therapist then introduces a given concept to the child (e.g., "It is important to *cooperate* when you play with Bobby") and follows the remaining steps in sequence for each concept.

2. The therapist probes the child's understanding of the concept by asking for specific behavioral examples. For example, the therapist might ask the child, "Do you know what cooperation is? (The therapist waits for a response.) Can you tell me how you can cooperate when you play the army men game with Bobby?"

3. If the child has difficulty responding, the therapist provides an example for the child. Alternatively, the therapist may need to rephrase the child's example(s) or suggest a shorter phrase if some clarification is needed. For example, if the child responded, "Share some men," the therapist might offer clarification by saying, "That's right. You would share the army men with Bobby. That's an example of how you could cooperate when you play with Bobby."

4. The therapist asks the child to provide specific examples of the opposite type of behavior. For example, the therapist might say, "Now, if you and Bobby were playing with the army men, can you also give me an example of what would not be cooperating?" Here the therapist should be prepared to provide the child with examples that are pertinent to the child's own difficulties in getting along with peers (e.g., hitting or yelling at the other child).

5. The therapist asks the child to say whether each of the behavioral examples (including the examples of cooperation) would result in making the activity fun or enjoyable for both the child and the other person. For example, if the child has responded that taking all the army men would be a way of not cooperating, the therapist might ask, "Would taking all the army men for yourself make the game fun to play for both you and Bobby?" After the child has responded to this question as it pertains to each example, the therapist helps the child to draw a conclusion about each of the different behaviors. "So, you wouldn't grab all the army men. You would cooperate by sharing them with Bobby."

6. The therapist asks the child to try some of these ideas in a subsequent play session with peers. Depending on the setting in which the therapist and child meet (e.g., school, clinic, home), the play session can be arranged by the adult (e.g., teacher, parent) who is responsible for supervising the child's activities.

7. A postplay review is conducted as soon as possible after the child's play activity. If for practical reasons the therapist has to wait several days to review the play session with the child, the therapist should train a parent to briefly review the play session with the child. For example, the parent can ask whether the child was able to try some of the ideas that were discussed with the therapist, and whether these ideas helped to make the activity enjoyable for the child and the other participant(s). The parent can also provide the child with substantial praise for trying out some of the new ideas and behaviors. Parental involvement has the additional advantage of promoting the generalization of behavioral improvements to the natural environment.

Variations on this coaching procedure have helped preadolescents to acquire skills and increase their sociometric status (e.g., Bierman & Furman, 1984). When teaching social skills to an older child or an adolescent, the therapist should focus on skill areas that are consistent with the child's capacity for more complex social understanding. For example, conversational skills such as self-disclosure (e.g., offering information about oneself), questioning (e.g., asking others about themselves), and leadership bids (e.g., giving advice) are especially relevant to the social functioning of older children (see e.g., Bierman & Furman, 1984). For these training procedures to be effective, the therapist must combine the training with structured opportunities to develop positive peer interaction. Again, these opportunities should occur in a context for social interaction that is consistent with the child's developmental status. Among older children, these structured interactions with peers provide both a context for the practice of new social skills and the opportunity for peers to recognize and accept the new competencies of the coached child. Toward this end, structured involvement with peers may be essential for changing the child's reputation among peers and for altering the negative responses of these peers. The following example highlights how the therapist can help the adolescent to improve his or her social skills within the context of age-appropriate social activities.

Janey was a 16-year-old girl who was referred to the therapist after completing an inpatient drug treatment program. She had been dependent on marijuana since the age of 13, had been sexually promiscuous, and had engaged in various antisocial activities with her drug-using friends. Now that she was in recovery, Janey realized that she could no longer associate with her problem peers. However, she was having considerable difficulty in establishing friendships with "straight" peers.

This difficulty could be viewed as a social skills deficit. Although Janey was very familiar with the social norms and behavioral styles of drug users, she had very little experience interacting socially with straight peers. For example, she had little knowledge of appropriate dating behavior. In the past, she and her date would "get high and party." Now, however, her date planned to take her out to dinner and a movie. What would they talk about during the meal? What should she wear? Should she offer to pay? How should she act on the way home?

The therapist helped Janey to develop a new set of social skills by discussing the peer-related problems that she had experienced during the week. Janey would bring a list of these problems to each therapy session, and the therapist and Janey would first examine the interpersonal dynamics that might be involved. Next, they would jointly develop alternative responses to the problems and evaluate the strengths and limitations of each response. Finally, the therapist and Janey developed a plan to use more viable social responses when similar problems arose during the upcoming week. Through a series of feedback and problem-solving sessions, Janey was able to develop a keener sense of social awareness and to respond with greater flexibility in social situations.

Educational Achievement

Academic achievement is positively associated with children's sociometric status (Green, Forehand, Beck, & Vosk, 1980), presumably due to the prestige that peers attach to good grades. Among younger children, however, the relationship between achievement and sociometric status may be spurious. The association may be due to a third variable (such as verbal skills or social effectiveness) that enhances both academic achievement and social competence.

Although relatively few researchers have addressed directly the association between peer relations and academic achievement among adolescents, at least two areas of research speak indirectly to this relationship. First, several longitudinal studies examine the association between early adolescent peer relationship difficulties and later dropping out of school. Although dropout status is not equivalent to academic achievement, it is similar to achievement in that it is a good predictor of future occupational success. In a recent review of this literature, Parker and Asher (1987) concluded that there is strong evidence of a link between the decision to drop out of school and earlier peer relationship difficulties. This link was clearest when low acceptance and aggressiveness were used as indexes of problematic peer relationships, and was less clear when shyness/withdrawal was used. Parker and Asher speculated that unpopular students may miss important opportunities to collaborate with their peers on homework, studying, and informal tutoring and may therefore suffer academically. They also postulated that low-accepted children may find school to be stressful and aversive, with few of the social rewards that constitute much of school's holding power for adolescents.

A second group of studies has examined the relative impact of parents and peers on adolescents' educational aspirations (Spenner, 1975). Although the relative strengths of family and peer influences have not been resolved, it seems likely that peer approval for academic accomplishments influences adolescents' educational aspirations and achievement. However, as Panella et al. (1982) have noted, this influence is apparently mediated by demographic variables such as social class, race, age, and gender. It also seems likely that a self-selection process may be operating (Kandel, 1978); that is, adolescents tend to select friends who have similar educational aspirations and accomplishments.

Interventions.   When the therapist determines that a younger child's educational difficulties are contributing to difficulties with peers, it is extremely important to determine the cause(s) of the academic problems. In some cases, such as those involving a neglected child with low intellectual abilities (see Chapter 6), retaining the child in his or her current grade can lead to significant changes in the child's peer status. The child may carry the stigma of being left back a grade but will also be higher on the academic achievement hierarchy, the physical size hierarchy, and the social maturity hierarchy of his or her new group of peers. In these instances, the therapist may need to help the parents (and perhaps the teacher) to appreciate how retention can be in the child's best interests.

Placement of an academically and socially deficient child in a resource class can also lead to increases in sociometric status as the child is shifted into a new group of peers (i.e., other children who are experiencing educational and social difficulties). However, this kind of placement is unlikely to improve that child's peer relations with children in regular classrooms.

As the child approaches adolescence, the nature of the association between achievement and peer acceptance is more complex. On the one hand, affiliating with adolescents who have at least modest academic aspirations and who approve of academic achievement may facilitate the adolescent's own academic performance. On the other hand, an adolescent need not have high educational aspirations to be accepted by peers. In fact, in certain peer groups, high academic aspirations and performance by an adolescent might result in peer pressure to perform otherwise. The following case exemplifies this process.

Gary Taylor was a tenth-grader who was referred by his parents at the recommendation of his high school counselor. Gary had been suspended from school for truancy on three different occasions during a two-month period, and he had received numerous detentions for skipping classes. During a conference with the parents and three of Gary's teachers, the therapist learned that Gary had an excellent academic record until the past year, when he began to skip school with a number of his friends on the football team. Although Mr. and Mrs. Taylor had disciplined Gary appropriately (e.g., "grounding" him for several weeks at a time and removing his television and stereo privileges), their efforts had not produced any positive changes in Gary's grades or discouraged his association with problem peers. Mr. and Mrs. Taylor were especially concerned with the fact that one of Gary's friends had recently dropped out of school, and they feared that it was only a matter of time before Gary would do the same.

After meeting with Gary and his parents, the therapist concluded that everyone in the family (including Gary) valued academic achievement and occupational success. Moreover, Gary was fully cognizant of the negative consequences associated with skipping school and ignoring his grades, including being grounded, being temporarily suspended from the football team, dropping off the honor roll, and disappointing not only his parents but also his teachers. Nevertheless, he was adamant in his refusal to meet his parents' request to give up his friends, whom he had known since elementary school. Gary argued that he had a right to choose his own friends, regardless of what his parents thought of them.

Although it is sometimes necessary to advocate the adolescent's withdrawal from a deviant peer group and to encourage affiliation with nonproblem peers, a number of factors weighed against using this therapeutic strategy in the present case. First, Gary's strong long-term allegiance to his friends, with whom he shared common talents (i.e., football and athletic skills), greatly reduced the likelihood that he would shift his allegiance to a new group of peers. In fact, Gary had already indicated that he was willing to endure whatever punishments his parents might use to discourage this allegiance.

Second, when meeting with Gary and three of his friends one day after school, the therapist learned that Gary's friends were hard workers even if they were not academically inclined. Each of these boys had a part-time job and engaged in rigorous physical conditioning programs. Moreover, these boys begrudgingly admired Gary for his ability to get good grades in school.

Third, although Gary's friends teased him about being a "mama's boy," it was clear that they cared a great deal about him and were aware of the fact that he was under considerable pressure from his parents not to skip school.

In light of the preceding factors, the therapist decided that the family's interests would best be served by teaching Gary to cope with peer pressures aimed at devaluing academic achievement and skipping school. Although Mr. and Mrs. Taylor would have preferred that Gary find a new group of friends, they were gradually able to appreciate the fact that Gary's current friends met important emotional needs in his life and that Gary feared being rejected by these friends. Because Gary already recognized the long-term benefits of receiving an education and did not enjoy the consequences imposed on him by his parents for skipping school, he was willing to follow the therapist's suggestions regarding ways of responding to negative peer pressure. Although Gary skipped classes on a few occasions during the course of therapy, his grades showed dramatic improvement and he noted that his peers no longer hounded him about skipping school. At a one-year follow-up, Mr. and Mrs. Taylor reported that Gary's grades remained quite high and that he had expressed an interest in attending the local community college after graduating from high school.

Physical Attractiveness

One of the most consistent findings in the literature on children's peer relations is the association between physical attractiveness and sociometric status. During the preschool and elementary school years, better-looking children are usually accorded higher status by their peers (e.g., Dion & Berscheid, 1974; Kleck, Richardson, & Ronald, 1974; Pope, 1953; Staffieri, 1967; Vaughn & Langlois, 1983; Young & Cooper, 1944). However, Dodge (1983) has suggested that the relationship between physical attractiveness and social status might not be as clear as commonly assumed. With a sample of second-graders, Dodge initially replicated the finding that physical attractiveness is positively associated with sociometric status. However, after controlling for several measures of behavioral interaction, the correlation between attractiveness and status became nonsignificant. Apparently, physically attractive children are also likely to be more socially competent, and it is this competence, rather than their attractiveness per se, that is linked with popularity in school.

During early adolescence, physical maturation and physical attractiveness are associated with the social and sexual activities of boys and girls. Physically mature boys and girls develop heterosexual social relations earlier than their less mature counterparts, and physically attractive adolescents tend to be favored socially throughout the junior high school years (Brooks-Gunn & Petersen, 1983; Faust, 1960; Lerner & Foch, 1987). Likewise, physical appearance is of considerable importance to most high school students. In fact, Eme, Maisiak, and Goodale (1979) found that the most worrisome problem of middle-class high school students was their physical appearance. This concern is realistic, because both physical attractiveness (Cavior, 1970; Hendry & Gillies, 1978) and conformity to the clothing mode of peers (Smucker & Creekmore, 1972) are related to peer acceptance. Finally, the link between physical attractiveness and popularity also extends to college students (Byrne, Ervin, & Lamberth, 1970; Coombs & Kenkel, 1966).

Interventions.   Although factors such as physical attractiveness, personal hygiene, and clothing apparel may not be the primary determinants of peer acceptance, these factors can clearly influence how peers respond to a child. For example, a child who is poorly clothed or who is dirty and unkempt may be avoided by peers and may miss important opportunities for the development of social skills. The child may also be extremely self-conscious about his or her physical appearance and may stay on the fringe of social activities in an effort to avoid further embarrassment by peers.

The therapist should follow several general guidelines when intervening in such cases. First, the therapist should assess the child's family situation before designing any interventions. For example, in cases involving a child with poor hygiene and/or filthy clothing, the therapist should determine whether these problems are indications of a broader pattern of parental incompetence or neglect. In cases of neglect, the involvement of social service professionals who can provide the parent(s) with basic education in childcare and homemaking is often essential. In other cases, however, a child's poor or inadequate clothing may be more a reflection of economic hardships in the family than of any parental indifference toward the child's needs. Here, the therapist should be sensitive to the fact that the parent may already feel bad about the child's physical attire and may view the therapist's offer to help the child as an affront. In these instances, the therapist may need to devote considerable effort to developing trust and to supporting the parent's competencies before addressing issues related to clothing, finances, and the like. In still other cases, the therapist may find that the child's unusual appearance (e.g., a fourth-grader who wears bright red lipstick to school) or clothing may simply reflect poor parental judgment and that the parents are quite open to suggestions regarding the child's physical appearance.

Second, in cases involving an older child or an adolescent, the therapist should avoid making suggestions about ways to enhance physical attractiveness or dress in the absence of a warm, trusting relationship with the child. If such a relationship does not exist, another adult who is close to the child should make these suggestions. On the other hand, when the therapist and child have developed a trusting relationship, we have found that issues related to appearance and dress invariably arise in the natural course of discussion. In these instances, the discussion of such issues can often involve sharing ideas and suggestions that the child may find helpful. For example, with adolescents who apparently possess little knowledge of attractive attire and hair styles, the therapist might recommend that the adolescent study the clothing styles of the five most popular peers in school. During the next therapy session, the therapist and adolescent can discuss these styles and decide upon one or more that fit the "character" of the adolescent.

Finally, the therapist should appreciate that issues related to adolescents' physical appearance and dress are ultimately a matter of personal preference and choice. Many adolescents maintain friendships despite showing an apparent disregard for physical appearance and hygiene. In these instances, requests for the therapist's opinions (e.g., from the parents) are best deflected back to the family for joint decision making with the adolescent. We have found that many adolescents do not discover dress and hygiene until they discover a specific member of the opposite sex.

FAMILY-PEER LINKAGES

Having examined some of the ways that children's personal characteristics are associated with their peer relations, we turn to a consideration of familial correlates of peer relations from early childhood through adolescence. From a systemic perspective, peer relations are assumed to influence children's development *in conjunction with* personal charac-teristics and other family relations, rather than as independent or conceptually additive components. This interplay of family, peer, and individual systems can be viewed as a "synergistic" relationship (Hartup, 1983) in much the same way that different organs or muscle groups in the body work together to produce a cooperative action or force.

Infancy Through Middle Childhood

Based primarily on comparative research, Hinde (1974) proposed an ontogenetic se-quence for the family-peer linkage that has received some support in the child develop-ment literature. The family, as the primary social system in which the infant is initially involved, forms the foundation for future social adaptations. During the first few years of life, the attachment bond with parents promotes feelings of security and facilitates environmental exploration. After this time, mothers increasingly provide opportunities for social engagements with others, particularly peers, outside the immediate family. Security in family relations leads to enhanced self-esteem and feelings of self-com-petence, which, in turn, continue to facilitate peer interactions. The view that family relations provide the affective and instrumental bases for the development of positive peer relations is consistent with the perspectives of other developmentalists. Bron-fenbrenner (1979), for example, hypothesized that mutually positive feelings and flexible rules and roles within parent-child relationships enhance the development of interper-sonal relations across developmental settings.

Longitudinal studies have provided support for the synergistic relationship between the family and peer systems. Easterbrooks and Lamb (1979) and Pastor (1981) found that infants with secure attachments were later more attentive to peers during the toddler period (18–24 months) than were infants who were anxiously attached. Waters, Wipp-man, and Sroufe (1979) and Jacobson and Wille (1986) reported similar links between early infant attachment patterns and peer relations during the preschool age period. Other studies with preschool and primary grade children have shown concurrent linkages between family relations and peer relations. For example, Roopnarine and Adams (1987) found that parents of popular preschoolers used more explanations and praise in helping their children to complete a puzzle task than did parents of moderately popular or unpopular preschoolers. Similarly, Putallaz (1987) reported that mothers of popular first-graders, compared to mothers of unpopular first-graders, interacted with their children in a more positive and agreeable manner, were less demanding, and were more concerned with their children's feelings.

Several researchers have also suggested that a major linkage between parent-child and child-child interactions lies in the child's acquisition of emotional encoding and decoding skills that are learned during family interactions (e.g., MacDonald & Parke, 1984; Sroufe, Schork, Motti, Lawroski, & LaFreniere, 1984). MacDonald and Parke (1984) found that, with 3- to 4-year-olds, affectively arousing styles of physical play with parents, especially fathers, were positively related to children's popularity with peers, and that paternal directiveness was negatively associated with children's popularity. These researchers concluded that playful interactions with parents may provide children with important opportunities to learn the social communicative value of their own affective displays as well as how to use these signals to regulate the social behavior of others. In turn, children may also learn to accurately decode the social and affective signals of other social partners. Thus, it is also assumed that children who have highly controlling parents probably have fewer opportunities to develop and practice the rudiments of these encoding/decoding skills. These conclusions are consistent with recent findings that children's popularity is associated with both the physical play of fathers and children's emotional decoding abilities (Burks, Carson, & Bietel, 1987).

Adults who play successfully with children possess considerable sensitivity to the affective cues of the child and to the desires of most children for affectively positive stimulation. It is possible that parents who are relatively unresponsive or highly directive in their interactions with their children have deficits in their own affective cue detection skills. In a study of 3- to 5-year-old boys, MacDonald (1987) found that the parents of sociometrically neglected children engaged in less affectively arousing, physical play than did the parents of sociometrically rejected and popular children. In addition, the play sessions of rejected children were characterized by more overstimulation and avoidance of stimulation (i.e., alternately approaching the source of overstimulation and then withdrawing from that stimulation) than was the case with popular children and their parents. MacDonald concluded that neglected children generally look to others to provide the lead in their social interactions and that their parents are similarly inclined. Thus, parents of sociometrically neglected children seem less able than other parents to engage their children successfully in physical play. On the other hand, the greater overstimulation and avoidance of stimulation observed among rejected children seem to indicate that the parents of these children are not sensitive to the child's signals (e.g., screaming or other comments that indicate affective overarousal) to lower the level of stimulation during physical play. It is also conceivable, of course, that the seemingly aberrant behaviors observed among the parents of neglected and rejected children are at least partially due to temperamental differences among the different groups of children in their sensitivity to stimulation.

As children move through the elementary school years, their relationships with peers of the same gender become increasingly important sources of emotional fulfillment. Nevertheless, in the fifth grade, children still view their relationships with parents as providing more companionship and intimacy than do their relationships with peers (Buhrmester & Furman, 1987). Given this fact, one might also expect to find that during middle childhood, the quality of children's interactions with their parents continues to play an important role in the development of their peer relations. In one of the few studies to address the linkage between family and peer relations during this period, Patterson, Kupersmidt, and Griesler (1987) found that third- and fourth-graders who were rejected by their peers reported that their relationships with their fathers were of a lower quality than were those of nonrejected children.

As children get older they also interact with peers and form friendships in a variety of different contexts (Epstein, 1986). During the middle childhood years, boys and girls interact with peers in a number of structured (e.g., school, church, clubs) and unstructured (e.g., the school playground, the neighborhood) settings. These different contexts demand different types of behaviors from the child, and the behaviors that lead to popularity in one setting may be quite different from those that promote popularity in another setting. Again, one might reasonably expect that the family has an important function in preparing the child for understanding and adapting in these different contexts.

This hypothesis was recently tested in a longitudinal study by Henggeler, Edwards, Cohen, and Summerville (1989). Specifically, linkages among family relations, children's perceptions of self-competence, and changes in children's popularity during the school year were examined in a class of 24 third-grade children and their parents. Children's popularity with peers was assessed in both the classroom and the playground settings. The results showed that self-competence in academic and social areas was related to concurrent measures of peer popularity but did not predict changes in popularity in either context. However, the family relations measures, while not related to concurrent measures of popularity, predicted changes in popularity: Family cohesion and marital satisfaction were linked with children's increases in popularity in the playground setting, while family adaptability was associated with increases in children's popularity in the classroom setting.

The findings from this study demonstrate that different aspects of family relations prepare the child for functioning in different types of social contexts. Mutually positive feelings in family relationships seem to enhance the development of positive peer relations in the unstructured, peer-controlled playground setting. Therefore, children whose families are less cohesive and interpersonally positive probably have had less opportunity to learn the types of interactional styles that are needed for positive peer relations. In a different vein, it appears that flexible family functioning prepares children to adjust to the variety of situational demands that occur in the structured, adult-controlled classroom setting. That is, classroom work sometimes requires autonomous functioning and other times requires cooperative behaviors. In families that are more structured and rigid, higher rates of child dependence and compliance toward adults may be fostered, and such behavior may result in lowered peer status (Bearison & Cassell, 1975; Markell & Asher, 1984).

In addition to parent-child interactions, another important aspect of family relations that can affect children's peer relations is the parents' marital adjustment. Belsky and Vondra (1985) conceptualize the marital relationship as a social support system that offers the emotional and instrumental provisions necessary for optimal parenting. Consistent with this perspective, recent longitudinal findings have demonstrated that new parents reporting high marital satisfaction subsequently described their relations with their infants as warmer and less negative, perceived their infants as less difficult temperamentally, and felt that their infants were less of an interference in their lives than did parents with less satisfying marital relations (Easterbrooks, 1987). Poor marital relations have also been linked with authoritarian parenting, which, in turn, has been linked with low child social competence (Dielman, Barton, & Cattell, 1977; Olweus, 1980). In addition, numerous studies (for a review, see Emery, 1982) have demonstrated an association between marital dissatisfaction and child behavior problems, such as aggression and withdrawal, that are correlated with difficulties in peer relations (French & Waas, 1985).

It is also important to note that older siblings can have a significant impact on younger children's peer relations. Vandell and Wilson (1987) observed that infants who had more extensive experience in exchanging social behaviors with a preschool-aged sibling at 6 months of age were more likely to initiate exchanges and used a higher proportion of coordinated social behaviors with an unfamiliar peer at 9 months of age. There was no evidence that the infants' exchanges with an unfamiliar peer at 6 months influenced sibling interaction at 9 months. These findings suggest that even preschoolers, through interactions with their infant siblings, can affect their younger siblings' peer relations.

Interventions.   In cases involving difficulties in young children's peer relations, it is essential to consider the linkages between these relations and each of the different subsystems in the family. Interventions that focus on peer relations only, ignoring these linkages, may prove to be only partially successful in changing the child's behavior. One common focus of intervention may pertain to the child's interactions with the parents. In some situations, it may be necessary to teach the parents how to engage in successful physical play with the young child in order to enhance the child's acquisition of emotional encoding and decoding skills. We have seen many parents whose work schedules and interests outside the home allow little time for interacting with their child. We have also seen parents who spend an inordinate amount of time lecturing to and disciplining their child but almost no time engaging in positive interactions with the child. In such cases, it is important that the therapist avoid blaming the parents for the child's difficulties with peers. Nevertheless, the therapist can tell the parents that they are not giving themselves enough credit for what they can teach their child about social interactions. The therapist can also emphasize to the parents that playing with their child is an extremely important activity that the child values and that can have many positive effects on the child's social relations outside the home.

A second focus of intervention may pertain to the parents' provision of opportunities for the child's peer interactions. Without early and regular interactions with peers, the child may increasingly lag behind his or her agemates in the development of social skills and may later come to dread situations demanding peer involvement (e.g., elementary school). Thus, when opportunities for peer interactions are not being provided, the therapist should encourage the parents to consider some different ways to promote the child's involvement with peers. For example, the parents can enroll the young child in a preschool for several half-days each week, or contact other parents about organizing a children's play group that meets at different homes on a rotating basis. Similarly, as the child becomes capable of engaging in organized social activities, the parents should encourage the child to join athletic teams and social organizations such as the Scouts. The child and parents should learn to be proud of these activities and to value them highly.

A third form of intervention pertains to how parents manage children's interactions when supervising peer activities. In some instances, the parents' frequent intrusions into the child's interactions with a peer may all but prevent the development of skills for solving conflicts, expressing an opinion, behaving assertively, and learning to cooperate. In other instances, the parents may be so removed from the child's interactions with an agemate that they miss important opportunities to reinforce prosocial behaviors such as kindness and generosity. Thus, the therapist may need to provide suggestions to the parents about ways to better facilitate their child's transactions with peers.

Preadolescence and Adolescence

For most boys and girls, the transition from childhood to adolescence is marked by significant changes in family and peer relations. As described by Steinberg and Silverberg (1986), these changes seem to involve a shifting of dependency on parents to dependency on peers. These researchers reported that the development of children's emotional autonomy vis-à-vis parents during early adolescence was accompanied by increasing susceptibility to the influence of agemates in both antisocial and neutral situations. Thus, eighth- and ninth-graders showed more dependence on peers than did younger adolescents. This finding is consistent with other recent data showing that peers are perceived as more important companions than are parents during the eighth grade but not during the fifth grade (Buhrmester & Furman, 1987). Interestingly, Steinberg and Silverberg also found that dependence on peers leveled off in the ninth grade. As they noted, this year may represent an important turning point in that adolescents begin to become more resistant to peer pressure.

Although the influence of peers becomes greater during early to middle adolescence, there is some evidence that this influence is more situation-specific than general. Investigators have found that adolescents tend to conform with their peers when making decisions concerning everyday living, such as those pertaining to leisure time and clothing styles, but that they are more likely to consult with their parents regarding important decisions, such as those involving educational plans (Brittain, 1967; Kandel & Lesser, 1969; Sebald & White, 1980). Likewise, favorable attitudes toward parents and peers are often coexistent (Musgrove, 1964; Niles, 1979; O'Donnell, 1976). Thus, for many adolescents, the shift toward a peer social orientation does not necessarily involve a rejection of parents' opinions and values. Instead, it seems that the peer group serves as a filter through which parental norms must pass before they are truly meaningful to the individual adolescent (Siman, 1977).

The adolescent's gradual differentiation from the parents engenders a sense of self-sufficiency that is necessary for independent functioning as an adult. However, early or excessive autonomy from the parents can undermine the adolescent's feelings of self-reliance and can place the adolescent in a position of dangerous susceptibility to peer pressure, especially in the domain of antisocial behavior. For example, Dornbusch et al. (1985) found that the degree of behavioral autonomy granted to adolescents by their parents was positively related to the adolescents' involvement in deviant behavior (ranging from truancy to arrests). Similarly, other researchers have indicated that adolescents who reported less emotional support from their parents (Poole & Regoli, 1979) and less involvement with their families (Elliott et al., 1985) were more susceptible to the influences of delinquent peers than were adolescents who reported more support from and more involvement with their families. Thus, although a moderate amount of behavioral and emotional autonomy from parents is necessary for adolescents to become increasingly responsible and self-sufficient, excessive behavioral or emotional autonomy from parents can leave the adolescent without the behavioral guidance and emotional support that are needed to discourage involvement in deviant activities with problem peers.

Early or excessive autonomy from parental influences can lead to other problems as well. In a review of the literature on adolescent sexual behavior and pregnancy, Hanson and Henggeler (1982) concluded that the *initiation* of sexual activity in heterosexual relations is a component of the adolescent female's accelerated emancipation from her family. They also noted, however, that the *frequency* of sexual activity and the regularity of contraceptive use are more closely related to the qualities of the girl's heterosexual relationship (e.g., a perception of mutual love) and of her same-sex peer relations (e.g., peer contraceptive use). In a similar vein, research in the area of teenage drug use has suggested that both negative parent-adolescent interactions (i.e., low warmth, high conflict) and adolescent involvement with peers who use drugs play an important role in the progression of the adolescent to more serious stages of drug use (Brook, Whiteman, & Gordon, 1983; Brook, Whiteman, Gordon, & Brook, 1984; Brook, Whiteman, Gordon, & Cohen, 1986).

Several family processes may promote adolescents' dependence on peers and increase the risk for involvement in problematic behavior. As noted previously, adolescents who do not perceive love and support from their parents, or who engage in extreme and prolonged conflict with their parents, seem more susceptible to the influence of deviant peers. Another factor that is associated with both antisocial behavior (Patterson & Stouthamer-Loeber, 1984) and susceptibility to antisocial peer pressure (Steinberg, 1986) is a lack of parental monitoring—both proximal or direct supervision and distal monitoring, such as through telephone calls, an agreed-upon schedule, or the power of internalized parental controls. Indeed, in a study of adolescents' after-school experiences, Steinberg (1986) found that "latchkey" adolescents (i.e., those whose parents are not at home after school) who had been raised authoritatively or whose parents knew their whereabouts were less susceptible to antisocial peer influence than were other "latchkey" adolescents. This distal monitoring effect was evident even when the children spent their afternoons in contexts of lax adult supervision and high peer pressure for deviant behavior.

On the other hand, some types of family relations can stifle the adolescent's pursuit of emotional and behavioral autonomy and can interfere with the development of successful peer relations. In this situation, the parents typically adopt an authoritarian parenting style that involves unqualified power assertion and restrictiveness. Such parents often do not allow the adolescent to have age-graded involvement in family decision-making activities or in peer group activities that are essential for maturation. Moreover, if the parent(s) and child have little emotional closeness, the child might fear total rejection by the parents if he or she challenges the parents' decisions or attempts to spend more time with peers. In contrast, inordinately close (i.e., enmeshed) family relations can lead the adolescent to feel that his or her desire for autonomy refutes or betrays the family. Here, feelings of guilt and a desire to avoid emotional turmoil may prevent the adolescent from developing intimate relations with peers and from emancipating from the parents. In cases of both very restrictive families and enmeshed families, the adolescent may be missing experiences that are critical to the development of feelings of personal responsibility, self-worth, and internal control. In such cases, as described in Chapter 3, the parents should be convinced to grant their children more freedom and responsibility.

When considering the linkages between adolescents' family relations and peer relations, the therapist should recognize that adolescents' peers are members of other social contexts that can influence the adolescent. Siman (1977) has suggested that adolescents contrast the behavioral norms of their parents with those of their peers' parents. Parental standards are then reinterpreted by the adolescent on the basis of this comparative appraisal. For example, in an effort to obtain parental approval for participation in some new or previously disallowed activity, the adolescent may attempt to bring the influence of peers' parents to bear on his or her own parents' decision making (i.e., the adolescent may comment, "Jim's parents let him do it"). This reappraisal process demonstrates how systems that are "external" to the developing adolescent (i.e., peers' families) can indirectly influence the adolescent's behavior and family relations. Although the norms of parents and those of peers' families might conflict at times, the resolution of these conflicts can provide important opportunities for the adolescent's emotional and interpersonal growth.

Interventions.   The therapist will often find that the adolescent's behavior problems are being reinforced by the attitudes and behaviors of peers and that the parents feel helpless in their efforts to control the adolescent's behavior. Often, the parents will express the hope that the therapist can "talk some sense into" the adolescent to prevent matters from getting even worse (e.g., the adolescent may be on the verge of being expelled from school or getting pregnant). In such instances, removing an adolescent from a deviant group of peers and establishing an affiliation with nonproblem peers is seldom a smooth process and may be met with considerable resistance from the adolescent as well as from the parents. Therefore, the family should be told that there are no guarantees that the adolescent's behavior problems can be resolved and that the situation is quite difficult. However, the family should also be told that their decision to seek treatment is a very positive step and that, with significant effort on everyone's part, it may be possible to help the family resolve the situation. By framing the presenting problem(s) in this light, the therapist prepares the family for the difficult tasks that lie ahead and increases the likelihood that the family will follow the directives that are given.

The therapist must initially decide between two general courses of action in the treatment of an adolescent who is involved with deviant peers. On the one hand, it may be necessary to remove the adolescent from the present group of peers and to promote the adolescent's involvement with a new, more socially appropriate network of peers. This course is generally recommended in cases where one or more of the following criteria are met: (1) the current peer group has little interest or involvement in *any* type of prosocial activity (e.g., maintaining passing grades in school; participating in an extracurricular club, team, or organization; holding down a part-time or full-time job); (2) the peers have a history of *continued* participation in illegal activities, especially those involving violent behavior or drug abuse; or (3) the peers have parents who provide little structure and monitoring, and who may themselves engage in illegal behavior. Of course, the therapist may find that these criteria apply to some of the adolescent's friends but not to others. In these instances, we recommend that the adolescent's ties with the deviant peer(s) be severed and that his or her involvement with the nonproblem peer(s) be strongly supported and encouraged.

A second general course of action involves keeping the adolescent in the current peer group. This course is usually recommended when none of the preceding criteria are met. In such cases, the adolescent's deviant behavior often represents a transitory pattern and can be effectively controlled with interventions at the family level (e.g., by helping the parents to develop effective discipline strategies or by improving parent-adolescent communication patterns). In other cases, however, such as when the parents are unwilling or unable to comply with therapeutic efforts to promote parental monitoring and discipline, we have found that certain types of peer-related interventions are often helpful in promoting adolescent change within the context of the deviant peer group.

The following discussion first describes a series of interventions designed to remove the adolescent from a deviant group of peers and to promote an affiliation with non-problem peers and then considers two types of interventions that can be used when the adolescent's current peer ties do not need to be severed.

As noted earlier, the adolescent's involvement with deviant peers is often associated with a lack of parental monitoring. In such instances, it is essential for the therapist to conduct a careful assessment of the factors that are maintaining the parents' lack of supervision. In some cases, the therapist may find that the parents simply lack knowledge of appropriate strategies for monitoring and correcting adolescent behavior. In other instances, marital problems (Emery, 1982) or the absence of a parent from the home (Borduin & Henggeler, 1987; Steinberg, 1987) may be contributing to negative parent-adolescent relations, a lack of parental monitoring, and adolescent involvement in deviant activities. On the other hand, the therapist should also give serious consideration to the possibility that the adolescent's deviant behavior may be influencing the parents' response to that behavior over time. For example, an adolescent who repeatedly engages in criminal activity with his peers may cause his parents to withdraw their affection and to abdicate their disciplinary responsibilities because parental disciplinary efforts have been ineffective (compare Blaske, Borduin, Henggeler, & Mann, 1989; Henggeler, Hanson, Borduin, Watson, & Brunk, 1985).

Assuming that the therapist has found that the adolescent's involvement with deviant peers is associated with a lack of parental monitoring, the first therapeutic task is to address those factors that are maintaining the parents' lack of supervision. The parents may need to be educated about appropriate types of adolescent discipline (see Chapter 3) or, in cases where marital problems are evident, the parents may need to temporarily set aside their mutual grievances so they can work together effectively in controlling the adolescent's behavior (see Chapter 4). In situations where marital interventions are not possible (e.g., the parents may refuse to work together despite the therapist's request), the therapist may first need to help the spouses to arrive at a decision about their marriage (i.e., whether to improve the marriage or whether to divorce) before helping them to improve their effectiveness as parents.

Removing an adolescent from a deviant group of peers can be an exceedingly arduous process and may be met with considerable resistance from the adolescent. In light of this fact, it is essential that the therapist prepare the parents for the likely hassles associated with disciplining the adolescent. We recommend telling the parents in no uncertain terms that changing the adolescent's peer affiliations will require a major investment of time, energy, and emotion on their part. The parents should also be told to expect that the adolescent will respond angrily to their sanctions and will utilize various ploys in an an attempt to change their decisions. However, we also remind the parents that their child's long-term adjustment, and perhaps their child's life, is at stake. This latter reminder is especially important for parents who are easily intimidated by their children or who see discipline as being equivalent to torture. With these parents, we spend considerable time spelling out the probable long-term negative consequences of the adolescent's behavior (e.g., incarceration, drug addiction, getting shot while committing a crime), and we have the parents weigh these consequences with the short-term but unpleasant task of preventing the adolescent's continued affiliation with deviant peers. We also assure the parents that we will do our best to help them through this difficult process, including making ourselves available for a few brief phone conversations during the week to provide advice and support for the parents' efforts. In some cases, the therapist may decide that meeting with the family several times a week is necessary to guide the parents through the early phases of the struggle that may lie ahead.

The therapist should help the parents to establish very unpleasant consequences for the adolescent's continued involvement with deviant peers. These consequences should include those that the adolescent is likely to find especially aversive and that, under more normal circumstances, would seem quite unreasonable. For example, after establishing a set of procedures and guidelines for monitoring the who, what, when, and where surrounding the adolescent's activities, the parents might respond to *any* violation of their guidelines by restricting the adolescent to the house and having him or her perform a five-hour work detail that includes the most unpleasant household tasks (e.g., cleaning the toilet, bathtub, sinks, and kitchen floor). The parents must ensure the adolescent's compliance by inspecting his or her work and by having the adolescent redo any work that does not meet the parents' standards. Other relatively aversive activities, such as washing and waxing the car, or vacuuming and dusting the entire house, can also be added to the adolescent's list of tasks should the adolescent continue to violate the parents' rules.

The above set of interventions represents only one of the critical therapeutic tasks that must be completed to facilitate the adolescent's withdrawal from deviant peers. However, we should note that it is not always the case that an adolescent's involvement with deviant peers is directly related to poor parental supervisory skills. In some instances an adolescent will continue to affiliate with problem peers despite the parents' best efforts to stop that affiliation. As the following example suggests, the therapist needs to consider a somewhat different set of therapeutic strategies in such cases.

Heather was referred by her father and stepmother, who were both physicians. She was an attractive and physically mature 15-year-old whose deteriorating grades and increasing sexual activity were of considerable concern to her parents. In order to deal with these problems, the parents had gradually implemented a series of increasingly restrictive disciplines. By the time that the family came for treatment, Heather was essentially a prisoner in her home and the parents functioned as guards. She had no phone privileges, was not allowed out after school, and was confined to her home during weekends. Despite these restrictions, she had managed to sneak her 18-year-old boyfriend through a second-story window into her bedroom one night. It was this action that prompted the parents to seek professional advice.

In discussing the situation with the family, several pertinent aspects of the situation became clear. First, Heather's boyfriend had no positive direction in his life. He had dropped out of high school, was unemployed, and lived with his divorced mother who was chemically dependent and extremely permissive. Second, Heather was deeply committed to her boyfriend. He was her first love, and he met emotional needs that had not been met by her parents, who had relatively distant emotional styles. Third, if Heather was forced to choose between her family and her boyfriend, she would probably choose the boyfriend. Fourth, the parents were bright, competent individuals who were genuinely concerned about their daughter's welfare. And fifth, although Heather was physically mature, her level of emotional functioning was not yet at age level.

The therapist prepared the family for his recommended course of action in the following ways. First, he emphasized that a home should not be a prison and that it was not in the best interest of any family member to live in such a restrictive environment. Heather needed to spend time with her friends, but her parents' concern about her sexual activity also needed to be addressed. Second, the therapist noted that although he could understand why Heather was in love with her boyfriend, he did not believe that this was a positive relationship in the long run. Quite honestly, the boyfriend had some serious problems. Moreover, Heather was an attractive, bright, and sensitive young woman who would soon have many chances for relationships with fine young men. Nevertheless, Heather was now only 15 years of age, and she was legally bound to comply with her parents' wishes. Although the therapist could appreciate Heather's feelings, he had to support the parents' decisions to terminate this relationship.

Next, a course of action was presented that was designed to return the home to normal, to terminate Heather's relationship with her boyfriend, and to allow Heather the freedom that an adolescent needs. Because the parents' reasonable efforts toward these goals had failed, the therapist decided to recommend strategies that were less reasonable. Heather would be granted age-appropriate privileges and freedoms. However, if she continued to see her boyfriend, the parents would file a criminal complaint (statutory rape, contributing to the delinquency of a minor) against the boy and would consider placing Heather in a more restrictive environment in which she could have peer interactions only with girls (a residential school for girls with behavior problems in which the required stay was one year). The therapist emphasized that this was not a course that either he or the parents wanted to take, but that it was preferable to converting the family's home into a jail and to constantly worrying about Heather's welfare. Thus, if Heather chose to continue seeing her boyfriend, the consequences would be extremely unpleasant. On the other hand, if she terminated the relationship, her freedoms would be restored.

The therapist also used cognitive, family-based, and peer-based interventions to help Heather maintain her decision to terminate the relationship. At a cognitive level, the therapist helped Heather to appreciate that she had many positive intellectual, personality, and physical characteristics and that she would have many opportunities to develop relationships with boys who had as many positive qualities as she did. The therapist also addressed emotional aspects of family relations, such that the parents were able to express their love and concern for Heather more openly. Finally, the therapist helped the family to develop ways for Heather to establish nonproblematic peer relations. For example, Heather was provided with the resources to engage in extensive activities with her church's youth group.

Sometimes the adolescent must be removed from the home to break the strong emotional ties that have been established with deviant friends. Although it was not necessary in this case, this course of action would have been a serious alternative had the girl continued to see her boyfriend. Indeed, we do not recommend discussing such a course of action with an adolescent unless the parents are fully committed to following through when necessary.

The second therapeutic task that must often be completed to facilitate the adolescent's successful withdrawal from the current group of peers is to convince the adolescent of the deleterious consequences associated with membership in the peer group. If this task can be accomplished, the negative contingencies established by the parents may be sufficient to motivate the adolescent to change the deviant behavior. To accomplish this task, the therapist and parents should avoid trying to convince the adolescent that the peers have no redeeming personal or social attributes. The use of such an approach is seldom effective because it ignores the fact that the deviant peers are likely to be providing the adolescent with emotional support and a sense of belonging. Thus, we recommend that the therapist and/or parents adopt a more deliberate and cognitively oriented approach with the adolescent when discussing the current peer group affiliation. This can be accomplished by first helping the adolescent to identify his or her educational and occupational goals as well as the necessary steps for achieving those goals. After the goals and steps have been delineated, the therapist can help the adolescent to examine some of the likely discrepancies between the goals and the adolescent's current lifestyle. For adolescents who report that they would "rather wait" until age 25, for example, to start pursuing their educational or occupational goals, the therapist's task becomes one of convincing the adolescent that this strategy has no hope of success. Waiting until age 25 to pursue educational or occupational goals can be likened to delaying one's start at the Boston marathon or Indianapolis 500 by several hours and still hoping to finish among the top competitors.

This discussion also provides an opportunity to examine some of the probable differences between the adolescent's goals and those of the current peers. Once the adolescent recognizes that these discrepancies exist, it is often possible to examine productive ways that the adolescent can go about meeting his or her goals. It is at this point that the issue of forming friendships with nonproblem peers can be addressed.

Using the above approach, the therapist can also discuss the type of social reputation that the adolescent would ultimately like to develop in the broader community (assuming that the adolescent would not like a reputation as a criminal). Again, discrepancies between the adolescent's social goals and current behavior can be examined, and ways to better meet these goals can be addressed. Given that most adolescents hold positive occupational and social goals for themselves, the idea of beginning to work toward (and not in opposition to) these goals can sometimes be used as a lever to convince the adolescent that withdrawal from the current peer group is necessary.

A third step in changing the adolescent's peer group is to assist the adolescent in identifying his or her talents and interests. These talents and interests can provide an important vehicle for promoting the adolescent's involvement with nonproblem peers. For example, adolescents with musical talents can be encouraged to participate in organized musical groups (e.g., the school jazz band); adolescents with literary talents can be encouraged to join the staff of the school newspaper; mechanically talented adolescents can be enrolled in special vocational programs and can work as apprentices in certain employment settings; and athletically gifted youth can be encouraged to participate in organized sports. Although it is important for the therapist and parents to require that the adolescent become involved in prosocial activity, the choice of the specific activity should be left up to the adolescent, thus providing an illusion of control.

Whatever the prosocial activity, it is essential that the parents provide reinforcement for the adolescent's participation in the activity. For example, the parents may need to provide the adolescent with certain resources (e.g., a musical instrument, athletic equipment), they may need to see that the adolescent has transportation to and from these activities, and they may need to show interest in those activities at which their attendance is encouraged.

In some cases the therapist will not be able to accomplish one or more of these therapeutic tasks. For example, the adolescent may refuse to end friendships with deviant peers despite the therapist's cognitive interventions and the parent's disciplinary efforts. As the following case suggests, removal of an adolescent from the home and community may ultimately represent the only viable intervention for preventing some adolescents from harming others and from engaging in self-destructive behaviors.

Kyle was an intellectually gifted 12-year-old boy who was referred by his mother and stepfather. Kyle was failing four of his five courses and was engaging in serious antisocial behavior. He and his friends had broken into a neighbor's home and had wrecked furniture and walls, they had tortured a cat, beaten another boy until he was unconscious, and started a fire in an abandoned house. Although these boys had little experience with drugs, they pretended to snort cocaine at school.

Kyle had seen three other therapists during his childhood, and the parents were now at wits' end. They feared that Kyle's problems were escalating and that his behavior was virtually out of control. In speaking with Kyle, the therapist learned that his friends had serious emotional and family problems, but that Kyle looked up to these boys and felt that they were "super cool." Kyle's professed goal in life was to move out to California and smuggle drugs in from Central America. In reality, he was making good progress toward this goal. During this conversation, the therapist also realized that Kyle's level of moral development was severely delayed. Kyle could not understand why his parents were so upset and felt that they just needed to "chill out."

After considering the severity and danger of the situation, Kyle's lack of moral development, his commitment to his friends, and the parents' frustration and fear, the therapist recommended that Kyle be placed in a more structured environment. This environment should force him to use his considerable intellectual skills to improve his academics, it should provide extensive contact with nonproblem peers, and it should develop his self-discipline. Neither psychiatric facilities nor correctional schools place a significant emphasis on academics, and both types of settings involve extensive contact with peers who have serious problems. Therefore, the therapist recommended a military school that specialized in the education of bright, underachieving children. The therapist's and family's hope was that this setting would provide the consistent external control that was needed for Kyle to develop internal control of his behavior, and that extensive exposure to a new peer group would facilitate development of moral values.

Peer friendships are extremely important to adolescents, and we do not advocate the severing of such friendships unless there is little likelihood that the adolescent's behavior problems can be otherwise ameliorated. When the adolescent shares a number of prosocial interests or talents with an otherwise deviant group of peers, it is often possible to reduce the likelihood that the adolescent will continue to engage in deviant behavior without removing the adolescent from the current peer group. This approach may also represent a workable strategy when the parents refuse to establish or to enforce firm limits for the adolescent's problematic behavior or to promote the adolescent's association with nonproblem peers. Such parental noncooperation is especially likely to occur if the parents have serious individual problems (e.g., psychiatric disturbance, chemical dependency) or if they are extremely egocentric and have never developed a meaningful emotional attachment to the adolescent.

When the therapist's goal is to keep the adolescent in his or her current peer group while reducing the likelihood of subsequent deviant behavior, the therapist can employ one of two types of therapeutic strategies, depending on the potential of the peer group for positive change. The following case exemplifies the first of these strategies.

Darla King was a 16-year-old girl who was referred for therapy following a series of arrests for shoplifting with her peers. Mr. King had abandoned the family three years earlier, leaving Mrs. King with the difficult task of raising Darla and her five younger siblings. Although Mrs. King was concerned about Darla's behavior, she was clearly overwhelmed by her parenting and financial responsibilities, as evidenced by her numerous somatic complaints and her recent psychiatric hospitalization for depression. Mrs. King stated that she had neither the time nor the energy to keep close tabs on Darla's behavior and that Darla would need to be placed in a foster home if her shoplifting continued.

After meeting with Darla and two of her closest friends, the therapist concluded that the girls' problematic behavior was largely motivated by their desire to have certain types of clothes and other basic provisions that their families could not afford. None of the girls received an allowance, and their families could not afford to provide them with one. During a subsequent meeting, the therapist reached an agreement with the girls (and their parents) that they were happy to accept. Specifically, the therapist would help the girls to find part-time jobs if they would agree to stop shoplifting. With the help of Mrs. King, the therapist taught the girls how to fill out employment applications and provided some ideas about likely places of employment. Three weeks later, each of the girls had obtained a part-time job that did not interfere with her responsibilities at school or at home. In subsequent sessions with Mrs. King and Darla, the therapist helped them to negotiate a number of rules regarding the management of Darla's paycheck, her performance and attendance in school, her household and babysitting responsibilities, and her time spent with friends. At an 18-month follow-up, Darla had graduated from high school, had obtained full-time employment at a better job, and had not been arrested again.

The above case demonstrates how it is sometimes possible to eliminate deviant peer group behavior without severing emotional ties with peers. However, when the therapist estimates that it would be extremely difficult to promote positive change in the peer group, either because the peers are not interested in such change or because there are few relevant opportunities for promoting such change, we recommend that the therapist follow the procedures described in Chapter 2 for developing a supportive and caring relationship with the individual adolescent. Within the context of this relationship, the therapist can often motivate the adolescent to give up his or her deviant behavior and can teach the adolescent effective strategies to cope with peer group pressure.

REFERENCES

Asher, S. R. (1983). Social competence and peer status: Recent advances and future directions. *Child Development, 54,* 1427–1434.

Asher, S. R., & Hymel, S. (1981). Children's social competence in peer relations: Sociometric and behavioral assessment. In J. D. Wine & M. D. Smye (Eds.), *Social competence* (pp. 125–157). New York: Guilford.

Asher, S. R., & Wheeler, V. A. (1985). Children's loneliness: A comparison of rejected and neglected peer status. *Journal of Consulting and Clinical Psychology, 53,* 500–505.

Aydin, O., & Markova, I. (1979). Attribution tendencies of popular and unpopular children. *British Journal of Social and Clinical Psychology, 18,* 291–298.

Bearison, D. J., & Cassell, T. Z. (1975). Cognitive decentration and social codes: Communicative effectiveness in young children from differing family contexts. *Developmental Psychology, 11,* 29–36.

Belsky, J., & Vondra, J. (1985). Characteristics, consequences, and determinants of parenting. In L. L'Abate (Ed.), *The handbook of family psychology and therapy* (Vol. 1, pp. 523–556). Homewood, IL: Dorsey.

Bierman, K. L., & Furman, W. (1984). The effects of social skills-training and peer involvement on the social adjustment of preadolescents. *Child Development, 55,* 151–162.

Bierman, K. L., Miller, C. L., & Stabb, S. D. (1987). Improving the social behavior and peer acceptance of rejected boys: Effects of social skill training with instructions and prohibitions. *Journal of Consulting and Clinical Psychology, 55,* 194–200.

Blaske, D. M., Borduin, C. M., Henggeler, S. W., & Mann, B. J. (1989). Individual, family, and peer characteristics of adolescent sex offenders and assaultive offenders. *Developmental Psychology, 25,* 846–855.

Borduin, C. M., Blaske, D. M., Treloar, L., & Mann, B. J. (1989). *Development and validation of a measure of adolescent peer relations: The Missouri Peer Relations Inventory.* Unpublished manuscript, University of Missouri–Columbia.

Borduin, C. M., & Henggeler, S. W. (1987). Post-divorce mother-son relations of delinquent and well-adjusted adolescents. *Journal of Applied Developmental Psychology, 8,* 273–288.

Brittain, C. V. (1967). An exploration of the bases of peer-compliance and parent-compliance in adolescence. *Adolescence, 2,* 445–458.

Bronfenbrenner, U. (1979). *The ecology of human development: Experiments by nature and design.* Cambridge, MA: Harvard University Press.

Brook, J. S., Whiteman, M., & Gordon, A. S. (1983). Stages of drug use in adolescence: Personality, peer, and family correlates. *Developmental Psychology, 19,* 269–277.

Brook, J. S., Whiteman, M., Gordon, A. S., & Brook, D. W. (1984). Paternal determinants of female adolescents' marijuana use. *Developmental Psychology, 20,* 1032–1043.

Brook, J. S., Whiteman, M., Gordon, A. S., & Cohen, P. (1986). Some models and mechanisms for explaining the impact of maternal and adolescent characteristics on adolescent stage of drug use. *Developmental Psychology, 22,* 460–467.

Brooks-Gunn, J., & Petersen, A. C. (Eds.). (1983). *Girls at puberty: Biological and psychosocial perspectives.* New York: Plenum.

Bruner, J. S., Jolly, A., & Sylva, K. (Eds.). (1976). *Play: Its role in development and evolution.* Harmondsworth, Middlesex: Penguin.

Buhrmester, D., & Furman, W. (1987). The development of companionship and intimacy. *Child Development, 58,* 1101–1113.

Burks, V., Carson, J., & Bietel, A. (1987, April). *Parent-child interaction and peer sociometric status: The role of emotional decoding.* Paper presented at the biennial meeting of the Society for Research in Child Development, Baltimore.

Byrne, D., Ervin, C. R., & Lamberth, J. C. (1970). Continuity between the experimental study of attraction and "real life" computer dating. *Journal of Social Psychology, 16,* 157–165.

Cavior, N. (1970). *Physical attractiveness, perceived attitude similarity, and interpersonal attraction among fifth and eleventh grade boys and girls.* Unpublished doctoral dissertation, University of Houston, Houston, TX.

Chandler, M. (1973). Egocentrism and antisocial behavior: The assessment and training of social perspective-taking skills. *Developmental Psychology, 9,* 326–332.

Chandler, M., Greenspan, S., & Barenboim, C. (1974). Assessment and training of role taking and referential communication skills in institutionalized emotionally disturbed children. *Developmental Psychology, 10,* 546–553.

Coie, J. D., & Dodge, K. A. (1983). Continuities and changes in children's social status: A five-year longitudinal study. *Merrill-Palmer Quarterly, 29,* 261–282.

Coie, J. D., Dodge, K. A., & Coppotelli, H. (1982). Dimensions and types of status: A cross-age perspective. *Developmental Psychology, 18,* 557–570.

Coombs, R. H., & Kenkel, W. F. (1966). Sex differences in dating aspirations and satisfaction with computer-selected partners. *Journal of Marriage and the Family, 28,* 62–66.

Cowen, E. L., Pederson, A., Babigian, H., Izzo, L. D., & Trost, M. A. (1973). Long-term follow-up of early detected vulnerable children. *Journal of Consulting and Clinical Psychology, 41,* 438–446.

Deluty, R. H. (1981). Alternative-thinking ability of aggressive, assertive, and submissive children. *Cognitive Therapy and Research, 5,* 309–312.

Dielman, T., Barton, K., & Cattell, R. (1977). Relationships among family attitudes and child rearing practices. *Journal of Genetic Psychology, 130,* 105–112.

Dion, K. K., & Berscheid, E. (1974). Physical attractiveness and peer acceptance among children. *Sociometry, 37,* 1–12.

Dodge, K. A. (1980). Social cognition and children's aggressive behavior. *Child Development, 51,* 162–170.

Dodge, K. A. (1983). Behavioral antecedents of peer social status. *Child Development, 54,* 1386–1399.

Dodge, K. A., Coie, J. D., & Brakke, N. P. (1982). Behavior patterns of socially rejected and neglected preadolescents: The roles of social approach and aggression. *Journal of Abnormal Child Psychology, 10,* 389–410.

Dodge, K. A., Murphy, R. M., & Bushbaum, K. (1984). The assessment of intention-cue detection skills in children: Implications for developmental psychopathology. *Child Development, 55,* 163–173.

Dodge, K. A., & Newman, J. P. (1981). Biased decision-making processes in aggressive boys. *Journal of Abnormal Psychology, 90,* 375–379.

Dodge, K. A., Somberg, D. R. (1987). Hostile attributional biases among aggressive boys are exacerbated under conditions of threat to the self. *Child Development, 58,* 213–224.

Dornbusch, S., Carlsmith, J., Bushwall, S., Ritter, P., Leiderman, H., Hastorf, A., & Gross, R. (1985). Single parents, extended households, and the control of adolescents. *Child Development, 56,* 326–341.

Douvan, E., & Adelson, J. (1966). *The adolescent experience.* New York: Wiley.

Dunphy, D. C. (1963). The social structure of urban adolescent peer groups. *Sociometry, 26,* 230–246.

Easterbrooks, M. A. (1987, April). *Early family development: Longitudinal impact of marital quality.* Paper presented at the biennial meeting of the Society for Research in Child Development, Baltimore.

Easterbrooks, M. A., & Lamb, M. E. (1979). The relationship between the quality of mother-infant attachment and infant competence in initial encounters with peers. *Child Development, 50,* 380–387.

Eder, D., & Hallinan, M. T. (1978). Sex differences in children's friendships. *American Sociological Review, 43,* 237–250.

Elliott, D. S., Huizinga, D., & Ageton, S. S. (1985). *Explaining delinquency and drug use.* Newbury Park, CA: Sage.

Eme, R., Maisiak, R., & Goodale, W. (1979). Seriousness of adolescent problems. *Adolescence, 14,* 93–99.

Emery, R. E. (1982). Interparental conflict and the children of discord and divorce. *Psychological Bulletin, 92,* 310–330.

Epstein, J. L. (1986). Choice of friends over the life-span: Developmental and environmental influences. In E. C. Mueller & C. R. Cooper (Eds.), *Process and outcome in peer relationships* (pp. 129–160). New York: Academic Press.

Faust, M. S. (1960). Developmental maturity as a determinant of prestige in adolescent girls. *Child Development, 31,* 173–184.

Field, T. M. (1981). Gaze behavior of normal and high-risk infants during early interactions. *Journal of the American Academy of Child Psychiatry, 20,* 308–317.

Field, T. M., & Roopnarine, J. L. (1982). Infant-peer interactions. In T. M. Field, A. Huston, H. C. Quay, L. Troll, & G. E. Finley (Eds.), *Review of human development* (pp. 164–179). New York: Wiley.

Fogel, A. (1980). Peer vs. mother-directed behavior in one-to-three-month-old infants. *Infant Behavior and Development, 2,* 215–226.

French, D. C., & Waas, G. A. (1985). Behavior problems of peer-neglected and peer-rejected elementary-age children: Parent and teacher perspectives. *Child Development, 56,* 246–252.

Furman, W. (1982). Children's friendships. In T. M. Field, A. Huston, H. C. Quay, L. Troll, & G. E. Finley (Eds.), *Review of human development* (pp. 327–339). New York: Wiley.

Furman, W., & Bierman, K. L. (1983). Developmental changes in young children's conceptions of friendships. *Child Development, 54,* 549–556.

Furman, W., & Bierman, K. L. (1984). Children's conceptions of friendship: A multimethod study of developmental changes. *Developmental Psychology, 20,* 925–931.

Furman, W., & Buhrmester, D. (1985). Children's perceptions of the qualities of sibling relationships. *Child Development, 56,* 448–461.

Gelfand, D. M., & Peterson, L. (1985). *Child development and psychopathology.* Newbury Park, CA: Sage.

Gottman, J. M. (1977). Toward a definition of social isolation in children. *Child Development, 48,* 513–517.

Gottman, J. M., & Mettetal, G. (1987). Speculations about social and affective development: Friendship and acquaintanceship through adolescence. In J. M. Gottman & J. G. Parker (Eds.), *Conversations of friends: Speculations on affective development* (pp. 192–237). New York: Cambridge University Press.

Green, K. D., Forehand, R., Beck, S. J., & Vosk, B. (1980). An assessment of the relationship among measures of children's social competence and children's academic achievement. *Child Development, 51,* 1149–1156.

Hanson, C. L., & Henggeler, S. W. (1982). The behavior disorders and problems of female adolescents. In S. W. Henggeler (Ed.), *Delinquency and adolescent psychopathology: A family-ecological systems approach* (pp. 117–138). Littleton, MA: Wright-PSG.

Hartup, W. W. (1983). Peer relations. In E. M. Hetherington (Ed.), P. H. Mussen (Series Ed.), *Handbook of child psychology, Vol. 4: Socialization, personality, and social development* (pp. 103–196). New York: Wiley.

Hendry, L. B., & Gillies, P. (1978). Body type, body esteem, school, and leisure: A study of overweight, average, and underweight adolescents. *Journal of Youth and Adolescence, 7,* 181–195.

Henggeler, S. W., Edwards, J. J., Cohen, R., & Summerville, M. B. (1989). *Examining family-peer linkages: Associations among family relations, self-perceptions of social and scholastic competence, and changes in children's popularity.* Manuscript submitted for publication.

Henggeler, S. W., Hanson, C. L., Borduin, C. M., Watson, S. M., & Brunk, M. A. (1985). Mother-son relationships of juvenile felons. *Journal of Consulting and Clinical Psychology, 53,* 942–943.

Hinde, R. (1974). *Biological bases of human social behavior.* New York: McGraw Hill.

Hymel, S. (1986). Interpretations of peer behavior: Affective bias in childhood and adolescence. *Child Development, 57,* 431–445.

Jacobson, J. L., & Wille, D. E. (1986). The influence of attachment pattern on developmental changes in peer interaction from the toddler to the preschool period. *Child Development, 57,* 338–347.

Kandel, D. B. (1978). Homophily, selection, and socialization in adolescent friendships. *American Journal of Sociology, 84,* 427–436.

Kandel, D. B., & Lesser, G. S. (1969). Parental and peer influences on educational plans of adolescents. *American Sociological Review, 34,* 213–223.

Kleck, R. E., Richardson, S. A., & Ronald, L. (1974). Physical appearance cues and interpersonal attraction in children. *Child Development, 45,* 305–310.

Lerner, R. M., & Foch, T. T. (Eds.). (1987). *Biological-psychosocial interactions in early adolescence: A life-span perspective.* Hillsdale, NJ: Erlbaum.

Lochman, J. E. (1987). Self- and peer perceptions and attributional biases of aggressive and nonaggressive boys in dyadic interactions. *Journal of Consulting and Clinical Psychology, 55,* 404–410.

Maccoby, E. E., & Jacklin, C. N. (1974). *The psychology of sex differences.* Stanford, CA: Stanford University Press.

Maccoby, E. E., & Martin, J. A. (1983). Socialization in the context of the family: Parent-child interaction. In E. M. Hetherington (Ed.), P. H. Mussen (Series Ed.), *Handbook of child psychology, Vol. 4: Socialization, personality, and social development* (pp. 1–101). New York: Wiley.

MacDonald, K. (1987). Parent-child physical play with rejected, neglected, and popular boys. *Developmental Psychology, 23,* 705–711.

MacDonald, K., & Parke, R. D. (1984). Bridging the gap: Parent-child play interaction and peer interactive competence. *Child Development, 55,* 1265–1277.

Markell, R. A., & Asher, S. R. (1984). Children's interactions in dyads: Interpersonal influence and sociometric status. *Child Development, 55,* 1412–1424.

Musgrove, F. (1964). *Youth and the social order.* London: Routledge & Kegan.

Nasby, W., Hayden, B., & DePaulo, B. M. (1980). Attributional bias among aggressive boys to interpret unambiguous social stimuli as displays of hostility. *Journal of Abnormal Psychology, 89,* 459–468.

Niles, F. S. (1979). Adolescent girls' perception of parents and peers. *Adolescence, 14,* 591–597.

Oden, S., & Asher, S. R. (1977). Coaching children in social skills for friendship making. *Child Development, 48,* 495–506.

O'Donnell, W. J. (1976). Adolescent self-esteem related to feelings toward parents and friends. *Journal of Youth and Adolescence, 5,* 179–185.

O'Donnell, W. J. (1979). Adolescent self-reported and peer-reported self esteem. *Adolescence, 14,* 465–470.

Olweus, D. (1980). Familial and temperamental determinants of aggressive behavior in adolescent boys: A causal analysis. *Developmental Psychology, 16*, 644–660.

Panella, D. H., Cooper, P. F., & Henggeler, S. W. (1982). Peer relations in adolescence. In S. W. Henggeler (Ed.), *Delinquency and adolescent psychopathology: A family-ecological systems approach* (pp. 139–161). Littleton, MA: Wright-PSG.

Parker, J. G., & Asher, S. R. (1987). Peer relations and later personal adjustment: Are low-accepted children at risk? *Psychological Bulletin, 102*, 357–389.

Pastor, D. L. (1981). The quality of mother-infant attachment and its relation to toddler's initial sociability with peers. *Developmental Psychology, 17*, 326–335.

Patterson, C. J., Kupersmidt, J. B., & Griesler, P. C. (1987, April). *Sociometric status and children's perceptions of their relationships with mothers, fathers, teachers, and friends.* Paper presented at the biennial meeting of the Society for Research in Child Development, Baltimore.

Patterson, G., & Stouthamer-Loeber, M. (1984). The correlation of family management practices and delinquency. *Child Development, 55*, 1299–1307.

Platt, J. J., Scura, W., & Hannon, J. B. (1973). Problem-solving thinking of youthful incarcerated heroin addicts. *Journal of Community Psychology, 1*, 278–281.

Platt, J. J., Spivack, G., & Altman, N. (1974). Adolescent problem-solving thinking. *Journal of Consulting and Clinical Psychology, 42*, 787–793.

Poole, E. D., & Regoli, R. M. (1979). Parental support, delinquent friends, and delinquency: A test of interaction effects. *Journal of Criminal Law and Criminology, 70*, 188–193.

Pope, B. (1953). Socioeconomic contrasts in children's peer culture prestige values. *Genetic Psychology Monographs, 48*, 157–220.

Putallaz, M. (1983). Predicting children's sociometric status from their behavior. *Child Development, 54*, 1417–1426.

Putallaz, M. (1987). Maternal behavior and children's sociometric status. *Child Development, 58*, 324–340.

Roff, M., Sells, S. B., & Golden, M. M. (1972). *Social adjustment and personality development in children.* Minneapolis: University of Minnesota Press.

Roopnarine, J., & Adams, G. R. (1987). The interactional teaching patterns of mothers and fathers with their popular, moderately popular, or unpopular children. *Journal of Abnormal Child Psychology, 15*, 125–136.

Sebald, H. (1981). Adolescents' concept of popularity and unpopularity, comparing 1960 with 1976. *Adolescence, 16*, 23–30.

Sebald, H., & White, B. (1980). Teenagers' divided reference groups: Uneven alignment with parents and peers. *Adolescence, 15*, 979–984.

Selman, R. L. (1980). *The growth of interpersonal understanding: Developmental and clinical analyses.* New York: Academic Press.

Selman, R. L., Lavin, D. R., & Brion-Meisels, S. (1982). Troubled children's use of self-reflection. In F. C. Serafica (Ed.), *Social-cognitive development in context* (pp. 62–99). New York: Guilford.

Siman, M. L. (1977). Application of a new model of peer group influence to naturally existing adolescent friendship groups. *Child Development, 48*, 270–274.

Smucker, B., & Creekmore, A. M. (1972). Adolescents' clothing conformity, awareness, and peer acceptance. *Home Economics Research Journal, 1*, 92–97.

Spenner, K. (1975). *Predicting levels of aspirations: A comparison of perceived and actual informational inputs from significant others.* (ERIC Document Reproduction Service No. ED 103 290).

Sroufe, L. A., Schork, E., Motti, F., Lawroski, N., & LaFreniere, P. (1984). The role of affect in emerging social competence. In C. Izard, J. Kagan, & R. Zajonc (Eds.), *Emotion, cognition, and behavior* (pp. 289–319). New York: Cambridge University Press.

Staffieri, J. R. (1967). A study of social stereotype of body image in children. *Journal of Personality and Social Psychology, 1,* 101–104.

Steinberg, L. (1986). Latchkey children and susceptibility to peer pressure: An ecological analysis. *Developmental Psychology, 22,* 433–439.

Steinberg, L. (1987). Single parents, stepparents, and the susceptibility of adolescents to antisocial peer pressure. *Child Development, 58,* 269–275.

Steinberg, L., & Silverberg, S. S. (1986). The vicissitudes of autonomy in early adolescence. *Child Development, 57,* 841–851.

Sullivan, H. S. (1953). *The interpersonal theory of psychiatry.* New York: Norton.

Vandell, D. L., & Wilson, D. S. (1987). Infants' interactions with mother, sibling, and peer: Contrasts and relations between interaction systems. *Child Development, 58,* 176–186.

Vaughn, B., & Langlois, J. H. (1983). Physical attractiveness as a correlate of peer status and social competence in preschool children. *Developmental Psychology, 19,* 561–567.

Waters, E., Wippman, A. J., & Sroufe, L. A. (1979). Attachment, positive affect, and competence in the peer group: Two studies in construct validation. *Child Development, 50,* 821–829.

Young, L. L., & Cooper, D. H. (1944). Some factors associated with popularity. *Journal of Educational Psychology, 35,* 513–535.

CHAPTER 6

The School System and
the Family-School Mesosystem

The school is a major social institution that has a pervasive influence on child development (for an excellent and comprehensive review, see Minuchin & Shapiro, 1983). Although the nature of this influence can vary with qualitative aspects of the school environment (e.g., physical setting, philosophy of education, resources of the community), certain meta-level functions of schools are found in almost all school contexts. These functions can be divided into domains that pertain to either social development or cognitive development.

The school environment provides children and adolescents with a milieu in which they have the opportunity to experience a variety of social roles. For many young children, teachers are the first adults besides their parents with whom they have extensive contact. Some of these children find that patterns of behavior that are permitted by their parents can be problematic when used with the teachers. Such children must learn to make accommodations to different styles of adult control and affective interaction. For many young children, school provides their first extended contact with a stable group of peers. These children must learn strategies for gaining entry into peer group activities, for responding to the friendly or unfriendly initiations of others, and for the development and maintenance of friendships.

During the junior and senior high school years, the social roles become even more complex. It is within the school context that boys and girls have most of their initial experience with the development of heterosexual relations. In addition, participation in clubs and organized sports provide opportunities to develop cooperative behavior as well as leadership skills. With more mature cognitive development, adolescents begin to view teachers and the school system more realistically, recognizing both the strengths and limitations of their present school context. Such understanding contributes to adolescents' differentiation of self and a desire to improve the existing social structure.

The school environment also has a strong effect on children's cognitive development and their subsequent vocational achievement. Children acquire strategies for learning in the classroom that can be used for the rest of their lives. It seems likely that children who learn that significant personal effort provides substantive payoffs are more likely to continue such efforts during adulthood than are children who are not rewarded for their efforts or who are in a school context that does not demand significant effort. Moreover, based on the association between educational success and socioeconomic success, school performance can have a strong influence on occupational and career opportunities. The realization of such opportunities, in turn, has a pervasive effect on the quality of the child's adult life. For example, the status, prestige, and income that are associated with an individual's occupation affect his or her place of residence, choice of spouse and friends, and recreational activities.

SOCIAL FUNCTIONING

In most cases in which a child is referred for therapy, the child is evidencing behavior problems at home. Although the parents are often aware of the poor quality of the child's social functioning in school, such functioning is typically of secondary importance to the parents (unless, of course, the referral was initiated by the child's teachers). Understandably, the parents' attention is usually focused on problem behavior at home that has an immediate and direct effect on the family (e.g., drug use, aggression, or noncompliance).

Although the parents might initially emphasize problems that the child presents within the family, we recommend that the therapist also evaluate the child's social functioning in school. Such an evaluation often provides information that is critical to understanding how the behavior problems are being maintained. In addition, information provided by the teachers can be used by the therapist to confirm or disconfirm impressions of the family. For example, if the therapist believes that the child's behavior problems are linked with family disinterest and disengagement, the therapist can assess the teachers' impressions of parental support for the educational process. Similarly, if the therapist suspects that the parents are exaggerating the child's misbehavior, an evaluation of the child's behavior in school can help to clarify the situation.

In general, information provided by teachers can enable the therapist to determine whether the child's difficulties are associated primarily with dysfunctions in the individual, family, or peer systems, or in some combination of these systems. The therapist will sometimes find that the primary dysfunction is closely associated with characteristics of the school system itself. Hence, the process and direction of treatment can vary considerably based on information that is provided by the teachers.

The therapist should obtain several types of information from the teachers regarding the child's social relations. The therapist should determine whether the child has close friendships with other children in the school. If the child has such friendships, the therapist should ask about the levels of social and intellectual functioning of these friends. This information will provide the therapist with a good general idea of the child's level of social competence. For example, if a child has few friends or associates primarily with socially rejected children, it is likely that the child possesses significant deficits in social competence. Or, if an adolescent associates primarily with friends who have reputations for drug use, drugs probably play an important role in the adolescent's presenting problems. On the other hand, a child who is popular and highly regarded by his peers probably possesses significant interpersonal strengths that can be used as levers for therapeutic change.

The therapist should also evaluate the child's relationships with the teachers. One important issue in this evaluation is how the child responds to authority. A child (especially a young child) who is openly rebellious to authority in school, has probably been given tacit approval for such behavior by the parents (assuming that the teachers possess the disciplinary competence to control problem behavior). On the other hand, if the child is responsive to authority, it may indicate that the child's behavior problems are, in large part, situationally determined. We have seen quite a few cases in which children present behavior problems at home but are very well behaved in school. In these cases, the parents are usually mismanaging the child's behavior problems and need to develop more effective discipline strategies.

In evaluating the child-teacher relationship, the therapist might also learn, for example, that the child has developed an overly dependent attachment to the teachers and prefers to interact with the teachers more than with other children. This information can help to clarify emotional aspects of the child's family relations. Children who are very adult oriented tend to be members of families that either foster excessive emotional dependence or are emotionally rejecting. Although the therapist would probably suspect that such circumstances exist based on interviews with the family, the information obtained from the school can, again, be used to validate the therapist's impressions.

As noted earlier, the child's future social and economic functioning are linked with social and academic performance in the school context. Thus, the therapist should always ask the teachers whether the child displays behavior problems in school and whether these problems present any special difficulties to the teachers. The therapist might learn that the child presented several behavior problems at the beginning of the school year but that, following interventions by the teachers, these problems decreased. In such cases, if the child is presenting behavior problems at home, the therapist might use the teachers' interventions to guide the implementation of family-based interventions. In other instances, the therapist might learn that the child's behavior problems in school emerged suddenly and without warning. In these cases, a family stress (e.g., marital conflict, problems with a sibling) or a peer relationship difficulty (e.g., rejection) has usually precipitated the behavior problems. In still other cases, the child may have presented serious behavior problems that have not responded to the teachers' usual repertoire of disciplinary actions. Here, it is common for the teachers to request the therapist's assistance in the management of the child's behavior problems. Such situations provide an excellent opportunity for the therapist to effect change across multiple systems.

Implementation of School-Based Interventions for Social Functioning

The therapist should use several procedural and process level guidelines when interacting with educational professionals such as teachers and principals. When these guidelines are followed, most teachers and principals are very cooperative with the therapist's suggestions for school-based interventions. On the other hand, if the guidelines are ignored, the therapist's suggestions may be resisted.

1. The therapist should go through normal administrative channels. In many schools, the principal wants to be informed of all contact that teachers have with outside professionals regarding a student. After obtaining a signed release of information from the parents, the therapist should call the principal and request a conference with the child's teachers. In some schools, a guidance counselor acts as the administrative liaison between

the teachers and outside professionals. In such instances, the principal will usually ask the therapist to contact the counselor to schedule a meeting with the teachers.

2. During these initial phone conversations, the therapist should behave in a non-threatening manner. The therapist should explain that the parents are concerned about certain problems that the child is presenting and that the therapist would greatly appreciate any information that would assist in the development of effective treatment strategies for the child. The therapist should stress that the teachers' information and impressions are very valuable because they are more objective than most other information. It is critical that the therapist not say or do anything suggesting that the school has a substantive role in the maintenance of the child's behavior problems, even if the therapist is almost certain that the problems are due to teacher mismanagement. If the therapist even implies that the child's problems are associated with teacher mismanagement, the educational professionals might become defensive and restrict the flow of information to both the therapist and the parents. In the face of perceived outside threat, most systems (family, school, governmental) respond by becoming less open.

3. The therapist should meet with the teachers, guidance counselor, and principal at the school and at a time that is convenient for them. This helps to communicate a message of therapist flexibility and responsivity. In addition, it is very important that the therapist treat the educational professionals as equal-status colleagues. Most mental health professionals have earned master's or doctoral degrees from highly competitive graduate or medical programs. Unfortunately, some mental health professionals look down on colleagues in education who may hold lesser degrees or who may have attended less competitive programs and behave with an air of superiority when interacting with those colleagues. Because most educational professionals are quite aware of this status hierarchy, a therapist who communicates a message of superiority may deter teacher cooperation with the therapist's school-based interventions.

4. During the therapist-teacher conference, the therapist should take a "one-down" position (i.e., convey respect to the teachers in their role as experts on the child's education), emphasize the gathering of information, and avoid giving unsolicited advice and interpretations. If the child is disrupting the classroom and/or if the parents are not fully supporting the teachers' educational and disciplinary efforts, it is very important that the therapist empathize with these difficulties. Even though the parents have consulted the therapist, the teachers should not be led to believe that the therapist is necessarily aligned with the parents. Rather, the teachers should learn that the therapist's and parents' primary goals are to ameliorate the child's behavior problems and to optimize the child's social and academic development. These goals are essentially the same as those of the teachers. Later in this chapter, we discuss strategies for resolving the difficulties that sometimes exist in the interactions between the parents and the school system.

If, during the conference, the teachers request advice regarding the management of the child's behavior, the therapist should feel free to give whatever feedback is appropriate. The therapist might have some specific suggestions or might require additional information before making suggestions. In either case, the therapist should try to respond to the teachers' requests. Finally, at the conclusion of the conference, the therapist should express appreciation for the teachers' assistance and ask if the teachers would be willing to assist the therapist in the implementation of interventions, if necessary.

The therapist should explain that teacher assistance would take two general forms. First, the therapist would appreciate feedback from the teachers regarding the logic and probability of success of recommendations for school-based interventions. Such feedback and the therapist's flexible response to the feedback will enhance the teachers' cooperation with these interventions. Second, the therapist should ask if the teachers would be willing to devote several minutes per day to assist in the implementation of therapeutic interventions. Because teachers are generally underpaid and overworked, most will hesitate to devote an inordinate percentage of their class time to the needs of one behavior problem student. Hence, the therapist's recommendations for school-based interventions should require as little of the teachers' time as possible. In fact, the therapist should place most of the responsibility for school-based interventions on the parents (e.g., by implementing contingencies at home that are based on the child's behavior in school). Such an arrangement fosters parental cooperation with the school and helps to assure the teachers' continued support of treatment efforts.

After the therapist has obtained the information needed to design the interventions, the therapist should recontact the teachers. If the therapist established good rapport with the teachers during the initial conference, a phone conversation might suffice. If, however, the conference did not go well or if the interventions are very complicated, the therapist should meet with the teachers in person. During this phone call or meeting, the therapist should provide a general overview of the presenting problems and of the therapist's intervention plans. This overview can pertain to family problems (assuming that the therapist has a signed release of information), but should do so in only a very general way. For example, the therapist might indicate that the family is currently under a great deal of stress and that treatment will attempt to help family members cope with this stress. The therapist does not need to specify the exact nature of the stress (e.g., parental separation, incest, alcoholism) but should attempt to elicit the teachers' empathy with the family's overall situation. In fact, the therapist may find that the teachers are already quite familiar with the family's problems, since some children (especially younger children) do not hesitate to discuss family difficulties with their teachers and classmates. Nevertheless, the therapist's communication to the teachers that the family is seeking professional help may play an important role in eliciting the teachers' empathy and cooperation. Previously, the teachers may have viewed the parents' failure to seek professional help, in the face of serious family problems, as an indication of their lack of support not only for the child but also for the teachers' efforts to educate the child.

After providing an overview of the presenting problems and intervention plans, the therapist should detail the exact nature of the recommended school-based interventions. Then, as noted above, the therapist should elicit feedback from the teachers and, if necessary, change the interventions so that a mutually agreeable treatment plan is formulated.

When presenting recommendations for school-based interventions, one of the most difficult situations that the therapist can encounter is when the interventions pertain to problems with the teachers' behavior-management practices. It is common, for example, for teachers to contribute inadvertently to child misbehavior by using inappropriate reinforcement contingencies in the classroom. In such cases, the therapist must be especially skillful in presenting recommendations to the teachers. Because professionals do not respond favorably to communications that suggest incompetence, the therapist must use positive terms whenever possible. The following two cases exemplify this process.

Albert was a third-grader who was referred by his mother at the recommendation of his teacher, Ms. White. The therapist's conference with Ms. White revealed that Albert had at least one aggressive outburst toward another child each day. The therapist expressed concern over the disruptive influence that these outbursts had on the class and asked Ms. White how she responded to them. Ms. White reported that following each outburst she would turn the class over to her aide, take Albert aside for about 15 minutes, and explain to him that his behavior was harming others as well as himself. Because Albert was quite fond of Ms. White, the net effect of her discipline was to reward Albert with 15 minutes of individualized attention.

Later, after the therapist completed her assessment, she framed her feedback to Ms. White in the following way. The therapist noted that for 99% of children, Ms. White's discipline strategy was optimal; it is critically important for children to learn to consider the needs and rights of others and the optimal context for such learning is child-adult discussions, rather than corporal punishment. For Albert, however, the discussions were having the opposite effect of what was intended. This was primarily because Albert liked Ms. White so much that he was willing to engage in aggressive behavior just to have some time alone with her. The therapist then guided Ms. White in developing alternative disciplines that would not reinforce Albert's aggressive behavior. The therapist and Ms. White jointly decided to use a 10-minute timeout procedure when Albert misbehaved, and to give him special attention (e.g., praise, a pat on the hand) when he was behaving appropriately.

In a similar case, John was a physically disabled 9-year-old who was referred by his mother for a variety of behavior problems. The therapist-teacher conference revealed that John also presented several problems at school. For example, about five times per day John would fall to the floor while walking with his braces, scream in agony, and disrupt the classroom for about ten minutes. When it was learned that John walked at home without falling and that he received considerable attention and sympathy for his falls at school, the therapist concluded that the falling behavior was manipulative and was being maintained by the attention from his classmates and teachers. In explaining this interpretation to the teacher, the therapist noted that it is almost humanly impossible to ignore the pleading cries of a disabled child. Thus, it was easy to understand how John had learned to manipulate his teacher and classmates. The therapist stressed, however, that if John was allowed to continue to control his environment by manipulating the sympathy of others, this would have very negative implications for the development of his future independence and self-reliance.

Within this framework, then, the therapist and teacher jointly developed school-based interventions that required his teachers and classmates to ignore John's falls and cries. Instead of being soothed and helped to his feet by others, John was to crawl to the nearest chair and get up by himself. After approximately ten more falls, this intervention eliminated John's manipulative behavior. Thereafter, John would fall only when an outsider was visiting the classroom. (The visitor would respond with dismay as the teacher and entire class ignored the pleading cries of the prostrate disabled child.)

The amelioration of behavior problems is an important emphasis of treatment, but it is not the only therapeutic goal. Teachers are also in a unique position to foster positive peer relations among children. Because the behavior of children tends to gravitate to the norm of their immediate peers, a problem child can be moved away from other disruptive children and seated in closer proximity to well-behaved children. Similarly, as described by Minuchin and Shapiro (1983), teachers can structure reading groups and class projects in ways that encourage cooperative behavior and enable shy children to contribute to the group process. Although such interventions might not be the primary focus, the therapist should always be sensitive to opportunities to enhance child development.

COGNITIVE DEVELOPMENT

Children and adolescents who present behavior problems often have poor grades and low academic achievement. Although parents' concerns about misbehavior may overshadow their concerns about low academic achievement, the therapist should still consider the child's academic functioning in the assessment of therapeutic needs. As noted previously, academic achievement is an important consideration because of its association with future socioeconomic functioning. Moreover, academic and social difficulties frequently reflect the same underlying systemic dysfunctions. Thus, an understanding of one area of difficulty can facilitate an understanding of the other area.

In this section, we briefly discuss some of the different causes of children's academic problems, and we offer several guidelines for assessing these causes. In the subsequent section, interventions that pertain to these causes are suggested. Before proceeding, however, it is extremely important to emphasize that this brief discussion is only intended to provide the reader with a cursory overview of the general issues and problems in the area of children's academic difficulties. Relatively inexperienced therapists and therapists with little knowledge of psychometric theory and psychoeducational assessment should always obtain consultation from professionals who specialize in the diagnosis and treatment of children with learning problems (e.g., school psychologists) when significant academic difficulties are suspected. In fact, even for the most experienced therapists, it is often necessary to obtain outside consultation for the assessment of children's academic problems.

Having offered this caution, we will now discuss several factors that can contribute singly or in combination to poor academic performance. These factors include low intellectual abilities, learning disabilities, inadequate learning environments, emotional problems, family disturbances, and sensory/motor handicaps. An evaluation of these factors requires a working knowledge of family and peer systems (as discussed in previous chapters) as well as a familiarity with commonly used educational tests and the resources that are available within the school system.

Low Intellectual Abilities

The most common cause of poor academic performance is low intellectual abilities. Though a comprehensive discussion of strategies for intellectual assessment and interpretation of test scores is beyond the scope of this chapter, we strongly recommend that therapists who work with children and adolescents become familiar with several important issues in the areas of intellectual and academic assessment. Such familiarity can be obtained by reviewing excellent texts such as Sattler (1988) and Anastasi (1987).

To highlight the importance of developing a working knowledge of intellectual and academic assessment, two of the many issues that are pertinent to this area are discussed. The first issue pertains to changes in the stability of IQ test scores during the life span. There is strong evidence that intellectual abilities are relatively stable after several years of age (Honzik, 1976; McCall, Appelbaum, & Hogarty, 1973). However, there is also considerable evidence that the intellectual abilities of individuals can change dramatically throughout their life span (Honzik, MacFarlane, & Allen, 1948; Wohlwill, 1980) and that IQ scores for young children can be quite unstable. Therefore, it would be quite erroneous to conclude that a 3-year-old who obtained an IQ score of 55 on the Stanford-Binet Intelligence Scale was mentally retarded. Although this child is at significant risk for future intellectual and academic difficulties, the child could evidence a spurt of cognitive development that would subsequently place the child within the average range of intellectual functioning. Moreover, tests that are used with young children have greater measurement error. The therapist who is not aware of these realities might design therapeutic interventions (e.g, helping parents to adjust to having a handicapped child) that are predicated on false assumptions.

The second issue pertains to the situational determinants of intellectual test performance. Situational determinants include factors such as the interpersonal qualities of the examiner, child sociocultural characteristics, child emotional and behavioral problems, and the presence of sensory/motor handicaps. The importance of understanding situational determinants is exemplified in the following case.

The psychologist, who was a member of a multidisciplinary pediatric team, was asked by the nurse to determine whether a $5^{1}/_{2}$-year-old girl, Tonia, was cognitively prepared for placement in first grade. Tonia lived in a low-income housing project with her unemployed mother and her siblings. The nurse referred Tonia because she evidenced little communicative competence during her visits to the clinic. The psychologist interviewed and tested Tonia in his office. Tonia gave only one-word responses to test items that required verbalization and was hesitant to respond to items that were nonverbal in nature. Overall, Tonia scored in the borderline range of intellectual functioning. Based on these data, the psychologist usually would have recommended that Tonia delay entry into first grade. However, because Tonia's mother felt that her daughter had not performed optimally on the tests, the psychologist agreed to observe Tonia's behavior at home. Here, the psychologist heard Tonia use compound sentences when playing with her siblings. The use of such expressive language showed that Tonia possessed considerably greater ability than was evident during the psychologist's formal evaluation. Hence, Tonia's cognitive abilities had most likely been underestimated because of the strange and unfamiliar setting in which she was tested.

To determine whether a child's poor academic performance is a direct product of low intellectual abilities, it is necessary to obtain at least two types of psychoeducational data. The first data set is obtained from the results of tests that assess the child's intellectual strengths and weaknesses. We strongly urge the therapist not to rely on a group-administered IQ test for this purpose. It is difficult to make accurate interpretations of test scores if the therapist is not certain that the child performed optimally during the administration of the test. Knowledge of the child's level of motivation during the test is usually not available to the supervisor of a group-administered test. Such information, however, can be obtained by the professional who gives the child an intelligence test that is designed for individual administration.

The therapist should choose an IQ test that determines the child's intellectual strengths and weaknesses, rather than one that simply provides an overall IQ score. An evaluation of strengths and weaknesses can be used to identify special problems (e.g., learning disabilities) and can facilitate the formulation of educational interventions. For example, a child with low verbal skills and high analytic/mechanical skills can be steered toward an academic curriculum that emphasizes the latter.

In our experience, the Wechsler Intelligence Scale for Children-Revised (WISC-R; Wechsler, 1974) provides the most useful evaluation of children's intellectual abilities. As described by Sattler (1988), the reliability and validity of the WISC-R are well established for both White and minority children. An important advantage of the WISC-R is that it provides a meaningful profile of children's intellectual strengths and weaknesses. Factor analytic research has shown that the subscales assess three primary dimensions of intellectual performance (Kaufman, 1975). The first factor, *verbal comprehension*, is comprised of the information, similarities, comprehension, and vocabulary subscales. Because of the highly verbal nature of most academic coursework, this factor is the strongest predictor of achievement in classes such as social studies and English. The second factor, *perceptual organization*, is comprised of the block design, picture completion, and object assembly subscales. This factor taps abilities that are nonverbal or analytic/mechanical in nature. The third factor has been labeled *attention/freedom from distractibility* and is comprised of the coding, digit span, and arithmetic subscales. Although there is some debate regarding the conceptualization of this factor (e.g., Ownby & Matthews, 1985), most investigators consider this factor to be an index of the child's ability to focus attention on a task and to not be distracted by extraneous stimuli.

When interpreting the WISC-R results, we recommend that the therapist ignore the verbal versus performance distinction that is made on the WISC-R record form. This distinction is based on the face validity of the subscales, rather than on empirical findings. Instead, we recommend that the therapist calculate extrapolated scores for each of the factor analytically derived dimensions (e.g., verbal comprehension total score = [information scaled score + comprehension scaled score + vocabulary scaled score + similarities scaled score] /4 × 10). As described shortly, these factor scores can be very helpful in determining the nature of a learning problem.

Achievement test scores are the second set of data that should be obtained when evaluating poor academic performance. The Wide Range Achievement Test-Revised (WRAT-R; Jastak & Wilkinson, 1984) provides an excellent estimate of the child's spelling, arithmetic, and word recognition skills. An advantage of the WRAT-R is that it requires the child to perform in a way that is similar to that required in the classroom (e.g., the child must actively calculate arithmetic problems). The Peabody Individual Achievement Test (PIAT; Dunn & Markwardt, 1970) also provides an excellent measure of academic achievement, and its multiple-choice format makes it useful for testing disabled children. In some cases, it may also be necessary to obtain more specialized evaluations of children's math skills (e.g., the KeyMath Diagnostic Test; Connolly,

Natchman, & Pritchett, 1971) and reading skills (e.g., the Gray Oral Reading Test; Gray, 1967).

When the child's intellectual skills and achievement levels have been assessed, it is then possible to determine whether the child is functioning at levels that are above, below, or commensurate with his or her intellectual abilities. In making such a determination, a general rule of thumb is that the child's level of academic achievement in verbal subjects (e.g., spelling, English, civics, history, science) should be consistent with the child's verbal comprehension skills. For example, a 10-year-old fifth-grader who has a 130 verbal comprehension IQ should be expected to achieve at an approximately eighth-grade level (i.e., mental age = IQ + chronological age; 13-year-olds are usually in eighth grade). Likewise, a 10-year-old with a 100 verbal comprehension IQ should be achieving at a fifth-grade level, and a 10-year-old with an 80 verbal comprehension IQ should be achieving at a third-grade level (i.e., this latter child's mental age is eight years, and 8-year-olds are typically in third grade). In developing these estimates, however, it is also important to consider the reliabilities of the test instruments (Reynolds, 1981) and the phenomenon of regression to the mean (Yule, Rutter, Berger, & Thompson, 1974). That is, achievement grade levels for a child with a high IQ should be slightly less than expected from the preceding examples, and achievement scores for a child with a low IQ should be slightly more than expected.

Returning to the main point of this section, poor grades and low achievement are often the direct result of low intellectual abilities. A 12-year-old seventh-grader with an 85 IQ is going to have much more difficulty with academic materials than a 12-year-old seventh-grader with a 115 IQ. The former child will probably be achieving 1.5 to 2.0 years below grade level and will have approximately a "C" average in a typical public school. Thus, if this child had been referred for low grades and the therapist determined that the child was achieving at a fifth-grade level, the therapist would probably conclude that the child's achievement was consistent with his or her abilities and that interventions seemed unwarranted. If, however, the child was earning "Fs" in school, the therapist would investigate the situation further because the child was probably capable of earning higher grades. Similarly, if the child was found to be achieving at a third-grade level, such achievement would be below expectations and the therapist would need to consider the role of other variables that are associated with academic difficulties.

Finally, it should be emphasized that low achievement is a relative term, and that judgments about achievement must always be considered within the context of the child's abilities and resources. If, for example, the 12-year-old seventh-grader had an IQ of 130, this child would be expected to achieve well above grade level and to earn mostly "As". In this case, achievement at a seventh-grade level or course grades in the "C" to "B" range would be cause for concern.

Interventions.   When low achievement is the result of low intellectual abilities, several therapeutic issues may arise in regard to the family system, the child, and the school system. First, it is important that the parents appreciate the realistic limitations of the child's intellectual abilities. Often, parents will be disappointed that their child's low achievement is simply the result of low intellectual abilities, rather than of a seemingly more complicated cause such as dyslexia. Parents must learn to accept that their child might benefit more from vocational training than from a college-oriented curriculum.

Similarly, parents must reward and respect the child's maximum academic achievements (e.g., grades in the "C" range) to the same degree that they might reinforce a more intelligent sibling's highest achievements (e.g., grades in the "A" range).

The therapist can promote acceptance of the child's academic limitations by emphasizing the child's psychosocial strengths and how these strengths are often more strongly associated with successful adult functioning than is academic achievement. For example, perhaps the child is well liked by peers and has maintained a high level of motivation despite academic difficulties. The therapist might note that success in many occupations is determined more by motivation and strong interpersonal skills than by intellectual abilities. Likewise, qualities such as kindness, generosity, and a sense of humor are more important than intelligence in the development of friendships and successful family relations. Many individuals who did not do well in school have rich and fulfilling lives as adults.

It is extremely important for the therapist to reframe the value of academic achievement when the parents equate such achievement with the child's (and perhaps their own) worth as an individual. We have seen parents who require their elementary school-aged child to study four to five hours per day. These parents are aware of the value of an education and are usually attempting to overcome their child's intellectual limitations through the force of effort. The therapist must teach such parents that there are more important aspects of childhood than course grades. It might be more beneficial in the long run, for example, if the parents encouraged their child to develop close friendships and to experience diverse aspects of life such as athletics and the arts. Similarly, the parents should be told that their intense educational efforts may have an effect that is the opposite of the one intended. It is possible that after several years of academic frustration and failure to achieve up to parental expectations, the child might rebel in a potentially destructive manner.

A second focus of intervention may pertain to the child's attitudes and self-efficacy. In some cases, low achieving children feel incompetent, especially if academic achievement is strongly emphasized by the family. In a treatment process similar to that described for the parents, it is important to provide the child with a broader view of his or her strengths and weaknesses. Although the child might not be gifted intellectually, the therapist should stress the significance of the child's emotional and interpersonal strengths. The child should learn to be proud of these strengths and to value them highly. Moreover, the therapist should emphasize to the child (and to the parents) that motivation and effort are often more important dimensions of behavior than outcome. If, despite reasonable effort, the child earns a poor grade, this should not be viewed negatively.

The third focus of intervention pertains to the school context. Because the child might fail more often than he or she succeeds, the teachers should be encouraged to reinforce the child's efforts rather than waiting to reinforce the successes. If the child's achievement is substantially below that of classmates, the child might also benefit from being placed in a resource class for one or more hours each day, or even retained for a grade. This is an especially viable alternative if the child is socially immature or does not have adequate peer relations with classmates. The child's self-esteem and social competence might benefit from placement with children who have similar levels of cognitive skill and social maturity.

Learning Disabilities

Barkley (1981) concluded that learning disabilities represent one of the most confusing and disorganized areas in the field of child psychology. An important aspect of this confusion pertains to the diagnosis of learning disabilities. The most widely used definition of a learning disability (LD) defines this term largely by the exclusion of other causes of academic problems (*Federal Register*, December 29, 1977).

> "Specific learning disability" means a disorder in one or more of the basic psychological processes involved in understanding or in using language, spoken or written, which may manifest itself in an imperfect ability to listen, think, speak, read, write, spell or to do mathematical calculations. The term includes such conditions as perceptual handicaps, brain injury, minimal brain dysfunction, dyslexia, and developmental aphasia. The term does not include children who have learning problems which are primarily the result of visual, hearing, or motor handicaps, of mental retardation, of emotional disturbance, or of environmental, cultural, or economic disadvantage.

The reader should note several points in regard to this definition of LD. First, it suggests that the child with LD is achieving below expectations. As Sattler (1988) has noted, however, the guidelines do not specify how wide the discrepancy between achievement and abilities should be. Second, this definition of LD also includes conditions such as minimal brain dysfunction and dyslexia. Minimal brain dysfunction, however, is regarded as a catch-all diagnostic category that is rarely used in the scientific community (Campbell & Werry, 1986). Similarly, conditions such as dyslexia have very little explanatory power, that is, a child may be diagnosed as dyslexic after showing severe retardation in reading and writing in the absence of intellectual or cultural handicaps. Then, the diagnosis of dyslexia is used to explain why the child cannot read or write. Finally, the definition of LD excludes children whose learning difficulties seem to be associated with physical handicaps, emotional disturbance, and sociocultural disadvantage. It seems quite possible, however, that such children can also present learning disabilities that are independent of their particular handicap or disadvantage.

There is also little consensus regarding the etiology of learning disabilities. During the 1940s and 1950s, the visual perception theory was very popular. Vellutino (1978), however, concluded that this perspective has little empirical support. In a review of the literature, Ross (1976) has suggested that the fundamental problem of LD is the delayed acquisition of selective attention skills. From this perspective, deficits in selective attention are thought to account for the tendency of LD children to be highly distractible and to make errors of omission and inclusion in academic work. These errors may appear to be misperceptions but are actually the result of inattention. Other reviewers (e.g., Black, 1976), however, have not supported the selective attention hypothesis. Moreover, Barkley (1981) has concluded that it is a fundamental mistake to regard LD as a homogeneous disorder. He suggested that LD should be viewed instead as a broad educational classification that subsumes a diverse group of disorders of reading, spelling, writing, and mathematics.

Based on our clinical experience, we have come to favor Ross's (1976) conceptualization of learning disabilities: Children with poor academic performance that has not been explained by other factors (e.g., low abilities, handicaps, family dysfunction, emotional problems, motivation, etc.) tend to have poor attention and concentration skills.

For example, we have observed that these children have usually scored much lower on the attention/freedom from distractibility factor of the WISC-R than on the verbal comprehension and perceptual organization factors. These clinical observations are consistent with Rourke's (1978) finding that the arithmetic, coding, information, and digit-span subscales tend to be low in LD children.

Although it is likely that some clinicians and researchers will disagree about the role that attention and concentration skills play in LD, there can be little doubt that attentional skills significantly contribute to children's capacity to benefit from academic instruction. We have observed that children who have considerable ability to concentrate often achieve somewhat higher than would be expected on the basis of their verbal comprehension and perceptual organization abilities alone. Likewise, children with poor attention skills often do not perform up to expectations based on their verbal comprehension and perceptual organization abilities; apparently these children are so easily distracted during school that they do not encode information that they are perfectly capable of learning. The following example highlights the salient role that attentional skills can play in children's ability to achieve in the classroom.

Bobby was a 13-year-old eighth-grader who was referred by a pediatric social worker. The social worker felt that Bobby was capable of earning much better grades than he was currently achieving. The therapist learned that, despite the family's impoverished living situation, Bobby's mother was very supportive of his educational efforts. She frequently bought paperback books for her son, and she often took him to the library. Bobby thoroughly enjoyed reading and read at least one book each week. Moreover, the teacher reported that Bobby was highly motivated and well behaved in the classroom, but that he was also highly distractible. Socially, Bobby was somewhat isolated, though he did have one close friend.

Intellectual testing revealed that Bobby had exceptionally high verbal abilities. His receptive vocabulary (Peabody Picture Vocabulary Test-Revised; Dunn & Dunn, 1981) was at a 19-year-old level (IQ = 145), and his verbal comprehension skills (WISC-R) were above the 130 IQ level. However, Bobby's performances on word recognition (WRAT-R) and reading comprehension (PIAT) were both at an eighth-grade level. This low achievement, relative to his high abilities, was probably the product of Bobby's very low attention and freedom from distractibility skills (70 IQ). Hence, Bobby had the verbal abilities of a much older adolescent, but his ability to concentrate was at the level of an average 9-year-old child. Bobby's gross impairment in attentional skills interfered with his capacity to attain maximum benefit from normal classroom instruction and resulted in an achievement level that was well below his verbal abilities.

Interventions.   Unless the therapist has considerable expertise in the diagnosis and treatment of learning disabilities, he or she should seek the consultation of an educational specialist. In seeking such consultation, however, the therapist should take a conservative and cautious approach. We have obtained recommendations from specialists that seemed more self-serving and idiosyncratic than based on extant knowledge. Some specialists, for example, diagnose every referral as LD and recommend placement in the private school or agency for which they consult. To guard against this type of problem, we recommend that the therapist become personally familiar with community specialists and develop a collaborative relationship with at least one of these professionals. For the therapist who has minimal contact with clients after an educational referral is made, we recommend that follow-ups always be conducted to determine family satisfaction with the specialist's interventions.

We also recommend that the therapist consider several systemic interventions in cases where the LD seems to be linked with an attention deficit. At the individual child level, we use treatment techniques derived from cognitive behavior therapy (e.g., self-instruction training) to improve the child's ability to concentrate and to ignore distractions. These interventions are described more extensively in Chapter 2 and by Keogh and Hall (1984). At the family level, we recommend that parents provide the child with a place to study that is free of auditory and visual distractions. Similarly, on the school level, it is helpful if the classroom is as free of distractions as possible. Perhaps the teacher can seat the child away from such distractions as windows, doors, and talkative classmates. The worst type of classroom environment for a distractible child would be the open classroom model that was popular in the 1970s and is still used in some locales.

Finally, most school systems provide special services for children who are diagnosed as LD. These services usually include individualized instruction from resource teachers for several hours per week. Although the availability of these services is often limited, we have found that if the therapist and parents are persistent in their requests, the child is more likely to receive the appropriate assistance. Another viable option is the use of professional tutors. We have collaborated with tutors who have used motivational and instructional techniques that have resulted in dramatic gains in achievement. We recommend, however, that the therapist take the same care in identifying competent tutors as in identifying LD specialists.

Inadequate Learning Environments

In some cases, a child's academic difficulties are associated with a school environment that does not fully promote the child's motivation and efforts to learn (see e.g., Coleman, 1966). Certain characteristics of teachers and of schools are linked with low achievement.

Low achievement can be the product of poor teaching. We have observed several cases in which teachers evidenced little commitment to their profession and were not flexible in their approach to teaching. A commitment to teaching is demonstrated by good class preparation, substantive review of class and homework assignments, and energetic and creative presentations of learning material. On a process level, these teacher behaviors convey the importance of learning to students and provide a model of enthusiasm for and commitment to the learning process. Teachers who interact with children in a responsive and flexible fashion are also more likely to motivate children's academic efforts. For example, some children who are extending minimal effort on academic tasks will respond positively to individualized supportive encouragement from the teacher, whereas other children might need a more forceful approach that may include the use of contingencies and parental involvement. In either case, the teacher should not passively permit a child to be "lazy" but should attempt remediation through all possible means. Unfortunately, some teachers extend minimal effort in the classroom and make as few demands on their students as possible. One elementary school teacher, for example, treated her class as if it was an after-school daycare program, devoting extensive time to recreational activities and very little time to basic education.

The therapist's assessment of the teacher's competence requires a great deal of tact and sensitivity. To accomplish this task, the therapist can ask a series of carefully framed questions within the natural flow of the therapist-teacher discussion regarding the child. By adopting an attitude of helpful interest toward the child's and teacher's classroom activities, the therapist can gather considerable information about the teacher's competencies. The therapist should determine (1) how the teacher structures the class day; (2) whether it is possible to accommodate to individual needs of the students (e.g., how the teacher instructs an especially bright child); (3) how classroom disruptions are handled; (4) whether the teacher is satisfied with his or her career choice and believes that the school is well run; (5) how much contact the teacher has with the children's parents; and (6) how important the teacher regards such contact. Of course, the therapist should also pursue lines of discussion that may yield additional pertinent information.

Although the teacher has the most direct contact with the student, the educational tone of the school is largely set by the principal. Many principals are superb educators and motivators who maximize teachers' and students' efforts, but some have essentially abdicated their leadership responsibilities. They fail to discourage teacher incompetence and laziness, they permit students to engage in disruptive behavior, they do not inform parents of truancy, and they refuse to acknowledge serious problems (e.g., the sale and use of drugs) that are pervasive in the school.

One index of a principal's competence is the willingness to cooperate with responsible professionals who are not employed by the school system. Competent principals are usually very cooperative with professionals who are working with one of their students. Although the therapist's meetings with school personnel may represent an inconvenience for the school and may consume valuable time, these principals recognize that the professional's goal is to promote the well-being of the student and that this goal is consistent with those of the school. Moreover, successful principals are often pleased to "show off" their school. On the other hand, when the professional encounters considerable resistance from a teacher or principal, it is usually a sign that the school is not functioning as well as it might. If the therapist is cordial and persistent, however, cooperation can usually be gained. Indeed, of the hundreds of school evaluations that we have either conducted or supervised, teacher/principal cooperation has been flatly refused in only two instances.

Interventions.   Teacher incompetence and principal indifference are not the types of problems that can be ameliorated by the therapist. Therapist and parent complaints regarding such problems to school administrators are likely to have little effect. Like most social institutions, schools systems are highly resistant to change and do not respond favorably to protagonists from outside the system. Thus, in situations where a child's low achievement is associated with teacher incompetence, we rarely recommend that this issue be addressed directly. Such tactics are unlikely to achieve positive results and may result in subtle forms of retaliation against the child.

We are not suggesting that the therapist *never* confront the educational system but that the decision regarding confrontation should be taken very seriously and should weigh the cost/benefit ratio of the possible outcomes. In situations more serious than those involving a child's low achievement, the cost of inaction can be very high, and the therapist should support and encourage the parents to strongly advocate for their child's rights. In one such situation, for example, the school system was refusing to provide appropriate, but expensive, educational services for an autistic child whose family was in therapy. The therapist gladly acted as an advocate on the child's and family's behalf. In another case, a teacher was verbally abusive to an 8-year-old girl, and the therapist supported the parents' efforts to seek a legal remedy to the situation.

If the therapist and parents do not address teacher incompetence directly, what should the parents do when such incompetence is linked with their child's low achievement? If it is the beginning of the school year, the therapist might provide the parents with strategies for convincing the principal to allow the child to change classrooms. If it is the end of the school year, the therapist might advise the parents that it is too late to effect any substantial change, and that they should attempt to insure that the child is placed with a competent teacher in the fall.

If it is the middle of the school year, the situation is more problematic. In such cases, we typically recommend that the parents establish frequent contact with the child's teacher and attempt to make this contact as cordial as possible. The professed purpose of this contact is for the parents to assist the teacher in educating the child. There are three unstated additional purposes, however: (1) periodic contact with the parents might encourage the teacher to feel more accountable for his or her performance; (2) positive parent-teacher contact may lay the groundwork for improved teacher effort, or may provide the parents with a better case if they ever choose to confront the school administration directly; and (3) frequent parent-teacher meetings may reduce the parents' anxieties and feelings of helplessness.

In rare instances, teacher incompetence is not an isolated phenomenon and, with the principal's tacit approval, a laissez-faire attitude toward education has been adopted by most of the school's faculty. In such cases, the only viable alternative is to enroll the child in a different school. Unfortunately, this alternative may present logistic and financial hardships for the family that are more problematic than the child's low achievement. Here, the therapist and parents may be forced to choose among several unsatisfactory alternatives.

Child Emotional Problems

A fourth cause of low academic achievement is psychosocial dysfunction in the child. Some children, for example, are extremely afraid of making mistakes and consequently do not answer test items unless they are certain of the correct response. The grades and achievement test scores of such children may suffer considerably because of this response bias. Other children are quite anxious and may be intimidated by the social and academic demands of the school context. Such anxiety can interfere with their achievement and can make these children the target of school bullies whose threats serve to exacerbate the children's fears. Still other children may present somatic complaints and may devote considerable effort toward attempting to create a medical excuse to leave school early. As discussed in Chapter 2, children and adolescents may also hold unrealistic expectations that impede their performance in school (e.g., "school should be fun"). The therapist can assess the nature of such problems during the usual clinical assessment of the child and family, and during the therapist-teacher conference.

Interventions.   In cases of serious emotional and behavioral difficulties, the treatment of the child's problems in the family, peer, and school contexts usually take precedence over the design of interventions for low academic achievement. In such cases, educational problems often decrease when the child's psychosocial functioning improves. In cases of mild to moderate emotional and behavioral difficulties, the therapist might consider addressing the academic difficulties using the same set of treatment strategies that he or she is applying to the other presenting problems. For example, with a fearful and anxious adolescent boy, the therapist might teach the adolescent to cope with an upcoming exam in the same way that he would learn to cope with asking a girl out for a date. Similarly, with a noncompliant and irresponsible girl, the parents might link after-school privileges (e.g., telephone, television, stereo) to the girl's compliance with both parental demands and school assignments.

Family Dysfunction

The academic achievement of many children is disrupted during times of family conflict and stress. It is difficult for children to concentrate on coursework when their parents are arguing at night, or when a parent is experiencing severe emotional problems. Similarly, if there has been an illness or death in the family, it is common for the child's classroom performance to deteriorate. In evaluating the association between family dysfunction and the child's academic difficulties, the therapist should weigh the information gathered during the family interviews and the teacher conference. Teachers are often quite perceptive in their ability to link changes in classroom behavior with possible family crises.

Interventions.   The therapist's first priority should be to help family members cope with existing crises and to ameliorate family dysfunctions. When such difficulties have been abated, it is usually much easier to ameliorate a child's academic problems. As noted in earlier chapters, the success of therapeutic interventions is often predicated on parental support of and cooperation with the interventions. In cases when family difficulties do not seem resolvable, we recommend that the therapist consider the use of individually oriented intervention strategies for the child (see Chapter 2).

Some children who show decreased academic performance during a period of prolonged family stress continue to evidence academic problems after family dysfunctions have been ameliorated. In most cases, the academic problems are associated with one or more of the other determinants of academic difficulties that are described in this chapter and can be treated accordingly.

Sometimes, however, the problems reflect a change in the child's attitudes toward school and motivation regarding classwork. During a long family crisis, it is common for parents to devote less attention to their child's academic performance. The child, who is also distracted by the crisis, may follow the parents' lead and devote less energy to coursework. As time passes, the child may learn that it is easier to play and watch television after school than to study. Such work habits may be difficult to change. In these cases, we recommend that the parents use several strategies to enhance their child's motivation. These strategies include the development of a structured daily study session and an increase in parental monitoring of homework and coursework. The parents should also implement appropriate contingencies for changes in the child's study habits and motivation.

Sensorimotor Problems

Low academic achievement can also be the direct result of sensory or motor problems. For example, extensive research has documented the learning difficulties of hearing impaired children (e.g., Meadow, 1980). Similarly, it is not difficult to appreciate the learning problems that children with physical disabilities, such as cerebral palsy or blindness, might experience. In varying degrees, these problems can interfere with the reception, internal processing, and expression of information.

In all cases, the therapist should consider the possibility that a sensorimotor problem is interfering with the child's ability to learn. Almost all school systems routinely conduct hearing and vision screenings. Especially with young children, the therapist should ask the parents about the results from recent eye exams or hearing tests. It is possible for a sensorimotor problem to have been previously misdiagnosed. For example, Mickey was a 7-year-old boy from a very poor rural family. Mickey had no receptive or expressive speech and was referred for educational recommendations regarding his presumedly severe mental retardation. By using nonverbal communications, the therapist asked Mickey to draw a picture of a man. Mickey's drawing was immediately recognized as Mr. Spock of the "Star Trek" television series. The therapist obtained specialized consultation and learned that Mickey was profoundly deaf and had average nonverbal intellectual abilities. Apparently, Mickey's hearing impairment had not been detected two years earlier because he had presented severe behavior problems during the audiological examination.

Similarly, it is possible to misdiagnose the intellectual abilities of children with motor disabilities. Patsy, for example, was a 10-year-old girl who was assumed to be severely mentally retarded. She had severe cerebral palsy, was confined to a wheelchair, had very limited use of her limbs, and had no speech. The special educational consultant, however, taught Patsy to blink her eyes to indicate response choices on the Peabody Picture Vocabulary Test. Patsy scored within the average range of intellectual functioning. Although she appeared to be severely mentally retarded, Patsy was actually receiving and processing information quite well. Unfortunately, her physical impairment had prevented her from communicating her intellectual abilities.

Interventions. In assessing the intellectual and academic capabilities of children with suspected or confirmed sensorimotor problems, the therapist should consult with specialists. We prefer to refer such children to pediatric facilities (e.g., a handicapped children's clinic) that have multidisciplinary evaluation teams. At such facilities, children are examined by numerous professionals (e.g., audiologists, pediatricians, educational specialists, psychologists, social workers, and speech therapists) who specialize in the diagnosis and treatment of sensorimotor problems. The staff of such facilities often takes a broad and systemic view of any identified problems, designing interventions that meet the physical, educational, and psychosocial needs of the child, as well as interventions that help the family to cope with the child's handicap and other extant difficulties. In light of the comprehensive expertise provided by the pediatric staff, we usually recommend that the therapist transfer management of the case to these professionals.

THE FAMILY-SCHOOL MESOSYSTEM

Parental involvement in the school system is an important determinant of the child's academic achievement and psychosocial functioning in school. Parental involvement includes activities such as monitoring homework assignments and exam grades, having periodic contact with teachers, supporting extracurricular school functions, using contingencies that are based on the child's efforts and performance, and providing overt support for teachers' educational demands and goals. Parents do not need to have a high level of education to make valuable contributions to the child's progress in school. In fact, Stevenson and Baker (1987) have shown that mothers' involvement in their children's school activities affects the children's school performance independent of maternal educational status.

We strongly recommend, then, that therapists encourage the parents' involvement in their child's educational experiences. In many therapy cases, the parents are already involved and may benefit from suggestions regarding the remediation of specific problems such as low child motivation or reading difficulties. In other cases, family members might not appreciate the significance of the family-school linkage. Here, the therapist can give concrete examples of the long-term effects of education on socioeconomic achievements. The therapist should also recommend that the parents take the initiative in developing the family-school linkage. The therapist might advise parents about how to develop positive relations with teachers, but positive outcomes are enhanced when teachers believe that parental overtures are self-initiated.

The development of the family-school linkage is also dependent on the responsivity of school personnel. Bronfenbrenner (1979, 1986) described several studies that demonstrate the reciprocity of the family-school linkage. Parental involvement in school is promoted when teachers actively enlist parental support for educational goals. Teachers can elicit such support by periodically informing the parents of their child's progress (rather than contacting the parents only when there are problems), by personally inviting parents to the school for conferences, and by occasionally sending brief progress notes home with the child. We know of several elementary school teachers who arrange brief visits with each child's family in their home just before the upcoming school year. Such teacher efforts communicate concern and caring to the parents and facilitate the development of open family-school communication channels. If academic or behavior problems arise during the school year, the teacher and parents have already established a groundwork that will facilitate their ability to resolve problems.

In general, the development of the family-school linkage is the parents' and teacher's responsibility. The therapist might make suggestions to both parties that are intended to facilitate this linkage, but the therapist's role usually precludes extensive direct involvement in this mesosystem unless the family-school linkage is functioning poorly. Difficulties in the family-school mesosystem are usually associated with either parental avoidance of the school system or overt parent-teacher conflict.

Parental Avoidance of the School System

Some children and adolescents achieve below their ability levels because academic achievement is not a high priority for their parents. Many parents do not appreciate the link between education and socioeconomic functioning. Several self-made and financially successful parents have told us that school is of minimal importance for their children because experience is the best education. Similarly, we have observed socioeconomically disadvantaged parents who, based on their own difficulties in school, have a negative bias toward school and show little interest in their children's education. It is unrealistic to expect a child to be interested in and excited about school when the parents are not. Much of the educational experience is hard work, and it is unusual for children to extend considerable academic effort in the absence of parental support and encouragement.

It is relatively simple for the therapist to assess parental support for the child's educational efforts. The therapist can determine (1) how often the parents have contact with the child's teachers; (2) whether the parents are involved in the child's extracurricular activities or school-related organizations such as the PTA; (3) whether the parents monitor the child's homework assignments, inquire about pending examinations, and require the child to bring home test grades; (4) whether the parents have set aside a block of time and a quiet place for the child to study after school; and (5) whether the parents have developed a reward system for good grades and a disciplinary structure for poor grades. This information will provide the therapist with a good idea of the parents' investment in and support for the child's academic achievements.

Interventions. It is often very difficult to change parental indifference toward education. The therapist should present the advantages of education as palpably as possible. In presenting these advantages, the therapist should reframe the parents' primary arguments in ways that decrease their validity. For example, to the self-made parents who feel that education is not an important component to success, the therapist might agree that for these parents that certainly seems to be true. However, the therapist might then ask the parents whether achieving their level of success has been something of a struggle, and whether they want their children to undergo the same struggles in their efforts to succeed. We have not yet met a parent who says "No" to the first question, or "Yes" to the second. The therapist might also ask the parents to indicate the percentage of individuals with their education level who have achieved their level of financial success. The therapist might conclude that although competence and hard work sometimes lead to success for uneducated individuals, these factors almost always lead to success for highly educated individuals.

Another major cause of parental avoidance of the school system is that parents feel intimidated by the school context. We have observed that avoidant parents are often illiterate, have low arithmetic skills, and poor vocabularies. In interactions with more highly educated teachers, the parents' pride may inhibit them from revealing their lack of understanding regarding the teachers' communications and recommendations. To avoid embarrassment in educational situations that involve their children, these parents either minimize the importance of education or avoid educational situations entirely. The teachers, in turn, often interpret the lack of parental involvement as an absence of concern for the child's welfare. In fact, the low achievement of economically disadvantaged children has often been attributed to family apathy toward education (Coleman, 1966).

In such cases, we emphasize to the parents that, in many ways, they can have a greater impact on their child's education than the teachers. The most influential way is to express a strong interest in the child's performance and to support the child's efforts. For example, the parents can inquire about what the child learned in school that day; ask to see the child's classwork; inquire about test results and impending exams; have frequent contact with the child's teacher; sit near the child while he or she is doing homework; and express joy in the child's efforts and achievements. The parents can also restructure home life in ways that promote education. For example, the parents can establish a study hour during which all outside distractions (e.g., music, telephone, television) are eliminated. The parents can also buy inexpensive used magazines and books for the children to read. We have found that such interventions can have considerable impact on children's motivation and achievement. Rodick and Henggeler (1980) identified the 56 lowest achieving seventh-grade students in an inner-city junior high school that served a predominantly Black, lower-income neighborhood. The achievement test scores for these children ranged from 2.0 to 5.8 grade levels. Hence, the highest achieving student was functioning 1.5 grade levels below grade placement.

The researchers randomly assigned these adolescents to one of four equal-size intervention programs (standard reading, nonintervention, SMART, and PUSH), which were conducted during a 10-week period. The adolescents in the standard reading group met for one hour per day with a highly competent school reading teacher who held an advanced degree in reading education. The students in the nonintervention group received no special reading instruction. The adolescents in the SMART (Staats, Minke, Goodwin, & Landeen, 1967) group received intense tutoring from university undergraduates for one hour per day. This tutoring program was highly structured and made liberal use of social reinforcers.

At school, the students in the PUSH group received the same training as those students in the standard reading group. At home, however, the parents implemented strategies that were similar to those advocated by Rev. Jesse Jackson's "PUSH for Excellence" program. The supervisor of the PUSH intervention met with the family of each adolescent in the family's home. The supervisor developed rapport with the family and emphasized the importance of parental involvement and support for the remediation of academic and motivational problems. After discussion, the supervisor asked the parents and adolescent to agree to work together for approximately one hour per weeknight to enhance academic progress. During this time, the television, radio, and other distractions were to be kept to a minimum, and the parents were to share any of a variety of high interest readings (e.g., sports magazines, fashion magazines) or school-related tasks with their child. In addition, the parents were encouraged to become more actively involved in monitoring their children's performance in school, completion of homework, etc. For example, the parents would routinely inquire about test preparation and subsequent performance and respond quite favorably to signs of effort or success. All of the families were cooperative, though some more than others. Following the agreement to restructure the home environment, the supervisor periodically called the family to provide encouragement and support.

The adolescents were given a battery of educational and psychological tests (e.g., PIAT, WISC-R Vocabulary subtest) shortly before the interventions were implemented, immediately after the interventions ended, and at a 6-month follow-up. At the end of the 10-week intervention period, adolescents in the SMART group evidenced considerable gains in vocabulary skills, reading recognition, reading comprehension, and need for achievement. The adolescents in the PUSH group showed moderate gains on these same measures, and the adolescents in the other groups evidenced little change. At 6-month follow-up, however, the gains of the adolescents in the SMART group generally deteriorated, though test scores remained above pretest levels. On the other hand, the adolescents in the PUSH group continued to show improved vocabulary skills, reading recognition, and reading comprehension. In fact, the adolescents in the PUSH group scored higher on these measures than the adolescents in the SMART group. The adolescents in the standard reading and nonintervention groups continued to show little change.

The results of this study demonstrate two important points. First, parents who might seem apathetic toward education are often very willing to make changes to facilitate their children's educational achievement. It is noteworthy that each family in the PUSH group was selected at random and that each family agreed to participate in the project. Moreover, at 6-month follow-up, more than half of these families continued with the PUSH program after the project was formally terminated. Second, these findings clearly show that parental involvement in the remediation of their children's academic and motivational difficulties facilitated academic gains that continued in the absence of outside supervision. This remediation required a restructuring of the family home environment and the initiation of parental participation in the child's learning process. It is important to note that the PUSH supervisor advocated these family changes during his initial contacts with the families within a framework that acknowledged and valued the parents' capabilities. Consistent with the therapeutic style discussed throughout this volume, the supervisor emphasized the strengths of the families.

Family-School Conflict

Children's school performance usually deteriorates when conflicts develop between parents and teachers. In such cases, it is often necessary for the therapist to resolve family-school difficulties and to provide a context for parent-teacher accommodation and cooperation. As the following case suggests, family-school conflicts are often a product of the miscommunications that can occur when parents and teachers are of disparate sociocultural backgrounds.

Bobbie Schiflett was a 7-year-old second-grader who was referred by her teacher, Ms. Withers, to the Department of Human Services (DHS). Bobbie and her family (mother, father, and seven siblings aged 1, 2, 4, 5, 9, 11, and 12 years) lived in a house-trailer in the foothills of rural Appalachia. The trailer had electricity but did not have running water during the winter months, an indoor bathroom, or a telephone. Ms. Withers, whose husband was a professor at a nearby university, referred Bobbie to DHS because she was extremely dirty and her clothes had a foul odor. Ms. Withers had sent several notes home with Bobbie requesting a meeting with Mrs. Schiflett, but had not received a response.

Following the referral from DHS, the therapist first met with the Schiflett family in their home. Mrs. Schiflett reported that the teachers at Bobbie's school looked down on her family and that she had had little contact with these teachers in recent years. The therapist knew that most of the children who attended this school were from relatively affluent middle-class backgrounds. In contrast, Bobbie and her siblings had few clothes and consistently scored at the bottom of their classes on indices of academic achievement.

Next, the therapist met with Ms. Withers at the school. He learned that Bobbie's odor and lack of cleanliness were eliciting ridicule and rejection from her classmates. Moreover, Ms. Withers reported that the Schiflett children received little parental support regarding educational endeavors and that Mrs. Schiflett had threatened a teacher several years ago. After the separate meetings with the parents and the teacher, the therapist concluded that the parent-teacher conflict was clearly impeding the cognitive and social development of the Schiflett children. As one step toward resolving this conflict, the therapist arranged a mother-teacher conference.

Because Mrs. Schiflett did not have her own transportation, the therapist drove her to the school. During the drive, the therapist suggested several strategies that might ease the family-school conflict. Mrs. Schiflett indicated a minimal willingness to follow these suggestions. Then, she pulled out a butcher knife and told the therapist that if his plans didn't work, she had something that would. The therapist indicated that he hoped that they could achieve their goals without cutting up Ms. Withers and that it probably would be a good idea to leave the knife in the car.

During the conference, it became evident to the therapist that Ms. Withers was afraid of Mrs. Schiflett and that Mrs. Schiflett was very intimidated by Ms. Withers' intelligence and relative affluence. The therapist devoted much of his energy toward helping Mrs. Schiflett and Ms. Withers to appreciate their communalities and to gain an understanding of each other's perspectives. For example, Ms. Withers explained that she reported the case to DHS because she was concerned about Bobbie's welfare (not because she wanted DHS to take Mrs. Schiflett's children) and because Mrs. Schiflett had not responded to her requests for a meeting. Similarly, Ms. Withers needed to appreciate that it was very difficult for Mrs. Schiflett to obtain sufficient water for her family's drinking and cooking needs, and that there was rarely enough water left to bathe more than the youngest children. The use of water to wash clothes was a low priority. Likewise, Ms. Withers did not know that Bobbie brought only one of the notes home and that neither Mr. nor Mrs. Schiflett could read. When Mrs. Schiflett realized that Ms. Withers was legitimately concerned for Bobbie's welfare and that Bobbie's lack of cleanliness was beginning to result in ostracism from her peers, her anger subsided, and she agreed that Bobbie's personal hygiene needed to become a higher priority.

This case included several factors that are commonly associated with family-school conflict and the resolution of such conflict. First, the parents and the teacher lived in very different worlds. This was clearly evidenced in their choice of problem-solving strategies: Mrs. Withers wished to discuss the problem and Mrs. Schiflett was ready to fight anyone whom she viewed as a threat to her family. Second, a situation that seemed unacceptable (i.e., Bobbie's filth) became easier to appreciate when the larger systemic context was revealed. Third despite their considerable differences, both Ms. Withers and Mrs. Schiflett had similar goals, that is, the optimal development of the children. Fourth, when individuals with similar goals were brought together by a therapist who valued and appreciated each of their perspectives, the probability increased that mutually satisfactory solutions could be developed.

In other cases of family-school conflict, we have observed exceptionally competent parents who undermined their child's teacher because they believed that the child was not being taught properly. Here, the parent-teacher roles are almost the opposite of the Schiflett case. The parents have high status and are angry about the teacher's alleged incompetence. The process of the therapist's interventions, however, is largely the same; that is, the parents may need to realize that the teacher has the same goals as the parents, but that the teacher has realistic limitations in regard to the attainment of these goals. For example, the teacher might have 25 students in her class, making it impossible to provide individualized attention to each child. Similarly, the child might be behaving in ways that contribute to the extant problem, and the parents might compound the problem by supporting their child rather than the teacher.

Indeed, many cases of family-school conflict are exacerbated by a child who has learned to play the parents and teacher off against each other. For example, the child may tell the teacher, "My mother told me that I don't have to do what you say." Or, the child may tell his father, who is a police officer, that his teacher said that most policemen are corrupt. Similarly, we have seen children who, as an excuse for poor grades or behavior problems, create elaborate stories to convince their parents that the teacher does not like the child and is discriminating against him or her. Parents and teachers are especially vulnerable to such ploys from the child when family-teacher communication channels are not open. In such cases, therefore, it is essential that the therapist bring the parents and teachers together to clear the air. Then, the parents and teachers can develop procedures to immediately and directly deal with any potential problems that the child might present. Open communication between parents and teachers eliminates the ability of the child to play one system against the other.

REFERENCES

Anastasi, A. (1987). *Psychological testing* (6th ed.). New York: Macmillan.

Barkley, R. A. (1981). Learning disabilities. In E. J. Mash & L. G. Terdal (Eds.), *Behavioral assessment of childhood disorders*. New York: Guilford.

Black, F. W. (1976). Cognitive, academic, and behavioral findings in children with suspected and documented dysfunction. *Journal of Learning Disabilities, 9,* 182–184.

Bronfenbrenner, U. (1979). *The ecology of human development: Experiments by nature and design.* Cambridge, MA: Harvard University Press.

Bronfenbrenner, U. (1986). Ecology of the family as a context for human development: Research perspectives. *Developmental Psychology, 22,* 723–742.

Campbell, S. B., & Werry, J. S. (1986). Attention deficit disorder (hyperactivity). In H. C. Quay & J. S. Werry (Eds.), *Psychopathological disorders of childhood* (3rd ed.). New York: Wiley.

Coleman, J. S. (1966). *Equality of educational opportunity?* Washington, DC: Office of Education.

Connolly, A. J., Nachtman, W., & Pritchett, E. M. (1971). *KeyMath Diagnostic Arithmetic Test.* Circle Pines, MN: American Guidance Service.

Dunn, L. M., & Dunn, L. M. (1981). *Peabody Picture Vocabulary Test—Revised.* Circle Pines, MN: American Guidance Service.

Dunn, L. M., & Markwardt, F. C., Jr. (1970). *Peabody Individual Achievement Test.* Circle Pines, MN: American Guidance Service.

Federal Register, December 29, 1977, p. 65083, 121a.541.

Gray, W. S. (1967). *Gray Oral Reading Test*. New York: Bobbs-Merrill.

Honzik, M. P. (1976). Values and limitations of infant tests: An overview. In M. Lewis (Ed.), *Origins of intelligence*. New York: Plenum.

Honzik, M. P., MacFarlane, J. W., & Allen, L. (1948). The stability of mental test performance between two and eighteen years. *Journal of Experimental Education, 17*, 309–324.

Jastak, J. F., & Wilkinson, G. S. (1984). *Wide Range Achievement Test-Revised: Administration Manual*. Wilmington, DE: Jastak Associates.

Kaufman, A. S. (1975). Factor analysis of the WISC-R at ll age levels between 6 1/2 and 16 1/2 years. *Journal of Consulting and Clinical Psychology, 43*, 135–147.

Keogh, B. K., & Hall, R. J. (1984). Cognitive training with learning-disabled pupils. In A. W. Meyers & W. E. Craighead (Eds.), *Cognitive behavior therapy with children*. New York: Plenum.

McCall, R. B., Appelbaum, M. I., & Hogarty, P. S. (1973). Developmental changes in mental performance. *Monographs of the Society for Research in Child Development, 38*, (3, Serial No. 150).

Meadow, K. P. (1980). *Deafness and child development*. Berkeley, CA: University of California Press.

Minuchin, P. P., & Shapiro, E. K. (1983). The school as a context for social development. In E. M. Hetherington (Ed.), *Handbook of child psychology, Vol. 4: Socialization, personality, and social development*. New York: Wiley.

Ownby, R. L., & Matthews, C. G. (1985). On the meaning of the WISC-R third factor: Relations to selected neuropsychological measures. *Journal of Consulting and Clinical Psychology, 53*, 531–534.

Reynolds, C. R. (1981). The fallacy of "two years below grade level for age" as a diagnostic criterion for dyslexia. *Journal of School Psychology, 19*, 350–358.

Rodick, J. D., & Henggeler, S. W. (1980). The short-term and long-term amelioration of academic and motivational deficiencies among low-achieving inner-city adolescents. *Child Development, 51*, 1126–1132.

Ross, A. O. (1976). *Psychological aspects of learning disabilities and reading disorders*. New York: McGraw-Hill.

Rourke, B. P. (1978). Reading, spelling, and arithmetic disabilities: A neuropsychological perspective. In H. R. Myklebust (Ed.), *Progress in learning disabilities* (Vol. 4). New York: Grune & Stratton.

Sattler, J. M. (1988). *Assessment of children* (3rd ed.). San Diego, CA: Jerome M. Sattler.

Staats, A. W., Minke, K. A., Goodwin, W., & Landeen, J. (1967). Cognitive behavior modification: "Motivated learning" reading treatment with subprofessional therapy-technicians. *Behavior Research and Therapy, 5*, 283–299.

Stevenson, D. L., & Baker, D. P. (1987). The family-school relation and the children's school performance. *Child Development, 58*, 1348–1357.

Vellutino, F. R. (1978). Toward an understanding of dyslexia: Psychological factors in specific reading disability. In A. Benton & D. Pearl (Eds.), *Dyslexia: An appraisal of current knowledge*. New York: Oxford University Press.

Wechsler, D. (1974). *Manual for the Wechsler Intelligence Scale for Children-Revised*. New York: Psychological Corporation.

Wohlwill, J. (1980). Cognitive development in childhood. In O. G. Brim & J. Kagan (Eds.), *Constancy and change in human development*. Cambridge, MA: Harvard University Press.

Yule, W., Rutter, M., Berger, M., & Thompson, J. (1974). Over- and under-achievement in reading: Distribution in the general population. *British Journal of Educational Psychology, 44*, 1–12.

CHAPTER 7

Issues and Interventions
with Nonnuclear Families

*T*he nuclear family has been generally regarded as the optimal unit for childrearing. However, the once-popular assumption that marriage is a permanent relationship seems more a myth than a reality. Despite a recent leveling off of the divorce rate (Hernandez, 1988), researchers have estimated that 45% of the children born in the late 1970s and early 1980s will experience their parents' divorce before reaching the age of 18 years (Glick & Lin, 1986). Because 75% of divorced mothers and 80% of divorced fathers remarry, it is also predicted that as many as 25% of all children will eventually have one or more stepparents (Glick & Lin, 1986). In light of these demographic trends, it is essential that mental health practitioners understand the issues that envelop family disruption and reconstitution.

The family unit has been traditionally defined in terms of the unique biological and interpersonal relationships that exist among its component members. Although the importance of these relationships has been emphasized in theories of child development, family systems theorists have suggested that families also follow a developmental sequence (e.g., Haley, 1973; Minuchin, 1974; Solomon, 1973). These authors have proposed that the developmental stages of the family include marriage, the birth of the children, the individuation of family members, the eventual departure of the children, and the parents' readjustment to a marital dyad. An implicit assumption in the writings of these authors is that the developmental tasks are best accomplished within the context of the nuclear family. These authors rarely discuss, however, how the loss of a parent might interfere with the successful completion of these tasks.

A central thesis of this chapter is that the nonnuclear family cannot meaningfully be understood outside of its dynamic developmental context. As in the nuclear family, this context is defined by the multiple interrelated systems in which the individual family members are embedded, as well as by the individual characteristics of the family members themselves. In contrast with the nuclear family, however, the nonnuclear family is usually formed as a result of a developmental crisis. The process of adjusting to this crisis becomes the first important developmental task for the new nonnuclear family. Successful adjustment is not easy, as evidenced by the high rates of psychosocial problems reported by family members during the divorce and postdivorce period.

The primary purposes of this chapter are to describe the special developmental needs of different types of disrupted nuclear families, and to present intervention strategies designed to meet these needs. A review of the child development literature suggests that several important systems impact on the psychosocial functioning of members in disrupted nuclear families (Borduin & Henggeler, 1982). Consequently, we feel that the multisystemic model is well suited for conceptualizing the assessment and treatment of dysfunctional nonnuclear families.

THE SINGLE-PARENT FAMILY

Although an increasing number of divorced parents share custodial responsibilities, mothers are awarded sole custody of children in 90% of divorce cases (Hetherington, Stanley-Hagan, & Anderson, 1989). This outcome in child custody adjudication undoubtedly reflects the popular assumption that the mother is best qualified to raise the children. Though this assumption has been challenged by developmentalists, it seems likely that the sex-of-parent bias will continue to influence custody decisions for the next few decades. Consequently, our focus is on issues that are particularly relevant to the single-mother family.

From the multisystemic perspective, multiple systems are associated with the behavioral functioning of members in the single-parent family. The role of these systems requires a careful assessment on the part of the therapist prior to implementing treatment interventions. Our goal is to develop an individualized treatment program to meet each family's specific needs.

Financial Issues

Most single-parent families experience financial problems. The loss of a parent, whether due to death or divorce, frequently leads to a reduction in family income. Although the noncustodial father is often required to provide child support, payments are often inadequate or are ignored by the father. The implementation of legal sanctions related to nonsupport is time-consuming and often fails to address the immediate financial crisis engendered by nonsupport. Even when support is forthcoming, the cost of maintaining a comparable standard of living usually necessitates that the woman who had previously been a full-time mother return to work. For many custodial mothers who lack employment experience and skills, the task of obtaining a job is particularly difficult. Moreover, other problems often develop in response to the reduction of family income. The following case exemplifies this point.

Wally, a 12-year-old boy, and Jennifer, a 14-year-old girl, who lived with their mother and three siblings, were referred for therapy by the local juvenile court. Wally and Jennifer had been arrested following a shoplifting incident in a department store. During the therapist's initial interview with the family, the mother reported that she and her husband had divorced ten months earlier. The husband had moved to another state and refused to pay child support despite legal sanctions. As a result, the family could no longer afford to pay the rent on their home and had to move to a less desirable neighborhood. This neighborhood was in another school district, and each of the children was forced to change schools at mid-semester. This move was particularly difficult for the children, both of whom were somewhat shy. The mother, who had previously worked as a housewife, now worked at two separate, low-paying jobs in order to support herself and her children. She complained that her children did not receive adult supervision many hours that she worked. She also noted that her job demands and limited financial resources did not allow her to engage in various social outlets with friends, leaving her lonely and depressed. The children reported that their mother was usually too tired to spend time with them and that she was often angry or complained about work. They stated that they no longer received a weekly allowance and as a result were not able to engage in certain peer and classroom activities that required money.

This example suggests that the financial impact of divorce may contribute to the development of many types of psychosocial problems in the family. Limited financial resources were related to the mother's depression and withdrawal from peers, the children's relative lack of interaction with peers, and disturbances in mother-child interaction.

If the therapist had failed to consider financial status as a relevant ecological variable, therapeutic interventions might have emphasized individual psychotherapy to alleviate the mother's emotional difficulties, or family therapy to enhance mother-child relations. The therapist concluded, however, that the psychosocial problems were due primarily to the dramatic shift in the family's financial status, rather than any individual or familial pathology. This conclusion was based on several observations. First, due to her 70-hour work week and childcare responsibilities, the mother had no choice but to limit her social contacts. Second, periodic depression and anger directed toward loved ones are typical responses of many parents placed in similar situations. Third, shy children are often slow in adapting to new situations, and opportunities for developing new friends were less frequent due to the financial limitations.

Based on the preceding analysis, the therapist promoted the initiation and coordination of social service assistance including financial and budgetary counseling, subsidized daycare, employment training, and government subsidized housing. As the family's financial situation improved and the mother's optimism about potential careers increased, the emotional and behavioral problems were attenuated. In this case the clinician served more as an administrator and family advocate than as a psychotherapist. Although the therapist had numerous telephone contacts with the mother and with social service agency staff, the therapist met with the family only once per month for several months.

The coordination of social services that are relevant to the family's financial status assumes that the clinician has a working knowledge of the social service delivery system. It is also assumed that the therapist is willing to act as an advocate for the family within the larger social service system. Unfortunately, many training programs do not include practicum experience with community social service systems. Such experience is usually viewed as irrelevant to the therapist's needs. As a result, many therapists are forced to "find their own way" through the social service maze when the needs of their clients so dictate. Although the absence of appropriate training frequently handicaps the therapist, such a handicap should not prevent the therapist from learning about those agencies that are most relevant to clients' financial and vocational needs. The motivated therapist who plans to work with single-parent families will find that efforts toward self-education are well spent.

The Family System

Several family developmental issues, if left unresolved, can lead to serious psychosocial problems for the members of single-parent families. The central developmental issue is the redefinition of family boundaries following the father's departure. This redefinition requires both behavioral and cognitive accommodations among the family members. Behaviorally, the members must assume many of the tasks and responsibilities of the absent parent. For example, the eldest boy in the family might be called upon to perform the physically strenuous household tasks that were formerly the father's responsibility, the mother may have to find a way to earn extra money, and the other children will have more chores and household responsibilities. At a cognitive level, it is important that each member clearly understands his or her role within the single-parent family. In families where the absent parent maintains contact with the family members, each individual should have a clear grasp of the nature of his or her relationship with the absent parent. Although all of the family members are involved in the redefinition of family boundaries, the orchestration of this process typically falls upon the shoulders of the custodial parent.

Several factors represent potential impediments to the mother's redefinition of boundaries within the single-parent family. Typically, the single mother must reestablish family rules and delineate responsibilities at a time when she is lonely and depressed. Indeed, the stress and conflict that surround divorce may precipitate emotional difficulties for the mother, who as a result, is less capable of facilitating the psychosocial adjustment of the children. The mother might also fail to recognize that her children's perspectives regarding the family boundaries are likely to differ from her own. For example, while she may relinquish her role as wife with little apparent difficulty, the children are not as likely to redefine substantially their relationship with their father. It is important that the mother appreciate her children's perspectives while also asserting herself as the custodial parent of the children. Another impediment to the redefinition of family boundaries is continued conflict and animosity between the ex-spouses. Such conflict is usually related to child support or child visitation, although previous areas of discord within the marriage can also continue to fuel disharmony. Regardless of the reason for the conflict, discord between the ex-spouses tends to interfere with the stability of the single-parent family and contributes to increased psychosocial difficulties among the children.

Another developmental issue that frequently arises in the single-parent family regards the management of child behavior. The single-parent role invariably includes the difficult task of assuming primary responsibility for decisions related to child discipline. For many single mothers, this responsibility seems initially overwhelming. These mothers report that the responsibilities for child discipline were formerly shared with or assumed entirely by their husbands. A complicating factor is that many children evidence increased behavioral problems in response to the stress and conflict that surround the divorce. These problems are often extreme and seem unmanageable even to those parents who have mastered basic child disciplinary techniques.

Several treatment strategies can be helpful in resolving the developmental crises of the single-parent family. The use of any treatment strategy always follows a careful multisystemic assessment of those factors that are associated with an identified problem. For example, the absence of clear family boundaries might relate to maternal psychosocial problems in one case, whereas in another case, continued conflict between the ex-spouses might exacerbate the problem.

Mrs. Jennings came for treatment six months after her husband had left her and filed for divorce. Mr. Jennings was currently living with a younger woman who was an employee in his company. Mrs. Jennings was a middle-class housewife and had two children, 8-year-old Marsha and 5-year-old Peter. Mrs. Jennings was extremely depressed, had suicidal thoughts, and had lost 30 pounds since the separation. Both children were presenting behavior problems at home and at school. Mrs. Jennings had not been able to deal effectively with these problems, as Mr. Jennings had been the primary discipline agent. Since the birth of Marsha, Mrs. Jennings had focused her time and energy on her family. She had been very dependent on her husband, and in turn, she had fostered her children's dependency on herself.

The presenting problems could be conceptualized as the family's failure to create new boundaries due largely to Mrs. Jennings' emotional turmoil and desire to manipulate her husband back into the relationship. Mrs. Jennings was not providing the structure and reassurance that her children needed, and she was hoping that her husband would return home when he saw how depressed she was and that the children were also experiencing problems. Instead of severing ties with her husband and initiating means to improve her financial and social situation, she was behaving in the excessively dependent fashion that had contributed to the marital difficulties (e.g., she would call her husband in tears at 2 A.M.). It should be noted, however, that these "dependent" transactions had also been implicitly encouraged by her husband and had provided considerable payoff for Mrs. Jennings in the past.

Therapeutic goals emphasized the development of Mrs. Jennings' maturity, especially regarding responsibility and independence. At a cognitive level, the therapist promoted an understanding of the negative consequences of depending on someone who may be permanently out of her life. Concomitantly, the therapist attempted to alleviate her self-doubts and build her confidence regarding her potential for social and vocational success. Behaviorally, Mrs. Jennings was encouraged to begin developing a social network with other adults, seek employment, and consider the possibility of returning to college. Regarding the children, she was taught relatively simple behavior management techniques that, combined with emotional support, greatly diminished the children's behavior problems.

These cognitive and behavioral changes were quite difficult for Mrs. Jennings because they were contrary to her "true" treatment goal, which was to find a way to manipulate her husband back into the family. However, the therapist convinced her to make these changes by pointing out that her present strategies were not winning him back, and that he might be more attracted to someone who was strong and independent. If she made such changes she would be in a no-lose position. If Mr. Jennings returned, that would be fine. If he did not return, she would still be in a much better position than she was presently. Three months after the initiation of treatment, Mrs. Jennings had made friends with several divorced women, was employed at a daycare center, and was enrolled in night courses at a university. Therapeutic support was no longer needed. Two months later, her husband asked her to take him back, and she refused. She was pleased with her newly found independence as an adult and sense of competence as a parent and had decided that her husband represented a threat to these changes in her life.

Treatment interventions within the single-parent family are also guided by other salient factors that influence family functioning. One such factor is the length of time since the onset of the parents' separation. Hetherington, Cox, and Cox (1976, 1978) reported that conflict between former spouses often peaks during the year following divorce. By the second year, however, many families seem to reach a period of stability. At that time, fathers play a significantly decreased role in their families, and mothers tend to demonstrate increased competence in both disciplinary and affective relations with their children. Although these findings are not viewed as rigid development guidelines, they provide a useful framework for evaluating psychosocial problems in the single-parent family. Using this perspective, we have found that many psychosocial problems that occur at the time of the divorce can be attenuated through simply educating the family members about the types of behavioral responses that are normative in families of divorce, and by providing general guidelines for dealing with them. These guidelines usually pertain to the clarification of boundaries and providing a more explicit delineation of family rules and individual responsibilities.

On the other hand, when problems persist over an extended time, the family has probably not accomplished its requisite developmental tasks successfully. With such families, we are less likely to employ an educative approach and more likely to identify and modify those transactions that are associated with problems in family functioning.

Another factor that influences treatment strategies is the quality and quantity of contact between the absent parent and the other family members. To ignore the impact of the absent parent on the family is to court therapeutic failure. Obviously, some absent parents have little or no contact with any of the family members. However, even in those families where a parent is deceased, the remaining family members' perceptions of the parent often exert a salient influence over family interactions. For example, the child's idealized image of a deceased parent often interferes with the single parent's efforts to establish a new heterosexual relationship. In families broken by divorce, continued conflict between the former spouses can have an adverse effect on the entire family system. Such conflicts often represent boundary problems where, years after the divorce, the children are still caught in the middle of parental conflicts.

Vinny Giordano, 14 years of age, was referred for therapy by his mother. He was frequently truant from school and had run away several times, presumably in response to his mother's strictness. Vinny's mother and father had been divorced six years earlier. The divorce was extremely bitter and neither parent had remarried. Each parent actively and covertly sought the boy's alliance and lobbied against the other parent. Mrs. Giordano referred to her ex-husband as a "drunken, no-good bum who didn't care about anyone except himself." Although she "encouraged" Vinny to love his father, she also communicated indirectly that it was foolish to trust such a man. Mr. Giordano, on the other hand, was extremely permissive during Vinny's visits and periodically lavished him with gifts. These actions served to accentuate the mother's strictness and lower standard of living. Mr. Giordano also gave Vinny the message that he desired full custody. However, this message was intended more to provoke his ex-wife than to acquire increased access to Vinny.

The continued conflict between the former spouses had an adverse effect on the family system, especially Vinny. Each parent was using the child to hurt the other in revenge for past grievances. In such instances, we have typically found it necessary to meet with the divorced parents, either singly or together, in an effort to resolve issues that directly affect the children. Frequently, the parents are willing to alter their behavior if they understand that this is in the best interests of the children. Sometimes, we need to explain firmly that the parents' behavior may have very serious long-term consequences for the children. Almost invariably our meetings with the divorced spouses avoid any discussion of previous marital issues and focus exclusively on issues that are relevant for the children.

Unfortunately, while Mr. and Mrs. Giordano each agreed on the need for change, they did not fully comply with our recommendation that each stop using Vinny to undermine the other. Thus, we employed a tactic that has been successful with divorced parents who continue to resist needed changes. The therapist told each parent individually that the undermining was their way of maintaining contact with their ex-spouse. We suggested that their continued conflict and failure to become involved with another heterosexual partner after six years of divorce were evidence that both parents were still emotionally invested in the relationship. Therefore, they were encouraged to become more open and direct in their positive feelings and to actively seek a reconciliation rather than continue sending messages of caring through their son. If our reframing contained much truth, it would open the door for the couple to consider the feasibility of reconcilia-tion. If the reframing was erroneous, the parents would stop undermining each other, lest they give the impression that they still love the other and want to become reinvolved. In either case, our therapeutic goal would be met: The parents would stop using Vinny as a weapon against one another.

The Single Parent

Individual characteristics of the single parent mediate the impact of divorce on the family. The coping skills and strategies that the single mother employs can significantly influence the quality of her interactions with her children. Hetherington and Martin (1986) and Rutter (1971) have suggested that children model the crisis-related behaviors of their parents. During times of stress, the children behave as they have observed their parents behave during such times. From this perspective, the high rates of psychosocial problems observed among children of single parents may more strongly reflect the children's modeling of this parent's coping strategies than the negative effects of one parent's absence. For example, when a single mother remains depressed for a long period of time, her social withdrawal can impact negatively on the children at several levels. Similarly, as the following case demonstrates, coping strategies that include prolonged periods of anger also take a psychological toll.

Mrs. Landon's husband left her when their 16-year-old daughter, Barbara, was 12 years of age. Throughout the divorce process, Mrs. Landon was extremely hostile and vengeful toward her ex-spouse. She felt betrayed and violated and was determined never to allow a similar situation to occur again. Consequently, she cut off all contact with males and covertly taught Barbara that men were rotten, untrustworthy, egocentric opportunists. Although this coping strategy helped Mrs. Landon to deal with her feelings of rejection, hurt, and loss, Barbara paid a costly price for her mother's method of coping. Barbara distrusted and rejected her male peers, and recently engaged in a sexual relationship with a female teacher.

Other characteristics of the single parent also mediate the effects of divorce on the family. The parent's personality characteristics or interpersonal style, for example, might not elicit support from relatives or other significant adults. For example, the mother might behave in an overly dependent or "clutching" manner toward anyone who expresses concern. Although such behavior is intended to elicit emotional support, it usually evokes the opposite. The parent's intellectual attributes, level of educational achievement, and physical abilities are also pertinent factors in the assessment of problems and the planning of interventions. The single parent needs to utilize his or her strengths to the maximum in order to optimize the probability of successful adjustment.

Problems experienced by single parents often occur in response to an absence of social support. Consequently, a central goal of many of our interventions with single parents is to provide a base of social support. Although we view the therapist as an invaluable source of emotional and social encouragement, we have found that the therapist can also enlist the assistance of individuals who are natural providers of such support, such as members of the extended family, friends, neighbors, fellow employees, and members of the church or some other social organization. The client is encouraged to seek interpersonal contact and to share concerns with individuals who are likely to respond favorably. We feel strongly that the therapist should fill primarily a problem-solving role rather than a supportive role in cases where a social network exists but is not being utilized.

In some families, however, the single parent does not have access to appropriate sources of social support in the environment. Clients in this situation have typically been isolated from their community and are not emotionally close with their family of origin. In such instances the therapist's role should be supportive. These single parents often need substantial ego boosting and assurance regarding their self-worth. They also need to develop a social network of understanding adults.

In response to this need, an increasing number of single-parent groups and organizations have been created. The goals of these groups range from the provision of supportive psychotherapy (e.g., Epstein, Borduin, & Wexler, 1985) to the organization of social events and recreational activities (e.g., Parents Without Partners). An important advantage of such organizations is that the members view each other as experts in dealing with the problems of single parents and readily share their anxieties and concerns. Moreover, these groups are often able to develop and implement effective problem-solving strategies that benefit the members. For example, in one group, the parents developed a program in which they regularly alternated as babysitters for each other's children. This allowed several of the parents to pursue their educational and career interests successfully and allowed other parents to increase their social outlets. Significantly, involvement in these pursuits also had a positive impact on the parents' self-esteem and on their interactions with their children.

The Children

Researchers have suggested that the primary long-term psychosocial difficulties of father-absent children are manifested by abnormalities in sex-role development (e.g., Biller, 1974; Nash, 1965). Theorists of sex-role development commonly assume that the child's identification as male or female is strongly influenced by the child's observation of the same-sex parent. Hence, one might expect that the absence of a father has a more detrimental impact on the sex-role identification of boys than girls. Indeed, most extant research suggests that father-absent boys have a more feminine sex-role identification than similar-aged boys from intact families; and that father absence has relatively little impact on the girl's sex-role identification (Borduin & Henggeler, 1982).

Interestingly however, both father-absent boys and girls evidence disruptions in their actual sex-role behaviors. These disruptions are most commonly observed during adolescence, and are more likely to emerge when the father's departure occurred early in childhood. The behaviors of father-absent male adolescents are typically less aggressive and competitive than those of father-present males. On the other hand, father-absent female adolescents tend to evidence heterosexual difficulties. Females with divorced parents tend to show more attention-seeking and sexual acting-out than females from intact families, whereas females with widowed mothers evidence more inhibition, rigidity, and social withdrawal than their father-present counterparts.

In light of the sex-role problems identified for many father-absent children, it is important for therapists to evaluate the possibility of such problems and intervene accordingly. Investigators have shown that maternal encouragement of masculine behavior can improve the father-absent boy's sex-role development (Biller & Bahm, 1971). Consequently, single mothers might be encouraged to support masculine behavior in their sons. Mothers can promote increased contact with male peers (e.g., Boy Scouts, athletic teams) and with adult role models. Older male siblings and their friends are often willing to devote time as "masculine models" for a younger brother. A male neighbor or the father of a peer might be asked to occasionally include the boy in activities that are likely to promote masculine identity. Male teachers can serve as valuable models, as well. If the mother advocates her child's needs prior to the beginning of the school year, she can often influence administrative decisions related to the placement of her child with a male teacher. Even for father-absent boys who exhibit high levels of aggressive behavior, regular contact with a responsible male adult can provide a much-needed model of self-controlled, ethical behavior.

Although we have emphasized the amelioration of sex-role development problems with boys, it is equally important to provide father-absent girls with similar experiences interacting with adult males. It seems that such experiences provide opportunities for the girl to develop social skills that are pertinent for successful heterosexual relations as a woman (Biller, 1976; Jacobson & Ryder, 1969; Johnson, 1975).

Each of the interventions that were just described can influence behavior at other systemic levels, in addition to sex-role development. For example, the child's participation on an athletic team may enhance his peer interactions as well as his masculine self-image. Similarly, a male teacher might have a substantial impact on the child's academic achievement, and in turn, on the child's self-confidence. Hence, in planning treatment interventions, the therapist needs to select carefully those interventions that are likely to have optimal impact on multiple problem areas. Moreover, it is necessary to consider the individual characteristics of the child that might facilitate or impede the efficacy of each intervention. A child with physical characteristics that promote failure in athletic events might make greater gains if intervention emphasized another type of peer-related activity. Conversely, the aggressive child might achieve greater peer status in sporting events that reward such behavior. We are not suggesting that the remediation of individual deficits is unimportant. For example, some children might require the development of better social skills as an adjunct to involvement in peer activities. To minimize repeated failures, however, it is often useful to build on the child's individual strengths rather than focus on weaknesses that might not be fully remediable (e.g., poor coordination, limited intellectual abilities).

Cognitive ability is another important individual characteristic of the parent-absent child. In a comprehensive review, Shinn (1978) concluded that compared with children from intact homes, father-absent children are more likely to show deficits in cognitive performance. It is critical that the therapist consider the relation between the child's cognitive abilities and any identified problems. For example, the child with low intelligence might find academic tasks unrewarding and as a result associate with a peer group that does not support educational achievement. In a study of juvenile offenders, we found that low intellectual abilities and association with deviant peers were strong predictors of serious and repeated criminal activity among father-absent, male adolescents (Hanson, Henggeler, Haefele, & Rodick, 1984). The pertinence of cognitive level within our multisystemic model is described in greater detail in Chapter 2.

The thoughts, feelings, and beliefs of the parent-absent child can also have a significant influence on individual affect and interpersonal behavior. The departure of a parent frequently engenders fears among younger children that relate to abandonment by the parent. Preadolescents often express feelings of neglect, anger, and confusion, and may openly discuss fantasies about parental reunion. Among adolescents, identity and relationship issues are common concerns. These issues often include anxieties that they experience over conflicted loyalties to the parents. While such responses are normative, these thoughts and feelings often give rise to behavior problems at home and school. Although treatment that includes contingency management might represent one important component in the amelioration of such problems, especially among younger children, it is also necessary to address the cognitions that are related to the behavior problems.

In assessing the child's thoughts and feelings, it is essential to consider the child's level of cognitive development. Preoperational children structure their knowledge from an egocentric perspective. Their fears and behavior problems are more likely to be reduced through parental affection and reassurance than through an explanation of the impact of their behavior on others (Henggeler & Cohen, 1984). On the other hand, concrete and formal operational children are increasingly able to understand that their parents have needs that are not necessarily the same as their own. An explanation that delineates the detrimental impact of the problem behavior on the parent often promotes behavior change by the child. Many children voluntarily change their behavior when they understand that their parent is already lonely or depressed and that their misbehavior makes the situation worse. Concrete or formal operational children also require expressions of parental warmth and support. It is important, however, that the parent continue to provide structure and make maturity demands.

In some families, the stress and conflict that surround the divorce process do not readily dissipate. The children's psychosocial needs may go virtually unnoticed in the face of family discord and parental emotional turmoil. To meet the needs of an increasing number of such children, therapists have been using self-help group therapy for children of divorce (e.g., Epstein & Borduin, 1984, 1985). These groups can provide a useful adjunct to interventions that focus solely on the family system. We suggest that such a group be limited to same-aged peers who are at least at the concrete operational stage of development. Our primary goals for these groups have been to increase each child's sense of efficacy and to provide the children with a better understanding of the divorce experience through the encouragement of social comparisons with their peers. The children learn that many of their problems and anxieties are common to most children in similar situations. Through these groups children can also learn about a variety of resolutions to problems surrounding divorce (e.g., through role plays or through the reports of other children). During this process, the children usually come to feel that they have peers who accept and support them. The therapeutic value of such support is often substantial.

Formal Social Systems

In the preceding sections we have referred to systems outside of the family that are associated with the behavior of single parents and their children. Systems such as the peer group, school, church, social service agencies, and the work setting are all examples of social contexts that should be considered when designing and implementing treatment strategies. Effective advocacy within each of these systems requires that the therapist understand the processes and norms by which these systems function.

The legal system, for example, has an important bearing on the single-parent family. Therapists should be familiar with the laws governing custody decisions and with the factors that weigh in such decisions. We are not suggesting that the therapist become a legal expert, but lack of understanding of custody negotiations and decisions can interfere with the treatment process and may even place the unwitting therapist in the midst of a heated legal struggle. For example, in cases of joint custody or where custody has not yet been established, treatment that is initiated by one parent may be terminated or undermined by the other parent. Often, parents who are separated or divorced must rely on legal counsels for guidance and advice related to childrearing and child custody arrangements. The child's psychosocial welfare is sometimes, at best, a secondary consideration. To the extent that the court encourages parents to determine their own custody arrangements, the therapist can facilitate both pre- and postdivorce parental decisions concerning child custody. At the least, the therapist who plans treatment for a single-parent family should be familiar with the family's custody arrangements. Where complex legal issues arise, the therapist should consult with a colleague or other professional who is expert in this area. Failure to understand legal ramifications can have a negative effect on the family system, as the following case suggests.

Mrs. King requested therapeutic assistance for her 7-year-old son, Jason, who displayed academic and behavioral problems following his parents' separation six months earlier. Mrs. King reported that she and her husband would soon be divorced and that it was tacitly understood that she would receive custody of Jason. The therapist initially conducted a comprehensive intellectual and academic evaluation to assess the nature of Jason's difficulties in school. The results indicated that Jason had a learning disability, which had become especially evident when he began the second grade that fall. The therapist also assessed the behavior problems that Jason manifested at home, and concluded that Mrs. King needed to learn more effective ways of disciplining Jason. (Before the parents separated, Mr. King had taken total responsibility for child discipline.)

The therapist had begun to implement relevant treatment interventions when he was contacted by Mr. King's attorney, who requested information related to Jason's problems. The therapist refused to provide any information and was subsequently issued a subpoena to appear in court for the custody case and to present records related to Jason's academic and behavioral evaluations. Despite the therapist's testimony that Mrs. King was a competent parent (i.e., she had initiated treatment) and was helping to ameliorate her son's academic and behavior problems, the court awarded custody to Mr. King, in part on the basis of his demonstrated ability to control his son's behavior and Mrs. King's evident lack of control.

In this case, the unwitting therapist should have assessed Mrs. King's understanding of the "tacit" agreement with her husband in greater detail. Indeed, the therapist later learned that Mr. King had called his wife on several occasions and had indicated that he desired custody of their son. However, Mrs. King was hesitant to discuss her husband's phone calls and had assumed that his stated intentions were merely a bluff. Had the therapist been aware of the impending custody battle, he might have postponed certain aspects of assessment and therapy until after the custody decision. Even more unfortunate was the fact that Mr. King was very neglectful of his son after custody was granted. Although custody was later awarded to the mother and treatment was reinitiated, the therapist did not fully understand the judicial process surrounding divorce, nor did he anticipate his possible role in the custody decision. While the therapist undoubtedly had the best interests of both mother and child in mind from the outset, these interests might have been better served through a more accurate understanding of predivorce legalities.

THE STEPFAMILY

Although remarriage often resolves many of the problems that accompany single parenthood, it also raises a new set of issues that some parents are unprepared to address. The transition from the single-parent family to the stepfamily encompasses several systemic changes that have a substantial impact on the development of parents and children. In the following sections we identify these important systemic issues and discuss strategies that have been useful in treating families who have not handled these issues successfully.

The Stepfamily System

The role definitions that accompany membership in the stepfamily are not as clearly delineated as those within the nuclear family. While the nuclear family uses biological ties to define parent and child role functions, the stepfamily cannot rely on this differentiation. In an effort to conceptualize the ambiguity of role prescriptions that occurs in many stepfamilies, Jacobson (1979) described the "myth of the re-created nuclear family." According to Jacobson, stepfamily members frequently assume that the remarriage signals the formation of a family unit that is similar to that composed of biological parents and their children. However, in contrast with the nuclear family, the members of the stepfamily have varying biological, emotional, and historical loyalties. These loyalties interfere with the redefinition of the stepfamily as a reconstituted nuclear family and engender confusion as family members attempt to fulfill their varied roles.

The new marital partners have the primary responsibility for defining the roles of the stepfamily members and for enhancing the stability of the new system. To accomplish this task successfully, the marital relationship must be cohesive and adaptable. However, in contrast to the marital dyad in the nuclear family, the spouses in the stepfamily have not had as extensive an opportunity to develop the norms of their marital relationship prior to establishing their roles as parents. Consequently, conflict over parenting issues can interfere with the process of mutual accommodation that must occur in establishing marital roles. Contrary to their expectations, the spouses may find that they have little time or energy to invest in their marital relationship. The frequent lack of adequate preparation for remarriage, coupled with the immediate and often intense demands of parenting, might account for the higher divorce rate in remarriage than in initial marriage (e.g.,Glick & Lin, 1986).

Parent-child relationship issues are of primary importance in the stepfamily system. The stepparent might be forced to assume the role of disciplinarian in the absence of a strong affective bond with the stepchild. In response, the stepchild may reject the stepparent and thus discourage the stepparent from initiating positive interactions. Differences in disciplinary strategies between the parents are also likely to promote parent-child conflicts. The children might play one parent against the other, or they might align with their biological parent against the stepparent. The division of family tasks may require that family members are forced to accept responsibilities that they do not wish to accept. Moreover, privileges and responsibilities that were considered appropriate in the single-parent family may be considered inappropriate in the stepfamily. For example, a new stepmother may attempt to assume many of the household responsibilities and child management decisions that were previously undertaken by her husband's adolescent daughter. The stepdaughter might refuse to relinquish her role as the parental child and engage in a struggle for power with her new stepmother.

The relationships among stepsiblings may also promote systemic problems within the stepfamily. Adolescents may resent the increased childcare responsibilities that accompany the presence of younger stepsiblings. The presence of same-aged stepsiblings may lead to unfavorable comparisons related to abilities, grades, appearance, and friends. Competition for parental affection and financial resources may result in feelings of animosity among stepsiblings. In addition, the stepsiblings may cooperate to develop strategies that foster discord between the stepparents. As Visher and Visher (1979, 1983) suggested, stepchildren often desire the reconciliation of their biological parents and attempt to accomplish this goal by promoting marital disharmony and conflict in the stepfamily. The absence of clear social sanctions against sexual relations between adolescent stepsiblings can also seriously disrupt the stability of the stepfamily.

Another source of stress on the stepfamily is related to contact with ex-spouses. Repeated interactions between the biological parents regarding custody and visitation arrangements can have a disruptive effect on the new marriage. Conflict may also arise between the stepparent and the biological parent over issues related to child education, the purchase of clothes and toys, vacation times, and church attendance. The remarriage of either biological parent often leads to the rekindling of dormant legal battles over child custody. In cases where joint custody has been awarded, the periodic alternations in living arrangements and disciplinary practices can have a negative impact on the stepfamily as well as on child psychosocial functioning.

Family Interventions

Many of the problems that emerge in the stepfamily system can be viewed within the context of the family's attempt toward self-definition. As noted earlier, members of the stepfamily often hold unrealistic expectations in their desire to establish a nuclear family. In treating the stepfamily, we often explain that the family's problems are common to a large proportion of stepfamilies. We address the uncertainty with which family members view their new roles and label this uncertainty as normal. It is often useful to explain that the family needs time to develop an identity, and that the development of such an identity will necessarily require effort and engender conflict. By reframing the thoughts and behaviors of the parents and children as natural components in the development of the stepfamily system, it is often possible to alter unrealistic expectations and to foster a sense of cooperation among family members.

Marital therapy is a common component of our treatment with stepfamilies. It is essential for the survival of a new stepfamily that the spouses form a coalition of emotional and instrumental support. As described in Chapter 4, specific marital interventions vary with the systemic parameters of a given case. With stepfamilies such therapy often involves teaching the spouses to separate their responsibilities to each other from their responsibilities to their children. In many cases, it is important first to address mutual needs within the marriage before turning to parenting issues or parent-child relations. When each spouse feels that the other is primarily committed toward the marriage and marital communication channels have been opened, the groundwork is set for solving difficult parent-child interaction problems.

Mrs. Ford and her 12-year-old son, Michael, had lived alone since Mr. Ford, a wealthy businessman, died when Michael was 3 years of age. Dr. Powers, a 42-year-old bachelor, was a successful research physician who was not highly socially skilled and had few friends. Following a 3-year, low-key courtship, the couple was married. They sought treatment 19 months later. Each partner felt that the marriage was confining, restricting, and possibly more trouble than it was worth. Each spouse believed that the other was inconsiderate, yet each also behaved in an egocentric, selfish manner. In addition, Michael's behavior had become almost uncontrollable; he was frequently truant from school and irresponsible around the house. Dr. Powers wanted to take a strong hand with Michael, but his wife would not allow him to do this.

Intervention aimed first at determining whether the couple had actually made a serious commitment to the marriage. The therapist observed that both spouses behaved as if they were still single. They competed with each other rather than sharing and giving. Following long careers as comfortable single adults, it was not easy to make the compromises and sacrifices that marriage required. The couple essentially had three choices: (1) seek a divorce and regain their nonconfining lifestyles; (2) maintain the status quo and learn to live with the concomitant conflict and hostility; or (3) learn to share, compromise, and solve conflicts in a straightforward, nonmanipulative fashion. The therapist emphasized that the third choice would require great effort and motivation, but that it was the only choice that might lead to long-term emotional satisfaction. The couple committed to the third choice and the therapist, using strategies described in Chapter 4, focused attention on developing a cohesive and flexible marital relationship. Once this was accomplished, it was not difficult to deal with Michael's misbehaviors.

Therapeutic interventions often need to address child behavior problems more quickly than in the preceding example. In some instances it is useful to teach more effective child discipline strategies to the parents. We usually advise, however, that the new stepparent does not become the sole disciplinarian with the children of the other spouse. In the absence of an emotional bond between stepparent and stepchild, disciplinary attempts are more likely to meet with failure and evoke long-lasting hostility in the child. Nevertheless, it is very important that the new stepparent actively demonstrates support for the other spouse's disciplinary efforts. Such support is appreciated by the spouse and has a positive impact on the marital relationship. In addition, the support discourages the children from playing one parent against the other. In families with younger children, it is easier for the stepparent to gradually assume an increased role in parenting behavior. With adolescents, interventions that open avenues of communication are an important precursor to stepparent involvement. For example, it is useful to address the adolescent's conflicted loyalties between the stepparent and the absent biological parent. Clarification of the roles and responsibilities of the stepparent, the present parent, and the absent parent often helps to resolve disciplinary issues, as the following case shows.

Margie was a 15-year-old referred by her mother and stepfather, Mr. and Mrs. Zweibel, because she was presenting several serious problems and was not responding to parental discipline attempts. Except for the difficulties presented by Margie, the Zweibels had been happily married for five years. Margie was in frequent contact with her father, an extremely permissive parent who lived a 1960s, dope-smoking lifestyle in the Wyoming Rockies.

Margie used several ploys to avoid yielding to her parents' maturity demands. She would threaten to move to Wyoming and live with her "real" father unless the Zweibels relaxed their demands. This was an effective way to handle her mother because Mrs. Zweibel felt guilty that she had subjected her daughter to the stresses of divorce, living in single-parent poverty, and integration into a new family. In addition, Mrs. Zweibel knew that her ex-husband would not provide the structure that Margie needed to stay out of trouble. In fact, she would probably become involved with drugs and risk pregnancy if she moved to Wyoming. Margie used the "you can't tell me what to do, you're not my real father" ploy to diminish Mr. Zweibel's influence in the situation. In a well-conceived strategy, Margie had disarmed the parental power of both her mother and stepfather.

Therapeutic interventions were geared to clarifying each participant's role in the family and to reestablishing boundaries. During discussions with Mr. and Mrs. Zweibel, it was decided that they should assume the role of parents and that Margie should be treated as a manipulative 15-year-old daughter who was misbehaving. Because Mrs. Zweibel's ex-husband continued to offer Margie freedom in Wyoming, his role was framed as the active subverter of the stepfamily. The strengths and weaknesses of two courses of action were discussed. (1) The parents could "lay down the law" and tell Margie that she needed either to improve her attitude and behavior at home and school or she would have to leave. This parental move would undermine Margie's manipulations, but it would also run the risk of Margie moving to Wyoming. Because of this risk, the Zweibels had to be fully aligned and Mrs. Zweibel had to be in full and complete agreement with this decision. (2) The only other option was to continue making the halfhearted attempts to deal with Margie that were failing. The therapist predicted that this course of action would be less traumatic in the short run, but would eventually lead to more serious problems and would have a low probability of success. In addition, it was necessary to rule out the possibility that Margie was chemically dependent, as described in Chapter 9.

The Zweibels chose the first option. Margie soon got into trouble and was sent to Wyoming. At first, Mr. and Mrs. Zweibel were upset, but later they came to enjoy the increased time they were able to spend with one another now that they no longer had to deal with Margie's constant emotional turmoil.

The therapist terminated the case, but two months later the Zweibels returned to therapy. Margie had requested that she be allowed to return home. Although her father provided much freedom, he gave little attention or emotional support. The Zweibels were ambivalent. On one hand, they loved Margie and knew that it would be in her best interests to return. On the other hand, they had come to prize their tranquility and time together and were afraid that Margie would disrupt their harmony again. The following decision was reached. Margie was told that she could return in three months if she demonstrated an increased sense of responsibility and maturity while living in Wyoming (e.g., improved grades and acquisition of a part-time job). In addition, she was told that she would have to maintain this improvement following her move, or she would go back to Wyoming. Margie returned three months later on the Zweibels' terms, knowing that they would follow through on any contingencies. Margie continued to behave in a relatively mature and responsible manner and later enrolled in college.

Conflicts between stepsiblings are another common problem in stepfamilies. The stepchildren may feel that they have been forced to live with each other, and in an attempt to reassert control within their environment, they may initiate conflict. Although their behaviors may be inappropriate and obnoxious, the reality of the situation is that the stepchildren usually have little choice in becoming members of the stepfamily. The therapist can best facilitate child behavior change if this reality is acknowledged. The parent and stepparent are encouraged to set limits for the children's behavior, provide sufficient structure, and maintain clear boundaries between themselves and the children. It is usually better for the stepsiblings to work out their own conflicts within this context. Parental involvement in stepsibling conflicts should be limited to serious situations. Otherwise, it is likely that biological boundaries will become stronger than adult-child boundaries, and that the new stepfamily will not develop successfully.

When one spouse remarries, the single spouse sometimes feels extremely threatened. Many still harbor a hope of reuniting with their former spouse. This hope is dashed with remarriage, and feelings of anger and bitterness may follow. In addition, the single spouse might be jealous of the former spouse's new mate and fear that his or her place with the children will be taken over by this stepparent. As a consequence, single spouses often go out of their way to evoke conflict in the new stepfamily. When the therapist can arrange a meeting between the former spouses, it is often possible to facilitate cooperation on issues that directly involve the children. In some instances, however, the absent biological parent is unwilling to meet. When such cooperation is not forthcoming, the therapist might adopt an alternative approach, which involves teaching the custodial parent various strategies for minimizing the negative impact of the noncustodial parent. The following case illustrates the use of a paradoxical strategy to achieve this end.

Mr. and Mrs. Downs reported that their 10-year-old son, Billy, had become increasingly anxious and withdrawn during the past few months. Mrs. Downs noted that her ex-husband, Billy's father, had angrily expressed his opposition toward her recent marriage to Mr. Downs. After years of minimal contact, the father began to visit Billy on a weekly basis and, by the child's report, encouraged him to defy family rules. Mrs. Downs stated that while Billy did not comply with his father's requests, Billy had become increasingly tearful and withdrawn following each paternal visit. With little success, Mrs. Downs had pleaded with her ex-husband to stop his undermining behavior. Subsequent efforts by the therapist to contact the father were met with profane language and no cooperation.

Inasmuch as legal actions (e.g., attempting to modify visitation rights) might have further exacerbated the problematic situation, Mrs. Downs asked if an alternative solution was available. The therapist instructed Mrs. Downs to stop pleading with her ex-husband to change his behavior. Instead, when her ex-spouse arrived to take Billy on his visit, she should inform him that she appreciated his interest and concern in Billy's welfare. She should also state that his visit provided her with time to relax from the responsibilities of childrearing and spend some private time with her new husband. She should thank her ex-husband for structuring Billy's time and avoid any criticism or mention of Billy's withdrawn behavior. Mrs. Downs carefully carried out this procedure for five weeks, during which time she observed both a diminution of her son's symptoms and a decrease in visitation by her ex-husband.

Extrafamilial Systems

The establishment of a stepfamily through remarriage may have a substantial impact on extrafamilial systems in which the family members are embedded. The children of one of the stepparents may be required to change schools and to establish new peer groups. Similarly, a change of residence may mean that one of the stepparents must now travel a considerable distance to and from work. The stepparent may decide to seek another job, or to stop working in order to meet increased childrearing responsibilities. Any of these changes require adaptations that can precipitate stress for the individual and the family system.

The influences of extrafamilial systems must be considered when designing and implementing treatment strategies. In some instances, it is helpful for the therapist to identify strengths within existing extrafamilial systems. For example, fellow church members might represent an important source of social and emotional support for the new stepparents. Similarly, stepchildren who lack positive peer activities might be encouraged to become involved in other extrafamilial systems, such as an athletic team, scout troop, crafts class, or other activity, to develop new friends.

Another source of support for stepfamily members is the extended family. Remarriage typically increases the size of the extended family network. Stepchildren frequently have interactions with grandparents, aunts, uncles, and cousins from both the previous and the current marriages of their parents. These relatives may be able to provide emotional and instrumental assistance for members of the stepfamily. Moreover, members of the extended family can have an important role in facilitating relations between former spouses on issues related to the children.

Elaine Bentley sought therapy in an attempt to resolve continued conflicts with her ex-spouse. Although divorced for three years, Elaine and her former husband still had intense arguments related to child discipline and education, as well as regarding their previous marriage. Although both individuals had remarried, they had retained joint custody of their three children and saw each other on a weekly basis when the children moved from one household to the other. Mrs. Bentley reported that the arguments with her ex-husband not only upset the children, but that her relationship with her new husband had been adversely affected as well.

Initial attempts by the therapist to meet jointly with the former spouses were repeatedly thwarted, despite statements by both individuals that they wanted their conflicts to cease. The therapist's impression was that each spouse was still attempting to make the other pay for the hurt that had surrounded the divorce. Rather than continue to urge a halt to the conflict, the therapist decided to enlist the aid of Mrs. Bentley's parents as treatment agents. These adults related well to both their daughter and her ex-spouse, and they were genuinely concerned about the impact of the continued fighting on their grandchildren. As a result, it was not difficult to establish the grandparents' home as a transition point between weekly alternations in parental custody. Specific times were established at which the children were to be dropped off and picked up and were scheduled such that the mother and father did not meet. The grandparents were allowed sufficient time to provide the children with a pleasant transition between homes. The therapist also requested that the former spouses communicate their disagreements only in writing and via the mail. This arrangement buffered the children effectively from further direct parental conflict and had a positive impact on the relationship between Mrs. Bentley and her new husband.

Individual Characteristics

The children.   Stepfathers can attenuate some of the negative psychosocial and cognitive effects of father-absence on children. In the area of sex-role development, it has been reported that boys with stepfathers show more masculine sex-role behavior than father-absent boys (Santrock, 1970). There is also evidence that the introduction of a competent, involved, supportive stepfather is associated with a decrease in behavior problems in boys (Peterson & Zill, 1983; Santrock, Warshak, Lindberg, & Meadows, 1982). Regarding cognitive development, researchers have consistently found that children (Santrock, 1975) and adolescents (Chapman, 1977; Lessing, Zagorin, & Nelson, 1970) with stepfathers obtain higher scores on cognitive performance tasks than their father-absent counterparts. Such findings have important implications for treatment. For example, the therapist can cite these research findings as evidence of the stepfather's importance in childrearing and by so doing facilitate the stepfather's confidence as a parent and encourage his active involvement with the children.

The therapist can also provide the stepfather with specific suggestions related to the enhancement of child sex-role development and cognitive development. These suggestions should include active tasks that maximize positive reciprocity and mutual enjoyment and also promote the stepparent-child bond. For example, a stepfather might coach his stepson's athletic team. Such a commitment would demonstrate the stepfather's interest in the boy and provide a framework for their interaction. This specific framework presents numerous opportunities to acknowledge the child's accomplishments and provide emotional support and constructive advice for the child's failings and shortcomings. In essence, the stepfather and stepson would have the opportunity to develop a father-son relationship.

The parents.   The individual characteristics of each parent have a direct bearing on interpersonal relations in the stepfamily. As in the single-parent family, parental coping skills, personality, interpersonal style, and self-esteem influence family functioning. For example, previous marital failures may contribute to negative expectancies regarding the long-term success of the new marriage. Similarly, the presence of several stepchildren may threaten the self-confidence of the new stepparent who has had no prior experience in parenting. In such instances, therapy might emphasize the development of more realistic expectations and the acquisition of parenting skills. Although the spouse would certainly be instrumental in facilitating these changes, therapeutic interventions might have an individual component as well.

THE SURROGATE-PARENT FAMILY

In some families, neither biological parent is present. Although the relative proportion of such families is low, the children in surrogate-parent families are at high risk for developing behavior problems. The members of surrogate-parent families are often forced to make accommodations and adaptations. In this section, several salient developmental issues that are relevant to therapeutic interventions with surrogate-parent families are reviewed.

The Family System

The circumstances under which children are placed in the custody of surrogate parents—child abuse or neglect, the death of a parent, teenage pregnancy, severe parental psychopathology, parental illness, and child abandonment—are frequently linked to child behavioral and emotional problems. Consequently, it is often difficult to find qualified adults who are willing to care for children who are at serious risk for presenting problems. Often, grandparents or other relatives may reluctantly assume custodial responsibility for the child. In fewer instances, foster care or adoption may be arranged.

The introduction of a child into an existing family system has a profound impact on that system. Grandparents may be forced to change their lifestyle in order to reassume their roles as parents. An aunt and uncle may find that their own childrearing plans are disrupted as they take custodial responsibility for their niece or nephew. Foster parents may alter their marital relations as they devote more attention to the foster child. Although some of these changes may be anticipated, and even welcomed, other adaptations are likely to raise feelings of resentment toward the child. Children who are already in the home may feel jealous of the attention that the new child receives at their expense. All family members may resent the strain on existing financial resources. In addition, the behavior of an absent biological parent may disrupt family relations. For example, in the grandparent family, the biological parent may undermine the grandparents' disciplinary authority or promote conflict during visits with the child.

The absence of a biological tie between parents and one or more children can raise unique issues. Despite statements to the contrary, the surrogate parents may convey negative attitudes about the absent biological parent to the child, who may strongly identify with this parent. The surrogate parents may also aim anger at the child that is really intended for the biological parent. Child behavior problems or undesirable personality traits may be interpreted by the surrogate parents as a predisposition that the child has inherited from the "no-good" father. In response, the child may refuse to accept the love and discipline of adults who are not viewed as the "real" parents.

There are several guidelines for dealing with surrogate parents who blame the child's problems on traits that may have been inherited from the biological parent. It is usually not productive for the therapist to engage the family members in a discussion concerning the genetic determinants of behavior or to attempt to convince the surrogate parents that their position is incorrect. Such attempts seldom facilitate change. It is more helpful for the therapist to address the meta-level fears and concerns that underlie such issues. For example, the parents' discussion of the child's biological predispositions probably reflects their underlying doubts concerning their abilities to handle the child's behavior. The child's statement that the surrogate parents are not really his or her own may indicate a low sense of self-worth and doubt as to whether parental love and attention will be forthcoming. Such statements might also represent the child's tactic for subverting the disciplinary strategies of the surrogate parents. By addressing the underlying issues through carefully planned interventions, the therapist is more likely to encourage cooperative parent-child interactions.

Tom and Karen Miller, a middle-aged, childless couple with very successful careers, had recently adopted a 14-year-old boy named Jerry. Despite the protests of his new parents, Jerry had little interest in academic achievement and was primarily invested in developing his athletic skills. Mr. and Mrs. Miller reported that Jerry had physically assaulted two of his classmates who had joked about his academic deficits. The parents brought Jerry to the therapist with the hope of curbing Jerry's aggressive behavior and cultivating his scholastic abilities so that he could go to a good college and eventually pursue a professional career.

During the initial session, Mr. and Mrs. Miller blamed Jerry's aggression on his "troubled childhood" and hinted that he might be genetically determined to become a "failure." To avoid a pointless argument, the therapist admitted her relative ignorance of genetic factors and suggested that the parents might consider consulting a "genetic expert." The therapist suggested that prior to pursuing such a complex evaluation, however, the family should explore other possible solutions to Jerry's aggressive behavior. During the next few weeks, the therapist helped the family to plan mutually enjoyable activities that were aimed at fostering positive parent-adolescent interactions and altering the parents' negative perceptions of Jerry. As the parents began to appreciate Jerry's positive qualities and strengths (including his athletic abilities), he was more willing to accept his parents' rules regarding behavior and school performance. Together, the family decided that Jerry should attempt to do his best both in school and on the athletic field. At the termination of treatment three months later, the therapist asked the parents whether they had decided to pursue a genetic evaluation of their son. The parents dismissed this question by noting that such an evaluation would probably be costly and serve little purpose.

As in the stepparent family and the single-parent family, a clarification of the roles and responsibilities of members in the surrogate-parent family is often a useful starting point for therapy. A factor that frequently impedes the delineation of parent and child roles is the uncertainty regarding the length of the child's stay. Except in cases of child adoption, the surrogate-parent family is often established as a temporary family arrangement. In some instances, there may be vague plans to eventually reunite the child and the biological parent. In other instances, the child may be expected to live in a series of surrogate-parent homes. Because of these uncertainties, many surrogate parents are lax in their structuring of child responsibilities. Also, the surrogate parents often feel sorry for the child and honestly believe that the implementation of demands and responsibilities could create traumatic stress for the child. In such instances it is important that the therapist help the family members to set short-term goals that are designed to improve the immediate quality of family interactions and promote child responsibility and independence. Such goals might relate to issues that include child discipline, parent-child affective relations, performance in school, chores and privileges, and the like. Moreover, the family members can be encouraged to share their feelings related to the possibility of eventual separation. Rather than ignore the uncertainty of the situation, the family members should learn to address their fears and concerns openly. They should be advised to make the best of their current situation, exert their best effort to cooperate in the present, and deal with future events as they come.

Individual Characteristics

The child. Children have many individual characteristics that can facilitate or impede the quality of their interactions with surrogate parents. One important variable is the age of the child. Surrogate parents are often more likely to accept an infant into their home because they feel that they can have a greater influence on the development of a young child. Older children, especially adolescents, are usually accepted with less enthusiasm because of the possibility of serious acting-out, such as drug use and sexual promiscuity. The physical characteristics and temperament of the child also affect family relations. Cute, even-tempered children receive more favorable responses than unattractive children who show little social responsivity. To the extent that the child possesses characteristics that resemble those of the surrogate parents, the parents may be more likely to respond favorably to the child. Child cognitive problems, such as a learning disability, may also impede positive family relations, especially when the surrogate parents hold high academic expectations.

The child often comes to the surrogate-parent family with inappropriate cognitive sets and behavioral styles that create problems for the family members. If the child's previous living situation was extremely permissive, the child might openly rebel when limits are set and responsibilities are required. A child who was sexually abused may respond with distrust and fear to expressions of affection from the surrogate parent. Many of these children have also learned to imitate the behaviors and attitudes of their disturbed biological parents. Such children can present a range of serious problems that make them less desirable. If they perceive a negative attitude among family members, they may present even greater difficulties. Interventions in such instances should follow the models presented elsewhere in this volume. Especially important are the clarification of roles, the development of open communication channels, and the teaching of appropriate interpersonal behavior.

The surrogate parent.   The role of surrogate parents is an exceedingly difficult one and differs in many respects from that of biological parents. Although the surrogate parents may convey warmth and acceptance toward the child, they may find that the child responds with rejection and continued behavioral problems. Financial problems may arise as the surrogate parents attempt to meet the child's physical and educational needs. With an unmarried surrogate parent, the presence of the child may reduce the parent's opportunities for heterosexual interactions and for social outlets with friends. In such instances, the ability of the parent to successfully resolve the problem is strongly dependent on individual factors such as coping skills, personality style, and emotional maturity.

The age and physical capabilities of the surrogate parents can have an important influence on parent-child interactions, as well as on the length of the child's stay with the family. These capabilities are an especially significant consideration when grandparents assume custody of the child. The grandparents may gradually find that they have little energy to meet the continued demands of childrearing. Their diminishing physical abilities may prohibit attendance at parent-child social events outside of the home as well as impede adequate supervision of the child's activities. A physical disability of one grandparent may also demand that the other grandparent assumes total responsibility for raising the child. Moreover, the increased healthcare costs that accompany physical disabilities may compete for the financial resources that the grandparents have available for childrearing.

To a large extent, the therapist's task is to support the generosity and kindness of the surrogate parents by providing them with advice that makes their tasks more efficient and successful. Childrearing can be an extremely rewarding experience. The emotional satisfaction for surrogate parents can be even greater with a child who initially presents behavior problems, but then begins to develop as a responsible and caring person. However, in some situations the greatest good is served by removing the child from the surrogate family home and finding another placement.

Monica was a self-abusive and severely mentally retarded 7-year-old daughter of Felicia Jackson. Because of Felicia's neglect and alcoholism, Monica was removed by the Department of Human Services to the custody of her grandparents, Mr. and Mrs. Rolling. The Rollings were an extremely accepting and loving couple who felt a strong familial responsibility toward Monica and were pleased to take care of her. However, Mr. Rolling had a serious heart condition and Mrs. Rolling had kidney problems that required frequent outpatient treatment. Upon placement in the Rollings' home, Monica continued to engage in screaming and head-banging behaviors. Although these behaviors were amenable to treatment with operant conditioning techniques, Mr. and Mrs. Rolling did not have the energy or capability to apply these techniques in a consistent fashion for a prolonged period of time. In fact, Monica's behavior was having negative effects on their own emotional and physical well-being. The therapist and attending physician were fearful that the stress added by Monica's presence would lead to another heart attack for

Mr. Rolling. In light of these conditions, intervention focused on convincing the Rollings that Monica could receive more extensive treatment in another environment. Because of the Rollings' self-sacrificing nature, the therapist emphasized that the move was more for Monica's benefit than for theirs.

Extrafamilial Systems

The influence of extrafamilial systems is an especially important consideration when assessing the behavior of children who live with surrogate parents. Children who experience repeated placements with surrogate parents often rely heavily on their peer groups for social and emotional support. Frequently, this identification with peers is so strong that the influence of the surrogate parents on child behavior is secondary, at best. As a result, the therapist might find it useful to direct intervention efforts toward the child's transactions with peers. Specific intervention strategies for altering peer group behavior are discussed in Chapter 5.

A frequent goal of treatment is the development of a close relationship between the child and an adult whose personal psychosocial functioning is adequate. Ideally, one of the surrogate parents should fill this role for the child. In some situations, however, an appropriate surrogate parent is unavailable. In such cases, members of the extended family or the parents of the child's friends might be recruited to provide support for the surrogate parents or the child. An older adult sibling, or a sibling who lives in another surrogate-parent family, might also enhance the child's identity and provide an important source of emotional support. In addition, it may be possible to enlist the cooperation of a neighbor, friend of the family, or fellow church member to serve as a role model for the child. Although the therapist may have to devote some time to searching for extrafamilial support, the establishment of a long-term positive relationship of the child with an adult in the natural environment could be the most productive intervention that the therapist makes.

Social service professionals who assist in the placement of children with surrogate parents might also be enlisted as agents in the child's treatment. In some cases, these professionals have had repeated contacts with the child over many years and have an excellent understanding of the child's strengths, weaknesses, and needs. Although it is always important to respect the role of the surrogate parents, the social service professional may agree to serve in a supportive role with the child and in an advisory capacity with the parents. Enlisting the assistance of such individuals can help to attenuate the negative effects of future separations from surrogate parents and may provide the child with an enduring adult figure during the course of his or her development.

REFERENCES

Biller, H. B. (1974). *Paternal deprivation: Family, school, sexuality, and society*. Lexington, MA: D.C. Heath.

Biller, H. B. (1976). The father and personality development: Paternal deprivation and sex-role development. In M. E. Lamb (Ed.), *The role of the father in child development* (pp. 89–156). New York: Wiley.

Biller, H. B., & Bahm, R. M. (1971). Father absence, perceived maternal behavior, and masculinity of self concept among junior high school boys. *Developmental Psychology, 4*, 178–181.

Borduin, C. M., & Henggeler, S. W. (1982). Psychosocial development of father-absent children. In S. W. Henggeler (Ed.), *Delinquency and adolescent psychopathology: A family-ecological systems approach.* Littleton, MA: Wright-PSG.

Chapman, M. (1977). Father absence, stepfathers, and the cognitive performance of college students. *Child Development, 48*, 1155–1158.

Epstein, Y. M., & Borduin, C. M. (1984). The children's feedback game: An approach for modifying disruptive group behavior. *American Journal of Psychotherapy, 38*, 63–72.

Epstein, Y. M., & Borduin, C. M. (1985). Could this happen: A game for children of divorce. *Psychotherapy: Theory, Research, and Practice, 22*, 770–773.

Epstein, Y. M., Borduin, C. M., & Wexler, A. S. (1985). The Children Helping Children Program: A case illustration. *Special Services in the Schools, 2*, 73–93.

Glick, P. C., & Lin, S. (1986). Recent changes in divorce and remarriage. *Journal of Marriage and the Family, 48*, 737–747.

Haley, J. (1973). *Uncommon therapy: The psychiatric techniques of Milton H. Erickson.* New York: Norton.

Hanson, C. L., Henggeler, S. W., Haefele, W. F., & Rodick, J. D. (1984). Demographic, individual, and family relationship correlates of serious and repeated crime among adolescents and their siblings. *Journal of Consulting and Clinical Psychology, 52*, 528–538.

Henggeler, S. W., & Cohen, R. (1984). The role of cognitive development in the family-ecological systems approach to child psychopathology. In J. B. Gholson & T. L. Rosenthal (Eds.), *Applications of cognitive-developmental theory* (pp. 173–189). New York: Academic Press.

Hernandez, D. J. (1988). Demographic trends and the living arrangements of children. In E. M. Hetherington & J. D. Arasteh (Eds), *Impact of divorce, single-parenting, and stepparenting on children* (pp. 3–22). Hillsdale, NJ: Erlbaum.

Hetherington, E. M., Cox, M., & Cox, R. (1976). Divorced fathers. *The Family Coordinator, 25*, 417–428.

Hetherington, E. M., Cox, M., & Cox, R. (1978). The aftermath of divorce. In J. H. Stevens & M. Matthews (Eds.), *Mother-child, father-child relations* (pp. 149–176). Washington, DC: National Association for the Education of Young Children.

Hetherington, E. M., & Martin, B. (1986). Family factors and psychopathology in children. In H. C. Quay & J. S. Werry (Eds.), *Psychopathological disorders of childhood* (3rd ed.; pp. 332–390). New York: Wiley.

Hetherington, E. M., Stanley-Hagan, M., & Anderson, E. R. (1989). Marital transitions: A child's perspective. *American Psychologist, 44*, 303–312.

Jacobson, D. S. (1979). Stepfamilies: Myths and realities. *Social Work, 24*, 202–207.

Jacobson, G., & Ryder, R. G. (1969). Parental loss and some characteristics of the early marriage relationship. *American Journal of Orthopsychiatry, 39*, 787–799.

Johnson, M. M. (1975). Fathers, mothers, and sex typing. *Sociological Inquiry, 45*, 15–26.

Lessing, E. E., Zagorin, S. W., & Nelson, D. (1970). WISC subtest and IQ score correlates of father absence. *The Journal of Genetic Psychology, 117*, 181–195.

Minuchin, S. (1974). *Families and family therapy.* Cambridge, MA: Harvard University Press.

Nash, J. (1965). The father in contemporary culture and current psychological literature. *Child Development, 36*, 261–297.

Peterson, J. L., & Zill, N. (1983, April). *Marital disruption, parent-child relationships, and behavior problems in children.* Paper presented at the meeting of the Society for Research in Child Development, Detroit, MI.

Rutter, M. (1971). Parent-child separation: Psychological effects on the children. *Journal of Child Psychology and Psychiatry, 12*, 233–260.

Santrock, J. W. (1970). Paternal absence, sex typing, and identification. *Developmental Psychology, 2*, 264–272.

Santrock, J. W. (1975). Father absence, perceived maternal behavior, and moral development in boys. *Child Development, 46*, 753–757.

Santrock, J. W., Warshak, R., Lindbergh, C., & Meadows, L. (1982). Children's and parents' observed social behavior in step-father families. *Child Development, 53*, 472–480.

Shinn, M. (1978). Father absence and children's cognitive development. *Psychological Bulletin, 85*, 295–324.

Solomon, M. A. (1973). A developmental, conceptual premise for family therapy. *Family Process, 12*, 179–188.

Visher, E. B., & Visher, J. S. (1979). *Stepfamilies: A guide to working with stepparents and stepchildren.* New York: Brunner-Mazel.

Visher, E. B., & Visher, J. S. (1983). Stepparenting: Blended families. In H. I. McCubbin & C. R. Figley (Eds.), *Stress and the family, Vol. I: Coping with normative transitions* (pp. 133–146). New York: Brunner-Mazel.

CHAPTER 8

Treatment of Delinquent Behavior

*D*uring the past decade we have devoted considerable time to the study of delinquent behavior. A systematic research program was developed to identify the systemic correlates of delinquent behavior and to formulate effective intervention strategies for delinquent adolescents and the systems in which they are embedded. From 1978 to 1982, more than 100 families of juvenile offenders were evaluated and treated in the Memphis State University Delinquency Project. In addition, more than 100 control families (i.e., families of juvenile offenders who received an alternative treatment and families of well-adjusted adolescents) were evaluated during this time. Similarly, from 1983 through the present, approximately 150 families of juvenile offenders have been assessed and treated in the University of Missouri–Columbia Delinquency Project. An additional 150 adolescents and their families have served as either delinquent or normal controls. The Missouri project is still in progress, and we are enthusiastic about findings that are continuing to emanate from it.

This chapter first provides a brief overview of research findings regarding the systemic correlates of delinquent behavior. Next, we describe the findings of investigators who have developed causal models of delinquent behavior. The results of our multisystemic outcome studies are then presented in conjuction with the findings of other investigations of therapeutic outcome. Finally, we describe the components of the multisystemic approach that may account for its relative success in treating delinquent behavior.

DEFINING THE PROBLEM

Delinquent behavior consists of acts that violate the law, but it is important to note that there is a very wide range in the seriousness of such acts. On one end of the continuum are *status offenses*, which are offenses such as truancy, running away, and possession of alcohol, that would not violate the law if committed by an adult. At the other end of the continuum are *index offenses*, including murder, rape, robbery, arson, and aggravated assault.

Although the definition of delinquent behavior is relatively straightforward, the classification of an adolescent as delinquent is problematic. This is because, as shown in self-report surveys (e.g., Hindelang, Hirschi, & Weis, 1981), a very high percentage of adolescents have committed delinquent acts at some time. The probability that a particular adolescent will be arrested and classified as delinquent varies as a function of the adolescent's social ecology (e.g., neighborhood), the frequency and seriousness of the offenses, and a variety of other systemic variables. Therefore, some adolescents who are officially labeled as delinquents have low rates of delinquent behavior, and many adolescents who have no arrest history have high rates of delinquent behavior.

The association between self-reported delinquent behavior and arrest rates has important implications for the interpretation of the results from our research projects. Specifically, the vast majority of the adolescents in our "delinquent" groups had at least two arrests that were not for status offenses. Although we recognize that arrest history is not an exact measure of delinquent behavior, it has been shown that a high percentage of adolescents with two or more arrests are identified as career offenders based on self-reports of delinquent behavior (Elliott, Huizinga, & Morse, 1985). Thus, the criminal behavior of the delinquent adolescents in our samples probably falls at the relatively serious end of the delinquent behavior continuum.

SERIOUSNESS OF THE PROBLEM

Mental health professionals must develop effective interventions for adolescents, especially males, who engage in repeated and serious criminal activity for several reasons:

1. Male adolescents commit a disproportionately high percentage of violent criminal acts. In 1984, for example, males under the age of 18 years accounted for 16.8% of all arrests for violent crimes, including 16% of forcible rapes, 25% of robberies, and 13% of aggravated assaults (Federal Bureau of Investigation, 1985). These arrest statistics are especially disturbing in light of findings that the offense/arrest ratio for male adolescents is approximately 25:1 for rape, 20:1 for robbery, and 100:1 for aggravated assault (Elliott, Huizinga, & Morse, 1985). The development of therapeutic interventions that can decrease recidivism may result in significant reductions in extremely serious criminal activity.

2. Considerable evidence shows that youths who display high rates of antisocial and delinquent behavior tend to maintain such behavior through adolescence and adulthood (Loeber, 1982; Olweus, 1979). For example, Elliott, Huizinga, and Morse (1985) found that while rates of delinquent behavior show age-related declines in the general adolescent population, rates of criminal behavior among chronic offenders may actually increase with age.

3. Serious juvenile offenders seem to be part of family systems that have an extremely detrimental impact on the community. Indeed, investigators have found that although repeat juvenile offenders and their families comprise a relatively small percentage of the population, they account for a large percentage of a community's crimes (Farrington, 1979; Hamparian, Schuster, Dinitz, & Conrad, 1978; Strasburg, 1978). Thus, interventions that are implemented at the family level may provide preventive benefits for the community.

CORRELATES OF DELINQUENT BEHAVIOR

A growing body of empirical evidence shows that adolescent criminal activity is related to important characteristics of the individual, family, and peer systems (for comprehensive reviews, see Henggeler, 1982; Henggeler, 1989; Loeber & Dishion, 1983; Quay, 1987). In regard to individual factors, several investigators have found that delinquent adolescents evidence lower levels of sociomoral reasoning than do their nondelinquent counterparts (Hains & Miller, 1980; Hudgins & Prentice, 1973; Jurkovic & Prentice, 1977). In a critical review of this literature, Blasi (1980) concluded that a high percentage of delinquents are at Stage 2 of Kohlberg's (1976) developmental typology. In Stage 2, the adolescent is primarily concerned with the gratification of his needs, whereas in Stage 3, the adolescent is more concerned with social conformity, approval, and meeting the expectations of others. In a recent investigation, Finger and Borduin (in preparation) found that the level of moral development among adolescents accounted for 22% of the variance in predicting rates of self-reported delinquency.

Researchers have also concluded that delinquent behavior is associated with individual adolescent factors, such as social skill deficits (Dishion, Loeber, Stouthamer-Loeber, & Patterson, 1984; Freedman, Rosenthal, Donahoe, Schlundt, & McFall, 1978), impulsivity and attitudinal bias (Camp & Ray, 1984), and low intelligence (Wilson & Herrnstein, 1985). In general, these researchers have concluded that delinquent adolescents evidence cognitive deficits that interfere with their ability to develop competent responses to problematic situations. For example, the delinquent might process interpersonal communications in a distorted manner, reach erroneous conclusions regarding the meaning of the communications, and fail to consider the strengths and weaknesses of possible responses to the communication.

Regarding the family system, numerous investigators have concluded that delinquent behavior is closely associated with problematic parenting strategies and family relations. Patterson and his colleagues (Patterson, 1986; Snyder & Patterson, 1987) have emphasized the roles that inconsistent parental discipline strategies, coercive interactions, and inadequate parental monitoring play in the development of delinquent behavior. In our research (Borduin & Henggeler, 1987; Borduin, Henggeler, Hanson, & Pruitt, 1985; Borduin, Pruitt, & Henggeler, 1986; Henggeler, Borduin, & Mann, 1987; Henggeler, Edwards, & Borduin, 1987; Henggeler, Hanson, Borduin, Watson, & Brunk, 1985; Rodick, Henggeler, & Hanson, 1986), we have found that delinquent behavior is associated with low rates of positive communication, high rates of hostile communication, and difficulties in family cohesion and adaptability.

The adolescent's association with delinquent peers is also highly predictive of criminal activity. As discussed subsequently, Elliott, Huizinga, and Ageton (1985) found that current involvement with delinquent peers was a powerful and direct predictor of delinquent behavior. Similarly, we found that the extent of the adolescent's association with delinquent peers was the most consistent and powerful predictor of serious and repeated arrests among adolescents and their siblings, when contrasted with several individual and family variables (Hanson, Henggeler, Haefele, & Rodick, 1984). Other extrafamilial factors that have been linked with delinquent and antisocial behavior include poor school performance (Hindelang, Hirschi, & Weis, 1981), neighborhood of residence (Gold, 1987), stress on single mothers (Patterson, 1986), and the family's social support network (Dumas & Wahler, 1983).

Although the above studies have contributed significantly to our understanding of the different factors that are associated with delinquent behavior, most of these studies possess two important methodological limitations. First, in light of the correlational nature of these studies, it is impossible to determine whether observed correlates of delinquency led to the delinquent behavior, or whether the delinquent behavior led to the correlates. For example, does parental rejection lead to delinquent behavior, does delinquent behavior lead to parental rejection, or is the relationship reciprocal? Second, most of the extant studies have tapped only a small subset of the correlates of delinquent behavior. Thus, it is not possible to examine the interrelations among the correlates of delinquent behavior to determine which variables have direct effects or indirect effects on delinquent behavior, or which variables are not linked with delinquent behavior when the effects of other correlates are controlled.

MULTIDIMENSIONAL CAUSAL MODELS OF DELINQUENT BEHAVIOR

In order to address the inherent limitations of correlational research, several investigators have begun to develop multidimensional causal models of delinquent behavior (Henggeler, in press). Two exemplary research projects have examined the causal linkages among several key correlates of delinquent behavior. Although the two projects differ significantly in design, sampling, and measurement, the findings from each seem quite similar.

In their National Youth Survey, Elliott, Huizinga, and Ageton (1985) used a longitudinal design with a representative national sample of adolescents to assess the psychosocial determinants of delinquent behavior. Endogenous and exogenous variables were derived from adolescent self-report data that were collected on a yearly basis. The predicted variables were self-reported delinquent behavior (general delinquency, drug use, index offenses) at time 2, and the predictor variables included measures of strain at time 1 (home, school), conventional bonding both at time 1 (family normlessness, school normlessness) and time 2 (family involvement, school involvement), bonding to delinquent peers at time 2 (attitudes toward deviance, involvement with delinquent peers), and self-reported delinquent behavior at time 1. Across sexes and types of delinquent behavior, the results showed that prior delinquency and current involvement with delinquent peers were the only variables that directly affected delinquent behavior. Two additional variables, conventional bonding to family and conventional bonding to school, indirectly influenced delinquent behavior by directly affecting adolescents' involvement with delinquent peers. Together, the four variables accounted for 52% of the variance in predicting general delinquency.

Elliott et al. also found a significant statistical interaction between conventional bonding to family and school and current involvement with delinquent peers in predicting delinquent behavior. Strong conventional bonds partially buffered the negative effects of involvement with delinquent peers. At present, this model is being refined through the examination of reciprocal relationships between variables (e.g., between conventional bonding and deviant bonding) and the inclusion of other measures (e.g., social disorganization, adolescent depression) that may tap additional variance in predicting delinquent behavior (Elliott, Huizinga, & Morse, 1985).

Patterson and his colleagues (Patterson, 1986; Patterson & Dishion, 1985; Patterson & Stouthamer-Loeber, 1984) used a cross-sectional design to test the hypothesis that delinquent behavior is directly linked to poor family management skills, involvement with deviant peers, and poor academic skills. The sample in this project included 136 adolescent boys and their families and was fairly representative of the population in Eugene, Oregon (e.g., 10.7% of the boys had a court record). In order to enhance the reliability and validity both of the exogenous variables (parental monitoring, social skills, academic skills) and the endogenous variables (deviant peers, delinquent behavior), the researchers used multiple measures of each variable and obtained data from multiple respondents (adolescent, mother, interviewer) across multiple settings (home, school, juvenile court, research center). Structural equation modeling revealed that parental monitoring, academic skills, and involvement with deviant peers were each directly linked to delinquent behavior, although each of the path coefficients was only of marginal statistical significance. Nevertheless, these variables accounted for 54.3% of the variance in predicting delinquent behavior. In addition, it was observed that parental monitoring and adolescent social skills were indirectly linked to delinquent behavior through their direct influence on the adolescent's association with deviant peers. Patterson and his colleagues are also refining their model through the use of a longitudinal research design and the consideration of extrafamilial variables, such as chronic stress, that may increase the predicted variance.

One of our studies addressed conceptual issues that are similar to those raised by Elliott, Huizinga, and Ageton (1985) and Patterson and Dishion (1985). In a cross-sectional design, Hanson et al. (1984) evaluated the relative contribution of demographic characteristics, individual characteristics, family relationship variables, and involvement with deviant peers to adolescent arrest history. Multiple regression analyses revealed that association with deviant peers was the most powerful predictor of adolescent arrest history, accounting for 28% of the variance. Age at first arrest contributed an additional 26% of the variance. Although these findings are mitigated by the fact that the design was not longitudinal and that adolescent arrest history may underestimate actual rates of delinquent behavior (Dunford & Elliott, 1984), it is noteworthy that the results are quite similar to those of Elliott, Huizinga, and Ageton (1985). That is, association with deviant peers and age of first arrest (which is probably significantly correlated with self-reported delinquent behavior) each contributed substantial amounts of unique variance. Moreover, similar to the findings of Patterson and his colleagues, we found that family variables contributed a substantial amount of variance. Combined, the variables in our study accounted for approximately 56% of the variance in predicting adolescent arrest history.

In summary, the results from correlational studies and causal modeling studies are consistent with the multisystemic model of child and adolescent behavior problems. Delinquent behavior is linked with individual adolescent characteristics and with various aspects of the multiple systems in which adolescents are embedded. Although different groups of investigators have emphasized the roles of different factors within these systems (e.g., within the family system, Patterson and colleagues emphasize the importance of parental discipline strategies, Elliott and colleagues address family bonding, and we stress family conflict, affect, and communication processes), it seems clear that each system makes a unique contribution to delinquent behavior. Moreover, it seems likely that the contributions of these different systems are not strictly linear and additive. The linkages between different systems frequently exert an impact on the adolescent's behavior (Bronfenbrenner, 1986). We believe that future studies will demonstrate these synergistic associations among systems in which delinquents are embedded.

Finally, it should be noted that the results from these causal modeling studies have important implications for the treatment of delinquent adolescents. Based on the findings of Elliott, Huizinga, and Ageton (1985), it seems crucial for treatment to promote the adolescent's disengagement from deviant peers and to build stronger bonds to such conventional groups as the family and school. Considering the findings of Patterson et al. (Patterson, 1986; Patterson & Dishion, 1985), it seems most important to enhance family management skills (monitoring and discipline) and to develop the adolescent's social and academic competence. Again, these implications are consistent with the multisystemic conceptual framework and approach to intervention.

OVERVIEW OF TREATMENT STUDIES

Reviews of treatment outcome studies with juvenile delinquents reveal that the development of effective intervention strategies has been an extremely difficult task (Blakely & Davidson, 1984; Lipsey, 1988). Some evidence, however, does point to the efficacy of treatment approaches that focus directly on the systemic contexts of which adolescents are members. In a peer group intervention study, for example, Feldman, Caplinger, and Wodarski (1983) found that behavior problem adolescents assigned to peer groups with a high percentage of prosocial peers showed long-term decreases in rates of delinquent behavior, whereas problem adolescents who participated in peer groups that were composed of deviant peers did not evidence decreased delinquent behavior. Similarly, Tolan, Cromwell, and Brasswell (1986) concluded that family-based interventions have shown considerable promise in reducing delinquent behavior. However, other reviewers (Gurman, Kniskern, & Pinsof, 1986; Kazdin, 1984) have noted that the promising results of family-based interventions have generally pertained to cases from the "soft" end of the antisocial/delinquency continuum (i.e., Alexander & Parsons, 1973; Klein, Alexander, & Parsons, 1977; Patterson, 1982). These reviewers also concluded that it is considerably more difficult to intervene in family systems that are characterized by minority status, high rates of poverty and father absence, and social disorganization. As discussed previously, chronic and serious offenders, rather than status offenders, are the delinquents who present the most significant problems for our society.

As noted earlier in this volume, the multisystemic treatment model has been applied especially to serious juvenile offenders and their families. Consistent with the findings from the causal modeling studies of delinquent behavior, multisystemic treatment attempts to change transactions within and among pertinent systems (family, peer, school) that are associated with the adolescent's problem behavior. As described next, the results from three outcome studies with "difficult to treat" families have been very encouraging. These studies have focused on the families of inner-city juvenile offenders (Henggeler, Rodick, Borduin, Hanson, Watson, & Urey, 1986), families charged with child abuse or neglect (Brunk, Henggeler, & Whelan, 1987), and a heterogenous sample of families of juvenile offenders (Borduin, Blaske, Mann, Treloar, Henggeler, & Fucci, in preparation).

Multisystemic Treatment of Juvenile Offenders: Effects on Adolescent Behavior and Family Interaction

A total of 116 families of juvenile offenders were referred for *multisystemic treatment* by the Memphis-Metro Youth Diversion Project (Henggeler et al., 1986). Although these families were not under court order to enter or complete treatment, only 25% of the families terminated treatment prematurely. Strategies used to promote family coopera-tion are outlined later in this chapter. The *alternative treatment* comparison group consisted of 40 juvenile offenders and their families, who were referred to other mental health agencies for services. Approximately 65% of these families completed treatment. To control for developmental maturation and to provide a frame of reference, 50 nonpathological adolescents and their families were recruited for participation as *normal controls*. The demographic characteristics of the three groups showed no significant differences: the mean age of the adolescents was 14.8 years, 65% of the families were Black, 75% were lower class, 62% were from single-parent families, and 84% of the adolescents were males. The delinquent adolescents averaged 2.1 arrests.

Multisystemic therapists, who were doctoral students in clinical psychology, used several interventions that have been developed by family therapists, developmental psychologists, and social-learning/cognitive-behavioral therapists. The therapists also used interventions that were originated by themselves or by other members of the multisystemic project. It is important to note that treatment was not given wholesale; rather, it was targeted at the identified dysfunction in a system or between two or more systems. Treatment was delivered in a variety of settings as needed (e.g., clinic, home, school, neighborhood). The total number of hours in treatment ranged from 2 to 47, with a mean of 20 hours. Interventions received by the alternative treatment group reflected the range of services that are provided to juvenile offenders and their families in the city of Memphis: family counseling, individual counseling, structured recreational and social experiences, and alternative educational programs. Youths in the alternative treatment group averaged 24 hours of intervention, and their therapists possessed relatively exten-sive experience.

Assessment sessions were conducted immediately before the beginning of treatment and within three weeks of the termination of treatment by an independent group of research assistants. Dependent measures assessed multiple systemic levels and vantage points, including self-reported personality variables (Eysenck Personality Inventory; Eysenck & Eysenck, 1963), parent ratings of adolescent behavior problems (Behavior Problem Checklist; Quay & Peterson, 1975)), family members' perceptions of family relationships (Family Relationship Questionnaire; Henggeler & Tavormina, 1980), and observer ratings of family interaction derived from an audiorecorded unrevealed differences task. Specific observational measures tapped family affect, conflict, dominance, and supportiveness-defensiveness.

Because the multivariate analyses and results are detailed in the research manuscript, the findings are only briefly summarized and several concrete examples are presented. As shown in Table 8-1, adolescents in the multisystemic group evidenced fewer behavior problems following treatment, and their mothers reported that these adolescents were less involved with deviant peers. Moreover, the mother-adolescent and marital dyads were warmer and more affectionate, and the adolescent was more actively involved in the family discussion following treatment. Such changes were not observed for the alternative treatment group. In fact, some family relations in the alternative treatment group had deteriorated.

Table 8-1   Examples of pre-post changes in mean scores

	Pre	Post
Mother-adolescent warmth		
Multisystemic	3.9	4.6*
Alternative	4.8	4.4
Normal control	4.7	4.8
Mother-father warmth		
Multisystemic	4.1	4.6*
Alternative	5.7	4.6*
Normal control	5.0	4.8
BPC-conduct problems		
Multisystemic	13.4	9.3*
Alternative	7.2	6.3
Normal control	5.2	5.7
BPC-socialized aggression (association with deviant peers)		
Multisystemic	4.0	2.2*
Alternative	2.7	2.1
Normal control	1.0	1.0

*Significant pre-post change.
Note: BPC = Behavior Problem Checklist. Warmth refers to a qualitative rating on a 7-point observational scale.

Overall, the results from this outcome study were quite favorable. Short-term success was demonstated with a client population that is typically regarded as quite recalcitrant to treatment. The methods used to achieve this relative success are outlined later in the chapter.

A Comparison of Multisystemic Therapy and Parent Training in the Brief Treatment of Child Abuse and Neglect

The second study to evaluate multisystemic therapy was directed by Dr. Molly A. Brunk, who is currently the Director of Psychology at the Virginia Treatment Center for Children. In this study (Brunk et al., 1987), we compared the effects of multisystemic therapy and parent training on families of abused children and on families of neglected children. Maltreated children are considered by many mental health professionals to be at risk for the development of antisocial and delinquent behavior (Lane & Davis, 1987). The theoretical foundations of multisystemic therapy and parent training are compatible with the two primary models of child maltreatment that have emerged in the literature. Multisystemic therapy is consistent with the ecological model of child maltreatment developed from systems theory (Belsky, 1980), and parent training is consistent with the social-situational model derived from the paradigm of learning theory (Parke & Collmer, 1975).

Forty-three families served as subjects. These families were composed of at least one parent who had been investigated for abuse or neglect and the child who was the target of the maltreatment. Families were randomly assigned to either *parent training* or *multisystemic therapy*, with type of maltreatment (abuse vs. neglect) counterbalanced across treatment conditions. Five families in each treatment condition terminated treatment prematurely. In the remaining 33 families, 55% of the maltreated children were male, 76% of the maltreating parents were female, 57% of the families were White and the rest were Black, and almost all of the families were of low socioeconomic status.

For both treatments, therapy sessions lasted for 1 1/2 hours and were held once per week for eight weeks. All therapists were M.A. level psychologists and were equally experienced in the use of their respective therapy techniques. Parent training was conducted with groups of parents in a clinic setting; in multisystemic therapy, each family was seen separately in either their home or the clinic. There were advantages to each context of therapy. For example, group treatment seems to enhance parental support systems, decrease the social isolation of maltreating parents, and provide immediate feedback from peers regarding the development of solutions for extant problems (Wodarski, 1981). On the other hand, meeting with families in their homes may facilitate the generalization of therapeutic progress and address family interaction problems more directly (Halperin, 1981).

Parent training groups, modeled after those developed by Wolfe and his colleagues (Wolfe, Sandler, & Kaufman, 1981), focused on instructing parents in normative child development and behavior management techniques. Topics for each session were derived from *Parents Are Teachers* (Becker, 1971) and *Living with Children* (Patterson, 1979). These topics included guidelines for the use of positive reinforcement and nonpunitive discipline strategies, an emphasis on the importance of parental consistency, descriptions of the negative effects of punitive methods of discipline, and suggestions for developing more positive parent-child relations.

The exact nature of the multisystemic interventions varied for each family, depending on the strengths and weaknesses of the pertinent systems. In all cases, however, therapists used joining and reframing techniques and prescribed tasks designed to change interaction patterns (Haley, 1976; Minuchin, 1974). Approximately 88% of the families also received informal parent education regarding child management strategies and expectations for normative child behavior. In addition, 88% of the cases involved some restructuring of the family system: Neglectful parents learned to perform executive functions, and abusive parents developed greater flexibility. In 25% of the cases, marital therapy was conducted, and in another 25%, the mother's relations with extended family were targeted for change. Coaching and emotional support were used to address peer relationship problems with 19% of the children and 31% of the parents. In approximately 50% of the cases, the therapist helped to resolve the family's difficulties with outside agencies. Finally, therapists attempted to enhance the social perspective-taking abilities of one or more family members in 38% of the cases.

Each family was assessed before entering treatment and within one week after the eighth therapy session. During each assessment session, the maltreating parent completed several questionnaires and interacted with the target child during a semi-structured interaction task. The questionnaires tapped three levels of systems that are related to child maltreatment: individual (SCL-90-R; Derogatis, 1983; and the Behavior Problem Check-list; Quay & Peterson, 1975), family (Family Environment Scale; Moos & Moos, 1981), and social system (Family Inventory of Life Events and Changes; McCubbin, Patterson, & Wilson, 1982). Therapy outcome questionnaires were used to quantify parents' and therapists' perceptions of the specific presenting problems for each family at individual, family, and social system levels. Parent-child interactions were examined with a sequen-tial coding system specifically designed to evaluate parental control strategies. The coding system was based on the research of Schaffer and Crook (1979, 1980) and yielded three-part sequences (antecedent child behavor—parent control—consequent child be-havior) that measured parental effectiveness, child passive noncompliance, and parental unresponsiveness.

The results showed that multisystemic therapy and parent training evidenced similar treatment effects on some measures, and showed different treatment effects on other measures. Maltreating parents (i.e., neglectful parents and abusive parents) in both treatment conditions reported decreased psychiatric symptomology, reduced stress, and improvement in the specific individual and family problems that parents reported at the beginning of treatment. The amelioration of these self-reported individual and family problems was generally corroborated by the therapists' reports of change. *Observational findings, however, showed that multisystemic treatment was more effective than parent training in restructuring parent-child relations.* Following multisystemic therapy, maltreating parents showed increased effectiveness in controlling their children's be-havior, maltreated children exhibited less passive noncompliance toward their parents, and neglecting parents became more responsive to their children's behavior. On the other hand, parents who received parent training reported a greater decrease in social problems such as isolation that had been identified by the parents at the outset of therapy.

It seems likely that the differential effects of parent training and multisystemic therapy on parent-child relations were a function of the different theoretical models from which these treatment approaches were derived. Behavioral parent training emphasizes relatively mechanistic and linear conceptualizations of behavior, whereas family therapy approaches stress circular causality and place greater emphasis on the ecological context of behavior problems. Although parent training is clearly an effective treatment in many situations, it may present certain limitations when applied as the primary therapeutic intervention for multiproblem families. Systemic models of change provide the flexibility needed to intervene at multiple levels and with issues that are cognitive, emotional, and/or instrumental in nature. It is also possible, however, that the advantages of multisystemic therapy were due to the fact that many of the families were treated in their homes, rather than in a clinic setting.

In conclusion, we believe that this study provides relatively strong support for the short-term efficacy of multisystemic therapy with maltreating parents and their children.

Methodological strengths of the study included random assignment to treatment groups, assessment of change from multiple perspectives and with multiple methods, and the use of a comparison treatment that has received considerable support in the therapy outcome literature.

Multisystemic Treatment of Juvenile Offenders: A Replication and Extension

As in our first outcome study in the area of delinquency (Henggeler et al., 1986), the purpose of this study was to compare multisystemic therapy with an alternative treatment for families of juvenile offenders. This investigation (Borduin, Blaske, et al., in preparation), however, differed from our earlier study in several important ways. First, the juvenile offenders and their families were from two rural Missouri counties with a combined population of approximately 125,000. Second, assignment to treatment conditions was random. Third, the interventions received by the alternative treatment group were relatively homogeneous in nature. Fourth, a broader range of individual and systemic variables was assessed. And, fifth, a follow-up evaluation was conducted.

A total of 210 families of juvenile offenders agreed to participate in the assessment and treatment components of the study. Following the initial assessment session, each family was randomly assigned to either *multisystemic therapy* or the *alternative treatment* group. Approximately 84% ($n = 88$) of the families in multisystemic therapy and 65% ($n = 68$) of the families assigned to alternative therapy completed treatment.

Within one week of the completion of treatment, a postassessment session was conducted by an independent group of research assistants. Forty-five nondisturbed adolescents and their families served as *normal controls*. For these latter families, the waiting period between pre- and postassessments ranged from three to five months ($M = 4.5$ months) and reflected a time frame that was similar to that of the families in treatment. The three groups did not differ significantly in their demographic characteristics, including adolescent age ($M = 15.1$ years) and gender (79% were males), race (68% were White and 32% were Black), social class (70% were lower class), intactness of family (59% were father-absent), and number of children per family ($M = 3.4$). All of the delinquent adolescents had multiple arrests ($M = 4.2$), with their most recent crimes ranging from shoplifting and vandalism to aggravated assault and attempted rape.

Multisystemic treatment was provided by second- and third-year doctoral students in clinical psychology and ranged in length from 5 to 54 hours ($M = 23$ hours). Although the interventions varied for each family, the following five types of interventions were most frequently used:

1. Family therapy (83% of the cases), which usually involved restructuring the family system and/or building cohesion and emotional warmth among family members.

2. School intervention (60%), including the facilitation of parent-teacher communication and assisting in remedial efforts and behavior management.

3. Peer intervention (57%), including coaching, emotional support, integration into prosocial peer groups such as scouts and athletic teams, and/or direct contact and intervention with relevant peers.

4. Individual therapy with a family member (28%), including cognitive-behavioral intervention, training in social skills and social perspective-taking, and/or education and support.

5. Marital therapy (26%).

The content of these interventions is described more extensively in the next section of this chapter.

Interventions in the alternative treatment group were provided by experienced M.A.-level therapists at local social service agencies and ranged in length from 15 to 72 hours ($M = 28$ hours). All of the adolescents in this group received individual counseling that focused on personal, family, and school-related issues. In 66% of the cases, the therapist and parent(s) had brief contact (at least once a month) to discuss the adolescent's progress at home and school. In 10% of the cases, the adolescent initially received a psychiatric evaluation at the therapist's request and was subsequently given medication.

During each assessment session, the parent(s), target adolescent, and siblings completed several questionnaires. Measures of individual psychosocial functioning included the SCL-90-R (Derogatis, 1983), the Defining Issues Test (Davison, 1979), and the Revised Behavior Problem Checklist (Quay & Peterson, 1987), which was completed by the parents only. Measures of family and marital relations were obtained with the FACES-II (Olson et al., 1982), the Family Relationship Questionnaire (Henggeler & Tavormina, 1980), and the Locke-Wallace Marital Adjustment Scale (Locke & Wallace, 1959), which was completed by parents only. Observational measures of family affect, conflict-hostility, and positive communication were derived from an unrevealed differences task that was videorecorded. Parent and adolescent ratings of adolescent peer relations were obtained using the Missouri Peer Relations Inventory (MPRI; Borduin, Treloar, Blaske, & Mann, in preparation). This inventory yields three factors: emotional bonding to peers, aggression toward peers, and peer acceptance. We also obtained teacher ratings of the adolescent's peer relations using the MPRI, and the therapist completed a series of 7-point bipolar scales that assessed adolescent and family psychosocial functioning.

Preliminary results, based on multivariate analyses of variance, are presented in Table 8-2. The findings indicate that following treatment, adolescents in the multisystemic group showed improved relations with peers and fewer behavior problems. The siblings of these adolescents also reported less symptomatology following treatment. Moreover, the mother-adolescent dyad showed increased positive communication, and family members reported that levels of family adaptability and flexibility had increased. Such changes did not emerge for adolescents in the alternative treatment group, and their family relations showed some evidence of deterioration.

In addition, some evidence, though not derived from the entire sample, suggested that multisystemic treatment may be effective in reducing rates of delinquent behavior. First, based on a measure of self-reported delinquency (Elliott & Ageton, 1980) that was added to our assessment well after the study had begun, we found that adolescents ($n = 16$ per group) who received multisystemic therapy showed a significant decline in reported offense rates, whereas adolescents who received the alternative treatment did not. Second, at a one-year follow-up for 120 of the subjects, official arrest records showed that 10 of 58 (17.3%) adolescents in the multisystemic group had been rearrested, in contrast to 16 of 40 (40%) adolescents in the alternative treatment group. None of the 22 adolescents in the normal control group had been arrested during the follow-up period.

Table 8-2 Pre-post changes on individual, peer, and family variables

	Pre	Post
Bonding to nondeviant peers		
Multisystemic	−0.54	−0.04*
Alternative	−0.49	−0.42
Normal control	0.67	0.58
RBPC-conduct problems		
Multisystemic	12.51	8.14*
Alternative	12.89	11.35
Normal control	5.48	5.65
Global symptom index-sibling		
Multisystemic	80.6	56.6*
Alternative	76.4	82.4
Normal control	47.0	43.3
Mother-adolescent positive communication		
Multisystemic	−0.37	1.13*
Alternative	−0.30	−0.24
Normal control	1.19	1.25
Family adaptability		
Multisystemic	43.2	49.1*
Alternative	44.6	39.1*
Normal control	51.3	50.6

*Significant pre-post change.
Note: RBPC = Revised Behavior Problem Checklist. Emotional bonding and facilitative information exchange are reported as standardized composite factor scores.

OVERVIEW OF SPECIFIC INTERVENTION STRATEGIES

As emphasized throughout this volume, child and adolescent behavior problems can be maintained by a range of intrapersonal and systemic factors. Because different combinations of these factors are relevant for different adolescents and families, treatment is directed only at those factors that are most pertinent. The findings we have just described suggest that the multisystemic treatment model is a promising approach for improving the relations of dysfunctional families and for decreasing the behavior problems of delinquent adolescents.

Following are some general strategies that we use in the treatment of delinquent behavior. Some of these strategies parallel the types of interventions that have been described elsewhere in this volume; others pertain more specifically to families of juvenile offenders and other involuntary client populations.

It should be remembered that the therapists in our treatment studies were relatively young doctoral students who were being paid from special grants and that the families were not charged for therapy. As such, some of the methods that we have used to promote cooperation with treatment (e.g., extensive home visits) might not seem applicable for private practitioners. Nevertheless, we have followed the process of these methods, varying the content somewhat in our own private clinical work, with considerable success. Moreover, the conceptualizations of delinquent behavior and the development of intervention strategies are the same whether the family is seen by the private practitioner or by a therapist in training.

Promoting Cooperation with Treatment

As discussed throughout this chapter, we have conducted much of our research and clinical practice with "difficult to treat" juvenile offenders and their interpersonal systems. A high percentage of these offenders have been from lower-income, single-parent families. In addition, these juveniles and their siblings have commonly had long histories of behavior problems, academic difficulties, and failure in various intervention programs. In light of the numerous problems in living faced by these juveniles and their families, together with their suspiciousness and occasional hostility toward middle-class service providers, it is not difficult to appreciate why this population of juveniles is generally considered "difficult to treat." Nevertheless, we have adopted several procedures that are of considerable value for dealing with impediments to treatment in this population. These procedures represent a central aspect of our treatment approach, and we believe that they are largely responsible for the excellent cooperation that we have been able to obtain from these adolescents and their families. Several of these procedures are now briefly described.

We usually begin treatment by meeting with the adolescent and all other family members living in the home. Despite the fact that the family has agreed to participate in treatment, family members are often extremely anxious about meeting with a therapist. This anxiety is often intensified when the family is also expected to meet with the therapist in an unfamiliar setting such as a mental health clinic. Therefore, we often conduct the initial family session, and subsequent sessions as well, at the family's residence. We have found that most families of serious juvenile offenders, when given a choice by the therapist, prefer to meet on their own "turf" rather than in an unfamiliar setting. We believe that the therapist's willingness to travel to the family's home conveys a high level of respect for the family members' participation in treatment and helps them to form an image of the therapist as a reasonable person.

Meeting the family in their home also serves several pragmatic purposes. In our experience, a high percentage of missed or canceled clinic appointments occur because the family does not have reliable transportation (many do not own an automobile, and public transportation is poor in many cities), or because the meeting time conflicts with the parent's work schedule. Consequently, the therapist's time is used most efficiently when sessions are conducted in the family's home, and often at night or on the weekend. A further advantage of our scheduling practices is that it is much easier for unmotivated families to ignore an appointment at a clinic that is five miles away than to ignore the therapist who knocks at their door at the scheduled time.

In those few instances when the family is not home at the scheduled time, the therapist often waits for up to an hour for the family to return. If that is not possible, the therapist will return later that day to meet the family briefly and to reschedule the appointment. Although such effort is time-consuming for the therapist, we have found that initial persistence in making contact with the family members helps to ease their apprehensions about meeting the therapist and starting treatment.

The persistence of the therapist also serves an important communicative function for the small percentage of families who have learned strategies for passively avoiding the attention of social service professionals. Some multiproblem families have little desire for contact with social service professionals. For one reason or another, however, family members have experienced problems that have come to the attention of governmental service agencies. When social service professionals contact these families, the families seem to be very agreeable to suggestions, but rarely follow through after the professional leaves. The family has learned to present a cooperative front as a strategy for minimizing contact with professionals. The professional, who is typically underpaid and has a very high caseload, is often satisfied with the family's apparent cooperation or does not have the time or resources to persist in engaging the family. The multisystemic therapist, however, indicates both verbally and behaviorally (in a friendly and nonpejorative manner) that he or she is willing to devote as much time as is needed to deal with identified problems. When highly resistant families realize that the therapist is very persistent, many decide to cooperate with therapy.

During the initial interview with the family it is necessary that the meeting room (kitchen, living room) be structured to minimize distractions. Accordingly, the therapist might need to ask the family to turn off the television and stereo, and to tell visitors and callers to return later. The therapist usually begins the session with a brief social stage in which an effort is made to help everyone to relax. The therapist makes a point of obtaining some social response from each family member to convey that everyone in the family is important and to define the therapy situation as one in which all family members can contribute. The therapist then shifts to a problem stage in which everyone in the family is asked to give his or her view of the presenting problem(s). This strategy provides important information about areas of agreement and conflict in the family and also helps to define therapy as a cooperative endeavor.

The last part of the first interview involves a goal-setting stage during which the family members are asked to specify what changes they seek in therapy. In this regard, the therapist's task is to help the family to develop a clear operational definition of the behaviors or complaints that they would like to have solved. By arriving at such a definition, the therapist and family members have essentially entered into a contract about the goals of therapy, and the therapist (and family) will have a yardstick for measuring change and for evaluating the success of the treatment. Additional goals for treatment may be added by the therapist after an assessment has been completed in other relevant systemic contexts (e.g., the peer group, school).

Parents of adolescents who have committed serious law violations tend to be very insecure about parenting and other personal issues. These insecurities are often long-standing and may have been reinforced by the behavior of other professionals (e.g., a teacher, a previous therapist) toward the parent. Thus, we believe that in most cases it is essential that the therapist align strongly with the parent(s) from the outset of therapy to alleviate the parent's fears of failure and to establish a cooperative, rather than an adversary, relationship. In fact, in our treatment process research with families of delinquents, we have found that when treatment initially emphasizes parental strengths (e.g., the parent's concern for the adolescent and ability as a provider), it is likely that positive changes in parent-adolescent interactions will follow (Mann, Borduin, Henggeler, & Blaske, 1989). On the other hand, if the therapist's efforts to align with the parent(s) are unsuccessful, subsequent interventions involving the parent(s) are unlikely to succeed.

Our clinical experiences have also suggested that it is often useful to define the adolescent's behavior problems in terms of the adolescent's extreme susceptibility to influence from others (e.g., peers). The therapist can then suggest that the parent may need to modify his or her behavior to benefit the susceptible adolescent. By focusing on the parent's ability to help the adolescent and on the long-term negative consequences of the adolescent's present behavior, parental cooperation in treatment is more likely to follow. In cases where parental discipline is lax, the clinician may need to devote substantial and continued effort to the maintenance of a therapeutic alliance with the parent(s). In the absence of therapist support, the parent(s) may quickly abandon disciplinary efforts when adolescent resistance mounts.

In many single-parent families with adolescent offenders, we have found that practical problems in living (e.g., long hours at work) may interfere with the parent's ability to supervise the adolescent, provide the adolescent with adequate emotional support, and assist with the adolescent's educational needs. Consequently, we believe that a working knowledge of the social service delivery system and a willingness to coordinate such services is a therapeutic necessity when working with these families. Otherwise, the well-intentioned therapist may fail to address the problems that are directly responsible for parent-adolescent difficulties. Only after such interventions have been completed are more traditional therapeutic procedures (e.g., communication skills training) likely to be effective. We should also emphasize that basic yet important issues such as transportation and childcare assistance may need to be resolved before lower-income parents can be reasonably expected to attend meetings with social service professionals. Demanding that the lower-income parent adjust his or her work schedule to attend a meeting at a social service agency does little to enhance cooperation or to convey an appreciation for the parent's life situation.

In some families maladaptive patterns of interaction may continue despite the therapist's best efforts. For example, the therapist might align strongly with the parent but find that he or she continues to resist a directive to engage in some desired set of behaviors. To resolve this stalemate, the therapist might ask the parent and adolescent to define the minimum behavioral change they would like to achieve. By avoiding a battle of wills with the parent, the therapist sets the stage for the family members to improve. One small change can lead to another, and substantial progress can eventually result.

The personal and interpersonal qualities of the therapist also represent critical levers for change. For our programs we have tried to select therapists who have experience with a range of human problems, and who are sensitive to important cultural and ethnic issues. In addition, these therapists must be able to adjust their interpersonal styles (e.g., from empathic and reflective to directive and confrontive) in response to changing therapeutic needs. For example, in some situations, a sense of humor and an appreciation of human foibles can promote an atmosphere that is most conducive to therapeutic progress. In other situations, such as when families members do not complete "homework" assignments and their efforts seem minimal, the therapist may need to take a more authoritative position. Always, however, the therapist is ready to praise the genuine efforts of family members and to congratulate them on their successes. The therapist does not take the credit for positive change, but notes that such change would not have been possible without the hard work of the family members.

Individual Therapy with the Adolescent

Individual therapy can facilitate behavioral change in adolescent offenders in several situations (see Chapter 2). Interventions in these situations are generally targeted at changing the adolescent's social perspective-taking skills, belief system, and motivational system.

The behavior problems of many adolescents are exacerbated by their attitudinal biases. For example, some juvenile offenders may believe that their parents, their teachers, and the police are "out to get them" and so are primed to expect hostility from others and are quick to respond aggressively. In turn, these adolescents' attitudinal biases often evoke hostility from peers and adults. This hostility then serves to reinforce the adolescents' belief that others are biased against them. From a treatment perspective, it is extremely important for the adolescent to learn that body posture, tone of voice, and behaviors play a pivotal role in this cycle of hostility. To promote this understanding, the therapist uses Socratic methods that enhance the adolescent's appreciation of the other person's perspective. For example, the therapist might encourage the adolescent to consider how his teacher felt when, in front of the class, the adolescent challenged the teacher's competence and authority. The therapist might ask the adolescent a number of different questions such as "What is the teacher's job?" "How do you think the teacher took your behavior?" "What choices did the teacher have in responding to you?" "How would you respond if you were the teacher and a student smart-mouthed you in front of the entire class?" In essence, the therapist attempts to teach the adolescent that, in many situations, his negative attitude and behavior force adult authorities to respond to him in a punitive fashion.

Adolescents who are able to understand the connection between their behavior and the responses of others are then capable of learning how to "play the game." If obnoxious adolescent behavior evokes punitive responses from adults, it follows that respectful and considerate adolescent behavior should evoke favorable responses from adults. This is especially likely to occur when the therapist primes the relevant adults to expect positive changes in the adolescent's behavior. In one case, for example, the therapist taught a 15-year-old boy, whose belligerence had seriously alienated his principal and teachers, how to win them over and thereby avoid some of the negative consequences (including permanent expulsion) that were on his horizon. Instead of making obscene gestures behind teachers' backs, he requested permission to sit in the front row of his classes and asked his teachers for extra homework so that he could catch up on the learning that he had missed. He also made a point of being friendly and making polite conversation whenever he saw the principal. The teachers and principal were initially quite skeptical of his behavior change, but because he maintained this change for several weeks, they began to respond to him quite favorably and he, in turn, came to appreciate the benefits of being liked by the principal and teachers.

Some adolescents, of course, cannot be motivated to make such a change, and others do not possess the level of cognitive maturity needed for the skillful use of social perspective-taking skills. Nevertheless, we have often used variations of this individual intervention with success in our clinical work. We should also note that it is important for the therapist to prime the relevant adults to expect positive change in the adolescent's behavior.

The behavior problems of some other adolescents can be associated more with social skill deficits than with attitudinal biases. These adolescents do not know appropriate ways of responding to peer pressures, dating situations, or the aggressive behaviors of others. In such cases, the therapist can discuss problem situations with the adolescent and provide a variety of possible solutions. Role play is often an effective strategy for developing more adaptive social responses. In a similar vein, the behavior problems of some adolescents are associated with their impulsivity. Individual therapy in such cases can be used to help adolescents develop a more reflective style of responding. Indeed, interventions described in detail by cognitive-behavioral therapists have shown promise in use with delinquent adolescents and, in our experience, can often serve a useful adjunctive role in therapy.

Individual therapy is probably the most viable treatment approach in situations where the parents are seriously disturbed or neglectful. In these situations, after it has been determined that parental involvement is counterproductive and that the adolescent's environment does not include other adults who might serve as surrogate parents, the therapist attempts to form a trusting one-to-one relationship with the adolescent. Once such a relationship has been established, the therapist uses the adolescent's emotional attachment as a lever for behavior change. The role of the therapist might be similar to that of a concerned aunt or uncle. The relationship is not "buddy-buddy," nor is it authoritarian. In essence, the therapist attempts to provide guidance, give emotional support, and instill a worldview that promotes positive behavior.

We should emphasize that we never use individual treatment approaches in isolation from the adolescent's systemic context. While we are attempting to change the beliefs and attitudes of the adolescent, we are also attempting to change the environment in ways that will reinforce the adolescent's progress.

A small percentage of delinquent adolescents will absolutely refuse to cooperate with any individual intervention. In such cases, we focus our energies on changing other pertinent systems to promote the therapeutic changes that are needed to minimize subsequent criminal activity. When full parental support for treatment goals is attained, adolescent behavior change usually follows, even if the adolescent remains resistant to individual treatment. When the parents are highly resistant to treatment and the therapist's attempts to develop a trusting relationship with the adolescent have failed, prognosis is very poor unless the adolescent develops a positive relationship with another adult in his or her natural environment.

Family Therapy

Because marital and family relations are almost always linked with adolescent behavior problems, the family plays a central role in the amelioration of delinquent behavior. In general our family-based interventions focus on instrumental and affective family issues.

On an instrumental level, the parents must have a clear and well-defined set of expectations and rules regarding the adolescent's school performance, household chores, and interpersonal behavior. Similarly, the parents should have a clear and well-defined set of positive and negative consequences that are contingent on the adolescent's adherence to the expectations and rules. These consequences should be in proportion to the importance of the rule or to the nature of the behavioral transgression. It is essential that the parents develop rules and consequences jointly, and that they be enforced consistently. The therapist's task is to help the parents set and reinforce appropriate limits on the adolescent's behavior.

In the development of family expectations, rules, and consequences for adolescent behavior, the therapist typically provides the parents with guidance and education regarding normative adolescent behavior and effective discipline strategies. Often, however, parents are unable to arrive at mutually satisfactory decisions because of concomitant marital conflicts. In such cases, the therapist's most immediate task is to address and to attempt to ameliorate the marital difficulties that are impeding the couple's ability to function as parents. Joining the spouses together to deal with problematic adolescent behavior often provides the initial context for building marital cooperation. Subsequently, issues such as resentment regarding the division of labor and dissatisfaction with their emotional relationship can be addressed in marital therapy.

On an affective level, family cohesion, warmth, and love play an extremely important role in both child development and the treatment of behavior problems. The therapist can emphasize the numerous ways of showing love. Some family members show that they care by giving gifts or doing chores, while other members might demonstrate their love by listening to another's problems and providing emotional support. In many families that have experienced high degrees of conflict, members tend to ignore or devalue expressions of love and concern. For example, delinquent adolescents often perceive parental rules as authoritarian impositions that are the outcome of parental hostility. The therapist might help the adolescent to understand that the rules are enforced because the parents love the adolescent and want him or her to develop into a mature and responsible adult. If the parents did not care about the adolescent, they would allow the adolescent to do as he or she pleased. Thus, the therapist reframes appropriate discipline as a sign of parental love.

Frequently, the therapist also needs to increase the rates of positive interactions among family members. The therapist might encourage the parents to spend more time together engaging in whatever activities they enjoyed with each other in the past. If no such activities exist, the couple should plan to develop some pleasurable conjoint interests. The therapist might emphasize that because the areas of conflict and disagreement will be addressed extensively in therapy, it is counterproductive for the couple to allow these conflicts to arise during the time that is set aside for recreation and mutual enjoyment. To increase positive interactions between the parents and adolescent, it is often necessary for the parents to take the initiative, due to their greater emotional maturity. The therapist should encourage parents to spend time with the adolescent engaging in activities that are enjoyed by all.

An important goal of multisystemic family therapy is the elimination of cycles of escalating negativity that can lead to intense and prolonged conflicts. When addressing this problem, the therapist should emphasize the development of perspective-taking and communication skills. When family members stop behaving stubbornly and express an accurate understanding of each other's perspectives, many areas of disagreement can be resolved. To achieve this end, however, it is critical that the therapist help the family members to develop conjoint problem-solving strategies that stress interpersonal cooperation rather than competition.

Finally, it is important to address the problems of individual family members that may attenuate positive therapeutic change. For example, many single mothers may be so overwhelmed by their workload (40 hours per week employment, household responsibilities, childcare responsibilities) that they have little energy to devote to handling their noncompliant adolescent. In such cases, the therapist might find a way to restructure the mother's workload or to provide the mother with additional social support. Similarly, in many families, children other than the delinquent adolescent also evidence behavior problems that must be addressed. In fact, the therapist's family interventions rarely pertain only to the delinquent adolescent and more typically involve at least one of the other children in the home.

Peer Interventions

The peer group is important to psychosocial development because it provides adolescents with a sense of belonging, emotional support, and behavioral norms. Within peer groups of many delinquent adolescents, the sense of belonging and emotional support are evident; however, the group behavioral norms often conflict with societal norms. Moreover, criminal activity frequently serves an adaptive function for these adolescents because it is collaborative and elicits continued peer support and acceptance. Therefore, as therapists, we believe that it is essential to obtain as much information as possible about the adolescent offender's peer relations. This information is then considered together with other pertinent information about characteristics of the individual adolescent (e.g., social skills) and the family (e.g., the parents' willingness to set firm and consistent limits for the adolescent's behavior), when deciding whether peer-related interventions are needed.

Useful information about the adolescent's peer group can often be provided by teachers, parents, and the adolescent. The therapist can ask the teacher about the general reputations of the adolescent's friends. The parents can be asked about their impressions of their child's friends. (It is a negative sign if the adolescent has kept the parents from having much contact with his peers.) Often, the adolescent will be quite open about his friends. He will describe the nature of their social activities, how they are performing in school, what their outside interests are, and what their families are like.

The content and direction of subsequent therapeutic interventions depends on the results of the peer assessement. It is a positive prognostic sign if the adolescent's peers (and the adolescent) are generally involved in prosocial activities (e.g., school sports, after-school jobs, and church). In such cases, the adolescent's delinquent behavior is often a transitory pattern and interventions should focus on the individual and family levels. On the other hand, if the adolescent is a member of a deviant peer group (e.g., friends have failing grades, engage in illegal activities, have little contact with prosocial activities, have parents who provide little structure and monitoring), it may be necessary to remove the adolescent from that peer group and to establish a new, more socially appropriate, network of peers. It is difficult to decide on the direction of therapy, however, when the information regarding the adolescent's peers is contradictory. Peer friendships are extremely important to adolescents, and we do not advocate the severing of peer relations unless we are certain that these friendships are directly linked with the adolescent's behavior problems. Therefore, when in doubt, we recommend that the therapist directly assess the peer group to obtain first-hand impressions and information.

To assess peer relations directly, the therapist should arrange to have two or more informal meetings with the adolescent and his peers. These meetings can be arranged in various ways depending on the interests of both the adolescent and the therapist. For example, the therapist might ask the adolescent to invite several of his friends to participate in a mutually enjoyed activity (e.g., basketball, video games, shopping). If such an activity cannot be arranged, the therapist might have informal conversations with the adolescent and some friends at a place and time when the peer group is usually together (e.g., at a fast food restaurant after school). Whatever the setting, we have had little difficulty in arranging meetings with the adolescent's peers, though we might sometimes have to "buy the burgers." These meetings can provide the therapist with considerable information regarding the antisocial/prosocial nature of the peer group as well as qualitative aspects of the adolescent's peer relations (e.g., leader vs. follower; shy vs. assertive). In fact, we have found that meeting with the adolescent's peer group also provides useful information in cases when the antisocial/prosocial nature of the peer group is already known.

When the therapist determines that the adolescent's behavior problems are being reinforced by the attitudes and behaviors of peers, our most common intervention strategy is to advocate the adolescent's withdrawal from the present peer group and to encourage an affiliation with nonproblem peers. The success of this intervention is based on the therapist's ability to accomplish three important tasks. First, the therapist (and/or parents) must convince the adolescent that some extremely negative or harmful consequences are associated with his current peer group affiliation. Second, the therapist must enlist parental cooperation in reinforcing the adolescent's involvement with nondeviant peers. This may involve providing the adolescent with transportation or resources to facilitate involvement in prosocial activities, and attending those activities at which parental attendance is encouraged (e.g., a sports event). The parents should also have a clear set of negative consequences ready to implement if the adolescent continues to associate with deviant peers. Third, inasmuch as the adolescent's association with nonproblem peers is more likely to occur if these peers have talents and interests that are similar to those of the adolescent, it is important that the therapist assists the adolescent and the parents in identifying the adolescent's strengths, current or potential interests, and academic/vocational goals.

In some instances, one or more of the three therapeutic tasks described above cannot be accomplished. For example, the adolescent may recognize that negative consequences are associated with membership in his present peer group, but may still refuse to break the strong emotional ties that have been established with these peers. The parents may also refuse to take the necessary steps to encourage the adolescent's involvement with nonproblem peers and to discourage involvement with deviant peers. Or, the adolescent may already share a number of common talents or prosocial interests with an otherwise deviant group of peers, thus hindering the therapist's efforts to shift the adolescent's allegiance to a new group of peers. In such instances, we have found that two types of interventions are often helpful in promoting positive change. First, the therapist can negotiate behavioral changes among the adolescent and his peers by assisting them in obtaining desired positive goals (e.g., job skills training; employment; a sponsor for a sports team, musical group, or automotive repair club). In these cases, the peer group can continue to provide the adolescent with a sense of self-worth and security without promoting deviant behavioral norms. In some instances, however, the therapist may judge that the peer group's potential for positive change is minimal. A second, alternative strategy is more likely to succeed in these cases. Using strategies similar to those described in Chapter 2, the therapist can develop a trusting relationship with the adolescent and use certain cognitive interventions within this relationship to motivate the adolescent to change his deviant behavior and to teach the adolescent effective ways to cope with peer pressures.

School-Based Interventions

An understanding of the broader social context of which the adolescent is a part can help the therapist to discern the parameters of behavior problems and to develop optimal interventions. School is an extremely important system because the adolescent's performance sets the stage for future vocational, social, and economic opportunities. Therefore, as needed, the therapist should develop strategies to facilitate the adolescent's academic performance and/or vocational training, as well as social relations.

In making decisions about educational interventions, it is important to have certain information about the adolescent's intellectual strengths and weaknesses and his level of academic achievement. Educational testing, using instruments such as the WISC-R and WRAT-R, can help the therapist to determine whether the adolescent is achieving up to his or her ability or whether he or she might have a learning disability that would require special educational interventions. Such tests can also evaluate whether the adolescent is in an appropriate grade placement. In addition, educational evaluations can assess whether the adolescent has a special intellectual strength that might have important implications for career choice. In one case, for example, we evaluated an adolescent who had modest language skills and was having great difficulty with his language-oriented courses (English, social studies). Once we found that this adolescent had very high perceptual organization (analytic-mechanical) skills, he was steered into mathematics and computer science courses.

The school setting provides the most important extrafamilial opportunity for the development of social relationship skills. Children and adolescents have a multitude of opportunities to learn to interact appropriately with authorities, same-sex peers, and opposite-sex peers. As therapists, we take full advantage of the controlled social microcosm that the school setting provides. As described in Chapter 6, adolescents can be taught how to make amends to teachers whom they have previously alienated and can learn how to avoid peer interactions that may lead to aggressive behavior.

School personnel also enable the therapist to obtain independent verification of the success of therapeutic interventions. After obtaining written parental consent, we recommend that the therapist maintain periodic contact with one or more of the delinquent's teachers. We have learned that the therapist may draw a false conclusion if he or she assumes that the adolescent and parents always provide an accurate and objective report of the adolescent's academic progress and behavior in school. Contact with the adolescent's teachers is very helpful because it can provide the therapist with information regarding the adolescent's academic and social functioning, and with feedback regarding the course of treatment. Teacher contact also enables the therapist to foster attitudinal change in the teacher regarding problematic aspects of the adolescent. For example, the therapist can stress that the adolescent and his family are making significant efforts toward resolving their difficulties. Moreover, the therapist can consult with the teacher about behavior management issues and provide the teacher with support and credit for his or her efforts on the adolescent's behalf.

Finally, the school system provides numerous opportunities for the adolescent to engage in prosocial peer group activities such as team sports and other academic/non-academic organizations. There are several ways in which these activities can promote more positive attitudes and behavior in the juvenile offender. First, athletics and other activities provide greater structure for the adolescent's after-school and weekend hours. Second, most extracurricular activities, especially team sports, stress the importance of self-discipline and responsibility. Group goals are usually superordinate to individual desires. Third, these activities provide the juvenile offender with the opportunity to develop friendships with adolescents who are not involved in criminal activity. Fourth, individual and group accomplishments can promote self-esteem and instill a sense of pride. And, fifth, in many communities, the privilege of participating in an extracurricular activity is contingent on adequate academic progress.

Interventions Involving Multiple Systems

The therapist may also need to provide interventions that target the transactions between two or more systems. A common focus is the interface between family and school. The parents may feel that their child is being persecuted by his teachers, and the teachers may feel that the parents are unsupportive of the school's efforts to correct the adolescent's problem behavior. Accordingly, an important therapeutic goal is to open intersystem communication channels and gain collaboration on mutually desired goals. Initially, the therapist takes responsibility for bringing the parents and teachers together and mediates parent-teacher interactions so that mutual goals can be defined (e.g., the adolescent's success in school). Often, parent-teacher cooperation can be established through the use of a daily homework assignment sheet for the adolescent that is signed by both parents. The parents can also call the teacher at scheduled times to check on the adolescent's behavioral progress. During this process, the therapist should monitor the participation of parents and teachers and should regularly provide reinforcement for continued cooperation.

The therapist can also assist the family members in their transactions with other community systems. For example, in low-income families, the therapist may need to teach the parents to negotiate the social service maze to obtain needed services for the adolescent or a sibling. In single-parent families, the therapist can encourage the parent to become involved in support groups and educational programs that are designed to meet specific needs that many parents face following divorce. Additionally, parents of chemically dependent adolescents and adolescents who present serious behavior problems may be encouraged to attend meetings of "tough love" and other support groups. These groups provide parents with constructive advice, emotional support, and the reduction of guilt when they realize that they are not the only parents whose children and adolescents present serious behavior problems.

Finally, as suggested earlier, it is very important that the therapist facilitate contact between the parents and the adolescent's peer system. In extreme cases, we encourage the parents to require that they meet and approve each of their adolescent's friends before the adolescent is allowed to associate with that friend. In all cases, we encourage parents to become familiar with their son's or daughter's peers and with the peers' parents. Such contact can provide important information regarding the parameters of extant difficulties.

REFERENCES

Alexander, J. F., & Parsons, B. (1973). Short-term behavioral intervention with delinquent families: Impact on family process and recidivism. *Journal of Abnormal Psychology, 81*, 219–225.

Becker, W. C. (1971). *Parents are teachers*. Champaign, IL: Research Press.

Belsky, J. (1980). Child maltreatment: An ecological integration. *American Psychologist, 35*, 320–335.

Blakely, C. H., & Davidson, W. S. (1984). Behavioral approaches to delinquency: A review. In P. Karoly & J. J. Steffen (Eds.), *Adolescent Behavior Disorders: Foundations and Contemporary Concerns* (pp. 241–283). Lexington, MA: Lexington Books.

Blasi, A. (1980). Bridging moral cognition and moral action: A critical review of the literature. *Psychological Bulletin, 88*, 1–45.

Borduin, C. M., Blaske, D. M., Mann, B. J., Treloar, L., Henggeler, S. W., & Fucci, B. R. (in preparation). Multisystemic treatment of juvenile offenders: A replication and extension.

Borduin, C. M., & Henggeler, S. W. (1987). Post-divorce mother-son relations of delinquent and well-adjusted adolescents. *Journal of Applied Developmental Psychology, 8*, 273–288.

Borduin, C. M., Henggeler, S. W., Hanson, C. L., & Pruitt, J. A. (1985). Verbal problem solving in families of father-absent and father-present delinquent boys. *Child and Family Behavior Therapy, 7*, 51–63.

Borduin, C. M., Pruitt, J. A., & Henggeler, S. W. (1986). Family interactions in black, lower-class families with delinquent and nondelinquent adolescent boys. *Journal of Genetic Psychology, 147*, 333–342.

Borduin, C. M., Treloar, L., Blaske, D. M., & Mann, B. J. (in preparation). Development of a self-report measure of adolescent peer relations: The Missouri Peer Relations Inventory.

Bronfenbrenner, U. (1986). Ecology of the family as a context for human development: Research perspectives. *Developmental Psychology, 22*, 723–742.

Brunk, M., Henggeler, S. W., & Whelan, J. P. (1987). A comparison of multisystemic therapy and parent training in the brief treatment of child abuse and neglect. *Journal of Consulting and Clinical Psychology, 55*, 171–178.

Camp, B. W., & Ray, R. S. (1984). Aggression. In A. W. Meyers & W. E. Craighead (Eds.), *Cognitive behavior therapy with children* (pp. 315–350). New York: Plenum.

Davison, M. L. (1979). The internal structure and the psychometric properties of the Defining Issues Test. In J. Rest (Ed.), *Development in judging moral issues* (pp. 223–245). Minneapolis, MN: University of Minnesota Press.

Derogatis, L. R. (1983). *SCL-90-R: Manual-II*. Towson, MD: Clinical Psychometric Research.

Dishion, T. J., Loeber, R., Stouthamer-Loeber, M., & Patterson, G. R. (1984). Skill deficits and male adolescent delinquency. *Journal of Abnormal Child Psychology, 12*, 37–54.

Dumas, J. E., & Wahler, R. G. (1983). Predictors of treatment outcome in parent training: Mother insularity and socioeconomic disadvantage. *Behavioral Assessment, 5*, 301–313.

Dunford, F. W., & Elliott, D. S. (1984). Identifying career offenders using self-reported data. *Journal of Research in Crime and Delinquency, 21*, 57–86.

Elliott, D. S., & Ageton, S. S. (1980). Reconciling race and class differences in self-reported and official estimates of delinquency. *American Sociological Review, 45*, 95–110.

Elliott, D. S., Huizinga, D., & Ageton, S. S. (1985). *Explaining delinquency and drug use.* Newbury Park, CA: Sage.

Elliott, D. S., Huizinga, D., & Morse, B. J. (1985). *The dynamics of deviant behavior: A national survey progress report.* Boulder, CO: Behavioral Research Institute.

Eysenck, H. J., & Eysenck, S. B. G. (1963). *Eysenck Personality Inventory.* San Diego, CA: Educational and Industrial Testing Service.

Farrington, D. P. (1979). Longitudinal research on crime and delinquency. In N. Morris & M. Tonry (Eds.), *Crime and justice: An annual review of research, Vol 1* (pp. 289–348). Chicago: University of Chicago Press.

Federal Bureau of Investigation, U.S. Department of Justice. (1985). *Uniform crime reports.* Washington, DC: Author.

Feldman, R. A., Caplinger, T. E., & Wodarski, J. S. (1983). *The St. Louis conundrum: The effective treatment of antisocial youths.* Englewood Cliffs, NJ: Prentice-Hall.

Finger, W. W., & Borduin, C. M. (in preparation). Correlates of self-reported delinquency among adolescents: An ecological-systems model.

Freedman, B. J., Rosenthal, L., Donahoe, C. P., Schlundt, D. G., & McFall, R. M. (1978). A social-behavioral analysis of skill deficits in delinquent and nondelinquent adolescent boys. *Journal of Consulting and Clinical Psychology, 46*, 1448–1462.

Gold, M. (1987). Social ecology. In H. C. Quay (Ed.), *Handbook of juvenile delinquency* (pp. 62–105). New York: Wiley.

Gurman, A. S., Kniskern, D. P., & Pinsof, W. M. (1986). Reseach on the process and outcome of marital and family therapy. In S. Garfield & A. Bergin (Eds.), *Handbook of psychotherapy and behavior change* (3rd ed.) (pp. 565–624). New York: Wiley.

Hains, A., & Miller, D. (1980). Moral judgement in delinquent and nondelinquent children and adolescents. *Genetic Psychology, 137*, 21–35.

Haley, J. (1976). *Problem solving therapy.* San Francisco: Jossey-Bass.

Halperin, S. L. (1981). Abused and non-abused children's perceptions of their mothers, fathers, and siblings: Implications for a comprehensive family treatment plan. *Family Relations, 30*, 89–96.

Hamparian, D. M., Schuster, W. J., Dinitz, S., & Conrad, J. P. (1978). *The violent few.* Lexington, MA: Lexington Books.

Hanson, C. L., Henggeler, S. W., Haefele, W. F., & Rodick, J. D. (1984). Demographic, individual, and family relationship correlates of serious and repeated crime among adolescents and their siblings. *Journal of Consulting and Clinical Psychology, 52*, 528–538.

Henggeler, S. W. (Ed.), (1982). *Delinquency and adolescent psychopathology: A family-ecological systems approach.* Littleton, MA: Wright-PSG.

Henggeler, S. W. (1989). *Delinquency in adolescence: Vol. 18. Developmental Clinical Psychology and Psychiatry*, A. E. Kazdin (Series Ed.). Newbury Park, CA: Sage.

Henggeler, S. W. (in press). Causal models of delinquent behavior. In R. Cohen & A. W. Siegel (Eds.), *Context and development.* Hillsdale, NJ: Erlbaum.

Henggeler, S. W., Borduin, C. M., & Mann, B. J. (1987). Intrafamily agreement: Association with clinical status, social desirability, and observational ratings. *Journal of Applied Developmental Psychology, 8*, 97–111.

Henggeler, S. W., Edwards, J., & Borduin, C. M. (1987). The family relations of female juvenile delinquents. *Journal of Abnormal Child Psychology, 15*, 199–209.

Henggeler, S. W., Hanson, C. L., Borduin, C. M., Watson, S. M., & Brunk, M. A. (1985). Mother-son relations of juvenile felons. *Journal of Consulting and Clinical Psychology, 53,* 942–943.

Henggeler, S. W., Rodick, J. D., Borduin, C. M., Hanson, C. L., Watson, S. M., & Urey, J. R. (1986). Multisystemic treatment of juvenile offenders: Effects on adolescent behavior and family interactions. *Developmental Psychology, 22,* 132–141.

Henggeler, S. W., & Tavormina, J. B. (1980). Social class and race differences in family interaction: Pathological, normative or confounding methodological factors? *Journal of Genetic Psychology, 137,* 211–222.

Hindelang, M. J., Hirschi, J. T., & Weis, J. G. (1981). *Measuring delinquency.* Newbury Park, CA: Sage.

Hudgins, W., & Prentice, N. M. (1973). Moral judgement in delinquent adolescents and their mothers. *Journal of Abnormal Psychology, 82,* 145–152.

Jurkovic, G. J., & Prentice, N. M. (1977). Relation of moral and cognitive development to dimensions of juvenile delinquency. *Journal of Abnormal Psychology, 86,* 414–420.

Kazdin, A. E. (1984). Treatment of conduct disorders. In J. Williams & R. Spitzer (Eds.), *Psychotherapy research: Where are we and where should we go?* New York: Guilford.

Klein, N., Alexander, J., & Parsons, B. (1977). Impact of family systems intervention on recidivism and sibling delinquency: A model of primary prevention and program evaluation. *Journal of Consulting and Clinical Psychology, 45,* 469–474.

Kohlberg, L. (1976). Moral stages and moralization: The cognitive-developmental approach. In T. Lickona (Ed.), *Moral development and behavior: Theory, research, and social issues* (pp. 31–53). New York: Holt, Rinehart & Winston.

Lane, T. W., & Davis, G. E. (1987). Child maltreatment and juvenile delinquency: Does a relationship exist? In J. D Burchard & S. N. Burchard (Eds.), *Prevention of delinquent behavior* (pp. 122–138). Newbury Park, CA: Sage.

Lipsey, M. W. (1988). Juvenile delinquency intervention. In H. S. Bloom, D. S. Cordray, & R. J. Light (Eds.), *Lessons from selected programs and policy areas.* San Francisco: Jossey-Bass.

Locke, H. J., & Wallace, K. M. (1959). Short marital adjustment and prediction tests: Their reliability and validity. *Marriage and Family Living, 21,* 251–255.

Loeber, R. (1982). The stability of antisocial and delinquent child behavior: A review. *Child Development, 53,* 1431–1446.

Loeber, R., & Dishion, T. (1983). Early predictors of male delinquency: A review. *Psychological Bulletin, 94,* 68–99.

Mann, B. J., Borduin, C. M., Henggeler, S. W., & Blaske, D. M. (1989). An investigation of systemic conceptualizations of parent-child coalitions and symptom change. Manuscript submitted for publication.

McCubbin, H. I., Patterson, J. M., & Wilson, L. R. (1982). Family Inventory of Life Events and Changes. In D. H. Olson et al. (Eds.), *Family inventories* (pp. 69–87). St. Paul, MN: Family Social Science.

Minuchin, S. (1974). *Families and family therapy.* Cambridge, MA: Harvard University Press.

Moos, R. H., & Moos, B. S. (1981). *Family Environment Scale Manual.* Palo Alto, CA: Consulting Psychologists Press.

Olson, D. H., McCubbin, H. I., Barnes, H., Larsen, A., Muxen, M., & Wilson, M. (1982). *Family inventories.* St. Paul, MN: Family Social Science.

Olweus, D. (1979). Stability of aggressive reaction patterns in males: A review. *Psychological Bulletin, 86,* 852–875.

Parke, R., & Collmer, C. (1975). Child abuse: An interdisciplinary analysis. In E. M. Hetherington (Ed.), *Review of child development research* (Vol. 5, pp. 509–590). Chicago: University of Chicago Press.

Patterson, G. R. (1979). *Living with children*. Champaign, IL: Research Press.

Patterson, G. R. (1982). *A social learning approach, Vol. 3: Coercive family process*. Eugene, OR: Castalia.

Patterson, G. R. (1986). Performance models for antisocial boys. *American Psychologist, 41*, 432–444.

Patterson, G. R., & Dishion, T. J. (1985). Contributions of families and peers to delinquency. *Criminology, 23*, 63–79.

Patterson, G. R., & Stouthamer-Loeber, M. (1984). The correlation of family management practices and delinquency. *Child Development, 55*, 1299–1307.

Quay, H. C. (Ed.). (1987). *Handbook of juvenile delinquency*. New York: Wiley.

Quay, H. C., & Peterson, D. R. (1975). *Manual for the Behavior Problem Checklist*. Unpublished manuscript.

Quay, H. C., & Peterson, D. R. (1987). *Manual for the Revised Behavior Problem Checklist*. Coral Gables, FL: Department of Psychology, University of Miami.

Rodick, J. D., Henggeler, S. W., & Hanson, C. L. (1986). An evaluation of the Family Adaptibility and Cohesion Evaluation Scales and the Circumplex Model. *Journal of Abnormal Child Psychology, 14*, 77–87.

Schaffer, H. R., & Crook, C. K. (1979). Maternal control techniques in a directed play situation. *Child Development, 50*, 989–996.

Schaffer, H. R., & Crook, C. K. (1980). Child compliance and maternal control techniques. *Developmental Psychology, 16*, 54–61.

Snyder, J., & Patterson, G. R. (1987). Family interaction and delinquent behavior. In H. C. Quay (Ed.), *Handbook of juvenile delinquency* (pp. 216–243). New York: Wiley.

Strasburg, P. A. (1978). *Violent delinquents*. New York: Monarch.

Tolan, P. H., Cromwell, R. E., & Brasswell, M. (1986). Family therapy with delinquents: A critical review of the literature. *Family Process, 25*, 619–650.

Wilson, J. Q., & Herrnstein, R. J. (1985). *Crime and human nature*. New York: Simon & Schuster.

Wodarski, J. S. (1981). Comprehensive treatment of parents who abuse their children. *Adolescence, 16*, 959–972.

Wolfe, D. A., Sandler, J., & Kaufman, K. (1981). A competency-based parent training program for child abusers. *Journal of Consulting and Clinical Psychology, 49*, 633–640.

CHAPTER 9

Adolescent Chemical Dependency

Milton Trapold

The purpose of this chapter is to provide a basis for the effective diagnosis and treatment of adolescent behavior disorders that are "driven" by excessive use of mood-altering drugs. Most people in the general population, and in the mental health and related professions, grossly underestimate both the prevalence and the seriousness of chemical abuse/dependence. There is a pervasive reluctance in our society to consider the possibility that an adolescent's problems may be related to the use of alcohol or drugs. There is also widespread ignorance among both lay people and professionals about the role of drugs in many kinds of behavior problems, and about the signs of drug abuse. As a consequence, misdiagnosis of this class of disorders is very common, especially in adolescents, where drug use is often a well-kept secret.

To make matters worse, many professionals still cling to the notion that drug abuse is only a symptom of underlying individual or family pathology or a behavior that is qualitatively similar to other kinds of deviant behavior. Therefore, even when drug use is recognized as an important element in a case, these professionals tend to employ treatment strategies based on erroneous assumptions regarding the nature of chemical dependency. Consequently, these strategies seldom produce important or lasting changes in the adolescent's problem behaviors.

We believe that chemical dependency is a problem that is qualitatively different from the other types of psychosocial difficulties discussed in this book, and that it requires a unique set of interventions. Before describing these interventions, we will first present some definitions and assumptions, describe some basic facts about the epidemiology of chemical dependency, and discuss its diagnosis.

DEFINITIONS

Chemical use and *drug use* are synonymously defined as the use of mood-altering chemicals (including alcohol) in any form, legal or illegal, whether by prescription or for "recreational" purposes. In practice, most use is recreational. Mood-altering drugs are those that make most people feel good or "high" and have the potential for inducing chemical dependence in at least some users. The most commonly used recreational drugs among today's youth are, in approximate order of prevalence, alcohol (first by a wide margin), marijuana/hashish, amphetamines (speed), methaqualone (Qualuude), barbiturates, minor tranquilizers (e.g., Valium, Librium, Tranxene), cocaine, opiates (e.g., codeine, morphine, heroin) and their synthetic relatives (Talwin, Percodan, Demerol, Dilaudid), phencyclodine (PCP), hallucinogens (e.g., LSD, mescaline), and a variety of inhalants (e.g., gasoline, freon, some paint thinners and organic solvents, some plastic glues, typewriter correction fluid).

Chemical dependency refers to a condition that develops in 10 to 20% of those who use mood-altering drugs. We employ a functional definition of chemical dependency very similar to that proposed for drug abuse in DSM III-R (American Psychiatric Association, 1987), by the World Health Organization (Kramer & Cameron, 1975) and many others (e.g., Goodwin, 1976; Johnson, 1980; Lawson, Ellis, & Rivers, 1984; Macdonald, 1984). An individual is chemically dependent if he or she (1) uses mood altering drugs, (2) suffers serious recurring life problems as a result of that use, and (3) nevertheless continues to use drugs. Those individuals whose drug use does not create serious problems are not chemically dependent; this includes the majority of recreational drug users of all ages. Those individuals whose drug use causes problems, but who then curtail their drug use so that the problems cease, are also not chemically dependent. Only those who continue their problem-causing drug use, despite these problems, are chemically dependent.

Note that this definition does not specify the amount, type, duration, or frequency of drug use. A once-a-month weekend drinker is chemically dependent if that use causes problems at any systemic level, and he or she continues to drink. On the other hand, it is possible, though unlikely, that a daily user of a quart of whiskey or several joints of marijuana would not experience any serious problems, and hence not be chemically dependent. Of course, in general, people who are chemically dependent use a greater variety of drugs, higher doses, and use with greater frequency than those who are not. For example, more than 85% of high school seniors who were classified "heavy drinkers" on the basis of their amount and frequency of alcohol use, were also classified "problem drinkers" on the basis of drinking-related problems in their lives. On the other hand, practically no "moderate drinkers" were classified as "problem drinkers" (Rachel, Guess, Williams, & Maisto, 1982). However, some chemically dependent youngsters show patterns of use that are well within the limits of their nondependent peers. Consequently, information about the amount, type, and pattern of a particular youngster's drug use is of only modest value in diagnosing individual cases of chemical dependency.

Note, too, that physical dependence on a drug is not a prerequisite for the diagnosis of chemical dependency. Chemical dependency can be strictly a psychological and behavioral phenomenon. The individual appears unable to stop using drugs despite the fact that using results in serious problems. This psychological dependency nearly always develops before any physical dependency. It is psychological dependency that keeps people "locked into" continued drug use and produces most of the deviant behavior in chemical dependency. Psychological dependence is the condition that must be treated if the deviant behavior is to be corrected. Physical dependence may or may not develop contingent on the pattern of drug use and the individual. When physical dependence does develop, it probably serves to strengthen the psychological dependence, but it is not necessary for the definition or diagnosis of chemical dependency. Physical dependence, however, can have important implications for the choice of treatment.

ASSUMPTIONS ABOUT CHEMICAL DEPENDENCY

The model that we use has its roots in the "disease model of alcoholism" (Jellinek, 1960; Ward, 1983), and in the more recent generalizations of that model to other forms of drug dependency in both adults and youngsters (Mann, 1979; Macdonald, 1984). This model assumes that at some point in their use of mood-altering drugs, individuals undergo a fundamental change in the way they react to these drugs; that is, they become dependent. The principal manifestation of this change is that the individual now appears to be in a "love affair" with drugs such that, regardless of the severity of the problems that may be created by the use of drugs, the person cannot (or at least does not) stop using them. The individual loses volitional control over the drug use.

Although there has been much speculation about the nature of this fundamental change, no one yet knows what it really entails. Many educated guesses relate it in some way to brain biochemistry. Others think it represents an exceptionally stable form of learning. Fortunately, for our purposes it is not important that the exact nature of this change be understood.

This individually oriented model of chemical dependency also makes a number of other assumptions that have important implications for the diagnosis and treatment of this disorder. These assumptions are briefly outlined as follows.

Drug Interchangeability

The various mood-altering drugs all function more or less identically in producing dependence. Some drugs (e.g., heroin) produce dependence more quickly and with greater certainty than other drugs. However, all the mood-altering drugs, including marijuana, can and sometimes do produce dependence, and most chemically dependent adolescents regularly use a variety of different drugs. Moreover, many individuals who have become dependent on one drug have tried to switch to some other "safer" drug. The result of this maneuver is that the individual either soon reverts back to the drug of choice or quickly becomes dependent on the new drug as well. Because of these facts, the model assumes that once an individual has become dependent on one mood-altering drug, he or she is for all practical purposes dependent on all mood-altering drugs, including those that have not yet been tried.

Some clinicians claim to know of cases in which individuals who presumably were dependent on drug A were able to switch to drug B in an unproblematic fashion. We have never encountered such a case ourselves, nor have we ever encountered a chemical dependency specialist who has encountered one. Moreover, even if such cases do exist, they almost certainly represent only a small minority of all dependent people. Furthermore, we do not presently possess any basis for identifying a priori the individuals who belong to this theoretical minority. Therefore, we believe that the only morally defensible goal for the treatment of chemical dependency is total abstinence from all mood-altering drugs. To recommend otherwise is to recommend that chemically dependent people perform a potentially lethal experiment on themselves.

Progressiveness

Dependence becomes progressively worse as long as the individual continues to use drugs. One does not "grow out" of chemical dependency; loss of control worsens. Early in dependence an individual might be able to go for weeks without using drugs or use them in a socially acceptable fashion most of the time. However, as the intensity of the "love affair" increases, the duration of periods of abstinence will become shorter, and the frequency of problematic use will increase. The overall frequency of drug-using episodes will also increase, as will the amount of drugs used per occasion. The hardness of the drugs used and the directness of the route of drug administration (e.g., injecting vs. ingesting) may also increase. The severity of the problems encountered as a result of using will get progressively worse as well.

The progressiveness of the dependence does not preclude short periods of improvement. Indeed, short-term improvements are common, especially when an individual is under pressure to "clean up his or her act." However, if the individual is truly dependent, the long-term progressive worsening of symptoms will soon become apparent.

Seriousness

Chemical dependency is a very serious and potentially fatal condition. A chemically dependent individual who does not get "unhooked" from drugs will probably die as a direct result of the dependency. This death can take many different forms: suicide (the suicide rate among chemical dependents is many times that in the "normal" population), vehicular accidents, house fires, fights, medical complications, overdoses, and drownings. Many teenagers die of chemical dependency. However, because the condition so often goes undiagnosed, or its role is unrecognized, we can only guess at the actual death rate. Moreover, chemical dependency is life-threatening to people other than the one who is dependent. In addition to the fatalities caused by the chemical dependency, it is often implicated in cases of abuse and in violent crimes.

Before an individual dies of chemical dependency, the disorder will often wreak enormous havoc. A very large percentage of all medical and psychological problems are due directly to chemical dependency (Macdonald, 1984; Talbott & Cooney, 1982; Ward, 1983). Many dependent people spend years in and out of mental institutions, or otherwise living on the fringes of society. Perhaps three out of four of those who occupy our jails and prisons have committed crimes that are directly traceable to chemical dependence (Talbott & Cooney, 1982; Health and Human Services, 1980). Adolescents who are chemically dependent frequently drop out of school and often lead lives of relative poverty.

Chemical dependency also has a tremendous impact on family and friends. It is impossible to be close to a chemically dependent person and avoid getting shredded emotionally and/or physically by his or her erratic, unpredictable, and irresponsible behavior. Parents and siblings often feel that they are to blame for the problems of a chemically dependent adolescent, and that they can "fix" him or her if only they can make appropriate changes in their own behavior. Parents may become overwhelmed with guilt and become overly permissive and indulgent. Siblings may learn to misbehave to gain attention, albeit negative, from their parents who are too consumed by the "problem" child to pay much attention to them (Cleveland, 1981). After numerous futile attempts to control the dependent adolescent's behavior, family members lose confidence in themselves and in their ability to change the situation, feeling helpless, distrustful, and bitter. It is not uncommon for another family member to start using drugs and to become dependent, or for marriages to break up under the strain.

Arrestibility

The progressively destructive course of chemical dependency can be halted, and much of the existing dysfunctionality reversed, when the individual completely abstains from all mood-altering drugs. This is not to say that all of the problems will vanish if one merely eliminates drugs. As discussed shortly, much of the dysfunctional behavior of the chemically dependent person requires specific therapeutic treatment over and above abstinence. The progression of the disorder can be checked, however, and some of the existing problems reversed by eliminating drugs from the system.

Irreversibility

Once an individual has become dependent, he or she cannot be nondependent again. The loss of the ability to regulate one's drug use is permanent. This assumption, in combination with the arrestibility assumption, yields the conclusion that successful long-term recovery from chemical dependency requires complete abstinence from all mood-altering drugs. Probably no other assumption of this model has been tested more often or with greater determination than this one. It is the fondest hope of all chemically dependent persons, including youngsters, to eventually resume using drugs "just a little" without serious repercussions. Furthermore, a large percentage of individuals, especially youngsters, who achieve some long-term sobriety, eventually feel that they have been abstinent long enough to have regained some control over their drug use. So they put this assumption to empirical test. The experiment always fails, even when preceded by years of abstinence. Sometimes it fails very quickly; there is an almost instantaneous loss of control over drug use and a resumption of drug-related "crazy" behavior. In other cases, the individual may be able to use "just a little" on multiple occasions before finally losing control.

Uninformed family members and friends may also believe that the dependent person can resume nonproblematic use of drugs following long-term sobriety. They may promote the use of drugs to reward the dependent person's good behavior and to demonstrate their renewed trust in the individual. They may also encourage drug use because they feel guilt about their past treatment of the dependent person.

The assumption that recovery requires total abstinence from mood-altering drugs is, of course, at variance with treatment strategies that attempt to return chemically dependent people to unproblematic "controlled" drug use. Such strategies have become increasingly popular in treating adult alcoholics (Marlatt, 1983, Miller, 1984). We have encountered numerous therapists who assume that a controlled-use strategy is, therefore, viable for adolescents. We do not agree for the simple reason that we know of hundreds of chemically dependent adolescents who have attempted controlled use, but we have never known one to succeed. Any resumption of use always results quickly in escalation of use, and in deterioration of psychosocial functioning.

Primacy

Chemical dependency is a primary disorder in at least four senses. First, chemical dependency must be the focus of therapeutic interventions and must not be seen as a secondary effect of other individual or systemic problems (e.g., disturbed family system, low self-esteem, depression) that will somehow magically go away if we treat these other conditions. This is not to say that individual or systemic problems do not play a role in the early use of drugs. Before becoming dependent, one might very well use drugs as a means of self-medicating the pain of depression or coping with family conflict. However, once an individual becomes dependent, the drug use takes on a life of its own, and will continue unabated regardless of what success we might have in ameliorating the depression or family conflicts.

Second, chemical dependency is primary because it causes collateral dysfunctions more often than vice versa. For instance, depression is common in chemically dependent individuals. So is poor self-concept and disturbed relationships among members of the individual's family. What causes what? Many therapists automatically assume that the drug problem must be caused by one or more of the other problems. In point of fact, however, the drug use is more likely to create the other problems. Heavy drug use nearly always induces depression. Constantly behaving in ways that violate one's own moral standards leads to erosion of self-esteem. The erratic, irresponsible behavior of the dependent almost always leads to massive disruption of the family system.

Third, because chemical dependency produces such a wide spectrum of collateral problems, it must be treated first. Only after the drug use and drug-induced dysfunctions have been removed is it possible to view the remaining problems with any clarity. In some cases there are none; treatment of chemical dependency per se may succeed in eliminating the observed collateral problems. In other cases, some problems will remain.

Fourth, drug use blocks the effectiveness of any treatment that might be directed at other systemic problems. Unknowingly, the therapist might attempt to resolve problems such as marital conflict, poor parent-child relations, or physical abuse. As important as such changes might be, however, they will not occur as long as the chemically dependent person is still using drugs. Things may improve for a short time, but they will soon deteriorate. It is impossible for people to make serious and lasting changes in close relationships while dependent on drugs.

EPIDEMIOLOGY

During the past 20 years, the recreational use of mood-altering drugs has become a quite commonplace and accepted part of the youth lifestyle in our culture. Virtually all (95%) of our young people experiment with mood-altering drugs by the time they are seniors in high school. Well over half of these will use at least weekly, with perhaps 20% using daily. Overall, about 30% of high school seniors are rated as "problem drinkers" on the basis of frequency of drunkenness and alcohol-related problems (Johnston, Bachman & O'Malley, 1982). Numerous adolescents are problem users of other drugs, but we are not aware of any reliable estimates of the actual number. Over the last two decades, the average age at which our young people begin to use drugs has progressively decreased. It is not uncommon to find high school freshmen who have already had extensive experience with recreational drug use (Johnston et al., 1982), and drug use among grade school children is by no means rare.

The available evidence shows some variations in these basic facts about drug use across different sociocultural contexts (Lowman, 1981, 1982; Johnston et al., 1982). However, in all cases the figures remain high enough to belie the common myths that drug use occurs only in certain geographical areas, in certain educational or socioeconomic groups, and among proponents of certain philosophies or religions. The simple fact is that today the odds are better than 50/50 that any randomly selected ninth-grader has already experimented with mood-altering drugs.

Solid data on the proportion of young drug users that become chemically dependent are not available. Estimates range from 5% to 20%. We believe the truth lies closer to the higher estimates. There is no good evidence that the incidence of chemical dependency varies dramatically with any of the common demographic variables. Consequently, information about socioeconomic status, educational level, place of residence, religious preference, and so forth are of little value in diagnosing chemical dependency. It may be true that males are more susceptible than females and that Whites have higher rates than Blacks, but this information does not assist in the diagnosis of the problem in any particular person. Chemical dependency must be diagnosed on a case by case basis, using as the primary criterion continued drug use in the face of negative systemic consequences.

SYMPTOMATOLOGY

The common symptoms of chemical dependency fall into four general categories: symptoms associated with (1) short-term (intoxicating) effects of mood-altering drugs; (2) long-term effects of chronic use; (3) acquiring, storing, and praising drugs, and with protecting one's ability to use; and (4) the delusional system that always accompanies chemical dependency.

Short-Term (Intoxicating) Effects of Mood-Altering Drugs

These symptoms vary, depending on the type, amount, and frequency of drug use, but generally include such characteristics as:

Slurred speech

Irrational thought processes

Loss of normal inhibitions over actions

Impaired motor coordination

Glassy eyes

Bloodshot eyes

Abnormally constricted or dilated pupils

Hypoactive speech

Hyperactive speech

Excessive sleeping

Blackouts

Intoxication, of course, does not necessarily mean chemical dependency; nondependent users become intoxicated too. Conversely, because a youth is never observed in an intoxicated state does not mean that the youngster is not chemically dependent. Most adolescents are careful not to be seen by their parents while intoxicated. Furthermore, only relatively severe intoxication produces readily observable symptoms. It is quite common for adolescents to be regularly intoxicated while in the presence of their parents (or their therapist) and never have their intoxication recognized.

Long-Term Effects of Chronic Drug Use

The symptoms of long-term use are largely a direct consequence of the physiological and biochemical changes that are caused by repeated chemical insult. Some of these symptoms are clearly medical (e.g., stomach and liver problems resulting from excessive alcohol use, infections caused by dirty needles, weight loss resulting from a chemically depressed appetite). When such symptoms are seen in adolescents, the problems with drugs are usually already so evident that diagnosis is not a problem. Much more important for diagnosis in adolescents are the deficits in intellectual and emotional functioning that are caused by repeated drug use.

Chronic use of mood-altering drugs impairs memory, concentration, information processing, judgment, and problem solving. These impairments often appear as a sudden loss of IQ points. Such adolescents become prone to forgetfulness and to drawing irrational conclusions. They become very poor at predicting the implications of current happenings, especially the implications of their own behavior. They often pull "dumb stunts" (major breaches of well-understood rules that will cause them a lot of trouble) and otherwise behave stupidly. Some, but not all, show an abrupt decrease in school performance along with these other symptoms.

Chronic use of mood-altering drugs also has major effects upon general emotional tone and lability. Chemically dependent youngsters tend to be depressed and apathetic much of the time, and they often sleep excessively. This is sometimes referred to as the "amotivational syndrome" (Macdonald, 1984). At the same time they display very unpredictable and volatile swings of mood, going from extreme anger and hostility to sadness, to ebullience, to relative normalcy in an abrupt fashion without apparent stimulus.

These symptoms generally disappear if the drug use can be stopped for a sufficient period of time. The length of time required is highly variable, depending on the individual and the type, amount, and frequency of drug use. An alcohol dependent adolescent might require a week for most of the cognitive impairment to fade and two weeks for most of the emotional impairment to disappear. A heavy marijuana-using adolescent, on the other hand, might require two to four times that long. In general, marijuana produces the longest lasting direct drug-induced impairments.

A problem of chronic drug use that does not automatically disappear with the mere passage of drug-free time is emotional immaturity. The mood-altering drugs, regardless of what other effects they might have, are all very effective in providing short-term reduction in both physical and emotional pain. Everyone who experiments with mood-altering drugs learns this very quickly; for at least some people, mood-altering drugs accomplish this pain reduction more quickly and reliably than any other means available. Consequently, these people learn to cope with discomfort by using drugs, rather than by using other healthier coping strategies. Adolescence is the period during which much of the learning of coping responses takes place. Emotional maturity is largely a reflection of the successful acquisition of such strategies. When an adolescent learns to use drugs as a means of coping, this generally precludes the learning of healthier alternatives that enhance emotional maturation. Consequently, most chemically dependent adolescents appear to be emotionally retarded. The simple passage of time is usually not sufficient to correct this acquired immaturity; amelioration requires specialized treatment. One major component of chemical dependency treatment is aimed directly at this remediation.

Symptoms Associated with Acquiring, Storing and Using Drugs, and with Protecting One's Ability to Use

Using drugs becomes one of the most important activities in the lives of chemically dependent people—adolescents or otherwise. They become preoccupied with maintaining a supply of drugs and with activities closely associated with using. They also become involved in activities that can best be described as "drug worship."

Drugs cost money, and in order to purchase drugs, adolescents often start to pressure their parents for larger allowances, or request money for various poorly defined special needs. When these tactics fail to work, the adolescents may steal from home, break into houses and businesses, shoplift, steal cars, or prostitute. With surprisingly high frequency, adolescents also become involved in selling drugs; this is one of the easiest ways to support a habit, and drug wholesalers actively encourage the practice.

A supportive environment for drug use is created by dropping relatively "straight" friends in favor of new drug-using friends, and by ceasing participation in healthy activities (e.g., scouts, sports, church) in favor of new activities in which drugs are an integral part. Because drug use is the dominant theme of these new friends and activities, parents often have difficulty learning much about them. When parents inquire about these new friends and their activities, adolescents often give responses such as: "I don't know his name," "I only know she lives on the other side of town," "They are poor and don't have a phone," "Oh, we just sit around and listen to records," "We just wandered around and window-shopped," "Oh, its just a party," and so on. Because the home and the school environment are usually not supportive of drug use, chemically dependent adolescents tend to withdraw from both. Truancy and cutting classes are common, as are long unexplained absences from home, and a loss of interest in family activities. Attempts to keep the adolescent at home more are met with hostility. Sneaking and running away from home are frequent.

Chemically dependent people like to keep drugs and related paraphernalia close at hand, which usually requires finding some way to hide them around the home. As a consequence, chemically dependent youth often become sneaky and secretive about their activities. They begin to make an issue of their right to privacy and the sanctity of their rooms and their belongings. They also become masters at manipulating, conning, and controlling parents and other adults, including therapists. They learn how to induce fear and guilt as a means of getting their way, and how to make parents back down from inspecting their room or monitoring their activities too closely. They learn how to manipulate with displays of aggression. They also become very adept at being sweet, loving, and conciliatory when it is to their advantage.

"Drug worship" can take many forms. Some of the most common are: talking a lot with friends about drugs and drug-related activities; writing notes to friends about drugs and getting high; doodling in notebooks about drugs, drug-related activities, and drug-worshipping rock groups; and assigning immense importance to being able to attend particular rock concerts and other events that are largely celebrations of drug use. In some areas, involvement with occult activities also appears as a form of drug worship.

Symptoms Associated with the Delusional System

Chemical dependency in both adolescents and adults is always accompanied by a strong, well-integrated, distorted picture of reality that we refer to as the "delusional system." This system is characterized by massive amounts of minimization, denial, and rationalization of the individual's drug use. Ask chemically dependent adolescents about the extent of their drug use, and they are likely to deny any use at all. At best, the answer will be only a fraction of the truth. Ask about the problems they are experiencing, and they are likely to overlook many of them, including major ones like being pregnant, trouble with the law, and suspension from school. Further, those problems to which they do admit are likely to be blamed on other people and circumstances. Ask about the relationship between their drug use and their problems, and they will usually deny any possibility of an association.

Undoubtedly, some of these false reports can be ascribed to lying. The youngster does not want the truth known because parents and other adults would then take steps to interfere with continued drug use. However, there is also no question that other false reports can be attributed to "sincere delusion." The adolescent really is not aware of the true extent of his or her drug use, cannot perceive the magnitude of some of the problems, and really does not see that drug use has anything to do with the problems. Another significant component of chemical dependency treatment is aimed at correcting this sincerely deluded picture of reality.

The issues of exactly how much of the delusional system is sincere, how this system develops, and why it is such a universal component of chemical dependency has not yet been adequately explained. However, we do know that we cannot get the truth by simply asking a chemically dependent adolescent how much he or she uses. Though this may seem too obvious to need emphasis, we have lost count of the number of chemically dependent adolescents who had previously been given a clean bill of drug health by a professional whose diagnostic routine consisted of merely asking how much they used, and then taking the answer as gospel. Diagnosis of chemical dependency requires sensitivity to other signs, and much detective work when it comes to verifying actual use.

The delusional system is also important to diagnosis because it is often one of the earliest tip offs to the possibility of chemical dependency. If the adolescent does not seem to fully appreciate the severity of the impending problems, shows no guilt or remorse over gross violations of rules, seems oblivious to the fact that everyone else in the family is tearing their hair out over his or her behavior, denies any and all drug use in the face of good evidence to the contrary, and seems to have somebody else to blame for all the problems, we should immediately suspect the possibility of chemical dependency.

This delusional system also means that an adolescent with a drug problem will very rarely admit that fact to a professional. Adolescents may concede that they have other problems for which professional consultation might be useful (bad parents are a common complaint of chemically dependent youth, and attempts to fix those bad parents are common responses from clinicians who are not sensitive to chemical dependency), but "certainly not a drug problem."

This delusional system is usually so strong that an individual (professional or otherwise) is unlikely to talk a chemically dependent adolescent into a more veridical picture of reality. This is one of the principal reasons why programs specializing in the treatment of chemical dependency rely very heavily on milieu and group therapy. Treatment requires extensive feedback from many people who will confrontatively reflect reality over a long time span. This feedback eventually replaces the distorted perceptions of the dependent individual with a more accurate and realistic self-appraisal.

The operation of a delusional system also has a very important implication about who the therapist must regard as the primary client when parents bring a minor in for evaluation. Because of the delusional system, and because drugs assume such overriding importance to the dependent person, chemically dependent adolescents are not likely to cooperate in efforts to get at the truth about their drug use. Parents will usually have to do some snooping, prying, and invading of the youngster's privacy (without his or her knowledge) in order to get the truth. Similarly, the adolescent is likely to be very resistant to any suggestion of treatment for chemical dependency. Consequently, parents will usually have to apply extreme pressure (*force* is often the better word) to "convince" the youth to enter, stay, and be cooperative in treatment. Counseling parents to invade their child's privacy, or to apply pressure, is very difficult if the therapist views the child as the primary client, but appropriate when the *family system* is viewed as the client.

DIAGNOSIS

The diagnosis of chemical dependency is a process that typically involves several steps and may require weeks to complete. In this section the major elements of this process are described.

Step One: Hypothesizing Chemical Dependency

Adolescents do not usually wear their drug use where it can be easily seen. Most parents, including those of chemically dependent adolescents, have never seen their youngster intoxicated, and many are convinced that their child would never "mess around" with drugs. When parents do admit that their adolescent may have experimented with drugs, they are still relatively certain that the use is light and certainly not abnormal for an adolescent of this age. Almost surely they do not believe that the drug use is related to the presenting problems, and quite often they have received "expert" support for this belief from therapists they have consulted.

Because the adolescent is not likely to tell the truth about drug use, and the parents are likely blind to the truth, how do we go about diagnosing a possible drug problem? Usually the first clues come from the presenting behavioral difficulties, and *include no reference to or information about actual drug use.* We have listed some adolescent behavioral changes that are a tip-off to possible chemical dependency and are likely to be reported during the first or second interview.

Increased incidence of abrupt, unpredictable mood swings

Increased secretiveness

Decreased involvement in family activities

Increased seclusion and isolation

Increased lying, stealing, conning, and manipulating

Increased defensiveness

Increased irresponsibility

Deterioration of intrafamily relationships

Deterioration of school performance

Deterioration of memory, thinking, problem solving, and other cognitive functions

Increased incidence of breaches of rules and authority

Emotional immaturity

Lack of guilt and remorse for wrongdoings

Increased incidence of "dumb stunts"

Running away

Suicide talk, gestures, or attempts

In addition, other family members often experience changes that suggest chemical dependency.

Increased marital conflicts, especially regarding how to deal with the adolescent's behavior problems

Increased guilt and blame of other family members for the problems

Increased cross-generational alignment of one parent with the problem child

Feelings of confusion

Feelings of failure as a parent

Some of these symptoms, of course, can result from individual or systemic difficulties other than chemical dependency. Indeed, it is probably rare for any family to survive adolescence without observing or displaying at least a few of these. What, then, differentiates the chemically dependent from the "normal" adolescent in terms of expressions of these symptoms? Principally the clustering, the persistence, and the progressive worsening of the symptoms. A chemically dependent adolescent typically displays several of these symptoms simultaneously. Moreover, the symptoms persist, and additional ones develop for as long as the youth continues to use drugs. They do not represent brief periods of adjustment difficulty with fairly quick resolution. Further, in chemically dependent youth who continue to use drugs, the symptoms generally worsen over time, even in the face of concerted efforts by parents, therapists, school officials, and juvenile justice officials to "correct" the problem behavior or treat the family system. Individual symptoms may show periods of temporary improvement, but these periods will be brief. The longer-term trend will still be progressive worsening. In our practice, we have come to follow the rule of thumb that if three or more of the above-listed symptoms are present for at least three months, we automatically consider chemical dependency.

In some cases, of course, parents will be aware that their child has experimented with drugs. Perhaps they have seen the adolescent intoxicated, or occasionally an adolescent will admit some (usually trivial) amount of drug use. In these cases, we automatically suspect chemical dependency, regardless of how many of the other symptoms are present.

Step Two: Confirming Drug Involvement

The most common situation at the end of the hypothesis stage is that we have an adolescent whose behavior suggests chemical dependency, but whose drug use and related activities are largely unknown. The next step of the diagnostic process is to collect more reliable information about the actual drug use. As suggested earlier, this will typically require that the parents conduct a campaign of snooping, prying, and spying. The parent(s) may have to: search the adolescent's room and other likely sites for drugs and paraphernalia; look through school books and papers for references to drugs; listen in on phone conversations (Radio Shack sells a $20 unit that plugs into any phone jack and converts any inexpensive tape recorder into a silent voice-actuated recorder of all conversation on that phone system, making it unnecessary for parents to spend hours waiting for an opportunity to eavesdrop); check on the youth's whereabouts when he or she is away from home; follow the adolescent to see where he or she goes; talk to teachers and school officials about the adolescent's friends, activities, and possible unexplained absences; check with other parents to see what they have observed (other parents often know about another child's drug activities but do not know how to broach the subject with the child's parents); and the like.

Of course, parents are often very resistant to taking such steps, and one of the therapist's most important tasks will be to overcome this resistance. One effective strategy is to have the parents talk with "expert" parents who have already investigated the activities of their chemically dependent youngsters. These parents can attest to their own original naiveté about their child's drug use and to the importance of getting the truth by whatever means necessary. In our work, we have relied heavily on one of several ongoing parent support groups. These are self-help groups of parents who are at some stage of contending with children who have behavior problems (mostly drug-related). When we suspect chemical dependency, we immediately encourage our clients to join and to participate actively in one of these groups.

If an adolescent is heavily into drugs, the snooping campaign will usually elicit clear evidence to that effect. Occasionally, it yields only equivocal results, often because the adolescent becomes suspicious and modifies his or her behavior before unequivocal data can be obtained. In these cases, we counsel parents to simply back off and wait. Chemically dependent adolescents tend to be careless. If parents know what to look for and remain vigilant, it typically takes only a few weeks for clear bits of evidence to appear.

Step Three: The Tough Love Test for Chemical Dependency

Assume that we have determined that an adolescent shows a pattern of behavior problems that is consistent with chemical dependency (step one), and that we have confirmed involvement with drugs (step two). Before we can satisfy the definition of chemical dependency, we must answer two additional questions: (1) Has the adolescent continued to use drugs despite serious problems related to drugs? (2) Assuming that the problems are judged to be serious, are they, in fact, caused by drug use?

The only way we have found to answer the second question is to do an experiment in which we eliminate drugs from the system and observe whether at least some of the problem-causing behaviors disappear. The strategies for doing this experiment are discussed later in this chapter. Here we concentrate on the first question.

In some cases, by the end of step two, both the parents and the therapist are convinced that the adolescent is probably chemically dependent and that appropriate intervention is necessary. In these cases, step three is unnecessary. However, in all cases in which there is uncertainty on the part of either the therapist or the parents, step three provides a means for resolving that uncertainty.

Sometimes it will not be clear at the end of step two whether an adolescent's drug-related problems are truly serious. In other cases, especially when an adolescent has already suffered major consequences as a result of drug-related activities (e.g., time in juvenile justice facilities, expulsion from school, serious injury), the therapist may need no further convincing that the youth is chemically dependent, but the parents are not convinced. Parents tend to be more resistant to a diagnosis of chemical dependency than to just about any other diagnosis. They often believe drug problems imply immorality or are a sign of parental failure. They may have difficulty believing that their child needs special help with such an apparently simple task as not using drugs, especially when they discover that the special help may require that their child spend several very expensive weeks in an in-patient treatment program, along with major lifestyle changes and regular participation in an ongoing recovery program for at least several years. Occasionally, a case arises in which the parents are persuaded at the end of step two that their child is chemically dependent, but the therapist requires more convincing.

The strategy we prefer for further testing the chemical dependency hypothesis is called the "tough love test." To perform this test, the adolescent is simply told by the parents: "Your use of drugs without our explicit knowledge and permission is unacceptable to us. We know that you have been using drugs, and you must stop immediately. If you use drugs even once more, then you will immediately receive consequence X." The critical aspect of this test is to choose a consequence such that, if it fails to deter further drug use, both the parents and the clinician will be convinced that the chemical dependency hypothesis must be pursued further.

What kinds of consequences should be selected? In general, if an adolescent is not chemically dependent, even a relatively mild consequence will be sufficient to put a stop to the drug use. However, if a mild consequence is used in the test, and it fails to deter further drug use, the parents or the therapist are likely to remain unconvinced that the adolescent is really dependent. Therefore, the test should use as stiff a consequence as the parents have the courage to implement. The consequence that we have found to be most effective is: "If you use drugs again, we will immediately take you to a chemical dependency treatment facility for a thorough evaluation, and if they decide you are chemically dependent, you will go through a treatment program."

Most parents find this consequence palatable. However, some consider it too stiff and insist on first trying some lesser consequence, even though in all probability they will remain unconvinced that the adolescent is chemically dependent when this lesser test fails to deter further drug use. In these cases, we simply let the parents try the lesser test. If it fails to stop the drug use, we insist that they impose the promised consequence and then urge them to move up to a more convincing version of the test. Most parents end up presenting the treatment program consequence before becoming convinced.

What if the adolescent does not believe that the parents will go through with the consequence threatened in the tough love test? This is very likely to happen, particularly because typically the parents have made many previous threats that they have not carried through. If the adolescent does not believe the threat, the test is less convincing. Therefore, we always encourage parents to wait until they are fully prepared to follow through on the consequence before they apply the tough love test. Their conviction will be evident to the child. We also encourage them to confront the child with the tough love conditions in the presence of other people (e.g., friends, family, therapist) who whole-heartedly support the action the parents are taking. The presence of supportive witnesses goes a long way toward convincing most adolescents that the parents are serious.

What if the adolescent continues to use drugs in such a way that the parents cannot detect it? This is theoretically possible, but it rarely occurs in practice. When parents have learned what to look for and how to look for it, it is very difficult for an adolescent to use drugs extensively without the parents finding out. However, because this might happen, we ask parents to use a slightly modified form of the tough love test in which the treatment program consequence will be implemented if the adolescent is detected using drugs, *or* if certain other specified unacceptable behaviors (e.g., skipping school, belligerency with parents, lying) persist. If these aspects of the adolescent's behavior remain unacceptable, the parents may still want to go through the chemical dependency evaluation, and they will find it easier to do if that contingency was spelled out initially.

Sometimes youth respond to the tough love test by using various fear and guilt-inducing tactics to get their parents to yield. Running away is one common gambit. Nothing works quite as well as running away to scare parents back into line, and most youth (at least most who are chemically dependent) know this. Suicide threats or attempts, physical violence, and other extreme forms of acting out are also effective. We routinely warn parents that these kinds of responses are possible. We also tell them that these responses are virtually foolproof indicators of chemical dependency, and that if they get any of these responses from their adolescent, they should cancel the rest of the tough love test and see that the adolescent immediately receives a thorough chemical dependency evaluation. If they are not comfortable with that course of action, we urge them to at least not back down from the conditions they stated prior to the test.

A Word about False Positive Diagnoses

Many therapists appear to be exceptionally concerned about the consequences of incorrectly diagnosing an adolescent as chemically dependent, with the result that they are very reluctant to make this diagnosis unless they are absolutely certain. We feel this extreme caution is dangerously placed. With chemical dependency, the consequences of a false negative diagnosis are very severe for the adolescent and include intense physical and emotional suffering, and possibly death. The consequences may also be dangerous for other members of the family, for friends, and even for bystanders. The consequences of a false positive diagnosis, on the other hand, are relatively benign. In the discussion that follows, we argue that effective treatment of chemical dependency can only happen in programs designed specifically and exclusively for the treatment of this problem. Therefore, in virtually every case the clinician will make a referral to such a program, and an expert second opinion will be forthcoming as a matter of course. Any false positives will be identified in short order, and the worst consequence of such an error will be that the adolescent will spend a few unnecessary days in a chemical dependency program. Simply stated, this will not happen very often. Chemical dependency treatment programs rarely get false positive referrals because the general reluctance to diagnose chemical dependency is so very high among both professionals and lay people.

INTERVENTION

As mentioned earlier, we believe the only sensible and ethically justifiable goal for the treatment of chemical dependency is complete abstinence from mood-altering drugs. Two general approaches are used to achieve this condition: The "jail approach" attempts to restrict an individual's access to drugs and to drug-related activities so that use is not possible. The "therapeutic approach," on the other hand, attempts to effect changes in the individual's cognitive structure, attitudes, family, peer relations, and lifestyle such that the adolescent does not use drugs even with the opportunity.

Quite often when parents finally become convinced that drug use is an important part of their youngster's problems, they are immediately inclined to try some variant of the jail approach to control the use. The parents may, as one father stated, try to "handcuff the kid to me so that she won't be able to do *anything* without my knowing about it." They may refuse to allow the adolescent to leave the house without supervision. They may also enlist the cooperation of school officials in maintaining close supervision over the youngster, or switch the child into a private school. Parents usually attempt these "jailing" maneuvers on the assumption that if they can just keep the adolescent from using drugs for a month or so, he or she will somehow "get over" the desire to use drugs. Unfortunately, this does not happen.

Jail tactics fail because it is not possible to monitor and control a chemically dependent adolescent closely enough to prevent drug use for very long. No matter how close the supervision and surveillance, the opportunity to use will arise and the youngster will take it. Parents will eventually tire of their role as warden. The adolescent will find a way to sneak out in the middle of the night or to have drugs slipped into the house. The futility of jail tactics becomes especially obvious when we stop to consider that despite very elaborate precautions and large staffs of paid employees, our jails, prisons, and juvenile training centers are awash in drugs. Drug dependent people who are not in recovery want very badly to use drugs, and they usually find a way to do it. In light of these facts, we actively discourage parents from wasting their time and energy on jail tactics, and encourage them to concentrate their efforts on forcing the adolescent to cooperate with a good treatment program.

Forcing Participation in Treatment

Chemically dependent people love drugs and do not believe that there is anything wrong with their drug use. Consequently, it is rare to find anyone who has truly volunteered for treatment. Even those people who on the surface may appear to agree to treatment usually turn out, on closer inspection, to have done so for reasons quite different from wanting to give up drugs. They may have been trying to avoid going to jail or losing a job or a spouse, but they almost certainly were not trying to deal with their drug problem. Fortunately, the treatment process appears to work fairly well regardless of the initial motivation for entering treatment (Macdonald, 1984; Pattison, 1979).

In the case of adolescents, the main reason for entering treatment is that the parents or the courts will impose serious consequences if treatment is avoided. Such consequences also provide motivation for staying in the program, for cooperating with it, and for at least the initial effort of trying to remain drug free upon return to the "real world." Because of the strength of the love affair with drugs, only extremely serious consequences will be effective in starting and keeping an adolescent in treatment. We know of only two consequences that are likely to be effective, and even these do not work 100% of the time: threat of incarceration, and threat of being ejected from the home and family.

Because the criminal justice system is still largely ignorant about chemical dependency, employing the threat of incarceration to force adolescents into treatment is, unfortunately, fairly rare. Therefore, in most instances, parents are left with only one lever with which to start and maintain their child in treatment—the threat of putting the youngster out of the home.

We recognize that threatening to eject an adolescent from home and family is a drastic measure for any therapist to recommend or for any parent to implement. If we knew of a less drastic measure that might work, we would suggest it. However, this measure appears somewhat more reasonable when we compare it with the alternative. Suppose there is no threat, or a threat which, from the adolescent's standpoint, is less severe. In either case, it is very likely that the adolescent will refuse to stay in treatment or to cooperate with treatment. Suppose the youth refuses to stay in treatment and receives the parents' permission to come home. What will happen? Regardless of what the adolescent says, which will probably entail a promise never to use drugs again, he or she will resume using drugs in short order. The dependency will become worse, and the adolescent's behavior will become even more unpredictable, irrational, dishonest, manipulative, and disruptive of the family. The adolescent will probably drain the family finances, cause severe emotional turmoil for everyone in the family, and may spur the breakup of the family. The adolescent may also cause serious physical harm to others in the family, and will certainly cause severe physical self-harm. Sooner or later, one way or another, the adolescent is likely to die from the chemical dependency.

On the other hand, consider the consequences of threatening expulsion from the home. First, the chances that the youth will leave treatment, or arrange to get thrown out, are greatly reduced. What will happen, however, if the youth does leave treatment and is not allowed to return home? Parents are often quite frightened, and realistically so, of the "bad things" that can happen to adolescents "out there." Nonetheless are these dangerous uncertainties worse than the consequences that are virtually guaranteed if the adolescent is permitted to come home? We think not. Further, our experiences suggest that the likelihood of serious emotional or physical injury to the adolescent while "out there" is quite low. In over 200 cases with which we are personally familiar, nothing serious has happened *so long as the door was kept open for the adolescent to return home when he or she decided to cooperate with treatment*. Indeed, it is very unusual for youth under 16 years of age to live independently for more than a few weeks. Moreover, most of this time is usually spent living in the homes of various friends who are willing to provide temporary food and shelter. Even though the adolescent may be living in the relatively protected environment of a friend's home, this lifestyle often comes to a halt because the friend's parents soon tire of feeding, clothing, and housing the adolescent in the absence of financial reimbursement. At this point, recovery begins to look like an attractive alternative and the adolescent agrees to cooperate with treatment.

Many parents are especially reluctant to use the "get out" threat on younger children because it is so clear that they will not be able to cope on their own. We argue just the opposite: Because younger adolescents are so unable to cope on their own, they are especially good candidates for this threat. They are likely to know they cannot cope, and therefore are much less likely to risk leaving or getting thrown out of treatment. If they do leave, they discover very quickly that being on their own is not what they expected.

We are familiar with more than a dozen 12- and 13-year-old youngsters who chose the "get out" alternative over cooperating with treatment. In no case did it take more than 48 hours for the child to call home and reopen negotiations to enter treatment. On the other hand, we also know of numerous cases in which adolescents who were 15 years of age and older managed to cope successfully enough on their own that they never got into treatment. We are also familiar with many cases in which the parents were unwilling to use the "get out" threat before the adolescent turned 18 years old, at which time it was too late. When an adolescent becomes 18 years of age, the parents lose their special legal status over the adolescent. In some cases, the parents also lose insurance coverage for payment of treatment that the adolescent might receive.

Chemically dependent adolescents who are accorded adult status by virtue of reaching age 18 often muddle through life on their own until they eventually kill themselves. Therefore, we urge parents to force their children into treatment at the earliest possible age, using the strongest lever they possibly can.

What about the legality of ejecting a minor from the home? Laws and law enforcement practices vary widely from locale to locale. The therapist needs to be familiar with the situation in his or her particular area. Where we practice, parents are legally obligated to support a child until 18 years of age. Failure to do so can result in prosecution for violation of the child welfare statutes. Accordingly, police and juvenile officials routinely counsel against ejecting a child. Parents are also technically liable for the actions of the minor, and are subject to civil suit for any damages caused by the child. Despite the fact that parents have this same liability when the child is living at home, this liability is often used as a basis for counseling against ejecting a child.

In our experience, however, there is a huge discrepancy between what the law states and actual practice. In the 200 or so ejection cases with which we are personally acquainted, no parent has ever been prosecuted for ejecting an adolescent who refused to cooperate with treatment. In those cases in which the ejection has come to the attention of juvenile authorities, the authorities have supported the parents, and in many cases have added the threat of incarceration as a consequence for the adolescent's noncompliance. In fact, if parents eject their child for refusal to cooperate, they can report their child as a runaway. This step protects parents from charges of abuse and abandonment, and increases the likelihood that (1) the adolescent will be detained and brought before a juvenile judge, (2) the parents will be able to tell the court about their child's condition and the necessity for treatment, and (3) the court will help get the adolescent into treatment. On the question of civil liability, in only one of our cases did the parents incur any financial liability as a result of the child's actions while away from home, and that case involved emergency medical expenses for the child.

Finally, a word must be said about possible legal problems a therapist might incur by counseling parents to adopt and follow through on the ejection threat. This is usually one of the first questions raised when we discuss this tactic with mental health professionals, particularly those who have little or no experience working with adolescent chemical dependency.

Certainly, the therapist runs a risk that a family might eventually sue if the ejection tactic doesn't work or if it results in harm to the youngster. Further, although we know of no data on the issue, we also suspect that a therapist's chances of being sued are greater in this situation than in many others, simply because this tactic is unusual and appears to many to be harsh. We can see no easy way around this problem. Ultimately, as with any course of treatment, the therapist must decide which is more important—increasing the client's chances for recovery, or avoiding a lawsuit. In the case of adolescent chemical dependency, those who are afraid of a lawsuit are advised to refer the case to someone else rather than try to deal with the chemical dependency in some seemingly safer but ultimately futile (and possibly counterproductive) way.

Although it is impossible to completely avoid the risk of being sued, a couple of tactics can reduce the risk. First is to make sure the parents understand their full range of options, the possible consequences thereof, and that the decision is ultimately theirs to make. Second is to make use of a parent support group to allow the parents to hear how the various options have worked in other families, and to help them come to their own decision about how to proceed.

GOALS IN CHEMICAL DEPENDENCY TREATMENT

In order to promote long-term abstinence effectively, any treatment program for chemical dependency must accomplish a number of basic tasks.

Detoxification

Some chemically dependent people become physically dependent on one or more drugs: Whenever they cease using drugs, they begin to show primary withdrawal symptoms. These symptoms are physiological reactions to the unaccustomed absence of the drugs from the body and may include profuse sweating, muscle cramps, nausea, hallucinations, and convulsions. The precise nature of the symptoms, their severity, and their duration vary with the type of drug and the history of the drug use (Shuckit, 1979). Because withdrawal from some drugs can be life threatening, and because some individuals refuse to report the exact drugs to which they are addicted, knowledgeable medical consultation should always be sought during the early stages of any program that intends to preclude drug use. (The average physician is not knowledgeable about withdrawal.) Although it is quite rare for an adolescent to display serious withdrawal symptoms, chemical dependency treatment facilities automatically provide this consultation.

Regardless of the specific drugs involved and the severity of observable withdrawal symptoms, withdrawal is always a painful process. Moreover, most chemically dependent individuals are well aware that drugs will make this pain go away. Therefore, the motivation to use drugs is especially intense during withdrawal.

As mentioned earlier, all mood-altering drugs, including those that produce minimal primary withdrawal symptoms (e.g., marijuana), also produce another class of symptoms that can last for weeks or months following cessation of drug use. These "extended withdrawal symptoms" include impaired cognitive functioning, large, unpredictable fluctuations in emotional tone, continued bouts of both physical and emotional pain, and continued episodes of intense cravings for drugs.

The chemically dependent person must get through primary withdrawal completely, and through the initial portions of extended withdrawal at least, before any real benefits from the cognitive and emotional components of treatment can be derived. With adolescents who have been heavy users of marijuana, for example, it often takes three or four drug-free weeks before they are fully able to comprehend what they read and hear. Moreover, complete abstinence from mood-altering drugs is an absolute prerequisite for this process. The person who manages to sneak in "just a little" drug use during withdrawal might as well not be considered in withdrawal at all, as far as cognitive and emotional functioning are concerned.

The detoxification phase of treatment is the one situation where "jail tactics" are useful. Indeed, we believe that the treatment of choice is a program designed specifically for chemical dependency that requires the youngster to live in the treatment facility on a 24-hour-a-day basis, and in which all contact with people from the outside world is carefully controlled and monitored. There are several reasons for this preference, but perhaps the major one is that such programs are better able to enforce a drug-free condition, especially during the crucial withdrawal periods.

Delusion Smashing

Chemically dependent people possess a radically distorted picture of themselves, their problems, their relationships with other people, their reliance on drugs, and the interactions among these factors. They minimize and deny both drug use and drug-caused problems. Frequently, they seem to have a bottomless capacity to spin fanciful rationalizations for the problems that have been happening in their lives. Before any therapeutic progress can be made, this delusional system must be replaced by a more accurate picture of reality.

Smashing delusions is a very difficult undertaking. It cannot be accomplished by any single individual (whether a therapist, parent, teacher, judge, drug counselor, or friend) on a one-on-one basis. The dependent's delusional system is simply too well developed and too strong. Rather, this task requires a group of people who work together over many hours to confront the omissions, the distortions of fact, and the inconsistencies in the delusional story. Confrontative tactics are required to break through the rigid defenses and to make contact with some honest emotional reactions. It helps enormously if the group contains some chemically dependent people who have only recently had their own delusions smashed. Such persons tend to be much more sensitive to the minimizing and rationalizing ploys of the dependent than are even many clinicians, and they tend to be less skittish about tough confrontation and expression of intense emotion.

Closely related to delusion smashing is the process of detecting and confronting attempts of the dependent adolescent to lie and con his or her way through the program. Virtually every dependent youngster will decide that the best way to deal with the treatment program is to "go along with the game and tell them what they want to hear." If this strategy works, the delusions are never destroyed. Consequently, much time and effort is devoted to detecting and confronting such superficial compliance. Again, other recovering dependents in the same treatment program tend to be particularly adept at identifying and challenging such ploys.

Education

When chemically dependent adolescents accept that drug use has been a major cause of their problems, they must then be educated about what they must do to avoid further problems. Therefore, treatment programs must include a large dose of education about drugs and chemical dependency. Individuals must be taught that they are different from "normal" people in regard to drug using, and that they can hope to lead a happy life only if they can achieve and maintain complete abstinence from mood-altering drugs. They must be convinced that theirs is a permanent, progressive, irreversible, and potentially fatal condition. Only then can they be expected to take other aspects of the treatment program seriously.

Adolescents must also learn that abstinence from mood-altering drugs is an achievable goal provided they are willing to follow certain fairly simple rules. These rules include avoiding the people, places, and things that were previously associated with using; avoiding situations that might present a temptation to use; and not becoming too confident about one's ability to refrain from using in the face of temptation. These rules also include one that most chemically dependent people, and for that matter most professionals and lay people, find especially difficult to swallow. Namely, long-term abstinence is most readily achieved by following an active, ongoing long-term recovery program, such as Alcoholics Anonymous (AA) or Narcotics Anonymous (NA). The possibility of relapse into drug use is an ever-present danger. Those who are most successful in avoiding relapse are those who become active in one of these very successful programs (Armor, Polich, & Stambul, 1976; Vaillant, 1983). For this reason, most treatment facilities work very closely with AA and NA programs. They provide instruction in the basic tenets of these programs and encourage or require patients to attend meetings of these programs while in treatment. In addition, they place great emphasis on the importance of continued participation in AA or NA programs after leaving treatment.

Attitude Change

The distinction between education and change of attitude is not sharp, but it is very important because education alone is not sufficient. Dependent persons must come to believe at an emotional level that these facts about chemical dependency are true and apply to themselves. They must develop a whole new set of attitudes about themselves in relation to drugs.

The development of these new attitudes is a long and slow process that seems to occur best in a milieu in which the process is reinforced many hours a day during interactions with others who are undergoing the same transition. Thus, changing these attitudes practically demands a group treatment mode. This is one of the main reasons why virtually every successful treatment program, and all of the self-help programs, operate predominantly in a group mode.

One component of this attitude change deserves special mention. Probably the most difficult fact for any chemically dependent individual to accept is that: "Drugs make me crazy. That is always the way it is going to be. I will never be able to use mood-altering drugs safely again." Without having accepted this "first step" (as it is called in the lingo of AA and NA), long-term abstinence is not likely. It is hard to overestimate the difficulty of maintaining such a belief when (1) one is madly in love with drugs, and (2) much of the population seems to be able to use these substances without serious problems. One of the best teachers of this reality about chemical dependency is to see other dependent people fail in their efforts to engage in nonproblematic use of drugs following a period of sobriety.

Problems with accepting the permanence and irreversibility of chemical dependency probably also account for the difference that is observed in the success rates of adult versus adolescent treatment programs. Many adult programs report success rates (i.e., proportion of clients finishing the program who remain abstinent for one year) of approximately 60% (Johnson, 1980; Laundegren, 1982). On the other hand, it is generally accepted that even the very best adolescent programs do not fare better than about 40%. Much of this difference probably stems from the fact that by the time many adults reach treatment, they have already failed numerous times to "use without getting crazy," whereas adolescents are much less likely to have already conducted these personal experiments.

Skill Development

Chemically dependent individuals are typically lacking in a variety of skills that are necessary to achieve a reasonably happy and fulfilling drug-free lifestyle. As a consequence, a major component of treatment is devoted to replacing dysfunctional behaviors with a healthier repertoire. The range of skills that requires remediation during treatment is too broad to be treated in any detail here. However, a few examples will be offered.

Ability to manage emotions.   As mentioned previously, drugs provide a method for dealing with unpleasant feelings that is faster and much more effective, in the short run, than just about any alternative. Chemically dependent people discover this and come to rely almost exclusively on drug use as their means of dealing with emotions. If successful recovery is to be achieved, they must learn new ways of managing and coping with their feelings. Therefore, much therapeutic effort is devoted to teaching individuals how to identify and label their feelings better, how to avoid situations that may evoke problematic emotions, and how to deal more effectively with those feelings that do occur.

Honesty. Most people who are chemically dependent learn to lie, cheat, con, and manipulate until dishonesty becomes a way of life. Indeed, such persons often cannot discriminate the truth from their own fabrications. If the individual is ever to develop normal satisfying relations with people in the "straight" world, this penchant for dishonesty must be changed. Therefore, considerable therapeutic effort is spent on teaching the person to be more honest with both self and others.

Interpersonal skills. Chemically dependent adolescents tend to associate primarily with other heavy drug users. Drugs become the focal point around which all peer activities revolve. Many chemically dependent adolescents have literally no experience dating or cultivating friendships while not under the influence of drugs. They have no idea what it means to "have fun" when drugs are not involved. Nor do they know what friendship means on an affective and realistic level. Most chemically dependent adolescents have a very extensive history of sexual activity, all while drugged. They have little experience dealing with sexual feelings without drugs, and they have only a minimal idea of what constitutes socially acceptable sexual conduct among nondrug users. Chemically dependent adolescents are also almost completely lacking in healthy skills for relating to others in the family. Much of treatment, then, is devoted to starting the development of more functional interpersonal skills.

Responsibility. In our society, whenever anyone, especially a youngster, begins to behave in a crazy manner, family, friends, and institutions all move in to "help." This assistance typically includes a minimization of the consequences of the crazy behavior, an assumption of responsibility for the individual and his or her actions, shielding the individual from normal pressures and expectations, and otherwise "padding the corners" and taking care of the individual. Chemically dependent adolescents quickly learn to take advantage of these tendencies. They become masters at getting others to take care of and protect them, with the consequence that chemically dependent youngsters tend to be exceptionally dependent on other people, skilled at getting others to do for them, and poor at assuming responsibility for themselves. Therefore, much of treatment consists of experiences designed to begin weaning people from their dependence on others and to encourage accepting responsibility for their own behavior.

Family Treatment

Although there is no reason to believe that families cause chemical dependency in any unidirectional fashion, families can have a very significant impact on the likelihood that an adolescent will achieve stable recovery. This impact can occur in many different ways.

To take only a few examples: If parents do not understand the importance of total abstinence, they may unwittingly encourage the adolescent to attempt nonproblematic use of drugs following a period of sobriety. If they do not understand the importance of ongoing participation in AA/NA, they may discourage such participation. If they do not understand the importance of fostering self-responsibility, they may unknowingly interfere with recovery by encouraging continued dependency and tolerating irresponsibility. If they do not understand drug dependency, they may continue to blame the child for previous unacceptable behavior, or they may continue to carry a crippling load of guilt for not having been "good parents."

In addition to educational components of family treatment, the therapist must also pay attention to family relations and communication patterns. In many instances the marriage has suffered as a consequence of the adolescent's chemical dependency. Spouses often disagree about how to handle the child's behavior problems, and the child is often effective at playing one parent off against the other. As one parent becomes strict, the other undermines disciplinary efforts in an attempt to shield an already hurting child from more pain. It is very natural for a parent to try to "help" the child with love and protection. Unfortunately, this is a counterproductive strategy when used with chemically dependent children. In other situations, the noxious behavior and trouble of the dependent adolescent has raised family tensions to a very high level. With heightened stress, family communication becomes more defensive, blaming increases, and problem solving becomes less efficient. Younger siblings can start to imitate the dependent adolescent's misbehavior, and family chaos is intensified.

Because of the importance of families in fostering stable recovery (among other reasons), many treatment programs now include a specific component that is aimed expressly at smashing delusions, educating, changing attitudes, and developing necessary skills in the family. Moreover, these programs attempt to structure the family in a way that both supports parental authority and opens communication channels. Mutual listening, discussing, and problem-solving strategies are developed. Spouses learn to work out disagreements between themselves, without pulling in the children. They also learn, on both emotional and instrumental levels, about the nature of chemical dependency and about the role that it played in family functioning. This learning can take place during individual family sessions with the program's therapist, and during multifamily group sessions. Advantages of these multifamily sessions are that couples come to realize that other parents have been in the same boat and there is an opportunity for mutual validation and support.

Aftercare

Recovery from chemical dependency is a long-term proposition. Inpatient or intensive outpatient treatment should be followed by some type of ongoing maintenance program for at least several years. Usually this maintenance program will be AA or NA. In order to further facilitate the transition from inpatient treatment back to the real world, many treatment programs also offer aftercare programs (to supplement AA/NA) in which patients and families are urged to participate after primary treatment is completed. The aftercare program may last from six weeks to two years and usually consists of weekly group meetings dealing with issues such as the development of new peer relations and more effective styles of family communication.

THE ELEMENTS OF A GOOD TREATMENT PROGRAM

Many different types of treatment are available for chemical dependency, and as the prevalence of chemical dependency becomes more widely recognized, additional programs will undoubtedly emerge. At present, therapists should weigh several major components of an effective treatment program when making a referral.

1. *The program must be specifically and exclusively for adolescent chemical dependency.* The educational and therapeutic needs of chemically dependent adolescents are sufficiently unique that they cannot be met in general psychiatric programs that cater to a wide range of emotional and behavioral problems. Even "multitrack" programs, in which some therapeutic activities are unique to specific problems while others are common to all problems, are not satisfactory because of the spillover from one problem to another. For example, it is very difficult to convince one child that his or her poor self-concept is due to the use of drugs, while a roommate who also has a poor self-concept is told not to worry about drugs, but to work on better communication with his or her parents. Therefore, we refer clients only to programs that are specifically and exclusively for adolescent chemical dependency.

2. *The program should subscribe to the abstinence model of chemical dependency.* In our experience, this is the only type of program that stands a real chance of getting an individual unhooked from drugs and into stable recovery, which is why most programs apply this model. However, there are some programs that do not follow the abstinence model. The therapist should check program philosophy carefully before making a referral, and, in our opinion, refer only to those that work from the abstinence model.

3. *The more intense the program the better.* One of the most common errors made by parents and therapists alike is to assume that a particular child's case is not so far advanced that he or she needs an inpatient program. We think this is an error. We believe that the best program for any chemically dependent adolescent, regardless of how heavy the drug use or how severe the problem, is the most intensive treatment that can be arranged and afforded. In the case of adult alcoholics, one of the best predictors of success in treatment is the sheer number of hours that the individual can be kept in contact with the treatment medium (Armor et al., 1978). The same appears to be true of adolescents. The efficacy of intensive treatment is, incidentally, not a new discovery. For years, AA has recommended to newcomers that if they are really serious about giving up drinking, they should commit themselves to attending a minimum of 90 meetings in the next 90 days.

4. *The longer the program the better.* It takes time to effect the changes in attitude and to develop the skills needed to maintain a drug-free existence, especially with youngsters. Therefore, while the inpatient phase of a typical adult program might average four weeks, similar programs for adolescents usually last six to eight weeks, and even then much work remains to be done. Hence, it is also quite common for adolescent

inpatient treatment to be followed by several months in a halfway house that deals exclusively with chemically dependent residents. If it were feasible, we would recommend a halfway house for all of our adolescent chemically dependent clients, regardless of how much progress they may have made in primary treatment. Again, we believe that the more structured help the individual receives, the more likely that person is to achieve a solid, stable recovery.

5. *The program should stress the importance of an active long-term recovery program.* In practice, this usually means that the program (a) introduces the dependent adolescent to AA/NA and places heavy emphasis on continued active participation following primary treatment, and (b) offers a separate outpatient aftercare program in which the individual and family are encouraged to participate for a period of time after primary treatment.

6. *The program should be sensitive to the family dimensions of chemical dependency.* Usually this involves (a) an educational/therapeutic component expressly for family members, (b) a component in which the individual and the family do therapeutic work together to heal some of the wounds caused by the drug-induced behavior, (c) an aftercare program for the family that meets separately from the dependent person's aftercare program, and (d) an emphasis on the importance of an ongoing recovery program for the family through organizations such as Alanon, Naranon, and Families Anonymous.

ALTERNATIVES TO INPATIENT TREATMENT

Inpatient treatment of adolescent chemical dependency can be a very expensive proposition. Hospital-based and privately operated programs can easily cost $20,000 or more, not including costs associated with aftercare or a halfway house. Moreover, some insurance policies do not cover treatment for chemical dependency. Consequently, many families simply cannot afford such programs. What alternatives are available in such cases?

Publicly Funded Programs

Some locales are fortunate enough to have fairly low-cost publicly funded programs. These programs can be excellent. They are usually operated on very tight budgets and are located in converted houses or other low-rent quarters. They tend to be short on amenities and to use more paraprofessional and fewer professional staff than their more expensive counterparts. They also make heavy use of volunteer staff, who are often former residents of the program. In the residential versions of such programs, the residents usually take care of cooking, cleaning, laundry, and other housekeeping chores.

We have encountered many professionals who have a strong bias against this type of program because of the low-rent facilities and the paraprofessional staff. Some therapists also assume that if a program does not charge much, it must not be very good. These biases are, in our experience, without foundation. The quality of a chemical dependency treatment program is measured by its ability to help individuals attain a stable recovery, and many low-cost programs do very well on that score. In fact, the best program we know of is of this low-cost publicly funded type. Again, we follow the general rules that, with other things equal, a residential program is preferable to an outpatient program, longer programs are preferable to shorter, and the more hours of treatment the better.

Very Light Outpatient Programs

School systems, mental health centers, and other agencies sometimes conduct drug abuse treatment programs that bring the adolescent in for an hour or two per week. Quite often the personnel that run such programs know little or nothing about chemical dependency. Generally, the content of the counseling in these programs is not directed at drug use (we know of one in which the adolescents are forbidden to talk about their drug use), but rather concentrates on developing more effective coping or communication skills, or some other futile task. If drug use is mentioned, it is often to encourage youngsters to use in a more controlled and socially acceptable fashion, or to switch to a drug that causes them less trouble than their current favorite.

Although such programs may be of some value with nondependent youngsters, they are ineffective with those who are chemically dependent. In fact, these programs may be downright dangerous because they add the weight of a professional opinion to the dependent child's (and family's) already strong belief that drugs are not at the heart of the problem, and that the child can, if he or she only tries hard enough, find a way to use drugs without problems.

AA and NA

Alcoholics Anonymous, along with its younger cousin, Narcotics Anonymous, have been responsible for more recoveries from chemical dependency than any other type of program, perhaps more than all the others combined. AA has existed since 1935, NA since 1953. Formal treatment programs of the sort discussed above did not become common for adults until the 1970s and for children until the 1980s. Prior to the development of formal treatment programs, AA and NA were basically the only places one could go for help with an alcohol or drug problem, and millions of people achieved stable recovery through these programs.

AA and NA continue to represent a viable primary treatment option; untold thousands of people continue to achieve recovery every year employing just the help offered by these programs. Exclusive participation in AA/NA is less likely to lead to stable recovery than is participation in a good inpatient program followed by participation in AA/NA. This is probably due to the fact that AA/NA cannot insure the physical isolation of the individual from drugs and from the opportunity to use, and because the client's treatment hours are at the rate of only one or two a day. Nevertheless, AA/NA has a higher success rate than any other type of program, except the intensive in-patient/residential program that we advocate, and AA/NA should be the treatment of choice whenever a more intensive program is not possible.

Among the many advantages of AA and NA, two are of extreme practical importance: price and availability. These programs cost nothing. Participants may, if they wish, contribute a small amount to help pay for the meeting room and the refreshments, but no other costs are required. These programs are widely available; there is at least one AA group in nearly every community in the country that has more than a few thousand residents. NA can be found in most communities with a population over 50,000.

NA developed because, in the 1940s and early 1950s before the essential similarity of all the drug dependencies was recognized, AA did not welcome anyone whose primary drug was not alcohol. Recently, that attitude has changed markedly. In many parts of the country, AA now welcomes chemically dependent individuals who use any type of drug. However, the change is not yet complete, and some chapters still do not welcome "other drug" people. Consequently, the therapist would be wise to become familiar with the situation in his or her locale. The simplest way to familiarize oneself is to call the AA phone number listed in the local directory, and ask how AA locally feels about "druggies" and polydependents. Some professionals are reluctant to refer adolescents to AA because they think that the adolescent will feel either unwelcome or out of place. This is really not a matter for concern. Virtually every AA group welcomes all comers, regardless of age, sex, race, religion, or any other factors. The average age of AA membership is dropping every year, and most AA groups have some very young members. In larger communities, some groups are predominantly composed of people under 18 years of age.

In our experience, most professionals are almost totally ignorant about what the AA and NA programs entail. However, that ignorance does not stop many of them from having a very firm negative opinion about these organizations, especially, it seems, when it comes to their own clients. We urge every therapist who is likely to encounter chemically dependent clients to reassess their attitudes. These programs have much to offer, including 24-hour crisis assistance, ready availability of good role models, new friends, and activities, and an easy-to-understand plan for living sober or "straight"—the features that most mental health professionals do not have at their disposal otherwise. Further, these programs are dedicated to working cooperatively with professionals and will go to great lengths to provide information, literature, and speakers to discuss the programs with interested professionals. We also encourage professionals to develop a solid personal contact with someone in these programs who has achieved a stable recovery. This contact person can serve as a source of information, as well as help introduce clients to the program. A client is much more likely to attend a meeting of AA if first introduced to an older member who can serve as a guide, than if left to find his or her own way to a meeting.

The therapist must also remember that the facts about chemical dependency are the same whether the adolescent receives treatment through AA/NA or through any other treatment program. The dependent youngster will not believe he or she is dependent and in need of help and will probably have to be forced to participate in these programs. Breaking through the resistance will generally have to take the same form as it did for a more formal treatment program—giving the child a very serious consequence for not cooperating, such as removal from the home. The therapist need not worry about what the folks in AA or NA will think about someone being forced into their program. They understand better than anyone that there are no true volunteers to recover from chemical dependency.

Relapse, Failed Treatments, Pain, and Recovery

It is a simple fact of life that even with today's techniques for treating chemical dependency, more than half of the adolescents who succeed in getting into treatment will not achieve a stable recovery right away. They will resume using, often almost immediately after leaving treatment, and begin to deteriorate again. Many will require a second, third, or fourth treatment before finally "getting sober." Some will die before they make it. We are acquainted with some professionals who, in light of these facts, have adopted a "what's the use of trying treatment, it isn't likely to work" attitude. While this may be understandable as a response to the frustration of working with this very difficult problem, it is not logical. Without treatment, these adolescents are going to hurt themselves and others, and eventually they are going to kill themselves with drugs. With treatment, they may recover. If not, they may recover with their next treatment or their next. We have no alternative but to keep trying the approach that stands the best chance of producing recovery.

What should we do when a child goes through treatment and then relapses? The answer to that will, of course, depend on the particular case. However, some basic dynamics of dependence bear heavily on the answer in any case. Ultimately, every chemically dependent person who receives the proper education about chemical dependency must make a choice between continuing to use drugs or making the changes that make it possible to give up drugs. Like everyone else, the chemically dependent person operates according to the "least pain" principle. That is, given a choice between two unpleasant alternatives, he or she will choose the one that promises to be least unpleasant. Drugs are extraordinarily important to dependent people, so the prospect of giving up drugs is extremely unpleasant. Hence, it is not surprising that many people choose not to give up drugs. If we wish to increase the probability that the individual will choose to give up drugs, we have to make the consequences of not giving them up even more unpleasant.

How can we do that? One way is for those close to dependent persons to cease covering for them, bailing them out, paying their bills, supporting them, loaning them money, overlooking their lying, cheating and stealing, and otherwise "enabling" their continued use of drugs. The goal of this change is to permit the dependent person to experience the full negative consequences of his or her drug using. A second way is for those associated with the dependent person to add some new consequences for his or her continued drug use, such as "if you continue to use drugs, you don't live here any more." Quite literally, recovery from chemical dependency, especially in adolescents, usually begins with the application of some heavy doses of "tough love."

Applying tough love is difficult for both parents and professionals. It appears cruel, heartless, and contrary to everything we have learned about the proper way to behave toward people we love, especially when they are in trouble. However, tough love is necessary. The old saying that "An alcoholic must hit bottom before he or she becomes ready to accept help" is basically true. "Bottom" is the point at which the prospect of continuing to use becomes more painful than the prospect of giving up the drugs. Unfortunately, a very high percentage of the chemically dependent people in this country never give up their drugs because (1) they die before they hit bottom, or (2) when they do hit bottom, they do not know where to go for help. The two best ways we can increase the percentage of persons who do eventually give up their drugs is to (1) increase the chances that they will hit bottom by refusing to enable their use and by applying tough love, and (2) make sure that help is available when they do hit bottom.

REFERENCES

American Psychiatric Association. (1987). Diagnostic and statistical manual of mental disorders (3rd ed., rev.). Washington, DC: Author.
Armor, D., Polich, J., & Stambul, H. (1978). *Alcoholism and treatment*. Santa Monica, CA: Rand Corporation.
Cleveland, M. (1981). Families and adolescent drug abuse: Structural analysis of children's roles. *Family Process, 20*, 295–304.
Goodwin, D. (1976). *Is alcoholism hereditary?* New York: Oxford University Press.
Health and Human Services (1980). *First statistical compendium of alcohol and health*. Rockeville, MD: U.S. Department of Human Services.
Jellinek, E. M. (1960). *The disease concept of alcoholism*. New Haven, CT: Hillhouse Press.
Johnson, V. (1980). *I'll quit tomorrow*. San Francisco: Harper & Row.
Johnston, L., Bachman, J., & O'Malley, P. (1982). *Student drug use, attitudes and beliefs, National trends, 1975–1982*. Rockville, MD: National Institute of Drug Abuse.
Kramer, J. F., & Cameron, D. C. (Eds.). (1975). *A manual on drug dependence*. Geneva: World Health Organization.
Laundegren, J. (1982). *Easy does it: Alcoholism treatment outcomes, Hazelden, and the Minnesota model*. Center City, MN: Hazelden Press.
Lawson, G., Ellis, D., & Rivers, P. (1984). *Essentials of chemical dependency counseling*. Rockville, MD: Aspen Systems Corp.
Lowman, C. (1981). Alcohol use as an indicator of psychoactive drug use among the nation's senior high school students. *Alcoholism Health and Research World, 6*, 41–46.
Lowman, C. (1982). U.S. teenage alcohol use in unsupervised social settings. *Alcoholism Health and Research World, 6*, 46–51.
Macdonald, D. (1984). *Drugs, drinking, and adolescence*. Chicago: Yearbook Medical Publishers.
Mann, G. (1979). *Recovery of reality*. San Francisco: Harper & Row.
Marlatt, G. (1983). The controlled drinking controversy. *American Psychologist, 8*, 1097–1110.
Miller, W. R. (1984). Controlled drinking: A history and critical review. *Journal of Studies on Alcohol, 44*, 68–83.
Pattison, E. (1979). The selection of treatment modalities for the alcoholic patient. In J. Mendelson & N. Mello (Eds.), *The diagnosis and treatment of alcoholism*. New York: McGraw-Hill.
Rachel, J., Guess, L., Williams, J., & Maisto, S. (1982). Alcohol misuse by adolescents. *Alcohol Health and Research World, 6*, 61–68.
Shuckit, M. (1979). *Drug and alcohol abuse*. New York: Plenum.
Talbott, G., & Cooney, M. (1982). *Today's disease: Alcohol and drug dependence*. Springfield, IL: Charles C Thomas.
Vaillant, G. (1983). *The natural history of alcoholism*. Cambridge, MA: Harvard University Press.
Ward, D. (1983). *Alcoholism: Introduction to treatment and theory*. Dubuque, IA: Kendall Hunt.

ADDENDUM

Many family systems theorists and clinicians would disagree with several aspects of the approach to treating chemical dependency that is described in this chapter. These theorists (e.g., Cleveland, 1981; Stanton & Todd, 1982) consider adolescent chemical use as a symptom primarily of family dysfunction. For example, Goldenberg and Goldenberg (1985) concluded that chemical-abusing adolescents are likely to: (1) carry the symptom of family dysfunction, (2) maintain family homeostasis, (3) deflect marital conflict, (4) model parental chemical use, and (5) engage in cross-generational alliances. From this perspective, chemical dependency is viewed more as an outcome of dysfunctional family structures (e.g., an enmeshed mother-adolescent dyad aligned against a disengaged father) than as the cause of such structures.

Trapold's view, and the views of many other specialists in the treatment of chemical problems, differ in significant ways from those of most family therapists. The most salient aspect of this difference is that chemical dependency is viewed as a disorder of individuals, which has a secondary impact on family systems. This means that chemical dependency, in contrast with most other types of behavior problems, has a very strong individual component. Furthermore, chemical dependency can "cause" marital problems, parent-adolescent conflicts, and emotional difficulties. This view also suggests that before such family problems can be effectively treated, it is essential that drugs be entirely eliminated from the family system. Therefore, a critical goal of treatment is complete abstinence from chemical use, not simply an increase in "drug-free" days as stressed by theorists such as Stanton and Todd (1982).

At first glance, the primary disorder view of chemical dependency advocated by Trapold may seem to run counter to the basic tenets of a systems approach to behavior and behavior change. We believe, however, that the primary disorder approach is entirely consistent with the multisystemic model presented in this volume. We have noted that one of the limitations of most family therapy approaches is their failure to appreciate the significance of certain individual characteristics (and extrafamilial systems) that are strongly associated with problem behavior. As detailed throughout this chapter, chemical dependency is an example of a problem that has a strong individual component. As also discussed throughout this chapter, adolescent chemical dependency is linked with peer and societal components as well. Although there is considerable evidence that family problems predate the use of drugs for many adolescents (Brook, Lukoff, & Whiteman, 1980; Jessor & Jessor, 1977; Kandel, 1982), the presence of family problems prior to drug use and the exacerbation of these problems following chemical abuse, does not negate the validity of viewing adolescent chemical dependency as a primary disorder.

In fact, the views of some family therapists have many similarities with those expressed in this chapter. For example, Usher, Jay, and Glass (1982) have noted that the confrontation of the chemical dependency is the therapist's first priority when working with the families of chemically dependent persons. When chemical use is removed from the family, it is then possible to address dysfunctional affective and interactional patterns within the family. In addition, Usher et al. (1982) and other family therapists (e.g., Kaufman & Pattison, 1981) typically refer family members to support groups such as AA, Alanon, and Alateen. Similarly, Anderson and Henderson (1983) concluded that chemical abuse will not cease by simply addressing family structural problems and communication problems. If chemical dependency is not recognized quickly by the therapist, family therapy can become just another way of avoiding actual change. Abstinence is seen as the essential first step toward improving individual functioning and family relations.

References

Anderson, S. C., & Henderson, D. C. (1983). Family therapy in the treatment of alcoholism. *Social Work in Healthcare, 8*, 79–94.

Brook, J. S., Lukoff, I. F., & Whiteman, M. (1980). Initiation into adolescent marijuana use. *Journal of General Psychology, 7*, 133–142.

Cleveland, M. (1981). Families and adolescent drug abuse: Structural analysis of children's roles. *Family Process, 20*, 295–304.

Goldenberg, I., & Goldenberg, H. (1985). *Family therapy: An overview*. Pacific Grove, CA: Brooks/Cole.

Jessor, R., & Jessor, S. L. (1977). *Problem behavior and psychological development: A longitudinal study of youth*. New York: Academic Press.

Kandel, D. B. (1982). Epidemiological and psychosocial perspectives on adolescent drug use. *Journal of the American Academy of Child Psychiatry, 21*, 328–347.

Kaufman, E., & Pattison, E. M. (1981). Differential methods of family therapy in the treatment of alcoholism. *Journal of Studies on Alcohol, 42*, 951–971.

Stanton, M. D., & Todd, T. C. (1982). *The family therapy of drug abuse and addiction*. New York: Guilford Press.

Usher, M. L., Jay, J., & Glass, D. R. (1982). Family therapy as a treatment modality for alcoholism. *Journal Studies on Alcohol, 43*, 927–938.

Understanding Insulin-Dependent Diabetes Mellitus (IDDM) and Treating Children with IDDM and Their Families

Cindy L. Hanson

*F*amilies of chronically ill children are faced with continuous treatment demands and emotional strains that can add considerable stress to family life. Many researchers and health care professionals have assumed that because of this additional stress, chronically ill children are at high risk for the development of psychopathology and the families of such children are vulnerable to the development of dysfunctional family relations. Most early investigators of the psychosocial correlates of chronic illness attempted to delineate the "deficits" of chronically ill children and their families by evaluating the factors that differentiated chronically ill children and their families from "normal" children and their families. In a landmark study, however, Tavormina and his colleagues (Tavormina, Kastner, Slater, & Watt, 1976) challenged the popular notion that chronically ill children are especially vulnerable to psychopathology. Subsequently, many other investigators have supported Tavormina and his colleagues' findings that individuals with a chronic illness are not especially vulnerable to psychopathology and do not possess specific personality traits that predispose them to specific emotional and physical illnesses (e.g., Anderson, Bradley, Young, McDaniel, & Wise, 1985; Dunn & Turtle, 1981; Jacobson, Hauser, Powers, & Noam, 1984; Jacobson et al., 1986; Kellerman, Zeltzer, Ellenberg, Dash, & Rigler, 1980; Simonds, 1977; VanderPlate, 1984; Zeltzer, Kellerman, Ellenberg, Dash, & Rigler, 1980).

In contrast to the deficit model adopted by early researchers, the adaptation model of chronic illness emphasizes the coping abilities and strengths of youths and their families. From this perspective, researchers examine the ways in which children and families use their strengths to cope with the stress and difficulties associated with a chronic illness. An excellent example of research from an adaptation model is the work of Garmezy and associates (1981, 1983) with "stress resistant" children. These children have demonstrated mastery and competence despite intense life stressors, such as having a parent with a severe mental disorder or living in conditions that are extremely deprived. Garmezy and his colleagues examined "protective" factors in the children's lives that fostered adaptation to stress. The identification of protective factors is also important in research with chronically ill children. A later section in this chapter, for example, describes how social competence can attenuate the detrimental association between chronic stress and the metabolic control of children with insulin-dependent diabetes mellitus (Hanson, Henggeler, & Burghen, 1987b).

In this chapter, our research program and clinical work with families who have adapted to a serious childhood chronic illness, insulin-dependent diabetes mellitus (IDDM), are discussed, and the adaptation model of chronic illness is emphasized. IDDM affects almost every aspect of daily living and requires continual adaptation by the child and his or her family to successfully cope with the illness. Many of the issues that face the families discussed in this chapter, such as the emotional strains, the time demands associated with treatment, the daily monitoring of the child's health, treatment disappointments, expense, and the periodic impairment of functioning also confront the families of children with other types of chronic illnesses. The treatment needs of families of children with IDDM can serve as a prototype for conceptualizing treatment related to problems of other families with chronically ill children.

THE NATURE OF IDDM

Therapists and other health care professionals who treat children with IDDM and their families must have a clear understanding of the nature of the disease and the demands that the illness and the treatment regimen place on the youth and family. Family members can quickly lose faith in health care professionals who do not understand the problems that arise in daily treatment. Without adequate knowledge, health care professionals may unknowingly prescribe an intervention that is harmful, and possibly life-threatening. In one case, for example, a family had sought psychological counseling from a local therapist who was unfamiliar with diabetes. The mother, who had IDDM, had become pregnant and was having difficulties controlling her diabetes. Her retinopathy (blood vessel changes in retina from IDDM) had become quite severe, and the possibility of blindness was present. The family also had an acting-out teenage boy who was in trouble with the law. Unfortunately, the therapist blamed the mother for her poor glucose levels and suggested that it was her way of escaping the family problems. One of the therapist's interventions had been to increase stress in the therapy sessions to force the mother to confront the family problems. The therapist was clearly insensitive to the difficulties associated with metabolic control during pregnancy and to the role that stress plays in exacerbating control. The unknowing therapist had created an even more stressful environment for the family and, under the circumstances, could have endangered the mother's eyesight, as well as the lives of the mother and baby.

A therapist who has a solid understanding of the disease process and treatment demands will also be better equipped to avoid triangulations with other health care professionals and between family members. For example, families may blame health care professionals (e.g., physicians, nurses) for mismanagement of the disease and for neglecting other needs of the family. Likewise, health care professionals may dismiss the family as noncompliant with their treatment recommendations. The therapist may be in the middle of an intense conflict between the family and the health care system without an adequate knowledge base to evaluate and rectify the concerns of both parties. Similarly, without an adequate knowledge base, a therapist would not be able to determine whether, for example, the parents are overprotective regarding treatment demands or whether the youth is not concerned enough about the treatment demands. Because an understanding of IDDM and its treatment is essential to avoid several undesirable outcomes in therapy, an overview of IDDM is provided as follows.

Types of Diabetes

There are four major types of diabetes: insulin-dependent diabetes mellitus (IDDM), noninsulin-dependent diabetes mellitus (NIDDM), gestational diabetes, and diabetes associated with or secondary to health problems (Harris, 1985). Each of these types shares the common underlying feature of abnormally high glucose levels due to either an insufficient amount of insulin in the body or impaired effectiveness of the insulin. This chapter focuses on IDDM (formerly called "juvenile onset diabetes"). The overt symptoms of IDDM usually occur during childhood or adolescence, but they can manifest themselves at any time. IDDM is characterized by low or no levels of endogenous insulin, so insulin injections are necessary for survival. As discussed shortly, the etiology of IDDM is probably only partially genetic. In contrast, the more common form of diabetes, NIDDM, seems to have a strong genetic component and occurs predominantly in people who are obese and over 40 years of age (Harris, 1985). Because obesity can cause deficiencies in the insulin binding sites on cells, which renders the endogenous insulin ineffective, treatment of NIDDM focuses on weight reduction, with oral agents and insulin if necessary. Both IDDM and NIDDM are associated with serious medical complications, but IDDM is more strongly associated with early mortality (Dorman & LaPorte, 1985) and major organ system complications, such as renal disease and blindness (Herman & Teutsch, 1985; Klein & Klein, 1985). Gestational diabetes occurs in 2 to 5% of all pregnancies; however, following the birth of the baby, almost all women return to normal glucose tolerance levels (Harris, 1985).

Epidemiology

In their review of the epidemiology of IDDM, LaPorte and Cruickshanks (1985) provide an excellent description of the incidence rates, possible causes, and risk factors for developing IDDM. They note that IDDM most often develops in childhood, affecting approximately 12 to 14 new cases annually per 100,000 children up to 16 years of age. The peak age for developing IDDM is during puberty. Approximately 120,000 youths in the United States have IDDM (LaPorte & Tajima, 1985). The risk of developing IDDM is much higher than the risk of developing other highly publicized chronic illnesses in childhood (e.g., cystic fibrosis, muscular dystrophy, rheumatoid arthritis, leukemia) and is similar to the risk of developing cancer in childhood. The incidence of IDDM is about equal for males and females, and is 1.5 times higher in Whites than in Blacks.

Although IDDM tends to run in families, the etiology of IDDM is not clearly genetically determined (LaPorte & Cruickshanks, 1985). The risk of developing the disease is associated with genetic markers related to the human leukocyte antigen (HLA) system, which appears to be associated with autoimmune diseases. IDDM is thought to be an autoimmune disease in which the body mistakenly identifies the insulin-producing beta cells in the pancreas as foreign, and the body produces islet cell antibodies (ICA) to destroy the cells. Most people with IDDM have ICA, as do some of their siblings who have later developed the disease. It is thought that the ICA of the nondiabetic siblings start to destroy the insulin-producing cells in their pancreases before the symptoms of the disease develop. Researchers have also hypothesized that certain viruses may interact with the immune system to produce damage to the pancreas, and the ICA are markers for tissue damage rather than destroyers of the beta cells in the pancreas. Although siblings of children with IDDM have a 7- to 18-fold greater risk of developing IDDM compared to the general population, only 1 in 50 develop the disease before age 20. In a study with 81 identical twin pairs in which one of the twins developed IDDM before 20 years of age (Barnett, Eff, Leslie, & Pyke, 1981), 42% of the co-twins did not have IDDM. Further research is needed to determine the combination of genetic and/or environmental factors that contribute to the onset of IDDM.

Short-Term Complications: Hypoglycemia and Hyperglycemia

Some low blood sugar (hypoglycemia) and high blood sugar (hyperglycemia) levels are caused by deviations from the treatment regimen (e.g., giving the insulin shot late, not eating dinner on time), some are caused by unexpected errors in the management of the disease (e.g., not eating enough food prior to or after exercise, misjudging how much additional insulin is needed to handle a high blood sugar or how much less insulin is needed to avoid an insulin reaction), and some undesirable blood glucose values are unexplainable and unavoidable (e.g., the youth adhered to treatment and took appropriate precautions but still experienced hypoglycemia several hours after exercise). As hypoglycemia and hyperglycemia can be very unpleasant, as well as dangerous, a major goal of treatment is the avoidance of both physiological states.

Hypoglycemia.   Hypoglycemia impairs cognitive and motor functioning and can cause symptoms such as extreme weakness, dizziness, fatigue, sweating, irritability, headache, anxiety, and shakiness. Loss of consciousness (and occasionally death) can occur if the insulin reaction is not treated promptly with a source of sugar. Often, the symptoms of hypoglycemia resemble drunkenness because the individual may exhibit unruly behavior or seem lethargic or unresponsive. Moreover, alcohol lowers blood sugar levels, so if the person has taken a drink, the smell of alcohol on the person's breath can contribute to a misdiagnosis of the hypoglycemic state. It is not unusual for the public to misinterpret hypoglycemic episodes, as the following scenario illustrates.

A recent newspaper article (*The Commercial Appeal*; Holbeck, 1987) described a 70-year-old woman who had diabetes and was arrested for public drunkenness. The normally well-mannered woman, who was very religious and abstinent, was taking a bus home from the store at supper time. During this time, she became disorderly and then was briefly unconscious from hypoglycemia (in severe hypoglycemia, counterregulatory hormones that raise glucose levels are sometimes released and the individual can regain consciousness). The bus driver called the police and the arresting officer erroneously indicated that the woman had a smell of intoxicant on her breath, slurred speech, and bloodshot eyes. The woman reported that the police would not let her explain about her diabetes. Although the police officers searched her purse, they ignored the vial of insulin in it, as well as the medical alert bracelet that she was wearing. The elderly woman was photographed, fingerprinted, and shackles were attached to her arms and wrists. She was not given a sandwich until over six hours later and was not allowed to call anyone. She was finally released 12 hours after the arrest by one of the jail officials, who apologized for the mistake. Fortunately, the woman did not die from her hypoglycemic state.

In light of the potentially serious consequences of hypoglycemia, several precautions are necessary. First, teachers, coaches, and friends need to be educated regarding the signs and symptoms of hypoglycemia so that the unknowing hypoglycemic youth can be treated promptly. Second, the youth must carry or wear identification that he or she has diabetes, and the youth should have a ready source of sugar available at all times. Third, families must keep a source of sugar available (e.g., at home, in the car) for hypoglycemic emergencies.

Although such precautions may seem self-evident, the therapist should never take it for granted that the child and family follow these guidelines. For example, while conducting a home visit with a family of low income, we tested the youth's blood glucose value with a blood-testing machine and found that his blood sugar was so low (below 25 mg/dl) that the machine was unable to read the actual value. We asked the mother what was typically done for the boy when he was hypoglycemic, and she indicated that the boy usually got something to eat. However, much to the mother's embarrassment, there was *nothing* in the house to eat. Consequently, she sent a sibling to the grocery store. We promptly treated the youth with a fast-acting form of sugar (i.e., glucose gel). Subsequently, the sibling brought home a cheeseburger from a fast-food restaurant. Without the glucose gel, the boy could have lost consciousness before the sibling returned. Moreover, the sibling's choice of food would have caused considerable delay in the rise of blood glucose levels because high-fat foods are slow to metabolize.

Hypoglycemia is a cause for realistic fears by both the youth and family. Appropriate coping with these fears is very important because the complete avoidance of hypoglycemia can result in hyperglycemia. For example, it is not uncommon for the youth and/or family to allow blood glucose levels to be elevated to undesirable levels in order to avoid hypoglycemia. Although this strategy prevents hypoglycemia, it has serious repercussions related to the negative effects of hyperglycemia.

Hyperglycemia.   The short-term effects of hyperglycemia include such symptoms as tiredness, increased thirst and dry mouth, headache, flushing, frequent urination, and nausea. Hyperglycemia of several hours to several days can produce ketoacidosis, which can result in coma or death. In many youths, mild to moderate levels of hyperglycemia can be tolerated by the body on a short-term basis (i.e., the child will not develop severe ketoacidosis). Unfortunately, these levels of hyperglycemia are deceiving because the youth may feel relatively healthy and may keep blood glucose levels too high in order to avoid hypoglycemic reactions. It is usually not until years later that the serious complications of the major organ systems, which are most likely the result of chronic hyperglycemia, become prominent.

The threat of future complications resulting from hyperglycemia is a double-edged sword. On one hand, it can help motivate families and youths to adhere to the treatment regimen. Most people, however, find it difficult to alter present behavior patterns to forestall poor health in the future. On the other hand, when youths and families are having difficulties maintaining optimal metabolic control, the threat of future complications can be an ever-present burden.

Long-Term Complications

Even with careful treatment, IDDM can lead to serious cardiovascular and other major organ system complications, including retinopathy and blindness, nephropathy, myocardial infarction, stroke, hypertension, arteriosclerosis, neuropathy accompanied by severe pain and frequent impotence, and peripheral vascular disease leading to ulcers, gangrene, and amputations. Compared to the normal population, renal and cardiovascular diseases are 56 and 13 times higher, respectively, among people with IDDM (Dorman & LaPorte, 1985).

The following brief discussion of the major complications of diabetes is based on the information provided in the book, *Diabetes in America*, sponsored by the National Diabetes Data Group (NDDG) of the National Institute of Diabetes, Digestive, and Kidney Diseases, National Institutes of Health (NDDG, 1985). Because most of the complications of diabetes do not become prominent until adulthood, the reader is referred to the aforementioned volume for a complete discussion of the complications of diabetes. Within the present chapter, four of the long-term complications are briefly discussed (i.e., diabetic ketoacidosis, renal disease, retinopathy, and growth/physical development).

Diabetic ketoacidosis (DKA).   One of the more frequent medical complications encountered by youths in poor metabolic control is DKA and coma. DKA usually occurs when the body has insufficient insulin, hyperglycemia, increased acidity in the blood from ketones, and dehydration from the loss of fluids associated with hyperglycemia. DKA occurs at the onset of diabetes in 20 to 30% of the cases and is the cause of about 10% of the deaths recorded on death certificates. In at least 50% of the cases, DKA is caused by illness, infections, and nonadherence to treatment. Mortality for youths between 0 and 9 years of age is primarily due to acute complications, such as DKA, which are largely preventable (Dorman & LaPorte, 1985).

Because illnesses can precipitate DKA, youths and their families must be in contact with their physicians and monitor ketone and blood glucose levels closely during illness. The early symptoms of DKA can mimic symptoms of the flu (e.g., nausea, weakness), which can easily confuse family members. For example, one family was traveling home from a trip and their daughter felt sick and was vomiting. The family assumed that she had the flu and delayed medical treatment. By the time the medical help reached the girl, she was in a coma. In addition to medical consultation during illness, youths need to consult with their physicians during times of high stress and hyperglycemia to prevent DKA.

Renal disease (nephropathy).   Renal disease is the leading cause of death of individuals with IDDM after the age of 20 years. After having IDDM for 15 years, one-third of individuals develop nephropathy (Herman & Teutsch, 1985). With the onset of persistent proteinuria, end-stage renal disease or death follows four to six years later.

The course is predictable in IDDM, though variations and other factors can alter the rates of decline between individuals. For the youth who develops IDDM, renal disease can strike early in young adulthood.

Retinopathy.   Diabetic retinopathy is the leading cause of new blindness in people 20 to 74 years of age (Klein & Klein, 1985). Early onset of IDDM and long duration of the disease are risk factors for retinopathy. By 25 years of age, 80% of young adults with IDDM have retinopathy. The prevalence of retinopathy five years after onset of IDDM in males is 14.5% and in females is 24.3%. *Proliferative* (or severe) *retinopathy* occurs in 50% of males and 33% of females after 19 to 20 years of IDDM. Treatment of proliferative retinopathy with the use of laser photocoagulation can reduce the incidence of blindness by about 50%.

Growth and physical development.   A complication in youths who are under poor metabolic control is delayed growth and maturation (Jackson, 1984). With proper treatment and improved metabolic control, accelerated growth can occur. Other potential problems related to the youth's physical development are obesity and the inappropriate use of insulin and glucose levels to change weight status. Overtreatment with insulin can cause weight gain because of the youth's increased food requirements. On the other hand, undertreatment with insulin can cause the youth to lose weight because the food ingested by the body is not utilized. There are reports of adolescents using this type of dangerous weight control strategy, as well as bulimic behaviors (LaGreca, Schwartz, & Satin, 1987; Wing, Nowalk, Marcus, Koeske, & Finegold, 1986).

Metabolic Control

One of the best measures of metabolic control is the glycated (glycoslated) hemoglobin (GHb) assay tests (for reviews, see Goldstein, Little, Wiedmeyer, England, & McKenzie, 1986; Service, O'Brien, & Rizza, 1987). A GHb test provides an estimate of the mean concentration of blood glucose in the blood for the two to four months preceding the test. GHb measures the blood glucose (G) that is attached to hemoglobin (Hb) in the blood stream. Hemoglobin is the substance in the red blood cells that is responsible for carrying oxygen from the lungs to cells and tissues in the body. Glucose attaches itself to the hemoglobin in the bloodstream by a process called glycosylation. The level of GHb in the blood depends on the amount of glucose available to the red blood cells. Because the life span of a red blood cell is 120 days, GHb levels indicate blood glucose levels over a three- to four-month period. Common GHb tests are called HbA_{1c} and HbA_1.

One shortcoming of GHb tests, however, is the inability to assess daily fluctuations in blood glucose levels. Because GHb levels indicate the mean level of blood glucose, swings in blood glucose can only be monitored with home glucose monitoring. For most youths, the ideal range for blood glucose is between 90 and 120 mg/dl. The ideal range for each youth can differ, however, based on the youth's age, his or her ability to detect hypoglycemia, the difficulty of maintaining appropriate blood glucose levels without extreme fluctuations (i.e., the brittleness of the disease), and mutual decisions made by physicians and families. If the youth has swings in blood glucose reflecting both hypoglycemia (usually defined as <65 mg/dl) and hyperglycemia (often designated as above 180 mg/dl), the GHb level reflects an averaged level of blood glucose. Practically speaking, the youth could have a "good" level of GHb, yet experience wide fluctuations in blood glucose.

It is important for professionals and parents to remember that a poor GHb level (e.g., $HbA_{1c} > 10\%$) does not necessarily indicate poor adherence to treatment. GHb assesses metabolic control, not adherence behaviors. Unfortunately, as Johnson (1987) pointed out, a majority of physicians use GHb to assess adherence (Clarke, Snyder, & Nowacek, 1985). Presently, no standardized, well-validated measures of adherence consistently relate to GHb. In fact, most studies that use well-standardized measures of adherence (e.g., Johnson, Silverstein, Rosenbloom, Carter, & Cunningham, 1986) report a low correlation between adherence and metabolic control. The multiple components of adherence are also not necessarily interrelated (Johnson et al., 1986). For example, the youth might adhere to insulin injections but not adhere adequately to the diet component. Although adherence is important in obtaining good metabolic control, the level of adherence that is necessary to maintain good control is unknown, and the necessary levels probably differ among individuals. Moreover, which components of the treatment regimen (e.g., diet, exercise) are most important and which other psychosocial factors relate to metabolic control are empirical questions that need further exploration. For present purposes, however, the following discussion describes the aspects of treatment that receive the most attention from researchers and clinicians.

Demands of Treatment and Adherence

Home glucose monitoring.   Prior to GHb tests, physicians and families were dependent on home glucose (urine or blood) monitoring for an indication of how well the disease was controlled. Although several problems associated with home glucose monitoring make it difficult to rely on for a measurement of overall metabolic control for clinical and research purposes, it is a necessary and integral part of treatment.

There are two types of home glucose monitoring, blood and urine. Blood glucose testing involves the use of reagent strips and/or machines that read the blood glucose level from a finger-prick of blood, which is ideal for individuals who want to try to keep tight control of their glucose levels because it gives a current reading of the person's blood sugar level. This technique is also helpful for parents of preschool children who are unable to inform their parents when they are feeling hypoglycemic. Although blood glucose testing has several important advantages, the expense is often too high for regular use by families of low income, especially those without health insurance coverage. Blood glucose testing machines range in price from $200 to $400 and the cost of individual test strips is approximately $.50, or $1 to $4 per day. Physicians can refer low-income families to agencies that can sometimes help the families obtain the necessary medical supplies. There are also strips available that can indicate blood glucose levels without the use of the machine. Youths who cannot afford daily blood glucose testing could possibly conduct blood tests at a few different times during the week and use urine tests for the other testing times.

There are several problems, however, with urine tests. First, the amount of glucose in the urine depends on the person's renal threshold. If the individual has a high renal threshold, the blood glucose may need to be quite high (e.g., over 200 mg/dl) before the glucose appears in the urine. Alternatively, if the individual has a low renal threshold, urine tests will indicate the presence of sugar even though the blood glucose is normal. If extra insulin is given because of these "false" positive urine tests, hypoglycemia could result.

Second, the amount of glucose in the urine does not reflect the amount of glucose in the blood because of the time lag for the glucose to show in the urine. Therefore, the urine test might indicate high levels of glucose, but the glucose in the blood may have already returned to normal levels. Again, in this circumstance, giving extra insulin based on the urine test could cause hypoglycemia. From a practical viewpoint, the urine test requires double voiding using the second specimen of urine for the test. It can be inconvenient and difficult for the youth to go to the bathroom twice in a 15- to 20-minute interval to complete the test. Although urine tests are often inaccurate and inconvenient for glucose testing, they are still a necessary part of the home regimen even if the youth uses blood testing. Urine tests are needed to test for ketones when the child has consistently high blood glucose levels (e.g., over 250 mg/dl) or when he or she is ill. Ketones are a by-product of the body's improper breakdown of fat in the liver when the body has insufficient insulin to metabolize glucose for energy. As noted earlier, ketoacidosis occurs when the ketonic acids raise the acidity of the blood to a certain level.

One of the practical problems with home glucose monitoring is the daily diligence that is required to perform the task and to record the results in some type of journal. Because daily glucose levels are a major component of discussion between the physician and family, there is considerable pressure on the family and youth to keep the log up-to-date. Because of the pressures involved in performing the task and the negative connotation of poor glucose values, some youths will falsify test results either by fabricating results when they do not test or by changing the results to a more acceptable value. The youth is likely to be suspected of this practice if the GHb values are not consistent with the log values. Other possible hypotheses, however, need to be ruled out. For example, the youth may not be using accurate testing techniques or the glucose monitoring device may read the youth's glucose results as lower than the true value. These types of problems commonly occur and must be evaluated before assuming that the youth is intentionally falsifying the results.

One way to help alleviate the falsification of test results is to discuss realistic expectations regarding the number and results of the daily glucose tests. Reframing aberrant glucose levels as a family problem is often helpful. For example, the family members could be told that they have a serious problem to tackle: how to get Jerry's glucose levels within an acceptable range. Each member of the family could then be asked how he or she could help solve the problem. Family members could, for example, volunteer to help Jerry with one of the daily glucose tests (e.g., getting the equipment, writing down the results) and/or the family could decide to have a problem-solving discussion each night for about ten minutes to decide if adjustments in insulin or food are necessary.[1] Family members could be told to support each other for the completion of

[1] The family's adjustment of insulin and food is under the supervision of the family physician. The physician frequently prescribes a sliding scale for insulin that is based on the results of the glucose test. Physicians typically discuss when and how families should make adjustments in this scale. If necessary, a phone call to the physician is often sufficient to verify appropriate changes in dosages.

the glucose tests and not to blame one another if the results of the tests are undesirable. It is important for the family to understand that keeping the glucose under control can be difficult and that continual problem solving and support are ways to help. It is also important for the family to have realistic expectations and to recognize the ambivalence that youths often have toward the IDDM treatment regimen. On one hand, for example, a youth might view glucose testing prior to exercise as valuable in preventing a dreaded insulin reaction. On the other hand, the youth might not want to be bothered with the task. There will be times when the glucose testing is skipped, for any number of reasons, including the youth's explanation that he or she "just didn't feel like it." The family and therapist should consider it a serious problem, however, when testing is skipped regularly for whatever reason (e.g., too busy, schedule didn't permit).

Insulin adjustment.   Both physicians and families use home glucose monitoring to adjust daily insulin dosages. Two to four daily checks of blood (or urine) glucose levels are usually used to determine adjustments needed in insulin dosages. Because different types of insulin have different rates of action and times of peak action, dosage changes are made according to the type of insulin used. For example, if a youth was consistently hypoglycemic in the late afternoons, the morning dosage of an intermediate-acting insulin, such as NPH or Lente, might be reduced since the peak action for these types of insulins is usually six to eight hours after injection. In contrast, if a youth was frequently hyperglycemic at noon, the morning dose of the short-acting Regular insulin might be increased since its peak action is typically from two to four hours after injection. The first insulin injection of the day is usually given early to avoid the "dawn phenomenon," which is characterized by a substantial increase in blood glucose levels that occurs in the early morning for some individuals, irregardless of food intake. If the youth likes to sleep in on Saturday mornings, he or she can get up early to test his or her blood sugar, give the insulin injection, eat breakfast, and then go back to bed.

Meal plan.   Dietary adherence involves consistency in the amount and nutrient composition of meals, the timing of meals, and accurate estimates of food portions. Foods with high levels of sugar and fat are avoided. The American Diabetes Association (ADA) provides a booklet that categorizes foods and amounts of foods that are relatively equivalent in terms of carbohydrate, fat, and protein composition (i.e., dietary exchanges). The youth chooses foods from those listed in the seven exchange lists (i.e., milk, bread, high-fat meat, medium-fat meat, low-fat meat, fruit, vegetable) that correspond to his or her meal plan. For example, a fruit exchange might be one small apple, one-half a banana, one-half cup of orange juice, or one-third cup of grape juice. All of these fruit exchanges consist of 15 grams of carbohydrate and are equal to 60 calories. A bread exchange, for example, is 80 calories, consisting of 15 grams of carbohydrate and 3 grams of protein. Foods that contain complex carbohydrates are encouraged because they take longer to digest, causing the youth's blood sugar to rise more slowly following ingestion. Foods that contain large amounts of simple sugars cause a sharp rise in blood glucose before the youth's insulin has a chance to work.

Exercise.   Exercise is encouraged for youths with IDDM because it may decrease the risk of coronary artery disease and improve cardiovascular functioning (Campaigne,

Gilliam, Spencer, Lampman, & Schork, 1984; Skyler, 1979; Stein, Goldberg, Kalman, & Chesler, 1984). Exercise programs may also increase the youths' sensitivity to insulin and thereby reduce the amount of insulin that is required (Felig, 1982; Landt, Campaigne, James, & Sperling, 1985). However, the presence of diabetes and its complications may alter the body's physiological response to exercise. For example, exercise can aggravate proliferative retinopathy by increasing blood pressure and the risk of hemorrhages; likewise, it can accelerate nephropathy by increasing blood pressure, decreasing the blood flow to the kidneys, and increasing proteinuria (Horan, 1985; Skyler, 1979). In addition, Baum and his colleagues (Baum, Levitsky, & Englander, 1987) found abnormal cardiac functioning following exercise in an otherwise healthy group of children and adolescents with IDDM.

The metabolic response to exercise depends on several factors, including such variables as the blood glucose level at the time of the exercise, the timing of the exercise relative to insulin action and peaks, and whether the body part that was injected with insulin is exercised (Felig, 1982). Exercise is encouraged when blood glucose levels are within the normal range. If blood glucose levels are too high, exercise can actually raise the blood glucose even higher because of the increases in counterregulatory hormones that occur to make glucose available for the muscles. If the individual is already lacking in insulin and is hyperglycemic, the blood glucose rise from the counterregulatory hormones will cause the blood glucose to rise even higher. Moreover, brief spurts of exercise are unadvisable for the person with diabetes because the increase in glucose from the counterregulatory hormones will not be offset by the small amount of glucose used by the brief exercise. Because exercise typically lowers blood glucose, however, appropriate precautions must be taken (e.g., testing blood glucose and eating a snack) prior to and after exercise. Special care must be taken when exercise is performed during a time of peak insulin action (e.g., 2 to 4 hours after an injection of a short-acting insulin and 6 to 8 hours after an injection of intermediate-acting insulin) as blood glucose levels will be lowered by both the exercise and the insulin action.

Finally, severe hypoglycemia can result from exercising a muscle in which insulin was recently injected. For example, if the youth injects insulin into his or her leg and then goes running, the insulin will work much more quickly than usual and can cause hypoglycemia. Hyperglycemia may also occur later when the insulin action was typically needed. Because of unexpected hypoglycemia, it is absolutely essential that the youth carry or have a source of sugar available when they exercise (as well as at other times).

In summary, IDDM is a serious and complicated disease that can impair every major organ system of the body. Current treatment involves adherence to a rigorous treatment regimen that includes the timely completion of several daily tasks, including blood tests, injections, and dietary restrictions. Short- and intermediate-acting insulins are often used in treatment and both need daily adjustment according to blood glucose levels, the exercise anticipated, and the types and quantities of food ingested. In addition to the completion of daily tasks, the youths and parents must have frequent regular contact (3 to 4 times per year) with their primary physicians and may need periodic consultation with other specialists as well (e.g., ophthalmology consultations for retinopathy evaluations). The treatment's complexity, lifelong duration, and interference with daily activities makes adherence difficult to achieve. In addition, the onset of puberty and the developmental changes that occur during adolescence can exacerbate metabolic control.

Unfortunately, many youths with diabetes are unable to achieve adequate metabolic control, even with diligent effort. Those who do achieve satisfactory control may still experience severe fluctuations in blood glucose levels.

OVERVIEW OF THERAPEUTIC PROCESS AND PROTOCOL

During the initial therapy session, there are at least four "generic" goals that the therapist should meet as he or she gains the information needed to formulate effective treatment strategies. First, the therapist should attempt to understand how the symptoms "fit" within the child's systemic context. Second, the therapist should actively communicate an appreciation for the perspectives of each family member. Third, the strengths of each family member, the family subsystems, and the family as a whole should be overtly identified. Fourth, the therapist should encourage positive expectations for change. The fulfillment of these process goals will expedite the course of therapy.

During the assessment phase of treatment, it is also frequently necessary to contact members of the extrafamilial systems in which the youth is involved, such as school personnel and health care professionals (e.g., physicians). When making such contact, the therapist should follow the procedural guidelines described in Chapter 6 and gather specific information about potential drug use, social/peer interactions, individual problems with concentration, homework, and other academic or behavioral problems. Teachers and health care professionals should be encouraged to discuss their "opinions" or "insights" about the problem because such opinions can often clarify the nature of the presenting problem or identify other problems that were not evident to the therapist. In addition, the opinions of teachers and health care professionals can provide the therapist with valuable information about their expectations for the child and possible misconceptions about the presenting problem. The therapist should also attempt to instill positive expectations by, for example, noting familial strengths and motivation.

In the development of treatment plans, the strengths and weaknesses of the child and the systems in which the child is embedded must be carefully weighed. To facilitate this process, we use an "intervention grid" on which the therapist depicts key information about the youth and his or her systemic context. As illustrated in Figure 10-1, the therapist should conceptualize goals on both process and content levels. Process goals are meta-level in that they reflect the overall organizational goals of the therapy. Content goals are specific strategies that may be used during therapy to facilitate the process goals. In Figure 10-1, for example, one process goal is to increase the youth's sense of control over IDDM. A content goal to facilitate this process goal is to set up a program that enables the youth, without parental supervision, to test her glucose throughout the day and ingest glucose tablets to correct hypoglycemic readings. Parenthetically, this content goal also facilitates another process goal of therapy, namely to increase the youth's independence.

Because each therapy session can focus on only a few of the process goals of therapy, it is helpful for specific process and content goals to be targeted for each therapy session. For example, a process goal of therapy might be to increase the positive interactions between the parent and child. Specific goals for a session might include improving the parent-child communication (a content strategy might be a perspective-taking task) or increasing parent-child supportive behaviors (a content strategy might be to encourage the dyad to engage in a fun activity twice a week).

THERAPY INTERVENTION GRID

THERAPIST NAME: *Jay Olson*

CLIENT'S FIRST NAME: *Sandy*

SESSION NUMBER: *3*   DATE: *3/5/88*

PRESENTING PROBLEM (PP): *Fear of hypoglycemia*

ONSET OF PP: *8 months ago*

PREVIOUS EFFORTS TO SOLVE PP: *Physician referral*

	Individual	Marital Relations	Parent/Child Relations	Siblings	Peer/Social	Extrafamilial (e.g., school, work, HCS)	Extrafamilial Relations (e.g., grandparents)	Therapist
STRENGTHS (+)	1.) Knowledgeable about IDDM 2.) Strong social skills 3.) Positive self-esteem 4.) Average intelligence	1.) Caring and supportive 2.) Willing to compromise	1.) Loving and supportive of Sandy 2.) Strong parental support for IDDM treatment 3.) Sandy very positive toward parents	1.) Close supportive relationship with older sister (18 yrs. old)	1.) Very active socially in prosocial activities 2.) Having grown up with Sandy, peers readily accept IDDM and treatment demands	1.) Family likes and trusts physicians 2.) Family participates in all IDDM education programs 3.) School personnel supportive/positive 4.) Family willing to travel 2-3 hrs. weekly to see therapist	1.) Supportive grandparents	1.) Strong knowledge about IDDM and psychosocial aspects 2.) Experience with family therapy and adolescents
WEAKNESSES (−)	1.) Somewhat immature for age 2.) Strong fears about passing out from hypoglycemia so she consumes lots of cokes and juice throughout the day 3.) Somewhat egocentric for age 4.) Tantrums	None noted	1.) Parents assume too much responsibility for IDDM treatment and other tasks (i.e., school, household) 2.) Inconsistent discipline and somewhat overpermissive	None noted	1.) Difficulty concentrating in school due to preoccupation with social activities and 18 yr-old boyfriend 2.) Both siblings have heavy social involvements, which creates stress for family	1.) Sandy missed at least half of her classes because school personnel would allow her to leave class if she felt hypoglycemic 2.) School personnel lack knowledge about IDDM	None noted	1.) Sandy was somewhat shy with therapist perhaps because therapist was relatively young male (i.e., mid-20's)

HISTORY

1.) Had IDDM since 4 yrs. old, no complications except skin disorders (warts, tough finger tips from finger pricks with inappropriate finger-pricking technique)
2.) Strong fears of hypoglycemia and overeats to avoid possibility of hypoglycemia
3.) Failing courses in school
4.) Has temper outbursts
5.) Intact family, middle upper middle SES

SESSION GOALS

PROCESS:
1.) Increase Sandy's sense of control over IDDM
2.) Encourage parents to give more responsibility to Sandy

CONTENT:
1.) Set up program whereby Sandy is allowed to test glucose throughout day without parental supervision and ingest glucose tablets according to sliding scale
2.) Have Sandy help design rules/structure at home to help her become independent in daily tasks (e.g., studying, getting up in the morning)
3.) Discuss with parents importance of allowing Sandy to take charge of IDDM and discuss glucose monitoring device with memory

OVERALL GOALS

PROCESS:
1.) Increase Sandy's sense of control over IDDM
2.) Encourage parents to relinquish more responsibility to Sandy
3.) Increase Sandy's independence
4.) Set up structure at home and school to facilitate academic achievement
5.) Decrease stress related to extracurricular activities

CONTENT:
1.) Allow Sandy to become more familiar with what her body feels like at different glucose levels using more frequent testing
2.) Use glucose tablets in controlled fashion vs. large quantities of liquid
3.) Structure home life to increase independence for self-care (and other) behaviors
4.) Have Sandy design "consequence" program to facilitate changes in her behavior (e.g., temper outburst)
5.) Increase school personnel's knowledge about IDDM, and not allow Sandy to leave class
6.) Set up tutor
7.) Help reorganize family life to decrease stress related to extracurricular activities

Figure 10-1 An illustrative example of the formulation of a multisystemic intervention with a youth who has difficulties related to IDDM management.

Figure 10-1 illustrates the use of the intervention grid with a family whose presenting problem was a female adolescent with poorly controlled IDDM. Sandy was a 15-year-old girl who had IDDM since she was 4 years of age. Sandy was under good metabolic control until she became an adolescent. With an increased awareness of the dangers of hypoglycemia and the social embarrassment associated with a reaction, she developed strong fears about hypoglycemia and passing out. Sandy felt symptoms of hypoglycemia (e.g., cold sweats, nervousness, dizziness), which also mimic feelings of anxiety, several times throughout the day and would consume large amounts of orange juice and Coke to relieve her fear of becoming hypoglycemic. Sandy missed at least half of her classes because school personnel would allow Sandy to leave the classroom if she felt hypoglycemic. (Sandy would also use the time away from class to visit with friends.) On some occasions, Sandy would call her mother and ask her to come to school so that she could test her blood glucose level to determine whether or not she was hypoglycemic. Mostly, however, Sandy just bought Cokes and candy from the school's vending machines.

At home, Sandy's parents limited her access to food and did not allow her to test her glucose frequently because they felt that such testing would encourage her unrealistic fears. This parental reaction increased Sandy's anxiety and caused her to become more covert in ingesting food. Because of the burden of her illness, Sandy's parents did not expect her to help with responsibilities at home. This parental "protectiveness" was reflected in some of Sandy's undesirable behavioral styles (e.g., immaturity, egocentricity, temper tantrums), and these behavioral styles further perpetuated the parents' reluctance to give Sandy more independence.

Some of the process issues that were important in this family, and in other families with children who have IDDM, are control over the disease, independence/dependence, responsibility for self-care behaviors, and treatment demands that interfere with school or social behaviors. Each of these process issues was targeted for change, and as Sandy became more independent, her fears of hypoglycemia diminished and her blood glucose levels improved substantially. The remainder of this chapter covers various systems that are important when intervening with families of children with IDDM.

MULTISYSTEMIC CORRELATES OF HEALTH AND THEIR IMPLICATIONS FOR TREATMENT

In the initial stages of our research, we sought to determine if there was empirical support for a multisystemic theoretical model of IDDM (Hanson & Henggeler, 1984). From our synthesis of the literature, we found that several studies supported our hypotheses that individual, family, and extrafamilial factors were important links in the health of these youths. Based on previous findings and questions in the literature, we began a multisystemic research program to identify factors that contributed to positive health outcomes in youths with IDDM (see Hanson, Henggeler, & Burghen, 1987c for an initial empirical model). Health outcomes included psychosocial adjustment and adaptation to the illness by family members, adherence to the treatment regimen, and metabolic control.

Demographic Characteristics

Although children with IDDM and their families are not generally at risk for psychosocial dysfunction, certain demographic characteristics may place particular families at higher risk than others. One of the first goals of our research program was to identify those children at high risk for poor health outcomes, and then identify factors that functioned in a protective fashion to promote positive health outcomes in these youths.

Father absence. One population that we hypothesized was at high risk was single-parent families. With the additional stress of living with a chronic illness, we felt that youths from single-parent families might be at high risk for poor health outcomes and low psychosocial functioning. Managing a chronic illness such as IDDM requires substantial time, energy, and financial resources—all of which are less available in the single-parent family. Youths from single-parent families are also more likely to have additional household responsibilities than youths in two-parent families, thus limiting the time that they can devote to adherence behaviors.

Subjects in this study were 30 intact families and 30 father-absent families of adolescents with IDDM (Hanson, Henggeler, Rodrigue, Burghen, & Murphy, 1988). The groups were matched on the adolescents' age, race, gender, duration of IDDM, family size, and socioeconomic status. Interestingly, we found that father-absent adolescents showed greater adherence to the treatment regimen than did their father-present counterparts. These findings are consistent with the developmental research showing that the loss of a father can promote the development of responsible behavior in adolescents. We also found that the metabolic control of father-absent adolescents did not differ from that of father-present adolescents. These findings demonstrate and support the adaptation model of chronic illness. That is, youth who were thought to be at risk actually performed better (with adherence behaviors) than the control group.

Race. A second population that was hypothesized to be at increased risk for poor health was Black youths and their families. Compared to Whites, the mortality rate from complications of diabetes is higher among Blacks (Roseman, 1985). The *Report of the Secretary's Task Force on Black and Minority Health, 1985* (Heckler, 1985) concluded that there is a serious disparity in the health status of Blacks and Whites and that most of this disparity was due to six diseases, one of which was diabetes.

We examined race and sex differences in the metabolic control of 27 Black and 27 White youths who were similar in age, age at diagnosis, duration of IDDM, relative weight, pubertal development, and socioeconomic level (Hanson, Henggeler, & Burghen, 1987a). Our analyses indicated that Black females had worse metabolic control than the other groups of adolescents. In an attempt to identify factors that placed Black females at high risk, we examined several multisystemic variables. Our results revealed that the poor metabolic control among the Black girls was not associated with problems in any of the following areas: knowledge about IDDM, adherence to treatment, self-concept, coping patterns, family functioning, chronic life stress, social support, or involvement in the health care system. These results led us to believe that the poor metabolic control among the Black females may be a result of biological or psychosocial factors that were not assessed in this study. We are currently conducting a follow-up investigation to replicate these results and to evaluate other variables that might account for the poor health status of the Black female adolescents.

Individual Characteristics

Several pertinent individual characteristics of the youths and their family members contribute to successful adaptation to the disease. In this section, developmental and/or maturational characteristics that have important treatment implications, knowledge about IDDM, and coping styles that promote positive outcomes are addressed. For additional information regarding developmental issues pertinent to youths with IDDM, readers are also referred to Hanson and Onikul-Ross (in press).

Cognitive development.   The youth's level of cognitive development affects his or her understanding of the causes of IDDM, adherence to treatment, efforts to prevent future complications, and adaptation to the disease. The following discussion is based on current theory and general findings regarding cognitive development during three stages of childhood (Harter, 1983; Flavell, 1977).

In *early childhood* (ages approximately 2 to 6 years), children conceptualize disease as resulting from misbehavior. For example, a 5-year-old child described how she got diabetes (Brewster, 1982):

> I was born with it. (How?) Your mommy has it in her stomach and you are born with it. (How?) You nibble on her, the inside of her stomach before I came out. (How come your brother did not get it and you did?) He didn't nibble on mommy's stomach (p. 360).

Similarly, children at this age might believe that treatment was punishment for being bad. A 6-year-old child, for example, reported that she was trying to bargain with God but was having some problems. Everyday she promised God that she would do something good if God would make her insulin injections easier for her and less painful. Because her bargaining was not working, she decided that she just had not found the right "good deed" to please God.

During early childhood, the child learns how to communicate information to others and to store and think about daily experiences (Flavell, 1977). Moreover, the child becomes increasingly able to control his or her own behavior. The beginnings of self-control are highly important in the child's ability to adhere to the IDDM treatment regimen, particularly the dietary components. Parents are unable to monitor everything the child eats, especially when the child does not want the parents to know (e.g., sneaking cookies from the cookie jar). During early childhood, the child's restraint from eating certain foods is controlled primarily by external forces, such as the parents' rules and structure. Internalized control of behavior usually does not emerge until middle childhood when the child has developed an ability to view others' perspectives and is motivated to please others. The development of internalization in the latter part of the early childhood years and during the middle childhood years is facilitated by discipline methods that include the use of person-oriented reasoning (Maccoby & Martin, 1983).

Because the treatment demands of IDDM require considerable self-control and discipline, as well as planning and structuring of time, the promotion of appropriate adherence behaviors by parents and therapists becomes highly important. In the early childhood years, parents need to provide the child with considerable structure in order for the child and parents to complete the various adherence tasks. Discipline strategies related to diabetes management need to be based on reinforcement principles. An emphasis on the positive is preferred because the child may already feel deprived and different from others (e.g., siblings, peers), and strategies that promote further deprivation or isolation may be counterproductive. For example, a reward system for the completion of glucose testing should be used rather than deprivation of privileges because of noncompliance with the task.

It is also important for the parents of young children to monitor their emotional responses to the child's disease. Young children are very sensitive to the emotions that their parents are experiencing (Harter, 1983) and often report experiencing the same emotions as their parents (e.g., "Mommy will be very happy to get a balloon after visiting the doctor," or "Daddy is scared that the shot might cause his skin to go away"). It is important for parents of young children to be as positive as possible regarding the management of the disease. Although parents might feel bad that their child has to comply with many of the aversive demands of the treatment regimen (e.g., injections, glucose testing, dietary restrictions), positive reframing becomes important in terms of the child's feelings about himself or herself. For example, the parent might tell a young child that the insulin injections are a special way to keep his or her body extra strong, and that glucose testing is to make sure the body has everything it needs to work right. The parents can also tell the young child that his or her body only wants sweet foods when it feels very weak; otherwise, the body needs other foods in order to keep it strong.

During *middle childhood* (about 7 to 11 years of age), developmental changes occur that enable the child to understand relationships between factors or actions (e.g., dietary intake and blood glucose) and to make hypotheses based on logical reasoning versus merely guessing or making simple perceptual inferences (Flavell, 1977). These new cognitive skills are very important in teaching children about IDDM and the various regimen-related tasks. For example, the child can understand that eating a small amount of a high caloric food (e.g., a slice of banana bread) will raise blood glucose levels more than a larger amount of a less caloric food (e.g., two cups of popcorn). Or, the child will be better able to understand that exercise in the early afternoon can cause hypoglycemia later in the day if proper precautions are not taken (e.g., food taken before or after exercise).

With the development of perspective-taking abilities during middle childhood, the child also begins to develop internalized control of his or her behavior. Self-control initially emerges from the desire to please others or avoid their disapproval. When a youth has developed a third-person awareness of the self, which usually does not begin until around 8 years of age, self-control can be used to meet the youth's own expectations and promote feelings of self-satisfaction. For example, the youth can develop a sense of competence about being able to take care of his or her body and follow important adherence behaviors.

Similarly, during middle childhood, children are better able to understand the motivations of others (Flavell, 1977). For example, a parent's reluctance to bring a young child to a favorite fast-food restaurant because the child's blood sugar is too high might be interpreted by the youngster as the parent's unwillingness or lack of desire to do so. Rather than just viewing the parent's decision as a result of the hyperglycemia, the young child overattributes the parent's motives to include disinterest in the child's wishes. During middle childhood, however, the child is more able to appreciate the parent's perspective. For example, the mother of an 8-year-old boy had promised to reward him for his good behavior at the hospital with a trip to a local fast food restaurant. After checking his blood glucose, however, the child learned that his sugar was very high. He turned to his mother and said, "OOPS, I guess no Taco Bell for me." If this child was at an earlier stage of cognitive development, he might have interpreted his mother's decision to reflect dissatisfaction with his behavior at the hospital.

During *adolescence*, the formal thought processes of abstraction occur. The elementary-aged child views the world in terms of concrete reality; problem-solving abilities are limited mainly to perceptions and inferences that are based on the observed reality of the situation. In contrast, during adolescence, speculations about the range of possibilities inherent in the situation are usually considered. For example, the adolescent might hypothesize about all the possible reasons for hyperglycemia and then proceed to discover which reason is most plausible. The younger child would most likely stick to the observed reality (e.g., I probably ate too much for dinner) and would be reluctant to consider other possibilities (e.g., too little insulin given, stressful argument preceding dinner, dietary composition of the foods eaten during dinner) as contributing factors. Similarly, adolescents recognize that diseases are caused by multiple factors; whereas, children in middle childhood typically believe that disease is caused by one factor, usually by germs (Brewster, 1982; Bibace & Walsh, 1979).

With the development of formal operational thought, the possibility of current behavior affecting future complications of IDDM can be fully understood. Other conflicting thought processes that occur during adolescence, however, make thinking about future complications difficult. Adolescents tend to think of themselves as invulnerable and often capable of extraordinary feats. This is largely because the new world of possibilities has opened up to them and their fantasy world is highly active. Such fantasies are adaptive and positive because they enable the youth to explore his or her potential. Feelings of invulnerability become harmful, however, when they are extreme and when the youth engages in dangerous behavior from a false sense of security. Although it is often difficult at any age to change current behavior because of future health benefits, such reasoning is especially difficult for adolescents even though they might possess the intellectual capabilities needed to fully understand the logic.

Knowledge about IDDM.   In our initial model of the interrelations among psychosocial variables and health outcomes, we demonstrated a direct link between knowledge about IDDM and adherence behaviors (Hanson et al., 1987c). The association between knowledge and adherence supports the findings of other investigators (e.g., Christensen, 1983; Lorenz, Christensen, & Pichert, 1985). Without adequate knowledge about the disease, the youth cannot adhere to all the necessary task requirements. Moreover, knowledge in one area does not necessarily relate to knowledge in another area of treatment (Johnson et al., 1982).

The child needs to learn several relatively complex tasks in order to adhere to the treatment regimen. For example, to adhere to a diet plan for lunch, the child first must remember the kind and number of diet exchanges on the plan (e.g., three meat exchanges, two bread exchanges, one fruit exchange, two fat exchanges, and one milk exchange).

Second, the child must remember how much of each specific food equals one exchange (e.g., 1/2 small banana equals one fruit exchange, 1/2 cup of corn equals one bread exchange, 1/4 cup of tuna equals one meat exchange). Third, the child must be able to measure or visually estimate the amount of food that is equivalent to the appropriate exchange.

Choosing appropriate foods from a restaurant menu is even more difficult because of the fats used in cooking, and the additional sugar and sauces that are added or served with the foods. Without nutritional knowledge about the food that a restaurant serves, the youths and parents can easily be deceived. For example, without prior knowledge, it is difficult to estimate that 12 to 15 small french fries at a fast-food restaurant could constitute the child's total allotment of bread and fat exchanges (i.e., two bread and two fat exchanges) for lunch.

Unfortunately, youths' and parents' knowledge about the disease is often inadequate for good adherence (e.g., Johnson et al., 1982; Lorenz et al., 1985). As might be expected, mothers and girls tend to know more about diabetes care than fathers and boys, and older children know more than younger children (Harkavy et al., 1983; Johnson et al., 1982; Lorenz et al., 1985). As discussed previously, health care system professionals need to consider the intellectual and developmental level of the youth before educating him or her about the daily management tasks. Otherwise, the youth is likely to misunderstand or forget important knowledge about the disease and its management.

Coping.   In their excellent discussion of coping with the crises of diabetes, Hamburg and Inoff (1983) described several typical reactions that individuals experience to the diagnosis of diabetes:

> (1) uncertainty about the outcome of the immediate situation; (2) feelings of intense guilt and/or anger about the occurrence of the diabetes; (3) feelings of incompetence and helplessness about the responsibility for management of the illness; (4) fears about future complications and early death; (5) loss of valued life goals and aspirations; (6) anxiety about planning for an uncertain future; and (7) recognition of the necessity for a permanent change in living pattern due to the illness (p. 411).

Hamburg and Inoff also describe the additional crises that the disease presents throughout the life span, such as the appearance of a major medical complication and failures to obtain desired medical outcomes. Therapists need to be aware of the continual pressures associated with diabetes and the various types of crises that can occur at different times during the course of the illness. To a large extent, the child's (and family's) ability to cope with and resolve these crises plays an important role in their psychosocial adaptation (LaGreca, 1987).

Coping can be conceptualized in several different ways. One approach has been to view coping as an end-product of the family's adaptation to the illness. From this perspective, researchers have examined the psychosocial adjustment of family members after diagnosis and the success of the youths' adherence to treatment. For example, Kovacs and her colleagues (Kovacs, Brent, Steinberg, Paulauskas, & Reid, 1986; Kovacs, Feinberg, et al., 1985; Kovacs, Finkelstein, et al., 1985) have conducted a longitudinal assessment of parents' and youths' psychological adjustment to IDDM. Their results have demonstrated the resiliency of families during the first year after the diagnosis of IDDM. By approximately six months after the initial diagnosis, most of the initial emotional distress and turmoil (e.g., anxiety, depression, worry) of the parents and youths were resolved. It is also noteworthy that the youths assessed themselves positively on psychological indices (e.g., self-esteem, depression, anxiety) at IDDM onset and one year later compared to normative data on healthy youths (Kovacs et al., 1986). Kellerman, Zeltzer, and their colleagues (Kellerman et al., 1980; Zeltzer et al., 1980) found similar results in their examination of the psychosocial factors associated with chronic illness in adolescents. Interestingly, these researchers found that 30% of the healthy adolescents in the control group reported a current acute illness and that the acutely ill and chronically ill adolescents did not differ in their perceptions of the impact of their illnesses. In fact, the acute illness group reported more disruption in peer activities and popularity than did the chronically ill group; whereas, the chronically ill group reported more problems with school activities and difficulties related to treatment. The researchers posited that chronically ill children have developed strategies to cope with the daily stressors and peer disruptions, but that the healthy youths (who were acutely ill) have not had the opportunity to develop adequate coping strategies. This is another example of the positive adaptation of youths with a chronic illness.

In addition to viewing coping as an end-product of adaptation to illness (e.g., the youths' psychosocial adjustment), coping has been viewed as a set of behaviors (e.g., seeking support from friends, obtaining information about IDDM from parents) and cognitions. For example, Kovacs et al. (1986) found that, in rank order, the most commonly reported cognitive coping styles at one-year post diagnosis were wishful thinking (e.g., "I wish I did not have it"; "If I do everything right, it will go away"), thoughts of forbidden food (e.g., thoughts about eating cookies, candies, sweets), positive future-oriented thoughts (e.g., "I hope they find a cure soon"), resentment and anger (e.g., "I don't want to be different," "Why can't I do...?" "I want people to stop hassling me"), and questioning or bewilderment (e.g., "Why me?" "I can't understand how it happened," "Why not my brother or sister?"). Most youths use several of these styles to some extent. For example, a young child in our research project was very excited to show a research assistant a large lollipop that he had tucked away in his closet for the time when diabetes is cured. This cognition links both "positive future-oriented thinking" with "thoughts of forbidden food." It is important to recognize that each of these cognitive styles is a normal way of coping with the disease. Kovacs et al. did not find that a particular cognitive style was associated with more positive psychosocial functioning or better adherence than another.

Dysfunctional coping styles may interfere with the youth's treatment goals and pose serious threats to the health of the child. For example, we examined the relations between coping styles and adherence to the IDDM treatment regimen in a sample of youths who were older than the children that Kovacs et al. studied (Hanson et al., in press). The frequent use of avoidance and ventilation coping (e.g., anger and blaming others for problems) related to poor adherence to treatment. We also found that high family stress and low family cohesion were associated with such maladaptive coping in the youths. Thus, the coping behaviors of the adolescents were associated with the family's functioning and adaptation to the disease.

Athough adherence to treatment, psychosocial adjustment, and coping are often interrelated, they represent distinct constructs that may not be associated with each other. For example, the youth might be coping adequately with the idea of having IDDM, yet fail to adhere to all the treatment regimen tasks. Alternatively, the youth might adhere diligently to all of the treatment demands, yet have a hard time coming to terms with the fact that he or she has diabetes. In another case, the youth might be well-adjusted in peer and social relations, but deny the presence of the illness and not adhere to treatment. It is important for the therapist to assess the ways in which family members cope with the disease and help both the youth and family redirect potentially destructive coping styles.

Family Functioning and Parental Support

Parental emotional functioning and guilt.   The contribution of genetics to the risk of developing IDDM or any other chronic illness is an issue that often arises in families of chronically ill children. Parents may feel guilty that they "caused" the disease and may respond by allowing the child to engage in activities that are counter to treatment goals. In helping parents resolve their feelings of guilt, the therapist might inform them that current research suggests that some families have a genetic predisposition to developing the disease and that in some cases this predisposition reacts with certain environmental conditions, which results in the onset of the disease. The therapist needs to emphasize that it is not purely genetics that cause the disease. It is also important to note, however, that many adults with IDDM chose to bear children even with knowledge of the increased risk of their offspring developing the disease. Parental guilt may be particularly salient in families with more than one child with the disease, and the therapist should suggest genetic counseling in such cases.

It is not uncommon for the parents of any child to feel some guilt about certain behaviors related to parenting (e.g., overreacting to a child's misbehavior when tired). When the child develops a chronic illness, however, it is easy for the parents to indulge their child because they feel that he or she has already been unfairly burdened by the illness. For example, in one case, the father allowed his adolescent son to forego the completion of his homework assignments because the father felt that the demands of treatment placed enough pressure on the boy. Because of a history of diabetes in the family, the father also felt responsible for his son's illness and he did not want to burden his son further by insisting that he complete his homework assignments. In addition to problems with schoolwork, the youth needed more guidance and structure in his life, but the father's guilt needed to be addressed before therapy could progress.

In addition to feelings of parental guilt, the demanding nature of IDDM treatment can contribute to feelings of blame between family members. When the youth is under poor metabolic control, for example, one parent might blame the other parent for not monitoring the child closely enough to avoid unusually high or low blood sugar values. The parent who has primary responsibility for the child subsequently feels frustrated, not only because the child's health was jeopardized, but because of the marital conflict that resulted. Similarly, because of the complicated nature of IDDM treatment and the need to feel a sense of control over the disease, parents, youths, and health care system (HCS) professionals tend to view the majority of poor blood sugar values as resulting from deviations from the treatment regimen and errors in the management of the disease. Many undesirable glucose values, however, are unexplainable and unavoidable. Despite optimal adherence, most children will sometimes experience poor blood glucose values. When they do, family members and health care professionals can get caught in a cycle in which they feel guilty or blame one another for difficulties that are essentially beyond anyone's realistic control.

Therefore, HCS professionals need to be sensitive to the family's efforts to control the disease and to the difficulties associated with this task. Even if the youth's adherence and/or the family's support of treatment could be improved, blame and guilt are destructive and countertherapeutic. Because these feelings can easily be reinforced by HCS professionals, they must be careful to avoid guilt-inducing and simplistic interpretations (e.g., the youth has poor metabolic control because he or she is just not doing what he or she should be doing).

Parent-child relations.   A frequent concern of therapists and families is the degree to which parents should monitor, supervise, and support certain adherence tasks for the youth. There is no easy solution to this issue because the degree and quality of parental involvement must change as the youth matures both cognitively and socially. An additional consideration is the age at which the child is diagnosed. Youths who are diagnosed at a younger age are usually able to take more responsibility for tasks at an earlier age than are youths who develop diabetes in later childhood (Allen, Tennen, McGrade, Affleck, & Ratzan, 1983). Moreover, youths who develop diabetes as teenagers have additional pressures associated with adolescence that may impede learning and integration of the tasks into daily life. For example, the teenager who usually joined his or her friends on Friday nights at 8:30 for pizza might find it difficult to eat supper earlier (corresponding to the late afternoon insulin peak) and then not eat any or at least substantially less pizza with his or her friends. Some youths are able to alter their insulin schedules to provide more flexibility, but this depends on the physician's recommendations, the cognitive maturity of the adolescent, and the stability of the diabetic control.

Kohler, Hurwitz, and Milan (1982) designed a four-stage curriculum for teaching diabetes self-care behaviors to youths aged 5 to 18 years. As a guide to the reader, each stage is briefly described and the self-care behaviors appropriate for each stage are listed.

Stage 1. This stage included children in kindergarten through second grade (5 through 8 years). Children are encouraged to try and practice insulin injections and glucose testing. They are taught about symptoms they might experience with hypoglycemia and hyperglycemia and how to seek help. Kohler et al. (1982) reported that 17% of the children in this stage were injecting their own insulin. All parents in this stage were responsible for keeping the log of the child's glucose levels.

Stage 2. This stage included children in third through the sixth grades (9 through 12 years). Technical skills related to glucose testing and injections are taught and mastered through repeated practice. Children are taught the relationships between insulin, diet, and exercise, and about making insulin dose adjustments based on home glucose testing, exercise, and eating. None of the children in this stage were primarily responsible for adjusting their own insulin, but 83% of the children were injecting their own insulin and 69% of the families made the insulin adjustments without physician consultation.

Stage 3. Junior high school children, aged 12 through 14 years, were included in this stage. Youths are taught problem-solving skills in the management of insulin, diet, and exercise. Metabolic control and long-term complications are introduced to the youths. In addition, the youths develop greater knowledge regarding the effects of environmental factors (e.g., stress, illness, social activities) on diabetes management and control. All children in this stage were giving their own insulin and 19% of the youths were primarily responsible for insulin adjustments.

Stage 4. Adolescents who were 15 through 18 years of age comprised this group. Changes in lifestyle, future planning (e.g., job possibilities, current research about medical treatment strategies, genetic transmission and pregnancy), long-term complications (e.g., prevention, symptoms, treatment), and resource help (e.g., specialists, importance of regular health care) are pertinent issues. All youths injected their own insulin, and 33% of the youths were primarily responsible for insulin dose adjustments.

Thus, most youths start injecting their own insulin at about age 10 years and by 13 years of age most have mastered this task. Other researchers report similar findings regarding the timing of the youths' mastery of insulin injections (e.g., Allen et al., 1983).

Although it is important to promote individual responsibility in children, giving a child too much responsibility too early can cause psychosocial and health-related problems. For example, Allen et al. (1983) found that children aged 11 years and younger who "usually" or "always" gave their own insulin injections coped less adequately and had worse metabolic control than children who gave their insulin injections "only sometimes" or "never." Most parents need to supervise the insulin injections (e.g., the amount of insulin in the syringe), particularly for children in stages 1 through 3. Errors in insulin dose are relatively easy to make, especially during times when the youth is tired and less attentive (e.g., early morning, late afternoon, before bed).

It is especially difficult for children to learn how to make appropriate insulin dose adjustments. Because such adjustments are potentially dangerous, youths who begin this responsibility early need close parental supervision. Glucose testing is also a difficult task because of the strict procedures that must be followed in order to obtain accurate results. Wing and her associates have found discouraging results regarding the accuracy of self-glucose monitoring in youths (Wing, Koeske, New, Lamparski, & Becker, 1986). Because insulin adjustments are made according to the results of the glucose tests, errors in glucose testing are also potentially dangerous.

In addition to age-appropriate parental monitoring and supervision of glucose testing and insulin dosage adjustment, parents can provide both instrumental and emotional support for their child in several other ways. For example, instrumental support might include exercising with the youth, providing consistent mealtimes, serving appropriate types of food, and inquiring about the results of the youth's glucose testing. Parents engage in some of these supportive behaviors less often with older adolescents because of the youths' growing independence and emancipation from parental control. Interestingly, this normative parental disengagement may be one reason that older adolescents evidence less adherence than younger adolescents (Hanson et al., 1987b). The parents might provide emotional support by showing a caring and understanding attitude when the youth is having difficulty with certain adherence behaviors. In contrast, parents can easily undermine the youth's adherence by providing ready access to unhealthy foods, scheduling erratic mealtimes, and otherwise showing disinterest.

An issue related to family support that often arises in treatment is whether other family members need to change their eating habits. Siblings may feel that it is unfair to prohibit them from consuming foods that are not a part of the normal diabetic diet (e.g., high sweet and fatty foods such as cakes, cookies, and potato chips). One way that we have successfully handled this issue is with reframing. Because family members love the member with IDDM and want him or her to live a long time without complications, the family can decide not to keep "forbidden" food in the house as a demonstration of their love and support. This is not to say that the other family members are not allowed to eat such foods, but the way in which they eat them is designed to help the youth with diabetes. For example, if the family wants to eat a cake for dessert, the family can buy a cake that can be eaten in one sitting (separate pieces of cake or pie can be bought for small families), or the family can dispose of or freeze leftover cake that poses a temptation to the youth. The family might also decide to go out and order dessert in a restaurant, and the youth with diabetes can pick something acceptable to eat or chose a different type of treat (e.g., choosing which movie the family will watch after dinner). In essence, the parents provide the child with acceptable alternatives that will not encourage nonadherence or interfere with the diabetic treatment regimen.

Marital and family relations.   In a series of reports, Minuchin, Baker, and colleagues observed that families of children with frequent episodes of ketoacidosis and multiple hospitalizations (averaging 12 hospitalizations per year) were characterized by excessive cohesion (enmeshment and overprotectiveness), rigidity in family structure and organization, and poor conflict resolution (Baker, Minuchin, Liebman, & Todd, 1975; Baker, Rosman, & Minuchin, 1982; Minuchin et al., 1975; Minuchin, Rosman, & Baker, 1978). These observations were based on family interviews and therapy sessions with a highly select group of children with superlabile diabetes. The results of Minuchin, Baker, and colleagues initiated other investigations of their hypotheses. Subsequent studies, however, have provided inconsistent findings regarding the links between global measures of family relations and health in youths with IDDM (Anderson, Miller, Auslander, & Santiago, 1981; Cederblad, Helgesson, Larsson, & Ludvigsson, 1982; Klemp & LaGreca, 1987).

Recently, we examined several pertinent issues regarding the associations between family relations and the health of youths with IDDM (Hanson, Henggeler, Harris, Burghen, & Moore, 1989). We also assessed the relationship between the metabolic control of the youths and the marital satisfaction of their parents. In addition to the youths' physical health, we identified factors relating to the youths' psychosocial well-being. Our results revealed the complex nature of the associations between family relations and health. The initial correlational results were relatively straightforward and consistent with findings in other investigations. Good metabolic control was significantly associated with marital satisfaction and family flexibility and was marginally associated with family cohesion. Although the relationship between adaptability and metabolic control supports the findings of Minuchin and colleagues, we did not find that high cohesion was related to poor metabolic control. These results changed substantially, however, when certain statistical controls were used. Marital satisfaction and family relations were strongly linked with metabolic control only under conditions of short duration of the disease. As duration of the disease increased, the relationship between family relations and the youths' metabolic control decreased substantially.

The interactions between the duration of IDDM and the quality of family relations may reflect two developmental processes. The decreased association between the youths' health and family relations with increased duration of the illness is consistent with the youths' developmental maturation. As the youths mature, family relations play a less important role in their psychosocial functioning (Maccoby & Martin, 1983). The declining influence of marital and family relations might also reflect overriding concomitants of the disease process (e.g., physiological changes that occur during puberty that contribute to poor metabolic control).

Because these data are correlational, it is not known whether poor control leads to a rigid family structure, or whether rigidity leads to poor control under conditions of short duration of the disease. In all likelihood, the two processes are reciprocal. The family may respond to the youth's poor metabolic control by making the family structure overly routine and rigid. Likewise, family rigidity might exacerbate metabolic control by decreasing the family's ability to cope with problems and by increasing parent-child conflict and stress. In either case, health care professionals should encourage families to develop a flexible supportive response to the physical and psychosocial stressors of youths, especially under conditions of short duration of IDDM. Such cohesion and flexibility in family relations also enhance the normal developmental processes of adolescents. Moreover, in support of the multisystemic view, our findings suggest that the quality of the parents' marital relationship is particularly important in youths with short duration of the illness.

Siblings of chronically ill children.   Consistent with early research on chronically ill children, most of the research on their healthy siblings has been based on a deficit model; that is, investigators have attempted to determine the detrimental effects of having a handicapped sibling. Although it is appropriate for clinicians and researchers to be concerned about the potentially negative effects of living with a sibling who is chronically ill, it is also important to study the adaptation of the healthy siblings and the positive effects that might result from having a chronically ill brother or sister. For example, Seligman (1987) noted that healthy siblings of cancer patients are often compassionate and empathetic, and have an appreciation of their own health. Moreover, healthy siblings of chronically ill brothers or sisters often choose careers in helping professions (Seligman, 1983). Although there is little empirical data regarding the role of sibling relations in chronic illness, clinical impressions suggest that there are both positive and negative aspects to living with a sibling who is chronically ill or handicapped.

In this section, four issues are discussed that are helpful in understanding the nature of sibling relations. Three of these issues (rivalry, power differences, and loyalty) pertain to all sibling groups. The fourth issue is the normative reactions of healthy siblings to their brother or sister with IDDM.

Sibling rivalry involves the processes of social comparison that begin early in the child's life (Bryant, 1982). An important aspect of social comparisons between siblings is whether the parents give preferential treatment to one or the other. An example of parental preferential treatment in healthy families is the differential treatment of first-born children by their mothers when the first-born child and mother are alone (Bryant, 1982). When a child perceives that his or her parents exhibit preferential treatment toward a brother or sister, the sibling relationship can become very conflictual. This conflict is usually associated with frustration over unmet needs (e.g., attention) and/or jealousy over the favored status of the sibling. Interestingly, it is not only the child with less parental attention who develops emotional discomfort, but the child with preferential treatment also behaves more negatively in the sibling dyad (Bryant, 1982).

Based on research with healthy siblings, it would seem that sibling rivalry might occur frequently in families where the chronically ill child receives increased parental attention because of treatment demands. The strong parent-child coalition that often develops when a parent has considerable responsibility for the medical care of the child can create rivalry between the siblings. Healthy siblings might also be expected to take on additional household responsibilities to help alleviate some of the parents' excessive workload arising from the treatment needs of their sibling. Healthy siblings might feel neglected, overworked, and unappreciated. The following example of sibling rivalry exemplifies the role that such rivalry can play within the larger systemic context.

Becky was a healthy 11-year-old sibling who attempted suicide largely because she felt neglected, and the stress in the family seemed overwhelming. There was considerable sibling rivalry because her 6-year-old brother, Jim, had IDDM that was difficult to control and the parents had to spend a lot of time with him. Jim had insulin reactions frequently, which naturally took priority over any other event that was occurring. Jim was also a finicky eater and the parents often had to fix several different meals before he ate what was needed. Because Jim fought insulin injections and glucose testing, treatment tasks took considerable time. Becky felt that her mother and father "babied" Jim and that he used his "special" relationship with them to isolate her from the family. For example, Becky reported that Jim often "tattled" on her and that her parents often sided with him. Because of the jealousy and anger she felt, the sibling relationship was highly conflictual.

In addition to sibling rivalry and conflict, the considerable time that was needed to care for Jim created stress and strain for the entire family, including the parents' marital relationship and their work schedule. The father had difficulty coping with the treatment demands and left his wife with most of the treatment responsibilities. This caused additional stress for the mother, strained the marital relationship, and created a strong mother-child coalition. The situation was further exacerbated by the fact that the parents had a weak social support system and were afraid to leave Jim with a babysitter because of the possible medical problems that could occur.

The children also had limited peer relations largely because of the parents' very high academic expectations. The children were in rigorous private schools that placed unusual amounts of pressure on them to perform in academic areas. The parents did not feel that extracurricular activities were a high priority for their children.

On a cognitive level, Becky had also developed perfectionistic attitudes regarding her performance and wanted to be the "best" at everything to gain more attention from her parents. Becky placed herself in an impossible situation, namely, she wanted to win her parents' attention by being perfect. This plan was doomed to failure within the present family context because her "perfect" behavior allowed the parents to be even less concerned about her and to devote more energy to Jim's difficulties. Feeling more isolated from her family, rejected by her parents, pressured at school, and neglected by her peers, Becky attempted suicide. The family was very surprised and sought professional treatment immediately.

This case is clearly an example of the extreme in sibling problems. It is presented not as a typical reaction of siblings, but as an unfortunate scenario that can happen. The multisystemic nature of this case is evident. Each of the following systems was involved in contributing to the problem: *individual* attitudes of perfectionism and poor coping abilities; conflictual *sibling relations* that were largely related to second-order sibling effects (i.e., the influences of third parties, such as parents, on the sibling relationship); poor *parent-child relations*; a stressful *marital* relationship; problems at *work*; a *school* that reinforced the child's unrealistic expectations for perfection; increased *stress* in the family due to the physical illness; and an inadequate *social support* system for both the parents and children.

As a final point about sibling rivalry, the chronically ill sibling might be jealous of parental rewards (e.g., a piece of chocolate cake) and social approval (e.g., being star of the football team) that are given to a healthy sibling and that might be difficult for the chronically ill child to obtain because of treatment demands and/or complications. Moreover, the chronically ill child might feel more parental disapproval compared to his or her sibling (e.g., "Why don't you eat what you're supposed to eat?" "Why haven't you tested your blood sugar?" "Why is your sugar so high?").

Before planning strategies for reducing sibling rivalry, the therapist should examine the *power structure* of sibling relationships. Older siblings are more likely to fill the role of caretaker because of their greater ability to provide support to younger siblings. Although helping and caretaking behaviors of older siblings can promote positive prosocial development, the power structure of the relationship can interfere with positive helping behavior (Bryant, 1982). Older siblings, especially girls, sometimes use controlling and dominating behavior, such as bossiness, when they "help" their younger siblings. Moreover, older siblings may try to foster dependency from their younger siblings (e.g., rewarding younger siblings by help-giving behaviors), which is not always welcomed or tolerated by the younger siblings.

Asking siblings to help with the disease management sometimes decreases sibling rivalry. This intervention strategy can teach prosocial behaviors and allows the healthy sibling to feel a part of an important family triad, namely the parents and ill child, and may lessen sibling rivalry for parental attention. The sibling will also gain a better understanding of the disease. Before implementing this intervention, however, it is essential to consider the power structure of the sibling relationship. In situations where the sibling is bossy or fosters dependency, this intervention may cause more sibling conflict and distress for the younger chronically ill sibling. Moreover, because it is important to foster independence in the chronically ill child, the dependency-seeking behavior of older siblings may not always be desirable. A sibling dyad that places the chronically ill child in an overly dependent role and the healthy sibling in the role of being in charge seems detrimental to both siblings' psychosocial development and may produce more conflict in the sibling relationship.

If the therapist decides that it would be therapeutic for the healthy sibling to become more involved in the management of the illness, the therapist and parents should supervise the negotiation of the caretaking roles between the siblings. The therapist is then able to help define the power structure of the relationship so that the caretaking roles are not overly dependent or independent. It is also useful to have the chronically ill child suggest sibling behaviors that might be of most help in order to reduce the likelihood that the child will become resentful of the siblings' help-giving behaviors. For example, the child might request that the sibling help with the glucose-testing task by bringing the testing equipment to the youth before dinner. Rather than viewing this behavior as the sibling hassling the child about testing, the chronically ill child will view it as supportive and helpful.

Sibling loyalty is the third important characteristic of sibling relations. In their review, Bank and Kahn (1982) describe intense sibling loyalties as involving a strong desire to be with each other; positive and helpful attitudes toward one another; a communication style that clearly facilitates closeness and is understood by each other but not necessarily others; protective behaviors toward each other, often as a reaction against hostile outsiders; and the open and quick resolution of conflict. Although parental abandonment or neglect can intensify sibling loyalties, nurturing parents can also serve as role models for such behavior. The following case exemplifies the intense loyalty of a younger sibling to an older sibling with IDDM.

Mickey was the healthy 10-year-old brother of Andy, who was 15 years old and had been diagnosed with IDDM at 11 years of age. Mickey deeply admired and respected Andy and the brothers were very close. When Mickey started to exhibit symptoms of IDDM (e.g., increased thirst, frequent urination, weight loss) and subsequently learned he had developed diabetes, Mickey evidenced little difficulty adjusting to the disease. Rather than fearing the disease, Mickey almost welcomed its onset because he wanted to be like his brother in every respect.

In some cases, pleasure with contracting an illness might be related to the healthy sibling's feelings that the chronically ill sibling receives more attention from family and others and that now, he or she will receive just as much attention. In the case of Mickey, however, his feelings reflected his extreme sibling loyalty. This example is also important because of the alternative view it presents; namely, the sibling may not have fears of developing the disease but rather view it as a natural course of events that is not to be dreaded.

Finally, it is important to discuss the *normative sibling reactions* and behaviors that can emerge in healthy siblings living with a chronically ill brother or sister. In addition to sibling rivalry, healthy siblings might fear that they will develop the disease. Depending on the cognitive stage of the child, the youth might believe that the disease is contagious or genetically determined and fear that he or she will soon contract it. Parents need to educate siblings regarding the etiology and treatment of the disease, with consideration given to the sibling's developmental level. Such education can also attenuate the healthy sibling's concern that the sibling with the illness will die. Fears for the ill sibling's life can arise when the healthy sibling interprets parental worries and concerns as an indication of the impending death of the ill sibling.

Another reaction that can occur in healthy siblings is embarrassment of their brother's or sister's illness. In general, youths do not want to be different from their peers. They want their mothers and fathers to behave like their friends' parents. If the parents behave differently (e.g., if the parents show up at cheerleading tryouts when no other parent does), the youth becomes painstakingly embarrassed. Similarly, youths do not want siblings to be "different." In one case of a sibling's embarrassment, an effective strategy was designed that utilized the strengths of the school system.

Tim was a 10-year-old child who had a difficult time accepting that his younger brother, Joey, had IDDM. Joey often did things with Tim and Tim's peer group. After Joey got IDDM, some of the social activities between the boys changed because of the IDDM treatment regimen. For example, Joey needed to test his blood glucose and eat a snack before engaging in excessive exercise with the other boys. Tim was expected to stop the activity and help Joey if he developed symptoms of hypoglycemia. Joey on occasion became hypoglycemic with Tim and his peer group, which was embarrassing to Tim. Joey also was not allowed to eat the donuts and cookies that the other mothers often provided for the boys. Some of the boys had teased Tim that Joey was a "druggie" because he used needles and "drew" blood (e.g., the finger-pricks of blood for glucose testing). Joey's hypoglycemic reactions were scoffed at as Joey "being high" and needing a "fix." This teasing greatly embarrassed and infuriated Tim.

The therapist and teacher planned a school assignment that involved all the children in the class. Students were divided into small groups to act in plays about what it is like living with a chronic illness or physical handicap and living with a brother or sister who is chronically ill or handicapped. The groups were each assigned a different illness or handicap. Tim was assigned to play the role of a boy with IDDM in the skit. The teacher worked with the children on perspective-taking and encouraged the children to discuss what it would be like to have the illness (e.g., feeling different, not being able to do everything that others can do) or to have a sibling with the illness (e.g., increased responsibility for the care of the sibling, teasing from peers about the siblings' illness).

This intervention was successful for several reasons. First, Tim's peers gained a better understanding of IDDM and Tim felt they were more accepting of Joey's illness. (In this case, the peer system had a major second-order sibling effect on the sibling relationship.) Second, Tim gained a better understanding and a more empathetic perspective of the problems Joey was experiencing in living with IDDM. Third, Tim's greater acceptance of the illness was also mirrored in his more facilitative and positive sibling interactions with Joey. Last, the school intervention reduced the conflict between Tim and his mother, who was very concerned with Tim's prior negative attitude toward Joey.

As a final note, the therapist needs to remember that the family environment of a chronically ill child may be very different from the family environment of their healthy siblings. In general, siblings experience different environments even though they live in the same household (Scarr & Grajek, 1982; Daniels, Dunn, Furstenberg, & Plomin, 1985). Parents treat their children differently because the children evoke different responses from their parents, and vice versa. In addition, siblings create different environments for each other.

Stress

From a multisystemic perspective, stress reflects the interactions among the systems in which the person is embedded, the attributes of the person, and his or her appraisal of the stressor. Families of chronically ill children are typically faced with daily time and treatment demands that can add considerable stress to family life. Stress can affect the child's health in at least two ways. First, stress can affect the youths' physiological functioning (e.g., the release of counterregulatory hormones that increase blood glucose). Second, stress can affect the youth's adherence to treatment, which in turn has an effect on metabolic control. Most professionals have assumed that stress is linked to metabolic control through its effects on adherence behaviors. For example, if the youth is under stress, he or she might not exercise, follow an appropriate diet, or consistently check blood glucose levels. Neglect in any of these areas could potentially cause problems in metabolic control.

In a recent study, we (Hanson et al., 1987b) investigated whether stress influenced metabolic control through its effects on adherence; and secondly, whether certain variables mediated the link between stress and metabolic control. Because both parental support and social competence are important in the adaptation of chronically ill children, the mediating effects of these variables were examined. Such a mediation could occur via two models: a main effect model or a buffering model (Cohen & Wills, 1985). In the main effect model, social competence and parental support have beneficial effects on health regardless of the level of stress in the youth's life. In a buffering model, social competence and parental support provide a sense of stability and well-being that attenuates the deleterious effects of stress on metabolic control during conditions of high stress, but is not associated with metabolic control during conditions of low stress. For example, the youth might benefit the most from parental assistance with the daily tasks of treatment during times of difficulty. Similarly, youths who have developed a strong sense of competence and who are well-adjusted in peer and family relations might be able to adapt more successfully during times of high stress.

The results indicated that the link between stress and poor metabolic control was not mediated by the youths' adherence behaviors. Rather, high stress was directly linked to poor metabolic control. The results also showed that social competence buffered the negative association between stress and metabolic control. Increased stress was not associated with poor metabolic control in youths with high social competence. In contrast, increased stress worsened metabolic control substantially in youths with low social competence. Parental support was associated with better adherence, but it did not mediate the effects of stress on metabolic control. This is not surprising in light of the developmental transitions that occur during adolescence. During the emancipation process, youths in general tend to rely less on parents for support, and instead, rely more on themselves or turn to peers for support and advice. In this respect, a strong sense of competence would enable the youth to cope more effectively during stress.

The link between stress and metabolic control suggests important treatment considerations. First, the youths' long-term health must be considered paramount. Families can become accustomed to living with high levels of stress, and maladaptive and adaptive coping patterns are developed in response to that stress. In some circumstances, these coping behaviors or interactional styles (e.g., a strong sense of social competence) are effective in buffering the effects of stress on the youths' metabolic control. In other cases, the youths' continued physiological adaptation to stress takes a toll on the youths' health. Professionals need to identify sources of conflict and stress in the youths' life (e.g., the parents' marital relationship, problems in peer relations) and work toward alleviating such stress. In addition, therapists can help the youth strengthen the buffering factors (e.g., self-esteem and positive social relations) that attenuate the negative effects of stress. Because adolescents are in the process of emancipating from parents, increasing parental involvement in treatment may be counterproductive for some youths. In situations where the parents are concerned and have appropriate expectations of the youths, increasing parental involvement may cause heightened conflict because of the youths' desire for autonomy. In this situation, an examination of the youths' peer system is essential.

Peers

Peer relations can be an important determinant of a youth's adherence to the treatment regimen. Peers are particularly important during adolescence when youths tend to spend more time with their peers than with their parents. In general, the peer system is important in the youth's overall psychosocial health (see Chapter 5), but there are additional concerns for children who are chronically ill. These concerns relate to the reactions of peers to the child with a chronic disease and to the types of peer relations that promote or hinder the health of the chronically ill child.

Healthy peers' reactions to children with a chronic illness depend on their stage of cognitive development, the information that has been given to them, and their previous experience (Bibace & Walsh, 1979, 1980; Brewster, 1982; Potter & Roberts, 1984; Redpath & Rogers, 1984). As discussed previously, peers' reactions may range from fear of "catching" the illness to understanding the multiple causal pathways that may trigger the disease process. Without a clear understanding of some of the more visible symptoms of the disease (e.g., hypoglycemia), peers may fear or be unable to help the youth when necessary.

The therapist should encourage the adolescent to discuss his or her treatment plan with a few close friends. The youth should tell his or her friends exactly how they can be helpful in certain situations. For example, the youth might say to his or her friends, "If I start to look a little pale and confused, it probably means I am hypoglycemic and need something to eat, so please remind me and make sure I eat something." Or, "I tend to eat too much pizza when we go out, so if you notice that I am eating a lot, would you just tell me to leave the rest for you or something like that." In this way the friends know what to do, and the youth chooses what he or she wants them to do.

Peer pressure and the youth's desire not to be different from peers can make adherence to treatment and good metabolic control difficult to achieve. Effective treatment of IDDM demands that specific behaviors occur at certain times during the day. This requires, for example, that the youth keep close track of the time and stop certain activities when it is time to test blood glucose. In addition, the youth may not be able to eat when others do, or may need to eat when others are not eating. Thus, the adherence regimen forces the youth to behave differently from his or her peers in certain respects. This can be especially difficult when the youth is on a date and is eager to please a companion. Fears of rejection are normal during adolescence, but are exacerbated when the youth feels different because of his or her treatment regimen.

In order to help youths (and parents) feel less isolated and "different" from peers, the therapist might recommend a family-oriented magazine, *Diabetes Forecast*, which is published by the American Diabetes Association (ADA) and contains articles written by professionals and individuals with IDDM. These articles address problems that can arise in living with diabetes and present adaptive strategies for coping with these problems. The magazine has sections for different age groups ranging from very young children to adults. The articles are highly informative and demonstrate a sensitivity to possible fears of parents and youths regarding serious issues related to IDDM. Presently, a one-year membership in ADA, which includes a subscription to *Diabetes Forecast* (12 issues), costs $20. If the family is unable to afford this cost, a free ADA newsletter, *Diabetes '90*, also provides valuable support and information. The therapist might also recommend a social activity group for youths with IDDM that may be sponsored by the local chapter of ADA. Unfortunately, social groups of youths with IDDM are relatively uncommon.

Often adolescents purposefully maintain higher than optimal levels of blood glucose because they fear embarrassment if they were to become hypoglycemic in front of their peers, during a class, or on a date. These feelings are understandable and are not entirely unfounded. It can be embarrassing to the youth when he or she becomes hostile or cries during a hypoglycemic epidsode. Likewise, some peers may reject or make fun of the youth because of his or her diabetes. Some dates may feel uncomfortable with or may not want to accommodate the youth's treatment plan. The therapist might discuss both realistic fears and problem-solving techniques for difficulties associated with peer relations.

Although some researchers have speculated that poor metabolic control relates to high satisfaction with social support (Kaplan, Chadwick, & Schimmel, 1985), there are no studies, to my knowledge, that demonstrate a significant relationship between poor metabolic control and high social support. It seems likely that overall peer support is beneficial, even though the social pressures associated with it can cause the youth to deviate from the adherence plan.

School System

School personnel can provide useful information to parents and therapists regarding the youth's ability to manage diabetes treatment away from home, as well as issues that surround peer interactions. In turn, families and therapists need to educate school personnel on how to help the youth adhere to treatment and how to manage any medical problems that might arise. Unfortunately, school personnel are usually not equipped to handle medical problems (Anderson, 1987; Walker, 1984; Weitzman, 1984). Although the school nurse may be qualified to provide instruction and education to appropriate school personnel for medical emergencies, the amount of training given to school personnel is often inadequate because of the nurse's time demands (Walker, 1984). Thus, parents must assume the primary responsibility for educating appropriate personnel.

It is essential that the therapist inform parents of their critical role as an advocate for their child in the school system. The school system needs to be flexible enough to accommodate to problems that may result from the illness (e.g., school absences, hypoglycemia during a school test, changing school schedules to meet the youth's treatment regimen for activities such as a physical education class or a class outing). Because of the serious consequences that can occur if school personnel forget important medical information (e.g., what to do if child is hypoglycemic), it is advisable to have parents schedule periodic meetings with key school personnel (e.g., teachers, bus drivers, coaches, playground supervisors, principals) to reiterate plans and procedures related to treatment. This recommendation is not meant to imply purposeful neglect or inattentiveness by school personnel, but rather the likelihood that such knowledge can easily be forgotten, especially if school personnel are not typically faced with these types of situations. Because of anxieties experienced during medical emergencies, teachers and other school officials may be less likely to remember proper treatment procedures when the emergency actually occurs. Such meetings may also alleviate some of the normal fears that parents have in trusting their child's medical care to school personnel. It is also important that the parents give school personnel the names and phone numbers of people, physicians, and hospitals to contact in an emergency.

Delamater, Bubb, Warren-Boulton, and Fisher (1984) addressed several parental concerns regarding the management of their child's diabetes during school hours. These are useful issues for both parents and therapists to discuss and clarify with school personnel.

> Will the child be able to inform his teachers when he or she is having an insulin reaction? Will the teacher recognize an insulin reaction and know how to treat it? If the child loses consciousness can a nurse inject glucagon (a hormone that raises blood glucose)? If not, can paramedics reach the school quickly and are they prepared to handle a diabetic emergency? Is it safe for the child to ride the school bus and does the bus driver know the symptoms and treatment of hypoglycemia? Is the child consuming all of his or her lunch and eating snacks so as to minimize the danger of hypoglycemia? Will the child accept candy, cookies, etc., from friends? If the child tests blood glucose levels during the day, where can she or he do it and who can help him or her? (p. 198)

These are just a few of the many questions and concerns that parents should address with the school system. An additional concern is whether the youth receives appropriate amounts of food before and after exercising during gym class or on the playground. Will the child's blood glucose be tested to insure he or she is not hyperglycemic or hypoglycemic prior to, during, or after exercise? (See discussion of exercise under "Adherence Behaviors" earlier in this chapter for more information.)

Because hypoglycemia can occur at any time, several key school personnel should be trained to recognize the symptoms of hypoglycemia and should know what to do in such an emergency. One procedure that teachers sometimes use when a child is feeling hypoglycemic is to send him or her to the nurse's office. It is appropriate to have the nurse check the child's blood glucose; however, it is not advisable for the teacher to instruct the child to go to the nurse's office. If the child is hypoglycemic, the additional effort required to walk to the nurse's office could worsen the hypoglycemia or the child could become confused and wander the halls. The personality changes that can occur with hypoglycemia (e.g., stubbornness, crying), and the possibility of the child becoming unconscious, also make it inadvisable to allow a peer to escort the child to the nurse. In this situation, the teacher could send another child to the nurse's office to request that the nurse come to the classroom. In addition, the teacher should have juice or glucose tablets available in the classroom for situations when the nurse cannot come to the classroom immediately. Some physicians and parents recommend giving the child some form of glucose immediately, rather than waiting the few minutes for the nurse to arrive. Either the child or the responsible school personnel (e.g., teacher, playground supervisor) should also have a source of glucose readily available (e.g., juice or glucose) when the youth is engaging in physical activity. Parents and therapists need to be very specific in their recommendations to school personnel regarding appropriate plans for treatment (e.g., hypoglycemia, exercise) while the child is in school.

One additional problem is related to the stress of tests or speeches that may be required as part of the child's coursework. Before an important test or speech, the youth may feel some normal anxiety. These symptoms (e.g., shakiness, nervousness, sweating, heart palpitations) can mimic the symptoms of hypoglycemia. It is advisable to have the youth test his or her blood glucose if these symptoms are evident before, after, or during an examination in order to rule out hypoglycemia. (In general, the youth needs to test his or her blood glucose whenever these types of symptoms occur.) Stress can lower or raise blood glucose, depending, in part, on the youth's blood glucose at the time of the stressor. Moreover, instances of severe hypoglycemia following a stressor such as an examination in school have been reported.

The teachers' interactions with the youth about the disease and treatment affect not only the child's attitude toward himself or herself, but also the attitudes of the child's peers. If the teacher singles out the youth and announces that the child is "different" because of the illness, the child might feel uncomfortable and isolated from the other children. A better approach would be for the teacher to discuss diabetes during a lecture about the body and how people can help their bodies to function appropriately. The teacher can discuss the importance of a well-balanced diet and exercise for everyone. The process message is that certain behaviors are essential for everyone's health, and that supporting these behaviors in each other is helpful. The child with diabetes then feels more a part of the group, and his or her treatment behaviors can be viewed as optimal health practices for everyone, with special treatment (e.g., insulin injections) that is necessarily added. This positive reframing can help the youth adhere to the treatment behaviors in front of his or her peers without feeling stigmatized.

Although school personnel must understand the basic information about IDDM (e.g., the interrelationships between food, insulin, and physical activity), school personnel should also be informed that, in general, the child's IDDM should not affect his or her schoolwork and that the child should not be limited in what he or she is allowed to do. Otherwise, school personnel might view the child as "sick," might not expect the child to perform up to his or her capacity, or might not allow the child to engage in healthy activities that are not precluded by the IDDM treatment regimen. Thus, school personnel must not only understand and accommodate the special precautions that are inherent with the child's IDDM (e.g., having glucose available, making sure the child eats lunch on time) but also recognize that the child with IDDM can with rare exceptions do everything that children without IDDM can do.

Health Care System

Periodic contact with the health care system is a necessary part of the youth's treatment. The family's interactions with the health care system can be stressful from both emotional and pragmatic perspectives. The length of time that families spend at clinics is considerable and often frustrating since most of the time can be spent in the waiting room. It is not unusual, for example, for a family to spend a large portion of the day for the clinic visit, considering the time driving to and from the appointment and the time spent in the physician's office. The expense of these visits is also very costly because of the finances lost from the parent missing work, in addition to the charges associated with the laboratory work and the physician's consultation.

Although several studies have examined the association between adult patients' perceptions of the health care system and health outcomes (e.g., DiMatteo, Hays, & Prince, 1986; Taylor, 1986), there are few investigations of the links between family members' satisfaction with the health care system and health outcomes in youths with a chronic illness. Recently, however, we examined the relationships between satisfaction with the health care system and health outcomes (i.e., adherence to treatment, metabolic control, and number of diabetes-related hospitalizations) in youths with IDDM (Hanson, Henggeler, Harris et al., 1988). Our results suggest that the youths' adherence to treatment was related to their satisfaction with physicians' personal qualities and to parental satisfaction with physicians' professional competence. Youths were more adherent when they perceived physicians as caring and their parents viewed physicians as skillful and competent. Although it takes more time during clinic visits, it seems important for physicians to show a caring attitude toward youths and convey their special knowledge and expertise to parents. Because our data are correlational, we cannot assume that family satisfaction causes better adherence; it is also possible that better adherence leads to family satisfaction. The importance of this study for our discussion, however, is that it demonstrates the association between extrafamilial factors, such as the health care system, and adherence behaviors of youths.

Role relationships between physicians and families.   Because of the extensive interaction with the health care system, especially during times of crisis, families often become dependent on health care professionals. Physicians may also become protective of and close to families by working through the struggles and "ups and downs" of management and treatment. Several issues can result from the dependency of family members on physicians. These issues include fears of disappointing the physician because of poor health, fears of addressing problems that might strain the physician-family relationship, dissatisfaction with the balance of power in the physician-family relationship, and fears about changing physicians.

One problem that often arises is the tendency of HCS professionals to blame the child or the family for the child's poor health or "noncompliance" to treatment. The word "compliance" has negative connotations because it implies a therapeutic process that is undesirable for both the family and health care professional. Compliance by definition denotes yielding to another's demands. With a chronic illness, compliance implies that the child or family is yielding to the demands of health care professionals. From a therapeutic perspective, placing the therapist or other HCS professional in a position of power over the family is inconsistent with a primary goal of therapy, namely, for the family to take primary responsibility for the daily care of the illness and successfully adapt to the demands of the illness. On the other hand, the term "adherence" denotes the process that both families and health care professionals seek: the family's act of adhering to and following treatment guidelines. If the family or child is not adhering to the treatment demands, it is the role of the health care professional to help the family and/or youth incorporate the demands of the treatment into family life. This collaborative approach utilizes the strengths of both health care professionals and families, and it also lessens feelings of helplessness and the potentially serious conflicts between HCS professionals and families.

The view that the physician is an "omnipotent expert" and that families should unquestioningly obey the physician's orders has been challenged by researchers and families (e.g., Deaton, 1985; Kirscht & Rosenstock, 1979). Clearly, the physician's medical knowledge is critical; however, the family's knowledge of the effects of daily management decisions is also important. Because of the many treatment decisions and the constant vigilance that are required by family members on a daily basis, parents and/or youth often become more "expert" than the physician in the daily management of the disease (e.g., the amount of insulin needed to lower blood glucose 50 mg/dl; the amount of food needed before engaging in 45 minutes of exercise). If the physician feels uncomfortable and/or is threatened by the family's assertion of knowledge and power in the daily control of the disease, conflict and stress can result. The physician may fear that the family wants to exert too much control over management decisions and endanger the health of the youth. The nature of the disease, however, requires that the family take considerable responsibility for daily management. The therapist can encourage the family members to use their own knowledge to actively evaluate the physician's recommendations rather than passively complying with whatever the physician recommends. It seems most desirable if a working relationship can be established whereby the family and health care professionals achieve a balance between self-reliance and mutual dependence. An illustrative example might clarify the delicate balance that exists between dependence and self-reliance on health care professionals.

Tom was an intelligent and mature 17-year-old adolescent who was hospitalized for poor metabolic control. His physician was widely respected for his expertise in diabetes and also had an extensive research background. Tom had taken great care in monitoring his blood glucose and adhering to treatment despite difficulties with daily glucose fluctuations and so had gained considerable knowledge about how his body responded to different amounts of insulin, food, and exercise. Tom was fearful of going into the hospital because of the control that would be taken away from him and his parents regarding daily management tasks (e.g., he had to rely on the hospital personnel to serve his meals on time; he was not allowed to check his own blood glucose or help prescribe the amount of insulin that was to be given to him). The physician was zealous in his eagerness to impress physicians-in-training with his diabetes management skills. He prescribed changes in the insulin schedule and doses that frightened Tom. Tom and his parents went along with the physician's orders until one occasion when the physician ordered a substantially higher dose of insulin. Based on his previous insulin dosages and reactions, Tom greatly feared a severe hypoglycemic reaction. The physician's rationale was that even if Tom did become hypoglycemic, it would not be a problem since he was in the hospital. Tom refused the insulin with his parents' permission. The physician was irate and angrily discharged Tom from the hospital because he would not follow the physician's orders. Although Tom's parents were extremely upset with the physician and wanted to confront him about his unprofessional behavior, they feared that he might prejudice his colleagues against Tom, and Tom would have little access to professional help that would be critically needed during a time of crisis.

Although Tom and his parents had asserted themselves, they were still dependent on the health care system. Tom was now on a new and unfamiliar insulin schedule that had been prescribed by his previous physician. Until Tom and his parents found another physician who was willing to work with them, they felt vulnerable and feared that if a diabetes crisis occurred they would have nowhere to turn. Older adolescents often have similar fears when they transfer from the pediatrician who has treated them for years to an internist who is unfamiliar with their management of the disease and views them as adults rather than as adolescents (Anderson, 1987; Barbero, 1982).

Although there are cases of nonadherence where families have irresponsibly relinquished their responsibility for care of the disease, most cases of nonadherence reflect environmental problems and the difficulties that both health care professionals and families share in assimilating the demands of treatment into the family's lifestyle. Physicians and patients, however, have different attitudes regarding the causes of adherence difficulties. House, Pendleton, and Parker (1986) examined physicians' and patients' attributions for nonadherence to diet and found that physicians tend to cite motivation as the primary cause for nonadherence to the IDDM dietary regimen (i.e., motivation was the reason 80% of the time). Environmental factors were only listed 5% of the time and informational factors 10% of the time. Individuals with IDDM had quite different views. They cited environmental factors (38%) slightly more often than motivational factors (34%), and somatic/physiologic reasons were given 26% of the time. Therapists need to recognize the environmental factors (e.g., instrumental, emotional, and economic burdens) that relate to problems with daily adherence in order to help families devise plans to successfully adapt to the disease and its treatment.

Because it is important for professionals to gain a clear understanding of the illness and the demands it places on families, how can this best be accomplished? One method is the enactment of the disease (e.g., pretending to have the illness for a few days). Although most HCS professionals may not have the time or desire to engage in a simulation of the disease, not to mention the inconvenience and disruption that it causes in daily routines, it is worthwhile to examine the experiences of some professionals who have chosen to undertake such an arduous task. I am aware of three studies that involve professionals simulating the experience of a person living with IDDM.

Welborn and Duncan (1980) recruited 12 hospital staff personnel (four physicians, three nurses, two dietitians, three occupational therapists) who agreed to simulate for seven days the lifestyle of a person with IDDM. These personnel were required to adhere to the basic components of an IDDM treatment regimen: two daily pseudo-insulin injections (one before breakfast and one before supper) with varying amounts of insulin (saline solution) required based on the results of two urine sugar testings that were recorded prior to each aforementioned meal (the urine samples were prepared with various levels of sugar without knowledge of the participants); three regular meals with three snacks; no additional foods; and complete avoidance of sweet foods. This regimen is the bare bones of an adherence program to IDDM treatment and does not involve many of the problems that arise in daily treatment. With this in mind, how well did the personnel succeed in adhering to treatment? Apparently, not very well: The group had 64 potentially serious or adverse outcomes because of nonadherence to the treatment.

> One subject abandoned the trial on the third day because of domestic tensions and an unsympathetic handicapped spouse. This was scored as the one case of "ketoacidosis." One subject missed a meal, a complete oversight due to work pressure, and another was one-half hour late eating two meals, even after taking the insulin injections, and without

taking the precaution of a snack. Thus, three episodes were scored as "major hypoglycemia" (in real life, major hypoglycemia can result in unconsciousness, and death in some cases). Between-meal snacks were omitted on an astonishing 32 occasions and all were scored as "minor hypoglycemic reactions." Sugar-containing foods were consumed on 19 occasions, 6 times accidentally and 13 times willfully or with premeditation. Only 3 of the 12 participants made the correct insulin dosage decisions, the remainder showed inaccurate urine test results, or misinterpreted them, or misunderstood the instructions about dosage. Bearing in mind the training and qualifications of the group, their overall performance as pseudo-diabetic patients can be rated only as fair (p. 680).

In the second study (Warren-Boulton, Auslander, & Gettinger, 1982), the 65 participants also had difficulty incorporating several aspects of the treatment regimen into their daily lives. On the first day, only 53% of the subjects "almost always" adhered to their diet; by the fourth day, only 42% were adhering to the diet. Glucose testing was even worse, with 48% "almost always" adhering on the first day to only 18% by the fourth day. This low rate of adherence is particularly interesting considering that these health professionals were being evaluated as a part of a continuing education program. In addition to specific changes that were recommended in education and training as a result of these studies, the participants in both studies gained a much better understanding of the problems that can impede adherence. They also had more realistic expectations of families and their need for support, and more empathy toward the families who live with the disease. The investigators in both studies highly recommended this type of simulation for health care professionals who work with people who have IDDM.

The third study dealt with the emotional aspects of living with the disease (Williamson & McCauley, 1984). For 48 hours the authors simulated the experience of being a newly diagnosed person with IDDM. The authors clearly described the burdens and intrusiveness of IDDM and the difficulties of assimilating the treatment demands into daily life. In a very interesting follow-up commentary to this study, Heyman and Bloch (1984) discussed their reactions to the emotions expressed during the simulation. Abigail Heyman has had diabetes for more than 35 years and her husband, Donald Bloch, is a physician and editor of the journal *Family Systems Medicine*. The dialogue between Heyman and Bloch is reprinted below as a conclusion to this chapter because it so readily captures the emotions and frustrations of living with IDDM. It is hoped that the issues discussed will be useful for therapists who work closely with families of youths who have IDDM.

Comment: A Diabetic Views the Simulation

Abigail Heyman is presently 42 years old and has been diabetic since the age of nine. She was interviewed about her reactions to the preceding article by her husband, Donald Bloch. They have an eight-year-old child.

A.H.: The article says something very meaningful to me. At one point she says, "I didn't think I had time to be a diabetic." Most people are not aware of the sense of constant time drain, of concentration that goes with being a diabetic. Keeping track of all the details and complications of daily management is seldom out of my mind.

D.B.: Doesn't that become automatic after awhile?

A.H.: No. I still think about it all the time. It takes a lot of time and still feels like a new problem every day. There is always a slightly new twist, a slightly new complication. The rest of my day meshes differently than it has before. A meal gets delayed in a different way, or there is a new kind of food served that I don't know how to evaluate, or my work is physically more active than I expected, or it's a cloudy day, so my child sleeps late, so I sleep late, and my insulin is delayed. There are thousands of variations, with hindsight I can usually figure out what went wrong and prevent *that* from happening again. But there's always something else I hadn't thought of.

D.B.: So you can't put that on automatic and simply consign it to routine because the physiological piece of it changes.

A.H.: Not only the physiological piece, the emotional piece—and the structure of outside life—I mean the structure of where you're having your meals, and what you're having, and who you're having them with, and how they get delayed, and what kind of exercise you get. How do you evaluate that?

D.B.: Why not make your life very routine then? Why not get up at the same hour, have exactly the same thing for breakfast, do exactly the same thing for exercise in the morning, have a measured lunch, have your meal precisely on time? Wouldn't that solve the problem?

A.H.: The ideal of leading a disciplined, routinized life is deceptive. In real life school buses break down, business lunches are delayed. As a photojournalist my working hours and the energy demands are variable and unpredictable. Unless one devotes oneself entirely to the management of the illness it is impossible to follow strict routines. I still could not possibly routinize my emotional state, or my infections, which also dramatically affect my insulin requirements.

D.B.: One of the things the authors talk about is being the mother of a diabetic. I wondered did that in any way tell you anything about what your own mother might have gone through, or your own parents might have gone through when you were first diabetic as a child?

A.H.: Not really. Somehow I was less involved in those issues as she wrote about them. One thing I think I'd be very involved in if I were the mother of a diabetic that she did not really go into because she hadn't had the experience perhaps, is what it's like to fear your child is going into insulin reaction and passing out. She never dealt with the actual anxiety of passing out yourself or knowing that that can happen, say, to a child. Knowing that can happen at any time if you're not careful, you feel that it's your responsibility not to let that happen. I think if I were a parent, that would be a really major concern for me that she doesn't really touch on.

D.B.: I recall that when we met with that group of families with diabetic members and some kids, that that was a big issue.

A.H.: Yeah, I think it's the biggest fear of diabetics, beside the long-range complications.

D.B.: Would you like to see all diabetologists undergo this experience?

A.H.: Yes, I really would. There was a lot of issues that became very real to her, that nobody else deals with, and I just think it's a wonderful experience for those health care professionals to go through. I obviously feel the limitations. A two-day simulation leaves a lot of issues untouched.

D.B.: Well, nobody is going to do it for 30 years, but what do you think would have been an appropriate stretch of time?

A.H.: When you talk about an appropriate stretch of time, it's what you can get health care practitioners to handle. I must say two days really feels like an interesting experiment but I wonder if in seven days, one might feel, "Boy this is really boring. It takes just as much attention, but it's really boring, whereas for two days I thought it was kind of interesting."

D.B.: I was struck by how involved the author got; it was really a very gripping experience right off.

A.H.: I was bewildered by how confused she was by the instructions. It was a little surprising that someone who knew a lot could be so confused, but maybe that's because I am so used to that equipment and issues and it just doesn't seem confusing anymore.

D.B.: I was impressed because I thought health care professionals were apt to provide a lot of information at a rate that is difficult for the person or family to absorb. Even as a physician, over the time you and I have been together, I have had to learn more and more about the illness. Presumably, I had some training to fall back on; but it was almost useless in learning how to cope with daily life and what was really called for.

A.H.: I suspect one of the things you have to learn is that when things go wrong, for instance a high blood sugar, and you think you know how much insulin you took, and you think you know what you ate, and how much exercise—you're still *wrong*.

D.B.: In other words, you have to give up something in controlling the blood sugar in order to get on with your life. You can devote your life to becoming the single-minded servant of the disease but that would be kind of a dumb way to live.

A.H.: Yes, but there is always a conflict for me in wondering which way you get more time to live; whether, if you spend a lot of time controlling, that gives you more time and energy, or whether it just takes more time and energy and doesn't pay off. I've never been very clear about that; it's not a clear answer.

D.B.: The other thing that struck me about the article was the importance of continued information coming from consumers, from patients and their families, back to the health care professionals, about what living with diabetes is like. In a funny way the professionals are very well informed, but the partnership has to be in both directions, it can't just be the experts providing the information.

A.H.: Coming back to the simulation for a moment, I found something a little vague about the way it was structured. I was curious to know more about how it was done, and I guess I could conceive of people going through the simulation without getting as involved as the authors.

D.B.: They could be cooler and more distant; it wouldn't grab them as much.

A.H.: Yeah, since, as she points out, it is not the injections that are the problem, it's the thinking about the possibilities that's the problem and taking the time to try to figure them all out.

D.B.: You may be doing something really bad to yourself but you don't know what it is.

A.H.: Yes, I was thinking as I was having an insulin reaction early this morning how that's really at the heart of the problem of daily control for me. It doesn't enter into a simulation and I don't know how to simulate it. What I was thinking this morning—I had an insulin reaction, or it seemed to be one and I didn't know how much to eat, or whether to eat.

D.B.: By the way, that was three o'clock in the morning.

A.H.: Right, and then we talked a little about how that could be simulated by giving insulin to somebody who was not a diabetic. Yes, that would give them a reaction, but it seemed to me a normal person could then know they could eat as much as they wanted and they would be out of the reaction. Whereas for me, I know if I ate too much I would be out of the reaction and into a high blood sugar that would make me wake up feeling terrible. So it was riding the fine line for me between eating enough to avoid reactions, and not too much, so that I didn't have a high blood sugar. I can't think of a way to simulate that, but it seems to me that's the essence of daily control.

D.B.: In effect the thing that you do to correct for the insulin reaction can so easily overcorrect and lead you then into another set of problems.

A.H.: The way they say to solve it now, I gather, is to take a certain measured amount of sugar and wait 20 minutes and then, if you're still having a reaction, take a little more and wait 20 minutes. Well to wait 20 minutes in the middle of an active day is really a problem. Last night I wanted to get a night's sleep. It's really a problem to stay up and wait 20 minutes and check it out again. It's a very time-consuming procedure and you remember through all that time-consuming procedure there is a lot of anxiety.

D.B.: And it interrupts your sleep, and in this instance, the sleep of your partner. That brings up another piece of it: What part does family play in terms of making this better or worse? For example, last night, it occurred to me that after you analyzed your blood sugar situation, it was useful to reach an agreement together that you would take a small amount of carbohydrate and protein to provide some protection against a rebound. The diabetic, by himself or herself, needs some outside person to use as a sounding board.

A.H.: Particularly because in the middle of an insulin reaction, it's a very confusing state of mind and it's real hard to concentrate on exactly what the problem is or all the considerations. So I feel it's extremely helpful to have someone else come in and focus the problem in a way when your mind is confused in an insulin reaction.

D.B.: I feel as if we function somewhat as a computer system; that is, that we're accumulating information over time as to what works and what doesn't work.

A.H.: This computer fails all the time, Donald. I really have to disagree with you. We overshot last night; I woke up with a high blood sugar again.

D.B.: OK, so it's very hard to simulate.

A.H.: I can't figure out a way to do it. Yet, you know it would be interesting to have a person doing this who then would be told, "You're feeling like you're having an insulin reaction so go lie down for 20 minutes." I mean that would be very interesting to say to you in the middle of your medical practice, "go lie down for 20 minutes." And, for you, to feel what that would do for your day.

D.B.: I'd like that a lot.

A.H.: I'm sure your office would love that and your patients, it would really be terrific. But I mean, do it in the middle of a meeting when people have been waiting to see you for three weeks and have to wait while you lie down for 20 minutes and try to figure out if you're out of the reaction or not.

D.B.: I'd just tell them I'm taking a nap. OK, but that's not true. Joking aside, the point is that it's often unpredictable and very disruptive.

A.H.: One of the difficulties is that some diabetics, particularly people who aren't concerned about their weight, will eat a pile of cookies and then, I guess, if they need more insulin, just take it, whereas people who don't want to eat endlessly have other problems. All the adult women in a group I belong to had that problem, whereas the young males seemed to have less difficulty.

D.B.: I think what this phase of the discussion illustrates is the limitations of the simulation, but I must say, despite all, that I was very impressed.

A.H.: I don't want to undercut the simulation at all because I also was very impressed with it. I just felt it also ran far short of the problem of what it was really like to be a diabetic. The other piece of it I wanted to bring up was that I felt that while she felt it was too time-consuming, while she felt a lot of the problems, I also felt it was an interesting thing to do for 48 hours. I feel as a life-long problem, it is really boring.

D.B.: Let's end on that note because that seems such a powerful statement. Thanks.

A.H.: You're welcome.

REFERENCES

Allen, D. A., Tennen, H., McGrade, B. J., Affleck, G., & Ratzan, S. (1983). Parent and child perceptions of the management of juvenile diabetes. *Journal of Pediatric Psychology, 8,* 129–141.

Anderson, B. J. (1987). Directions for pediatric diabetes research and care. *Newsletter of the Society of Pediatric Psychology, 11*, 3–7.

Anderson, B. J., Miller, J. P., Auslander, W. F., & Santiago, J. V. (1981). Family characteristics of diabetic adolescents: Relationship to metabolic control. *Diabetes Care, 3*, 696–702.

Anderson, K. O., Bradley, L. A., Young, L. D., McDaniel, L. K., & Wise, C. M. (1985). Rheumatoid arthritis: Review of psychological factors related to etiology, effects, and treatment. *Psychological Bulletin, 98*, 358–387.

Baker, L., Minuchin, S, Liebman, R., & Todd, T. (1975). Psychosomatic aspects of juvenile diabetes mellitus: A progress report. *Modern Problems of Pediatrics, 12*, 332–343.

Baker, L., Rosman, B., & Minuchin, S. (1982). Diabetes management in context: The psychosomatic diabetic. In C. M. Peterson (Ed.), *Diabetes management in the '80s* (pp. 152–167). New York: Praeger.

Bank, S., & Kahn, M. D. (1982). Intense sibling loyalties. In M. E. Lamb & B. Sutton-Smith (Eds.), *Sibling relationships: Their nature and significance across the lifespan* (pp. 251–266). Hillsdale, NJ: Erlbaum.

Barbero, G. J. (1982). Leaving the pediatrician for the internist. *Annals of Internal Medicine, 96*, 673–674.

Barnett, A. H., Eff, C., Leslie, R., & Pyke, D. A. (1981). Diabetes in identical twins. *Diabetologia, 20*, 87–93.

Baum, V. C., Levitsky, L. L., & Englander, R. M. (1987). Abnormal cardiac function after exercise in insulin-dependent diabetic children and adolescents. *Diabetes Care, 10*, 319–323.

Bibace, R., & Walsh, M. E. (1979). Developmental stages in children's conceptions of illness. In G. C. Stone, F. Cohen, N. E. Adler, & Associates (Eds.), *Health psychology—a handbook: Theories, applications, and challenges of a psychological approach to the health care system* (pp. 285–301). San Francisco: Jossey-Bass.

Bibace, R., & Walsh, M. E. (1980). Development of children's concepts of illness. *Pediatrics, 66*, 912–917.

Brewster, A. B. (1982). Chronically ill hospitalized children's concepts of their illness. *Pediatrics, 69*, 355–362.

Bryant, B. K. (1982). Sibling relationships in middle childhood. In M. E. Lamb & B. Sutton-Smith (Eds.), *Sibling relationships: Their nature and significance across the lifespan* (pp. 87–122). Hillsdale, NJ: Erlbaum.

Campaigne, B. N., Gilliam, T. B., Spencer, J. L., Lampman, R. M., & Schork, M. A. (1984). Effects of a physical activity program on metabolic control and cardiovascular fitness in children with insulin-dependent diabetes mellitus. *Diabetes Care, 7*, 57–62.

Cederblad, M., Helgesson, M., Larsson, Y., & Ludvigsson, J., (1982). Family structure and diabetes in children. *Pediatric and adolescent endocrinology, 10*, 94–98.

Christensen, K. S. (1983). Self-management in diabetic children. *Diabetes Care, 6*, 552–555.

Clarke, W. L., Snyder, A. L., & Nowacek, G. (1985). Outpatient pediatric diabetes—I. Current practices. *Journal of Chronic Diseases, 38*, 85–90.

Cohen, S., & Wills, T. A. (1985). Stress, social support, and the buffering hypothesis. *Psychological Bulletin, 98*, 310–357.

Daniels, D., Dunn, J., Furstenberg, F. F., & Plomin, R. (1985). Environmental differences within the family and adjustment differences within pairs of adolescent siblings. *Child Development, 56*, 764–774.

Deaton, A. V. (1985). Adaptive noncompliance in pediatric asthma: The parent as expert. *Journal of Pediatric Psychology, 10*, 1–14.

Delamater, A. M., Bubb, J., Warren-Boulton, E., & Fisher, E. B., Jr. (1984). Diabetes management in the school setting: The role of the school psychologist. *School Psychology Review, 13*, 192–203.

DiMatteo, M. R., Hays, R. D., & Prince, L. M. (1986). Relationship of physicians' nonverbal communication skill to patient satisfaction, appointment noncompliance, and physician workload. *Health Psychology, 6*, 581–594.

Dorman, J. S., & LaPorte, R. E. (1985). Mortality in insulin-dependent diabetes. In *Diabetes in America* (pp. XXX 1–9). (NIH Publication No. 85-1468, August). Washington, DC: U.S. Government Printing Office.

Dunn, S. M., & Turtle, J. R. (1981). The myth of the diabetic personality. *Diabetes Care, 4*, 640–646.

Felig, P. (1982). Exercise and diabetes. In C. M. Peterson (Ed.), *Diabetes management in the '80s* (pp. 118–124). New York: Praeger.

Flavell, J. H. (1977). *Cognitive development*. Englewood Cliffs, NJ: Prentice-Hall.

Garmezy, N. (1981). Children under stress: Perspectives on antecedents and correlates of vulnerability and resistance to psychopathology. In A. I. Rabin, J. Aronoff, A. M. Barclay, & R. A. Zucker (Eds.), *Further explorations in personality* (pp. 196–269). New York: Wiley.

Garmezy, N. (1983). Stressors of childhood. In N. Garmezy & M. Rutter (Eds.), *Stress, coping, and development in children* (pp. 43–83). New York: McGraw-Hill.

Goldstein, D. E., Little, R. R., Wiedmeyer, H. M., England, J. D., & McKenzie, E. M. (1986). Glycated hemoglobin: Methodologies and clinical applications. *Clinical Chemistry, 32*, 64–70.

Hamburg, B. A., & Inoff, B. A. (1983). Coping with predictable crises of diabetes. *Diabetes Care, 6*, 409–416.

Hanson, C. L., Cigrang, J. A., Harris, M. A., Carle, D. L., Relyea, G. & Burghen, G. A. (in press). Coping styles in youths with insulin-dependent diabetes mellitus. *Journal of Consulting and Clinical Psychology*.

Hanson, C. L., & Henggeler, S. W. (1984). Metabolic control in adolescents with diabetes: An examination of systemic variables. *Family Systems Medicine, 2*, 5–16.

Hanson, C. L., Henggeler, S. W., & Burghen, G. A. (1987a). Race and sex differences in metabolic control of adolescents with IDDM: A function of psychosocial variables? *Diabetes Care, 10*, 313–318.

Hanson, C. L., Henggeler, S. W., & Burghen, G. A. (1987b). Social competence and parental support as mediators of the link between stress and metabolic control in adolescents with insulin-dependent diabetes mellitus. *Journal of Consulting and Clinical Psychology, 55*, 529–533.

Hanson, C. L., Henggeler, S. W., & Burghen, G. A. (1987c). A model of the associations between psychosocial variables and health outcome measures of adolescents with IDDM. *Diabetes Care, 10*, 752–758.

Hanson, C. L., Henggeler, S. W., Harris, M. A., Burghen, G. A., & Moore, M. (1989). Family system variables and the health status of adolescents with insulin-dependent diabetes mellitus. *Health Psychology, 8*, 239–253.

Hanson, C. L., Henggeler, S. W., Harris, M. A., Mitchell, K. A., Carle, D. L., & Burghen, G. A. (1988). Associations between family members' perceptions of the health care system and the health of youths with insulin-dependent diabetes mellitus. *Journal of Pediatric Psychology, 13*, 543–554.

Hanson, C. L., Henggeler, S. W., Rodrigue, J. R., Burghen, G. A., & Murphy, W. D. (1988). Father-absent adolescents with insulin-dependent diabetes mellitus: A population at risk? *Journal of Applied Developmental Psychology, 9*, 243–252.

Hanson, C. L., & Onikul-Ross, S. R. (in press). Developmental issues in the lives of youths with insulin-dependent diabetes mellitus. In S. B. Morgan & T. M. Okwumabua (Eds.), *Child and adolescent disorders: Developmental and health psychology perspectives*. Hillsdale, NJ: Erlbaum.

Harkavy, J., Johnson, S. B., Silverstein, J., Spillar, R., McCallum, M., & Rosenbloom, A. (1983). Who learns what at diabetes camp. *Journal of Pediatric Psychology, 8*, 143–153.

Harris, M. I. (1985). Classification and diagnostic criteria for diabetes and other categories of glucose intolerance. In *Diabetes in America* (pp. II 1–10). (NIH Publication No. 85-1468, August). Washington, DC: U.S. Government Printing Office.

Harter, S. (1983). Developmental perspectives on the self-system. In E. M. Hetherington (Ed.), *Handbook of child psychology: Vol. 4. Socialization, personality, and social development* (pp. 275–385). New York: Wiley.

Heckler, M. M. (1985). *Report of the secretary's task force on Black and minority health, 1985. Executive summary. Vol. 1.* Washington, DC: U.S. Government Printing Office.

Herman, W. H., & Teutsch, S. M. (1985). Kidney diseases associated with diabetes. In *Diabetes in America* (pp. XIV 1–31). (NIH Publication No. 85-1468, August). Washington, DC: U.S. Government Printing Office.

Heyman, A., & Bloch, D. (1984). Comment: A diabetic views the simulation. *Family Systems Medicine, 2*, 416–419.

Holbeck, L. (1987, November 2). Diabetic is jailed after becoming ill. *The Commercial Appeal*, pp. B1–2.

Horan, M. J. (1985). Diabetes and hypertension. In *Diabetes in America* (pp. XVII 1–22). (NIH Publication No. 85-1468, August). Washington, DC: U.S. Government Printing Office.

House, W. E., Pendleton, L., & Parker, L. (1986). Patients' versus physicians' attributions of reasons for diabetic patients' noncompliance with diet. *Diabetes Care, 9*, 434.

Jackson, R. L. (1984). Growth and maturation of children with insulin-dependent diabetes mellitus. *Pediatric Clinics of North America, 31*, 545–567.

Jacobson, A. M., Hauser, S. T., Powers, S., & Noam, G. (1984). The influences of chronic illness and ego development on self-esteem in diabetic and psychiatric adolescent patients. *Journal of Youth and Adolescence, 13*, 489–507.

Jacobson, A. M., Hauser, S. T., Wertlieb, D., Wolfsdorf, J. I., Orleans, J., & Vieyra, M. (1986). Psychological adjustment of children with recently diagnosed diabetes mellitus. *Diabetes Care, 9*, 323–329.

Johnson, S. B., Pollak, R. T., Silverstein, J. H., Rosenbloom, A. L., Spillar, R., McCallum, M., & Harkavy, J. (1982). Cognitive and behavioral knowledge about insulin-dependent diabetes among children and parents. *Pediatrics, 69*, 708–713.

Johnson, S. B., Silverstein, J., Rosenbloom, A., Carter, R., & Cunningham, W. (1986). Assessing daily management in childhood diabetes. *Health Psychology, 5*, 545–564.

Johnson, S. G. (1987). Childhood diabetes: The role of the pediatric psychologist. *Newsletter of the Society of Pediatric Psychology, 11*, 7–12.

Kaplan, R. M., Chadwick, M. W., & Schimmel, L. E. (1985). Social learning intervention to promote metabolic control in type I diabetes mellitus: Pilot experiment results. *Diabetes Care, 8*, 152–155.

Kellerman, J., Zeltzer, L., Ellenberg, L., Dash, J., & Rigler, D. (1980). Psychological effects of illness in adolescence. I. Anxiety, self-esteem, and perception of control. *Journal of Pediatrics, 97*, 126–131.

Kirscht, J. P., & Rosenstock, I. M. (1979). Patients' problems in following recommendations of health experts. In G. C. Stone, F. Cohen, N. E. Adler, & Associates (Eds.), *Health psychology—a handbook: Theories, applications, and challenges of a psychological approach to the health care system* (pp. 189–215). San Francisco: Jossey-Bass.

Klein, R., & Klein, B. E. K. (1985). Vision disorders in diabetes. In *Diabetes in America* (pp. XIII 1–36). (NIH Publication No. 85-1468, August). Washington, DC: U.S. Government Printing Office.

Klemp, S. B., & LaGreca, A. M. (1987). Adolescents with IDDM: The role of family cohesion and conflict [Abstract]. *Diabetes, 36,* 18A.

Kohler, E., Hurwitz, L. S., & Milan, D. (1982). A developmentally staged curriculum for teaching self-care to the child with insulin-dependent diabetes mellitus. *Diabetes Care, 5,* 300–304.

Kovacs, M., Brent, D., Steinberg, T. F., Paulauskas, S., & Reid, J. (1986). Children's self-reports of psychologic adjustment and coping strategies during first year of insulin-dependent diabetes mellitus. *Diabetes Care, 9,* 472–479.

Kovacs, M., Feinberg, T. L., Paulauskas, S., Finkelstein, R., Pollock, M., & Crouse-Novak, M. (1985). Initial coping responses and psychosocial characteristics of children with insulin-dependent diabetes mellitus. *Journal of Pediatrics, 106,* 827–834.

Kovacs, M., Finkelstein, R., Feinberg, T. L., Crouse-Novak, M., Paulauskas, S., & Pollock, M. (1985). Initial psychologic responses of parents to the diagnosis of insulin-dependent diabetes mellitus in their children. *Diabetes Care, 8,* 568–575.

LaGreca, A. M. (1987). Children with diabetes and their families: Coping and disease management. In T. Field, P. McCabe, and N. Schneiderman (Eds.), *Stress and coping across development* (Vol. 2., pp. 139–159). Hillsdale, NJ: Erlbaum.

LaGreca, A. M., Schwarz, L. T., & Satin, W. (1987). Eating patterns in young women with IDDM: Another look. *Diabetes Care, 10,* 659–660.

Landt, K. W., Campaigne, B. N., James, F. W., & Sperling, M. A. (1985). Effects of exercise training on insulin sensitivity in adolescents with type 1 diabetes. *Diabetes Care, 8,* 461–465.

LaPorte, R. E., & Cruickshanks, K. J. (1985). Incidence and risk factors for noninsulin-dependent diabetes. In *Diabetes in America* (pp. III 1–12). (NIH Publication No. 85-1468, August). Washington, DC: U.S. Government Printing Office.

LaPorte, R. E., & Tajima, N. (1985). Prevalence of noninsulin-dependent diabetes. In *Diabetes in America* (pp. V 1–8). (NIH Publication No. 85-1468, August). Washington, DC: U.S. Government Printing Office.

Lorenz, R. A., Christensen, N. K., & Pichert, J. W. (1985). Diet-related knowledge, skill, and adherence among children with insulin-dependent diabetes mellitus. *Pediatrics, 75,* 872–876.

Maccoby, E. E., & Martin, J. A. (1983). Socialization in the context of the family: Parent-child interaction. In P. H. Mussen (Ed.), E. M. Hetherington (Vol. Ed.), *Handbook of child psychology: Vol. 4. Socialization, personality, and social development* (pp. 1–101). New York: Wiley.

Minuchin, S., Baker, L., Rosman, B. L., Liebman, R., Milman, L., & Todd. T. C. (1975). A conceptual model of psychosomatic illness in children. *Archives of General Psychiatry, 32,* 1031–1038.

Minuchin, S., Rosman, B. L., & Baker, L. (1978). *Psychosomatic families.* Cambridge, MA: Harvard University Press.

National Diabetes Data Group (1985). *Diabetes in America.* (NIH Publication No. 85-1468, August). Washington, DC: U.S. Government Printing Office.

Potter, P. C., & Roberts, M. C. (1984). Children's perceptions of chronic illness: The roles of disease symptoms, cognitive development, and information. *Journal of Pediatric Psychology, 9,* 13–27.

Redpath, C. C., & Rogers, C. S. (1984). Healthy young children's concepts of hospitals, medical personnel, operations, and illness. *Journal of Pediatric Psychology, 9,* 29–39.

Roseman, J. M. (1985). Diabetes in black Americans. In *Diabetes in America* (pp. VIII 1–24). (NIH Publication No. 85-1468, August). Washington, DC: U.S. Government Printing Office.

Scarr, S., & Grajek, S. (1982). Similarities and differences among siblings. In M. E. Lamb & B. Sutton-Smith (Eds.), *Sibling relationships: Their nature and significance across the lifespan* (pp. 358–382). Hillsdale, NJ: Erlbaum.

Seligman, M. (1983). *The family with a handicapped child: Understanding and treatment.* Orlando, FL: Grune-Stratton.

Seligman, M. (1987). Adaptation of children to a chronically ill or mentally handicapped sibling. *Canadian Medical Association Journal, 136,* 1249–1252.

Service, F. J., O'Brien, P. C., & Rizza, R. A. (1987). Measurements of glucose control. *Diabetes Care, 10,* 225–237.

Simonds, J. F. (1977). Psychiatric status of diabetic youth matched with a control group. *Diabetes, 26,* 921–925.

Skyler, J. S. (1979). Diabetes and exercise: Clinical implications. *Diabetes Care, 2,* 307–311.

Stein, R., Goldberg, N., Kalman, F., & Chesler, R. (1984). Exercise and the patient with type 1 diabetes mellitus. *Pediatric Clinics of North America, 31,* 665–673.

Tavormina, J. B., Kastner, L. S., Slater, P. M., & Watt, S. L. (1976). Chronically ill children. A psychologically and emotionally deviant population? *Journal of Abnormal Child Psychology, 4,* 99–110.

Taylor, S. E. (1986). Patient-practitioner interaction. In S. E. Taylor (Ed.), *Health psychology* (pp. 240–263). New York: Random House.

VanderPlate, C. (1984). Psychological aspects of multiple sclerosis and its treatment: Toward a biopsychosocial perspective. *Health Psychology, 3,* 253–272.

Walker, D. K. (1984). Care of chronically ill children in schools. *Pediatric Clinics of North America, 31,* 221–233.

Warren-Boulton, E., Auslander, W. F., & Gettinger, J. M. (1982). Understanding diabetes routines: A professional training exercise. *Diabetes Care, 5,* 537–541.

Weitzman, M. (1984). School and peer relations. *Pediatric Clinics of North America, 31,* 59–69.

Welborn, T. A., & Duncan, N. (1980). Diabetic staff simulation of insulin-dependent diabetic life. *Diabetes Care, 3,* 679–681.

Williamson, P. R., & McCauley, E. (1984). On being a diabetic patient: A simulated experience. *Family Systems Medicine, 2,* 409–415.

Wing, R. R., Koeske, R., New, A., Lamparski, D., & Becker, D. (1986). Behavioral skills in self-monitoring of blood glucose: Relationship to accuracy. *Diabetes Care, 9,* 330–333.

Wing, R. R., Nowalk, M. P., Marcus, M. D., Koeske, R., & Finegold, D. (1986). Subclinical eating disorders and glycemic control in adolescents with Type I diabetes. *Diabetes Care, 9,* 162–167.

Zeltzer, L., Kellerman, J., Ellenberg, L., Dash, J., & Rigler, D. (1980). Psychologic effects of illness in adolescence. II. Impact of illness in adolescents—crucial issues and coping styles. *Journal of Pediatrics, 97,* 132–138.

CHAPTER 11

Interventions with Incestuous Families

Pamela C. Alexander

*T*he effects of father-daughter incest are long-term, pervasive and severe. Incest victims are at risk for the development of poor self-concepts, loneliness, depression, and for subsequent victimization and interpersonal problems with both men and women (Alexander & Lupfer, 1987; Browne & Finkelhor, 1986; Herman, 1981; Meiselman, 1978). Moreover, the long-term effects of incest are reflective of the problems of trust, lack of empathy, cognitive distortions, denial, rigidity, and isolation that are characteristic of the incestuous family.

A wide range of intervention programs have been developed to deal with the serious problems presented by incest. Most of these programs are consistent with one of two very different treatment philosophies—the victim-perpetrator model or the family systems model (Alexander, 1985). The victim-perpetrator model focuses on the adult who aggresses against innocent children as a result of his pathology or deviant sexual attraction to them. The family systems model views incest as the product of a dysfunctional family system in which all family members are both victims and perpetrators.

As Trepper and Barrett (1986) have pointed out, although both the victim-perpetrator and family systems models are widely used by mental health professionals, each holds certain limitations. For example, the victim-perpetrator model is quite simplistic and allows a therapist to distance himself/herself from the sick or deviant perpetrator in treatment. Although the victim-perpetrator model is often considered a "victim advocacy" approach, this model can preclude empathy with and support of victims, such as daughters, who are emotionally attached to the perpetrator. On the other hand, the family systems model frequently fails to evaluate important individual characteristics of the perpetrator, including his history of sexual contacts with children outside the home.

Neither of these models has fully acknowledged the extreme complexity of incest by thoroughly assessing the individuals involved, the family subsystems, the family system, and the family's relations with extrafamilial systems. Consequently, treatment interventions arising from both models have been narrow in focus. Further, neither model has emphasized the fact that, aside from the complexity of the systems implicated by the incestuous behavior, the incest act itself is not a homogeneous behavior pattern. Depending on the perpetrator and the family environment, incestuous behavior may vary from a misguided attempt at affection, to inappropriate eroticism, to sexualized anger and aggression, to a psychotic expression of rage (Larson & Maddock, 1986). Moreover, because each model tends to frame incest as a behavior consistent with the philosophical tenets of that model, variations on the behavior are ignored or misinterpreted.

Incest, therefore, must be evaluated within a theoretical framework that assumes a diversity of etiologies, and that allows treatment to be tailored to the specific needs of the child, the perpetrator, and the family. It is argued that a multisystemic approach provides the degree of flexibility and comprehensiveness that are needed to deal with this very serious problem.

This chapter presents a systemic approach to the conceptualization and treatment of incest (Alexander, 1985). Common characteristics of incestuous families are described with consideration of the different components potentially contributing to and certainly affected by the incest—the individuals, the family subsystems, the family system, and the extrafamilial systems. A discussion of treatment objectives emphasizes how aspects of individuals and systems not only contribute to the occurrence of the incest, but are themselves maintained by the incest through the effects of secrecy and role reversal. Therefore, treatment objectives must not only focus on stopping the incest and encouraging the adult to acknowledge his responsibility, but also on preventing its recurrence in existing and future generations. Finally, assessment and treatment intervention strategies are presented in a way that reflects the importance of the individuals and the interactions within the family subsystems, family system, and extrafamilial systems. Case examples are presented throughout the chapter to illustrate the diversity of personalities, dynamics, and environmental conditions that may confront the therapist.

For several reasons this chapter focuses on father-daughter incest rather than sexual abuse per se. First, although extrafamilial abuse is common in chaotic incestuous families in which children are not protected, not all extrafamilial abuse is indicative of family dysfunction. Second, although it is not uncommon for sons to follow the example set by their fathers and to sexually abuse their younger sisters, sibling incest can also occur in families in which father-daughter incest has not been modeled. Such families are certainly dysfunctional; nevertheless, they are quite distinct from the father-daughter incestuous household (Smith & Israel, 1987). Finally, fathers are more likely to be perpetrators than are mothers, and daughters are more likely to be abused than are sons. However, father-son, mother-son, and mother-daughter incest does occur. Further, mother's boyfriend, a grandfather, or an uncle may interact with the victim in a manner that is functionally similar to that of a father. Therefore, examples of parent-child incest other than between fathers and daughters are also included. Most of the assessment and treatment considerations apply to all types of parent-child incest.

CHARACTERISTICS OF INCESTUOUS FAMILIES

Incestuous families typically display a wide variation in their behaviors. Characteristics of individual family members (the father/perpetrator, the child, and the mother/nonabusing parent) are presented first. Discussed next are the common structural characteristics in the incestuous family, as evidenced in the family subsystems and the family's interactions with extrafamilial systems.

Individual Characteristics

The abuser.   Incest offenders do not differ from the general population with respect to any major demographic characteristics. They are comparable in age, race, intelligence, level of education, socioeconomic status, and mental status (Groth, 1982). The one noticeable manner in which they do differ is in their sexual abuse of children in response to stress. According to Groth, incest perpetrators can be divided into two types on the basis of their primary sexual orientation. Fixated offenders have a primary or exclusive sexual orientation to children. Their sexual behavior is compulsive and marked by a persistent interest in children. Although they may marry (and thus may constitute a small portion of fathers who abuse their daughters), these marriages either result from social pressures or are motivated by attempts to gain easier access to stepchildren. Regressed offenders, on the other hand, display a primary sexual orientation to agemates, but may turn to children as a result of conflict in adult relationships and a variety of precipitating stresses. The regressed offender thus replaces his conflictual adult relationship with a sexual relationship with a child. Although his lifestyle is more conventional than that of the fixated offender, relationships with peers are usually underdeveloped.

The psychological motivations of the incest perpetrator are varied and include validation of self-esteem; compensation for feeling rejected by the spouse; a restored sense of power and control; gratification of a need for attention, recognition, or affiliation; and a strengthening of his sense of identity (Groth, 1982). Finkelhor (1984) referred to these motivations as emotional congruence between the adult's emotional needs and the child's characteristics. Like Groth, he also noted the importance of sexual arousal to children and a blockage in the adult's ability to achieve normal gratification in peer relationships.

However, Finkelhor (1984) also noted that the motivation to initiate sexual contact with one's daughter does not in and of itself differentiate men who abuse from those who do not. For most men, even those who are emotionally immature and sexually frustrated, a number of factors (ranging from empathy for their children to a fear of getting caught) preclude them from acting on any sexual fantasies toward their children. It seems that a common characteristic of abusive fathers is a temporary or long-term deficit in internal inhibition.

The internal inhibition of incestuous desires can be circumvented through a variety of serious emotional or characterological difficulties. Although the prevalence of psychosis is low, the contribution of alcohol abuse is well supported (Finkelhor, 1984). Further, a patriarchal belief that a man's home is his castle and that his wife and children are ultimately his property could attenuate concerns about whether outsiders would approve or whether there would be any ill-effects on his family. In addition, a perpetrator's ability to empathize might be so primitive or nonexistent that he may be able to justify the abuse as protection of his daughter and as a benevolent initiation into the facts of life. Finally, his ability to empathize with his daughter might be severely diminished because of a lack of bonding with her. For example, she may not be his natural child; there may have been long absences on his part; or his adherence to a patriarchal belief system may have precluded his involvement in childcare or in interaction with his children when they were young.

Hence, according to Finkelhor (1984), sexual abuse occurs only when all four factors—emotional congruence, sexual arousal to children, blockage of other sources of gratification, and a reduction of internal inhibitions—are present.

The child.   Very little is known as to why certain children within a family are chosen as targets of abuse while others are not. However, several factors have been identified that seem to predict involvement in an abusive relationship (given a perpetrator's motivation to sexually abuse, his overcoming of internal inhibitors, and inadequate maternal protection). These factors include a young age; naiveté or lack of knowledge regarding sexuality; a special relationship with the abuser such as being his daughter or even his favored daughter; the use of force by the father; and environmental or emotional circumstances that promote the child's feelings of insecurity and emotional need (Finkelhor, 1984).

At times, certain personality characteristics of the daughter may interact with the emotional demands of the rest of the family so that it is difficult to determine whether the daughter was selected to fulfill her role because of her preexisting personality characteristics, or whether she developed those personality characteristics as a result of having to meet the emotional needs of her family. An example of this is the oft-noted "pseudomaturity" observed in abused daughters. On one hand, pseudomaturity may result from being initiated so early and so inappropriately into the adult world of sexual relations. On the other hand, the daughter's sensitivity to the emotional needs of her parents may have helped to make her initially more vulnerable to the abuse. In either case, a role reversal with her parents results, and she is relied upon for emotional nurturing and decision making, as well as for meeting the sexual needs of the father. Her feelings of responsibility for her family's well-being may also make it difficult for her to disclose the abuse and thus to risk the breakup of the family unit. Further, some children are actually given special privileges as a function of their sexual involvement. These special privileges may be either an initial factor in the selection of the target or may serve merely to promote the continuance of the abuse.

The nonabusing parent.   The incest victim's mother has frequently been described as a weak and submissive woman who is emotionally distant from her family and incompetent as an adult woman. Feminist therapists have been understandably offended by such characterizations. However, for whatever reason, sexual abuse of children does seem to be associated with inadequate maternal protection (Finkelhor, 1979). The absence or incapacitation of the mother or stepmother may be due to death, sickness, long work hours, or shift work. The mother may be emotionally absent and withdrawn because of her own depression or her own experience of abuse and intimidation by her husband. If she is socially isolated from other people (a frequent occurrence in a strong patriarchal household), she may lack the social and economic resources necessary to defend herself and her children. If she was sexually abused as a child, she may never have had an adequate role model for how to be a nurturing parent. Finally, she may view the breakup of her marriage as so unacceptable that she would rather dismiss any suspicions or disclosures of abuse than risk the consequences to her marriage of actually acknowledging the abuse. In any case, long-term sexual abuse is indicative of the inability of the mother to provide protection.

Whether the mother's inaccessibility is clear or only inferred, it is important to remember that many incest victims perceive their mothers as either absent or unable to handle a disclosure of abuse even if the victims have never attempted to tell their mothers about the ongoing abuse (Alexander & Follette, 1987). Further, it is important to emphasize that many women act immediately upon discovery of the abuse and assure the child's continuing safety. The fact that the children of these mothers are much less likely to experience long-term effects of the abuse demonstrates the critical role that mothers play in incestuous families.

Family Structure

Interactional patterns within a family can be described in terms of structural variables including boundaries and hierarchies. Boundaries refer to the rules of participation in any interaction (i.e., who interacts with whom under what conditions). For example, in a normal family, the rules characterizing parents' interactions are different from those characterizing the interactions of parents with children or of siblings with each other. Hierarchies refer to the rules of power. This concept implies a differentiation of roles for parents and children as well as boundaries between generations (Simon, Stierlin & Wynne, 1985). According to Sluzki (1983), boundaries and hierarchies can be evaluated as to whether they are clear or unclear, predictable or variable, adaptive (to meet the specific needs of the situation) or rigid, appropriate for the developmental stage of the participants, and balanced or skewed in terms of the distribution of power between the parents. Although families, including incestuous families, vary greatly along all these dimensions, the family interactions and the meanings associated with the interactions can be better understood if the therapist conceptualizes these processes within the context of the family structure.

The endogamous or functionally incestuous family is a very common family structure associated with father-daughter incest. This structure is characterized by a lack of respect for individual boundaries, blurred subsystem boundaries, a tight external boundary, and an extreme imbalance of power between the parents. It should be emphasized that the incestuous behavior serves to reinforce and maintain the underlying structure. Moreover, incest is only one of a series of problematic interactions that can result from the endogamous family structure.

Individual boundaries.   A lack of respect for individual boundaries (i.e., differentiation or separateness) is readily apparent in the father's physical and sexual intrusiveness with his daughter. However, this lack of respect for individual boundaries can also be observed for other family members in more mundane areas such as physical privacy and private ownership. The Brown family, for example, was referred for treatment after it had been discovered that two of the four daughters had been sexually abused by their father for several years. Although both parents were employed and maintained a stable income, the four girls shared two twin beds. The three older girls shared one bra. The entire family shared one toothbrush. The lack of differentiation and separateness also extended to roles and developmental stages. Mrs. Brown reported that she had married her husband when she was 13 years old and he was 25. Consequently, he still regarded her as "one of the kids." Although the girls ranged in age from 11 to 19, the 11-year-old had as much power and decision-making authority as her older sisters. Thus, the behavior of incest in this family was consistent with the lack of respect for physical and emotional boundaries experienced by all family members.

Subsystem boundaries.   Again, the blurring of subsystem boundaries is readily apparent in the act of father-daughter incest. The sexual act, however, is only one example of the myriad of ways in which generational boundaries are crossed. Even in those instances when incest perpetrators *do* experience sexual arousal to children, and empirical evidence is inconclusive as to whether they generally do (Abel, Becker, Murphy & Flanagan, 1981; Marshall, Barbaree & Christophe, 1986; Murphy, Haynes, Stalgaitis & Flanagan, 1986; Quinsey, Chaplin & Carrigan, 1979), the pertinent emotions are just as likely to be affection, dependency, anger, or even rage as sexual arousal per se (W. Murphy, personal communication, March 15, 1988). In other words, the role reversal between parents and children characterizing the majority of incestuous families (Conte, 1985) is revealed in the parents' emotional expectations of their children. The daughter is used by the father to meet the emotional needs of intimacy, dominance, and reassurance that he is not able to satisfy in relationships with his wife and other adults. The mother also frequently relies on her daughter for nurturance, advice, and support.

As the following example illustrates, this parent-child role reversal sets the stage for inappropriate sexual behavior between children and adults. Mrs. Johnson had been repeatedly sexually abused as a child by her stepfather, her uncle, and several older cousins. She had received extensive treatment to deal with the effects of this abuse and was determined that her 7-year-old daughter would not be exposed to a similar experience. However, the structural characteristics of the mother-daughter relationship had not been addressed in treatment and showed no indication of spontaneous change. For example, while Mrs. Johnson participated in individual therapy, her daughter demanded that the door between the therapy room and the waiting room remain open so that she could hear the interchange between her mother and the therapist. This request mirrored the living situation at home. Doors in the house were never closed, and the family's meeting room—the parents' bedroom—always remained accessible to the children. Mrs. Johnson, who was rather petite in stature, shared all clothes and possessions with her daughter and interacted with her daughter more as a peer than as a mother. Therefore, in spite of the extensive individual psychotherapy that Mrs. Johnson received, the norms of the household and the lack of generational boundaries kept her daughter at risk for an eventual sexual violation of boundaries.

The blurring of subsystem boundaries is also associated with a lack of cohesion within subsystems, as evidenced both by empirical (Alexander & Lupfer, 1987) and clinical descriptions of incestuous families. One example is the extreme conflict and lack of emotional intimacy that almost always characterizes the marital subsystem in an incestuous family (Edwards & Alexander, 1989). However, the lack of cohesion can also be detected in the sibling subsystems. Although low sibling cohesion may result in part from the secrecy and rivalry of one sibling being selected for a special relationship with the father, low cohesion can also contribute to the maintenance of the incest. Mary, for example, reported that she had shared a room with her sister during adolescence. Although their stepfather made a habit of slipping into their room in the early morning hours and fondling either Mary or her sister, the sisters had never discussed the matter. Because of their lack of closeness, the sisters were not able to join together to stop the abuse through either confrontation of their father or disclosure to their mother. In this way, the lack of cohesion within the sibling subsystem both resulted from and contributed to the abuse.

      Power imbalance.   Another structural problem commonly found in the function-ally incestuous family is an extreme power imbalance between the parents. To use Sluzki's (1983) terminology, the family structure is "skewed." This power imbalance is usually consistent with a patriarchal/authoritarian structure in which the division of labor follows traditional sex-role stereotypes. Empirical evidence for the presence of rigid and patriarchal values within the incestuous family is ample (Alexander & Follette, 1987; Harter, Alexander & Neimeyer, 1988). Clinical impressions also suggest that the father typically uses his power capriciously, and the mother believes that the marriage must be preserved and that her duty is to serve and passively endure (Herman, 1981). It is possible, however, for the power imbalance to be reversed (i.e., matriarchal). In such cases, the father's exploitation of his children may be viewed as an expression of hostility against his domineering wife (James & Nasjleti, 1983). In either direction of power imbalance, it may be more useful to view the problem in terms of a boundary imbalance. That is, if either the mother or the father is of clearly lower status, then she/he cannot participate in a well-defined parental subsystem and marital subsystem.

The Family-Community Mesosystem

Endogamous incestuous families are also characterized by boundary problems at the interface of the family system with its environment. Whether due to physical or social isolation, incestuous families tend to have few contacts with people outside of the immediate family. The Mason family, for example, had been reported to the department of human services several times for allegations of sexual abuse. The children were not allowed to have friends outside the home and tended to be ostracized at school because of the bad reputation associated with their family name. The family was habitually in such intense conflict with community authorities (school, police, welfare) that these authorities were intimidated by the Masons. On one occasion, for example, the police had actually failed to investigate the shooting death of an extended family member. Similarly, the department of human services was more than willing to quickly drop their investigation when the children reneged on their claims of abuse. With such a tight external boundary, the children had little opportunity to realize that family behavior norms were deviant. In addition, the tight boundary made it highly unlikely that behavior within the family could be monitored from the outside. Further, even if Mrs. Mason had decided to leave her abusive husband and protect her children and herself, she was effectively cut off from the social support that would have facilitated this move.

      In other incestuous families, secrecy and isolation are maintained through a facade of role competence. For example, when Linda Smith reported to juvenile court that her stepfather had been sexually abusing her for several years, the judge dismissed her claim because Mr. Smith was a widely respected citizen in the community.

As also noted for individual boundaries and subsystem boundaries of the functionally incestuous family, incestuous behavior both results from and contributes to the impermeability of the external boundary and, thus, the isolation of the family. On one hand, the daughter may be kept at home for her father's convenience and thus be cut off from peers. On the other hand, the abuse itself frequently causes girls to feel very different from peers and disrupts their ability to relate to peers who do not live in abusive families. In other cases, because of the family's negative reputation, other parents may not allow their children to associate with children from the abusive home. Therefore, the social isolation so typically experienced by the abused daughter has the double effect of precluding normal social interactions with peers and of allowing the abuse to continue because of a lack of monitoring from the outside.

TREATMENT

The discussion of treatment strategies for incestuous families is divided into four sections. First, an overview of treatment goals and objectives is provided. Second, assessment and intervention strategies that may be used for the individual family members are described. Third and fourth, interventions with family subsystems and with the family-community mesosystem are presented.

Treatment Goals and Objectives

In contrast to the major goal of many family therapy approaches, therapeutic success with incestuous families does not require that the family remain united. It is recognized that the level of pathology of some individuals is so great, the potential for emotional bonding of some family systems is so minimal, and the impact of disclosure on some families is so stressful, that it may not be in the best interests of family members to remain together. If the family does remain united, many therapeutic objectives will pertain to the protection of the child and the restructuring of the family system. However, even if the father is permanently removed from the family, there will remain important therapeutic tasks that pertain to the dysfunctional family norms and structures as well as to the attitudes and cognitive sets of individual family members. Irrespective of the father's presence in the family, these dysfunctional individual and family processes can be transmitted through different generations and across different partners.

Because the behavior of incest is only one component of the circular processes that characterize the structure of the family, treatment must focus simultaneously on two goals: (1) the incestuous interactions must be stopped and prevented from recurring, and (2) the structural characteristics that preceded and followed the incest behavior must be altered.

Three specific objectives are associated with the goal of stopping the incest and preventing its recurrence:

1. *The child must be protected.* Such protection might require the temporary removal of the perpetrator from the home. However, it is important to remember that separation

of a perpetrator and victim does not assure that the child is protected from emotional abuse, blame, or ostracism that frequently accompany the disclosure of incest and the resulting crisis in the family. Nevertheless, the therapist must define the active protection of the child as the major priority of the family.

2. *The secrecy that surrounds the problem must be eliminated.* Incest is absolutely dependent on an atmosphere of secrecy that usually exists within the family and certainly exists in the family's relations with the environment. This secrecy not only assures the maintenance of the abuse, but is also responsible for many of the severe long-term effects of the abuse—social isolation from one's peers, the development of communication and emotional barriers between the child and the rest of the family, and, finally, the pervasive cognitive distortion and denial that occur when the child experiences an overt sexual act that is either denied or labeled as something distinctly different. Therefore, since secrecy is the *sine qua non* for the incest, the prevention of any future incestuous behavior requires the elimination of secrecy.

3. *The perpetrator and perhaps the nonoffending spouse must be encouraged to accept responsibility.* Family members must learn that one of the parents' primary responsibilities is the protection of their children from harm and exploitation. Moreover, the victim should learn that she was not responsible for her father's exploitation nor for the family crisis that resulted from her disclosure.

Although this delineation of responsibility seems evident to an outside observer, the sexually abused child has typically grown up in a family in which children are considered to be more responsible for their parents than vice versa. Therefore, one of the most significant long-term effects of incest on the victim is a feeling of overwhelming guilt for the abuse to have occurred in the first place. Such guilt is especially common when the father has communicated that he was seduced by his daughter and when he extracted a pledge of secrecy from her. In such cases, the victim essentially becomes defined as a co-conspirator. By placing the adults in the position of responsibility, the therapist not only absolves the incest victim of the guilt of her own involvement but also provides a clear model of how she is to later assume an adult's responsibility when raising her own children.

The second important set of objectives in working with the incestuous family involves a restructuring of the family system. As described previously, the family structure is not only maintained by the incest behavior but also seems to have preceded it. Further, because the family structure often bears no overt resemblance to the behavior of incest, it is frequently ignored by therapists. However, if the structure is not altered sufficiently, other incestuous interactions are likely to emerge in the family and in succeeding generations. The mitigation of long-term effects also requires a change in this structure.

Much of the process of therapy involves the restructuring of the family system.

1. Physical boundaries need to be established both physically and emotionally. These boundaries can be enhanced by the development of respect for personal space and personal property, and through greater role differentiation on the basis of age and competence.

2. Appropriate boundaries need to be established for the parental, marital, and sibling subsystems.

3. External boundaries must be altered to allow increased extrafamilial monitoring and social support.

Assessment and Intervention with Individual Family Members

As noted previously, the therapist's first consideration should be the immediate protection of the child from further abuse. Such protection often requires the temporary separation of the perpetrator and the victim as mandated by the legal system. It might also be necessary to have the court order treatment for the family. Although many families seek treatment voluntarily, others may be so accustomed to the use of denial and so threatened by any change in the status quo that they minimize or even question the occurrence of the abuse. In cases where the nonoffending parent resists the separation, the therapist should explain that the primary purposes of the separation are to allow the child time to develop trust in the parent's ability to protect her, and to protect the father from the temptation to engage in similar behavior before treatment progresses.

The second step in the treatment of the incestuous family is a multidimensional assessment of the pertinent individuals (i.e., perpetrator, victim, nonoffending parent, and siblings).

The offender.   Upon disclosure of the abuse, the perpetrator may react in several ways. He may rage and behave violently, accusing the victim of lying and of attempting to split up the home. If his daughter is an adolescent, he may accuse her of attempting to divert blame from her own sexual acting out. On the other hand, the offender may deny remembering the alleged abuse, but may also acknowledge feelings of guilt or threaten suicide. Although his distress may be sincere, it may also have the function of rallying the family's support around the father and of encouraging his daughter to renege on her claim. Regardless of the father's response, it is essential that the therapist firmly, but calmly, indicate to the family and to other agencies that the investigation of the abuse must proceed.

An early and extremely important therapeutic issue is a determination of the probability that the incest will be repeated. According to Groth (1978), the key to determining the likelihood that the perpetrator will repeat his offense lies in assessing the degree to which the offense was the result of external situational factors as opposed to inner psychological determinants. For example, if the perpetrator had a long history of abusing children, the prognosis would be much poorer than if he had just recently regressed in sexual orientation. Similarly, Groth noted that it is important to assess environmental conditions that might have contributed to the offense (e.g., marital difficulties, vocational and economic stress, alcohol and drug use, social isolation, and unmonitored access to his children) and determine whether these conditions are still problematic.

An assessment of the perpetrator should also address his degree of impulse control. This can be done, in part, by assessing his history of sexual assaults and other impulsive acts such as driving recklessly, quitting jobs, spending money freely, and abusing alcohol and drugs. Although psychosis is the exception rather than the rule among men who sexually abuse children, the therapist must assess the perpetrator's contact with reality.

For example, the therapist should examine distortions of the perpetrator's report of the offense and intrusions of fantasy, such as the suggestion that his 3-year-old daughter actively attempted to seduce him.

Groth (1978) also noted the importance of assessing the perpetrator's frustration tolerance, his emotional stability, and any adaptive strengths. The perpetrator's style of relating interpersonally can indicate the degree to which he can be characterized as manipulative, narcissistic, ineffectual, or malicious. These interpersonal characteristics are important predictors of the perpetrator's ability and motivation to develop normal and satisfying adult relationships to replace the incestuous relationship with his daughter.

Finally, one of the most important indicators of potential success or failure of treatment efforts concerns the individual's self-awareness. Is he willing to accept complete responsibility for his behavior? Does he show evidence not only of guilt and remorse, but of insight into his own behavior and empathy for the child? These are often very subtle and difficult characteristics to assess because fear of the authorities and of breakup of the family unit can at times be mistaken for an internalization of responsibility; that is, some offenders are more depressed and remorseful over being caught than over engaging in behavior that was damaging to the child.

When the father openly acknowledges his responsibility for the abuse, it changes his position from a pseudopartner of the daughter to that of a parent. It also gives his wife and the other family members a clear and realistic portrayal of the abuse, which it is hoped will engender more support for the victim. Such acknowledgement puts an end to the norm of secrecy established within the family. While increased openness is essential for subsequent work within family subsystems and the family unit, it is frequently found that openness can be established only through the initial use of individual and group therapy.

Depending on the results of the assessment and on the perpetrator's willingness to acknowledge his behavior, his treatment may begin with a combination of individual and group therapy. Options for the setting of treatment may include outpatient therapy for the regressed offender whose abuse is associated with external factors and who seems cognizant of his behavior; residential treatment for the perpetrator who is suicidal or chemically dependent; or a security institution in the case of a severely pathological pedophile. Regardless of treatment setting, the actual interventions should be broad-based and utilize strategies that address multiple aspects of the perpetrator's difficulties.

A behavioral approach might be used to directly alter the individual's deviant sexual arousal. Relevant behavioral techniques include covert sensitization in which the therapist describes fantasies of sexual interactions with children to the relaxed subject and then pairs those fantasies with aversive imagery such as nausea and vomiting (Murphy & Stalgaitis, 1987). Another behavioral technique is masturbatory satiation, which requires the patient to masturbate to orgasm using nondeviant fantasies (in order to reinforce those fantasies) and then to continue masturbating for 30 to 45 minutes while verbalizing the deviant fantasies. Other types of classical conditioning can be used to increase sexual arousal to appropriate stimuli.

Cognitive behavioral interventions might also be included to serve several purposes. First, such treatment can be used to confront the perpetrator's cognitive distortions surrounding the abuse. Second, cognitive behavior therapy can help the perpetrator establish more effective impulse control by assisting him to develop an increased sensitivity to the thought patterns leading to his sexual involvement. Third, cognitive interventions can help the perpetrator develop a more empathic awareness of the effect of his behavior on his daughter. Moreover, Murphy and Stalgaitis (1987) have found that a review of the deviant sexual fantasies produced during masturbatory satiation can be extremely useful in allowing the therapist to confront the perpetrator's denial system.

In addition, an interpersonal treatment approach such as group therapy can be used to promote the perpetrator's acceptance of responsibility for the abuse. Group therapy can also set the stage for family therapy in which the perpetrator learns alternative and more appropriate forms of self-expression and gratification of his needs. A group therapy setting can help to break through the secrecy and denial in much the same way that the group serves this function in Alcoholics Anonymous. Furthermore, Groth (1982) has noted that, like AA, an offender's group may be used to support the perpetrator in a life-long effort to control his sexually abusive behavior.

The victim. Although a child may initially experience relief when the abuse is stopped, many other reactions are sure to follow. Although some children truly feel contempt and hatred for the father who abused them, many children are also very emotionally attached to him. Further, in her typical role as "parentified" child, the daughter often feels responsible for meeting her father's emotional needs as well as those of other family members. Therefore, when the daughter witnesses the extreme stress and disruption that her family is experiencing as a function of her disclosure, she might feel extremely guilty and be tempted to renege on her claim. It is essential that, at this point, the mother and therapist reassure the daughter that her disclosure was important not only for her own safety but also for the long-term welfare of her father and the other family members.

In addition to guilt, many children experience fear, anxiety, nightmares, phobias, regressive behavior, and somatic complaints. Anxiety may generalize to other stimuli, such as males or certain surroundings. If the abuse has been especially prolonged or severe, older children may experience repression of the event or even a dissociative response. Berliner and Wheeler (in press) have emphasized the utility of helping children master their fears through such strategies as gradual direct confrontation with the feared stimulus, cognitive restructuring, assertiveness training, systematic desensitization, and stress inoculation.

To the extent that ruminative and avoidant reactions to the abuse can interfere with the child's peer relations, relations with other adults, and performance in school, the child's development can be further impaired by her emotional response to the abuse and to its revelation. Therefore, other treatment strategies focusing on the development of social skills and the integration of the child within her peer group and classroom setting may also be necessary.

Sexually abused children are also at risk for developing maladaptive and inappropriate social behaviors associated with and learned from their sexual experience. For example, abused children may approach other children in a sexually explicit manner or may become flirtatious and seductive with adults. Such behaviors are frequently learned in order to acquire reinforcement or to avoid punishment from their father. Moreover, inappropriate sexual behaviors can lead to social ostracism, ridicule from peers, increased risk for further victimization by other adults, and greater risk for victimizing other children (Berliner & Wheeler, in press). Therefore, when abused children display inappropriate sexual behaviors, it is critical that they be addressed therapeutically.

As noted previously, sexual abuse and the interactions surrounding it (e.g., social isolation and precocious interactions with adults) often interfere with normal developmental processes and socialization. The deleterious effects of the abuse, however, are mediated by the developmental stage of the child at the time of the abuse. For example, Gomes-Schwartz, Horowitz and Sauzier (1985) found that children who were abused as preschoolers experienced significantly less clinical disturbance than children who were abused during middle childhood. It is likely that the relative lack of guilt and awareness of the implications of the abuse protected the younger children from an important source of long-term distress.

The developmental stage of the child affects *how* the abuse is experienced. A preoperational or concrete operational child, for example, may be more disturbed by the violation of personal safety and less vulnerable to the guilt of participation experienced by the formal operational adolescent. On the other hand, because physical coercion may not be needed to abuse the young child (as opposed to an older child), the issue of physical safety is sometimes more relevant to the experience of the older child. It is therefore essential that assessments and interventions give consideration to the child's developmental stage and the specific experiences surrounding the abuse.

The use of individual and group therapy may be recommended for the child, depending on the strength of other family resources available to the child. If, however, the mother is able to provide reassurance regarding her daughter's feelings of guilt and betrayal, can help her daughter deal with subsequent anxiety, and can provide consistent correction of sexualized behaviors, the therapist is advised to work with the parent-child dyad in order to treat these effects of the abuse. In other words, the therapist might proceed directly to interventions with the mother-daughter dyad in cases where the mother is relatively competent.

However, in many cases of abuse, the lack of bonding between the mother and the child is apparent through the mother's minimization or denial of her daughter's claims. Because of the danger in such cases that the mother could effectively convince her daughter either that the abuse was only imagined or that it was the daughter's own fault, therapy with the mother-daughter dyad would be premature and possibly destructive. Instead, individual and group therapy with the daughter should be used to reduce the girl's guilt and increase her confidence in eventually confronting her mother.

Adolescents in particular often respond favorably to groups in which they can make some meaning of the experience for themselves, and both give and receive support and validation regarding their role in the abuse. Blick and Porter (1982) noted that some of the benefits of group treatment for adolescents include: opportunity to ventilate anger about the abuse; socialization with a peer group (albeit a sexually abused peer group); and sex education. If groups are used, however, it is recommended that they be time-limited so that they do not become a major substitute for the normal socialization with peers that sexual abuse victims often lack and so desperately require. In one regrettable incident, a social services agency required an adolescent girl to return home from her freshman year of college for long-term therapy when it was discovered that both she and her younger sister had been sexually abused by their father. In this case, the cure was as disruptive to the girl's social development as was the sexual abuse itself.

It would be unfortunate and irresponsible to intervene on the assumption of trauma when reassurance and family reorganization to assure future protection would suffice. Sexual abuse is one area in which the treatment provided by professionals is sometimes more traumatic and disruptive than the original abuse.

The nonoffending parent.   The mother may show a wide variety of reactions to the disclosure of abuse. She may accuse her daughter of lying or of chafing under the behavioral limits set by the father. For example, many sexually abusive fathers may accuse their adolescent daughters of being promiscuous with peers and may prohibit them from dating, from wearing makeup, and from attending parties. The mother may support these rules rather than question her husband's motives. Further, the mother's failure to believe her daughter's disclosures is especially likely if the daughter has already displayed a number of behavior problems or conflicts with the father. If the mother believes her daughter, she may initially support her daughter and even become enraged at her husband. Sometimes, however, the mother slowly changes her attitude and begins to deny any family problems because of her fears of living alone. The mother may suggest that the girl alter her story for the authorities, or may minimize the abuse by labeling it as mere physical affection. Denial and minimization seem to be common reactions among women who were themselves abused as children by their fathers.

Although the therapist can appreciate the mother's fears at having to deal with the implications of the abuse, her reaction to the disclosure and support of her daughter are important determinants of her daughter's short-term and long-term adjustment. In fact, many adolescents and adult women who were sexually abused as children display more pervasive mistrust and feelings of betrayal toward the nonoffending parent who did not believe their story than toward the perpetrator. Therefore, one of the main goals in assessing the mother is to determine the degree to which she believes her daughter and can provide her with adequate protection in the future.

The therapist should also consider the mother's emotional response to the situation. The mother may feel simultaneously betrayed by her husband and guilty for not being aware of the abuse. When the mother also feels that she has been betrayed by her daughter, it usually indicates a reversal in the mother-daughter roles that has been described previously. Such role reversal should become a major focus of therapy.

Individual and group therapy is also useful for the nonoffending parent. Two primary purposes of these therapeutic approaches are to sensitize the mother to the effects of the abuse on her child and to help the mother deal with her own guilt for not being aware or acting on her knowledge to protect her child. In addition, if the mother had been abused herself as a child, she may need to deal with the effects of her own experience before she can adequately empathize with and protect her child. For example, several adult victims of father-daughter incest who participated in a group treatment program casually recounted that they routinely relied on their parents to babysit their children even though these were the very individuals who had abused and/or failed to protect them as children. In other words, victims often compartmentalize their own abuse from the potential for abuse of their children; this kind of segregation can greatly interfere with an abused woman's ability to protect her own children. Individual and group therapy may be needed to help such women integrate these experiences.

Finally, both individual and group therapy have been found to be invaluable in helping the mother develop the personal resources that assure her ability to protect her children in the future. For example, Sgroi and Dana (1982) have discussed the importance of concurrent individual and group therapy in providing a safe arena to deal with pent-up anger, to develop assertiveness, to encourage increased communication with one's children, and to improve social skills.

Interventions with Family Subsystems

The blurred subsystem boundaries characteristic of the incestuous family are indicative of deficient communication, poor conflict resolution skills, and lack of cohesiveness within the subsystems. Therefore, the therapist is faced with the tasks of building the integrity of the subsystems as well as defining boundaries and improving communication between subsystems. For these reasons, it is recommended that work with the family proceed with specific dyads and subsystems before therapy with the whole family unit is initiated. Although therapy with the dyads and subsystems may be conducted concurrently, the probability of positive outcome is increased when priority is placed on the mother-daughter and parental/marital dyads before addressing the father-daughter dyad.

Before treatment of the family subsystems is described, it should be noted that intervening with the family is essential whether or not the family intends to stay united. In examining more than 150 cases of sexual abuse in which the parents divorced, Sirles (1987) found that the offending parent was usually allowed unsupervised visitation rights, placing the child at even greater risk of abuse. Further, family-based interventions are needed to address dysfunctions in the mother-daughter relationship and to enable the mother to better protect her child from potential perpetrators in subsequent relationships.

Mother-daughter dyad. There are two primary reasons why the mother-daughter dyad is the most important relationship for the therapist to address. First, the mother's presence, both physical and emotional, is essential for the protection of the child. Finkelhor (1979) noted that one of the most significant risk factors for either intrafamilial or extrafamilial sexual abuse was the absence of the mother or stepmother. Therefore, the mother and child must establish a strong emotional bond to guarantee that future abuse can be averted.

The second reason for urgent therapeutic attention to the mother-daughter dyad is that many of the long-term and pervasive effects of abuse seem to be mediated by the mother-daughter relationship. For example, many abused children have as many negative feelings toward their mothers as they do toward their fathers. In fact, Alexander and Follette (1987) reported that adult victims of father-daughter incest tended to blame their mothers for the destructive and conflictual family environment more than they blamed their fathers. This is not meant to imply that the mother should be held responsible for the abuse. However, it is important to recognize that many incest victims can more easily resolve their father's overt abuse than their mother's more passive lack of protection. The following example illustrates one woman's reactions to her abuser and to the nonoffending parent.

Roberta was subject to brutal physical and sexual abuse by her mother from infancy until she left home at 18 years of age. Her mother was later diagnosed as manic-depressive and her psychosis was characterized by religiosity, paranoia, and severe delusions. Roberta experienced substantial anxiety and described classically conditioned fears to a variety of stimuli associated with her mother's abuse (e.g., fears of cold weather associated with being locked in the attic during the winter; fears of rock music associated with being abused while her mother played the radio loudly; anxiety around Halloween when her mother would practice witchcraft; and, of course, fears of sex). However, Roberta also experienced a pervasive self-doubt and feelings that she was crazy. She attributed these feelings to having been told repeatedly by her father (the nonoffending parent) that she had simply imagined her mother's abuse. Independent corroborations by Roberta's sister, who had also been abused; by personnel at the mental institution at which her mother was now a resident; and even by her father (who acknowledged an incident during which his wife kept Roberta hostage for hours while threatening to kill them both) could not erase Roberta's questioning of her own sanity.

Because overt abuse may at times be easier for the victim to understand and to reconcile than the subtle invalidation stemming from the nonoffending parent's minimization or denial of the abuse, it is important that the therapist encourage the nonoffending parent to acknowledge to the child that the abuse has occurred. An admission by Roberta's father that he believed her report of the abuse would have reduced her guilt and helped mend their relationship.

In addition to the need for the mother to protect her daughter and to validate her daughter's experience, several other issues are likely to arise in therapy with the mother-daughter dyad. The daughter may be angry with her mother, justifiably or not, for not providing sufficient protection from her father. As noted previously, both mother and daughter may have mutual feelings of betrayal and guilt. In cases of long-term abuse characterized by role reversal within the home, the mother-daughter relationship may be competitive or even complementary. Here, the daughter may feel the need to protect her mother from the effects of her disclosure, and the mother may see herself, rather than her child, as the victim of the abuse. In such cases, the therapist's goal is to help the mother and daughter assume more appropriate roles in their relationship with each other.

Parental/marital dyad.   The next important dyad to work with is the parental subsystem. In the treatment of the incestuous family, the mother's and father's roles as parents should take precedence over their roles as husband and wife (Furniss, 1983). Not only does this emphasize the priority of the children in families that frequently evidence parentification of the children, but it is also the clearest way to establish intergenerational boundaries. Further, it is often less threatening for the couple to focus on communication and conflict resolution around the more concrete issues of parenting than around the more emotionally loaded marital issues of sex and intimacy. It may also be useful at this juncture for the couple to explore their own childhood experiences and their parents' roles in their families of origin.

The couple's marital conflict cannot, of course, be ignored if the problem of incest is to be resolved. Their sexual conflict and poor communication probably have been compounded by their emotional immaturity and dependence; therefore, some prior success in negotiating decisions about their children will be useful in helping the couple tackle the very complicated marital issues. It is also important for the therapist to address extant marital conflicts because of the possibility that the parents will scapegoat the daughter in an attempt to avoid their own conflict. Further, the therapist should address the dominance hierarchy in the family. The wife's status must change from her daughter's equal (or lesser) to that of her husband's equal and a legitimate authority figure. The therapist must engender the wife's ability to confront her husband and to deal with him directly and assertively.

Siblings and other family members.   Because incest occurs within a family context, it influences more people than just the perpetrator, the victim, and the nonoffending parent. The victim's siblings and other family members have been affected by the family structure associated with the incest and by the public disclosure of the father's behavior. The therapist's first priority in addressing the effects on siblings and other family members is to determine whether any other children in the family have been abused. If such is the case, the therapist must assess their experience and provide necessary treatment for them as described above.

However, even children in the family who have not been abused may be undetected victims. These children might experience self-doubts and confusion as to why they were spared. For example, Meg was the only one of her three sisters who had not been approached by her father, and she viewed this as a shortcoming in herself. Although the therapist speculated that Meg was probably spared because she was more assertive than her sisters, the therapist found it very difficult to resolve Meg's doubts about her attractiveness and desirability.

It is also common for the siblings to feel resentment toward the abused child because of her apparently favored position. For example, Angie recounted that her brothers and sisters would throw rocks at her while calling her "Daddy's girl." Thus, not only was she prevented by her father from having playmates so that she would be more accessible to him, but she was also effectively isolated from her siblings by her father's obvious preference for her.

Another typical sibling interaction is additional sexual abuse of a girl by her older brother if he has witnessed his father doing so. This scenario is more common in a patriarchal household where the sons, by virtue of their gender, are endowed with excessive authority over their sisters.

Finally, if the siblings are not informed as to the reason for their family's disruption, it is likely that they will blame their sister for the disruption of the family or for their father having to leave home. Unification of the sibling subsystem can promote normal peer socialization and help to maintain generational boundaries. Therefore, it is essential for the eventual unity of the family (with or without the father) and for the protection of all the children within the home, that the siblings be included at some point in the treatment process. As noted by Sirles (1987), in cases of divorced couples, a strong sibling subsystem may be the primary reliable protection against future abuse.

Father-daughter dyad.   The father-daughter dyad should be treated only after the integrity of the other subsystems has been established. This subsystem is treated last because both father and daughter must be clear in their roles before they can face their relationship successfully. The father needs to have acknowledged his responsibility for the abuse, and must understand his roles as father to his children and husband to his wife. Only then can he learn to relate to his daughter in a new and appropriate manner.

Similarly, the daughter must feel confident that she is being protected by her mother, and that she is an integral part of the sibling (and not the parental) subsystem. Finally, it is important for the therapist to realize that the daughter may have strong feelings of attachment and loyalty toward her father. Occasionally, a therapist may be so appalled by the abuse that he or she may fail to see this attachment. As noted previously, this oversight tends to be a particular problem for therapists who adhere to the victim-per-petrator model of incest.

Interventions with the Family-Community Mesosystem

Therapy with specific dyads and subsystems is generally aimed at developing the integrity and cohesiveness of the subsystems, establishing clear boundaries between subsystems, and improving communication and conflict resolution skills both within and between subsystems. Although therapy with the whole family unit is concerned with cementing these gains, therapy must also address the interface of the family with its environment. As mentioned previously, social isolation both precedes and results from incest in the functionally incestuous family. Therefore, an evaluation of the family's social network and its interactions with the community is an essential part of treatment.

The disclosure of incest means that at least two different social systems—the legal system and the department of human services—will become involved with the family. The therapist must be aware that these social systems might be vulnerable to the family's typical style of interacting with its environment. It is acknowledged that, under the best of circumstances, social agencies frequently exhibit competitiveness, incompatible goals, and poor communication with each other. The incestuous family is often quite expert at fostering even more secretiveness, deception, and conflict among these agencies. Consequently, the very agencies or treatment providers charged with the task of addressing the problem of incest may themselves develop a conflictual, though stable, interaction pattern with the family and with each other. Not only is change precluded, but the child is frequently left unprotected and the family experiences even more unresolved disruption than before the disclosure was made. The effect, of course, is to reinforce the family's justification of its need for secrecy and isolation.

On the other hand, when agencies work closely and openly with each other, the family is provided with a model of effective communication and conflict resolution among parties with different interests; diffusion of conflict is minimized; and the norm against secrecy is established. At this point, the strengths of the family can be explored. The following case study demonstrates some of these processes.

Hal Jones was a 38-year-old minister who was married and had a 14-year-old son. Mr. Jones was the third of six children, with two older sisters, two younger sisters, and a younger brother with whom he was particularly close. He and his wife were in the process of adopting a baby girl and were several months away from the end of the probation period. When Mr. Jones fondled an adolescent niece, who pretended to be asleep, she later told her mother, who then told Grandfather Jones. This apparently had not been the first example of sexual acting out between Mr. Jones and his nieces. Grandfather Jones, who was also a minister, decided to handle the situation himself and told the rest of the family to remain quiet about the abuse. Grandfather Jones forced his son to enter an inpatient psychiatric program for 30 days. Mr. Jones's therapist in the hospital, who also happened to be the consultant to the adoption agency, decided not to inform the adoption agency about why Mr. Jones was receiving treatment. The therapist also instructed Mr. Jones to have no further communication with his siblings. As a result, the siblings not only felt cut off from their brother, Mr. Jones, but also from their father, Grandfather Jones, who had developed feelings of increased loyalty and protectiveness toward his son. One of Mr. Jones's in-laws subsequently informed both the adoption agency and Mr. Jones's employer about the abuse, and the amount of conflict in the family and between the therapist and the adoption agency increased precipitously. It was at this point that Mr. Jones and his whole extended family were referred for family therapy.

The case is especially interesting for its illustration of the dynamics within the incestuous family as well as how the family's alliance with the therapist was used to avoid resolution of conflict with the adoption agency and with each other. The facade of role competence was very important even before Mr. Jones entered treatment, helping to account for Grandfather Jones's emphasis on keeping the fondling a secret. In addition, Grandfather Jones was so central in his family that the siblings apparently had never learned how to confront each other directly and resolve conflicts without him. The family was also characterized by a very strong tendency to see issues in absolute terms (e.g., good/bad, sick/well, moral/immoral), further decreasing the likelihood of resolving conflicts.

The original therapist's attempt to keep the abuse a secret not only reinforced the norm of secrecy within the home, but also created conflict with the adoption agency (to the point that it was no longer willing even to consider rehabilitation) and increased the degree of mistrust among the siblings. Further, the conflict led the siblings to scapegoat their brother, which then allowed Mr. Jones to externalize the blame for the abuse. Subsequent demands by the siblings that their brother accept responsibility for his behavior were ignored by him and by Grandfather Jones as being self-serving. Without face-to-face contact with Mr. Jones, the extended family was precluded from monitoring his behavior in the future. Finally, because of Grandfather Jones's protectiveness of his son, which increased in response to the conflict between him and his siblings, the other family members were effectively cut off from their father.

As can be seen by this case example, problems that contribute to the occurrence of abuse can also parallel the role that a therapist is enlisted to play in the system. If the family is successful in engaging the therapist in this manner, the conflict is likely to increase exponentially. Moreover, the potential strengths in the family that might preclude future abuse will not be identified and enlisted.

CONCLUSION

In conclusion, it is important to recognize the diversity of factors involved in the problem of father-daughter incest. A multisystemic model provides a framework for systematic and thorough evaluation of the perpetrator, the child, the nonoffending spouse, and the rest of the family. In addition to individual characteristics and developmental considerations, it is critical that the therapist understands how the family structure contributes to and is affected by the incest behavior. Similarly, the therapist should consider the interaction of the incestuous family with its environment. Only by precluding further secrecy and isolation from systems outside the family can the future protection of the children in the family be assured.

REFERENCES

Abel, G. G., Becker, J. V., Murphy, W. D., & Flanagan, B. (1981). Identifying dangerous child molesters. In R. B. Stuart (Ed.), *Violent behavior: Social learning approaches to prediction, management and treatment* (pp. 116–137). New York: Brunner/Mazel.

Alexander, P. C. (1985). A systems theory conceptualization of incest. *Family Process, 24,* 79–88.

Alexander, P.C., & Follette, V.M. (1987). *The clinical implications of incestuous family structures.* Paper presented at the annual conference of the American Association for Marriage and Family Therapy, Chicago, IL.

Alexander, P. C., & Lupfer, S. L. (1987). Family characteristics and long-term consequences associated with sexual abuse. *Archives of Sexual Behavior, 16,* 235–246.

Berliner, L., & Wheeler, R. (in press). Treating the effects of sexual abuse on children. *Journal of Social Issues.*

Blick, L. C., & Porter, F. S. (1982). Group therapy with female adolescent incest victims. In S. M. Sgroi (Ed.), *Handbook of clinical intervention in child sexual abuse.* Lexington, MA: Lexington Books.

Browne, A., & Finkelhor, D. (1986). Impact of child sexual abuse: A review of the research. *Psychological Bulletin, 99,* 66–77.

Conte, J. R. (1985). *The effects of sexual abuse on children: Preliminary findings.* Unpublished manuscript.

Edwards, J., & Alexander, P. C. (1989). *The contribution of family background and sexual abuse factors to the long-term adjustment of child sexual abuse victims.* Manuscript submitted for publication.

Finkelhor, D. (1979). *Sexually victimized children.* New York: Free Press.

Finkelhor, D. (1984). *Child sexual abuse: New theory and research.* New York: Free Press.

Furniss, T. (1983). Family process in the treatment of intrafamilial child sexual abuse. *Journal of Family Therapy, 5,* 263–278.

Gomes-Schwartz, B., Horowitz, J. M., & Sauzier, M. (1985). Severity of emotional distress among sexually abused preschool, school-age and adolescent children. *Hospital and Community Psychiatry, 35,* 503–508.

Groth, A. N. (1978). Guidelines for the assessment and management of the offender. In A. W. Burgess, A. N. Groth, L. L. Holmstrom, & S. M. Sgroi (Eds.), *Sexual assault of children and adolescents.* Lexington, MA: Lexington Books.

Groth, A. N. (1982). The incest offender. In S. M. Sgroi (Ed.), *Handbook of clinical intervention in child sexual abuse.* Lexington, MA: Lexington Books.

Harter, S., Alexander, P.C., & Neimeyer, R. A. (1988). Long-term effects of incestuous child abuse in college women: Social adjustment, social cognition, and family characteristics. *Journal of Consulting and Clinical Psychology, 56,* 5–8.

Herman, J. L. (1981). *Father-daughter incest.* Cambridge, MA: Harvard University Press.

James, B., & Nasjleti, M. (1983). *Treating sexually abused children and their families.* Palo Alto, CA: Consulting Psychologists Press.

Larson, N. R., & Maddock, J. W. (1986). Structural and functional variables in incest family systems: Implications for assessment and treatment. In T. S. Trepper & M. J. Barrett (Eds.), *Treating incest: A multiple systems perspective.* New York: Haworth Press.

Marshall, W. L., Barbaree, H. E., & Christophe, D. (1986). Sexual offenders against female children: Sexual preferences for age of victims and type of behaviour. *Canadian Journal of Behaviour Science, 18,* 424–439.

Meiselman, K. C. (1978). *Incest: A psychological study of causes and effects with treatment recommendations.* San Francisco: Jossey-Bass.

Murphy, W. D., & Stalgaitis, S. J. (1987). Assessment and treatment considerations for sexual offenders against children: Behavioral and social learning approaches. In J. R. McNamara & M. A. Appel (Eds.), *Critical issues, developments, and trends in professional psychology, Vol. 3.* New York: Praeger.

Murphy, W. D., Haynes, M. R., Stalgaitis, S. J., & Flanagan, B. (1986). Differential sexual responding among four groups of sexual offenders against children. *Journal of Psychopathology and Behavioral Assessment, 8,* 339–353.

Quinsey, V. L., Chaplin, T. C., & Carrigan, W. F. (1979). Sexual preferences among incestuous and nonincestuous child molesters. *Behavior Therapy, 10,* 562–565.

Sgroi, S. M., & Dana, N. T. (1982). Individual and group treatment of mothers of incest victims. In S. M. Sgroi (Ed.), *Handbook of clinical intervention in child sexual abuse.* Lexington, MA: Lexington Books.

Simon, F. B., Stierlin, H., & Wynne, L. C. (1985). *The language of family therapy: A systemic vocabulary and sourcebook.* New York: Family Process Press.

Sirles, E. (1987). *Structural interventions for work with divorcing child sexual abuse cases.* Paper presented at the annual conference of the American Association for Marriage and Family Therapy, Chicago, IL.

Sluzki, C. (1983). Process, structure and world views: Toward an integrated view of systemic models in family therapy. *Family Process, 22,* 469–476.

Smith, H., & Israel, E. (1987). Sibling incest: A study of the dynamics of 25 cases. *Child Abuse & Neglect, 11,* 101–108.

Trepper, T. S., & Barrett, M. J. (Eds.). (1986). *Treating incest: A multiple systems perspective.* New York: Haworth Press.

NAME INDEX

Abel, G. G., 329, 343
Adams, G. R., 150, 167
Adelson, J., 133, 164
Affleck, G., 299, 318
Ageton, S. S., 7, 29, 131, 165, 221, 222, 223, 230, 242, 243
Ainsworth, M., 76, 86, 90
Alexander, J. F., 224, 244
Alexander, P. C., 17, 28, 324, 325, 328, 329, 330, 338, 343
Allen, D. A., 299, 300, 318
Allen, L., 176, 193
Allen, T. W., 38, 60
Allman, L. R., 21, 28
Altman, N., 139, 167
American Psychiatric Association, 247, 275
Amirkhan, J., 39, 59
Anastasi, A., 176, 192
Anderson, B. J., 301, 309, 314, 319
Anderson, E. R., 195, 217
Anderson, K. O., 278, 319
Anderson, S. C., 276, 277
Aponte, H. J., 8, 28
Appelbaum, M. I., 176, 193
Arend, R., 76, 90
Ariel, S., 16, 29
Armor, D., 266, 270, 275
Asher, S. R., 131, 139, 142, 144, 146, 152, 163, 166, 167
Attneave, C. L., 4, 8, 32
Auerswald, E. H., 4, 8, 29

Auslander, W. F., 301, 315, 319, 323
Aydin, O., 139, 163

Babigian, H., 131, 164
Bachman, J., 251, 275
Bahm, R. M., 202, 217
Baker, D. P., 187, 193
Baker, L., 301, 319, 322
Baldwin, A. L., 84, 90
Baldwin, C. P., 84, 90
Bank, S., 305, 319
Barbaree, H. E., 329, 343
Barbero, G. J., 314, 319
Barenboim, C., 138, 164
Barkley, R. A., 11, 31, 38, 59, 180, 192
Barnes, H., 244
Barnett, A. H., 281, 319
Barnhill, L. R., 63, 90
Barrett, M. J., 324, 344
Barton, K., 152, 164
Bateson, G., 20, 29
Baum, V. C., 288, 319
Baumrind, D., 65, 66, 76, 90
Bearison, D. J., 152, 163
Beavers, W. R., 62, 90, 91
Beck, S. J., 146, 165
Becker, D., 300, 323
Becker, J. V., 329, 343
Becker, W. C., 227, 242
Bell, R. Q., 15, 29, 77, 90
Bell, S. M., 86, 90
Belsky, J., 2, 29, 152, 163, 227, 242
Benigni, L., 12, 32

Berger, M., 178, 193
Berliner, L., 335, 336, 343
Berscheid, E., 148, 164
Bertalanffy, L. von, 13, 29
Bibace, R., 295, 308, 319
Bierman, K. L., 132, 144, 145, 163, 165
Bietel, A., 151, 164
Biller, H. B., 201, 202, 216, 217
Bishop, D. S., 62, 91
Black, A. E., 66, 90
Black, F. W., 180, 192
Blakely, C. H., 224, 242
Blasi, A., 221, 242
Blaske, D. M., 3, 17, 29, 31, 135, 157, 163, 225, 230, 234, 242, 244
Blehar, M., 76, 90
Blick, L. C., 336, 343
Bloch, D., 315, 321
Bogdan, J. L., 4, 29
Borduin, C. M., 1, 2, 3, 6, 17, 29, 30, 31, 74, 84, 90, 135, 157, 163, 166, 195, 201, 202, 204, 217, 221, 225, 229, 230, 234, 242, 243, 244
Bousha, D. M., 3, 29
Bradley, L. A., 278, 319
Brakke, N. P., 142, 164
Brasswell, M., 224, 245
Brent, D., 296, 322
Brewster, A. B., 293, 295, 308, 319
Brion-Meisels, S., 133, 167

Brittain, C. V., 154, 163
Bronfenbrenner, U., 4, 29, 150, 163, 187, 192, 224, 242
Brook, D. W., 155, 163
Brook, J. S., 7, 29, 155, 163, 276, 277
Brooks-Gunn, J., 148, 163
Browne, A., 36, 59, 324, 343
Bruner, J. S., 132, 163
Brunk, M. A., 2, 15, 29, 42, 59, 77, 90, 157, 166, 221, 225, 226, 242, 244
Bryant, B. K., 302, 304, 319
Bubb, J., 310, 319
Buhrmester, D., 133, 143, 151, 154, 163, 165
Burbach, D. J., 84, 90
Burghen, G. A., 8, 30, 278, 291, 292, 301, 320
Burgio, L., 40, 61
Burks, N., 6, 30
Burks, V., 151, 164
Burton, R., 66, 92
Bushbaum, K., 139, 164
Bushwall, S. J., 91, 164
Byrne, D., 164

Cameron, D. C., 247, 275
Camp, B. W., 221, 242
Campaigne, B. N., 287, 288, 319, 322
Campbell, J. D., 66, 92
Campbell, S. B., 38, 59, 180, 192
Caplinger, T. E., 224, 243
Carel, C. A., 16, 28
Carle, D. L., 320
Carlsmith, J. M., 91, 164
Carrigan, W. F., 329, 344
Carson, J., 151, 164
Carter, E. A., 9, 16, 29
Carter, R., 285, 321
Cassell, T. Z., 152, 163
Cattell, R., 152, 164
Cavior, N., 148, 164
Cederblad, M., 301, 319
Chadwick, M. W., 309, 321
Chandler, M., 138, 164

Chaplin, T. C., 329, 344
Chapman, M., 211, 217
Chesler, R., 288, 323
Christensen, K. S., 295, 319
Christensen, N. K., 295, 322
Christophe, D., 329, 343
Cigrang, J. A., 320
Clarke, W. L., 285, 319
Cleveland, M., 250, 275, 276, 277
Cohen, P., 155, 163
Cohen, R., 7, 9, 12, 30, 35, 60, 152, 166, 203, 217
Cohen, S., 307, 319
Coie, J. D., 142, 143, 164
Colapinto, J., 21, 22, 29
Cole, R. E., 84, 90
Coleman, J. S., 182, 189, 192
Collmer, C., 2, 31, 227, 244
Conners, C. K., 34, 38, 59
Connolly, A. J., 177, 192
Connors, K., 86, 91
Conrad, J. P., 220, 243
Conte, J. R., 329, 343
Coombs, R. H., 148, 164
Cooney, M., 249, 275
Cooper, D. H., 148, 168
Cooper, H. M., 1, 30
Cooper, P. F., 6, 31, 132, 167
Coopersmith, S., 66, 91
Coppotelli, H., 142, 164
Cowen, E. L., 88, 91, 131, 164
Cox, M., 199, 217
Cox, R., 199, 217
Coyne, J. C., 22, 29
Craighead, W. E., 11, 31, 39, 40, 41, 60
Creekmore, A. M., 148, 168
Cromwell, R. E., 224, 245
Crook, C. K., 228, 245
Crouse-Novak, M., 322
Cruickshanks, K. J., 280, 322
Cunningham, C. E., 38, 59
Cunningham, W., 285, 321

Dana, N. T., 338, 344
Daniels, D., 306, 319
Dash, J., 278, 321, 323

Davidson, W. S., 224, 242
Davis, G. E., 227, 244
Davison, M. L., 230, 242
Deaton, A. V., 313, 319
Delamater, A. M., 310, 319
Dell, P. F., 6, 16, 21, 29
Deluty, R. H., 139, 164
Denner, B., 22, 29
DePaulo, B. M., 139, 166
Derogatis, L. R., 228, 230, 242
deRosnay, J., 12, 29
Dezen, A. E., 1, 32
Dielman, T., 152, 164
DiMatteo, M. R., 312, 320
Dinitz, S., 220, 243
Dion, K. K., 148, 164
Dishion, T. J., 221, 223, 224, 242, 244, 245
Dodge, K. A., 139, 142, 143, 148, 164
Donahoe, C. P., 5, 30, 221, 243
Dorman, J. S., 280, 283, 320
Dornbusch, S. M., 64, 91, 154, 164
Dotemoto, S., 38, 61
Douvan, E., 133, 164
Dreyer, A. S., 63, 92
Dubey, D. R., 39, 59
Dumas, J. E., 222, 242
Duncan, N., 314, 323
Dunford, F. W., 223, 243
Dunn, J., 306, 319
Dunn, L(eota). M., 181, 192
Dunn, L(loyd). M., 177, 181, 192
Dunn, S. M., 278, 320
Dunphy, D. C., 133, 164
D'Zurilla, T. J., 40, 59

Easterbrooks, M. A., 150, 152, 165
Eder, D., 133, 165
Edgar, M., 36, 60
Edwards, J. J., 7, 30, 152, 166, 221, 243, 329, 343
Eff, C., 281, 319
Eisenberg, L., 85, 91

Elkaim, M., 16, 29
Ellenberg, L., 278, 321, 323
Elliott, D. S., 7, 29, 131, 154, 165, 220, 221, 222, 223, 224, 230, 243
Ellis, D., 247, 275
Eme, R., 148, 165
Emery, R. L., 62, 88, 91, 152, 157, 165
England, J. D., 284, 320
Englander, R. M., 288, 319
Epstein, J. L., 143, 151, 165
Epstein, N. B., 62, 91
Epstein, Y. M., 201, 204, 217
Eron, L. D., 66, 91
Ervin, C. R., 148, 164
Eysenck, H. J., 225, 243
Eysenck, S. B. G., 225, 243

Falzer, P. R., 22, 29
Farrington, D. P., 220, 243
Faust, M. S., 148, 165
Federal Bureau of Investigation, 220, 243
Federal Register, 180, 193
Feinberg, T. L., 296, 322
Feld, S., 93, 129
Feldman, R. A., 224, 243
Feldman-Summers, S., 36, 60
Felig, P., 288, 320
Felner, R. D., 88, 91
Field, T. M., 132, 165
Finegold, D., 284, 323
Finger, W. W., 221, 243
Finkelhor, D., 36, 59, 324, 326, 327, 338, 343
Finkelstein, R., 296, 322
Fisch, R., 10, 18, 32
Fisher, E. B., Jr., 310, 320
Flanagan, B., 329, 343, 344
Flavell, J. H., 293, 294, 319
Foch, T. T., 148, 166
Fogel, A., 132, 165
Follette, V. M., 328, 330, 338, 343
Forehand, R., 146, 165
Freedman, B. J., 5, 30, 221, 243
French, D. C., 152, 165
Friedman, J. M., 115, 130

Fucci, B. R., 3, 29, 225, 242
Furman, W., 132, 133, 143, 145, 151, 154, 163, 165
Furniss, T., 339, 343
Furstenberg, F. F., 306, 319

Gammon, G. D., 92
Garmezy, N., 278, 320
Gelfand, D. M., 133, 165
George, C., 76, 91
Gettinger, J. M., 315, 323
Gholson, J. B., 39, 59
Gilliam, T. B., 288, 319
Gillies, P., 148, 166
Glass, D. R., 276, 277
Glick, P. C., 194, 206, 217
Gold, M., 222, 243
Goldberg, N., 288, 323
Golden, M. M., 131, 167
Goldenberg, H., 13, 16, 17, 18, 30, 276, 277
Goldenberg, I., 13, 16, 17, 18, 30, 276, 277
Goldfried, M. R., 40, 59
Goldsmith, H. H., 5, 30
Goldstein, D. E., 284, 320
Gomes-Schwartz, B., 336, 343
Goodale, W., 148, 165
Goodwin, D., 247, 275
Goodwin, W., 189, 193
Gordon, A. S., 7, 29, 155, 163
Gossett, J. T., 62, 91
Gottman, J. M., 132, 142, 165
Gove, F. L., 76, 90
Grajek, S., 306, 322
Gray, W. S., 178, 193
Gray-Little, B., 6, 30
Green, K. D., 146, 165
Greenspan, S., 138, 164
Griesler, P. C., 151, 167
Gross, R. T., 91, 164
Groth, A. N., 326, 333, 334, 335, 343
Guess, L., 247, 275
Gurin, G., 93, 129
Gurman, A. S., 1, 2, 22, 30, 224, 243

Haefele, W. F., 7, 30, 203, 217, 221, 243
Hains, A., 221, 243
Haley, J., 11, 19, 30, 31, 44, 46, 59, 60, 104, 111, 129, 194, 217, 227, 243
Hall, R. J., 182, 193
Hallinan, M. T., 133, 165
Halperin, S. L., 227, 243
Hamburg, B. A., 296, 320
Hamparian, D. M., 220, 243
Hannon, J. B., 139, 167
Hanson, C. L., 2, 7, 8, 19, 30, 36, 60, 74, 80, 90, 91, 98, 130, 154, 157, 165, 203, 217, 221, 223, 225, 242, 243, 244, 245, 278, 291, 292, 293, 295, 297, 300, 301, 307, 312, 320
Harbin, F., 74, 90
Harkavy, J., 296, 321
Harris, M. A., 312, 320
Harris, M. I., 280, 321
Harter, S., 293, 294, 321, 330, 343
Hartup, W. W., 6, 7, 17, 30, 131, 150, 166
Hastorf, A. H., 91, 164
Hauser, S. T., 278, 321
Hayden, B., 139, 166
Haynes, M. R., 329, 344
Hays, R. D., 312, 320
Hazelrigg, M. D., 1, 30
Health and Human Services, 249, 275
Heckler, M. M., 292, 321
Helgesson, M., 319
Henderson, D. C., 276, 277
Hendry, L. B., 148, 166
Henggeler, S. W., 1, 2, 3, 6, 7, 8, 9, 12, 15, 17, 18, 19, 23, 30, 31, 32, 35, 36, 42, 59, 60, 74, 77, 80, 90, 91, 98, 130, 132, 152, 155, 157, 163, 165, 167, 189, 193, 195, 202, 203, 217, 221, 222, 225, 229, 230, 234, 242, 243,

Henggeler, S. W. (continued) 244, 245, 278, 291, 292, 301, 312, 320
Henker, B., 34, 38, 39, 60, 61
Herman, J. L., 324, 330, 343
Herman, W. H., 280, 283, 321
Hernandez, D. J., 194, 217
Herrnstein, R. J., 221, 245
Hetherington, E. M., 62, 63, 76, 77, 84, 85, 91, 195, 199, 200, 217
Heyman, A., 315, 321
Hinde, R., 150, 166
Hindelang, M. J., 220, 222, 244
Hirshi, J. T., 220, 222, 244
Hoffman, L., 12, 19, 20, 21, 30
Hoffman, M. L., 66, 91
Hogarty, P. S., 176, 193
Holbeck, L., 281, 321
Hollon, S. D., 39, 60
Honzik, M. P., 176, 193
Horan, M. J., 288, 321
Horowitz, J. M., 336, 343
Horst, L., 66, 91
Horton, P. J., 66, 91
House, W. E., 314, 321
Hudgins, W., 221, 244
Huizinga, D., 7, 29, 131, 165, 220, 221, 222, 223, 243
Hurwitz, L. S., 299, 322
Hymel, S., 139, 142, 143, 163, 166

Inoff, B. A., 296, 320
Israel, E., 325, 344
Izzo, L. D., 131, 164

Jacklin, C. N., 133, 166
Jackson, D. D., 18, 30, 104, 130
Jackson, R. L., 284, 321
Jacobsen, N. S., 96, 129
Jacobson, A. M., 278, 321
Jacobson, D. S., 205, 217
Jacobson, G., 202, 217
Jacobson, J. L., 150, 166

James, B., 330, 343
James, F. W., 288, 322
Jastak, J. F., 177, 193
Jay, J., 276, 277
Jellinek, E. M., 248, 275
Jessor, R., 276, 277
Jessor, S. L., 276, 277
Johnson, M. M., 202, 217
Johnson, S. B., 285, 295, 296, 321
Johnson, S. G., 285, 321
Johnson, V., 247, 267, 275
Johnson, V. E., 114, 130
Johnston, C., 38, 60
Johnston, L., 251, 252, 275
Johnston, M. B., 40, 61
Jolly, A., 132, 163
Jurkovic, G. J., 221, 244

Kahn, M. D., 305, 319
Kalman, F., 288, 323
Kandel, D. B., 146, 154, 166, 276, 277
Kantor, D., 21, 31
Kaplan, H. S., 114, 115, 129
Kaplan, R. M., 309, 321
Kastner, L. S., 278, 323
Kaufman, A. S., 177, 193
Kaufman, E., 276, 277
Kaufman, K. F., 39, 59, 227, 245
Kazdin, A. E., 2, 23, 31, 39, 60, 224, 244
Keeney, B. P., 18, 20, 21, 31
Kellerman, J., 278, 297, 321, 323
Kendall, P. C., 39, 60
Kenkel, W. F., 148, 164
Kennedy, R. E., 40, 60
Keogh, B. K., 182, 193
Kidd, K. K., 92
Kirscht, J. P., 313, 321
Kleck, R. E., 148, 166
Klein, B. E. K., 280, 284, 321
Klein, N., 224, 244
Klein, R., 280, 284, 321
Klemp, S. B., 301, 322
Klesges, R. C., 39, 60
Kniskern, D. P., 1, 2, 22, 30, 224, 243

Koeske, R., 284, 300, 323
Kohlberg, L., 36, 60, 221, 244
Kohler, E., 299, 322
Kovacs, M., 296, 297, 322
Kramer, J. F., 247, 275
Kupersmidt, J. B., 151, 167

L'Abate, L., 4, 5, 31
LaFreniere, P., 150, 168
LaGreca, A. M., 284, 296, 301, 322
Lamb, M. E., 150, 165
Lamberth, J. C., 148, 164
Lamparski, D., 300, 323
Lampman, R. M., 288, 319
Landeen, J., 189, 193
Landt, K. W., 288, 322
Lane, T. W., 227, 244
Langlois, J. H., 148, 168
LaPorte, R. E., 280, 283, 320, 322
Larsen, A., 244
Larson, N. R., 324, 343
Larsson, Y., 301, 319
Laundegren, J., 267, 275
Lavin, D. R., 133, 167
Lawroski, N., 150, 168
Lawson, G., 247, 275
Leckman, J. F., 92
Lederer, W. J., 104, 130
Lefkowitz, M. M., 66, 91
Leiderman, H., 91, 164
Lerner, R. M., 24, 31, 148, 166
Leslie, R., 281, 319
Lesser, G. S., 154, 166
Lessing, E. E., 211, 217
Levin, S., 62, 91
Levitsky, L. L., 288, 319
Lewis, J. M., 62, 91
Liebman, R., 301, 319, 322
Lin, S., 194, 206, 217
Lindbergh, C., 211, 218
Lipsey, M. W., 224, 244
Little, R. R., 284, 320
Lochman, J. E., 139, 166
Locke, H. J., 230, 244
Loeb, R. C., 66, 91

Loeber, R., 3, 31, 220, 221, 242, 244
LoPiccolo, J., 115, 130
Lorenz, R. A., 295, 296, 322
Lowman, C., 252, 275
Ludviggson, J., 301, 319
Lukoff, I. F., 276, 277
Lupfer, S. L., 324, 329, 343

Maccoby, E. E., 6, 31, 43, 56, 60, 63, 76, 91, 133, 166, 293, 302, 322
Macdonald, D., 247, 248, 249, 253, 262, 275
MacDonald, K., 150, 151, 166
MacFarlane, J. W., 176, 193
Maddock, J. W., 324, 343
Madge, N., 77, 92
Main, M., 76, 91
Maisiak, R., 148, 165
Maisto, S., 247, 275
Mann, B. J., 3, 17, 29, 31, 135, 157, 163, 221, 225, 230, 234, 242, 243, 244
Mann, G., 248, 275
Marcus, M. D., 284, 323
Margolin, G., 96, 129
Markell, R. A., 152, 166
Markova, I., 139, 163
Markwardt, F. C., 177, 192
Marlatt, G., 250, 275
Marshall, W. L., 329, 343
Martin, B., 62, 63, 76, 77, 84, 85, 91, 200, 217
Martin, J. A., 6, 31, 43, 56, 60, 63, 76, 91, 293, 302, 322
Mash, E. J., 11, 31, 38, 60
Masten, A. S., 1, 31
Masters, W. H., 114, 130
Matthews, C. G., 177, 193
McCall, R. B., 176, 193
McCallum, M., 321
McCartney, K., 5, 16, 32, 34, 60
McCauley, E., 315, 323
McCubbin, H. I., 228, 244
McDaniel, L. K., 278, 319

McFall, R. M., 5, 30, 221, 243
McGillicuddy-DeLisi, A. V., 63, 92
McGoldrick, M., 9, 16, 29
McGrade, B. J., 299, 318
McKenzie, E. M., 284, 320
Meadow, K. P., 186, 193
Meadows, L., 211, 218
Meichenbaum, D., 39, 60
Meiselman, K. C., 324, 343
Merikangas, K. R., 92
Mettetal, G., 132, 165
Meyers, A. W., 11, 31, 39, 40, 41, 60
Milan, D., 299, 322
Miller, C. L., 144, 163
Miller, D., 221, 243
Miller, J. G., 12, 31
Miller, J. P., 301, 319
Miller, W. R., 250, 275
Milman, L., 322
Minke, K. A., 189, 193
Minuchin, P. P., 4, 12, 13, 14, 16, 19, 31, 169, 175, 193
Minuchin, S., 17, 19, 31, 50, 60, 194, 217, 227, 244, 301, 319, 322
Mitchell, K. A., 320
Montalvo, B., 11, 31, 44, 60
Moore, M., 301, 320
Moos, B. S., 228, 244
Moos, R. H., 228, 244
Morgan, S. B., 33, 60
Morse, B. J., 220, 223, 243
Motti, F., 150, 168
Murphy, R. M., 139, 164
Murphy, W. D., 292, 320, 329, 334, 335, 344
Musgrove, F., 154, 166
Muxen, M., 244

Nachtman, W., 178, 192
Nasby, W., 139, 166
Nash, J., 201, 217
Nasjleti, M., 330, 343
National Diabetes Data Group, 283, 322

National Institutes of Health, 322
Neal, J. H., 21, 31
Neimark, E. D., 16, 31, 107, 130
Neimeyer, R. A., 330, 343
Nelson, D., 211, 217
New, A., 300, 323
Newman, J. P., 139, 164
Nichols, M., 8, 31
Niles, F. S., 154, 167
Noam, G., 278, 321
Nowacek, G., 285, 319
Nowalk, M. P., 284, 323

O'Brien, P. C., 284, 323
Oden, S., 144, 167
O'Donnell, W. J., 132, 154, 167
O'Leary, S. G., 39, 59
Olson, D. H., 62, 91, 98, 130, 230, 244
Olweus, D., 64, 66, 91, 152, 167, 220, 244
O'Malley, P., 251, 275
Onikul-Ross, S. R., 293, 320
Orleans, J., 321
Osofsky, J. D., 86, 91
Ownby, R. L., 177, 193

Panella, D. H., 6, 31, 132, 138, 146, 167
Parke, R., 2, 31, 150, 166, 227, 244
Parker, G., 86, 91
Parker, J. G., 131, 142, 146, 167
Parker, L., 314, 321
Parsons, B., 224, 242, 244
Pastor, D. L., 15, 167
Patterson, C. J., 151, 167
Patterson, G. R., 4, 7, 31, 32, 55, 60, 63, 64, 67, 74, 92, 155, 167, 221, 222, 223, 224, 227, 242, 245
Patterson, J. M., 228, 244
Pattison, E., 262, 275, 276, 277

Paulauskas, S., 38, 59, 296, 322
Pederson, A., 131, 164
Pendleton, L., 314, 321
Pepper, S. C., 12, 32
Petersen, A. C., 148, 163
Peterson, D. R., 225, 228, 230, 245
Peterson, J. L., 211, 217
Peterson, L., 133, 165
Phillips, V. A., 62, 91
Pichert, J. W., 295, 322
Pinsof, W. M., 1, 30, 224, 243
Platt, J. J., 139, 167
Plomin, R., 306, 319
Polich, J., 266, 275
Pollak, R. T., 321
Pollock, M., 322
Poole, E. D., 80, 92, 154, 167
Pope, B., 148, 167
Porter, F. S., 336, 343
Potter, P. C., 308, 322
Powers, S., 278, 321
Prentice, N. M., 221, 244
Prince, L. M., 312, 320
Pritchett, E. M., 178, 192
Pruitt, J. A., 221, 242
Prusoff, B. A., 92
Putallez, M., 138, 150, 167
Pyke, D. A., 281, 319

Quay, H. C., 221, 225, 228, 230, 245
Quinsey, V. L., 329, 344

Rachel, J., 247, 275
Ransom, D. C., 22, 29
Ratzan, S., 299, 318
Ray, R. S., 221, 242
Redpath, C. C., 308, 322
Regoli, R. M., 80, 92, 154, 167
Reid, J., 296, 322
Relyea, G., 320
Reynolds, C. R., 178, 193
Richardson, S. A., 148, 166
Rigler, D., 278, 321, 323
Ritter, P. L., 91, 164
Rivers, P., 247, 275

Rizza, R. A., 284, 323
Roberts, M. C., 308, 322
Rodick, J. D., 2, 6, 7, 31, 32, 98, 130, 189, 193, 203, 217, 221, 225, 243, 244, 245
Rodrigue, J. R., 292, 320
Roff, M., 131, 167
Rogers, C. S., 308, 322
Romig, D. A., 2, 32
Ronald, L., 148, 166
Roopnarine, J. L., 132, 150, 165, 167
Roseman, J. M., 292, 322
Rosenbloom, A., 285, 321
Rosenstock, I. M., 313, 321
Rosenthal, L., 5, 30, 221, 243
Rosenthal, R. H., 38, 60
Rosenthal, T. L., 39, 59
Rosman, B. L., 301, 319, 322
Ross, A. O., 180, 193
Rourke, B. P., 181, 193
Russell, C. S., 62, 91, 98, 130
Rutter, M., 77, 92, 178, 193, 200, 217
Ryder, R. G., 202, 217

Saltzstein, H. D., 66, 91, 92
Sanchez, V. C., 39, 60
Sandler, J., 227, 245
Santiago, J. V., 301, 319
Santrock, J. W., 211, 218
Satin, W., 284, 322
Sattler, J. M., 176, 177, 180, 193
Sauzier, M., 336, 343
Scarr, S., 5, 16, 32, 34, 60, 306, 322
Schaefer, E. S., 63, 92
Schaffer, H. R., 228, 245
Schimmel, L. E., 309, 321
Schlundt, D. G., 5, 30, 221, 243
Schork, E., 150, 168
Schork, M. A., 288, 319
Schuster, W. J., 220, 243
Schwartz, G. E., 12, 18, 32
Schwartzman, J., 21, 22, 32
Schwarz, L. T., 284, 322
Scura, W., 139, 167

Sebald, H., 136, 154, 167
Seligman, M., 302, 323
Sells, S. B., 131, 167
Selman, R. L., 35, 60, 132, 133, 138, 167
Service, F. J., 284, 323
Sgroi, S. M., 338, 344
Shapiro, E. K., 169, 175, 193
Shinn, M., 62, 92, 203, 217
Shrier, D. K., 86, 92
Shuckit, M., 265, 275
Sigel, I. E., 63, 92
Silverberg, S. S., 154, 168
Silverstein, J., 285, 321
Siman, M. L., 154, 155, 167
Simon, F. B., 328, 344
Simonds, J. F., 278, 323
Sirles, E., 338, 340, 344
Skyler, J. S., 288, 323
Slater, P. M., 278, 323
Sluzki, C. E., 18, 20, 32, 328, 330, 344
Smith, H., 325, 344
Smucker, B., 148, 168
Snyder, A. L., 285, 319
Snyder, J., 221, 245
Solanto, M. V., 38, 60
Solomon, M. A., 194, 218
Somberg, D. R., 139, 164
Speck, R. V., 4, 8, 32
Spencer, J. L., 288, 319
Spenner, K., 146, 168
Sperling, M. A., 288, 322
Spillar, R., 321
Spivack, G., 139, 167
Sprenkle, D. H., 20, 21, 31, 62, 91, 98, 130
Sroufe, L. A., 76, 90, 92, 150, 168
Staats, A. W., 189, 193
Stabb, S. D., 144, 163
Staffieri, J. R., 148, 168
Stalgaitis, S. J., 329, 334, 335, 344
Stambul, H., 266, 275
Stanley-Hagan, M., 195, 217
Stanton, A. L., 39, 60
Stanton, M. D., 276, 277
Stayton, D. J., 86, 90
Stein, R., 288, 323

Steinberg, L., 154, 155, 157, 168
Steinberg, T. F., 296, 322
Stevenson, D. L., 187, 193
Stierlin, H., 328, 344
Stolberg, A., 88, 91
Stone, B., 86, 92
Stouthamer-Loeber, M., 64, 92, 155, 167, 221, 223, 242, 245
Strasburg, P. A., 220, 245
Sullivan, H. S., 133, 168
Summerville, M. B., 7, 30, 152, 166
Sutherland, J. W., 13, 32
Sylva, K., 132, 163

Tajima, N., 280, 322
Talbott, G., 249, 275
Tavormina, J. B., 225, 230, 244, 278, 323
Taylor, S. E., 312, 323
Tennen, H., 299, 318
Teutsch, S. M., 280, 283, 321
Thompson, J., 178, 193
Tobin, F., 86, 92
Todd, T. C., 276, 277, 301, 319, 322
Tolan, P. H., 224, 245
Treloar, L., 3, 29, 135, 163, 225, 230, 242
Trepper, T. S., 324, 344
Trost, M. A., 131, 164
Tsai, M., 36, 60
Turtle, J. R., 278, 320
Twentyman, C. T., 3, 29
Tyano, S., 16, 28

Urey, J. R., 2, 18, 31, 32, 225, 244
Usher, M. L., 276, 277

Vaillant, G., 266, 275
Valsiner, J., 12, 32
Vandell, D. L., 153, 168
VanderPlate, C., 278, 323
Vaughn, B., 148, 168
Vellutino, F. R., 180, 193
Veroff, J., 93, 129
Vieyra, M., 321
Visher, E. B., 206, 218
Visher, J. S., 206, 218
Vondra, J., 152, 163
Vosk, B., 146, 165

Waas, G. A., 152, 165
Wahler, R. G., 222, 242
Walder, L. O., 66, 91
Waldron, S., 86, 92
Walker, D. K., 309, 323
Wall, S., 76, 90
Wallace, K. M., 230, 244
Walsh, M. E., 295, 308, 319
Ward, D., 248, 249, 275
Warren-Boulton, E., 310, 315, 319, 323
Warshak, R., 211, 218
Waters, E., 76, 90, 92, 150, 168
Watson, S. M., 2, 31, 157, 166, 221, 225, 244
Watt, S. L., 278, 323
Watzlawick, P., 10, 18, 32
Weakland, J., 10, 18, 32
Wechsler, D., 177, 193
Weis, J. G., 220, 222, 244
Weissman, M. M., 84, 92
Weitzman, M., 309, 323
Welborn, T. A., 314, 323
Wells, K. C., 34, 38, 59
Wells, R. A., 1, 32
Werry, J. S., 180, 192
Wertlieb, D., 321
Wexler, A. S., 201, 217

Whalen, C. K., 38, 39, 60, 61
Wheeler, R., 335, 336, 343
Wheeler, V. A., 142, 163
Whelan, J., 2, 29, 34, 42, 59, 225, 242
White, B., 154, 167
Whiteman, M., 7, 29, 155, 163, 276, 277
Whitman, T., 40, 61
Wiedmeyer, H. M., 284, 320
Wilder, C., 22, 32
Wilkinson, G. S., 177, 193
Wille, D. E., 150, 166
Williams, J., 247, 275
Williamson, P. R., 315, 323
Wills, T. A., 307, 319
Wilson, D. S., 153, 168
Wilson, J. Q., 221, 245
Wilson, L. R., 228, 244
Wilson, M., 244
Wilson, M. N., 83, 92
Wing, R. R., 284, 300, 323
Wippman, J., 76, 92, 150, 168
Wise, C. M., 278, 319
Wodarski, J. S., 224, 227, 243, 245
Wohlwill, J., 176, 193
Wolfe, D. A., 227, 245
Wolfsdorf, J. I., 321
Wynne, L. C., 328, 344

Yarrow, M. R., 66, 92
Young, L. D., 278, 319
Young, L. L., 148, 168
Yule, W., 178, 193

Zagorin, S. W., 211, 217
Zeltzer, L., 278, 297, 321, 323
Zill, N., 211, 217

SUBJECT INDEX

Academic achievement,
146–148
  cognitive functioning,
175–187
  family dysfunction,
185–186
  intellectual abilities,
175–179
  learning disabilities,
180–182
  peer acceptance, 146–148
  teaching, 182–184
Assessment:
  academic, 175–179
  incestuous families,
333–338
  initial sessions, 24–28
  marital, 98–103
  peer relations, 133–137

Chemical dependency:
  definitions, 246–247
  diagnostic assumptions,
248–251
  epidemiology, 251–252
  family treatment, 268–269
  intervention, 261–264
  outpatient treatment,
271–275
  symptoms and diagnosis,
252–261
  treatment goals, 264–270
Child abuse and neglect,
2–3, 36–37, 48–50,
226–229
Circularity, 14

Cognitive behavior therapy,
39–41
Cognitive development, 35–
38, 138–141, 293–296

Delinquency:
  causal models, 222–224
  correlates, 221–222
  epidemiology, 220
  family therapy, 236–238
  individual therapy,
235–236
  motivating change,
232–235
  multiple system interventions, 241–242
  peer interventions,
238–240
  school interventions,
240–241
  treatment studies, 224–231
Diabetes:
  adherence to treatment,
285–289
  coping, 296–298
  cognitive development,
293–296
  complications, 281–284
  epidemiology, 281–282
  family functioning,
298–306
  health care system,
311–315
  metabolic control, 284–285
  multisystemic treatment,
289–291

  peers, 308–309
  school system, 309–311
  siblings, 302–306
  stress, 306–308

Families, single-parent:
  children, 201–204
  extrafamilial systems,
204–205
  family system, 197–200
  financial issues, 195–196
  parent, 200–201
Families, step:
  children, 211–212
  extrafamilial systems,
210–211
  family system, 205–210
  parents, 212
Families, surrogate parent:
  children, 214–215
  extrafamilial systems, 216
  surrogate parent, 215–216
Family-peer mesosystem,
150–162
Family-school mesosystem,
187–192

Health care system, 311–315
Homeostasis, 15–16, 21

Incestuous families:
  assessment, 333–338
  characteristics, 325–330
  family interventions,
338–341

family-community inter-
ventions, 341–342
family-community
mesosystem, 330–331
models of, 324–329
treatment goals, 331–333
Individual Therapy, 41–59,
235–236

Marital relations:
abuse, 125–127
affect, 98–114
commitment, 123–125
conflict resolution,
107–114
diabetes, 301–302
extramarital affairs,
122–123
in-laws, 127–129
instrumental issues,
117–121
sexual dysfunctions,
114–117
Motivating change, 55–59,
103–104, 232–235
Multisystemic therapy:
distinguishing features,
4–12

outcome studies, 2–4,
225–231

New epistemology, 20–23

Parental:
commitment, 81–83
consistency, 74–75
exploitation, 47–50
psychopathology, 45–47,
83–85
rejection of child, 43–45
skill deficits, 79–81
Parent–child relations:
affect, 76–88
conceptual models, 62–63
control and discipline,
64–75
diabetes, 299–301
emotional neglect, 77–85
modeling, 88–90
overprotection, 85–88
Peer acceptance, 137–150
behavioral skills, 142–146
cognitive processes,
138–141
educational achievement,
146–148

physical attractiveness,
148–149
Peer relations:
assessment, 133–137
delinquency, 238–240
development, 132–133,
150–156
diabetes, 308–309

School:
cognitive functioning,
child, 175–187
delinquency, 240–241
diabetes, 309–311
intervention guidelines,
171–175
social functioning, child,
170–171
teachers, 182–184
Social skill deficits, child,
53–55
Systems theory, 12–18
Therapist-parent alliance,
70–73